Coming
Apart

William L. O'Neill

Coming Apart

An Informal History of America in the 1960's

With a New Introduction by the Author

IVAN R. DEE, PUBLISHER, CHICAGO

Library of Congress Cataloging-in-Publication Data:
O'Neill, William L.
  Coming apart : an informal history of America in the 1960's / William
L. O'Neill ; with a new introduction by the author.
       p. cm.
  Originally published: Chicago : Quadrangle Books, 1971.
  Includes bibliographical references (p.) and index.
  ISBN 1-56663-613-2 (acid-free paper)
  1. United States—History—1961–1969. 2. United States—Politics
and government—1945–1989. I. Title.
  E839.O5 2005
  973.923—dc22
                                        2004052731

To our daughters Catherine and Cassandra

Ivan Dee, my friend and editor, talked me into doing this book and so shares the blame for it. Margaret Moore typed the manuscript and corrected my spelling. I am indebted to the thousands of students who have taken courses from me in this decade, as much as to pollsters, for my sense of the public response to various issues. A special note of appreciation to the Department of History of the University of Pennsylvania, whose generous provision for visitors gave me time to write. Especially I am grateful to the many brilliant journalists cited later, without whom a book like this could not be made. The press was frequently criticized in the sixties, no doubt often justly. Journalists, like the rest of us, should do better. Yet no decade has produced such rich and varied reporting. Because of it my task has been easier than that of any earlier writer attempting to chronicle times just past. Most of all, as always, I am thankful for Carol.

Contents

CONTENTS

Introduction to the 2005 Edition

O NE DAY IN 1969 my editor at Quadrangle Books suggested that the 1960s were so insane that I should write a book about the decade. I leapt at the chance since, without knowing it, I had been preparing myself for just such an opportunity, clipping newspaper and magazine articles and reading books on contemporary issues that had no obvious bearing on my work as an historian. I was angry and disillusioned at the time, as the causes I believed in, and had worked for in some cases, already lay in ruins. The civil rights movement had been destroyed by Black Power even before the assassination of Martin Luther King. The New Left had disintegrated in a welter of bombings, violence, and hysterical rhetoric. The Great Society had become a casualty of the Vietnam War, as had Lyndon Johnson. Richard M. Nixon, the politician liberals—myself included—hated most, was now president of the United States.

Coming Apart wrote itself, the pages pouring out of my typewriter. From beginning to end, research included, it took only eighteen months for me to turn in a complete manuscript. Had I been in less of a hurry, the text would be more polished. But what it might have gained from fine-tuning would not, I think, have made up for what would have been lost. This book is not just about the period, it is *of* the period, a time of intense experiences, great expectations, and dashed hopes, mine along with millions of others. I knew then that these feelings would pass, and wanted to finish *Coming Apart* before they did. I tried to be accurate and fair, even to Richard Nixon, and believe that I succeeded in the former, if not the latter. Most of all I wanted to present the decade as I saw it, while my memories were fresh and my heart still broken. That sense of immediacy is responsible, I believe, for the long life of *Coming Apart,* which now, to my immense pleasure, appears under the imprint of the man who conceived it, Ivan R. Dee.

In the main this book has stood the test of time, but there are some factual errors and, of course, much that I would treat differently if I were writing it today. To my knowledge I was the first historian to argue that Dwight D. Eisenhower had been an effective president. Many still dispute this, although revisionist books, notably Fred I. Greenstein's *The Hidden-Hand Presidency: Eisenhower as Leader* (1982), and the opening of Eisenhower's personal correspondence and diaries, have made belittling his leadership more a matter of partisanship than anything else. I did err in writing that after Nixon's Checkers speech in 1952 Eisenhower welcomed him with open arms. Technically that is correct, but it was an act put on for the media's benefit. In actuality Nixon infuriated Eisenhower by calling on Adlai Stevenson and his running mate to disclose their finances, as he had just done. That meant Eisenhower, a very private man, would have to disclose his own as well, which he subsequently did. His relationship with Nixon, weak to begin with, never recovered from this incident. It helps explain why Eisenhower tried to get Nixon off the ticket in 1956, and why, during the 1960 election when asked at a press conference if he could think of a "major idea of his [Nixon] that you had adopted," the president, angry because he heard that question so often, replied, "If you give me a week I might think of one. I don't remember."

The only important event I got wrong is the Cuban Missile Crisis of 1962 because crucial information about it did not become public until after the Cold War ended. Only then did participants on both sides hold joint public gatherings to discuss their roles in the crisis. Among the documents opened in the 1990s is a transcript of what was said at meetings held by the Executive Committee of the National Security Council (ExCom), which President Kennedy secretly audiotaped. It is now clear that while Khrushchev sent missiles to defend Cuba, he also intended to establish a Soviet military force of such proportions that it would narrow a little America's enormous (by a ratio of 17 to 1) lead in intercontinental ballistic missiles (ICBMs). If fully executed, the Soviet plan would have deployed the following elements in Cuba: 50,000 military personnel; 1 MIG-21 fighter wing; 42 IL-28 light bombers; 2 cruise missile regiments; 12 SA-2 anti-aircraft units with 144 launchers; a squadron of 11 submarines, 7 equipped with nuclear missiles; 36 SS4 medium-range ballistic missiles (MRBMs) with a range of 1,100 miles; 24 SS5 intermediate-range ballistic missiles (IRBMs) with a range of 2,200 miles. Perhaps the scariest aspect of this buildup, considering that a few of Kennedy's advisers wanted to invade Cuba, is that it also included 12 FROG short-range nuclear missiles that the Soviet commander in Cuba was authorized to use on his own initiative if communications with Moscow were cut off.

In short, the Soviets presented the United States with a genuine offensive threat that, while it would not reduce the American strategic advantage by much, compelled Kennedy to make a strong response. The threat was even greater than we knew at the time, both because of its scale and because a Soviet general had the authority to start a nuclear war under extreme circumstances. Given this new evidence Kennedy's response seems to have been just about right. Kennedy's tapes show that in virtually every instance he took the most conservative options available to him. They show, too, that Robert Kennedy did not play as consistent a role as I believed he had when I wrote about the crisis. One of the most important figures in ExCom who did not receive much attention then was the recently replaced ambassador to Russia, Llewellyn Thompson, who accurately predicted how Khrushchev would react to any move and foretold how the negotiations would play out. Throughout the crisis ExCom was a genuine forum for discussion and debate that provided Kennedy with a wide range of choices. In contrast, Khrushchev did not consult with anyone and made all his decisions on the basis of impulse and instinct. Both sides, but especially the Soviets, learned much from this crisis and so, while the nuclear arms race continued, the risk of a nuclear exchange receded.

An odd footnote has to do with the obsolescent Jupiter missiles in Turkey. Contrary to what I wrote, Kennedy had not ordered the missiles removed before the crisis. He had tried to retrieve them, but Turkey, for domestic political reasons, wanted to keep the missiles in place. Khrushchev tried to save a little face by publicly asking that in return for withdrawing his missiles from Cuba the United States do the same with its missiles in Turkey. This was resolved by a secret oral agreement. Robert Kennedy told Soviet Ambassador Dobrynin that America would remove the Turkish missiles, but that this must be kept secret, and it was not a quid pro quo. The last condition was because America had only fifteen missiles in Turkey. A quid pro quo would have required the United States to match the much larger Soviet missile force being withdrawn from Cuba.

I erred again in writing that the American promise not to invade Cuba never had to be made because Castro clung to his Soviet light bombers. In fact the last one left Cuba on December 6, 1962, some six weeks after the resolution of the crisis. In a sense, then, Khrushchev did salvage something from the crisis: there has been no invasion of Cuba since the Bay of Pigs.

The Camelot myth has proven to be far more durable than anyone writing in 1970 could have imagined, even though the secret life of John F. Kennedy is now an open book. That JFK had extramarital affairs has been public knowledge since 1978 when Judith Exner published *My Story*, which provided numerous details about her affair with the president. Since then many others have come forward, including former Secret Service agents, all confirming that Kennedy was a sexual addict who seems to have had hundreds of women during his presidency alone, sometimes two or more at a time since he enjoyed orgies—especially in the White House swimming pool. When traveling, if no amateurs made themselves available, he settled for hookers. Republicans knew about Kennedy's sex life but at the time of his death had not yet found a way to exploit his infidelities. Neither had reporters, since press conventions in those days banned writing about the sexual indiscretions of public figures except when they became news—for example, embarrassing disclosures revealed by divorce suits. Still, given his incredible foolhardiness, and the many people who knew about Kennedy's sexual habits, it appears probable that, had he lived, the secret would have gotten out before the end of his second term.

Kennedy's other secret, which would seem to belie the first, concerns his wretched health. The public knew about his bad back, and reporters, based on close observation, suspected he had other problems, but he lied about them, as did his family, close associates, and doctors. In 2002, after decades of speculation, the Kennedy family and the committee that controlled access to his medical records allowed Robert Dallek, a noted historian, and Dr. Jeffrey A. Kelman, a physician, to examine the records—which are by no means complete and cover only the last eight years of his life. According to the *New York Times*, they found that his back condition was much worse than the public knew. As a result of osteoporosis, three of his vertebrae were fractured so that, far from being vigorous, he could not put on his left sock and shoe without help. He also had severe intestinal problems. From 1955 to 1957 he was secretly hospitalized nine different times because of these two ailments alone. And, although he specifically denied it, Kennedy had Addison's disease, a deficiency of the adrenal gland, which, according to Nigel Hamilton, a Kennedy biographer, almost killed him twice.

The *Times* had this to say of his medications: "The records show that Kennedy variously took codeine, Demerol and methadone for pain; Ritalin, a stimulant; meprobamate and librium for anxiety; barbiturates for sleep; thyroid hormone; and injections of a blood derivative, gamma globulin, presumably to combat infections. In the White House, Kennedy received 'seven to eight injections of procaine in his back in the same sitting' before news conferences and other events, Dr. Kelman said." When he lost weight because of his maladies he was given the male hormone testosterone to build up his muscles. To combat his Addison's disease, for which there was no better treatment at the time, he had been given steroids in the 1930s, and they probably accounted for his premature osteoporosis. Other sources had already revealed that Dr. Max Jacobson, known as "Dr. Feelgood" to the Secret Service, regularly visited the White House and the Kennedy homes in Hyannis Port and Palm Beach. In 1975 Jacobson lost his medical license for misuse of amphetamines, or "speed." The presumption is that Jacobson not only injected Kennedy with a cocktail of drugs but left loaded hypodermic needles for self-administration, as he did with other patients. The list of ailments experienced and drugs taken by Kennedy in this eight-year period alone goes on, but the point is obvious. Or, rather, two points are obvious. Friends and family argue that since he experienced pain every day, his concealment of it, even from staff members, exhibited courage and grace. The other equally valid point is that he was physically unfit to be president. If the Democratic party had known about his frail health, it is doubtful that he would have been nominated, if only because Republicans would have exploited the issue.

Most of what I would change, given my present knowledge, is not very important.

—Lieutenant Colonel John Vann, who resigned his commission because he did not believe the Viet Cong could be defeated by using heavy guns and air power, later changed his mind. He returned to Vietnam as a civilian with the putative rank of major general. At the time he was killed in a helicopter crash in 1972, Vann was controlling military operations in the II Corps sector and directing B-52 strikes.

—That births surged in New York nine months after the great power failure of November 9, 1965, turned out to be an urban myth.

—Ralph Nader is an egomaniac and has always been one.

—The Black Panther party was more like a criminal gang than a political movement.

—*Bonnie and Clyde* remains a distinguished film, but had I known that it would open the door to unbelievable quantities of graphic movie violence, I would have been less enamored of it.

Although the New Left had not completely vanished when I finished my manuscript, it did disappear as expected. What neither I, nor anyone else, knew is that it would rise from the grave and take control of a large part of academia. In the 1980s former New Leftists and their sympathizers and allies, having acquired doctorates, began rising through the ranks. By the 1990s they controlled the humanities, liberal arts, and social science departments in most leading universities, and also the related academic professional bodies, notably the enormous Modern Language Association. Some became administrators, or intimidated administrators into promoting their agenda. Unlike the New Left, which really meant to change the world, academic leftists have been content to rule higher education, promoting multiculturalism, affirmative action, and similar policies, as also various arcane theories such as postmodernism. Since they have no outside ambitions, the damage to society at large has been minimal. Undergraduates have not suffered much either as brainwashing them is very difficult, contrary to popular opinion. Many graduate students do toe the line, out of conviction, self-interest, or some combination of the two. Faculties are divided, but ideological differences matter less than the relentless underfunding of public colleges and universities that has been going on since the 1970s. Little did I know as I wrote this book that I was living at the end of the golden age of higher education.

My pages on the Tet Offensive of 1968 still hold up, with one exception: the Viet Cong never recovered from the losses sustained during Tet. It seems they actually believed that the urban masses would rise up alongside them. When this failed to happen, the Viet Cong's destruction became inevitable. This made little difference in the long run as North Vietnamese regulars simply replaced them.

I would have muted my admiration for Eugene McCarthy had I known that he was far less serious about winning the Democratic presidential nomination in 1968 than he appeared to be. Despite losing the nomination to Humphrey he still had a strong following, which in later years he frittered away by giving up his Senate seat and subordinating politics to other interests. Every now and then he embarrassed himself by throwing his nonexistent hat into the ring, causing some pain to those who had voted for him in 1968.

It transpired that Richard Nixon really did have a plan for ending the Vietnam War. The speech by Henry Kissinger that I quote from in my text genuinely reflected both his views and those of President Nixon. Vietnamization was not, as I thought then, a way of making war on the cheap; it was a cover story to justify abandoning South Vietnam. More than twenty thousand Americans lost their lives there in 1968, the worst year of the war. By his rapid withdrawal of troops, Nixon cut that number by more than half in 1969. In 1971 he reduced the figure to 1,381, and in 1973 American losses amounted to zero. This process seemed slow at the time, but in retrospect it is clear that he pulled troops out of Vietnam as quickly as he dared. Nixon concealed the redeployments with militant rhetoric, and, more important, by increased bombing attacks. On June 7, 1969, he explained his policy of a phased retreat to military leaders in Honolulu, ordering them to stop saying that events in Southeast Asia represented a threat to America's national security. The bombing raids were front-page news while falling casualties and troop drawdowns did not receive anything like the same attention for several years.

Nixon planned from the start to establish direct contact with Communist China, the key to which was getting out of Vietnam. In July 1971 Henry Kissinger secretly visited China to make preparations for Nixon's unprecedented visit the following year. In 2003 declassified transcript fragments of Kissinger's conversations appeared in the *New York Times*. During one meeting he spoke to Prime Minister Zhou Enlai as follows: "I would like to tell the prime minister, on behalf of President Nixon, as solemnly as I can, that first of all we are prepared to withdraw completely from Indochina and to give a fixed date, if there is a cease-fire and release of our prisoners. Secondly, we will permit the political solution of South Vietnam to evolve and to leave it to the Vietnamese alone. . . ." Later in the conversation Kissinger made the point even more clearly. "If the government [of South Vietnam] is as unpopular as you seem to think, then the quicker our forces are withdrawn the quicker it will be overthrown. And if it is overthrown after we withdraw, we will not intervene." That was the real meaning of Vietnamization.

Events played out much as Nixon and Kissinger hoped they would. China obviously took Kissinger at his word because it tolerated a great deal of violence over the next few years. In March 1972, less than a month after Nixon left China, North Vietnam launched a major offensive. On April 10 the United States began heavily bombing both North Vietnam and its forces in the South. On May 8 Nixon announced further bombing attacks and the mining of Haiphong harbor and other ports in North Vietnam. China did little about this and, revealingly, anti-war demonstrations in the United States were very small. Several reasons account for the peace movement's collapse. Huge troop withdrawals would bring the number of men still in Vietnam down to 24,000 by year's end. Accordingly, casualties fell sharply as well. Only 300 Americans died in Vietnam in 1972. Nixon believed that the anti-war movement revolved around young men afraid of being drafted. By 1972 draft calls were so small, and limited to nineteen-year-olds chosen by lot, that the war had ceased to be a campus issue. Nixon appears to have been right: self-interest more than anything else had driven the student movement.

This sketch makes getting out of Vietnam seem much easier that it was. The government of North Vietnam had its own agenda and did not take orders from China or the Soviet Union, the North's chief supplier. There were plenty of ups and downs in Vietnam and in Paris where negotiations between Kissinger and North Vietnam's Le Duc Tho took place. Nixon desperately hoped for a "decent interval" between America's withdrawal and South Vietnam's fall, and in the end North Vietnam obliged him. In January 1973 Nixon announced that a peace accord had been reached, to take effect on the 27th. That same day the draft came to an end. In February North Vietnam began releasing American POWs. On March 29 the last American troops left South Vietnam. On April 8, 1975, North Vietnam launched its final offensive. Saigon fell on April 30, the last American civilians helicoptering out to the waiting Seventh Fleet, along with every Vietnamese ally with access to a chopper. They came in such numbers that empty helicopters were pushed over the sides of carriers to make room for incoming aircraft.

Nixon had fulfilled his promise to get America out of Vietnam—dishonestly, dishonorably, with repeated outbursts of violence and suffocating blankets of obfuscation. Only Nixon could have pulled this off, and he did so in the only way possible since the American people could not have handled the truth. He had to make it seem that by abandoning South Vietnam the United States was saving it. When Saigon fell, most people no longer cared cared enough about South Vietnam to protest its collapse—Nixon's final achievement.

My remarks at the end of this book about the liberal failure of nerve have proven more prescient than I imagined they would be. New Deal–Great Society liberalism never recovered from Lyndon Johnson's failures and the success of Richard Nixon, Watergate notwithstanding. President Gerald Ford vetoed almost every significant Democratic bill. President Jimmy Carter, hardly a flaming liberal in any event, spent much of his term performing damage control. President Ronald Reagan made conservatism popular, and his policies continued under President George H. W. Bush. Bill Clinton won his two terms by appropriating Republican issues, such as welfare reform, being tough on crime, producing budget surpluses, and the like. These benefited him but not the Democratic party, which lost both the House and Senate during his presidency. As I write, President George W. Bush is pushing an agenda even more radically right wing than that of Ronald Reagan. Meanwhile, Democrats are divided over racial and other issues that weaken the party and strengthen conservatives.

I wanted to call this book *Good Riddance*, and the galley proofs bore that title. But Ivan Dee and I finally agreed that it was a bit too dismal. In time we came to regret our decision. The greatest accomplishments of the decade, such as the Civil Rights Act of 1964, the Voting Rights Act of 1965, Medicare and Medicaid, continue to bear fruit. But the pleasure principle, epitomized in the sixties by the odious mantra "Do your own thing," has flourished beyond belief, raising divorce and illegitimacy rates, lowering marriage rates, as also standards of taste and behavior. In polls the public claims to want more money spent on health, education, the environment, and other good things. But it votes for tax cuts and to hell with public services, most of which have deteriorated since the 1970s. In this respect selfishness is the principal bequest of the sixties.

W. L. O.

Highland Park, New Jersey
September 2004

Coming
Apart

1 PROLOGUE: EISENHOWER'S YEAR

W<small>HO CAN DO JUSTICE</small> now to the 1950's? For liberals and intellectuals it was a dull, sad time, the age of television (ten thousand sets in 1947, forty million ten years later), tract houses, garish automobiles, long skirts, and bad movies. Arthur Godfrey was the biggest thing in show business; Norman Vincent Peale the country's most popular ordained moralist. People still joked about Brooklyn, the mere mention of which, for some forgotten reason, induced laughter. Charcoal grey suits went with pink shirts and black knit ties. Trousers had ornamental buckles in the back, an especially curious fashion since when worn with a coat they could not be seen. Men kept their hair very short, except for aspiring juvenile delinquents whose long sidehairs met at the back. This was called a "D.A." haircut. College students had no politics and were best known for sporadic "panty raids" in which men tried to break into women's dormitories to steal underwear.

Such customs could not but invite contempt even then. When the sixties arrived with its theatrical fashions and events, the fifties seemed worse still. The 1960's enjoyed the longest period of sustained economic growth in modern history, making the unemployment and Eisenhower recessions of the previous decade seem inexcusable. The politics of the fifties were equally shoddy, being dominated by five men—Truman, Taft, Eisenhower, Joseph McCarthy, and Adlai Stevenson—only one of whom, Stevenson, had any grace or wit. At least half the period was preoccupied with a wholly false issue: the supposed menace of American communism. Foreign policy was hardly better. Secretary of State John Foster Dulles's moralistic approach was laughable when not sinister.

3

There were plenty of critics who made these and other points. Liberal magazines like the *Nation*, the *New Republic*, and the *Progressive* exposed the shortcomings of foreign and domestic policies, though to little effect. David Riesman's *The Lonely Crowd* described how rugged individualism had given way to the modern American's pathetic need for peer-group approval. From John Keats's *The Crack in the Picture Window* and *The Insolent Chariots* people learned that their new homes and cars were shameful evidences of weakness and gullibility. Materialism and conformity prevailed everywhere, it was said, though few outside the intellectual community seemed to mind. John Kenneth Galbraith in *The Affluent Society* argued brilliantly for a redistribution of income to end the poverty of public services. Most people still expected economic growth alone to meet the country's needs. William H. Whyte showed how the corporation made its officers toe the company line. College graduates went on planning to become junior executives. A flood of books condemned the quality of public education. Schooling failed to change much. Domestic pleasure became the highest good. The birthrate rose; the age at which people married fell. So, after peaking in 1946, did the divorce rate. Everyone went to church more. The fifties remained an age, as the novelist Herbert Gold sardonically put it, of happy people with happy problems. Historians celebrated the value of unity and moderation. Daniel Bell observed with satisfaction that the fifties witnessed *The End of Ideology*.

Without suggesting the critics were wrong, it seems clear now that the fifties were better than they thought. The arts—painting, architecture, the dance—flowered. Despite several recessions, inflation was brought under control. At the end of his eight years President Eisenhower noted that the output of goods and services was up 25 per cent, average family income 15 per cent, and real wages 20 per cent. One-fourth of the country's housing as of 1960 had been built in the preceding decade. The population went up by 28 million, yet nearly everyone was better fed and housed than before. Schools expanded rapidly enough to keep up with the baby boom. It was true that the popular culture was unexciting, the new subdivisions ugly and poorly planned, and the family-oriented, suburban style of living wanting in charm or distinction. The fact remains that these were years of real progress for ordinary Americans.

Probably nothing in the fifties was so poorly understood as the Eisenhower presidency. At the time his friends were misled and his foes baffled. His popularity was based on rectitude and his apparent openness and geniality. He was thought to be the common man writ large. His critics believed he was too dependent on bad advisers like John Foster

Dulles to properly conduct foreign policy, and too uninformed to handle domestic affairs. In 1960 Senator John F. Kennedy announced that the country had been so mismanaged that he must run for President to save it. Henry Luce, the great publisher, wrote that "more than anything else the people of America are asking for a clear sense of national purpose." Adlai Stevenson said, "We seem becalmed in a season of storm and drifting in a century of mighty dreams and great achievements." Political columnists like James Reston and Walter Lippmann blamed Eisenhower for not providing vital leadership as Franklin D. Roosevelt had, and so did political scientists like Hans J. Morgenthau and Richard Neustadt.

Eisenhower was very different from what he seemed. He was a man of drive, intelligence, ambition, and ruthlessness. These are essential qualities in great military leaders. People sometimes appeared to think that he got his stars through luck or charm. But they were not why General George C. Marshall, the greatest military executive in American history, jumped him over hundreds of senior officers when it came time to appoint a Supreme Commander in Europe. Marshall saw in Eisenhower a man with abilities like his own. Even when young, Eisenhower had enormous self-discipline. Though not much of a student, he did well enough at West Point because he had to. Burdened with a hot temper, he learned not to lose it in public. As a junior officer he became good at bridge because that was what people played in remote Army posts, and his salary didn't, as Murray Kempton points out, cover losing money to civilians. He could take risks when he had to. His choice of June 6, 1944, as D-Day was one of World War II's great gambles. If the weather had not cleared briefly, his invasion force would have been destroyed. The key here is not that he made the right decision but that he made the hard one. A lesser man would have waited another month to be certain—and probably seen all Germany later occupied by the Soviets.

But Eisenhower did not believe in taking unnecessary risks. When he saw that the Korean War could not be won at a fair price he liquidated it. When Dien Bien Phu was about to fall in 1953 he was under heavy pressure to intervene, but saw that the odds were bad and refused to. When Lebanon asked for help in 1957 he sent it just enough men to secure the capital. If the government had popular support the troops would free it to crush the rising. If not, the small American force could be easily removed. People laughed when the Marines charged ashore at Beirut to be met by refreshment vendors and girls in bikinis. The landing was a low-risk venture which paid handsome dividends all the same. Eisenhower followed the same strategy in South Vietnam, where President Diem was given all the material help a viable regime needed. Though later Presidents said Eisenhower's aid to Diem justified their policies, it seems unlikely he would have acted as they did. He was willing to take small risks for small gains and big risks for big gains. He didn't like to chance a lot to win a little.

These remarkable qualities of mind and will were disguised by a boyish grin and homely face, still more by what can only have been deliberate stratagems. Arthur Larson, one of his speechwriters, says that though Eisenhower was famous for having said he never read the papers, he in fact did so carefully. He rarely picked up Westerns but let everyone think them his favorite reading matter. Though capable of composing a good speech himself (those he wrote for General MacArthur before the war were much admired), he insisted that his own writers do bad ones. He scrupulously edited out the phrases they liked best. Eisenhower knew he had to say something from time to time, but he meant to convey as little as possible. His press conferences, notorious for obfuscation and mangled syntax, were not so artless as they seemed. He admitted as much once when his Press Secretary James Hagerty asked what he would say about the sticky Formosa Straits issue. Eisenhower replied, "Don't worry, Jim. If that question comes up I'll just confuse them."

Equally confusing was his habit of allowing a hundred flowers to bloom. His underlings were always contradicting him and one another, or so it seemed. Everybody talked a lot but made little sense. The President spoke of peace, John Foster Dulles of brinkmanship. Eisenhower assured farmers of his concern for their profits; Secretary of Agriculture Ezra Taft Benson, a Mormon leader of antique views, threatened to do away with price supports. This practice not only made it hard to know what administration policy was, but provided Eisenhower with plenty of scapegoats when things went wrong. Failures abroad were always blamed on Dulles. There were legions of fall guys from Nixon on down to take the rap at home. When people irritated or compromised Eisenhower, he denied the claims of loyalty. Sherman Adams, his most valuable aide, was fired for having accepted embarrassing gifts. Nixon was kept dangling in both 1952 and 1956 before being assured of the vice-presidency.

This is not to exaggerate either Eisenhower's personal merits or his policies, but only to say that the first were different from what people thought then, and the second more useful than critics are yet willing to admit. He had profound limitations. His views on both foreign and domestic matters were wholly conventional. He ran for President in the first place chiefly, he said at the time, to keep Taft out of the White House. He feared that "Mr. Republican" would turn the country back to isolation. Eisenhower wished only to preserve the Cold War containment policies he had helped create. This kept him from securing the détente Russia was so eager to achieve. His domestic position was even more commonplace. On the one hand it meant paying lip service to free-enterprise capitalism, local government, and other traditional Republican fetishes. On the other he accepted the New Deal commitment to welfare liberalism and got more help from the Democrats in Congress than from his own party. This effort to reconcile opposites was called by Eisenhower "modern Republicanism," though no one else knew quite what that meant, or could be sure which half of the formula would be applied next. Eisenhower was not sympathetic to the civil rights movement (he reluctantly sent troops to Little Rock in 1957 to insure the integration of Central High). He had no feel for the poor. The President was not a daring or innovative politician and never pretended to be.

He said later that his chief accomplishment as President had been "to create an atmosphere of greater serenity and mutual confidence." Under his benign guidance the feverish witch-hunts and polemics of the McCarthy era gave way to something like business as usual. This was no small thing, and by the late sixties—when discord was even greater than when Eisenhower took office—it seemed all the more impressive. True, America needed more than business as usual. But if the country cannot have progress, it at least deserves stability, as under Eisenhower. After 1965 there was precious little of either.

It was typical of President Eisenhower that his greatest achievements were all negative. He ended the Korean War, entered into no new ones, and kept military spending down. People were grateful for the first, took the second for granted, and, often as not, attacked him for the third. Yet they were equally difficult and worthwhile accomplishments, though it is much easier now than then to see why. Halting the Korean War meant accepting defeat, for when a lesser power stalemates a greater one it comes off best. Only a man with supreme self-confidence could have terminated the war, as became clear in 1969 when Richard Nixon, confronted with the same opportunity, declined to take it. Eisenhower's second term was the only one since 1937–40 when the country was not at war somewhere. If people took that for granted then, we can hardly afford to do so at a time when staying out of war has become the great test of presidential fitness. And holding the line on defense costs now appears so remarkable a feat as of itself nearly to guarantee Eisenhower's place in history.

At first he did not find this hard. After Korea Eisenhower cut military spending (causing a recession in the process) to some applause. Then on October 4, 1957, Russia sent Sputnik aloft. The Russians issued only a routine announcement saying they had orbited a small earth satellite. But in America the shock was profound. It appeared that national self-confidence was based mainly on the assurance of technological superiority in every field. Demands for an expanded arms race multiplied. Russia had to be surpassed everywhere, especially in "science." The shortage of consumer goods in the Soviet Union, once thought to be evidence of communism's weakness, now appeared a mark of strength. Russia's Spartan vigor exposed American affluence for the enfeebling thing it was. Even Russia's schools were found to be models of efficiency. The practical consequences of Russia's success were twofold: at home Americans were urged to achieve what was always called "excellence"; in foreign and military affairs the mandate was again for dominance.

Because Eisenhower misunderstood the panic he handled it badly at first. Wernher von Braun sent up an American satellite to show how easily the thing was done. But it was too late and too small to help much.* Eisenhower appointed a commission on national goals; the demand for aggressive leadership continued. He appointed another body, the Gaither Commission, to review his defense policies, and instead it repudiated them. He pronounced the report "useful" and promptly suppressed it. Some of its proposals (like tunneling Strategic Air Command runways into the sides of mountains) appalled him. He said later that he tabled the report because "we could not turn the nation into a garrison state." Once it became clear that the storm was not going to blow over, the President organized his imposing resources. First among them was his great popularity. It was mainly among intellectuals, journalists, and the foreign policy establishment that his prestige declined. The people never doubted Eisenhower, and throughout these difficult years their confidence sustained him. His office was a potent weapon too. The White House had gotten nearly absolute authority over military and foreign affairs. However lax he may have been elsewhere, General Eisenhower retained that power.

By the beginning of 1960, though his foreign and defense policies were under attack from every quarter, the old man had given no ground. More than that, he had gained a little. Relations with the Soviets were better. The "Spirit of Camp David," inspired by Premier Khrushchev's strange visit to America, flourished. The Geneva talks on arms limitations, which Eisenhower had launched in 1958, were still dragging along, but the informal test ban established by the talks remained in effect. The President had begun it even before the U.S. test series was completed, despite the objections of hawks like Dr. Edward Teller (who was never called the Mother of the H-Bomb, though he gave birth to it). The ban eased tensions and saved infant lives. At the same time missile technology progressed encouragingly. On January 7, 1960, the President re-

---

* This was done by taking a Redstone rocket off the shelf and fitting it with an improvised satellite. The launching could have been accomplished successfully well before Sputnik had the government thought it worthwhile.

vealed that American ICBM's had landed within two miles of their targets after five-thousand-mile flights. His cuts in Army manpower had made it possible to develop missiles without enlarging the military budget. Pacifists wanted arms reduction, but by holding the line on defense spending while creating a nearly invulnerable nuclear deterrent the President hoped to stabilize the arms race. It was a better deal than later Presidents would offer.

In his last State of the Union Message President Eisenhower said his budget would provide a surplus of $200 million in fiscal 1960 and $4.2 billion the following year without jeopardizing national security. On January 19, 1960, Defense Secretary Thomas S. Gates, Jr., told the Senate Armed Services Committee that the nuclear arms race "showed a clear balance in our favor." Hardly anyone seemed to believe them. This was partly because of the hundred-flowers policy. The next day Army Secretary Wilber M. Brucker told the Senate that Russia's armed forces were splendidly equipped and vastly more numerous than America's. General Thomas Power of SAC warned the American Legion that Russia would soon be able to wipe out America's deterrent force in thirty minutes. According to Senate Majority Leader Lyndon B. Johnson, CIA director Allen Dulles expected a huge Soviet lead in missile-striking power to develop soon. These internal betrayals lent credibility to attacks from outside the administration. The easiest way to view this assault is to look at Walt Whitman Rostow's *The United States in the World Arena*, which appeared early in 1960. Though little noticed then, it was an important clue to the future. Rostow would soon be able to implement his views and, despite some idiosyncrasies, they were widely shared.

Rostow saw the fifties as dominated by General Eisenhower's fear of another Korea and by a "Great Equation" which balanced the cost of strategic forces against the need for a vigorous economy. In consequence Eisenhower stayed out of the Indochina war, failed to put teeth in the Southeast Asia Treaty Organization, and rarely sent U.S. troops into underdeveloped countries. He gave a fair amount of military aid, but in support of conventional forces. Meanwhile, the communists were turning to subversion, infiltration, and other unconventional methods against which standing armies were not much use. The President refused to assemble units that could be quickly moved to fight small wars anywhere in the world.

Worse still, he wouldn't speed up the arms race. General Eisenhower was willing to accept Soviet parity in strategic weapons. Even modest Russian leads didn't frighten him so long as his second-strike (retaliatory) capability was safe. The President defied nearly every important sector of the national elite on this point. On January 7, 1958, Senator

Lyndon Johnson's Preparedness Subcommittee issued a fourteen-point defense program which the President ignored entirely. He gave the (Nelson) Rockefeller Panel Report No. 2 equally short shrift. He suppressed the Gaither Report. Thus, while the foreign policy establishment agreed on the need for more arms, the military budget failed to grow. When corrected for price rises, military spending in 1958 was lower than in 1957. In the entire post-Sputnik period to 1961, arms costs increased by no more than 2 per cent.

This baffled Rostow. Most strategists agreed on the need for more missiles and a mobile task force to fight limited wars. Eisenhower refused to budge. He worried instead about the economy—and with reason, for unemployment kept going up. The President also feared that a runaway arms race might produce a world war. On the other hand, he had met many Russian leaders and they didn't scare him at all. Thus, because he was afraid of the wrong thing, Rostow concluded, Eisenhower accepted a Russian lead in strategic weapons that might induce Soviet leaders, through overconfidence, to bring on the war his policy was supposed to prevent.

Other critics were less charitable. General Maxwell B. Taylor reflected the dismay of Army officers who saw their position steadily erode during the late 1950's. President Eisenhower relied on the big nuclear punch ("massive retaliation") to deter aggression. The Army favored a strategy of "flexible response" that offered more military options. Flexible response demanded a large Army whereas massive retaliation made the Army redundant. Hence in 1955 and 1956 the Army shrank while the Air Force expanded. The so-called "new look" precluded intervention during the battle of Dien Bien Phu. "This event," Taylor pointed out, "was the first, but not the last, failure of the New Look to keep the peace on our terms." General Ridgway while Chief of Staff resisted the New Look so vigorously that he was forced to retire in 1955. As military costs grew, the Joint Chiefs planned to eliminate the Army altogether except for modest National Guard and civil defense units. This projected cutback to a 200,000-man force was blocked, but the Army kept dwindling anyway.

Equally trying for the generals was Eisenhower's contempt for their more extravagant ideas. Despite the Army's German V-2 genius Wernher von Braun, he increasingly assigned missile development to the Air Force. The Army's intermediate-range ballistic missiles, Thor and Jupiter, were cut back. Its anti-ballistic missile system was never deployed at all. The President thought it would be too expensive, might not work, and would lead to further increases in Soviet offensive missile strength. (As it turned out, the Nike-Zeus would have been obsolete before it was fully developed anyway.)

Eisenhower had so little sentiment about his own service that he thought of abolishing it several times, once, as we saw, by eliminating its functions, and once by merging it with the other services. He failed both times, so the Defense Reorganization Bill of August 1957 left the three-service structure largely intact. The President was still proud of it as a step toward full centralization. Since he had had to get along with separate services, he turned their rivalry to advantage. He set a ceiling on military spending, then assigned each service a percentage of the whole. If a service wanted money above its quota, it had to raid another's budget. In practice this meant that the Navy and Air Force ganged up on the Army.

Each service advanced whichever strategic doctrine gave it the most to do. The Air Force liked massive retaliation and a continental air-defense system based on fighter planes. The Army preferred flexible response and air defense using its ABM. The Navy and Marines thought flexible response desirable if it left the fighting to them. Massive retaliation was appealing when it stressed Polaris submarines. Eisenhower diverted the services' fire from him to each other. If they could not make him enlarge the whole pie, they could at least try to broaden their slices. The Air Force and Navy were strategic rivals, but each was strong enough to make protracted conflict between them costly. The cheapest tactic was to carve up the Army between them, and so they did. Maxwell Taylor was convinced, though, that if there were enough money for everyone the other services would take a more "objective" view of the Army's role. Later events proved him right.

The most famous attempt to discredit Eisenhower's defense policy was Herman Kahn's *On Thermonuclear War*. Kahn's 250-pound body mounted the fastest tongue and most agile mind in the strategy business. His critics detested him for his wit ("I can be really funny about thermonuclear war," he once remarked) and apparent inhumanity. With careful planning only twenty or thirty million Americans would be killed in a nuclear attack, he thought. But this happy prospect required more defenses, including civil defenses. Kahn's importance was hard to gauge. Outside the defense establishment *On Thermonuclear War* probably had little impact. It bristled with intimidating jargon (counterforce, preattack mobilization base, finite deterrence) and could hardly be read without a glossary. The reader who survived its language found himself trudging through countless "scenarios" (anticipated situations) each more incredible than the last. Few people had the stamina for such an enterprise, fewer still found Kahn's prescriptions believable. If wars were fought by computers his precise scenarios would have been useful. In the real world, though, they are fought by men, which is to say mainly by luck and muddle. Still, the military seemed to profit from his speculations, enabling him to leave the RAND thinktank (research institute) and found his own, the Hudson Institute.

Since the military was the only real buyer for their product, most strategists were appropriately belligerent. *A Forward Strategy for America* by Robert Strausz-Hupé, *et al.*, outdid all the rest. While Herman Kahn was too difficult for most generals and politicians to follow, Strausz-Hupé *et al.* had the common touch. By forward strategy they meant "a strategy of active pressures . . . designed not only to contain communism, but to emasculate its disruptive power." The authors hoped to win the Cold War by getting more weapons, putting pressure on the Soviet Union and China, freeing the "captive nations" of Eastern Europe, defeating national liberation movements with paramilitary, antiguerrilla forces armed with tactical nuclear weapons, and so on. Russia was to be ruined by a more costly arms race. "Economic offensives" would help too. The current of world affairs would thus be reversed and Western civilization and the Free World saved from communist tyranny.

Serious people dismissed this book (as most did) at their peril. Intellectuals thought it vulgar and silly. Liberals found it vicious. To all but rightists it was beyond the pale. They mistook packaging for product, however. Except for its menacing rhetoric the book was closer to the mainstream than it seemed. Liberal strategists were less adventurous than Strausz-Hupé *et al.* Yet they meant to defeat national liberation movements, expand the military, and put communism on the defensive. In their honest if demented way, the Strausz-Hupéians foreshadowed what was to come as liberals did not. Liberals suggested that people could have their cake and eat it too. The country was to win the Cold War, solve its domestic problems, and prosper all at once. Conservatives knew better. Sometimes, though, liberalism and reaction converged, as when Senator Kennedy made Strausz-Hupéistic appeals for sacrifice, leadership, and victory. President Eisenhower's critics were much in favor of sacrifices, especially those borne by others—young men of draft age, the poor, and small taxpayers. No one suggested that the military give up their privileges or industrialists their profits. General Eisenhower didn't ask anyone to give up anything—save dreams of well-armed glory. So he naturally excited the scorn of patriots.

The "great debate" on national strategy was critical to the 1960's because it led to the Kennedy-Johnson military programs which dominated them. But it had little effect on most Americans at the time. They were concerned with more homely matters. No single subject or mood prevailed as Korea had before and Vietnam would later. The old era was ending, the new one was yet to begin. At such times the future seems especially hard to read and men's attitudes peculiarly fragmented. The editors of *Fortune* probably reflected middle-class American views best at the end of the fifties. They worried little about military gaps, still less about a flagging sense of purpose. Instead optimism was carried to the edge of madness. Their book *America in the Sixties* predicted that by 1969 prosperity would be so great as to make the fifties seem deprived. "Real poverty will be largely abolished in the U.S." Mechanical marvels (few of which materialized) would astound the world. It is easy to expose false prophets after the fact. What was important about *America in the Sixties* was not its mistakes but its field of vision. To the editors, poverty scarcely existed. Only a million families "still look really poor," they said. Young people functioned as a highly specialized group of consumers. Minorities were generally invisible. Everything in the country (except public transportation) was getting better and better. The most interesting thing about Americans was how they exhibited status differences.

So *Fortune* read the future as the past. The post–World War II era had been a time of physical reconstruction. People were tired of the constant challenges they had faced since 1929. President Eisenhower could not abolish crises; he could make them seem less serious. As the fear of communism declined, confidence returned. In 1960 few people wished to sacrifice their new ease of mind, however much liberals, intellectuals, and strategists insisted on it. Wanting things to go on as before, most Americans believed they would. Hence the manic cheerfulness of *Fortune*. Hence also the Democrats' uncertainty.

They knew that prosperity was not so secure as it appeared. They suspected poverty was still widespread. They believed the country to be in mortal peril. Their problem was to win over that majority of Americans for whom General Eisenhower was the man of the year every year. Fortunately for them, he could not succeed himself, and his heir apparent was the most distrusted man in American politics. Governor Rockefeller had the best chance of beating the Democrats. Though 1958 had been a Democratic year he took the governorship of New York away from Averell Harriman. Polls showed him to be the Republican most likely to succeed in 1960. But regular Republicans thought him too liberal. General Eisenhower was angry at Rockefeller for criticizing his defense policies. Richard Nixon, on the other hand, was loved by the regulars, especially for his defects. The President was less enthusiastic, but as Nixon was obliged to run on the Eisenhower record he had to support him anyway. As so often before and after, vanity, prejudice, and ideology combined to make the GOP put its worst foot forward. Dedicated Republicans would almost always rather be Right than President.

Not so the Democrats. Generally they preferred to win. To be nominated, a Democrat had to show that he could best exploit Nixon's reputation. This disqualified Adlai Stevenson. Though liberal Democrats still loved him, the bosses never had. His wit and intellect carried no weight with them. They had accepted him twice before as a suitable lamb for the slaughter. Now that they had a chance to win, the bosses wanted someone untainted by defeat, however inevitable, honorable, or even necessary. Senator Stuart Symington wanted the job, but apart from former President Harry Truman he had little support. Lyndon Johnson had a better chance. As Senate Majority Leader he was famous and successful. Johnson was, with Speaker Sam Rayburn, one of the two most powerful Democratic officeholders. And he had Rayburn's support. But he was not well liked, even in Texas, and he was from the South. Southerners, like Jews, Catholics, and Negroes, were thought incapable of winning national elections. Senator Hubert Humphrey had many friends but little money. Except for some labor unions, he lacked the powerful connections other candidates enjoyed. And many considered him too liberal, for all his enthusiastic anti-communism.

Senator John F. Kennedy was the front-runner. Rich, handsome, and a genuine war hero, he had done brilliantly in the desperate world of Massachusetts politics. After two terms in the House he had unseated Henry Cabot Lodge, who was also rich, handsome, and talented, and who came from what was then an even more distinguished political family. In 1958 Kennedy was re-elected to the Senate by the largest margin of any candidate in Massachusetts history, and the largest of any Democratic Senator that year. Kennedy had unlimited funds and friends, a great organization, and, best of all in the electronic age, the ability to project conviction on camera. All that he lacked were convictions to project, or so his enemies claimed. He was never much interested in civil rights or civil liberties. He ducked the Joe McCarthy issue (McCarthy was a friend of his conservative father). After his best-seller *Profiles in Courage* was published, Eleanor Roosevelt said that presidential decisions ought not to be in the hands of "someone who understands what courage is and admires it, but has not quite the independence to have it."

This was not much of a handicap to Kennedy. Ardent liberals preferred Stevenson, but they would not control the convention. The bosses would, and all they cared about were work and welfare issues, which Kennedy was sound on. And his magnetism attracted the power-oriented liberals who liked a candidate more for the opportunities he offered than the principles he professed. Liberals who had swallowed President Truman would not find Kennedy hard to take. Kennedy only had two real weaknesses: he seemed a cold fish, and he was a Roman Catholic. His reputation for coolness irritated Kennedy men. James MacGregor Burns wrote the best campaign biography of modern times for Kennedy, but the Kennedy people never forgave him for describing their candidate as an unemotional technocrat. What he considered coolness they called self-control. To offset these defects, Kennedy had to run well in the primaries. All that prevented him from doing so was Hubert Humphrey. Kennedy's glamorous image was already such that most Democrats shrank from electoral combat with him. But Humphrey had reason to try. The first primary was in Wisconsin, where Humphrey had an edge. In the 1950's, when both its Senators were Republicans, Humphrey was called the third Senator from Wisconsin for the help he gave its Democrats. Most Wisconsinites live on farms or in small towns, and Humphrey remained a small-town boy at heart. He liked and got along best with people like himself. The biggest concentration of Democrats was in Milwaukee, a good union town. Humphrey had helped the unions before and now he expected their help.

These assets, though real, were not enough. Humphrey toured in a bus while Kennedy's private plane moved him comfortably from point to point. Humphrey had offices in only two of the state's ten congressional districts; Kennedy in eight. Humphrey depended on party leaders and union chiefs who owed him favors, but politicians don't like to commit themselves in primaries, and few gave Humphrey the support Kennedy got from his family, friends, and employees. Humphrey talked too much, as always, and too much about specific issues; Kennedy concentrated on making a good impression. It amounted to trial by television, and Kennedy had every advantage there. By election day Kennedy was expected to win handsomely. In fact, while he won 56 per cent of the vote on April 15, and carried six congressional districts, the margin of his victory was in Roman Catholic areas. In the Protestant districts he did poorly. The Kennedys were depressed. Now they would have to win all the other primaries to prove that their candidate's religion was no real handicap. Humphrey was elated. Having done moderately well in Wisconsin with its many Catholics, what might he do in West Virginia where 95 per cent of the population was Protestant? Humphrey was no bigot and scrupulously avoided the religious issue. But it did exist and was a fact of political life that no candidate could ignore.

Humphrey misread the Wisconsin experience. His own candidacy was finished. Democratic bosses were not about to support a man who couldn't carry the one state where, except for Minnesota itself, he was best known. By campaigning in West Virginia, Humphrey gave Kennedy a chance to undo the harm done him in Wisconsin. For Kennedy to win unopposed in West Virginia would prove nothing; beating Humphrey there would show he appealed to Protestants. The Kennedys poured money and talent into West Virginia and buried the pathetic Humphrey effort. Humphrey withdrew and thereafter Kennedy had a clear track to Los Angeles and the Democratic convention.

All men are vulnerable to events, but politicians especially. Nixon had hardly begun to run on General Eisenhower's record when the U-2 affair came along to tarnish it. Damaging enough in itself, it was all the more so for making the administration seem unable to deal with great affairs. It began on May 5, 1960, when Premier Khrushchev announced that an American military aircraft had been shot down over the Soviet Union. The timing could not have been worse, as a summit meeting was to be held in Paris on the 16th. It was hard to say which party to the fiasco was more compromised by it. If President Eisenhower had forgotten to cancel flights which if discovered might wreck the summit, he was incompetent. If he ordered them he was mischievous. Premier Khrushchev was embarrassed by the suspicion, soon confirmed, that there had been overflights before.* Even so, he was careful to leave President Eisenhower (whom he had earlier called a "courageous" and "sincere lover of peace") a way out. It was the militarists and not the President who were at fault, he suggested. This charge was entirely plausible according to Harold Stassen, former disarmament adviser to the President. He told reporters that the U-2 flight was meant to wreck the summit. (As perhaps it was. Fearing that a successful meeting would end the U-2 program, the CIA accelerated it, thus increasing the risk of exposure.)

The government succumbed to confusion at first. The National Aeronautics and Space Administration, which provided cover for the CIA, claimed that the U-2 was merely a weather plane off course. This alibi collapsed when Russia announced it had the pilot. Secretary of State Christian Herter apparently decided then to follow Premier Khrushchev's lead. NASA issued a vague statement admitting the flight but absolving Washington of responsibility for it. This was acceptable to Russia, and even more so to the Democratic party. Both wanted the President to appear weak, if amiable. Between seeming inept or belligerent, President Eisenhower preferred the latter. On May 9 the State Department admitted that U-2 flights over Russia had been going on for years, though Russia was to blame for them on account of its secretiveness. The President's authority was preserved. The summit conference was destroyed. Vanity prevailed over hope. Yet, the summit

---

* They began after Russia rejected Eisenhower's "open skies" proposal in 1955. As U.S. skies were already open, Russia had nothing to gain by it. Because of the flights, President Eisenhower knew there was no missile gap, though for secrecy's sake he could not say why he knew. Russia feared to negotiate an end to the flights because doing so would force it to admit weakness. In effect, it conspired with America to keep them secret. This was a self-defeating policy which added duplicity to impotence. The ultimate revelation was thus more harmful than an early one would have been. Neither country learned much from this; both continued to make a fetish of secrecy.

could not have accomplished much anyway. General Eisenhower lacked confidence in summit meetings. Like all Presidents, he wanted better relations with the Soviets, but on his own terms. He had nothing new to offer Russia at Paris. The summit was arranged because Premier Khrushchev needed it and Prime Minister Macmillan of England, for whom hope sprang eternal, wanted it. Premier Khrushchev's domestic policy hinged on curbing the arms race, for the Soviets could not afford both guns and butter on the American scale. As a starter Khrushchev had reduced his army by 1.2 million men, throwing sullen officers out of work. Without an American response he could go no further. But President Eisenhower had already cut the U.S. arms budget all he dared, so he couldn't respond to this initiative.

Yet while nothing could have come of the summit except more hot air —which is what summits usually produced anyway—it needn't have been a disaster. It cost Premier Khrushchev the most. He came to Paris and stormed and raged, as he had to. The party leadership was not impressed. He had shown weakness twice, first when he allowed the overflights to go unchallenged, then when he offered the U.S. a loophole after the fact. His power began to fade that May. Eisenhower got off easier. It is hard for an American politician to lose by offending Russia, however clumsily. Though President Eisenhower's place in diplomatic history suffered, his popularity did not. Neither, probably, did Nixon's. The Democrats were buoyed all the same. Few of his admirers thought Eisenhower gained stature from the affair. Even had the President's decision been right, he had arrived at it wrongly.

A feeling grew that events were slipping out of control. The U-2 seemed proof of that. Castro's Cuba did too. Student riots kept General Eisenhower from visiting Japan. Polls showed that the public believed there was a missile gap. Relations with the Soviets got worse. Premier Khrushchev threatened to sign a separate peace with East Germany, thus renewing the Berlin crisis. In June communist delegates walked out of the reconvened disarmament talks at Geneva. All this made foreign affairs seem more desperate and eroded the trust on which Republicans depended. Nixon could not fight an election on Eisenhower's popularity. It was his policies that counted, and people were losing faith in them. By wrecking the summit to save face, President Eisenhower lost the best chance of saving his programs. A détente, however fragile, would have preserved public confidence in them. Instead, Eisenhower's critics got a mouthful of new arguments with which to discredit his policies. They were essential to Kennedy's victory. So in protecting his image Eisenhower sacrificed the foreign and military policies that were his best claim on posterity's gratitude. It was a bad exchange for him, a worse one for the country.

The Democrats came to Los Angeles with more hope than to any nominating convention since 1944. And their enthusiasm survived the convention itself, though it was most notable for the efficiency with which Kennedy's rivals were disposed of. Only Johnson and Stevenson had survived the early skirmishes. Johnson hoped to be the compromise candidate after Stevenson and Kennedy neutralized each other. But Stevenson had waited too long before committing himself. Liberal Democrats still loved him best, but when he failed to raise his standard many took service elsewhere. The rest were disorganized and uncertain. Stevenson sounded out Mayor Richard Daley of Chicago, without whom no candidate from Illinois could succeed, and learned that the bosses were going for Kennedy. It was all over but the shouting then. Stevenson's supporters did a lot of it, staging that rarity, a genuinely spontaneous demonstration. Senator Eugene McCarthy nominated him, saying, "Do not reject this man who has made us all proud to be Democrats. Do not leave this prophet without honor in his own party." All was in vain, as Stevenson knew better than anyone. He hardly lifted a finger to save himself. Kennedy won easily, with legions of floormen and a mass of electronic equipment sweeping the opposition before him.

The main surprise at Los Angeles was his choice of a running mate. Many were astonished that Kennedy picked Lyndon Johnson to run beside him, many more that Johnson proved willing. Not only had their factions been rivals before, but the clash of styles between them was very sharp. Kennedy men were Eastern, intellectual, and swingers. Johnson men were Southern, uncultivated, and square. Some think Kennedy made the offer believing that Johnson would refuse it. Thus he would get credit for trying to bind up the party's wounds without actually having to do so. Others think he appreciated how much Johnson would help the ticket and simply made the politically wisest choice. In fact it was an astute move. The votes Johnson won in the South were vital to Kennedy's victory. Nor was it all that remarkable for Johnson to accept the vice-presidency. He had made a great name for himself as Senate Majority Leader, but if the ticket won in November, as seemed likely, that job would become less important. As leader of the opposition, Johnson had had much freedom of action; as leader of the President's party he would have very little. Since he could add nothing to his reputation by staying in the Senate, there was no reason not to become Vice-President. Then too, after eight years in a national office he might overcome his sectional reputation. Thus Johnson had nothing to lose and enough prospect of gain to make the shift worthwhile. The convention ended with Kennedy proclaiming the New Frontier. It was, perhaps, the most meaningless tag ever given an administration. The New Frontiersmen quickly tired of it. They were stuck with the title all the same.

The Republican convention was even more of a foregone conclusion than the Democratic. Richard Nixon had only one serious rival for the nomination, Governor Rockefeller, and he had said the previous December that he would not run. Then he changed his mind—sort of. By playing Hamlet so often in the sixties, Rockefeller appeared peculiarly indecisive. Actually he was stronger than his presidential bids suggested. Though heir to a great fortune, he had entered the public service while still young (thirty-two), and held offices under three Presidents.* He was even more successful in politics, where his rough good looks, coarse voice, and homely manners went down well. He easily wrested the governorship of New York from Averell Harriman, who had the misfortune of seeming to be what he actually was, a brilliant aristocrat. Rockefeller was an aristocrat too, but he didn't look like one, so people identified with him. He was an outstanding governor, hence a logical candidate for the presidency. The polls said he could have beaten Kennedy. He was certainly as well qualified to run as any Republican. But the regulars distrusted him. Nixon had been an organization man from the start. Rockefeller was a maverick who resigned from the Eisenhower administration so as to criticize its defense policies. And he had expensive ideas about what the country needed. When Rockefeller learned that both business and the professional politicians opposed him, he withdrew. Yet he went on thinking Nixon too conservative on domestic issues and too penurious on defense.

On June 8, 1960, he suddenly announced that Nixon must accept nine anti-administration propositions to have his support. Rockefeller then toured the country on their behalf, widening once more the GOP's split between its liberal amateurs and conservative professionals. This division, which had existed since 1912 when Theodore Roosevelt led the Progressives to disaster, was the party's curse. General Eisenhower's chief service to the GOP had been to narrow it for a time. Now Rockefeller threatened to reopen all the wounds the President had so carefully taped over. No one ever knew if this was essential to Rockefeller's strategy, or a by-product of it. In either case, there was nothing that Richard Nixon needed less than a divisive platform fight. So in two days of secret meetings he agreed to have Rockefeller's basic propositions written into the platform. No doubt he was sorry to repudiate the administration's foreign and domestic policies, but he would regret a platform struggle even more. As it turned out, the "Fourteen-Point Compact of Fifth Ave-

---

* Rockefeller was successively Coordinator of Inter-American Affairs, Assistant Secretary of State for Latin America, and head of the International Advisory Board under Presidents Roosevelt and Truman. He served President Eisenhower as Under Secretary of Health, Education, and Welfare, and as Special Assistant for Foreign Affairs.

nue" was unenforceable. President Eisenhower was outraged by its rejection of his foreign and defense policies, the regulars by its liberalism on domestic matters. In the end the platform, though more liberal than it would otherwise have been, was shaped mostly by the Eisenhower-regular coalition. This hardly mattered to Nixon. He had secured his own nomination and bought off the liberals cheaply. Like Jim Fisk, he might well have said, "Nothing was lost, save honor."

The ease with which Nixon disowned General Eisenhower to be nominated, and then invoked him again to be elected, was the measure of the man. No one in public life was more nakedly ambitious than Richard Nixon. Few cared so little for specific principles. For most of his public life Nixon was known as "Tricky Dick." This was because he early developed a safe way of slandering his opponents. In his first campaign for Congress he did not charge the incumbent with being a communist. What he did was attack "lip-service Americans" and high officials who fronted for "un-American elements, wittingly or otherwise." His headquarters issued a statement by a former lieutenant governor of California charging Nixon's opponent with voting the "Moscow-PAC-Henry Wallace" line. At a time when anti-communist hysteria was advancing, Nixon's opponents were helpless before this guilt-by-insinuation tactic. When accused of smearing them he could say correctly that he had not actually questioned their loyalty. And in refuting his implications, opponents gave them additional circulation. So he was elected to the House in 1946, and to the Senate in 1950.

In 1952 the GOP had seen him as a perfect complement to General Eisenhower. His youth offset the candidate's age, his political experience made up for what was thought to be the General's lack of it, and his reputation as a gut-fighter usefully supplemented Eisenhower's as a statesman. It worked out very nicely. Nixon did have one bad moment, though. During the campaign he was said to have improperly used a small campaign fund while a Senator. The charge was trivial even if true, but it hurt Nixon because the GOP was making great capital out of the supposed contrast between Republican honesty and Democratic corruption. Many party leaders thought Nixon ought to withdraw. Instead he went on network television and staged a melodrama. He described his modest finances, pointed out that his wife wore a plain cloth coat, and announced that his children had been given a dog named Checkers which he would never surrender. He also asked trusting viewers to write the Republican National Committee. A million did so. General Eisenhower was satisfied and welcomed Nixon back with open arms, inspiring a rush of grateful tears.

Nixon went on using the red scare for a time. He blamed the Democrats for twenty years of treason in 1952, and in the next congressional elections he accused the Communist party of working against the GOP because "the candidates running on the Democratic ticket in the key states are almost without exception members of the Democratic party's left-wing clique which has been so blind to the Communist conspiracy and has tolerated it in the United States." But as the furor subsided he used this line less frequently, unlike Joseph McCarthy who could not see that the red threat was played out and so was destroyed. Nixon traveled a great deal, often to political advantage. One tour of Latin America found him the target of anti-American assaults which he endured bravely and profited enormously from. He visited the Soviet Union and got into a shouting match with Premier Khrushchev. The "kitchen debate" was, like the Checkers speech, bad theater but splendid politics.

As candidates, Nixon and Kennedy were well matched for all their differences. Kennedy was handsome, sophisticated, intellectual, and charismatic. Nixon was plain ("I'm no pretty boy," he used to say), square, poorly read, and uninspiring. He was much better known than Kennedy, but also more disliked. His years of red-baiting, his role as the Eisenhower administration's official mucker, as well as his unfailing want of taste made many enemies. Few people genuinely hated Kennedy. Many loved him. The opposite was true of Nixon. But if he was not loved he was admired by Middle Americans. Republican candidates and officeholders everywhere owed him debts and would work hard to discharge them. The Eisenhower record of peace and plenty gave him solid support. He was not rich like Kennedy, yet as the candidate of big business he didn't have to be. Nixon was thought to be conservative. In reality, while he retained his small-town prejudices, he did not indulge them unless all other things were equal—which was rarely. He was prepared to take almost any position if gain was to be had from it. And he was not a Catholic. More than anything else, Kennedy's religion compromised his political assets and made the 1960 campaign unusually close.

But Nixon possessed weaknesses that were ultimately fatal to him. By trying to run everything himself he demoralized his staff and confused his supporters. He mishandled the press, thus offsetting the advantage Republican candidates have in a country where most forms of communication are owned by Republicans. He promised to campaign in all of the fifty states, then stuck to it even after a knee infection put him in the hospital for ten days. He literally wore himself out. Worst of all, he agreed to debate Kennedy on television. Nixon had fancied himself an expert on television ever since the Checkers speech. He told his admiring biographer Earl Mazo before the debates that "sincerity counts above everything else on television. This is something, unfortunately, that many of the public relations experts simply don't understand. They put too much emphasis on how a man is going to look or sound instead of bringing out his basic character and his beliefs." He was soon to learn otherwise.

When Nixon had his first TV debate with Kennedy he was in poor shape. He had lost weight in the hospital, and more after getting out. He was tired and understrength and looked it. He disdained makeup except for a light face powder, and this worsened his appearance because he had unusually translucent skin. TV cameras always made him look unshaven unless his skin was rendered opaque. And Nixon suffered from being a lawyer. He was not only a lawyer by profession, but he thought like one. He always tried to win arguments and score points. On television, however, it is the audience that counts, not the opponent. Kennedy knew this; Nixon did not. Thus, while Nixon did well with the radio audience, Kennedy impressed viewers more. Polls taken later showed that people who only heard the debate thought Nixon had argued best. And his deep, firm speaking voice was more impressive than Kennedy's high-pitched, rapid delivery. But most people viewed the debate, and on TV Kennedy had the edge. According to a Roper poll, of four million Americans who were decisively influenced by the debates, three million voted for Kennedy. Everyone agreed that Nixon recovered in three subsequent encounters. Yet none attracted so large an audience as the first. Nixon's only chief personal advantage over Kennedy, the presumption of his "experience" as against JFK's "immaturity," was lost. So was the election.*

Though Nixon failed to recover his early lead in the polls, he nearly won anyway. He finished with a strong series of telecasts. President Eisenhower, whom he had hoped to win without, was finally asked to campaign and did so effectively. But Nixon played his ace too late. Another mistake was his inability to grasp what Dr. Martin Luther King, Jr., meant to Negro voters. When King was sentenced to four months in the Georgia penitentiary, John Kennedy immediately called Mrs. King and offered his sympathies. His brother Robert did even better by helping secure King's release on bond. Whites paid little attention to the event, blacks were profoundly affected. Dr. King's father, a Baptist minister previously committed to Nixon on religious grounds (which

---

* The debate offered a classic example of what makes people despair of electoral politics. Kennedy favored aid to anti-Castro exiles in the hope they would overthrow the regime. The administration publicly took a moderate line on Cuba while it was secretly organizing an invasion force. Nixon believed Kennedy knew this (as apparently he did) and that Kennedy took unfair advantage of him by criticizing the government for failing to do what in fact it was doing but could not admit. This made Nixon angry, so he accused Kennedy of wanting to intervene illegally in Cuba. Liberal commentators gave Nixon high marks for advocating due process. Kennedy was cautioned against adventurism. But Nixon never forgave Kennedy for making him defend moderation when he favored excess.

prompted JFK to observe philosophically that we all have our fathers), now swung to Kennedy. Fortuitously, a million pamphlets describing the incident went out. Negroes provided the margin of Kennedy's victory. 250,000 voted for him in Illinois, which he carried by 9,000 votes. The same number supported him in Michigan, where he won by 67,000 votes. Nixon lost these states not because he opposed civil rights, but because the winning gesture was so foreign to him. It was not his style, and style was what the election was all about.

To bad judgment was added bad luck. Arthur Burns, a leading Republican economist, predicted a recession for late 1960 and urged more government spending to avert it. President Eisenhower ignored him and the recession developed on schedule, reaching its lowest point in mid-October when it would hurt Nixon most. So Kennedy became President, but by a hair. If 4,500 more voters in Illinois and 28,000 in Texas had gone against him, Nixon would have won by two electoral votes..

Kennedy's victory assured the realization of his dark prophecies, though his manner would make the confrontations to come seem less frightening than they were. Because of him the early sixties would also be remembered as more hopeful than they were. Richard Nixon could not have managed such a feat, yet he might not have needed to. He admired General Eisenhower's habit of avoiding conflict when possible. Hope could not wither because of him, since he never encouraged it to bloom. John Kennedy was abler and more liberal than Nixon, but not necessarily better prepared or attached to more useful propositions. Like most men, he lived in the past. He called on Americans to face great challenges, but the ones he meant had come and gone already. Russia was no longer a threat to American survival, if indeed it had ever been. China was comparatively weak and would remain so. Cuba was a trivial wound, and a largely self-inflicted one at that. Kennedy was mostly blind to what would dominate American life in the sixties. So, of course, were other public men.

They worried about the missile gap when it was the arms race itself that mattered. They warned the civil rights movement against asking too much too soon, though it was really a case of too little too late. They were preoccupied with affairs abroad while it was conditions at home that wanted attention. Every President since 1940 had been chiefly concerned with foreign policy. The country had prospered all the same. But those problems that did not solve themselves got worse. The economy flourished; the cities decayed. Airports and highways were built; railroad passenger service collapsed. Science and technology solved old difficulties while creating new ones—pollution, congestion, and contamination followed each advance. Kennedy had promised new leadership and new departures, yet his ideas were commonplace. The New Frontier at home was only the New Deal writ small. Overseas it meant the same expansive internationalism that was already too familiar. A new age was coming which these formulas did not provide for. Few administrations ever took office with more self-assurance than Kennedy's; few had less reason for it. Confidence is no substitute for wisdom, though men would have it so. If it were, the next several years would have turned out differently.

PROFILE:
The Supreme Court

THE SUPREME COURT, once revered by conservative patriots, lost status throughout the decade. Its desegregation decisions since 1954 had aroused hostile passions, in the South first and then later in the North. The Court threw out many of the worst legislative and judicial deeds of the McCarthy era. But nothing so aroused Middle Americans as the Court's 1962 decision that compulsory prayer in public schools was unconstitutional. This ruling was, perhaps, of all its unpopular decisions in the sixties the most frequently disregarded. Many schools carried on with prayers as usual, and few local officials were rash enough to interfere. On the national level it provoked such outbursts of devotion as had not been seen since the war. Former President Hoover said the ruling represented the "disintegration of a sacred American heritage." General Eisenhower remarked that he "always thought that this nation was essentially a religious one." Cardinal Cushing of Boston said it would make good propaganda for the Reds. Congress fulminated for three days. Representative Frank Becker got chairman Emanuel Celler of the Judiciary Committee to hold hearings on the matter. Becker favored a bill to restore prayer, and also to gain constitutional authorization for the phrases "under God" in the Oath of Allegiance, and "In God We Trust" on the coinage. There were 146 other congressional proposals along these lines. Gerald Ford of

Michigan declared that he received more mail about prayer than any other subject. One Congressman presented Chairman Celler with a petition bearing 170,000 signatures asking that God be restored to his rightful place in the classroom.

A host of politicians appeared before the Committee on prayer's behalf. A stream of ministers praised the Court and demanded that the schools remain free of worship. Congressman Becker said, "Invocations, duties, oaths taken on the Bible are as American and as universal as a taste for apple pie, or ice cream or watermelon. . . ." Congressman Wyman wanted the states to make applicants for driver's licenses express their belief in a supreme being (the God of their choice, naturally). Governor Wallace of Alabama took time out from his presidential campaign to testify. He noted that God is love and prayers promote goodness. This spectacle inspired Murray Kempton to say that all Congress really needed to do after its hearings was to draft a single sentence: "The people and the Congress of the United States hereby repeal and make void the doctrine that God is not mocked."

The Court did not, however, offend only conservatives. On March 21, 1966, it upheld the conviction of Ralph Ginzburg, publisher of *Eros* magazine. Previously the Court had ruled that a publication or film was obscene if it (1) appealed to a "prurient interest in sex," (2) was "patently offensive" by "contemporary community standards," and (3) was "utterly without redeeming social value." In practice this meant that almost any published writing was acceptable, while films and pictures could not show copulation—though even here there was some leeway. Ginzburg's conviction seemed to throw the whole matter into the air again. *Eros* was less racy than other magazines. What the Court objected to was not so much its contents as the way it was promoted. Ginzburg applied for bulk-mailing privileges in towns with suggestive names (Intercourse, Climax, Blue Balls). His advertising campaign as a whole, the Court declared, was permeated by "the leer of the sensualist." This introduced an exceptionally difficult standard for judging obscenity. Sensual leering was out. But what was a leer and what a mere smirk? And how could a thing, not obscene in its own right, become so by promotion? Solomon himself would have found this criterion trying. Most judges, lacking divine assistance, found it impossible to apply.*

Prayer was the Court's most unpopular area of decision-making. Obscenity was its greatest failure. Instead of clarifying the confusion, the Court compounded it. Even so, the Warren Court remained the most outstanding of modern times, and one of the greatest in American history. When Chief Justice Earl Warren resigned in 1969, everyone agreed it was the end of an era. Not that Warren had been a singularly powerful chief justice on the order of John Marshall. He had not pressed his views unduly. Even if he had, the Court changed so much in his sixteen years (a total of seventeen justices were involved) that even a more forceful man could not have shaped its course. But Warren symbolized the period of judicial activism that began in 1954 with the passage of *Brown v. Board of Education.* The John Birch Society acknowledged this by putting up "Impeach Earl Warren" billboards everywhere. After striking down school segregation, the Warren Court went on to expand civil rights. The rights of suspected criminals were more firmly established. The one-man, one-vote principle was extended. (Warren himself considered *Baker v. Carr,* which struck down malapportionment in Tennessee, the most far-reaching decision.) The Court, and Warren in particular, were roundly condemned. School desegregation was widely resented. The police were thought to have been unbearably handicapped.

But the *Gideon* decision only extended the right of legal counsel to the minority of states that lacked such statutes. In practice, *Miranda* and *Escobedo* had little effect on police work. The Court upheld stop-and-frisk laws that allowed police to make searches without showing cause. Here, as elsewhere, the Court was made the scapegoat for social problems its critics could not deal with.

President Johnson tried to replace Warren by elevating Justice Abe Fortas, a liberal, to his seat. Fortas was not well liked by the Senate, which refused to confirm him. Later he was found to have taken money

* Upholding Ginzburg's conviction settled nothing. Years later he was still out on bond pending various complex legal maneuvers, and publishing a new magazine, *Avant-Garde,* that was sexier than *Eros.* In the meantime community standards, in large cities anyway, changed so much that Ginzburg was left behind. If he did finally go to jail it would be for violating obsolete taboos.

from a foundation, somewhat irregularly it was said, and driven from the bench. President Nixon finally appointed Warren Earl Burger chief justice. He was a little-known federal jurist whose principal qualification appeared to be that he was a judicial inactivist. Nixon tried twice to replace Fortas with obscure Southern judges whose views were thought congenial to Senator Strom Thurmond. The Senate denied confirmation to both, and Nixon had to settle for a Northern judge whose position resembled Chief Justice Burger's. In a fit of pique the President declared that his first two choices had been turned down for coming from the South.

The Senate did not much like being called bigoted. Nor did it agree with the President that its constitutional role was to rubber-stamp his nominees. The Constitution provided that the President was to appoint justices with the advice and consent of the Senate. As he did not seek the Senate's advice, it withheld its consent. Nixon went on believing in Executive omnipotence all the same. And he did succeed in putting two moderately conservative judges on the Court. Of the remaining liberals, Justice Black was old and Justice Douglas in ill health. Nixon would soon be able to replace them with conservatives. They would then outnumber the liberals, and the age of Supreme Court activism would be over. The Warren Court's great record was safe, but it was not likely to be improved on for a while.

2 BUILDING CAMELOT

On JANUARY 17, 1961, President Eisenhower closed the old era with his Farewell Address; three days later President Kennedy opened the new one at his inaugural. The two speeches, like the men and their times, could not have been more different. Each perfectly reflected its author. Eisenhower's ponderous language eased the shock of his warning against the military-industrial complex. "The potential for the disastrous rise of misplaced power exists and will persist. . . . The prospect of domination of the nation's scholars by federal employment, project allocations, and the power of money . . . is gravely to be regarded."* Kennedy sounded better: "We observe today not a victory of party but a celebration of freedom. . . . Now the trumpet summons us again" to "forge against these enemies a grand and global alliance." His affection for verbal tricks, though, was never more pronounced: "If a free society cannot help the many who are poor, it cannot save the few who are rich. . . . Let us never negotiate out of fear, let us never fear to negotiate. . . . Ask not what your country can do for you; ask what you can do for your country."

President Eisenhower's last speech in office became his most famous and widely disregarded address. Everyone remarked on the old patriot's good sense. The demand for new weapons did not abate. President Kennedy's inaugural statements won even more praise. The shift from blandness to bombast in presidential oratory was so startling that few bothered to ask what the slogans meant. People were enjoined to struggle and

---

* The *New York Daily News* headlined his speech: BEWARE OF EGGHEADS, MUNITION LOBBY: IKE.

sacrifice. But who was to sacrifice, and for what? Menace and promise were mixed together, the one giving spice to the other. This was good theater, perhaps even good politics, but what sort of future did it imply? The President's State of the Union Message which followed soon after was not much more illuminating. It had a little something for everyone. Anti-communists were placated when Kennedy said, "We must never be lulled into believing that either [Russia or China] has yielded its ambition for world domination." Pacifists were warmed by promises of fresh overtures to the Soviets. The Peace Corps would make foreign aid more human and attractive. Militarists were offered new arms, liberals money to relieve ignorance and poverty. It was nice to think that you could have plenty of guns and butter too, nicer still to believe that you could have both another arms race and a settlement with Russia. But in the real world one must choose between opposites, and President Kennedy had already done so.

His appointments hinted at the direction he would take. Outstanding liberals like John Kenneth Galbraith, the distinguished historian Edwin Reischauer, and Adlai Stevenson were made ambassadors (to India, Japan, and the United Nations). But ambassadors do not make policy. In Kennedy's administration the men who did were people like Theodore Sorensen, Dean Rusk, McGeorge and William Bundy, Maxwell Taylor, and Walt Whitman Rostow. They were not so much liberals as technocrats, men of power rather than passion. Unsentimental, except about the President (and sometimes each other), they made a fetish of energy and style. The Cold War, it seemed, would be won on the squash courts and dance floors of Washington. Robert McNamara was the supreme example of this type. Though less sociable than many, he was characteristically brilliant, hard-working, competitive, and athletic. He was the most able and confident man ever to be Secretary of Defense.* At the time few guessed that such men would become legendary figures. Technocrats, however graceful and witty, do not a round table make. President Kennedy seemed too opportunistic ever to be King Arthur. Which only shows how life surpasses art. Out of these unlikely materials history would fashion a national legend equal to any that had gone before.

But first the reality. President Kennedy meant to win the Cold War

---

* Robert Strange McNamara was an expert at applying statistical analysis to management problems. After receiving an M.B.A. from the Harvard Business School in 1940, he was appointed to its faculty. During the war he was a staff officer. Afterward he joined a group of independent business analysts called the whiz kids. His first assignment with them concerned the Ford Motor Company. It was so challenging that he stayed with Ford and fourteen years later became the first man outside the family to be its president. Having exhausted Ford's possibilities, he resigned to join the Kennedy administration. His hair lay flat, inspiring President Johnson to call him the man with the sta-combed hair.

and restore order to the world. This was to be done by taking the lead in strategic weapons and building mobile strike units to suppress wars of national liberation. Having a strategic advantage would enable the U.S. to bargain with Russia from strength.* Counter-insurgency forces would preserve the status quo everywhere else. Thus America's dominant position would be sustained. To this end McNamara began building a military establishment theoretically capable of fighting one minor and two major wars at once. And he greatly expanded the strategic weapons arsenal, though the need for it soon vanished. On taking office McNamara learned that, as President Eisenhower had said, the missile gap was a "fiction." He made this public, only to have the White House contradict him. Having just campaigned on the missile gap, President Kennedy could not immediately admit it never existed. But the truth had to out finally, and by October the Pentagon was confessing parity with the Soviets in missiles. Soon it would have a clear lead, for Russia had scrapped its liquid-fueled ICBM while the U.S. had gone on deploying its own. When Russia began emplacing its solid-fuel missiles the U.S. would long since have put hundreds of first-generation ICBM's into service. The administration pressed on regardless. The Polaris submarine program was stepped up by half. A 100 per cent increase in the production of solid-fuel Minuteman missiles was ordered. The number of nuclear bombers on fifteen-minute alert grew by 50 per cent. Soon the U.S. lead was embarrassingly great, and getting more so by the month.

The strategic weapons program thus required a new rationale. Massive retaliation was a second-strike doctrine. It assumed a nuclear force that could survive an enemy first strike and wipe out his cities in return. The cost of attacking the U.S. would thus be prohibitive while the American force, since clearly defensive, would not provoke attack. This could be accomplished, it was thought, by a force approximately equal to the Soviets'. A modest lead over Russia was consistent with the older doctrine, a huge one was not. And what was the point of being able to destroy a possible aggressor many times over when once or twice would do? To justify the expense, McNamara therefore began talking about *counterforce*. This new doctrine aimed at destroying the enemy's strategic arms. McNamara suggested it was more humane because directed

---

* "Bargaining from strength" was one of the Cold War's most delusory concepts. Both sides aimed for strength, and the U.S. sometimes got it. Negotiations rarely followed. Strong nations need not bargain, and weak ones dare not. Real negotiation assumes equality, otherwise there is nothing to bargain over. A rough parity in strategic weapons between the U.S. and Russia existed at the beginning and end of the 1960's. Nothing happened either time because America insisted on an overwhelming lead. "We arm to parley," people said, echoing Churchill, but the one precluded the other. Being strong, America saw no reason to compromise; being weak, Russia could not afford to.

at weapons rather than cities. It was certainly more ambitious. Counter-force was a first-strike theory because to take out the enemy's planes and missiles you had to hit them on the ground. It made sense only if you intended a pre-emptive strike. Counterforce was thus both offensive and provocative. The enemy was threatened with a Pearl Harbor and incited to hit the U.S. first. Though counterforce was a very dangerous propo-sition, in the end little came of it. The government never embraced it directly. The Soviets were not frightened into launching a pre-emptive strike. Probably it was just another case of the lag between technology and theory. Major weapons systems were often built simply because the capacity for making them existed. The reasons for doing so were devised later. So it was with strategic missiles. They were desirable in the first place because they stabilized the balance of terror. Manned aircraft were dangerous because of their vulnerability. They could not really be pro-tected on the ground, and their limited flight capacity meant that, once airborne, decisions about them had to be made quickly. Not so with mis-siles. When land based they could be dispersed, concealed, and pro-tected. In Polaris submarines they were even more secure. Hence they allowed more time for reflection and reduced the chances of accident or error.

But the advantages missiles created were wasted. First the U.S. was panicked by Sputnik, then it overreacted. President Kennedy developed an "overkill" capacity that panicked the Russians in turn. They resolved to catch up and began doing so by the decade's end, when the whole cycle started repeating itself. The chance to stabilize the arms race was lost. Billions were spent only to make the risks worse. In 1960 each side had fewer than a hundred long-range missiles; in 1970 each had perhaps a thousand more powerful ones. "Better safe than sorry," the Kennedy administration had implied. In the end, everyone was no safer and a lot sorrier. Short of actual disarmament, Americans were most secure when the U.S. and Russia deterred each other equally. But that condition gen-erated feelings of insecurity. Getting ahead of Russia relieved them while tipping the balance of terror dangerously. The worse things got the better people felt, and vice versa. On this emotional reflex the stra-tegic arms race was built. All the elaborate strategies used to justify it were only the tribute fear paid to reason.

Defense contractors were well equipped for the Kennedy arms race. In the Eisenhower years they had made an art of milking the Treasury. In 1962 Senator John L. McClelland's investigating committee showed how this brand of "socialism for the rich" worked. The committee found cases where contractors made profits of 40 per cent or more. The sub-contracting system by which the subcontractors' profit was added to the main contractor's costs helped greatly. The Nike ABM system was a case in point. Western Electric, the prime contractor, made a seemingly modest profit of $112.5 million on a total contract of $1.545 billion. But the $1.4 billion worth of costs included the subcontractors' profits. Douglas Aircraft was paid $644.5 million for producing missiles. This sum included Douglas's own profit of $45.6 million, 7.6 per cent of the total. But Douglas actually performed only 17.2 per cent of the work. Thus the profit on what it actually did amounted to 44.3 per cent. Moreover, its sub-subcontractors' profits were included in the bill they submitted to Douglas, again in the bill Douglas sent to Western Electric, and finally in Western Electric's bill to the government.

Other favorite devices included padding the overhead (on which no taxes were paid, whereas profits were taxed at fifty cents on the dollar). The McClelland Committee found that Douglas Aircraft was still charging off to overhead on its Nike missile contract the development costs of the DC-3. Companies that made design or production errors often got new contracts to repair them—making a profit both times. If they ran short of cash they sometimes got advance payments. The government then provided their operating capital besides paying them a profit. Excessive design changes were deliberately made to exploit a system that rewarded error and penalized efficiency. Meanwhile, the bidding system declined so that most contracts were simply negotiated, often between military officers and their retired colleagues now working for the very companies they had once negotiated with while on active service. There were other abuses too, all tolerated because the military did not complain, the contractors were enriched, and the communities they worked in got fat payrolls. Military procurement was the most perfectly realized pork barrel in the history of a nation rich with them.

The spending boosts presided over by McNamara—$7 billion additional in 1961, $10 billion more over the next two years—ought to have made him popular with the military-industrial complex. That they didn't was due equally to his strengths and weaknesses. He was impatient with ignorance, which offended Congress. His extraordinary grasp of facts showed up the military. No one likes to be beaten at his own game, and McNamara was always doing that to the brass, who missed their old superiors, "those dumb bastards," as one general affectionately called them. And McNamara tried to offset the new costs by making savings elsewhere. This was universally resented, for waste was an essential feature of the system. He closed redundant military installations. Worse still, he tried to institute strict accounting and management procedures.

President Eisenhower had never been able to control waste. He had actually increased it by cutting back the government's own research and manufacturing capability in favor of private contractors, even though the government's shipyards, arsenals, and other facilities did the work cheaper and often better. They also provided yardsticks for measuring the performance of private contractors. But Eisenhower disliked them for ideological reasons and thought the private sector showed more initiative, as indeed it did—especially when it came to maximizing profits. All he did to curb waste was to cancel programs when they got out of hand. Hence, $1.5 billion was wasted on the Nike ABM system. But had Eisenhower not canceled it another $12 billion at least would have gone down the drain.*

As its finest product, McNamara was no less devoted to capitalism than Eisenhower was. He didn't think profiteering was essential to it, though. Hence he tried to institute cost-efficiency as the chief procurement goal. Not the best possible weapon but the best combination of cost and performance was his ambition. To fulfill it he brought in efficiency experts like himself and transformed the Pentagon's bookkeeping and management techniques. This too was resented. The brass couldn't understand the new methods. Contractors had to work overtime thwarting them. In the end, McNamara's reforms made little difference. He periodically announced fresh savings. The arms budget swallowed them up. Profiteering went on. McNamara was the smartest and most imperious man ever to challenge the Pentagon. It defeated him anyway, as it had all who went before him. This reinforced the Eisenhower doctrine that the military-industrial complex could not be mastered, only contained. Not human frailty but the system itself was at fault. Once its assumptions were granted, no amount of talent and drive could alter its course. The Kennedy administration thought sophistication a match for power. It planned to make the military greater than before, and yet more docile. Eisenhower knew better, as later events proved.

That President Kennedy's military program was a disaster could not be seen clearly until afterward. His domestic failures were immediately evident. While modest by comparison with his other efforts, Kennedy's internal program faced trouble from the start. He had a big congressional majority in theory only. Of 261 Democrats in the House, 101 came from Southern and border states. Mostly conservatives, they were closer on many issues to the GOP than to their own party. It was barely possible that a coalition of liberal Democrats and liberal Republicans could offset the conservative elements in both parties. And, for a moment, it did. The Rules Committee, an obstacle to liberal measures, was reformed by enlarging it, but only by a margin of five votes. That this was

---

* There was no end to the contracts disposed of in this way. The Army spent $300 million on a missile system that never met performance standards and proved unusable. The Navy spent $500 million on a seaplane contract that never produced a serviceable aircraft. The ill-fated Navaho missile project cost $750 million, the nuclear-powered aircraft $1 billion, a nuclear rocket engine $2 billion, and so on.

not a workable minority soon became apparent. President Kennedy sent down a minimum-wage bill and lost it. He later got the minimum raised by the Senate, whose liberal majority assured passage. Then the bill went to a House Conference Committee chaired by Adam Clayton Powell who steered it through. But this did not restore President Kennedy's lost prestige.

He lost still more when his education bill went down. Catholics were irritated by his aid-to-education proposals which excluded parochial schools. Kennedy then sent over three separate bills, one of which provided forty-year loans to private and parochial schools. All three were killed in the Rules Committee when a Northern Catholic member defected. When James J. Delaney learned that conservatives meant to kill the bill aiding parochial schools, he joined with them to kill the other two. After this the President had less influence in the House. Liberals were irritated that he made deals with conservatives who wouldn't stay bought. (By proposing a bill to make grants to all states, whether their schools were racially integrated or not, for example.) He didn't punish Delaney, thus showing weakness again. Some Congressmen lost their respect for him, others their fear. As a result, while Congress put up billions more for defense, a few dollars for the Peace Corps, and half a billion for the Alliance for Progress, it turned Kennedy down on Medicare, federal aid to education, tax revision, postal increases, and long-term foreign aid appropriations. When urged to go to the people over Congress's head, he had an aide say, "The President feels that there is never an appropriate time for opening a cold war with Congress." So much for the New Frontier at home.

While President Kennedy's domestic policy was dismal rather than disastrous, his foreign policy was both. This was not entirely his fault. Eisenhower had left him several sticky problems, but he contrived to worsen them—Cuba especially. Though Castro was much admired in the U.S. when he came to power, the applause soon ended. His regime was scarcely seven months old when *Life* magazine wrote, "What was glory and noble purpose in January has turned into demagoguery in July." President Eisenhower cut the Cuban sugar import quota by 95 per cent. In October 1959 he declared an economic embargo against Cuba. The CIA began training Cuban exiles in the arts of war.

Why had Cuban-American relations reached this low point so soon? It became dogma that Castro had gained power through American benevolence by posing as a liberal democrat. Later it was asserted that he had been a lackey of Moscow all the while. What seemed ingratitude soon proved to be treachery. America erred only in seeing the threat too late and reacting too mildly. As this view met the needs of both countries, it persisted. Castro used it to show the communist world's debt to him, Washington to excuse the errors of three administrations. But only those who had to believed it. Castro was quite open from the start. When Herbert Matthews of the *New York Times* met Castro in the Sierra Maestra on February 17, 1957, he described Fidel as nationalistic, socialistic, anti-American, and noncommunist.* The U.S. had been a good neighbor to Cuba's President Batista. The American ambassador to Cuba, Earl Smith, thought Castro merely a "ruffian" and a "bandit." The U.S. Air Force decorated a Cuban general after he bombed the town of Cienfuegos, causing thousands of casualties (in fairness, he didn't get the award for this atrocity). The U.S. military mission went on instructing Batista's forces until he fell. Washington did restrict the flow of arms to Batista in 1958. He had more than he could use by then anyhow. It never allowed the rebels to buy arms in America. Castro had every reason to be anti-American, the *New York Times* notwithstanding. Castro planned a socialist revolution and said so. He also claimed it would be democratic, perhaps honestly. Yet the one precluded the other, as events soon showed.

Castro won power not because he was strong but because Batista was weak. The peasants did not flock to Castro. The general strike called on the eve of victory failed for want of proletarian support. The Communist party denounced Castro for "putschism" and only joined in at the end. Such backing as he had came mainly from the business and professional classes alienated by Batista's cruelty and incompetence. They wanted a liberal revolution, Castro a radical one. When he began implementing his radical revolution they turned against him. Castro had then to attract a new base of support and devise a new ideology. He talked vaguely at first about something called "humanism." When the middle class began deserting him he dropped it in favor of Marxism-Leninism, but not as defined by Moscow. Having won power as guerrilla fighters, he and his most visible ideologist Che Guevara naturally thought rural warfare important. In developing his revolutionary thesis after the fact, Guevara, Theodore Draper points out, argued that since guerrillas must fight in the countryside they must have the support of peasants. "Thus, Guevara does not derive guerrilla warfare from the nature of an agrarian revolution; he derives the agrarian revolution from guerrilla warfare."

As Castro replaced the middle class with the peasantry, its role in the fight against Batista was suppressed and the peasantry's exalted. The past was revised to conform with the present. Democracy was forgotten too. Bourgeois subversion made it inconvenient. Peasant apathy ren-

---

* This interview made Castro famous. William Buckley blamed Matthews for the revolution's success in an essay called "I Got My Job Through the *New York Times.*" But though powerful, the *Times* was not that powerful.

dered it superfluous. The logic of internal events thus drove Castro toward authoritarianism. As Draper put it: "Castroism is a leader in search of a movement, a movement in search of power, and power in search of an ideology." Castro took power with one ideology and held it with another. This would probably have happened even had the U.S. reacted with wisdom and grace. In the event, Washington guaranteed the collapse of democracy in Cuba while forcing it into the communist bloc.

Like all satisfied powers, the U.S. wanted to keep its sphere of influence stable. Latin America's historic duty was to provide the U.S. with raw materials and a market for finished goods. In return Washington promised to keep the area from being exploited by anyone else. The U.S. liked the rulers it dealt with to be progressive and democratic. There being few such in Latin America, it had to get along with many dictators and oligarchs. Though ethically and ideologically repugnant, they usually had the virtue of being hospitable to American business. Thus, while in theory the U.S. was pledged to advance democracy everywhere, in practice a regime could hardly be too squalid so long as it retained the confidence of investors and voted right in the UN. The main exceptions were in countries so insignificant as to invite contempt— Haiti and the Dominican Republic, for example. America could take a lofty moral position on the cheap in such places, and sometimes did. Small and weak governments that became odious were occupied or, more frequently in later years, subverted. (Like the Guatemalan regime overturned by the CIA in 1954.) Larger countries were more troublesome. Revolutionary Mexico gave continuing offense to the U.S. oil industry for more than twenty years. Perón's pro-fascist Argentina also hampered inter-American unity. In the end, though, the U.S. usually got what it wanted, if not always all it wanted.

By definition, then, no radical government in Latin America could avoid conflict with the U.S., Cuba least of all. Americans had many interests to protect there. They owned 35 per cent of the sugar industry, 90 per cent of the public utilities, and with Royal Dutch Shell all of the oil refineries. The U.S. Navy had a great base at Guantanamo Bay. To get and keep these advantages the U.S. had repeatedly intervened in Cuba, a privilege allowed it by the Cuban constitution until 1934. Avarice sustained this policy, though rarely in public. "I am doing my best to persuade the Cubans that if only they will be good they will be happy; I am seeking the very minimum of interference necessary to make them good," Theodore Roosevelt observed while suppressing an insurrection. Later Presidents felt the same, agreeing that what was good for business was good for Cuba.

As a radical nationalist Castro had two reasons for confiscating American-owned property. The socialist revolution required it, so did independence. Cuba would never be free as long as Americans played a crucial role in its economy. Castro was prepared to buy them out, but not at their own figure and not in cash. Mexico had paid for the American-owned property it confiscated after its revolution with long-term state bonds. Castro offered to do the same and was refused. Nor were American owners amused when he suggested payment on the basis of assessed value. Under Batista their property had been assessed at only a fraction of real value. Castro was prepared to bargain, the owners refused. All or nothing was their position. Nothing was what they got. Matters came to a head when American-owned refineries wouldn't process Russian oil. This left Cuba with no choice except to take them over. Cuban-American relations then collapsed.* American trade with Cuba was embargoed. The CIA began trying to undermine Castro's regime. Communist countries offered him guns and aid. Castro had to accept them. In 1959 he repeatedly denied being a communist, in 1960 he no longer bothered. Later he announced that not only was he now a communist but always had been, thus "proving" his detractors to have been right all along. What this really proved was how self-fulfilling prophecies work. By treating him as a communist the U.S. forced him to become one.

Fidel paid a big price for communist aid, but it was not so much as the U.S. demanded. America would have had him call off the revolution. Instead he preserved it and his independence too. Russia was too far away to dominate him. Yet Russia could not abandon him after Cuba went communist, which was probably why it did. The Soviets got an expensive, useless, and truculent ally. The Cuban people were faced with years of austerity and struggle. The U.S. lost some money and more face. What began as a self-serving policy turned out to be self-defeating as well.

When President Kennedy took office, people believed relations with Cuba could hardly get worse. This was an error he soon corrected. On April 17, 1961, he launched an invasion of Cuba so poorly planned that Castro needed only four days to destroy it. The administration was led to disaster partly through inexperience. The CIA presented it with a

---

* Castro didn't help matters by executing some of Batista's men. They were tried secretly for a time, then publicly. Americans complained that the trials were too secret at first, too public later, and too vindictive throughout. Such criticisms baffled and outraged revolutionary Cubans. No one doubted that the men were guilty. In the event, only about five hundred were executed, whereas Batista had killed many times that number. Compared with other revolutions, Cuba's was nearly bloodless. And had there been any fewer executions, the Cubans maintained, Batista's surviving victims would have resorted to lynch law. Americans continued to attack the executions. Cubans were therefore persuaded that Yankee hypocrisy would always impede justice.

plan guaranteed to overthrow Castro with a landing force of Cuban émigrés. The Joint Chiefs agreed. As they had been subverting governments and winning wars for so long, President Kennedy believed them. Had he looked at their records more closely he might not have. The CIA did indeed help overthrow the governments of Iran, Guatemala, and Laos. But they had also tried and failed in Costa Rica, Burma, and Indonesia. The Joint Chiefs, Kennedy would discover, automatically favored every hostile act. Their consent meant less than nothing.

A more suspicious President might have gone along anyway. Having taken a tough line on Cuba as a candidate, Kennedy feared having his bluff called. And so many in Washington knew of the CIA's plan that he could not stop it without being embarrassed politically. The CIA assured him that while Castro was a grave threat to the inter-American system, he lacked support in Cuba and could be easily overthrown. That Castro could hardly be both a menace and a pushover seems not to have occurred to anyone except Senator William Fulbright. His appeal for isolating Cuba rather than invading it moved no one but Arthur Schlesinger, Jr. And Schlesinger was the author of a white paper explaining why Castro had to go.* He was not much help to Fulbright, nor was anyone else on the President's staff. A further difficulty was that the administration didn't understand the plan it authorized. President Kennedy thought the landing force could fade into the mountains if the Cuban people did not respond. But the landing site was many swamp-filled miles from the mountains. Though in theory easily defended, it was not a good place from which to jump off. Which suggests that the CIA meant the émigrés to stay there, establish a provisional government, and call on the U.S. for military support. That was certainly the émigrés' impression.

So the operation proceeded in strictest secrecy—outside of Washington, Miami, Guatemala, and Cuba. Washington knew because the CIA had to drum up broad support in the government for it. Miami knew because the CIA had done everything but take out classified ads to get volunteers. Guatemala knew because the exile brigade was training there, as a local newspaper pointed out. And Castro knew because everyone else did—except the American people. As they were the only ones who could have stopped the invasion, the CIA's security program was adequate to its needs. When Cuba told the UN that America was preparing to attack it, no one was more genuinely indignant than Ambassador Stevenson. Security could hardly do more. American journalists helped out too. Some printed information about the Guatemalan training camps. But though both the *New Republic* and the *New York Times* learned of

---

* Not because the U.S. was against the revolution (though it was), Schlesinger insisted, but because Castro was a communist (which he was not).

the invasion in advance, neither said so. President Kennedy was not especially grateful. First he blamed the *Times* for printing its story about the training camps. (Castro, it seems, depended on the *Times* for military intelligence.) Afterward he blamed it for not telling the whole truth and making the landing impossible.

In the event, the *Times* did not restrain President Kennedy. On April 15 Cuba's airfields were bombed. These raids were supposed to destroy Castro's air force but didn't. The President was told they had, so he canceled the second strike hoping to ease such fears as the first had raised abroad. The brigade went ashore at the Bay of Pigs on Monday, April 17. Castro's six operational aircraft, including two T-33 jet trainers, knocked out the brigade's air force and sank the ship carrying its reserve ammunition. Castro personally organized a counterattack that soon cleared the beach. Of fifteen hundred invaders all but three hundred were taken, along with four of their five tanks. The Cuban people failed to rise. Most stayed loyal, or at least scared. The rest were imprisoned, a routine precaution that seems to have taken the CIA unawares.*

The publicity campaign went no better. When the invasion began a press agent announced that it was being directed by something called the Cuban Revolutionary Council. There was a Cuban Revolutionary Council, but it was being held incommunicado by the CIA. The U.S. went on denying responsibility for some days. No one except Ambassador Stevenson believed this. And he was pressed so hard in the UN that he descended finally to arguing that the invasion's failure proved America had not staged it. Then the President confessed, making Stevenson seem either a cynic or a fool. He was neither, just uninformed. Knowing he would disapprove, the administration did not tell him of what was planned. Later it misled him, thinking, no doubt, that he could lie better if he believed what he was saying. That a diplomat lies or says half-truths does not make him less worth hearing. He may let the truth slip. Omissions may suggest it. But there is no point in attending a man who is himself ignorant. The Bay of Pigs showed that far from making policy, Stevenson didn't even know what it was. He went on speaking as well as before. There was no longer much reason to take him seriously.

The Bay of Pigs fiasco, as everyone now called it, had other consequences. It removed any chance of further dealings with Castro. When the Cuban government made overtures to the State Department afterward, it was told only that "communism in this hemisphere is not ne-

---

* The genuine resistance movement in Cuba got little help from the CIA. It thought some members too left wing. And it favored an invasion anyway. The underground was thus too weak to rise when the landing started. Much of it was caught in Castro's dragnet. What was left resorted to futile acts of terror during the next several years.

gotiable." Henceforth American policy toward Cuba would be to have none. In accepting responsibility for the affair President Kennedy prevented Russia from blaming it on the CIA, thus forcing Premier Khrushchev to take a harder line. As a candidate Kennedy had criticized President Eisenhower's handling of the U-2 incident. Now he acted the same way, and for much the same reason. Having less face than Eisenhower to begin with, he was all the more eager to save it. So the Cold War got worse. Not until the President's image was sufficiently repaired could things improve. The Berlin crisis showed that. And President Kennedy's reaction to it was influenced as much by the Bay of Pigs as by conditions in Europe.

All the Berlin crises had a shadowy quality, mostly because American policies in Europe were so indistinct. They hinged on the need to defend Western Europe from a Soviet attack. But the Soviets never did attack, or even threaten to. This was explained as a consequence of the North Atlantic Treaty Organization's armed might. But NATO was a figment of the diplomatic imagination, as few member countries met their troop quotas. Between crises NATO was reviled for its inadequacies. After each it was hailed for having once more deterred Soviet aggression. The American stand on Germany was vaguer yet. Germany was divided in fact though not in theory. Bonn and Washington agreed that East Germany was only a temporarily detached fragment. One day West Germany would reabsorb it. Russia had indicated before, notably in the Austrian settlement, what it would take to effect this: Germany would have to be disarmed and neutralized. Washington, like Bonn, insisted on an armed and partisan Germany. Though favoring reunification, they rejected the means of getting it.

Unlike Germany, NATO was a harmless delusion, even perhaps a useful one. Being weak it didn't threaten Russia. It was a convenient dumping ground for surplus American arms. And it was said to keep West Germany from going Nazi again, or, even worse, selling out to Moscow. The German question itself was another matter, thanks chiefly to Berlin. As West Berlin was encircled by communists it was easily harassed. And as it was an outlet for East German refugees the communists had reason to harass it. East Germany would never be a viable state so long as Berlin drained off its best people. For a time this made little difference, since Russia didn't think it would last. Moscow exploited East Germany for years as if there would be no tomorrow. But at some point it was decided that the division of Germany was permanent. East Germany was finally brought into the East European common market, COMECON. The flow of refugees had to be arrested then. This could have been done unilaterally. It wasn't, because Premier Khrushchev apparently hoped for a general settlement of the German question. The U-2 frustrated his

41

first efforts. He tried again after President Kennedy took office. The Russian position then was that if some kind of agreement on Berlin was not reached it would sign a peace treaty with East Germany. The agreement itself was not specified in advance, though Premier Khrushchev said it might include making Berlin an open city. What a separate treaty with East Germany meant was equally unclear. East Germany might be emboldened by it to close the access routes to Berlin. Then again, it might not. It would remain tied to Russia anyway, and who could believe that a mere document would give East Germany what Russia had previously denied it?

Britain's Prime Minister Macmillan wanted to negotiate. The refugee flow would be ended one way or another. It might as well be done in the way that best protected Western interests. But West Germany would concede nothing. It lavishly subsidized West Berlin precisely because it drained the East. Berlin was not economically viable. People lived there because Bonn paid them to. Even so, it had an old population. The young left. The pensioners stayed on. Bonn considered the money well spent anyway. Though garish, West Berlin sucked in the discontented. Whether they came for liberty or luxury or both didn't matter so long as they kept coming. Even had Bonn known this could not go on forever, no German administration could admit reality and stay in power. As for the danger involved, the Allies were obliged to cope with it since Berlin was still nominally under Four-Power control.

Berlin was thus a high-risk, low-yield investment for America. At best the U.S. got nothing but trouble from it. If things went wrong, America even more than West Germany would foot the bill. Yet President Kennedy meant to stand pat in Berlin. On taking office he had Dean Acheson study the question.* He predictably brought back a list of possible military responses to future Russian overtures. Ambassador Stevenson was aghast. So were Macmillan and his Foreign Secretary Lord Home. They thought military answers were what you fell back on, not what you began with. And they wanted to negotiate over Berlin. The State Department held that there was nothing to discuss. President Kennedy agreed, especially after his meeting with Premier Khrushchev in Vienna on June 3 and 4, 1961.

The President was defensive even before meeting Khrushchev. He feared that the Bay of Pigs had made him look weak. After meeting Khrushchev he was certain of it. The two men got along badly. Their translators made errors that gave unintentional offense. Premier Khru-

---

* Acheson had been Secretary of State under Truman. Though accused at the time of being soft on communism, he was actually a determined Cold Warrior. Age had not mellowed him. He still felt that Russia understood nothing so well as a kick in the teeth.

shchev threatened again to sign a separate peace treaty with East Germany. The President felt bullied. The Premier thought himself insulted. On July 8 Russia announced that the American arms buildup was forcing it to do likewise. The U.S. viewed this as a hostile act against Berlin, not as a response to its own arms increases. Acheson and Vice-President Johnson wanted a state of national emergency declared. White House advisers were less militant. Henry Kissinger of Harvard argued for diplomatic as well as military responses. Otherwise, when negotiations some day took place, agreeing to have them would seem like a defeat. The President decided on a military reaction anyway. On July 25 he called for another $3.5 billion for defense and mobilized some reserve units. They were needed, he explained, because Berlin was "the great testing place of Western courage and will."*

In a way this meant nothing. Hostile powers test each other constantly, probing for weaknesses or signs of change. The process goes on regardless of how any single crisis is handled. A country may seem firm one time and evasive another. Britain failed the test on Czechoslovakia in 1938 and passed the one on Poland in 1939. Thus it is usually nonsense to call any particular challenge decisive. But doing so is significant all the same. When a crisis is defined as a test of will, compromise becomes impossible. In saying that Berlin was a test of will (and perhaps even believing it), President Kennedy burned his bridges. Russia took the point. On August 13 a wall went up between East and West Berlin. Nothing could be done to stop it. A handful of American troops were sent to Berlin. So were Lyndon Johnson and General Lucius Clay, formerly the American proconsul there. The one made a speech pledging "our lives, our fortunes, and our sacred honor" in defense of West Berlin. The other stayed on as a reminder of past glories. The crisis was over at that point, though it dribbled on a while longer.

In August the Soviets announced they would resume testing nuclear weapons, perhaps on account of Berlin, more likely because of the quickening arms race. Later Russia stopped threatening to sign a peace treaty with East Germany. It was a famous Cold War victory for America, if an empty one. East Germany was saved. The West got nothing in return. West Berlin lost its assets while retaining its liabilities. The reservists President Kennedy had called up remained on active duty, though there was little for them to do. Some people thought this unfair. The President replied that life is unfair, which, while true, was beside the point. His standing in the polls increased anyway. He might well have

---

* Not that he denied Berlin any value of its own. In a single memorable sentence he called it a showcase, a symbol, an island, a link, a beacon, and an escape hatch. As a candidate he had predicted that Berlin would be where the Allies' will was tested most.

43

said, as he did after the Bay of Pigs, "It's just like Eisenhower. The worse I do the more popular I get."*

The Berlin crisis generated one of the period's more bizarre domestic controversies. Though the crisis took place mainly in the headlines, as Prime Minister Macmillan observed, it scared people all the same.† The media covered each act with appropriate solemnity. Post-Munich emotions were revived. Experts discussed the probable effects of a nuclear attack on the United States. Schoolchildren were drilled to hide under their desks in case of one. This did not seem entirely adequate. In his July 25 TV special, President Kennedy asked for an expanded civil defense program. Stuart L. Pittman, later made Assistant Secretary of Defense for CD, advanced the case for a national fallout-shelter program. It cost little compared with air defenses, and was thought to save more lives per dollar than any other measure. The Russians would not be provoked, as fallout shelters didn't lessen the explosive force of attacking missiles, only their radioactive side-effects. They were an easy way of organizing the population in a time of crisis. These were sound arguments. The program failed spectacularly all the same.

President Kennedy erred first in trying to make fallout shelters a personal as well as a national responsibility. People were urged to build them at home. Personal responsibilities create personal anxieties. Home shelters were more frightening than remote public ones. Then too, many feared the program would not be cheap at all. The government estimated that a national system would cost $20 billion. Dr. Teller thought a combination of blast and fallout shelters would run to $37 billion. Gerard Piel, publisher of the *Scientific American,* believed that $150 billion was more like it. Nor was there agreement on the shelters' effectiveness. President Kennedy and *Life* magazine said they would save 97 per cent of the population. Dr. Willard Libby, a Nobel Laureate in chemistry, claimed 90 to 95 per cent would survive in modest shelters like the one he built in his backyard. Dr. James Van Allen, who discovered the

---

* In fact, though, he took pride in his handling of the crisis. In 1963 he was tumultuously welcomed in West Berlin and gave his *"Ich bin ein Berliner"* speech, asserting that all free men were automatically citizens of Berlin. Afterward he made the curious remark to Sorensen that he would leave a note for his successor "to be opened at a time of some discouragement." It would read: "Go to Germany." During World War II he had fought in the Pacific.

† This remark was attributed to Macmillan's famous composure. His being "unflappable" did not, however, make it less true. Russia went ahead with its planned troop reductions during the early stages. The Soviet garrison in East Germany was not enlarged, neither was it deployed in offensive positions. The only Russian threat was to make peace with East Germany. Having few ICBM's, it did not brandish them. The danger came mainly from America's insistence, as President Kennedy told the President of Finland later, that Russia meant to take over Western Europe. Most Europeans thought otherwise, which to Washington only showed how little they knew.

44

Van Allen radiation belt, and other physicists disagreed. Their case was strengthened when Dr. Libby's backyard shelter was destroyed by a brush fire. The government then discovered a shelter gap. Unlike weapons, however, shelters could not be concealed. Their usefulness depended on easy access. Travelers in the Soviet Union found no evidence of a massive Russian shelter program. This was proof that none existed.

The government was poorly served by its friends. A Jesuit priest advised people who built shelters to shoot their neighbors if necessary. A CD official told Nevada businessmen to form a militia that could turn back refugees from California. An Idaho housing subdivision planned a shelter with armed guards to keep out nonmembers. All this discredited the program. Even if useful, some thought it too costly. Others felt it caused moral damage in excess of any possible gain. Scientists took out advertisements to say it wouldn't work anyway. Their case gained from Russian tests that showed there was no limit to a weapon's power. It was possible to orbit a thousand-megaton bomb capable of setting six Western states afire in one great blast. This made fallout shelters seem both fraudulent and pathetic. The fallout-shelter program was quietly dropped. The anxieties it aroused were not so easily disposed of.

The renewal of atmospheric testing was also frightening. The Eisenhower test suspension had been resisted by the Atomic Energy Commission and the military. They believed Russia was making secret underground tests undetectable by Western instruments. This view was later proven false. Far from concealing explosions, underground tests often made them easier to spot. These fears did not prevent President Eisenhower from negotiating for a test ban. They did keep him from getting one. The military demanded safeguards that Russia would not agree to. The Congress's Joint Committee on Atomic Energy insisted that all U.S. security regulations be scrupulously observed. So the talks dragged on fruitlessly. The informal test ban was worth having anyway. It reduced tensions and saved lives. This last was a disputed point, however. The AEC did not quite say that radioactive fallout was good for you. It did set the acceptable levels of radiation exposure so high as to make unlimited testing seem harmless. Many scientists thought general levels meaningless since radiation tended to gather in "hot spots." A body might thus be damaged by exposure that would be safe if uniformly absorbed. Certain elements, like Strontium 90, were particularly dangerous as they persisted through the food chain. In cow's milk they were a threat to children especially. Later a positive correlation between atmospheric testing and infant and prenatal death rates was clearly evident. Even at the time, common sense suggested that fallout was undesirable. President Kennedy, a great milk drinker it was said, did not enjoy having Strontium 90 for breakfast. Nor did he wish to injure babies.

All the same, when the Soviets resumed testing in August 1961 the pressure for American tests was irresistible. Kennedy denounced Soviet "hypocrisy" and prepared to order an American series. He was dissuaded by Edward R. Murrow of the United States Information Agency and others. They pointed out that a valuable propaganda advantage would be lost by immediate resumption. Let the hostile world reaction to the Soviet tests run its course first, they argued. The U.S. would then seem less culpable, and criticism of Russia would not be diluted or diverted. They were quite right. Everyone denounced Russia for a time. Later the U.S. quietly resumed underground testing. It did not start testing in the atmosphere until 1962. By then people were exhausted from attacking Russia, and the American response had come to seem inevitable. The U.S. got only a fraction of the blame Russia earned, though it was nearly as guilty. This showed again what advantages free countries have over totalitarian ones.

These crises and controversies were alarming enough. The administration's theatrical reactions made them seem worse. People supported the government anyway, more out of fear than confidence, partly also from habit. The Cold War had inspired a reflexive patriotism that turned blunders abroad into votes at home. Among those who did criticize the government's policies, few were liberal or left wing. For one thing, there were hardly any leftists by then. The Old Left had been ruined by the Communist party and the Cold War. What remained included a few radical scholars like William Appleman Williams and C. Wright Mills, the democratic socialists clustered around Norman Thomas and *Dissent* magazine, and assorted Trotskyists and unreconstructed Stalinists. Most liberals still identified with Democratic administrations, however inept. They too had been conditioned to accept the government line on foreign affairs. What thought they gave it was mainly devotional. There was a peace movement, more distinguished by weight of intellect than numbers. A daring handful climbed aboard nuclear submarines and picketed missile sites. The average pacifist was content with educational work and an occasional small demonstration. This meant that attacks on government policy came mainly from the right.

American conservatives were an odd lot. Most were not very conservative to begin with. Hardly anyone who claimed to be one revered tradition, established institutions, or the status quo. There was no aristocracy to rally round, no shared philosophy. The very documents conservatives professed to admire—the Constitution, the Declaration of Independence, the collected works of Andrew Carnegie—were essentially liberal. Conservatives were against change and in favor of what caused it—technology, corporate growth, and such. In ordinary speech a conservative meant someone attached to an obsolete principle, like the gold standard or Social Darwinism. In practice what defined them were prejudices held in common. Conservatives opposed liberal administrations, civil rights, and being taxed for nonmilitary expenditures. They liked private property, religion, and General MacArthur. Most of all, they hated communism. This was lucky for them, as otherwise they could scarcely have gotten along with one another. Conservatives were as sectarian as radicals, and being more numerous suffered accordingly. They were also more demented. Hard times had reduced the left to a sensibly depressed few, but paranoia flourished on the right.

On April 17, 1961, the same day that Cuba was invaded, Major General Edwin A. Walker was removed from command of the 24th Infantry Division in Germany. Walker had commanded the troops that kept order during the integration of Central High School in Little Rock, Arkansas, in 1957. The mission was so repugnant to him that it affected his reason. He had been indoctrinating his troops with extreme right-wing propaganda and had tried to influence their votes in the 1960 elections. To his mind even moderate journalists like Walter Lippmann and Eric Sevareid were "confirmed communists." The government itself was full of traitors. Conservatives retaliated by charging Secretary McNamara with "muzzling the military." Senators investigated the case but got nowhere as McNamara possessed documented evidence of Walker's extravagances. General Walker testified before them, made his customary wild charges, and punched a reporter in the eye. In November 1961 he resigned his commission. The next year he would be arrested for insurrection, conspiracy, and other offenses committed during the Meredith riots at the University of Mississippi.

General Walker was the most notorious right-wing senior military officer, but not the most important. Air Force General Curtis LeMay believed in preventive war with everyone. The manic General Buck Turgidson in the film *Dr. Strangelove* was probably modeled on him. Other officers developed or attended right-wing activities with names like "Project Alert" and "Strategy for Survival." They promoted militarism at home and abroad in the name of anti-communism. McNamara found rightist officers hard to muzzle, as is always the case when disloyalty masquerades as patriotism. Corporate extremism was harder yet to cope with. H. L. Hunt, the Texas oil billionaire, spent perhaps a million dollars a year on right-wing causes. His radio program "Life Line" was carried by 212 stations in twenty-eight states. For a time he sponsored the Dan Smoot Report which was carried by seventy radio and forty TV stations. Dan Smoot supported the independence of Katanga (a separatist province of the Congo much admired by American rightists for relying on white mercenaries and international business consortiums). He wanted to invade Cuba, impeach Chief Justice Warren, and pull out of Germany. This last would lead to war between Germany and Russia. If Germany won, so much the better. If not, Russia would be so damaged as to insure American supremacy. While not a common view, it was typical of what passed for geopolitical thought on the right. There was no end to corporate involvement in right-wing activities. The Coast Federal Savings and Loan Association of Los Angeles, third largest in the country, sent out two million pieces of anti-communist and pro-capitalist literature in 1961. Its president, Joe Crail, liked to expose the myth that "human rights are above property rights." He also had more homely motives. "Anti-communism builds sales and raises employee performance," he often remarked. The Allen-Bradley Company of Milwaukee worked both sides of the street even more successfully. Allen-Bradley promoted the American free-enterprise system in public while secretly undermining it. The company was a member of the great electrical price-fixing conspiracy. Competition was a splendid thing—for others, it believed. For itself it chose security—as, perhaps, would most businesses given the chance. Dozens of other companies contributed to the radical right. Hundreds more supported anti-communist propaganda efforts, ranging from the malign to the absurd.

The most visible of these in the early sixties was Fred Schwarz's Christian Anti-Communist Crusade. It held "schools" of anti-communism, mostly in California, that frightened many. After one, several ministers critical of the CACC had their homes bombed. The publisher of *Life* magazine was humbled before a mass audience in the Hollywood Bowl. He confessed his error in having previously spoken ill of the Crusade. If Schwarz could bring mighty *Life* to its knees, what else might he not do? Liberal magazines detected a Hitler in the making. When his Crusade came to Oakland, California, early in 1962, the spectre of Nuremburg accompanied it. But Oakland became his Waterloo instead. Bishops, Congressmen, and other notables denounced the school. State Attorney General Mosk called it a "fly-by-night promotion." The school went ahead in its usual way. The customary assortment of hysterics and demagogues attacked liberalism and communism. They warned of the red plot to corrupt youth with pornography. The rights of Katanga were upheld. The Crusade started fading all the same. Corporate sponsors were less willing to pay for television time. The fear of Schwarz declined when he failed to silence his critics. Soon Schwarz and the panic associated with him were forgotten. The radical right always seemed more powerful than it was anyway. The corporations that actively supported it were usually small or middle-sized. Large corporations commonly were more moderate. Some bad experiences with rightists, and the waning enthusiasm for anti-communism, reduced their interest further. When it became clear that the U.S. had a great lead over Russia in strategic arms, the hysteria on which radical rightists fed abated. The right would go on providing the background noise for American politics. It would continue vetoing certain domestic and foreign initiatives. But it would not be so visible again for a while.

President Kennedy's decision to have a manned space program was perhaps the most far-reaching of any made during his first year in office. There was nothing inevitable about it. Earlier President Eisenhower had turned down schemes for going to the moon. He thought them dubious and expensive. Even if successful they would only lead to fresh demands for flights to Mars or wherever. "Anybody who would spend $40 billion in a race to the moon for national prestige is nuts," he said after retiring. Most scientists agreed. James R. Killian told President Eisenhower that "the really exciting discoveries in space can be realized better by instruments than by man." Jerome Wiesner of MIT, who advised President Kennedy, thought the same at first. Instrumented exploration, though meanly funded, had already brought great rewards.

What compelling reasons produced this decision? Foremost among them was the need to beat Russia. The Soviets had bigger rockets and were doing all the spectacular things first. This was thought to have bad effects on American prestige and morale. It certainly depressed Kennedy's. Worse yet, capitalism was made to look bad. After the Bay of Pigs, national, or at least presidential, prestige needed reinforcement all the more. Then too, as national leaders were determined to have booster rockets as strong as Russia's, a reason for them had to be found. The military rockets—Atlas, Minuteman, Polaris, Titan—were quite adequate. Only manned flights justified the building of vastly more powerful ones. Economics played a part too. The military rocket programs were nearing completion, and unemployment would follow if new projects were not devised. The moon race meant additional jobs and profits for the aerospace industry. Like the arms race, the space race involved a kind of perverted Keynesianism. Congress would not stimulate the economy for economic reasons. But it would make appropriations for national defense and prestige that had stimulating effects. So President Kennedy decided to go to the moon. 1967 became the initial target date because, as it coincided with the fiftieth anniversary of the Russian Revolution, it was thought to be the Soviets' goal. A vast new pork barrel was thus opened.

Naturally, more uplifting justifications for a moon race had to be found.

President Kennedy explained to Congress that "we go into space because whatever mankind must undertake, free men must fully share." Senator Kerr of Oklahoma assured scientists that the moon flight would add ten years to the life of every American under fifty. In this manner the base was laid for Apollo 11, which a scientist would someday call "the smallest but most expensive pyramid in history."

President Kennedy's first year in office was marked chiefly by frustration at home, crisis abroad, and waste everywhere. People had not been so scared in years. Yet it soon would be remembered as the start of a golden age. In America hope not only springs eternal, it becomes retroactive.

PROFILE:
Space

On May 6, 1961, Commander Alan B. Shepard, Jr., made a three-hundred-mile suborbital flight from Cape Canaveral. On May 25, in a special message to Congress, President Kennedy committed America to put a man on the moon before 1970. Partly this was because it would never do to have the Russians get there first, partly for the sake of national grandeur, partly because "whatever mankind must undertake, free men must fully share," vicariously at least. There was no thought then or later of giving allied countries a piece of the action. Except for the arms race itself, no other Cold War enterprise in the 1960's cost Americans so much money. But in contrast to most Cold War events, which were remote, impersonal, and frequently ambiguous, space flights were dramatic, straightforward, and immediate. Thanks to television, their entertainment value was incalculable. Agreeably short periods of suspense were almost always climaxed by success. In the astronauts people gained a new set of folk heroes appropriate to the conditions of modern life, who yet manifested the simple, winning virtues of an earlier and less complicated time. They made everyone think better of test pilots as a class. As the Soviet lead was first diminished and then overcome, patriotic contentment was added to the other gratifying emotions engendered by the moon race.

The President's decision to beat Russia to the moon meant that the space program would subordinate science to engineering even more than it already did. The Mercury program was opposed by influential scientists—Linus Pauling, of course, but also men like James R. Killian, one of President Eisenhower's chief science advisers. Killian wanted to concentrate on instrumented flights and said, "We should pursue our own objectives in space science, and not let the Soviets choose them for us." President Kennedy's own science adviser, Jerome Wiesner, was dubious about Mercury, and more so about the moon race. But when the decision was made he supported it on military and political grounds, though not for its scientific prospects, which still seemed to him negligible compared with what unmanned programs might accomplish. Other scientists went along for poetic reasons. Harold Urey cited man's need to build cathedrals. Others had only slightly less splendid metaphors. There were plenty of moral and aesthetic excuses for going to the moon when science was not enough.

No one expected the military-industrial complex to oppose such a bonanza as the moon race promised to be. It was more surprising that scientists did not resist much, for even though science had been a hitchhiker on the early space probes, its accomplishments were great. The very first American satellite, Explorer 1, discovered the Van Allen radiation belts. Vanguard 1, also launched in 1958, was only a six-inch sphere, but it stayed in orbit for more than six years and taught scientists many new things about the earth, including the fact that it is slightly pear-shaped. The definition of the magnetosphere (to which the Van Allen belts belong) that surrounds the earth was the early space program's finest achievement. The experiments that produced this knowledge were merely tacked onto what were essentially engineering tests. They cost very little (the four shots that positively identified the Van Allen belts cost only $16 million) and were richly productive.

Later space probes, both American and Russian, discovered the great wind blowing off the sun and filling the solar system with low-energy protons. Its existence had been predicted by scientists, since otherwise certain natural phenomena could not be explained, but it was never actually identified until instruments were put into space. These probes demonstrated that the "vacuum" of space contained all sorts of matter and energy interacting in complex and not yet fully understood ways.

The manned flights provided little new knowledge by comparison with the instrumented flights, yet throughout its history the space program favored the former over the latter. The mass media came to call manned launchings "space spectaculars," which aptly described their function. But while science remained a stepchild of the space race, without it science would probably have been even worse off. The money spent for the Mercury, Gemini, and Apollo programs would not have been available for scientific research in any case. On the contrary, it was precisely because these programs were so vast that it was possible to slip in scientific projects that enlarged man's knowledge of the universe. This was hardly a sensible way to go about the search for truth, but it is often how the thing gets done. Critics quite properly condemned the space race for hokum, waste, and pretensions to grandeur. But by comparison with the arms race, the space race at its worst was the very epitome of sanity and good will. Except for the war in Vietnam, it was John F. Kennedy's chief legacy to the 1970's.

On February 20, 1962, at 9:47 A.M., a Marine officer, Lieutenant Colonel John H. Glenn, was fired into space from Cape Canaveral. He flew around the world three times and landed in the Caribbean that same afternoon. Three days later President Kennedy arrived at the Cape to praise him. On February 26 Glenn spoke to a joint session of Congress. The next day he touted the space program before a House committee. All this recognition came not so much because of his skill and courage, although he had plenty of both, but because he was the first American to be put into orbit. Originally NASA (the National Aeronautics and Space Administration) had planned to make six suborbital flights in the Mercury project. After the crafty Soviets put their second man in orbit, however, the government decided that American honor required something more impressive to sustain it. Glenn's three orbits did not compare with Titov's eighteen, but they were much better than none at all. They were also important because for the first time a man actually took control of his spacecraft. During the flight an automatic control malfunctioned causing the ship to yaw. Glenn was able to correct this manually and complete his mission as scheduled. Advocates argued that this showed the value of having a human pilot aboard space vessels. This was true, but redundant. Friendship 7 was designed to carry a human pilot and without one would have been only partially equipped. A craft designed to pilot itself would have had different equipment and characteristics. All the same, it was an impressive flight, despite a variety of equipment failures.

It was followed later in the year by two other flights of three and six orbits respectively. The second, piloted by Scott Carpenter, was especially gripping because the spacecraft lost radio contact after landing two hundred miles further downrange than expected. This was nerve-wracking for the flight controllers, and for the public as well since these flights, like all the big NASA productions, were shown live on TV. The public was thereby exposed to thrills and dramatic moments more gripping than any devised by the networks as pure entertainment. The success of these flights, and the public-relations benefits they brought, helped reconcile Americans to the Soviets' continued lead in space. In August Russia launched two ships at once; they maneuvered to within a few kilometers of each other, demonstrating that linkups in space were feasible. They landed only minutes apart, having completed forty-eight and sixty-four orbits respectively.

Although most of NASA's money and glamour was tied up in the manned shots, the unmanned space probes continued to produce information. In August 1962 Mariner 2 was sent outward bound to Venus. On December 14 it passed within 21,000 miles of that mysterious planet, radioing signals back to earth over the longest distance ever transmitted from a spacecraft. Other objects put into orbit that year included Telstar, the first commercially developed communications satellite. It and its successors were among the most immediately useful products of the space program since they made live transoceanic TV possible. Fears that this meant only that the whole world would watch "The Beverly Hillbillies" together proved premature. As a practical matter, only live sports and news events were transmitted by the communications satellites. Other constructive space efforts included several joint scientific launchings with England and Canada, and three launchings in the Tiros series of weather satellites. The Ranger series of moon probes was a considerable failure: several missed the moon, and the one that did impact malfunctioned. The Air Force continued secret launchings of its Samos and Midas spacecraft. Although seemingly the most odious fruits of the space program, these "spy" satellites served a useful purpose. Unlike so much of what came under the rubric of "security," the spy satellites did help make the country more secure by improving its early warning system. And, since both the U.S. and the USSR developed such crafts, each side knew more about the other's capabilities, thus reducing the chances of miscalculation. They also reduced the need for on-site inspections in the event arms-control agreements were ever reached. Distasteful though it was, bilateral aerial espionage offered the promise of a slightly safer world.

The Mercury program survived its technical problems without loss of life thanks to brilliant piloting. The next series of flights in two-man Gemini capsules was more thrilling yet. On March 16, 1966, Gemini 8, with astronauts Neil Armstrong and David Scott, was the first American spacecraft to link up with another in flight. After Gemini 8 was made fast to the Agena rocket with its four thousand pounds of fuel, both began to roll and yaw uncontrollably. Armstrong broke free of the Agena, but Gemini then began tumbling end over end. Working furiously (their hearts beating at twice the normal rate), the astronauts found what was wrong. One of their sixteen thrusters had turned on by itself. In regaining control afterward the astronauts were forced to use their re-entry rockets. This reduced their margin of safety for returning and the mission had to be aborted.

Gemini 9, after weeks of delay, lifted off on June 3, 1966. It was unable to link up with another craft that failed to lose its protective shroud. Astronaut Thomas Stafford said it looked "like an angry alligator." Astronaut Eugene Cernan then took a walk in space that ended when his helmet visor fogged over so he could scarcely see. Vision was a problem with Gemini 10 in July also. At one point the astronauts' space suits filled with fumes, obliging them to close the hatch. During the flight of Gemini 11 in September, Astronaut Richard Gordon got so hot working in space that his vision was obscured. Gemini 12 had its radar fail, and the primary propulsion system on the Agena malfunctioned. But the problems of space-walking were solved, and NASA declared the flight an "unqualified success." Project Gemini had sent twenty astronauts into orbit in twenty months. Now the stage was set for Project Apollo which would take men to the moon.

Apollo started badly. Its first flight was scheduled for November 15,

1966, but too many things went wrong. Rockets blew up in tests. A power inverter, an oxygen generator, and other devices malfunctioned. The first manned flight was set back to December. More trouble developed with the life-support system. A water line cracked. The flight was set back to January. In December the Manned Spacecraft Center reported that more than twenty thousand failures had already occurred in the Apollo program. Most were trivial, yet they were warnings of what was to come. The whole problem was simply that NASA was working at the far edge of its technical capacity. The safest thing would have been to wait until a spacecraft was developed that could both take off and land under power. But that might take decades. The moon could have gone communist by then. To avoid that prospect the nation proposed to offset its lack of power with technical ingenuity.

A big, self-sustaining vessel, such as science-fiction writers always envisaged, would have had plenty of margin for error. The tiny Apollo had none. And yet the very complexity occasioned by its being so small and weak made error all the more likely, as Mercury and Gemini had shown. People were awed by the intricacy of these space vessels. Few realized that this was a consequence of their primitive state. The internal-combustion engine was complex indeed compared to its successors—the gas turbine, the jet engine—which were both simpler and more powerful. Apollo bore the same kind of relation to its descendants. It would do the job, but only just. Had the government been willing to wait for more advanced power systems, men would have gone to the moon in relative ease and safety. Some argued this but to no avail. What made their caveats irrelevant was that Apollo was designed not so much to get to the moon as to get there first. So an infant technology was dangerously extended that it might accomplish earlier what if done later, however safely, would have less propaganda value.

On January 27, 1967, Lieutenant Colonel Virgil I. Grissom, Lieutenant Commander Roger B. Chaffee, and Lieutenant Colonel Edward H. White entered an Apollo capsule for routine tests. After a series of equipment malfunctions the tests had nearly been called off, then it was decided to go ahead with a mock countdown. Seconds later fire broke out and within minutes all three were dead of carbon monoxide poisoning. Critics of the space program were hardly surprised. In 1963 Dr. Vannevar Bush, director of the Office of Scientific Research and Development during World War II, wrote the *New York Times* to protest the program's risk and cost. "To put a man on the moon is folly, engendered by childish enthusiasm. It will backfire on those who drive it ahead." Others who supported manned flights hoped NASA would wait until space technology was further advanced. A rocket that could take off and land on its own power would be best. Next best was the earth-orbiting method proposed by Dr. Wernher von Braun and many scientists. It called for the development of a manned space station in earth orbit, from which a moon vehicle could be launched. Some thought EOR would be ten times as safe as the lunar-orbiting method actually chosen. But EOR involved a vehicle twice as heavy as the Apollo, and with two boosters instead of one. It would take much longer to develop. So naturally it was decided to go with the LOR which, though dangerous, could be executed before 1970. The government was fixated on this deadline for no good reason except that President Kennedy had once thought it a reasonable target date.

The three dead astronauts, then, were victims of a deliberate high-risk policy. They accepted the danger cheerfully, it must be said. Earlier Gus Grissom himself had expressed the hope "that if anything happens to us, it will not delay the program. The conquest of space is worth the risk of life." That is, of course, the stuff of which heroes are made. It remained to doubt if a heroic space program was more vital to the national interest than a sensible one. Besides the general rush, actual delinquencies were involved. In December 1964 Lockheed had proposed that a combination "vacuum cleaner and fire extinguisher" be used on space capsules. It would have suppressed the fire that killed Grissom and his crew. But NASA considered it too heavy, so it was never built. The underpowered Apollo could not accommodate all the safety features that might be desirable. Beyond that, NASA had gotten careless after so many casualty-free flights. Even though Gemini had been plagued with technical errors, NASA had given its employees two Distinguished Service Medals, five Exceptional Service Medals, three Outstanding Leadership Medals, one Exceptional Scientific

Achievement Medal, seventeen Public Service Awards, seven Group Achievement Awards, and eight Superior Achievement Awards at the project's end.

Apollo was even more complex, "an engineering nightmare," some called it, yet NASA remained complacent. It failed even to build a quick release hatch into Apollo 1, though both Mercury and Gemini had had them. Such a hatch would probably have saved the three astronauts' lives. Then too, the combustible materials in Apollo 1 had never been tested under high pressure. It turned out later that they burned five times faster than expected. And so it went. James E. Webb, NASA's administrator, first tried to blame the accident on Congress for giving him such an "austere budget." But NASA's own investigative body thought otherwise. Its lengthy report criticized NASA and North American Aviation, the prime contractor, for poor management, carelessness, negligence, and much else. Repeated examples of defective design and engineering work, manufacture, installation, and workmanship were cited. Lastly, NASA and North American failed to realize that tests were dangerous and neglected the astronauts' safety. Congressional committees reproved NASA also. Apollo went ahead all the same; nothing had really been learned.

On July 20, 1969, Neil Armstrong became the first man (that we know of) to walk on the moon. Live TV broadcasts enabled a quarter of the world's population to watch him. It was an intensely thrilling moment, the climax of man's technological progress to that date. The most extravagant self-acclaim followed it. Winning the moon race showed the merits of free enterprise, the American way of life, and, perhaps, Christianity. More generous observers extended credit to all mankind. President Nixon thought it the best week's work since the creation. Walter Cronkite of CBS News believed it put the hippies and other dissidents in their place. The three astronauts—Armstrong, Edwin Aldrin, and Michael Collins—became international heroes and seemed destined to spend the rest of their lives getting and giving honors. It was NASA's finest moment, perhaps also its most self-destructive. This seeming paradox derived from its primary mission—beating Russia to the moon. Having done so, what else remained? Vice-President Agnew tried to promote a Mars race. NASA argued for human settlements on the moon. Either would be vastly expensive.

Most scientists had gone along with the moon race for unscientific reasons. Others who wanted to reach the moon were disenchanted by NASA's emphasis on engineering and public relations. Little money was spent on basic research. None of the astronauts were scientists. The Apollo program, for all its expense ($25 to $35 billion), was a technically marginal operation barely able to launch a round-trip vehicle. Each moon trip cost around half a billion dollars. Yet the spacecrafts were so small that only the simplest experiments could be made. NASA had grand rationales for manned space voyages. They gave mankind a new self-image. The human consciousness was expanded. NASA spokesmen fell into mystical raptures at the mere sight of a reporter. But the government's intent had always been more homely. NASA's budget was cut even before Apollo 11 reached the moon, as it became clear Russia wasn't going to make it. The decline continued afterward. The number of future Apollo launchings was sharply reduced.

A few scientists complained that cutting back NASA retroactively discredited the whole moon program. Most welcomed the end of manned space flights. Dr. James Van Allen said that Apollo's success freed the country to develop a "more rational" program of space exploration based on unmanned flights. According to Dr. Philip Abelson of *Science* magazine, their scientific cost-effectiveness was one hundred times that of manned flights. With all the solar system to explore and the moondoggle finally over, Ralph Lapp thought it time to trade "a space project that provides spectacles for one that serves science." Should that happen, Apollo might have been worthwhile, if only to have it done with.

Still, it was hard to fault General Eisenhower's initial remark that anyone who wanted to spend so many billions of dollars to get to the moon was nuts. Here, as so often where national-security affairs were concerned, Eisenhower was a prophet without honor in his own time. But also as so often before, he reflected that common sense which ordinary people possessed though policy-makers seemed not to. When President Kennedy first announced his moon plan, polls showed that

58 per cent of the public opposed it. After Apollo 11 a great majority favored scaling down the manned space program. This provoked some bitterness among astronauts. Armstrong was later to express regret that the "spirit of Apollo" lasted so short a time. But the "great cathedral" having been built, there was no reason for endlessly embellishing it. It was not a true cathedral anyway, being in such large part a monument to the vanity of public men and the avarice of contractors. This made it a good symbol of the sixties.

3 COMPLETING THE MYTH

THE ADMINISTRATION's fortunes began improving in 1962. In reality, things were about as bad as ever. The economy remained sluggish. Congress was still unresponsive. The Cold War worsened. But a string of apparent victories created at least the illusion of progress. Big steel provided the first of these. On April 10, 1962, Roger Blough, chairman of the board of United States Steel, gave President Kennedy a mimeographed announcement of his company's decision to raise prices. Other producers followed suit. The President and his Secretary of Labor, Arthur Goldberg, were furious. Only days before, the United Steelworkers Union had signed a contract with big steel widely hailed as noninflationary. Goldberg had persuaded the union to accept modest wage increases in return for an industry pledge not to raise prices. The promise was not legally binding, however, so U.S. Steel broke it. Blough cited the profit principle in explanation.

It was clear enough why big steel felt obliged to cheat, though why it did so stupidly was not. Profits were down sharply, especially in relation to assets. In the postwar years steel had grown fat, but in the late fifties conditions changed. Competition from other sources—plastics, concrete—increased, as did pressure from German and Japanese producers who made better steel for less than American manufacturers with their aging plants and conservative research and development programs. In 1957 the U.S. had enjoyed a favorable balance of trade in iron and steel of $781 million. By 1961 this had shrunk to only $7 million. Plant utilization declined accordingly, from 93 per cent in 1955 to 60 per cent in 1958. Profits fell less sharply because productivity increases enabled steel to get along with 118,000 fewer workers, and because its goods were overpriced. Steel prices had risen 120 per cent from 1947 to 1958 while industrial prices as a whole went up only 39 per cent. Even so, this cushion was wearing thin. The administration wanted steel to hold prices steady and modernize so as to meet foreign competition. But the price rise of April 10 showed that U.S. Steel meant to go the other way and maintain its profits in a shrinking market by raising prices. This meant even fewer jobs at a time of high unemployment, and a worsening of the balance-of-payments deficit just when the outflow of gold was becoming painful. U.S. Steel compounded its error by showing bad faith. The President felt obliged to protest steel's mistake. Blough's arrogance made it politically essential for him to do so.

Kennedy began by attacking the industry in a press conference. As Presidents always do, he compared its "the-public-be-damned" spirit to the sacrifices of American reservists called up over Berlin, and of soldiers sent to Vietnam. Congressional leaders threatened to investigate the industry's price structure. Government officials asked their friends in business to appeal to the steel industry's better nature. Secretary McNamara announced that Defense would try to buy steel only from companies that did not raise prices. This strategy worked, but only just. The administration could bluster and threaten and send FBI agents snooping round, as it did. It had no authority to do much more. Luckily, Inland Steel, an unusually well-managed and efficient company, was persuaded to hold steady. Other small companies lined up behind Inland, and with the industry's united front broken the big companies had to give way.

The President's victory was a costly one. Business was confirmed in its dislike of him, and in the board rooms and country clubs of America he became the most unpopular President since Franklin D. Roosevelt. This did not lose him many votes. It did make the corporate establishment's support in the future more problematical. Business had never forgiven President Roosevelt, as Averell Harriman pointed out, for moving the center of power from Wall Street to Washington. They would not forgive President Kennedy for humiliating Roger Blough, and, even more, for allegedly saying afterward, "My father always told me that all businessmen were sons of bitches, but I never believed it till now." Businessmen, like other people, need love, and the less lovable they are the more they need it. Business did well under President Kennedy, better than under President Eisenhower in fact. Eisenhower admired businessmen, John Kennedy did not. So businessmen liked the one and distrusted the other, all apart from whatever material gains each brought them.

The stock market break in May 1962 didn't help matters. In three days 35 million shares changed hands. The Dow-Jones index swung wildly from 611.78 at closing on Friday the 25th, to a low of 563.24, then back to a high of 613.36 at closing the next Thursday. Business blamed it on the administration's economic policies. Some of the President's aides thought it was a business plot to discredit him. Probably the main reason was that prices were too high. In any case, Kennedy considered it the proper occasion to talk sense to capitalists. At Yale University in June he suggested that widely held views about the economy were untrue. Government expenditures were not rising in relation to the GNP. Budget deficits were not always a bad thing. The speech backfired. However ignorant they may be, businessmen don't care to be lectured on economics by politicians. And, thinking themselves hardheaded and practical, they like even less to be told that what they believe is wrong.

President Kennedy gave up trying to improve their minds, but he never despaired of winning their affections. He offered business many plums, something that was all the easier for his being a Democrat and thus presumed by liberals to be pure of heart. One of his first acts was to secure an investment tax credit worth a billion dollars a year. Labor opposed it because with so much plant already idle the likely result was that business would use the money for labor-displacing machines. Businessmen were indifferent. The President grew angry with labor for resisting his giveaway; with business for not appreciating it. The administration decided to tie as much as 80 per cent of foreign aid to the purchase of American-made goods. Only a Democrat could have made such blatant protectionism acceptable to liberals. Only a Democrat could have gotten so little credit from business for doing so. When Kennedy filled key positions with eminently conservative men, like Secretary of the Treasury Douglas Dillon and Federal Reserve Board Chairman William McChesney Martin, business blamed him for making the liberal Walter Heller chairman of his Council of Economic Advisers, though an adviser would seem less consequential than a Treasury Secretary.

Perhaps the most important economic decision made during the Kennedy years was to cut taxes. The way this came about shows how the economy was managed. Walter Heller argued for a cut in the summer of 1962 on Keynesian grounds. Unemployment was high and growth slow in the early sixties, as in the late fifties. Kennedy had promised to get the economy moving again, but after taking office found it easier said than done. Heller felt it was time to apply Keynes's theory that government should lower taxes and increase spending during business lows, and raise taxes and reduce spending during business highs. This had seemed daring in the 1930's. By the 1960's most economists had accepted the proposition. The average voter was thought not to. Congress remained unpersuaded. Business was not quite ready to abandon the nineteenth-century theoretical precepts it had done so much to erode in practice. All the same, Heller insisted that tax cuts and public works programs would lower unemployment and promote growth. Lawrence O'Brien, the President's chief congressional aide, assured him that Congress would not go along. Secretary Dillon wouldn't either. So nothing happened in 1962.

As the economy continued to flag, the President decided on action. Heller talked him out of raising taxes to pay for the Berlin crisis. The President did insist on a balanced budget, but it was subverted by the overestimation of tax revenues for fiscal 1963. The budget was supposed to produce a billion-dollar surplus but actually generated a $6.2 billion deficit. Thus while the government did not make matters worse, it did not help them much either. The administration finally approached the tax cut in something of a gambler's spirit. All else having failed, why not try a little dose of Keynes? But the effort was made so halfheartedly that it probably had no important results. It was not accompanied by a public works program. Tax reform was supposed to complement the tax cut, but as usual the one was sacrificed to get the other. The tax cut itself was mildly regressive, thus benefiting the frugal rich rather than the spend-thrift poor. This was not so much immoral as un-Keynesian. Tax cuts for the rich meant money diverted into savings and investment. Money saved was money lost so far as stimulating the economy went, or so Keynesians believed. Additional investment meant more redundant plant expansion and labor-displacing machinery leading to fewer jobs. Extra money for low-income earners would have been immediately spent, thus invigorating the economy. Besides being regressive and unreformed, the tax cut was too small to begin with, and smaller still in effect thanks to increased social security and other deductions withheld from payrolls.

When it finally went through in 1964, the tax cut was hailed as a successful attempt at "fine tuning" the economy. It was supposedly the most liberal aspect of President Kennedy's economic policy. If true, this did not say much for either. The tax cut was mutilated at the outset and delayed so long that the economy had already begun recovering when it took effect. That so weak a step was thought important only demonstrated how feeble was the administration's grasp of problems. Just before he died the President reminded business that while the national debt had equaled 120 per cent of the Gross National Product in 1945, by 1963 it was only 53 per cent of the GNP. He did not point out that the price paid for small annual deficits had been the continuing poverty of millions of Americans and the neglect of great public needs.

John Kenneth Galbraith had argued in 1958 that relying on growth alone made the contradiction between private affluence and public squalor more acute. Yet the President kept worrying away at such tired and abstract questions as the size of the national debt. Growth alone was to solve the public's problems, though somehow it never did. If growth was the answer it was not promoted vigorously enough. If Keynesianism was the proper mechanism it was not applied with sufficient conviction. If spending for public needs was the correct solution it was largely neglected. Such a policy was not much better than no policy at all. Still, the President's admirers talked of the "new economics" as if the government's approach had greatly changed since General Eisenhower's day. The President went on courting business. He played his liberal advisers off against his conservative ones, splitting their differences where possible. The result was a policy that was not so much liberal or conservative as incomprehensible.

In 1962, as in 1961, foreign affairs eclipsed domestic ones. They were not all so mismanaged as before, however. Laos became an apparent success story. This tiny country was lavishly subsidized. It received more aid per capita than any other country in Southeast Asia, and with fewer results. The chief threat to the Royal Laotian government was the Pathet Lao, a revolutionary movement dominated by an odd collection of aristocrats, schoolteachers, and tribal chieftains. It was modeled on the Viet Minh and led by a member of the royal family, Prince Souphanouvong. To deal with its insurgent potential, Laos needed a counter-guerrilla force. What it got was a conventional army paid and trained by the U.S. The Royal Laotian Army was even given an armored reconnaissance battalion, though the country had few roads, none of them usable all year round. Most Laotians were mountain tribesmen. The RLA consisted mainly of lowlanders. Its payroll was the only important source of currency in a largely barter economy. The result was runaway inflation, curbed only by an American program financing the importation of durable goods to sustain the purchasing power of the Laotian *kip*. It cost several million dollars a month, and promoted black marketeering and currency speculation. Between 1955 and 1963 about $480 million was pumped into Laos. Only $1.9 million went to agriculture, though 96 per cent of the population lived off it. Things went from weird to worse, especially after December 31, 1959, when the RLA seized power.

American involvement in this strange place was not a consequence of deep-seated national interests. Laos owned no important natural resources. American businessmen had no money invested there. Nor was Laos of much strategic value. It was an isolated mountain country, not a key, a gateway, or even a domino. Indeed, it was not a nation in any real sense, only a collection of peasants and tribesmen joined together by the Royal Laotian Army. Laos was seen as a vacuum to be filled, by the communists if not by the CIA, but the CIA came in not so much because it was necessary as because it was easy. The army welcomed it, and no one else had the power to object effectively. CIA support encouraged the army to seize power and drive the Pathet Lao underground. And it alienated the few genuine noncommunist nationalists, especially Captain Kong Le of the RLA's Second Parachute Battalion. His unit was the only one to actually fight the Pathet Lao. The 25,000-man Royal Laotian Army disliked combat and rarely saw any. On August 9, 1960, Kong Le and his three hundred men overthrew the government of General Phoumi Nosavan and asked the former civilian premier, Prince Souvanna Phouma, to form a coalition government including the Pathet Lao, as had been done before. This was probably the only solution, if there was any, to the Laotian problem. U.S. Ambassador Brown supported it, the CIA did not. General Phoumi owed his power to the CIA, and the CIA was always loyal to its mistakes. Thus encouraged, Phoumi regrouped and recaptured the capital, Vientiane, in December. Kong Le then allied his forces with the Pathet Lao and took the strategic Plain of Jars, where in February Prince Souvanna Phouma established a government in exile supported by the Soviet Union and North Vietnam.

President Kennedy's first thought on taking office was to retrieve the CIA's blunders by force. Secretary McNamara was obliged to inform him there were no troops available for an invasion of Laos. Some in the Pentagon favored using nuclear weapons instead. But the Bay of Pigs had undermined presidential confidence in their advice. (A few months later Kennedy told an aide that "if it hadn't been for Cuba we would be fighting in Laos today.") His indecision was resolved by Ambassador Harriman. Unlike most diplomats who had been avoiding responsibility since the McCarthy era, Harriman was accustomed to it. The most distinguished and experienced man in the service, he took advantage of that fact by arranging to speak with Prince Souvanna Phouma. Souvanna assured Harriman that Laos could be neutralized by a coalition government that included the Pathet Lao. Harriman persuaded President Kennedy to take that chance. A cease-fire was arranged and negotiations begun in Geneva. It took all Harriman's great skill to bring it off, but eventually the talks bore fruit. On July 21, 1962, agreement was reached in Geneva on a neutralized Laos with a tripartite government.

The Geneva agreement was a tribute equally to Harriman's strength and America's weakness. It was possible because the U.S., and Russia even more, wanted Laos eliminated as a great-power issue. But it did not change conditions on the ground much. The Royal Laotian Army and the Pathet Lao remained incompatible. The RLA was still backed by the CIA and the Pentagon, and the Pathet Lao by North Vietnam.

The main result of Geneva was that it made Souvanna Phouma dependent on the CIA. The coalition government soon collapsed and fighting resumed, but with a difference. The Pathet Lao was now a comparatively large and well-equipped force. This led the U.S. to intervene more directly than before, chiefly from the air. In the early years few suffered from the struggle between Vientiane and the Pathet Lao. The most sanguinary engagement was Kong Le's expulsion from Vientiane by General Phoumi. Six hundred or so died then, mostly civilians caught between the two sides. But from 1965 on many died and more were displaced as the Pathet Lao expanded and the U.S. retaliated with air attacks. By the decade's end perhaps a third of the population had been uprooted and unnumbered thousands killed with inconclusive results. As was to be the case in Vietnam, in order to save the country it became necessary to destroy it.

The ruin of Laos was all the easier because it mattered so little. The President wished to save face, the CIA its playground. Few outside the government cared much one way or another. Cuba was quite another case. It had humiliated the President in 1961. It was a standing offense to the American sense of order. For both reasons the government needed to do something that would eliminate Cuba as a public question. In 1962 Russia provided a way to accomplish that by sending missiles to Cuba. It is still not clear why. The official American view is that it was done to bridge the missile gap. Russia's first generation of ICBM's had turned out badly and were never fully deployed. Until the next generation was ready, Russia was stuck with a handful of ICBM's in unprotected sites. Its medium-range ballistic missiles couldn't reach the U.S. It had few strategic bombers and missile-firing submarines. Putting MRBM's in Cuba would, it was thought, redress the balance of terror.

This was a useful interpretation because it justified the American response. But it was probably not true. Jane's *All the World's Aircraft*, the standard authority, said in its 1964–65 edition that the missiles deployed in Cuba had a range of 220 miles. This was hardly enough to change the balance of terror. It was quite adequate to defend Cuba, however. Cuba's problem was that with conventional weapons it could never stop a serious American invasion. But a handful of nuclear armed missiles might do the job, and more cheaply. This explains why Cuba wanted the missiles, not why Russia donated them. Perhaps Premier Khrushchev hoped to reduce the expense of arming Cuba. Or maybe he thought that as the U.S. had IRBM's in Italy and Turkey it could hardly protest Russia's doing likewise in a smaller way. Whatever the reason, Premier Khrushchev miscalculated. No administration could expect to keep the existence of missiles in Cuba a secret, if only because the Joint Chiefs or the CIA would leak the news. And once made public no administration could fail to react, especially one in so weak a political position as President Kennedy's, and certainly not just before a congressional election.

Kennedy had trouble believing that Khrushchev could be so foolish. The Soviets had never deployed nuclear weapons outside of Russia before. Premier Khrushchev was not adventurous. When Senator Kenneth Keating began saying there were missiles in Cuba he was not believed, except by the anti-Castro faithful. He offered no hard evidence, and the anti-Castro forces had cried wolf too often before. But on October 14 U-2 flights showed that missile sites were being built in Cuba. Though the CIA's record did not inspire instant agreement, this time it was right. President Kennedy then bypassed the national security bureaucracy and established an informal body of advisers later called the Executive Committee of the National Security Council. Ex Com consisted mostly of Kennedy loyalists.* They could be trusted to protect the President's interest as the national security people could not. The military naturally wanted to bomb or invade Cuba. Some asked for a nuclear strike. Attorney General Kennedy was their chief antagonist. Later he would write: "I thought, as I listened, of the many times I had heard the military take positions which, if wrong, had the advantage that no one would be around at the end to know." People changed sides and positions throughout. Robert Kennedy remained moderate and practical. He was the key figure in the Ex Com and, after the President, the man most responsible for the crisis's nonviolent resolution.

At first some thought the crisis was really over Berlin. Others believed the Russians' plan was to trade off its Cuban missiles for U.S. missiles in Turkey and Italy. Most believed the Cuban missiles threatened American security. McNamara did not, but appreciated their threat to American prestige, especially in Latin America. President Kennedy saw them as yet another test of will. In order to pass the test before election time he resolved to have the crisis in public. It would have been easy to give Russia a private warning. Foreign Minister Gromyko was scheduled to meet the President on October 18 and could have been instructed then. But secret negotiations ran the risk of exposure before matters could be settled, perhaps even before the election.

The next question was what sort of pressure to use. An immediate air strike was ruled out because, as the Attorney General put it, "My brother

---

* They included Vice-President Johnson, Secretaries Rusk, Dillon, and McNamara, Attorney General Kennedy, General Taylor, Roswell Gilpatric, George Ball, McGeorge Bundy, Theodore Sorensen, Ambassador Bohlen, and others. Director McCone of the CIA soon joined it. When Bohlen left for Paris he was replaced by Llewellyn Thompson, newly arrived from Moscow.

is not going to be the Tojo of the 1960's." (Dean Acheson left Ex Com in disgust at this.) Most members were persuaded to start with a naval blockade by Secretary McNamara's celebrated "maintaining the options" argument. If one began with the least violent alternative, it was always possible to escalate should it fail, he pointed out. But beginning with the most violent act left nothing but nuclear war to fall back on. Despite the congested emotional atmosphere, common sense prevailed. The Joint Chiefs' final plea for a Pearl Harbor was rejected. But everyone agreed that if the blockade didn't work, air strikes and an invasion would have to follow. Accordingly, 156 ICBM's were readied for launch. Strategic bombers were either airborne or on fifteen-minute alert. The Navy organized a fleet of 180 vessels; 250,000 troops were assembled for the invasion. The creation of this great striking force on short notice was the first dividend from President Kennedy's rearmament program. Then, as later in Vietnam, flexible response permitted steps that could not have been taken before.

On October 22 Kennedy informed the cabinet and a congressional delegation of the crisis and his plans to meet it.* At 6 P.M. he received Ambassador Dobrynin and ordered the Soviet missiles removed. At seven he went on television and told the country what had happened and what to expect. The people were assured that he would run any risk, including thermonuclear war, on their behalf. TV newsmen displayed maps with sweeping arcs showing every large city but Seattle to be in range of Cuba's missiles. Schoolchildren practiced hiding under their desks again. Each day tension grew as missile-bearing Russian ships approached the blockade line. Would they try to cross it? Would they be stopped or sunk? Would Russia strike back then? On retiring no one knew if he would live to see the morning. Was the country, perhaps the world, to perish now?

It was the most dangerous moment in the Cold War. Yet few people complained. Most went about their work as usual. Russian perfidy was denounced, the government's resolution applauded. Years of indoctrination had done their job. Men agreed that genocide or suicide was better than allowing Russia to do in Cuba what the U.S. had done in Turkey. A handful did protest. A tiny band of peace leaders including Norman Thomas, A. J. Muste, and Carey McWilliams called on the U.S. to end its blockade, Russia to withdraw its missiles, and Cuba to declare its neutrality. Secretary General U Thant of the UN asked the great powers to stand down for a few weeks. President Kennedy never for a moment considered doing so. The whole of his policy was to make Russia choose

---

* The congressional leaders irritated him by wanting to invade Cuba. Not having shared in the group dynamics that produced the blockade, they could hardly appreciate how irrelevant their advice was.

surrender or destruction. Suspending the blockade would ruin it. In any case, he could not wait that long as the elections were only two weeks away.

For the same reason he could not consider a trade-off. Earlier Ambassador Stevenson had urged the President to consider withdrawing the Jupiter missiles from Italy and Turkey if Russia would do the same in Cuba. In fact, Kennedy had ordered the Jupiters out months before because, being vulnerable to a first strike, they would be useless in an emergency. (The same was of course true of Russia's missiles in Cuba, even if they had had a long range, which they didn't.) But if he were to arrange now for diplomatic reasons what he had ordered before on military grounds he would be charged with "appeasement." Nor did he want to fortify General de Gaulle's prediction that in a crisis the U.S. would abandon Europe. When Walter Lippmann made the same proposal in a column, Russia, thinking it an official trial balloon, responded favorably. Naturally, nothing came of it.*

On the 24th the crisis began easing. A dozen Soviet vessels on the way to Cuba were diverted or halted. This inspired Dean Rusk's most memorable statement in office: "We're eyeball to eyeball and I think the other fellow just blinked." Conditions remained dangerous, however. Construction of the missile sites continued. The Navy was in contact with six Russian submarines, and forced all of them to surface at one time or another. No one could be sure what the Navy would do if a Russian ship tried to run the blockade. McNamara attempted to explain to Admiral Anderson, Chief of Naval Operations, that the function of the blockade was not to kill Russians but to communicate with the Kremlin. It was unclear whether Admiral Anderson ever grasped the distinction, which was probably why he was not reappointed when his first term expired.

On the 26th a solution began to emerge. First through an unofficial emissary, then in a long emotional letter, Premier Khrushchev started backing off. While insisting that the Cuban missiles were purely defensive, he admitted that President Kennedy would not believe that. He implied that an American noninvasion pledge would enable him to remove the missiles. President Kennedy liked the idea. His advisers feared a Russian trick. Before anything could be done another letter from Moscow arrived offering to trade off Russia's Cuban missiles for America's Turkish and Italian ones. This was, of course, unacceptable, so Ex Com

---

* Stevenson suggested the trade-off because he knew it would go down well in the UN. But his doing so made Attorney General Kennedy think him insufficiently tough. When Stevenson returned to the UN John McCloy went along to insure his resolution. This doubtlessly confirmed Dean Rusk's belief that it was a mistake to represent one's constituency in such matters. Thereafter Rusk's preference for military as against diplomatic solutions was if anything more distinct.

began talking of an air strike again. Then Robert Kennedy produced one of those strokes of genius so obvious in retrospect, so difficult to find when needed. He suggested responding to the first Khrushchev letter and ignoring the second. Accordingly, Ambassador Dobrynin was given a letter accepting the implied proposal to exchange missiles for promises. He was told that if no answer was forthcoming in two or three days Cuba would be bombed. The device worked. On the next day, Sunday, October 28, Radio Moscow announced that the missile sites were being dismantled. President Kennedy insisted on his full pound of flesh all the same. He would not give a noninvasion pledge until Cuba returned its few Ilyushin jet bombers to Russia. These were directly under Premier Castro's control and he would not give them up. Nor would he allow UN observers to determine that Cuba was free of "offensive" weapons. Some on Ex Com wanted to forget the bombers as they were obsolete anyway. But the President persisted and Dr. Castro gave way. He never did allow UN observers into Cuba though, so the U.S. was not obliged to give a no-invasion pledge. Hence the administration got everything it wanted and gave nothing in return, not even a paper promise.

Having driven Moscow to the wall, Washington now began explaining that it had not. It was soon official dogma that the administration had shown incredible restraint and a keen sensitivity to Premier Khrushchev's political situation. Arthur Schlesinger, Jr., later wrote: "It was a combination of toughness and restraint, of will, nerve, and wisdom, so brilliantly controlled, so matchlessly calibrated, that it dazzled the world." And the President himself drew this moral from the crisis: "Above all, while defending our own vital interests, nuclear powers must avert those confrontations which bring an adversary to the choice of either a humiliating retreat or a nuclear war." In fact the President had stripped Premier Khrushchev bare, denying him even the fig leaf of a missile swap to cover his nakedness. The U.S. never negotiated. It merely issued ultimatums backed by an overwhelming display of force. Yet the crisis was said to be a triumph of American craft and subtlety. Crisis management had become an exact science, it was claimed. Ambitious men hoped to emulate the legendary figures in Ex Com, and feared only (though wrongly) that there would be no more great crises to manage.*

* One of the few to dispute the official line was I. F. Stone, who argued that the risks run seemed disproportionate to the threat posed. "How would the historians of mankind," he wrote, "if a fragment survived, have regarded the events of October? Would they have thought us justified in blowing most of mankind to smithereens rather than negotiate, or appeal to the UN, or even to leave in Cuba the medium-range missiles which were no different after all from those we had long aimed at the Russians from Turkey and England? When a whole people is in a state of mind where it is ready to risk extinction—its own and everybody else's—as a means of having its own way in an international dispute, the readiness for murder has become a way of life and a world menace."

The crisis had many effects. President Kennedy was at last persuaded that his will and courage were no longer in doubt. This enabled him to consider serious negotiations with Russia and led to the test-ban treaty. Some were sobered by the experience. Robert Kennedy would later write that if any one of six other men on Ex Com had been President, "I think the world might have been blown up." The President benefited politically from his handling of the affair. On election day Democrats held their own in the House and picked up a few more Senate seats. As the party in power nearly always loses ground in the off-year elections, this was considered a victory. The Camelot myth was well launched.

Premier Khrushchev was ruined by the missile crisis. For him, as Michel Tatu points out, it was a Bay of Pigs in reverse. He was criticized both for having launched the adventure, and for failing to see it through. His decline, which dated from the U-2 affair, accelerated. This was not so happy an event as men thought then. It was fashionable in America to depict the Premier as a Prince of Darkness and a worthy heir of Stalin. But though a brutal man (he could not have survived Stalin's reign had he been otherwise), his policies were hardly contemptible. For whatever selfish reasons, he stood for de-Stalinization at home and détente abroad. He would be replaced by men of sterner views. There was no profit and some loss for America in the exchange. Afterward, destroying his prestige would not seem to have been quite the shrewd move it first appeared.

Surprisingly, all chances of an accommodation with Cuba were not lost. Several weeks before the crisis President Dorticos had offered to demilitarize his country in return for a nonaggression pact with the U.S. Ambassador Stevenson wished to follow this up, but was obliged to answer Dorticos with the usual formula that "the maintenance of communism is not negotiable" (though, of course, not reversible either). The crisis showed Cuba that Russia was not an entirely reliable ally. Russia had, in effect, sold Cuba out to protect itself. Perhaps that was why Premier Castro signed an agreement on December 21 to release the prisoners taken at the Bay of Pigs. President Kennedy did not exploit this overture. On the contrary, he went to Miami and gave an emotional address to the wretched survivors assuring them that their flag "will be returned to this brigade in a free Havana." Mrs. Kennedy hoped that John Kennedy, Jr., would grow to be half as brave as they.

The missile crisis illuminated several curious aspects of America's foreign policy in the early sixties. One was the isolation of decision-makers from reality. Ex Com and the senior officials connected with it lived in a closed environment where it was entirely in order to propose not only Pearl Harbors but Doomsdays as well. Whatever evil resulted, they mostly agreed, would be Russia's fault. This disposed of the moral question. Speaking only to one another, sharing the same assumptions and values, governed by abstract conceptions of will, power, and prestige, Ex Com (and its counterpart in the Kremlin probably) showed how thin a line divided strategy from insanity. In this feverish atmosphere Robert Kennedy's chief virtue was displayed to particular advantage. What distinguished him from his fellow crisis managers was not so much intellect, or courage, or even common decency, but manhood. This was not always an agreeable trait. It gave him more than his share of the family's showy machismo. It was responsible for his notorious "ruthlessness." But it kept him in touch with the more ordinary concerns of humanity— the passion for life, the sense that a man is answerable for what he does. Thus anchored, Kennedy was able to resist the Strangelovian militarists and geopoliticians who cared more for glory than the interests of mankind.

Finally, the crisis showed again the limits of power. Though mighty beyond belief, the U.S. was unable satisfactorily to coerce small but stubborn nations. It wouldn't do to drop an H-bomb on Cuba or North Vietnam or East Germany. Invading them was not much more practical. This seemed to exhaust the alternatives. Hence Washington's response when faced with a small problem concerning a truculent little power was to magnify it into a big problem so that great-power solutions could be applied to it. Instead of dealing with an East Germany or a Cuba, the U.S. tried to involve Russia (sometimes even China). If Cuba wasn't awed by the bomb, Russia was, or so the reasoning seemed to be. Perhaps Washington thought it degrading to negotiate with Havana or Hanoi on equal terms. Maybe it really believed that Russia called the tune in every communist country. In any case, however emotionally satisfying it was, this strategy rarely worked. Premier Castro and President Ho were not puppets. Conflicts in Southeast Asia and Latin America could not be resolved in Geneva or Vienna, especially when all the parties did not participate. Elevating a crisis to the great-power level made it more dangerous and no less soluble. The missile crisis turned out differently than most, but only because the great power involved was actually responsible for it. Otherwise, the U.S. went on denying the fact of its impotence in Cuba and elsewhere. It kept on trying to match international problems with predetermined solutions. Yet American policy was called "pragmatic," and its makers described as hardheaded, nononsense men of affairs.

After the missile crisis came the Meredith crisis. That too was a triumph for the President. It began the year before when James Meredith applied for admission to Ole Miss, as the University of Mississippi was fondly called. Meredith had been born in Mississippi, graduated from a Florida high school, and served eight years in the Air Force. At the time of his application he was a student at Jackson State College. Meredith integrated Ole Miss for several reasons, but especially because he genuinely wanted to study there. Mediocre as it was, Ole Miss was still the best institution of higher learning in a desperately poor and backward state. Meredith was an ambitious man, a principled man too. He knew his rights and meant to have them, whatever the cost.

By the end of September 1962 all the University's attempts to prevent his enrollment had failed. Though urged to say that students who violently resisted his admission would be punished, the University administration feared to do so. Ross Barnett, governor of the state, was equally unstrung. He had been elected on the customary segregationist platform, and his only ambition now was to save face. In secret negotiations with Attorney General Kennedy, who had taken personal charge of the Meredith case, he tried to make a deal. After a token resistance, he would step aside and allow Meredith to be brought on campus. The Attorney General was willing to cooperate if the governor would keep order on the campus. Barnett was evasive. If he did protect Meredith from violence he would be compromised locally, if he didn't Kennedy could reveal their secret talks to the same effect. Though bargaining with the governor was probably necessary, it contributed to the confusion that followed when Barnett tried to keep Meredith from registering for classes. Meredith was finally registered on September 30. That evening President Kennedy went on television and asked Mississippians to obey the law. Even as he spoke rioting broke out at Ole Miss. Attacks by four thousand students and outsiders were met by a small force of U.S. marshals. General Walker was there to encourage the studentry, and may even have led one charge. The rioters were further heartened by their traditional college cheer which went "Hotty toddy, God A'mighty/ Who in the hell are we/ Flim flam, bim bam/ Ole Miss, by damn." When the fighting ended the marshals still held their ground, and though many were injured none died. Casualties among the students were numerous but not serious. However, a newsman and a bystander were shot to death.

Troops were brought in to maintain order, and several hundred remained until Meredith graduated. He was harassed in various ways until the worst offenders were expelled. The next year thirty-nine professors resigned, and some who helped integrate Ole Miss were later forced out, most notably the distinguished historian James Silver. Meredith got his degree and went on to New York where he studied law and began what was to be a peculiar career in politics and civil rights. Governor Barnett was convicted of civil contempt by a federal court and heavily fined.

The next Negro to enroll at the University was given no protection, and when he provided his own was expelled for carrying it. Two more did enroll successfully after him, however, so the integration of Ole Miss seemed assured. The affair probably made no difference to the administration's fortunes. Few votes were lost since the South was largely hostile to it already. Nor could it have gained many as Negroes had nowhere else to go politically in any case. But if the practical consequences of the Meredith case were slight, its symbolic importance was very great. New luster was added to the Kennedy legend, and the pleasure they derived from seeing white racist power humbled in Mississippi helped reconcile many Negroes to the slow pace of integration, to the administration's inability to get a sweeping civil rights bill, and to its failure to protect rights workers in the South from intimidation and assassination. Here, as elsewhere, public relations bridged the gap between promise and performance.

By the end of 1962 the administration had some grounds for satisfaction. The missile crisis had been a triumph of brinkmanship. In Asia President Diem was still hanging on, while the undeclared Sino-Indian War diminished the appeal of China to some nonaligned nations and made the U.S. seem more attractive. Congress gave the President sweeping new powers to negotiate with the European Common Market countries. This advanced what some friendly journalists were calling his Grand Design for American-European relations. As they saw it, the U.S. was trying to take advantage of Western Europe's new prosperity and relative harmony. Europe would be asked to bear a larger share of the NATO burden, and to contribute more to the underdeveloped nations. The U.S., in turn, would help supply Europe with some kind of modern nuclear deterrent of its own, acceptable to both France and Germany, and would reduce tariffs on European exports. As Joseph Kraft put it, "The inner meaning of the Grand Design is partnership in growth. The United States will be plugged into the dynamism of Western Europe. The Old World will be called in to redress the balance of the New." There were setbacks of course, especially in Latin America where the Alliance for Progress bogged down. Latin governments were happy to accept American help; reluctant to make the internal reforms thought necessary to its proper application. Congress continued to take a dim view of foreign aid, and the President had his request for funds pared down from nearly $5 billion to less than $4 billion.

Congress was stubborn about other matters too. Medicare failed in the Senate. A program for federal aid to higher education was in the main rejected. A proposed Department of Urban Affairs stalled after the President indicated he would make a Negro, Robert C. Weaver, head of it. But the administration did get most of its bills through, if not always in the form it wanted. Congress passed its communications' satellite bill, despite a filibuster by Senate liberals who objected to having private groups profit from what had been developed with the public's money. As usual, Congress considered the rich more deserving of aid than the poor. Handouts for the poor were considered degrading and destructive; for the rich they were declarations of faith in the free-enterprise system. The administration was further encouraged when it broke even in the off-year elections, and by the defeat of H. Stuart Hughes in his bid for a Senate seat. A professor of history at Harvard, Hughes ran on an independent platform which featured unilateral American disarmament. Though he had some three thousand volunteer workers, he secured only fifty thousand votes, a mere 2 per cent of the total. There was still no room in American politics for left-wing and pacifist critics of the government. Even more heartening was Richard Nixon's failure to win the governorship of California. He told reporters they wouldn't have Nixon to kick around any longer and announced his retirement from public life. Unemployment continued at a high rate. The balance of payments showed another deficit, so did the budget. But all in all 1962 was a good year for the administration.

1963 was President Kennedy's best year in office, despite its bad start on January 2, 1963, when the Viet Cong won the war in South Vietnam. As the year opened Ap Bac, a village in the Mekong Delta, was invaded by the Viet Cong's elite 514th Battalion. Saigon moved four battalions and an armored company against it. The 514th chewed them up, then made a clean escape. The government claimed victory. American newsmen and military advisers knew better. Ap Bac demonstrated that the recent arms buildup had accomplished nothing. The South Vietnamese army (ARVN) was as incompetent as before and the VC stronger. Barring further U.S. intervention, the war was lost.

To understand why, we must go back to 1954 when what had been French Indochina was divided into four parts. Laos and Cambodia became independent, and Vietnam was partitioned. The northern half became the Democratic Republic of Vietnam with its capital in Hanoi. Saigon presided over what became the Republic of Vietnam in the South. Although it had been agreed at Geneva that there were to be elections in 1956 on reunification, they never took place. Saigon, knowing it would lose to Hanoi, if only because of Ho Chi Minh's prestige as the father of Vietnamese independence, refused to hold them. The French maxim that nothing is so permanent as the provisional was once more borne out. Both states proved to be viable. The DRV became an efficient communist state led by "Uncle" Ho and his disciplined veterans. North Vietnam had never been able to feed itself, so the regime concentrated on industrial development. The bulk of the population, which did not immediately benefit from this policy, was reconciled to it in several ways. The ethnic minorities (including seven major tribes) were given partial self-government. Land vacated by the nearly 900,000 Roman Catholics who moved south before partition was distributed among the peasants. The Catholic migration was helpful in other ways too. It removed potential subversives and spared the country a bloody purge of anti-communists. The regime was not without its horrors, notably in land reform, which was conducted with great brutality. Bernard Fall estimated that fifty thousand landlords, often very small ones, were killed. President Ho called off the land program in 1956, too late to prevent an uprising in his own home province. Perhaps six thousand farmers were executed or deported before the uprising was suppressed. Thereafter agricultural change was promoted more tactfully. The foundation of an industrial economy was laid. Living standards were maintained at about their old levels. Despite its shortcomings, no one doubted that the government enjoyed the respect, and in Ho's case probably the affection as well, of its people.

In the South things were more complex. The French puppet, Emperor Bao Dai, was replaced by Ngo Dinh Diem, a Roman Catholic aristocrat with excellent American connections. He crushed the warring religious sects and established Saigon's authority. To everyone's surprise, the communization of Indochina was arrested. Even a degree of prosperity obtained, though Vietnam never regained its prewar status as an exporter of rice. Diem's success entitled him to American support, and he got it. Appearances were never more deceptive, however. Diem's regime was dominated by Catholics and Northerners who were isolated from the native population on both counts. The North Vietnamese traditionally viewed Southerners as lazy, backward, and inefficient. The vaguely Buddhist majority of the country was ruled, therefore, by an alien and arrogant caste. The government promised land reforms but failed to deliver. Its program of buying surplus lands for redistribution was slow and expensive. In seven years only one million hectares were purchased, of which barely a quarter went to landless peasants. Traditional abuses went untouched for the most part. The government treated the mountain tribesmen even worse. The Vietnamese were deeply prejudiced against the tribesmen to begin with. Accordingly, the Diem regime implemented a brutal colonization policy that cheated the tribes of their ancestral lands. Since this was how the West had been won, the U.S. had trouble protesting it.

Americans could speak with greater conviction on South Vietnam's economy, but, as it turned out, no more successfully. Trade and construction flourished without regard for social needs or future consequences. Between 1957 and 1960 a building boom increased the country's usable space as follows: 47,000 square meters were devoted to cinemas and dance halls, and 6,500 square meters to hospitals; 56,000 square meters to churches or pagodas, and 3,500 square meters to rice mills; 425,000 square meters to high-rent villas and apartments, and 86,000 square meters to schools. Imported goods produced a trade deficit of $185 million in 1961 alone, an amount equal to two-thirds of all the currency in circulation.

The insurrection began as early as 1957 when scattered groups of Viet Minh partisans concluded that President Diem would neither permit reunification with the North nor preside over a social revolution in the South. They dug up arms cached during the partition, then gradually re-equipped themselves with captured weapons. Their operations expanded until in some areas the Viet Cong (which meant simply "Vietnamese Communists," a label they rejected) became the effective government. The insurrection was largely self-sustaining. A few advisers and liaison people from Hanoi filtered down to them, but mostly their reinforcements consisted of native Southerners who had moved north during the partition. The VC offered land to the peasants and some autonomy to the tribes. Everywhere their energy and dedication contrasted favorably to the corruption and arrogance of government officials. Mostly the VC were indigenous while officials were often strangers to the districts they governed. It was customary for South Vietnam's civil and military officers to purchase those appointments that graft made profitable. They earned plenty of money, but little respect and less loyalty.

Such a government could hardly cope with serious revolutionaries, and it didn't. President Diem had his secret police, trained by experts from Michigan State University, to no avail. The prison camps filled up. His visible opposition was silenced. But repression only bred further resentment to the Viet Cong's advantage. President Diem's position was untenable. The Viet Cong could only be defeated by overwhelming force, or sweeping reforms which would undercut their popular base (or, perhaps, some combination of the two). Neither alternative was open to him. His army was too corrupt, demoralized, and inept to find and destroy the elusive foe. His support came from the very people who profited by those abuses that demanded reform. All he could do was authorize fresh repressions which bought him time while further alienating his countrymen.

President Diem was poorly served by American policies which abetted his delusions. At first the American military mission (MAAG) adhered to the "last remnant" theory which held that the rebels were merely Viet Minh leftovers. Even when it became clear that the insurrection was more broadly based, MAAG clung to its old ways. The ARVN had been established as a conventional force because what the American generals feared most was another Korea. To prevent it they wanted a South Vietnamese army capable of repelling an invasion from North Vietnam. To transform the ARVN into a counterinsurgency force would be terribly difficult. Worse still, it would leave the South open to attack, which could involve the U.S. Army itself in another futile Asian war. Officers conditioned from birth to believe that American arms always prevail found stalemate intolerable, defeat unthinkable. The ARVN was designed, then, to meet American rather than Vietnamese needs, and though conditions on the ground changed, those needs did not. Hence when the insurrection broke out the Army had to blame it on North Vietnam because a threat from the North was the only one it was prepared to meet.

As with MAAG, so with the nonmilitary American advisers in South Vietnam. American aid was based on the notion that President Diem was fairly popular and effective. To admit that the rebellion was largely indigenous would be to confess the failure of American policies, and the principles on which they rested. It was much easier to blame everything on the North. Thus the American commitment to President Diem, which began as a kind of low-risk gamble, began to escalate. President Eisenhower left office before the situation deteriorated to a point where the crucial decision had to be made. Chances are that he would not have intervened directly. After all, the Viet Minh had really won the Indochina war in 1954, only to be denied all the fruits of that victory at Geneva. Everyone had expected North Vietnam to win the referendum scheduled for 1956. South Vietnam had been written off in advance. At first President Diem offered the U.S. a chance to salvage something from the wreckage at little cost. If he succeeded in his unlikely enterprise, so much the better. If he failed, nothing was lost save money. By 1961 this was no longer true. Now more than money was at issue; men would be needed too. And once American blood was spilled no President could abandon Vietnam, for to do so would mean that American boys had died in vain.

Considering the gravity of this decision, it was surprising how casually President Kennedy made it. Partly, it seems, he enlarged the American presence to impress Premier Khrushchev with his resolution, and partly because he didn't want to be charged with having "lost" Vietnam. Here again, the decision was made on the basis of American rather than Vietnamese needs. And, once more, aggression from the North was invoked to sanction it. In support of this proposition yet another dreary

State Department document (a "blue book" rather than a "white paper" this time) was ground out. It charged that sheer frustration in Hanoi over the South Vietnamese "miracle" had prompted it to stir up contented villagers. In support of this fiction a handful of captured weapons were displayed. The Kennedy administration was not, of course, wholly captive to its own propaganda. President Diem was encouraged to broaden his base and enact some reforms. Great weight was placed on counterinsurgency techniques, especially those of the U.S. Special Forces, President Kennedy's favorite soldiers. The administration thus admitted in practice what it denied in principle. Generally, however, it perpetuated old errors while committing fresh ones. The ARVN was given new equipment, but it remained a conventional force. Its officers continued to be chosen for political and commercial reasons. The enlisted men were still dragooned, demoralized, and impoverished. President Diem grew ever more paranoid and suspicious. By the end of 1962 there were perhaps ten thousand U.S. troops in South Vietnam.

On January 14, 1963, during his third State of the Union Message, President Kennedy observed that "the spearpoint of aggression has been blunted in South Vietnam." This was less than two weeks after the battle of Ap Bac. A little later Admiral Harry Felt, who commanded the Pacific theater, said that the "South Vietnamese should achieve victory in three years." In March MAAG's commander, General Paul D. Harkins, announced that "victory is in sight." General Harkins went to extraordinary lengths to preserve his innocence. After the ARVN's 7th Division had been beaten at Ap Bac, its American adviser, Lieutenant Colonel John Vann, sent Harkins a report detailing its corruption, incompetence, and reluctance to fight. Vann himself was a conservative, almost a reactionary. But he was a brilliant soldier and an expert on unconventional warfare. In Vietnam, he often said, the best weapon was the knife. The rifle was next best, because at least you knew whom you were shooting at. The airplane, a promiscuous destroyer, was the poorest weapon of all.* As divisional adviser Vann walked through an operation every week in an effort to inspire the ARVN's officers. He never quite understood that the whole point of being an officer in the South Vietnamese army was that you didn't have to go into the field. All the same, he suffered from few of MAAG's illusions. His report had a predictable affect on General Harkins. Harkins was a conventional soldier. His job was to get along with President Diem, and one got along with the President by going along

---

* David Halberstam, who has written on Vann at length, offered an incident from his own experience that illustrates this point. On his first trip to the Delta Halberstam noticed that the peasants below froze when helicopters went over them. It was explained to him that the gunners were in the habit of firing at anyone who ran. Having learned this, the farmers held their place and generally survived. Though that day a gunner in Halberstam's craft shot one anyhow out of nervousness.

with him. Since Vann's report indicted both American policy and the delusions on which it rested, General Harkins decided to fire Vann, though his aides talked him out of doing so. When Vann's tour of duty ended he came back to Washington with proof of the ARVN's incompetence. He was not even debriefed, and soon resigned in despair.

As with the military, so with the American political mission in Saigon. Having staked everything on President Diem's success, the mission had to ignore evidences of his decline. It treated every handout from the presidential palace as gospel truth, every critical newspaper story as malicious nonsense. It turned a blind eye to President Diem's increasing reliance on his unscrupulous brother Ngo Dinh Nhu. When the President's beautiful sister-in-law, the amazing Madam Nhu, banned divorce, dancing, and the singing of romantic or sad songs, the mission said nothing. It did feebly resist Nhu's campaign against the Buddhists, which turned out to be the final nail in President Diem's coffin. On May 8, when the Vietnamese celebrate Buddha's birthday, they were forbidden to fly the customary flags. A protesting crowd was fired on by government troops and nine people were killed, seven of them children. This triggered a deadly struggle between the regime and the bonzes (monks), who fell heir to all the political discontent the government had suppressed. On June 11, 1963, Thich Quang Duc, an elderly bonze, set himself on fire in protest. The next day U.S. Ambassador Frederick E. Nolting declared that "South Vietnam is on its way to victory." In July and August there were more self-immolations. Madame Nhu said that she clapped her hands in pleasure whenever a bonze "barbecued" himself, and hoped only that David Halberstam of the *New York Times* would do likewise. (Even President Kennedy had only wanted the *Times* to recall him.) Halberstam was one of a small band of reporters in Vietnam who were telling the truth in dispatches home. Though a credit to their profession, they profoundly embarrassed their government. A policy based on fiction could, as it turned out, withstand the truth, but not comfortably. Readers of the *New York Times* knew what was happening in Vietnam, even if the government didn't. They could not, however, change the government's direction. Washington could neither win the war in Vietnam nor withdraw from it. Faced with a choice between the impossible and the impolitic, Washington evaded both and soldiered grimly on with President Diem.

It was, finally, the Buddhists, and not the press or public opinion at home, that forced a change. On August 21, at Nhu's insistence, President Diem ordered an attack on the pagodas. Hundreds of bonzes and nuns were arrested. Martial law was declared. Wholesale arrests of the discontented, including many teen-age boys and girls, followed. Next day the unfortunate Nolting's successor, Henry Cabot Lodge, arrived in Saigon. Lodge was one of President Kennedy's happier appointments. A former Senator and ambassador to the United Nations, Richard Nixon's running mate in 1960, Lodge brought to Vietnam the distinction of his great name, much experience in politics and government, and formidable abilities. The only mystery about his appointment was his acceptance of it since Vietnam was already becoming the graveyard of reputations. If he did well, President Kennedy would get the credit. If he did badly, the Republican party would have a share of the blame. To go there was a serious, probably a fatal, political risk.

With Lodge came many changes. He won reporters over and detached the embassy somewhat from the regime. He personally supervised all the mission's work and took no one into his confidence. Lodge was poor with small groups (though eloquent in formal speeches), but he wrote beautiful reports to Washington where it counted. One of his subordinates—no admirer—later wrote of him: "In the barracuda world of government service, Lodge's protective shell was an invaluable asset, enabling him to operate as he thought best with serene ruthlessness— which is exactly what it often requires to get anything done in the government. Right or wrong, he knew what he wanted. He crushed the spirits of many of us, but he also disengaged the operations of the U.S. Mission from the endless, agonized soul-searching that prevailed before his arrival. He was a commander by instinct, in a situation where resolute commanders had been hard to come by. Lodge expected to be judged on performance, not on the affection of his staff."

He was the perfect choice for the new policy of coercion which the U.S. government gradually arrived at. President Kennedy had made a mistake in not exacting concessions beforehand when he rescued Ngo Dinh Diem in 1961. Now, at Lodge's prompting, he attempted to repair that error. It is still not clear whether the administration meant to overthrow President Diem if he remained obdurate, though that was certainly the ARVN high command's impression. But the administration was determined to have the anti-Buddhist campaign called off and substantial reforms enacted. The Voice of America began to criticize Diem's regime while specifically exempting the Vietnamese military. White House interpreters in Saigon drew the appropriate conclusions. President Kennedy then ended certain kinds of aid to South Vietnam, notably the vital Commercial Import Program. Madam Nhu helped the administration immensely by going around America denouncing it. On November 1 President Kennedy's efforts bore fruit. A military junta seized power after murdering President Diem and his brother. (In the curious official language of South Vietnam, their deaths were pronounced "accidental suicide.") Madam Nhu went to Europe with her equally beautiful daughter and bought a Paris bank. The regime's fall compelled Washington to face reality. As late as October 2 Secretary McNamara and General Taylor were still saying that the U.S. mission would no longer be needed after 1965. McNamara had just ordered the withdrawal of a thousand troops. But the new regime, eager to stay in power and now able to blame everything on Diem, was soon to admit what the press had been saying all along: the war was indeed being lost. President Kennedy would again have been forced to choose between escalation and withdrawal. Before he could do so fate intervened. In one of those odd coincidences by which life mocks art, the American President soon followed his Vietnamese opposite number to the grave, and in the same way. The guns of November took both their lives.

Official Washington worried as much about General de Gaulle as Vietnam in those days. What Arthur Schlesinger, Jr., would call the administration's "Not So Grand Design" wobbled from the start. On January 14, 1963, de Gaulle declared himself against British entry into the European Economic Community. The administration seemed surprised at this, though de Gaulle's distrust of the "Anglo-Saxons" was well known. He feared British entry would make France No. 2 in the Common Market. He thought that Britain was not yet truly European. It still cherished the Commonwealth, if less so every day. And it kept hanging on to its "special relationship" with America. A few weeks earlier this had been underlined by the Kennedy-Macmillan talks in Nassau, where the U.S. agreed to supply Britain with Polaris missiles. This gave President de Gaulle an excuse to keep England out of the Common Market. Washington took the news badly. George Ball spoke of nameless European leaders dominated "by a nostalgic longing for a world that never was," who sought to revive the "vanished symbols of beglamored centuries." Privately officials were more intemperate. One State Department man described the general as a "bastard who is out to get us."

Partly such abuse was a measure of de Gaulle's greatness, partly a consequence of Washington's shortsightedness. To Americans greatness was based on material power. Having little, the French were supposed to stay in their place. But General de Gaulle's whole career refuted this thesis. During the war, though dependent on Allies who disliked him, he made himself master first of French North Africa, then of France. Afterward he won parity in the occupation of Germany, despite France's negligible contribution to victory. Later still, when the Algerian War seemed about to ruin France, he saved his country again, and then made it a force in world affairs once more. During the sixties he remained the most commanding figure in the noncommunist world.

Few Americans admitted that. De Gaulle's arrogance and vanity, however merited, sat poorly with a people who prefer false modesty to none at all. It was thought unbecoming for one whose country was free and prosperous because of American arms and American aid to speak so meanly of Uncle Sam. His attachment to the present honor and past glory of France baffled Americans, to whom the patriotism of others is always incomprehensible. His purposefulness made American policy in Europe seem even more muddled than it was. President de Gaulle believed England and the U.S. wanted to keep France down. He meant instead to have France pre-eminent in Western Europe, and Western Europe itself a third force holding the balance of power between East and West. And he hoped that one day his strategy might produce a Europe of federated states extending from "the Atlantic to the Urals."

Compared with de Gaulle's splendid confidence, American policy was embarrassingly uncertain. Its German policy was absurd, NATO was more so. Yet though meaningless except as a trip-wire to the American deterrent, NATO had been so hard to build that Americans were attached to it beyond reason. When Greece became a military dictatorship later, some argued that nothing could be done for fear it would abandon NATO. Greece's military were fully occupied in repressing their own citizenry. If driven out of NATO Greece would not be missed. Besides, it had nowhere else to go. Yet for the sake of its puny contributions to a largely mythical defense structure the U.S. tolerated, even assisted, the first noncommunist European dictatorship initiated since World War II. This was not so much *Realpolitik* as obsessiveness. NATO counted for more in American eyes than the purposes it was meant to serve.

The Nassau agreement showed another contradiction in America's European policy. Earlier Britain had contracted to buy the U.S. Skybolt missile. When finished it was to be fired from a bomber, and would, it was hoped, extend the life of Britain's obsolescent V-Bomber force. Then in 1962 Secretary McNamara canceled Skybolt as too unreliable and expensive. This was a blow to the English, and all the more so as Polaris missiles were not immediately substituted for Skybolt. The delay was suggested by some American diplomats who thought Britain would have to give up her independent deterrent to get into the Common Market. If Skybolt were merely replaced, General de Gaulle might take that as a sign of British insincerity. They were right, and he did.

The Nassau agreement was self-defeating in other respects. The U.S. wanted England in the Common Market to offset France and restrain Germany. Selling Polaris to Britain frustrated that hope. Yet it also raised the question of why the U.S. was so eager to see Britain retain nuclear capabilities that added little to American security while compromising its plans for Europe. Perhaps Washington felt that the Anglo-American alliance legitimized the Pax Americana and showed the U.S. to be England's proper heir as world policeman. But this policy encouraged Britain to live beyond her means. It aggravated the balance-of-payments problem and nourished the illusions that helped create it. America needed an England prosperous enough to play a strong role in Europe. This meant more than the slight military advantage to be gained from arming her. Wavering between guns and butter weakened the economy without adding markedly to England's military strength nor even to her prestige, probably the main reason why missiles were wanted. England was to blame for putting status ahead of profits, but so was the U.S. for sustaining this delusion.

Equally self-defeating, perhaps more so, was America's enthusiasm for the Common Market. Partly this was a tribute to American altruism. Then too, a richer Europe might become a better-armed Europe, enabling the U.S. to bring some troops home. This was a vainer hope than most. Europe showed little enthusiasm for diverting additional capital to weapons. The Soviets displayed no interest in invading Western Europe. If they did the U.S. would have to intervene anyway. France alone made sacrifices for weaponry, and then only to subvert American policies, not support them. Moreover, what assurance did the U.S. have that over time the Common Market would not harm American interests? It was intensely protectionist to begin with, and already a formidable competitor in some areas. Japan was pressing harder every year. American businessmen scarcely needed even more competition abroad, especially from an area with such imposing potential. And what guarantees did the U.S. have that a powerful Europe would follow its lead? The modest foreign policies of most European states reflected their modest capacities. It was reasonable to suppose that if merger made them strong, their foreign policies would change accordingly, especially if France had her way, and no one could say she would not.

The Multilateral Force was a perfect example of Washington's obsession with Europe in the Kennedy years. It was conceived in 1962 as a way of stopping European countries from developing independent deterrents. It might inspire the French to abandon their own *"force de frappe."* Germany would get the illusion of nuclear equality but not its substance. The MLF was aimed, then, less against Russia than France, and perhaps Germany. Germany was made to want the MLF, France was not. The proposal was for twenty-eight surface vessels, with crews drawn from at least three nationalities and armed with eight Polaris missiles, each of which the U.S. would control. German participation would supposedly ease the humiliation any big country not in the "nuclear club" was thought to feel. But France already had nuclear weapons and was working on thermonuclear ones. It did not need the MLF. Even if it did, France would not contribute to weapons systems controlled by the U.S. In fact, the "multilateral farce," as some West Europeans called it, only confirmed General de Gaulle's theory that Washington meant to keep France down. It seemed a crude effort to trick the French and make Europe all the more dependent on an ally of doubtful reliability. The MLF thus increased the fears it was meant to allay. Opposition to it became so great that President Kennedy finally dropped the scheme, though the State Department kept on trying to revive it for years.

The MLF, the hatred of General de Gaulle, the countless speeches calling for European unity, Atlantic partnership, interdependence, and the like all showed a poor sense of what the U.S. could get in Europe. Europe was no longer helpless and easily manipulated. Yet if America could not direct West European affairs any longer, it had nothing to fear from them. Western Europe and America shared fundamental interests that, fortunately, diplomatic meddling could not much impair. Even France, though it left NATO finally, remained loyal to the West and supported America during the Berlin and Cuban crises. No doubt the worst consequence of Washington's obsession with Europe was that it diverted attention from places like Latin America, where U.S. interests were less secure. This preoccupation was partly a legacy of the two world wars, partly a consequence of the Cold War. Perhaps also it was because dealing with Europe was more enchanting. European assignments were usually elegant and agreeable. They conferred more status. Who would not rather be ambassador to Great Britain than to some difficult Latin country, though the one post was largely ceremonial and the other challenging and responsible? And what Congressman would not rather make a junket to Paris than to Lima? So Western Europe, where things went as well for America as human nature permitted, was fussed over endlessly, and Latin America, where things went from bad to worse, was ignored—except briefly during revolutions.

People soon forgot the MLF, and most other setbacks the Kennedy administration suffered abroad. What they remembered was the nuclear test-ban treaty. Disarmament talks had dragged on pointlessly for years while people became more radioactive. Both sides went on filling the atmosphere with poison. Infant and prenatal mortality rates climbed. Then in 1963 the break came. Russia did not so much want a test ban as a broad agreement stabilizing, perhaps even reducing, the arms race. Premier Khrushchev was desperate to ease military pressure on the sagging Russian economy. He needed a diplomatic *coup* to offset the damage done his reputation by the series of American rebuffs. An arms-limiting agreement of some sort was his last chance to retain power. As relations with China worsened, Russia needed a détente with the West all the more. Khrushchev had been trying for one since 1955 without much luck. President Eisenhower's interest was real if fitful. President Kennedy meant to win the arms race first. Even if he had wanted to negotiate with Russia, the Bay of Pigs made that impossible. But after the missile crisis Kennedy had more room to maneuver. His will was no longer in question. He could not easily be charged with appeasement.

Public opinion apparently made him exercise this newly won option. The threat of nuclear war was too remote to bother people much. No matter how intense the arms race, relatively few worried about it. But atmospheric testing was another matter. Every rain brought the fallout down. It concentrated in adults, and even more dangerously, in children. Fears of it grew, and on June 10, 1963, at American University the President addressed himself to these fears. In a speech notably free of his customary portentousness, he said, "If we cannot end now all our differences, at least we can help make the world safe for diversity. For, in the final analysis, our most basic common link is that we all inhabit this small planet. We all breathe the same air. We all cherish our children's future. And we are all mortal." A test ban would not provide absolute security, but would offer "far more security and far fewer risks than an unabated, uncontrolled, unpredictable arms race." It was his finest address. Khrushchev thought that no President since Franklin Roosevelt had spoken so well. The President did not call for an end to all testing, only to tests above ground or in the water. Moscow wanted a general ban because to permit underground tests would continue the competition in an area where Russia was least proficient. Yet Premier Khrushchev was so eager to begin that on July 2 he agreed in principle to a partial ban.

As a sign of earnestness President Kennedy sent Averell Harriman to negotiate the treaty. The State Department was reluctant in those days to let Harriman deal with Russia, though he had more experience at it than any man and was the living American most respected by Russians. Envy was no doubt the cause—if he were absent from talks with the Russians, no one would be outshone by him. Harriman drove a hard bargain, as he was expected to. At one point Lord Hailsham, the British delegate, feared the talks would fail if Harriman didn't ease up. But Moscow gave way in the end and accepted a limited ban without any other binding stipulations. It was a victory for mankind in the abstract, and for President Kennedy in particular. Russia agreed to let tests continue underground where its technology was far behind America's. In return for this concession it got absolutely nothing except the false hope that agreement on larger matters would follow. It was a defeat for Premier Khrushchev, about the last one before his fall.

Instead of improving, the nuclear arms race got worse. The U.S. conducted more tests after the treaty than before, 210 tests as of this writing as against 98 in all the years before August 5, 1963. These produced the MIRV (Multiple Independently Targeted Re-entry Vehicle) which destabilized the balance of terror in the late sixties. From the military standpoint this was the whole reason for having a partial test ban. At first the Pentagon had endorsed test-ban talks thinking they would fail. When they succeeded the Joint Chiefs balked, until Secretary McNamara persuaded them that far from narrowing America's lead in the nuclear arms race a partial test ban would enlarge it. Russia had gained on the U.S. from unlimited testing. Putting tests underground, where the Soviets were less prepared to operate, insured American supremacy for years to come. Many in the Senate agreed. Some voted yes on the treaty to retard the arms race, others to advance it. At one point Senator McGovern observed, more prophetically than he knew, that "the Administration has been called upon to give so many assurances of our continued nuclear efforts after treaty ratification that a casual observer might assume that we are approving this treaty so that we can accelerate the arms race and beef up the war-making facilities of our country."

Still, though the arms race worsened, radioactive fallout declined. When Harriman returned to his home in Georgetown after negotiating the treaty, his neighbors welcomed him with a torchlight parade. One carried a small baby, a symbol of all those infants yet unborn who would live because of the agreement. Perhaps they would all perish later in a nuclear holocaust brought on by the failure to exploit this modest détente. Yet it was worth celebrating, for the treaty was more than a bitter joke, if also partly that. Though it benefited them, there would have been no treaty had the militarists prevailed. The country might have ended up with an accelerated arms race and aerial testing too. President Kennedy averted that possibility. If the treaty was less admirable than it seemed at the time, it is not entirely wrong to remember him warmly for it. Man would go on adding poisons to the atmosphere. Thanks to the test ban, radioactive fallout might no longer be among them. (Except for the little from French and Chinese tests.)

Cuba, Vietnam, and Congress continued to trouble Kennedy in 1963. But thanks to the missile crisis and the test-ban treaty, American prestige abroad was never higher. At home the administration was functioning smoothly, especially the Justice Department. When the President made his brother Attorney General people complained. He was too young, too ruthless, too inexperienced. He had been an admirer and employee of Senator Joseph McCarthy. Most thought it a shocking display of nepotism. Everyone except his relatives was surprised when Robert Kennedy became an outstanding Attorney General. No intellectual, conspicuously lacking in fixed principles, disheveled in speech and dress, loyal to a fault, he yet possessed important virtues. His taste in people was catholic and productive. He saw problems in terms of their human element, and he liked to confront those involved personally. He was a tireless worker, persistently attentive to detail. His moral vision lacked subtlety. "I believe there is a right and a wrong," he once said. But, he added, "I also believe that it is a sin to be uncharitable and unforgiving." He was properly cautious in dangerous or delicate situations.

The Attorney General surrounded himself with brilliant men, many of whom—Nicholas Katzenbach, Burke Marshall, and Ramsey Clark among others—went on to have distinguished careers in government. Robert Kennedy was more deeply committed to the civil rights movement than anyone in Camelot. After the Freedom Rides it was the Justice Department that made sure every major terminal, bus depot, and airport in the South was desegregated. Through private conversations Robert Kennedy helped desegregate public schools in Memphis, Atlanta, Dallas, and New Orleans. He saw to it that Negro voting rights were secured in dozens of counties. Though much remained undone, Justice still did more for blacks than any department of government. Kennedy also stepped up the fight against organized crime. Thanks to him the Internal Revenue Service had ten times as many men working on crime as before. He set up a special intelligence unit to monitor racketeers. In the Teamsters Union alone eighty-one officials were indicted, and fifty-eight convicted—mostly for embezzlement and extortion. Kennedy was careless about civil liberties, particularly those of the odious teamster boss Jimmy Hoffa, whom he persecuted mercilessly and, some said, vindictively. Nor did anti-trust work engage his sympathies. Still, he was splendidly effective in the areas of his concern. These included not only Justice's traditional responsibilities but various odd jobs, like ransoming the Bay of Pigs survivors. This last, Operation Habeas Corpus, was a task of such peril and delicacy that no other arm of government could probably have accomplished it. Camelot's domestic achievements were largely administrative: no department had more of them than Justice.

Despite everything, then, the President had grounds for satisfaction when he began a tour of the West on September 24, 1963. That very day the Senate, which some had feared would reject it, ratified the partial test-ban treaty by a handsome margin. President Kennedy expected to speak on conservation. In the West, as it soon became clear, this was a matter of carrying coals to Newcastle. Then, in Billings, Montana, his listeners caught fire for the first time at his mention of the test ban. This led him to speak of it everywhere. It was important, he said, "not because things are going to be easier in our lives, but because we have a chance to avoid being burned." The trip reached a climax in Salt Lake City. He was nearly mobbed by enthusiasts at his hotel. That night he spoke on peace to a wildly cheering audience at, of all places, the Mormon Tabernacle. So jubilant a reception in the very heartland of his conservative opposition could not fail to cheer the President. It proved that the right wing was weaker and the test ban more attractive than anyone had guessed. It showed what his strategy would be in 1964 and how well he could do with it. If, as seemed likely, the Republicans were foolish enough to nominate Senator Goldwater, Kennedy might even get a liberal majority in Congress. Then his legislative program would be unlocked and the promises of his first campaign redeemed.

Such thoughts must have sustained him on his trip to Texas in November. The Democratic party was in deep trouble there. While the Republicans gained strength daily, the Democrats wasted themselves feuding with one another. Lyndon Johnson had barely saved Texas for the party in 1960. Next time it would be even harder if Texas Democrats could not somehow come to terms. Of the four cities President Kennedy was to visit during his peacekeeping mission, Dallas was easily the strangest. There the tensions between the old Texas and the new were especially marked. It was a center of modern commerce, rich, cultivated to a degree, and efficiently managed by a tight ruling clique of big businessmen. At the same time it nourished the most virulent strains of right-wing fanaticism. The bigotry and violence of historic Texas—racist, fundamentalist, lawless—lived on in the persons of General Edwin A. Walker and his admirers. To them John F. Kennedy—urbane, liberal, cosmopolitan, Eastern, Catholic—personified all that was hateful and alien. Adlai Stevenson, who had been struck and spat on in a recent visit to Dallas, nearly advised the President not to go there. But the President could not visit Texas and avoid Dallas. And it was not his nature to take such precautions. He often remarked, and did so again in Fort Worth, that any desperate man with a rifle who wanted to kill him could. The risk went with the job, and he refused to worry about it. He was shot to death that very afternoon.

Everyone knows what happened in Dallas. Millions followed the events from beginning to end on television. Because of TV, the President's assassination and its aftermath made a deeper impression on the American people than any earlier tragedy. The presidential party was extensively photographed. His alleged killer, the pathetic Lee Harvey Oswald, was on camera when murdered two days later. Television made the funeral unbearably poignant. To sit before the screen day after day exposed Americans to such images as no people had ever seen. Films of the President's life punctuated the chronicle of somber events. The terrible moments were shown again and again, so were the great ones, and most touching of all, the merely happy. Shots of his lovely wife Jacqueline, radiant at some public event, alternated with ghastly pictures of her stricken face and bloodstained clothes. John F. Kennedy was alive and vigorous on some film clip in one instant, and lying in state the next. The drums rolled, the bells tolled, the heads of state marched in grim procession, and all the while his familiar voice and figure filled the air.

Television is not ordinarily an affecting medium. The screen is so small, it competes with so much else in the room, that one rarely is absorbed by it. But the cumulative effect of countless hours spent watching such memories and events as followed the assassination was indescribably powerful. In that short time President Kennedy passed from history into legend.* What had taken decades in Abraham Lincoln's case required only days in his. And, what is more remarkable, it was done by the generation that knew him. Lincoln was enshrined by posterity, Kennedy by his contemporaries. But though television was indispensable to this process, it could not have happened had the President himself not been so gay and witty and gallant a man. His death elicited remarkable expressions of grief, and not just in the West. Marshal Tito was moved beyond words. Premier Khrushchev was first to sign the Moscow embassy's condolence book. Ben Bella of Algeria phoned the American ambassador in tears; Guinea's Sékou Touré said, "I have lost my only true friend in the outside world." If people who saw him rarely and owed him little felt so strongly, what was it like for the Americans who had seen him, it often appeared, every day for three years?

The emotional burden Kennedy's death placed on most Americans still makes it nearly impossible to weigh his presidency. And it was so short that comparisons with others are hard to draw. Few Presidents now considered great would be so regarded had they died in the third year of their first term. If he had gotten a friendly Congress for his second term, and somehow escaped disaster in Vietnam, his administration might have been above average. But he was killed before its mediocre record could be redeemed. Few important bills were passed, and these accomplished little.

Appalachia was a case in point. Senator Kennedy had been touched by the highlander's plight during his primary campaign in West Vir-

---

* No one could have guessed that Kennedy would become the center of a maudlin cult. Only days before his murder James Reston had written in a column that the President "has touched the intellect of the country, but not the heart." Reston thought Kennedy would be re-elected out of inertia rather than affection.

ginia. Once elected he set up the President's Appalachian Regional Commission to save the region, headed by Franklin D. Roosevelt, Jr., the Under Secretary of Commerce. PARC apparently decided that it was more important to conciliate the eleven state governments involved than to have an effective program. Each state was allowed to veto any measure it disliked. This demonstration of Washington's belief in regional autonomy had but one flaw: the greed and ineptitude of its governments were the cause of Appalachia's ruin. Any program that depended on their wisdom and benevolence was assured of failure. And so it turned out. By 1965 about a billion dollars had been spent in Appalachia. Eighty per cent of the money went to highway construction, a boon to the region's absentee owners who were trucking out its remaining assets. The rape of the land went on. The people's tragedy continued.

The foreign equivalent of PARC was the Alliance for Progress. Here too the money was handled chiefly by the very people whose misrule made it necessary in the first place. The ruling classes in Latin America paid lip service to the need for internal reforms, but they were not about to use Washington's money to finance their own removal. Hence the Alliance guaranteed the frustration of such hopes as it created.

Elsewhere the President was hardly more successful. The less said of his Cuban policy the better. He maintained the notion that China was really a small island off the coast of a large, unidentified land mass. Much time and energy were spent in Africa, the Near East, and Europe to little effect. The seeds of disaster were sown in Vietnam. His military policy was an expensive folly. The arms race was pointlessly raised to a higher order of magnitude. An army was formed capable of fighting a land war in Asia, thus creating the irresistible temptation to have one.

Yet one cannot evaluate the Kennedy years solely in these practical terms. No mere bookkeeper's calculation can explain his hold on the world's imagination. At home his impact was even greater. Critics often complained that his dazzling style obscured the thin substance of his government. But while true, that also was beside the point. Shared fictions are more potent than truths denied. The President's style created its own reality, his dash its own momentum. Little progress was made, yet the illusion of it persisted. And it was not all illusion. The test ban was real if misleading. So was the government's commitment to civil rights.

When John Kennedy ran for the presidency, the novelist Norman Mailer struggled to decide which of the candidates merited his support. From Mailer's own radical standpoint, the Democratic nominee left much to be desired. Mailer decided to back him all the same and wrote a magazine essay called "Superman Comes to the Supermarket" explaining why. With characteristic modesty, Mailer later claimed that by glamorizing Senator Kennedy, and making him intellectually respectable as it were, his piece provided Kennedy's margin of victory. That may be (since his margin was so slight, everything contributed to it), but what remains instructive about Mailer's contribution was that he supported Kennedy for nonpolitical reasons. Writing about it later he recalled, "I knew that if he became President, it would be an existential event: he would touch depths in American life which were uncharted. . . . *Regardless of his overt politics* [my italics], America's tortured psychotic search for security would finally be torn loose from the feverish ghosts of its old generals, its MacArthurs, and Eisenhowers—ghosts which Nixon could cling to—and we as a nation would finally be loose again in the historic seas of a national psyche which was willy-nilly and at last, again adventurous." Mailer was to get more adventure than he bargained for, still he had no reason to change his mind later. To Mailer, the candidate's wit and charm, his attractive wife and glamorous family, were not just happy adjuncts but important new political facts. Together the entire complex of attributes that made up the Kennedy image had an oddly liberating effect. A new order was struggling to be born; John F. Kennedy became its midwife. Such a thing cannot be proved. Perhaps American life in the sixties would have been much the same had Nixon been elected instead. No one believed this. President Kennedy's politics were hardly less conventional, and not much more liberal, than Nixon's. Yet he was, in Mailer's sense, an existential figure, and he opened the door through which all had to walk, however reluctantly.

When such a man is cut down senselessly in his prime, the shock is terrible. Americans, unaccustomed to tragedy, hardly know how to cope with it. The best way was probably Daniel Patrick Moynihan's, who was then Assistant Secretary of Labor. Few of the Kennedy men made a better adjustment afterward than he. One can guess why from his immediate response to it. He said, "I don't think there's any point in being Irish if you don't know that the world is going to break your heart eventually." But such fatalism is alien to most Americans (though not to the Kennedys). If we cannot have a happy ending, we must at least have the promise of one. Out of this need was born the legend of Camelot, whose doomed Prince gave the nation a moment of glory before dying for its sins, but who also created the possibilities of change and left behind the means of effecting it. Camelot was to have great consequences. It made the lot of President Johnson—himself not quite the stuff of legends—a hard one. None of his successes would please the Knights of the Round Table as Kennedy's failures had. He aggravated their determination to re-create the past: to have another Camelot whatever the price. Much was sacrificed to this dream, especially by the Kennedys.

PROFILE:
The Warren Report and After

ON SEPTEMBER 27, 1964, the Warren Commission issued its
report on the assassination of President John F. Kennedy. It found the
President to have been killed by Lee Harvey Oswald, a lone crank. No
other individuals were involved, either as assassins or conspirators. In
his introduction to a *New York Times* edition of the report, Harrison
Salisbury pronounced it "exhaustive" and the evidence for its
conclusions "overwhelming." Most Americans agreed. Yet before long
many were calling the report a "whitewash." Numerous articles and
books to this effect were written, at least one of which (Mark Lane's
Rush to Judgment) became a best-seller. By 1968 the critics and their
theories were so numerous that *Esquire* magazine published "A Primer
of Assassination Theories" as a public service. There were at least
twenty-one different explanations in this vast literature. Among the
more colorful was the "Manchurian Candidate Theory" (after the
popular novel), which held that Oswald had been conditioned in
Russia as a "sleeper" assassin, for other purposes, but had been turned
on accidentally. Another argued that Oswald was a decoy set up by
the real assassins. A third held that he was really an agent of some U.S.
government agency like the FBI or the CIA. An enormous folklore
was built up on these speculations.*

---

* It is satirized by the movie *Greetings,* one of whose characters is a Kennedy

The late President was so mythic a figure that his shocking death was certain to provoke fantasies. They were blocked initially by the august stature of the Warren Commission. Within a week of the assassination, President Johnson had insured this by appointing a distinguished (largely conservative) body of public men to report on the crime.* Their prestige alone guaranteed the report's success, at first anyway. So did the twenty-six volumes of testimony and evidence later released by the Commission, the product, it was assumed, of ten months of comprehensive inquiry. Finally, their report said what people wanted to hear. Solitary maniacs who assassinate Presidents are a national tradition. The idea of a conspiracy, so logical to European minds, was alien to Americans. Then too, if even one more suspect was uncovered the whole ghastly matter would have to be reopened with unpredictable consequences. No one wanted that. It was much better all around to accept the Warren Report.

Unfortunately, the Commission, wanting to reassure the public, did just the opposite. For all its bulk, the report was a sloppy piece of work, carelessly researched and based on *a priori* judgments. Among the many damning points unearthed by Edward Jay Epstein in his book *Inquest,* the most sober and widely accepted critique of the Commission's work, the following are especially important. Though it took ten months to publish the report, the investigations on which it was based lasted only ten weeks. Of its staff of investigating attorneys, half worked only part time. A handful of young lawyers was responsible for most of it. The crucial matter of determining the actual facts was assigned to one man (Arlen Specter, later the district attorney of Philadelphia). The staff was so small and worked on such a tight schedule that it was hardly able to cope with the voluminous official reports given it. The FBI alone provided a mass of data too great for any one man to grasp in its entirety, and so filled with trivia as to make the truth harder, not easier, to determine. The Commission refused to hear many witnesses. Those it did hear were not challenged in any serious way. Its generosity to Oswald's widow Marina, whose

<hr>

assassination buff. In one scene he gets so carried away with his own theory that he ends up drawing bullet tracks to illustrate it on the nude body of his female bedmate.

* Besides Chief Justice Earl Warren they were Representatives Gerald Ford and Hale Boggs, Senators Richard Russell and John Sherman Cooper, John J. McCloy, a director of the Eastern Establishment, and Allen Dulles, former chief of the CIA.

testimony was full of contradictions, led some Commission attorneys to call their act "Snow White and the Seven Dwarfs." The Commission heard testimony for forty-nine days, but 43 per cent of this time was taken up with discussions of Oswald's life, and less than a third with the assassination itself. Evidence that cast doubt on the single-killer hypothesis was ignored, so was material pointing to other possibilities.

After the report was issued, about all the public could be certain of were these facts. President Kennedy was hit twice at 12:30 P.M. while his motor caravan went through downtown Dallas on November 22, 1963. Governor John B. Connally of Texas, who sat in front of him, was also struck. The President died at 1 P.M. Less than an hour later Lee Harvey Oswald was arrested for the murder of a Dallas police officer. Oswald had a remarkably checkered past for a young man. Though only twenty-four years of age, he had served in the Marines, spent three years as a laborer in the Soviet Union, married a Russian girl, and returned with her to the U.S. He then lived in various places, including New Orleans, where he organized what seemed to be a chapter of the pro-Castro Fair Play for Cuba Committee. Just before the assassination he had made a mysterious trip to Mexico. After two days of interrogation by the Dallas police, during which he admitted nothing, he was killed by Jack Ruby, a night club operator and police buff.

The Commission resorted to many dubious expedients in hopes of establishing Oswald's sole responsibility for President Kennedy's death. For Oswald to have hit a small moving target sixty yards from his supposed vantage point in the Texas Schoolbook Depository where he was employed would have required him to be a brilliant marksman. In later tests no expert rifleman, using the cheap weapon with its faulty sight attributed to Oswald, was able to duplicate this feat. Some were unable even to get off three shots in the brief time established by a home movie of the murder (the Zapruder film). There was no proof that Oswald was such a marksman, considerable evidence that he was a poor shot, yet the Commission insisted that he was expert and the shot itself an easy one. Some witnesses believed shots to have been fired from other sites, notably a "grassy knoll." The Commission disregarded them. But the weakest and most controversial point in the

Commission's case was the "single-bullet theory." The Zapruder film showed that Governor Connally was hit no more than 1.8 seconds after the second, fatal shot struck the President. Oswald's alleged weapon could not be fired twice in less than 2.3 seconds—not including aiming time. The only way Oswald could have shot both men was if his second bullet had passed through the President's body and into Connally's. Subsequently *a* bullet was found on *a* stretcher. If it was on the President's stretcher then it could not also have hit the governor. In the absence of any real evidence, the Commission decided it had been found on Connally's stretcher. The bullet which struck the governor left fragments in his wrist. When these fragments were added to the bullet supposedly found on his stretcher, they added up to more weight than the bullet could have had before it was fired. Connally himself believed he had been hit by another bullet; so did all of the one hundred witnesses who testified on the point. Nonetheless, the Commission decided both men had been struck by the same shot. There was much reason to doubt this point, little to believe it, yet the Commission clung to it desperately for an obvious reason. It was the only theory consistent with the lone-assassin hypothesis.

When the Commission was first announced, Norman Podhoretz, the editor of *Commentary* magazine, warned that given the rumors already circulating it must undertake a model investigation and file "a lengthy report in which every question involved in the assassination is examined with microscopic thoroughness and according to the highest standards of judicial impartiality. The Warren Commission ought to know that anything less would only reinforce the ugly suspicions circulating through the air, and would only compound the shame and disgust that all of us should be feeling still." But the Commission took the easy way out, thus insuring what it was supposed to prevent. Its failure generated a mass of lurid speculation so rich, sinister, and inventive as to defy summary. Many young people had their faith in authority undermined. The young were especially ardent consumers of assassination lore, and as their passion for it grew, so did their suspicion of the government. The Warren Commission relied chiefly on its prestige to make the report a success. Its failure drove another nail into the coffin of the old order. Many people took this fiasco as evidence of the Establishment's incompetence or malevolence, or both. At the very least, the Warren Report was hardly calculated to inspire respect for the system that produced it.

The Kennedy family did not help much to allay suspicion. First they denied access to certain medical evidence, for reasons of good taste probably. This made some feel they had things to hide. When finally released the evidence added little to public knowledge, but by then assassination buffery was too far advanced to be much affected. Then Mrs. Jacqueline Kennedy decided to have an authorized version of the tragedy written. Her choice was a little-known journalist, William Manchester, whose principal qualification was that he had earlier written a "relentlessly flattering" biography of President Kennedy. It was characteristic of the Kennedys, as of other great families, that they had little perspective on themselves. They had disliked James MacGregor Burns's *John Kennedy,* the best campaign biography of modern times, for its judiciousness. They loved Manchester's book for lacking it. The rationale for choosing Manchester was that he would produce a "work of accuracy and good taste." But if his selection did not rule out accuracy, it was itself in bad taste—besides being a harbinger of worse to come.

The Kennedys thought to protect themselves by insisting on the right of the President's widow and Robert Kennedy to censor Manchester's manuscript. This was easier said than done. The first draft was 300,000 words. So large a document made censorship physically difficult. Moreover, so many people were previewing it that bits and pieces leaked out from the start. It was also a valuable commercial property. Even before publication, *Look* magazine paid $665,000 for serialization rights, the Book-of-the-Month Club $250,000, and Dell a flat million dollars for paperback rights. Part of this money was pledged to the Kennedy Library at Harvard. Even so, sums this great generate their own momentum. The family found much of the manuscript objectionable. Certain confidences, they felt, had been betrayed. President Johnson was put in the worst possible light. No doubt this was how they saw him, yet it was impolitic to have their views broadcast. They asked for many changes and got quite a few.

But Manchester was developing delusions of grandeur. He was not so much a greedy as a vain man. Having interviewed five hundred people associated with the tragedy, and spent years familiarizing himself with all its details, he saw himself as the repository of a sacred trust, not for the Kennedys but for posterity. After months of negotiation he finally decided to go ahead without their approval. On December 16 they petitioned the court to enjoin the book's publication. The flood of publicity this loosed was so unnerving that the Kennedys soon backed down. On December 27 it was announced that amicable negotiations were in progress. The book was duly published the next year without Mrs. Kennedy's more intimate revelations.

No one but President Johnson emerged with any credit from this affair. Though maligned before and after the book's publication, he kept his peace. Most people still believed he had managed the transition with grace and tact. Mrs. Kennedy, who was thought to have forced the family's hand, declined in popularity. Manchester went about justifying himself tirelessly. In his apologia for *Look* he claimed that history would absolve him. No one doubted that he had suffered as much as he said. Few believed it had been to any great purpose. However pure his motives, they could not make his book any less meretricious. It was unfailingly sentimental about the Kennedys, and consistently malicious toward the Johnsonians. Even as a species of court history, it left everything to be desired.

Most critics agreed that never before had so bad a book gotten so big a promotion. Edward Jay Epstein said that before being censored it was even worse. Epstein had seen the original draft, then called *Death of Lancer,* after the Secret Service code name for President Kennedy. According to him it was a "mythopoeic melodrama" organized around the notion of a struggle for power between JFK and LBJ. President Kennedy was cast as D'Artagnan and Johnson as Richelieu. This draft was apparently not so much a historical document as a black fairy tale, complete with ritual hunts, saturnalias, and fictitious episodes created for dramatic effect. *Death of Lancer* was dangerous to the Kennedy family not so much because it slandered President Johnson (now virtually a national pastime) but because it did so with the Kennedy seal of approval. Thus the

Kennedys had to censor the book, especially by cutting out the fiction and the most scurrilous anti-Johnson material.

These cuts made the book more accurate but reduced its theatrical impact. Without the implication that Lyndon Johnson was somehow responsible for Kennedy's death, much in the book made little sense. Manchester agreed to cuts that left part of the manuscript incomprehensible, but stubbornly insisted on retaining minor scenes the family thought in bad taste. The result was a mass of tedious detail on the one hand, and on the other substantial errors of fact. Walter Lippmann pointed out that "in the mistakes I know about there is the same pattern: always the mistake is a fiction which intensifies the drama of the story." And Elizabeth Hardwick drew the appropriate moral by remarking that "few people with power and money realize that the eulogist blackens more reputations than the liar."

Bad as it was, the Manchester affair was not so damaging as the one staged by Jim Garrison, the district attorney of New Orleans. Garrison was a particularly flamboyant man, even by contemporary standards. In February 1967 he announced, "My staff and I solved the case [Kennedy's assassination] weeks ago. I wouldn't say this if we didn't have evidence beyond the shadow of a doubt. We know what cities were involved, we know how it was done, in the essential aspects: we know the key individuals involved, and we are in the process of developing evidence now." A little later Garrison arrested Clay Shaw, a prominent local retired businessman, and charged him with conspiring with Oswald and others to assassinate President Kennedy. The national press soon zeroed in on Garrison. The *New York Times* and the *Washington Post* were hostile, so were *Newsweek* and the *Saturday Evening Post*. NBC did a critical documentary on Garrison while CBS aired a four-hour defense of the Warren Report.

This aroused sympathy for Garrison. The more he was attacked, the more people suspected he was onto something. Official noncooperation helped him too. The FBI and the CIA refused to open their files. Ohio, Texas, and Iowa wouldn't extradite witnesses for him. Of course, Garrison gave them no real reason to. He claimed to have solid evidence, but would not make it public for fear of prejudicing the Shaw trial. He was trusted not only by assassination fanatics but by many average citizens as well. A Harris poll showed that 60 per cent of the public believed President Kennedy to have been killed by conspirators.

The Garrison affair had its roots in the arrival of Lee Harvey Oswald in New Orleans on April 25, 1963. There he got an unskilled job and sent for his wife and child. But soon he became discontented and had Marina write the Soviet embassy about getting repatriated. Then Oswald lost his job and became involved with the Fair Play for Cuba Committee. Though never recognized by the national office, he seems to have founded a one-man chapter of the FPCC. Once he was arrested by the police, perhaps intentionally. Another time he hired several men to help him hand out pro-Castro material in front of the International Trade Mart (which Shaw managed). In short, he made great efforts to become identified as a Castro sympathizer. On September 24 he sent his family back to Dallas. The next day he went to Mexico and tried vainly to get from there to Cuba. In October he returned to Dallas. This is about all that can be said with any certainty of his stay in New Orleans.

The next figure in Garrison's case was David Ferrie, a bizarre figure who was hairless owing to an exotic disease called alopecia. He wore a wig and false eyebrows of such lushness that witnesses compared them to carpet strips. He was a licensed pilot who had tried to get an Air Force commission in 1950 so as to kill communists, as he told officials in an emotional letter. Ferrie was also a bishop in a quasi-underground cult called the Orthodox Old Catholic Church of North America. And he was involved in a grotesque variety of anti-Castro activities. After the assassination Ferrie was questioned by the FBI, having been accused of planning to fly Oswald to safety. The FBI concluded this was a false tip, but Garrison picked it up and started his own investigation. Garrison kept Ferrie in protective custody for a time, then let him go on February 21, 1967. The next day he was found dead, apparently of natural causes, though assassination buffs called it murder. Garrison then turned up another witness, Perry Russo, who claimed to be a confidant of Ferrie. He said that Ferrie had shown him a picture of a fellow conspirator by the name of Clay Bertrand. Russo then identified Clay Shaw as Bertrand, on the strength of which Garrison had Shaw arrested.

Things rapidly got worse. Assassination theorists flocked

to Garrison's side, including not only people who had written books such as Mark Lane, Harold Weisberg, and others, but also entertainers like Mort Sahl. Garrison began making peculiar statements. At one time he said President Kennedy was shot by a man in a sewer manhole. Another time he blamed a fourteen-man Cuban guerrilla team. After talking with Professor Richard H. Popkin, he adopted the latter's celebrated "second Oswald" theory, which held that a man posing as Oswald did the killing. He steadily expanded his list of supporting characters. At first the conspirators were merely a band of sexual perverts and anti-Castro Cubans. To them he later added Minutemen, CIA agents, oil millionaires, Dallas policemen, munitions exporters, the Dallas establishment, assorted reactionaries, White Russians, and elements of "the invisible Nazi substructure." He kept on even after Russo admitted to the grand jury that he had perjured himself by falsely identifying Shaw as Bertrand. Every attack on Garrison gave him opportunities for fresh charges, thanks to equal-time rules and fair-coverage procedures. When Edward Jay Epstein published a hostile article on him in the *New Yorker* magazine, Garrison denounced it as part of a CIA plot to discredit his investigation. Garrison made many charges against the CIA, his clincher being that the government had not given him any material linking the CIA with the assassination. To ordinary men this might seem a point against his theory. But Garrison triumphantly celebrated it as evidence that the government was hiding the truth from him. It says something about the government's credibility that by then millions agreed.

Garrison was so strongly established as a gutsy loner bucking the power elite that his reputation even survived the trial itself. When Clay Shaw came to court Garrison had no evidence beyond what was already known, and Shaw was easily acquitted.* This shattering failure, and the ridicule poured on him for having boasted so much of so little, had small effect in New Orleans. He hardly campaigned at all, seemingly depressed by events, but was handily returned to office anyway. His populist image remained intact, though no one knew if it

---

* Garrison's malice knew no limits. After Shaw was acquitted Garrison charged him with perjury. Shaw took this persecution urbanely. Defense costs having taken his savings, he went back to work remarking, "The French have a proverb, 'the wounds that come from money are not fatal.' I hope it's true."

would carry him as far as he once hoped. Assassination folklorists were undiscouraged by this affair. Some even concluded that the debacle was proof that Garrison was a CIA agent seeking to discredit them. Like UFO's, it seemed the assassination of John F. Kennedy would always puzzle us.

4 JOHNSON IN POWER

LYNDON BAINES JOHNSON was as well equipped for the presidency as any living American. He had been in public life for thirty years. As Vice-President he had understudied the star. Upon his accession his record became an object of anxious scrutiny, especially the crucial Senate years. Johnson had become party leader in 1953 while still a junior member of the Senate club. Partly this was because few wanted to be Minority Leader, partly because he was sponsored by the powerful Richard Russell of Georgia. But mainly it was a tribute to his own adroitness. His relations with Republican Senators were good. As he usually supported important administration bills, Johnson got on well with President Eisenhower. The only Senators he failed to please were liberal Democrats. He was close to Hubert Humphrey, though, and thus had an opening to the left when he needed it. Johnson used his assets so shrewdly, and the Republican majority was so slender, that sometimes he even beat the Majority Leader, William Knowland of California.

When the senatorial balance shifted slightly, allowing him to become Majority Leader, Johnson flowered. His handling of Joseph McCarthy was especially revealing. Knowing, as he put it, that "Joe will go that extra mile to destroy you," he did not join liberals in direct attacks on the Wisconsin Senator. He waited for McCarthy to overreach himself and was rewarded with the Army-McCarthy hearings. Johnson made certain they were televised. Obligingly, McCarthy ruined himself on TV, which showed him for the bully and fraud he was. When the Senate moved to censure McCarthy, Johnson stacked the special committee with important conservatives who had not previously taken strong positions on McCarthy. They had the freedom to censure him and the power to make it stick. Though he took no public credit for it, the McCarthy censure was a Johnson *tour de force* and foreshadowed the system he would perfect as Majority Leader.

This system was made up of two parts: the Johnson Network and the Johnson Procedure. The Network consisted of his allies in the Senate, about a quarter of the whole including members of every persuasion. They provided the balance of power on most issues. The Johnson Procedure involved endless turning of stones, information gathering, and personal contacts. When necessary, he resorted to The Treatment, which George A. Smathers, the young Senator from Florida, described as "a great overpowering thunderstorm that consumed you as it closed in around you." The Treatment could last for ten minutes or four hours. Rowland Evans and Robert Novak say of it: "Interactions from the target were rare. Johnson anticipated them before they could be spoken. He moved in close, his face a scant millimeter from his target, his eyes widening and narrowing, his eyebrows rising and falling. From his pockets poured clippings, memos, statistics. Mimicry, humor, and the genius of analogy made The Treatment an almost hypnotic experience and rendered the target stunned and helpless." Added to this was his unlimited capacity for small favors, courtesies, and attentions.

Johnson transformed the Senate. His use of "unanimous consent" to limit debates made the cloakroom horsetrading at which he excelled all-important. Night sessions became common too. When LBJ wanted something badly he kept the heat on until his opposition collapsed from exhaustion. He developed a stop-and-go technique in which business was alternately pressed and suspended. Thus formal debate gave way to intricate, and mostly subterranean, maneuverings. The crowning achievement of the Johnson system came in 1957 when he passed the first civil rights bill since Reconstruction without a filibuster and without splitting the party. It did not have much practical influence, but it was a stunning triumph for Johnson all the same. The big Democratic victory in 1958, paradoxically, made life for LBJ more difficult. The swollen majority with its large liberal bloc was harder to handle than the smaller, more conservative body that preceded it. When the newly elected Senator Eugene McCarthy was asked if LBJ would bend to the liberal wind in consequence, he said, "Lyndon doesn't lean *with* the wind; he leans *ahead* of it." And he did. But he was never as happy with the new majority as with the old. Johnson's talents were uniquely suited to a narrow margin; with a large one he was less adroit and sure of himself. Even so, when he left the Senate he was still the most powerful Majority Leader in modern times.

The vice-presidency was an unhappy experience for him, though why he thought it would be anything else remains a mystery. In the Senate he had been one of the chief men in the country. As Vice-President he was only the President's shadow, subject to petty indignities by Kennedy men. The President's deportment toward him was always correct; not so that of many aides. They never forgave Johnson his hard fight for the nomination. The Johnson style clashed with theirs. LBJ's conduct in office was impeccable, his loyalty to the President never wavered, but the strain on him was enormous. He was a giant being stung to death by gnats. The great career built with all that strength, cunning, and resolution was fading away. TV comedians made fun of him. "Whatever became of Lyndon Johnson?" they would say.

Then, in one awful moment, everything changed. Having been nought, he became all. The man was truly matched to the hour. He was powerful and confidence-inspiring at a time when the country needed reassurance. Never a handsome man, he had achieved a certain distinction and presence in his middle age that proved useful now. The people needed a father figure, and President Johnson turned out to be it. To the stricken Kennedy family he extended all the help and sympathy he could. His first letter as President was written to the Kennedy children. Toward the Kennedy entourage he was more tactful and considerate than, even in its sorrow, it perhaps deserved. Most of all he took control so masterfully that panic was averted. The people were assured that things would go on, if not exactly as before. Some of the Kennedys' following thought it unseemly of Lyndon Johnson to have himself sworn in when the late President's body was scarcely cold. Yet when Air Force One, which brought John Kennedy's remains to Washington, landed at Andrews Field in the dusk, it was the President of the United States who emerged from it. Not just the desolate mourners gathered there but the whole country needed to know that. They could be secure even in their grief. The President was dead, the presidency was not. In that sad time no one needed to wonder where the power was.

President Johnson added dignity to the solemnities. Immediately afterward he demanded of Congress that it honor the fallen President by enacting his program. When the House tried to adjourn for Christmas without passing a suitable foreign aid bill he brought the members back and, by judiciously applying The Treatment, made them see reason. When the year ended it was still not clear what sort of President he would be, but there were grounds for hope. C. Vann Woodward, the great Southern historian, summed it up best for the *New York Review of Books*. Noting the President's talents, remarking that he was the first important Senator to become the chief executive, and considering that he was a Southerner at a time when the worst domestic problems were in the South, he concluded: "What eventualities or future disclosures may handicap him or embarrass him in the use of his capabilities it is impossible to foresee. One can only say that he has displayed them before, that they are formidable engines indeed, and that there is a need for them now."

Lyndon Johnson was hardly settled in the White House when the election year began. He could go slowly as he was certain of nomination, but Republican aspirants had to start early. Thus January found Governor Rockefeller opening his campaign in New Hampshire. Rockefeller was the most popular Republican in the country at large during the 1960's. He was not well liked by party regulars, however, which was why he never won the presidential nomination. Then too, Rockefeller made mistakes, and showed indecisiveness at crucial moments. In 1960 he wobbled badly; in 1968 he would so again. In 1964, though, he was the first to announce his candidacy and the first to begin running. He continued as long as hope remained. All the same his prospects were dim, for the previous year he had divorced his wife and married another divorcee whose former husband had gained custody of her children. Before his divorce the Gallup poll showed that 43 per cent of all Republicans wanted Rockefeller to be their candidate in 1964, as against 26 per cent who favored Senator Barry Goldwater of Arizona. Afterward only 30 per cent favored Rockefeller as against 35 per cent for Goldwater. Regardless of the facts (and they were less damning than they seemed), Rockefeller's divorce and remarriage had ruined his chance of being nominated in 1964. His power in the party was largely a consequence of his demonstrated vote-getting capabilities. These were now seriously impaired. Everyone told him not to run. But his organization was finely tuned and ready to roll, he had prepared for years for this moment, and he was not going to stop now just because the polls said to. Still, from the outset the real question was not how much good he could do himself but how much harm he could inflict on Goldwater. It proved to be quite a lot.

Rockefeller's candidacy was based on talent and ambition, Goldwater's on neither. Apart from certain technical skills (photography, aviation), the only ability Goldwater ever demonstrated was a knack for winning elections in Arizona. He did not much want to be President, and there is a rule that to win the highest office one must lust after it. Many wished to see him President nonetheless. For one thing, he was a strikingly handsome man, even at a time when good-looking politicians were commonplace. And, politics aside, he was a likable man too. Goldwater had many public enemies but few personal ones. Most of all, however, he was wanted as leader of the right. After the death of Senator Joe McCarthy he had become the chief spokesman for what was always known as "conservatism." In fact there was nothing conservative about Senator Goldwater. He held no brief for existing institutions, he did not accept the force of history, nor did he favor balance, moderation, or the golden mean.

On the contrary, he was an ideologue who hoped to replace the limited welfare state with an unlimited warfare state. He advocated militarism abroad and unrestrained capitalism at home. Goldwater's peculiar vision of the good society was attributed by Theodore H. White to the fact that he had only lately been introduced to the world of books and ideas. "Thus, ideas for him seemed to have a vigor and validity and virulence strange to those inoculated by learning earlier in life. His outrage was that of a man who could perceive all things with the brittle certainty of the frustrated intellectual . . . as if he were a Trotsky of the far right." One need not accept White's philosophy of education to take the point. Goldwater's intellectual reach greatly exceeded his grasp. He was possessed by ideas while lacking the means to order them. Hence his formulations were crude, inexpressive, and frequently contradictory. That he was thought conservative despite all these handicaps only shows how impoverished American conservatism had become. No real conservative had held high office since Charles Evans Hughes except, possibly, for Robert Taft. Even certified right-wing intellectuals like Russell Kirk and William Buckley had to take what they could get, and all they could get were the likes of Joe McCarthy and Barry Goldwater. Small wonder that conservatism was thought so dismal a profession that for every intellectual on the right there were a hundred on the left.

If Goldwater lacked intellectual allure, he was not entirely wanting in political sex appeal. Millions of Americans swore by him, and their naive affection was a resource that shrewder men coveted from the start. Goldwater's presidential campaign was actually launched by one of them, long before the candidate himself had given any thought to it. In 1961 Clifton F. White of New York, national boss of the Young Republicans (a weightier group in politics than its Democratic counterpart), met with like-minded friends, and they resolved to capture the party for Goldwater. The Senator himself did not share their enthusiasm. He believed that to run a poor race against President Kennedy would do the cause great harm. Thus, he reasoned, it would be better not to seize control of the GOP than to do so in such a way as to compromise his movement. On the other hand, if he could come within 5 per cent of JFK's popular vote the race would be worth running. Undaunted, White's group went ahead and by the fall of 1963 Goldwater was persuaded that he could get the nomination and make a strong race. The President's assassination almost changed his mind. He had rather liked President Kennedy and looked forward to challenging him. He loathed President Johnson. Running against him would be no fun. But by this time Goldwater's candidacy had gone so far, so many people were committed to it, that he had little choice. He believed that to turn his back on them at this late date would damage the cause even more than a weak race. So, with more genuine reluctance than any candidate since Eisenhower, he followed Rockefeller into New Hampshire.

As everyone knows, the New Hampshire primary is important because it comes first. Victory there puts a candidate ahead of the game, defeat puts him behind. Complaints are frequently made that a small state should not exert so great an influence. But it is a better place for campaigns to begin than many. If New Hampshiremen are cautious in the old New England way, the state itself is the second most heavily industrialized in the country. Though it has no real urban center, a variety of ethnic groups work its mills and factories. And its voters are notably independent. In 1945 it held a referendum on whether the U.S. should join the United Nations, the only state to do so, and in their town meetings New Hampshiremen voted 20 to 1 for American entry. They have always been proud of that.

At first Senator Goldwater was way ahead in the polls. But by January his lead had slipped badly. His criticism of the UN did not go down well, as anyone familiar with the state's history ought to have known. Nor, in a state with the fourth highest percentage of old people in the country, did his attacks on social security. Goldwater claimed to want a voluntary social security system. But most people thought a voluntary system unworkable, believing the young would not support it.

Goldwater was used to addressing the indulgent faithful. Skeptical or uncommitted auditors were less likely to give him the benefit of the doubt. Heedless of this, Goldwater roamed the state criticizing social security, impugning the reliability of American missiles, saying that the jobless were unintelligent or lacking in ambition, and calling for Marines to make Fidel Castro reopen the water lines to Guantanamo Bay. Often he did not mean what he seemed to say, or say what he seemed to mean, but New Hampshiremen weren't to know that. The press corps had not yet learned the trick of uncovering his real intent. Thus his raw observations were broadcast around the country with deadly effect. In the normal course of events Goldwater's blunders would have made it easy for Rockefeller to win in New Hampshire. He might then have swept the other primaries and secured the nomination in spite of being divorced. At this point one of those accidents occurred that make politics the chancy business it is. A tiny group of Henry Cabot Lodge supporters from Massachusetts (only two men and two girls, according to Theodore White) opened a write-in campaign for Lodge in New Hampshire. Their candidate was fully occupied in Saigon. They had no organization and relied entirely on direct mailings. But they won the primary. Lodge rolled up a handsome plurality against Goldwater, Rockefeller, and Nixon (who got a substantial write-in vote also). New Hampshire Republicans couldn't stand Goldwater, but they couldn't stomach Rockefeller's divorce. The Lodge write-in offered them an alternative, and enough took it to finish off Rockefeller.

Rockefeller then launched the most gallant effort of his political career. Knowing himself to be finished, he felt that if he ran well in Oregon and California he could knock out Goldwater and enable a moderate to win the nomination. He did win in Oregon, but to no avail. Goldwater refused to fight there. The Goldwater forces put everything they had into California, and after an exhausting, costly campaign their candidate squeezed out Rockefeller with 52 per cent of the vote. Had Goldwater gone to the convention without winning a single primary it would have been hard to nominate him, even though his organization had locked up most state delegations. California allowed them to claim a popular base for their candidate. Now it was all over except the shouting. At this late date Republican liberals, who had given Rockefeller little help when it was still possible to beat Goldwater, became alarmed. At a governors' conference in June, William Scranton, the amiable governor of Pennsylvania, was urged to make a final kamikaze attack on Goldwater at the convention. After dithering a bit, he agreed, thus enabling one of the more grotesque political happenings in recent history to go forward.

San Francisco was an unlikely site for the Goldwater convention. A liberal community with a relatively sane public temper, it was still very beautiful (though, as Norman Mailer pointed out in his account of the convention, it was losing the struggle to stay that way). Into this cool, windswept city by the bay came the strangest assortment of political kooks ever assembled in one place. They crammed the galleries in the aptly named Cow Palace where the more staid convention delegates assembled, and gave a perfervid quality to the rites enacted there. Their screams and chants dominated the convention and made watching it on television a singular experience. The slightest remark would set them off. General Eisenhower was persuaded to give the affair his benediction. During it he urged the delegates to ignore sensation-seeking journalists who cared nothing for the GOP. This triggered a rapturous demonstration, in the course of which one leaping delegate was heard to cry "Down with Walter Lippmann!"

The main target of this venom were the Rockefeller-Scranton forces. Rockefeller gave a tough speech on the party platform that drove his auditors mad. Though nearly prevented from finishing his remarks, Nelson Rockefeller relished the tumult. Despite his wealth he was an uncommonly rough man. With his gravelly voice and heavy features he looked more like a longshoreman than a patrician. Unlike Lyndon Johnson, for example, Governor Rockefeller was not at his best in complex or ambiguous political situations. But given a straight fight he could be superb. He had taken great abuse during his long drive to stop Goldwater; now he made that experience pay. His subject was extremism and in his speech he told the convention what that meant: anonymous threats, obscene letters, strong-arm tactics, totalitarian methods. The more the galleries raged, the cooler he got. None of the millions who saw his address on television will ever forget its mixture of disdain and belligerence, nor the ravings it inspired. The TV audience missed plenty of little details (like the woman who kept screaming "you lousy lover" at him), but they got the picture well enough. Goldwater's fanatic supporters, whom Norman Mailer described as " a convention of hangmen who subscribe to the principle that the executioner has his rights too," drove the biggest nail of all into what was already an extensively studded political coffin.

The rest was anti-climax. Goldwater's disciplined machine cranked out his nomination. In accepting it he spoke the lines that were to haunt him ever after: "Extremism in the defense of liberty is no vice . . . moderation in the pursuit of justice is no virtue." Like so many of his delphic observations, its intent was obscure. But it was taken to mean that good intentions justified any excess. Earlier Goldwater had shown his colors by choosing Congressman William Miller of New York as his running mate. His reactionary views were the sole qualifications for high office of this deservedly obscure figure.*

---

* It was so hard to explain why Goldwater selected Miller that Norman Mailer claimed it could only be as a deterrent to assassination. Anyone who hated Goldwater enough to try to kill him would find the thought of Miller's becoming President even more repugnant.

🏴

While the Republicans slaughtered one another, Lyndon Johnson was organizing the greatest victory ever enjoyed by a modern President. His triumph was built of many elements, not the least of them being his enviable presidential record. The same Congress that had given his predecessor so much trouble was no obstacle to President Johnson. To get the tax cut moving he promised an economical administration. His State of the Union Message on January 8 announced that an anticipated budget of $103 billion had been pared down to less than $98 billion. Impressed with these savings, Congress not only approved an $11 billion tax cut but gave him another billion for the war on poverty which he announced in the same message. Thirty million Americans lived in families earning less than $2,000 a year, an intolerable condition he proposed to remedy. In May he gave a name to his ambition by calling on the country to help build the "Great Society." In June he extracted from Congress the most sweeping civil rights bill in history.

By then, the essential Johnson was fully on display. In some respects he was unappealing. A man of boundless vulgarity, he could not prevent his more colorful expressions from becoming public knowledge.* He was harder on his personal staff than any President in memory, humiliating them one moment, lavishing attention and praise on them the next. Few could stand this for long, and the turnover among his aides was very great. He lived by the telephone. No official knew at what hour of the day or night he might hear from the President. Lyndon Johnson was on the job every waking minute and expected the same of his men. Whether in the pool or on a hammock he always had a phone at hand.† He was vain, arrogant, and suspicious to boot. No flattery was so shameless that he did not revel in it, no criticism so well founded that it could not be dismissed. He delighted in wrapping his least decision in suspense. If news of an appointment leaked out in advance he was likely to cancel it. Presidential travels began unexpectedly. The reporters who covered him hardly knew from one hour to the next where they would be.

These traits, bad enough by themselves, seemed all the worse when

---

* They were always picturesque. Of one high official the President remarked that "he can't reach his ass with his right hand." And he was wont to decry the "piss-ant" questions with which "piss-ant" reporters wasted his time.

† The telephone had by then replaced the pen and the sword as a symbol of power. Magazines seeking to emphasize the potency of great men invariably show them speaking on it. Many look uncomfortable in this pose, President Johnson never did. No gunman ever held a Colt .44 so easily.

compared with President Kennedy's. People—liberals and newsmen in particular—were so charmed by JFK that his most partisan acts often escaped them. But everything President Johnson did, however altruistic, was called "merely" political, as if, somehow, this demeaned the most political office of all. The historian Eric Goldman, who succeeded Arthur Schlesinger as White House intellectual-in-residence, offers a telling example of how this worked. Goldman proposed a Presidential Scholars program in which high school graduates of special distinction were honored. Later Goldman corresponded with some of them and found that most attributed the program to cynical political motives, or believed it had actually been conceived by President Kennedy. One wrote Goldman that he agreed with a friend who said to him, "It's too bad you couldn't have gotten the award from Kennedy. It would have meant more then." This was one of President Johnson's most legitimate complaints: that political skill, the very thing which was his chief qualification for office, was held against him—sometimes maliciously by people who had played a hard political game to less effect in the previous administration, and were glad to savage him for his accent or his homely manners if nothing else would do.

All the same, President Johnson played his role with deftness and gusto. He invoked his predecessor's martydom on every occasion that would profit by it. He carefully tailored the Kennedy (now rapidly becoming Johnson) bills to fit the Congress's requirements. He struck ingenious attitudes to advance them. As proof of his frugality, for example, he explained how he went about the White House at night turning out lights. His critics sneered, but it went down well in most places because it was the kind of economy that ordinary people could understand. And it all helped build the great consensus that was his chief contribution to political life. While Goldwater inflamed the populace, President Johnson soothed it. Strange as it seemed later, remembering the bitter years of his decline, President Johnson's harmonic qualities seemed the most important thing about him in 1964. In April when a rail strike threatened, the President averted it by giving everyone concerned The Treatment, then virtually locking them up in the White House for a marathon bargaining session. Afterward he summed up his position on these matters by saying, "There wasn't a bad man on either side—well, hardly any, except one or two. The point is they've got problems, you've got problems, I've got problems, and somehow we have to work them out without messing up each other too much." As a philosophy of government it lacked elegance, but it worked.

Congress reluctantly came around. The business community, frightened by Goldwater's rejection of the entire post–New Deal settlement, began to fall in line also. Though nominally Republican, and ostensibly practitioners of competitive enterprise, most big businessmen were loyal to the corporate society which had emerged during World War II. Its workings were complex, to be sure, but in essence the corporate state was based on the common admission of big business, big labor, and big government that they needed one another. Organized labor secured higher wages and broader benefits for its members. In turn, it provided a disciplined labor supply for the corporations, reduced the incidence of strikes, and, with the increase in the members' purchasing power, expanded the market for consumer goods. The federal government (and the larger state governments) narrowed business's freedom of maneuver to a degree, yet this irritant was offset by heavy subsidies that made the exchange a profitable one. Sometimes directly (to airlines, railroads, and shipping companies), more often indirectly through defense contracts, tax loopholes, and the like, government changed the business communities' view of it. The result was what might be called the limited welfare state. Large groups were excluded from the new order—racial minorities, working women, small farmers and merchants among others. Many within it sought to change the balance of rewards and penalties. Still, the majority of middle- and upper-class Americans were satisfied with the system, however much they complained. Few wished to see the Darwinian aspects of nineteenth-century free enterprise restored. Goldwater's utopian capitalism was a dream fit for heroes, but the great corporations were in business to maximize profits and minimize risks, not to win medals. Goldwater's inherited wealth permitted him to fantasize about a golden age of enterprise that never was. The average businessman felt more comfortable with Lyndon Johnson, a self-made millionaire who knew how the money was really made.

Big businessmen joined the National Independent Committee for Johnson and Humphrey in droves. Farmers who needed Rural Free Delivery, TVA, electrical co-ops, and other forms of government assistance joined the Rural Americans for Johnson-Humphrey. A procession of great names (including Dr. Benjamin Spock, whose word on babies was law to millions) enlisted in the ranks of Scientists and Engineers for Johnson-Humphrey. There was a committee for everyone with a stake in the present or a hope for the future. For the first time in modern history a Democratic presidential nominee was the candidate of both the established and the deprived. Neither had anywhere else to go. This left only the bigots, profiteers, and superpatriots to Goldwater. As it turned out, there were not many of them. The hidden conservative vote which Senator Goldwater's candidacy was supposed to materialize never surfaced. In 1965 a poll indicated that only about six million of his 27 million votes came from dedicated extremists. The rest were Republican partisans who would not vote for a Democrat if their lives depended on it (as many believed they did in 1964).

By early summer President Johnson's position was an enviable one. He had staked out the entire center of American life for himself. He had racked up a string of victories in the Congress. Private polls showed that no Democrat would add or detract from the strength of his ticket, so he had a free hand in selecting his Vice-President. The first thing he did was knock out Attorney General Kennedy. The two had disliked each other for years. Yet, for some odd reason, Robert Kennedy seemed to want the vice-presidency. President Johnson, in a wounding interview, told him he couldn't have it, then leaked a story putting Kennedy in the worst possible light. He justified his decision on the grounds that no member of the cabinet or regular participant in its sessions could be spared. Since these were mostly John F. Kennedy appointees, the Attorney General remarked wryly, "I'm sorry I took so many nice fellows over the side with me." The President had probably decided early that Hubert Humphrey, his old Senate protégé, a good friend, and a man of stature among Northern liberals, would properly balance the ticket. But, as was his custom, he kept everyone in suspense while he dangled the prize before other men. Among them was Senator Eugene McCarthy, who recognized what was happening in time to withdraw his name. President Johnson would later pay for the fun he had with McCarthy. At the time, though, everything seemed to be breaking his way, and he looked forward to the nominating convention in Atlantic City with pleasure.

Where the Republican convention had been bizarre, the Democratic convention was, with a few exceptions, merely sordid. Atlantic City, a sleazy resort town, was the perfect setting for it. Lyndon Johnson's shameless manipulations degraded the affair. Mostly, however, the convention's moral tone was established by its treatment of the Mississippi Freedom Democratic party. The MFDP was one product of the great effort then going on to politicize black Mississippians. Unlike the racist regular party delegation, it was integrated. And it could properly claim to be the only delegation from Mississippi loyal to the national party. Its members, Mrs. Fannie Lou Hamer in particular, had suffered much to reach that moment of truth in Atlantic City. Most Democrats outside the South accepted the righteousness of their case in principle. The problem was how to implement it, for discipline had never before been exerted in a Democratic convention against those Southerners who so regularly deserted the ticket during election years. It was finally decided to give the MFDP two delegate votes at large, and to deny racist delegations a seat at future conventions. No one contributed more to this arrangement than Hubert Humphrey. Most Democrats were quite satisfied with it, though not of course the MFDP. When the frustrated MFDP delegation attempted to take its seats on the floor anyway, others were aghast. Theodore White wrote later that the delegation "stained" its honor by this act. What few appreciated was that many black Americans regarded this refusal to seat the MFDP as final proof of the system's perfidy. While black militancy was nourished from many sources, no other event contributed so much to it.

Lyndon Johnson was nominated by acclamation and made a dull speech. Hubert Humphrey received the crowd's benediction and gave a lively one. "Only an ebullient idealist like Humphrey," I. F. Stone wrote, "could show such extremism in the pursuit of moderation." Stone described the elements which made Humphrey, once thought a dangerous liberal, such a perfect choice for Vice-President. "It's not just that the rich like Lyndon and the poor like Hubert. It's that they're turning into Siamese twins. Johnson, the faithful Janissary of the oil-depletion millionaires, is crusading against poverty, while Humphrey, the darling of Americans for Democratic Action, is chucking chairmen of the board under their double chins. While the twin on the left moves right, the twin on the right moves left. How can poor Goldwater out-maneuver this dazzling political choreography?"

On its last day the convention honored President Kennedy. When his brother Robert took the stage the applause lasted twenty-two minutes. He gave a moving tribute to their fallen leader, ending with these words from *Romeo and Juliet:*

> . . . when he shall die
> Take him and cut him out in little stars,
> And he will make the face of heav'n so fine
> That all the world will be in love with Night
> And pay no worship to the garish Sun.

As if this were not enough, a filmed biography of the late President was shown. And, says Theodore White, "we all wept."

In the meantime, Barry Goldwater was busily completing his ruin. Earlier he had urged that NATO commanders be given control of tactical nuclear weapons. Wanting to help the public overcome its unseemly fear of atomic bombs, he coined the phrase "conventional nuclear weapons" to put them in a more homely light. No doubt this was a further effort to make "nukes," as he liked to call them, socially acceptable. But it only confused the public. Which weapons and which commanders, they asked? Goldwater didn't really seem to know. Remarks like this gave the Democrats rich opportunities which they did not fail to exploit. President Johnson set up what was called the "anti-campaign," a small group of Washington intellectuals who made "black propaganda" out of Goldwater's looser expressions. The Democrats came up with in-numerable variations on Goldwater's themes, including the slogan, "In Your Heart, You Know He Might" (a takeoff on the GOP motto "In Your Heart, You Know He's Right"). Doyle Dane Bernbach, the Demo-crats' advertising agency, also took advantage of Goldwater's vulner-ability. One of their TV ads (known as the Daisy Girl spot) had a little girl picking petals from a daisy that dissolved into a mushroom-shaped cloud. Another had a girl eating an ice cream cone while a motherly voice talked about Strontium 90 and pointed out that Goldwater had voted against the test-ban treaty. Still another merely showed two hands tearing up a social security card.

If the Democrats went too far sometimes, it was because Goldwater invited them to. He not only said ridiculous things, he allowed every kind of nonsense to go out over his signature. His battery of ghost writ-ers had churned out thousands of speeches and three books over the years, some of which Goldwater seemed not to have read. He was, as Richard Rovere put it, "a casual student of his own works." Once he did attempt to get some kind of information-retrieval system that would en-able him to review by subject everything said in his name. The effort was hopeless, so Goldwater had no choice but to deny the more embar-rassing parts of his corpus. Still, by mid-October he was so far behind in the polls that the GOP canceled its polling service. Who needed more bad news? Later Goldwater was to say that he knew the election was lost in August, and ought to have known it sooner. Mostly, of course, he should have known better than to run at all.

If Goldwater gave the President every advantage, Lyndon Johnson improved on them. Afterward some writers were to accuse him of going for political overkill, as if that were unsporting. But vanity apart, Presi-dent Johnson had two good reasons for wanting to run up the biggest margin possible. He intended to discredit Goldwater's kind of conserva-tism so thoroughly that the Republicans would never be tempted by it again. And he meant to carry a congressional majority with him big enough to build the Great Society. Time will tell if he accomplished the one; the wave of legislation that roared through Congress in 1965 proved the other. By September nothing was left to do except the President's own campaigning. Everything was running smoothly, only his personal-ity remained a problem. Even at the peak of his glory unfriendly people continued to exploit his rough edges. He always felt their jabs were the product of malice or misunderstanding; if they knew the real Lyndon they would behave differently. At one point a senior adviser tried to set him straight. Mr. President, he explained, you are just not a very likable man. This information seems not to have helped the President much.

When Johnson hit the campaign trail in September, a surprising thing happened. Though he was no more lovable than before, vast crowds turned out to cheer him. Goldwater had so terrified the people, and President Johnson was running the government so masterfully, that they took to him, warts and all. He was, as he often pointed out, the only President they had. He had maintained the continuity of power when John F. Kennedy was killed, then used his skill and the martyred President's memory to get things moving again. Come, let us reason together, he said, bringing harmony out of discord. And when the spectre of Goldwaterism darkened the land, President Johnson dispelled it with his bright confidence and radiant promises. The great throngs that came out to see him turned him on, and the President, a mighty campaigner to begin with, surpassed himself. He would stand up in his auto and urge the crowds to "come down an' hear the speakin'." When they got to the meeting place none knew which Johnson would confront them, for the President had an extensive repertoire to draw on. Theodore White gave names to them. "Mr. President" was the statesman. At his convention he had been "Imperial Lyndon," arrogantly surveying his dominions, but on the trail he was more apt to be "Kindly Lyndon," with a heart as big as all creation. "Fair-Shares Johnson" would see to an equitable distribution of the wealth. "Ole Doc Johnson" had a cure for whatever ailed you. "Lonely Acres Johnson" was a careworn figure, weighted down by the burdens of his office. "Sheriff Johnson," steely eyed and firm of jaw, was determined to see justice done.

These were not merely poses. Each showed one aspect of an infinitely various and complex man. And though President Johnson tailored himself to fit the occasion, he rarely pandered to local prejudice. Sometimes he did the opposite. His best speech on integration was given in New Orleans to an audience that largely opposed it. He explained how racism was the curse of the South, the chief reason for its backwardness, and the main obstacle to its advance. The President concluded with an anecdote told to him by Speaker Sam Rayburn. When Rayburn was a young man he visited a Texas Senator who had been born in Mississippi. The Senator spoke to Rayburn of its poverty and degradation, and said that if he weren't so old and tired he would like to go back and speak the truth for once. "Poor old state, they haven't heard a real Democratic speech in thirty years. All they ever hear at election time is nigra, nigra, nigra." Altogether a remarkable address to be given in that time and place by a candidate for public office. The President's hatred of racism was the best part of him, and a point on which he never wavered. Himself as much a Southerner as a Westerner, he knew firsthand the price Southerners paid for their prejudice, how it was used to divide them, destroy their best leaders, and pervert their finest instincts. When he was still a regional politician Lyndon Johnson had been forced to compromise with it. But once he became a national leader he never stopped trying to make clear to his own people their folly. Perhaps only a few were converted, yet some must have respected, however grudgingly, a man who told them the hard truth in such familiar accents. And many who would never admit it, even privately, must have known in their hearts that he was right.

The Deep South remained hostile, though the President's wife was politely received in most places during her Southern swing on the Lady Bird Special. But in the North Johnson's crowds became, if anything, more rapturous. Even New England, the very antithesis of all that Lyndon Johnson embodied, was won over. In some places more people came out to see him than had rallied to John F. Kennedy, their native son. Providence, Rhode Island, with a population of 208,000, saw half a million people line his parade route. Nothing like it had ever happened before. In retrospect it was clear that Goldwater's campaign had been doomed from the start. Probably even his election would not have been the disaster everyone predicted. Yet in the strange atmosphere of those days the Goldwater threat made President Johnson seem messianic. He played the part beautifully. No one who saw him then will ever forget his commanding presence, what comfort was taken from his homely, reassuring phrases. Everyone knew those great hands would never press the button. Against the background of Goldwater's negative polemics, the President's consensus shone ever more brilliantly. In Providence he climbed up on his car, grabbed a bullhorn, and shouted out, "I just want to tell you this—we're in favor of a lot of things and we're against mighty few." That was what the people came to hear, and that was what he gave them.

In November President Johnson got 61 per cent of the popular vote and carried all but six states. 43 million people voted for him, as against 27 million for Goldwater. Twenty-eight Democratic Senators and thirty-seven new Congressmen were borne along on the tide, giving the party huge majorities in each house. Many said in print that the GOP would pay for this ideological binge with its life. Such obituaries were premature. Though few noticed it then, the party did well enough in the South to become, for the first time in its history, a national party. The key event was George Wallace's decision not to campaign as a third candidate. He ran strongly in several Democratic primaries, then withdrew in Goldwater's favor so as not to split the conservative vote. Had he continued he would surely have carried the five Southern states that ultimately went Republican. As it was, the conditions for a Republican comeback were established. Four years later Nixon would carry the Upper South and outpoll Humphrey in many of the states that went to Wallace.

In 1964, though, with the opposition in eclipse and the President fully in command, the question was, What would the Great Society be like? It was already clear that welfare liberalism would prevail at home. It was not so easy to tell what the President's foreign policy would be. The signs were there, but Goldwater kicked up so much dust that few could see them. Goldwater's prescription for Vietnam was drastic enough to enable President Johnson to run as the peace candidate even while waging war. The temptation to have it both ways was irresistible. No doubt President Kennedy would have succumbed to it too had he lived. Goldwater's proposals for nuclear defoliation and instant victory alarmed women especially, and women normally voted for Republican presidential candidates. In 1964 a majority of them voted Democratic for the first time. The Johnson strategy paid off handsomely in that respect. Meanwhile, conditions in Vietnam deteriorated as *coup* followed *coup* in Saigon. Six thousand more Americans were sent over to no avail. Escalation was the obvious response. Nearly all the Kennedy men still in office urged President Johnson to raise the ante in Vietnam. At the same time, for political reasons he could not seem to be doing so, nor even to be entertaining the prospect. These conflicting imperatives led to the famous "credibility gap." They would have been as compelling for President Kennedy as they were for President Johnson. The chief difference was that Lyndon Johnson's predecessor would surely have handled the play more cleverly. The Kennedy administration was no more truthful than Johnson's, yet it did not suffer from a credibility gap. (One Kennedy appointee even spoke of the public's "right not to know.") Charming people are always more believable than oafs. The good con man makes theft a pleasure, even for his victims. Johnson, though devious, lacked panache. So the people he misled never forgave him for it. And he compounded his future difficulties by going so much further than he needed to.

Thus all through 1964 official cheerfulness on Vietnam was carried to the point of mania. In February both Rusk and McNamara asserted that the South Vietnamese could fight the war by themselves. In March, Taylor and McNamara went to Vietnam and declared that General Khanh, the current dictator, was a "truly remarkable" national leader. In May the Secretary of Defense said again that American strength in Vietnam was not likely to increase. In June, when Ambassador Lodge resigned to join the stop-Goldwater movement, he said the war was "on the right track." Finally, in language reminiscent of Franklin Roosevelt's under similar circumstances in 1940, the President said, "We are not about to send American boys nine or ten thousand miles from home to do what Asian boys ought to be doing for themselves." These were not outright lies. There remained hope for divine intervention. But they were disingenuous remarks at best, and plainly dishonest before long. The day was to come when people would take for granted that any official statement on Vietnam was false.

The Gulf of Tonkin affair was costly too. On August 2, with the presidential campaign barely underway, North Vietnamese torpedo boats allegedly struck at U.S. destroyers patrolling the Gulf of Tonkin. Two days later this perfidy was supposedly repeated. The President then ordered a retaliatory attack that wiped out the DRVN navy, or the better part of it anyway. He also asked Congress for a resolution endorsing this and any other steps he might take. The President easily obtained his blank check. But even then the Gulf of Tonkin affair aroused suspicion. When I. F. Stone went to New York to cover the UN Security Council debate over it, newsmen were cynically recalling Ambassador Stevenson's statement four months earlier that the U.S. disapproved of "retaliatory raids, wherever they occur and by whomever they are committed." During the brief congressional debate Senator Wayne Morse asked why the tiny North Vietnamese fleet dared attack the world's strongest navy. Morse pointed out that on July 31, when the South Vietnamese navy shelled Northern territory, U.S. vessels were in attendance. If they were providing cover for aggression against the DRVN, then the Northern response was purely defensive. Senator Fulbright answered that it was merely a coincidence that U.S. naval ships were around during the bombardment. When Senator Gaylord Nelson attempted to amend the resolution to rule out further escalation, Fulbright assured him that no further action was contemplated.

The government's case was even weaker than Morse suspected. The administration never proved that the alleged DRVN attack took place. The American warships in question sustained no damage. The DRVN torpedo boats they allegedly sank with counterfire left no debris. The "battle" was guided entirely by radar sightings so unreliable that one U.S. destroyer nearly fired on its sister ship. Though Hanoi freely admitted pursuing American vessels that had violated its territorial waters on August 2, it denied making any later assaults. No serious evidence to the contrary has ever been put forward. Senator Fulbright came to believe that he had been gulled by the President into sponsoring a resolution susceptible of unlimited abuse. No other incident tried the Congress's faith in President Johnson so severely. He never enjoyed the full confidence of its liberal members again.

Whatever the actual facts, the Gulf of Tonkin affair became a dry run which showed military escalation in Vietnam to be a politically viable policy at home. And, since the excuse for it was so feeble, it suggested that almost any pretext would do. The President was free after his re-election to take whatever action he pleased. He knew it. Before long the country would too.

PROFILE:
Ralph Nader

ON SEPTEMBER 9, 1966, President Johnson signed the Highway Safety Act and the Traffic Safety Act. They allocated large sums for state and local traffic safety programs and applied safety standards to vehicle manufacturers. Afterward a distinguished body of interested figures lined up to shake the President's hand. Among the last to file by was a tall, dark, intense-looking lawyer. There is no evidence that the President recognized him, but Ralph Nader had done more to secure those bills than anyone. His book, *Unsafe at Any Speed,* had generated public support for auto safety. His research and lobbying had been indispensable to its congressional advocates.

Nader was one of the age's most remarkable men. He did not own a car, nor was he an expert on automotive affairs, but rather a graduate of the Harvard Law School who wanted to make a career of defending the public interest. There was no one else like him at the time. Lawyers of good conscience either went into government or politics, or tried to turn their private practice to the public's advantage. No one had ever thought of making a practice out of representing the public. Where was the money to come from? The public interest was a concept, not an institution with funds and resources. Nader solved this problem by creating his own support. *Unsafe at Any Speed* made a lot of money, and he used it to further his work. He lived in a rooming house and spent practically nothing on himself. This became evident when General Motors put a private detective on his trail in hopes of uncovering dubious vices and practices. But Nader's life was so austere nothing could be found against him, nor could he be entrapped. He found out what was going on and told Congress. In consequence the president of GM was called before a Senate committee where he apologized. This satisfied the committee but not Ralph Nader. He sued GM and two detective agencies for $26 million. (They later settled out of court for nearly half a million.)

The publicity, the indignation, and the congressional hearings which attended these proceedings made the two safety bills into law. They also established Nader's reputation as a public-interest specialist. He went on to investigate other abuses and outrages. And he began to get help. A little foundation money came his way, as did student volunteers. He put them to work on his investigations, and "Nader's Raiders" became a familiar sight in Washington. He also inspired young people to become lawyers like himself. Before Nader, altruistic youths had scorned the law. Nader showed them that the legal sword cut both ways. This created opportunities for the talented young who wanted to move beyond protests and demonstrations which, though worthy in themselves, were not enough to build a life on. Thereafter, the corporations' ramparts had to be continuously strengthened. To leave a gate unguarded was to risk finding Nader's Raiders pouring through it. Being a captain of industry was never quite so much fun again.

Still, the corporations gave ground slowly. The auto industry was a case in point. The gasoline-powered automobile was the country's pride and its curse. Americans loved their vehicles beyond reason. Though the cars changed but little over time, it was the dream of most adult males to have a new one every year. Most autos were much alike, whatever the make or price, but men developed brand loyalties anyway. It was hard to see why. They all got bigger, faster, and more expensive. Still, marginal differentiation, as social scientists call it, was something Americans were bred to. Even as children they learned to distinguish between virtually identical products and to think these differences important. Thus while in many areas, cars among them, product variety diminished, consumer enthusiasm appeared not to. A car by any other name was still a Chevrolet. Few Americans seemed to mind.

An encouraging minority did buy foreign cars, many of which (the robust Volkswagen, for example) remained distinctive at a time when even European and Japanese vehicles were coming to resemble American ones. Foreign cars were socially more desirable because of their size. Most were small, hence they did not clog the streets as American cars did. Their tiny engines did not pollute the air so badly. They used less of the earth's irreplaceable resources. But their virtue was their defect too. Because of their light weight they were even more dangerous to passengers than U.S. autos, and American cars, as Nader pointed out, were rolling death traps. Bumpers could not withstand an impact of three miles per hour. Head-on collisions at speeds as low as twenty-five miles per hour were often fatal. Much had been done to make highways safer; the cars themselves were ignored. Thus in 1965 nearly fifty thousand Americans died of the automobile. It was the principal cause of death for people under thirty-five years of age. Half of all adult Americans could look forward to being injured by one at some point in their lives.

The manufacturers were to blame, of course. If they had spent as much on safety as on styling ($700 per car), many thousands more would be alive today. But the public was guilty too. Once the Ford Motor Company had launched a safety campaign that failed utterly. Market research showed that by stressing safety, Ford discouraged buyers. In purchasing a car people also bought an image of themselves. Men wanted power and status, women looked for luxury. Nobody wanted to be reminded that his life was at stake when driving. When seatbelts were installed in all new cars, people could not be made to use them. They were too awkward or uncomfortable, it was said. Mostly, no doubt, they announced one's mortality.

The manufacturers' greed and the consumers' weaknesses combined to make America a victim of its transportation system. Cars polluted the air, wasted resources, jammed the cities, and decimated the population. When existing roads became inadequate, larger ones were built. These encouraged more people to buy and drive cars. Hence more land was taken from productive use and turned into freeways and parking lots. The more people drove, the more public transit decayed, making people even more dependent on automobiles. It was as if the country were addicted to the motor car and required ever larger doses of it. That the cars themselves became more lethal was only one part, though an important one, of the total problem. Lewis Mumford and other social critics had been complaining of it for years. But not until 1966 did the government take notice of them. Then, thanks to Ralph Nader, Senators Ribicoff and Nelson, the government's own purchasing agent—the General Services Administration, which began specifying safety items for the cars it bought—and others, the problem was confronted.

Even so, very little happened. Cars did become slightly less dangerous. They did not pollute the air quite so much. Money was spent to improve public transit services, though it was hard to get people to use them. A few high-speed commuter lines showed it could be done if a big enough investment was made. Few private firms were willing to do so. The government moved sluggishly in this area, partly because of the cost. Another reason was the huge existing investment in roads, cars, and the network manufacturing and sustaining them. If auto use did decline, so would profits and employment, it was feared. In a way, automobiles were central to the national economy precisely because they were so costly and wasteful. Public transit was cheaper, safer, and more efficient, but however widespread it became it could never, for just those reasons, puff up the economy as autos did. American prosperity was based on waste—disposable containers, annual model changes, and planned obsolescence. Even a change from internal-combustion engines to other forms of automotive power would threaten it. The very fact that electric- or steam-powered automobiles would be simpler and cheaper to operate told against them. No manufacturer wanted to make propulsion systems that would earn him less money. And even if by some miracle a suitable vehicle were devised, how could people be induced to use it? Over and over again consumers had shown that what they wanted in a car was size, power, and luxury. To be competitive other types of autos would have to be just as big, fast, and costly as the present ones.

So at the decade's end the transportation problem still seemed insoluble. Commuter lines improved in a few cities. Popular opposition and rising costs slowed the pace of urban freeway construction. The Penn Central's Metroliner showed that good passenger train service paid, at least in the densely populated Northeast corridor. But the automobile continued its deadly work. People could not be weaned from it by even the most ingenious experiments. In Flint, Michigan, the federal government spent $1.6 million over a three-year period for a "maxicab" service that transported workers from home to factory at low rates. The maxicabs offered coffee, music, newspapers, and other amenities. Even so, only 320 people a day used them, half the number needed to show a profit. In *Brave New World* Huxley's characters speak of living in the time of Our Ford. But they had, at least, freed themselves of his machines. Those who lived in the world Ford actually made were not so fortunate, though in their way they worshiped him too.

None of this discouraged Ralph Nader. He was the kind of reformer, once common in America (Florence Kelley, Jane Addams, Paul Kellogg, and so on) but latterly quite rare, who signed on for life. He went on living in a drab furnished room and created a reform industry. There were nine Nader's Raiders in 1968, one hundred in 1969. Another of his operations was called simply "Auto Safety." It continuously monitored the automobile industry and relevant federal agencies, putting the heat on them where it could. A third was The Center for the Study of Responsive Law, which with a staff of six lawyers and one political scientist pushed forward Nader's concept of the public-interest law firm. It would do for the public what the great Washington firms did for private interests. Then there was the "Nader network," a largely secret corps of experts that Nader could call on for help. They made possible those detailed reports on corporate outrages that Nader used so effectively. And Nader's impact was multiplied by those who studied under him and then went off on their own, like the group that tried to get GM to put public-interest representatives on its board of directors in 1970. No one could remember when a single man had had such impact on the corporate society. If the country could be saved it would be by people like him.

5 THE DESPERATE YEARS BEGIN

WHEN LYNDON JOHNSON started his first full term as President in 1965, almost no one guessed what lay ahead. The war in Vietnam was small and distant. To most people, Watts only stood for units of electricity. President Johnson had handled the succession crisis brilliantly, suppressed the Goldwater rebellion, and squeezed a tax cut and a civil rights bill out of Congress. Now that he had a liberal majority, what might he not accomplish? These expectations were well founded. Johnson's performance in 1965 and into 1966 refuted those who feared that the constitutional process was obsolete. Every modern President had been frustrated by Congress in domestic matters. Even Franklin Roosevelt had found it responsive only for a time. In foreign affairs, where the separation of power no longer applied, Presidents usually got their way, but in domestic matters only rarely.

Congressmen felt obliged to see the public interest much as the folks back home in Middle America did. Middle Americans would pay taxes for war, and for what benefited them directly, but for little else. A powerful lobby could overcome this where deep feelings were not aroused. Hence the special-interest legislation benefiting growers, shippers, munitions makers, and the like. But the needy were, by definition, powerless. Those who spoke for them had also to challenge the general feeling that the poor deserved no more than they got. The Protestant Ethic never really died among Middle Americans, who continued to think their prosperity, however slight, the reward of virtue, and other's poverty, however great, the penalty of vice. To overcome these views, and the locally oriented federal system that enshrined them, required not so much a President as a magician, it was thought. Lyndon Johnson did not agree. In 1964 he had task forces make policy recommendations in fourteen areas. These were distilled into a single volume of legislative proposals. Knowing that he would never again be as strong in Congress as he was now, the President moved quickly to implement them.

In October 1965 he presented a glass case containing fifty pens to the White House press corps. Its plaque read: "With these fifty pens President Lyndon B. Johnson signed into law the foundations of the Great Society, which was passed by the historic and fabulous first session of the Eighty-ninth Congress." There was some hyperbole here, but not much. The list of bills included trivia like the silver coinage act. It also contained the bills that established Johnson's place in history. He got federal aid for public and parochial schools by tying the bills to his war on poverty. When Selma blew up he was irritated by the Negro leadership at first. Confrontation politics was not his style. But he seized the chance given him nonetheless. On March 15, 1965, he went personally to Congress and made the best speech of his presidency. He talked about the Mexican-American children he had taught thirty-seven years before. He invoked the American dream. He ended by quoting the civil rights movement's anthem "We Shall Overcome"—and so the Congress did. Voting rights were secured, as were immigration reform, federal scholarships for college students, anti-poverty programs, and a new Department of Housing and Urban Development. There were bills to fight cancer, heart disease, strokes, air pollution, water pollution, roadside billboards, and auto junkyards. Among the best was Medicare.

America was the only developed country without some kind of national health program. This was because the American Medical Association had as strong a lobby as any in Washington. Organized physicians used their monopoly of health care to restrict competition, maintain high piecework rates, and keep laymen out of medical affairs. The AMA inveighed ceaselessly against the notion that health care was a right. Its press releases depicted physicians as veritable Robin Hoods, robbing the rich to help the poor. They did indeed soak the rich, and the middle classes too, but this didn't seem to do the poor much good. The AMA was probably not the most sinister organization going, but many thought so because it held to ransom the very stuff of life. Medicare was the AMA's first defeat. If President Johnson had done nothing else he would still be remembered for that. It was not a perfect bill. It helped only the old, and then in a cumbersome and limited way. In obedience to the great payoff principle it was made acceptable to physicians by giving them control over fees. Many scandals resulted.

These defects hardly mattered. The AMA's mystique was damaged. The aged got immediate relief. Everyone could look forward to a time when health care would be a matter of right, when serious illness would not lead to bankruptcy, and when the American health delivery system would be as good as Western Europe's. And, thanks to a little-noticed rider called Medicaid, funds were soon available for the states to help poor people not covered by Medicare. Even the abuses were helpful. Profiteering physicians drove the costs up, creating pressure for reform. Congress thought of limiting fees, a first step toward public supervision of the health industry. After President Nixon took office he announced that the country faced a medical crisis. Reform began at last to seem inevitable. If so, that would be because Medicare and Medicaid showed how great the need was, and how unfit the medical establishment was to meet it.

Things did not go quite so well for President Johnson in 1966. As expected, Congress got harder to manage. This happens to every administration, no matter how shrewd. Time and events whittle away its majority. More important, the war in Vietnam began costing real money. Since the government's policy hinged on making the war painless, inflation resulted. To keep the war from being inflationary required tax increases, or lower expenditures at home, or price and wage controls, or some combination of all these. But any of them would make the war unpopular. So the administration gambled on a short war and did nothing. In the early sixties consumer price increases averaged only 1.2 per cent a year. After escalation of the war in 1965 they rose by 3.7 per cent in twelve months. When the President failed to act, the Federal Reserve raised interest rates on loans to member banks. Johnson grumbled at this. His solution, such as it was, involved delays in projected tax cuts and speedups in corporate tax collections. The Tax Adjustment Act of 1966 was supposed to remove $4.8 billion from circulation. Increased social security levies would take $5 billion more. This scheme failed. Food prices went up causing short-lived consumer revolts. Corporations planned to spend 16 per cent more than the previous year on plant expansion. President Johnson called one hundred business leaders together and got them to reduce their expansion plans by 10 per cent. But though most kept their word, and the Federal Reserve Board pushed interest rates up, these efforts failed too. Interest rates were the highest in nearly forty years. The Treasury found itself paying 6 per cent on government bonds, an extraordinary rate for these safest of all securities. The increase in wages, prices, and capital investments continued.

The President soldiered on. "Inflation need not be the price of social progress, nor should it be the cost of defending freedom," he told Congress. In this spirit the Office of Economic Opportunity, Johnson's main weapon in the war on poverty, had its budget increased slightly. Yet this war did not seem to be going well either. Under Sargent Shriver the

OEO supported a staggering variety of programs—Head Start for preschoolers, a Job Corps for dropouts, Upward Bound for college students, a domestic peace corps (VISTA), a Neighborhood Youth Corps, and a Community Action program featuring neighborhood centers, among others. The results were not impressive. For one thing, $1.6 billion, however carefully expended, didn't go far toward meeting the needs of thirty or forty million poor people. And some of it was wasted. Much of the criticism given OEO was partisan or captious. Conservatives hated to spend any money on poverty. They especially disliked OEO's attempt to involve the poor. "Maximum feasible participation" was the program's aim. Conservatives found it bewildering, perhaps immoral. The poor sometimes bit the hand that fed them. The Mississippi Head Start program was so bumptious that Shriver denied its request for more money, charging it with conflicts of interest, nepotism, payments to people outside the state, and misuse of government automobiles. Admirers of the Mississippi Group for Child Development thought its main offense was irritating the state's two powerful Democratic Senators, Stennis and Eastland.

In fact, many errors were made. The programs were often hastily assembled. Sometimes they were based on false principles, as was Head Start. Though a fine program, it assumed that intensive training for impoverished preschoolers would carry over into their school years. Generally that didn't happen. In a few more years evidence would accumulate that the disadvantaged, once out of the program, tended to fall behind again. But the main problem was always money. OEO had $50 million to help 150,000 migrant workers, $32 million for over 200,000 reservation Indians. Sargent Shriver, who headed the war on poverty, put the best possible face on things. "I think we've turned the corner and are on our way," he said. But as in that other war, where the corner was always being turned too, victory stayed out of reach.

The disaster began on February 7, 1965, when fighter-bombers from three U.S. aircraft carriers attacked what was described as a Viet Cong staging area near Dong Hoi, North Vietnam. The raids were ostensibly in retaliation for a VC attack on American installations at Pleiku. But they proved to be only the first of many during the next three years. When they ended, President Johnson's career lay in ruins, as did much of Vietnam. They destroyed the Great Society and made Richard Nixon President. They divided the country as nothing had since the struggle over American entry into World War II. The administration insisted then and later that only the gravest reasons pushed it to such desperate actions. The raids and the troop buildup that accompanied them were essential to sustain faith in American commitments elsewhere. Escalation was needed to repel North Vietnam's invasion of the South. If South Vietnam went communist, other Asian states would fall like dominoes. Negotiations were impossible, any peaceful settlement would be another Munich. The raid on Pleiku, and the "aggression from the North" even more, was, as Secretary McNamara put it, yet another "test of will."* Should the U.S. flunk it, China and/or Russia would be emboldened to fresh adventures. The communist theory of world conquest through "wars of liberation" had to be disproved. At the very least, the innocent people of South Vietnam must be saved from a bloodbath such as followed communist victory in the North. Their right to determine their own destinies became America's moral responsibility.

If all this made little sense at the time, it made less later. Far from sustaining confidence in American commitments, escalation undermined it. The price was so great that few believed America would pay it another time. When President Nixon took office he proclaimed the Guam or Nixon doctrine which was taken (wrongly perhaps) to mean never again. President Nixon might indeed launch such a war of his own sometime, somewhere, but only the rashest ally could count on that.

There was no invasion from the North. Men trickled down from it, but they were mainly displaced Southerners rejoining old comrades from the Viet Minh. The National Liberation Front, a communist-dominated political coalition which sponsored the VC, got little material help from outside. The State Department white paper justifying the raids admitted that of 15,000 weapons taken from the VC to date (February 27, 1965), only 175 were manufactured in communist countries. In the same period the VC had captured 27,000 ARVN weapons. These, together with what it made itself, were quite enough to sustain operations. Only afterward did North Vietnam send in troops and supplies on a large scale. Escalation thus provoked the invasion it was supposed to deter.

The domino theory was just that, a theory. There was no evidence to support it, only faith. Cuba had gone communist without toppling the dominoes around it. In Indonesia later, communism would be destroyed without U.S. help, and without much effect on other countries. To all but Cold War metaphysicians it seemed obvious that each country had to be judged on its own terms. Solid political structures would survive (barring outright attack on them, which was not at issue), rotten ones

---

* Recognizing a test of will was not so easy as it seemed. North Korea was also insolent throughout the decade. Once it even captured a U.S. naval vessel, the *Pueblo*, on the high seas. This was not a test of will, only piracy, so President Johnson let it go unpunished. Ordinary people found the distinction hard to grasp.

might not. Laos and South Vietnam could hardly stand on their own feet, regardless of what North Vietnam did. Cambodia was doubtful. The rest of Southeast Asia had a good chance of surviving, especially if the war ended soon. The longer it lasted, the greater the risk that other states would be drawn into it.

The Munich syndrome and the test-of-will hypothesis were equally fanciful. Ho Chi Minh was not Hitler. South Vietnam was not Czechoslovakia. The world arena was not a schoolground where boys dared each other to fight, though Washington seemed to think so. If it were, the U.S. would be the school bully for beating up North Vietnam which, even if provocative, was so much smaller. Nor was it clear who was testing whose will. Washington kept talking about the war as if China were fighting it. But though involved, China was not a combatant. Escalating the war only made Chinese involvement greater. Pounding North Vietnam made it more, not less, dependent on China. The chances of a reunified, independent Vietnam becoming a buffer between China and Southeast Asia, good at first, declined. And to Hanoi it must have seemed that the U.S. was testing *its* will with the bombing raids.

As China and Russia were so little engaged in Vietnam to begin with, it was never clear why bombing the North was supposed to discourage them. Invading North Korea had not kept China from rising to its support. Why should China react differently to events in Vietnam? The spectacle must, at the very least, have inspired mixed reactions in Moscow. Escalation was so irrational as to seem a kind of madness. True, the powerful and insane do command a certain respect. Russia might well have been moved to greater caution. Yet it had been cautious anyway in Southeast Asia, and got progressively more adventurous in the Near East. So it was hard to see what lessons it learned from the war in Asia. Some believed that Russia welcomed American involvement there. It was costly in men and lives, destructive of America's standing in the world, and a political cancer at home. In the event, no one really knew what either country thought. To say that by making war in Asia the U.S. was preventing war elsewhere was to call upon Americans for still more of that blind faith upon which the country's foreign policy increasingly depended.

Nor did escalation show that wars of liberation wouldn't work. The VC and the North Vietnamese were bombed more heavily than Germany and Japan had been in World War II. They were pitifully weak compared with the United States. Yet they kept on coming. As Henry Kissinger pointed out later, in a guerrilla war "the guerrilla wins if he does not lose. The conventional army loses if it does not win." So it was in Vietnam. Of course the enemy suffered terribly to accomplish this. Who knows but that somewhere a potential uprising might be deterred, not for fear of losing, but for fear of what it would cost to win? On the other hand, who knows but that threatened countries, viewing the wreckage in South Vietnam when the big guns and bombers had done their work, might not think twice about asking for that kind of help?*

The humanitarian excuses were most pitiful of all. It was said that the VC committed atrocities, especially by murdering government officials, while the North Vietnamese were even worse. After partition in 1954 they slaughtered dissidents by the thousands. This was a lie. There was no slaughter after partition because most dissidents had left. Many were slain in a peasants' revolt later, though the policies that produced it were then reformed. Which is not to excuse the communists, only to say that they weren't habitually bloody-minded as charged. If Vietnam was reunited the law-abiding Southerner would have little to fear.† It was true that the VC committed atrocities and murdered their enemies. So did the U.S. and the South Vietnamese. American troops butchered civilians at close quarters in My Lai and elsewhere. Project Phoenix, a program for assassinating suspected rebels, was organized by the U.S. and executed by Saigon with such enthusiasm as to claim perhaps more lives than the VC did. The difference between the two sides in this respect was that the VC needed popular support and Saigon didn't. For the NLF to govern and the VC to fight, a degree of acceptance was required. This made them careful about whom they killed. Saigon had no popular support to lose, so whom it killed was of no great moment. Moreover, the ARVN and American forces shelled and bombed vast areas indiscriminately. It was thought less reprehensible to kill civilians at long distance than by hand. Hundreds of thousands died this way. The distinction eluded the dead no doubt, perhaps also those whose "mind and heart" the government proposed to win. Such random slaughter did not leave the "allies" (as the U.S. and its client state forces were quaintly called) with much to be morally superior about.

* Alas, this was a forlorn hope. When in 1970 Prince Sihanouk of Cambodia was overthrown, his military successors asked for U.S. aid. American troops invaded the border zones where the VC hid out. This forced them to disperse and they soon occupied half the country. As in Vietnam, the U.S. began indiscriminate bombing raids. The country's ruin seemed assured. It was worth the price to the country's new leaders if it kept them in power. South Vietnam was destroyed because it might go communist; Cambodia because it was neutralist. There appeared no limit to what Indochinese militarists would do to gratify their ambitions, nor to what America would do in support of them. No one asked the peasantry which ideology, if any, they wished to die for. They died just the same.

† Of course the Saigon regime and its followers would have to be evacuated as in 1954. Honor would compel the U.S. to admit and resettle all refugees who wished to emigrate, preferably in those American communities where support for the war had been highest. This would provide numerous opportunities for patriotic citizens, especially in the South, to display those benevolent feelings for the Vietnamese that justified America's war policy.

The U.S. kept insisting too that it was in Vietnam to preserve the people's freedom of choice. This also was false. American policy was to prevent the Vietnamese from choosing wrongly. The U.S. sustained President Diem's decision not to allow a vote on reunification in 1956 for fear that Hanoi would win. Every regime from then on jailed its critics and suppressed its opposition. America kept saying that freedom of choice was all it wanted in Vietnam. The less of it there was, the louder Washington invoked it. Most Southerners seemed to want a neutralized, Buddhist state. What they got was a pro-Western military dictatorship operated by Roman Catholics and displaced Northerners. The worst fears of what a communist victory would mean for South Vietnam were less than what American intervention actually produced. In the name of liberty and life, America gave it tyranny and death.

What then were the true reasons for American involvement? Strictly speaking, there weren't any. American policy in Indochina was not a considered one in the sense of people weighing the pros and cons of this step or that. The original commitment was slight and tentative. It was made mostly from habit. In those days whoever asked for help against communism got some. Aid was given with little thought at first, then increased out of sheer momentum when conditions worsened. At some point the process came to be seen as irreversible. This may have been when President Kennedy sent the first troops, more to impress Russia than North Vietnam it will be recalled, or perhaps when President Johnson was given a free hand by the Tonkin Gulf resolution. The point was reached because each step taken forced another. If the communists won, all the aid previously given would have been wasted, and the careers of those responsible damaged.

This last was especially important. Washington did not wish to be politically embarrassed by a defeat, however minor. Everyone with a stake in the policy was determined to preserve it, and the worse things got the more determined they became. One way they showed this was by denying reality. When the ARVN was beaten at Ap Bac, it claimed victory and Washington agreed. President Kennedy asked the *New York Times* to recall David Halberstam not because he lied, but because he didn't. Those who spoke the truth, like Colonel Vann, were ruined. Those who denied it got promoted. Higher echelons could not admit error, lower echelons could not report it. The bigger a man was, the greater the pressure to tell him what he wished to hear. Thus while for years each Saigon regime was weaker than the last, each was described as stronger. Every new pacification device was hailed as the ultimate weapon. Few minded, or even remembered, that the same was said of all the earlier plans before they collapsed. Military and political solutions failed alike. But as military actions required less thought and had more advocates, failure did not discredit them. Political setbacks encouraged despair; military defeats led to escalation. Americans paid lip service to political reform while putting their money into weapons. Everyone agreed that guerrilla warfare was more political than military. Chairman Mao and President Ho were politicians of genius, not great soldiers, it was freely admitted. Yet being ill-equipped for political action the U.S. met each new crisis with a military response. These bought time. The time was always wasted, so each crisis was graver than the last. This was because politics were neglected, and also because the military buildup was wrongly done.

The U.S. Army talked a good counterinsurgency game but played a bad one. American generals remained fixated on Korea. Though they liked jumping out of airplanes, and recognized in theory the need for counterinsurgency tactics in Vietnam, they kept ordering more heavy equipment and calling for bigger battalions. This was the easiest course to take. The American Army, and the ARVN even more, were unprepared for guerrilla war, and conventional forces were best for repelling an invasion from the North. The generals wanted to make South Vietnam so strong that American troops would not have to become involved in yet another squalid Asian land war. The means used defeated the ends. The ARVN, though heavily armed (*because* heavily armed), could not cope with an insurgency. This was clear by the end of 1964. But instead of confessing their own error and the ARVN's incapacity, the generals blamed everything on North Vietnam. If only the infiltration routes were bombed and the DRVN made to pay for its sins, Saigon would prevail. Hence the bombing raids. When these failed to work a miracle, nothing remained but to pull out or go in in strength. Retreat was unthinkable. So the generals got what they dreaded most, another Asian land war to be fought under even worse conditions than before.

Though needed to save military face, President Johnson had other reasons for ordering the bombing raids. As an old Cold Warrior he naturally subscribed to its metaphysics. All the nonsense about Munichs, dominoes, and tests of will came easily to his lips. His chief advisers were like-minded. Secretary Rusk had, with General MacArthur, called for total victory over China in 1951. He was still warning against the "Sino-Soviet Bloc" long after it had collapsed. The President was urged on by strategists and crisis managers eager to practice their professions. He feared withdrawal would strengthen rightists and blow the Democrats out of office as in 1952. He did not wish to become the first President to lose a war.* Bombing was his natural response to bad news from

* Of course the U.S. had not won all its wars. Two, the War of 1812 and the Korean War, had been draws at best. It was never entirely clear why having a perfect record was so important anyway. Would losing one matter less if there was a

Vietnam. He did not want to commit troops until everything else had been tried. Even the largest raids hazarded few lives compared to what ground action would take. This calculation was as much political as moral. Bombing meant the random slaughter of Vietnamese, civilian and military alike. As luck would have it, the Vietnamese did not vote in American elections. It didn't hurt Democrats much to kill people in a small distant country. But it would go hard with the party if American boys began to die there.

Then too, President Johnson shared the general faith in air power. North Vietnam was so underdeveloped that there was little in it worth hitting. Even if "bombed back to the stone age," as General LeMay said, the DRVN's capacity to fight would not be much impaired, nor, as the experience of Germany and Japan in World War II suggested, its will to resist diminished. The U.S. had enjoyed complete air supremacy over North Korea, flattened every structure of note, and still failed to win though it also had a great army in the field. There was little reason to think that bombing alone would do in Vietnam what greater force had not accomplished in Korea. Yet the air-power mystique flourished all the same. Perhaps this was because the Air Force had such good propagandists, mostly on the outside. More likely it was a consequence of the American faith in technology, that reverence for machines which is so salient a national trait. Then too, people naturally like to do what they are good at. In war, what Americans do best is aerial bombing. It was pretty much an irrelevant skill in Vietnam. This fact discouraged few in Washington, and as President Johnson had nothing else at hand when he decided on escalation, there was all the more reason to use it. So the raids began, and when they failed, as they had to, the troop buildup that followed brought the war home to Americans.

The raids were launched amidst the usual fakery. "We seek no wider war," President Johnson said after widening it. "Whether or not this course can be maintained lies with the North Vietnamese aggressors." The Soviets replied in kind. Premier Kosygin announced, "We sternly declare that the Soviet Union will not remain indifferent to the destiny of a brotherly Socialist country and is ready to give . . . all necessary assistance if aggressors dare to encroach upon the sovereignty of the Democratic Republic of Viet Nam." By then the great powers not only followed the same policies but used the same language to obscure them. When either committed aggression, the victim was to blame. Cuba and North Vietnam were at fault for making the U.S. attack them. Czecho-

---

precedent? If so, that might be a good reason for accepting defeat. Then, perhaps, the reality principle would overcome the sporting principle. Yet it seems unlikely that Johnson (or Nixon later) would have felt much different about being the second President to lose a war than he did about being the first.

slovakia and the Dominican Republic were invaded later by Russia and the U.S. respectively for their own good. Each side gave the same empty warnings when unable to deter the other. Russia could not keep the U.S. from attacking North Vietnam, however stern its promises. America could not stop Russia from invading Czechoslovakia, though the military was alerted and equally stern warnings issued. This disproved the theory, held by intellectuals in both countries, that since the two countries were coming to resemble each other convergence would lead to peace. There was indeed little difference between their foreign policies, but peace stayed as distant as ever. Their domestic policies did not converge at all. Russia remained a closed society, America a relatively open one. The convergence theory was, therefore, partly false and wholly pathetic. Those who drew comfort from it showed only how desperate they were.

Though the bombing raids were born of panic and muddle, they were naturally attributed to calculation. Elaborate planning was said to lie behind them. Perfect control was supposedly exercised throughout. Yet the raids began when Premier Kosygin was visiting Hanoi. Their targets included, as Harrison Salisbury among others would later report, schools, churches, and hospitals. A number of raids took place even as peace feelers were being extended. If the raids were precisely orchestrated, as claimed, they seemed intended to avert a settlement. If not, then the fighting continued from sheer maladroitness. Neither explanation encouraged faith in the government's ability to secure peace. But the latter was no doubt preferable to the former. A democracy is healthier when it goes to war by accident rather than design. Popular confidence survives ineptitude better than malice—up to a point anyway. What would finally cost the administration so dearly was precisely the feeling, inspired by repeated errors, and even more by their denial, that bad faith, not human frailty, was at work.

The President was encouraged in his folly by the Dominican crisis. He practiced gunboat diplomacy then and got away with it. Afterward, bullying North Vietnam seemed an even better idea. Though few recall it now, the Dominican affair was a triumph for the Johnsonian system (which is probably why it was forgotten—Johnson was one of those Presidents whom people remember for their failures). In a sense the Dominican intervention hardly requires explanation. The U.S. had been dominant in the Caribbean for so long that people naturally expected it to overthrow unfriendly governments and sustain cooperative ones. Lately American power had grown so great that direct intervention was seldom needed. Thus when the CIA overturned an unfriendly Guatemalan regime in 1954 the stroke was made to seem indigenous. Cuba got the same treatment in 1961, if less successfully. But whether gloved or not, the mailed fist was always there. The use of it declined somewhat when the Alliance for Progress was unveiled. But immediately after President Kennedy's death Thomas C. Mann, a veteran of the Guatemalan *coup*, was appointed Assistant Secretary of State for Inter-American Affairs. In choosing so unrepentant an imperialist, President Johnson showed rebellious Latins what they could expect from him.

The Dominican Republic offered an especially complex challenge to American power. When its odious dictator, Rafael Trujillo, was destroyed in 1961, Washington was not displeased. His crimes were so monstrous they made even the State Department uneasy. To show good will President Kennedy sent a benevolent journalist, John Bartlow Martin, as ambassador to the newly liberated Republic. Though he meant well, Martin's job was more proconsular than ambassadorial. When discouragement led him to consider resigning, he decided against it for fear of injuring President Kennedy. "We would hold this place for the President, our President," he wrote later. What made holding the country for Washington particularly trying was its leading citizen, Juan Bosch. Bosch was not only the foremost living Dominican but a chief spokesman in Latin America for that democratic revolution which the U.S. was ostensibly committed to advance. A quarter-century in exile and a lifetime spent in Caribbean politics had not made Bosch an easy man to deal with. All the same, Martin helped secure a free election in 1962 which put Bosch in power. After seven months he was overturned by a military *coup*. The U.S. withheld recognition for a time to no effect. The *golpistas* hung on. Sporadic guerrilla fighting broke out. So Washington backed down and recognized the military junta. Martin was not much interested in holding the country for President Johnson and resigned soon afterward.

Despite the bankruptcy of American policy there, the democratic impulse survived in the Dominican Republic. On April 24, 1965, an odd coalition of democrats, radicals, and junior military officers launched a counter*coup* to restore constitutional government under Bosch. At first it went badly, and the rebels asked Ambassador William Tapley Bennett to mediate. He refused. Then the military began to crumble. The embassy panicked and asked President Johnson for American troops to back it up and avert "another Cuba." Washington complied by stages. On April 28 the President announced troop landings to protect the embassy and evacuate foreign nationals. Later a cease-fire was enforced which kept the military in power and the constitutionalists out.

All this was rationalized in the most extraordinary way, as Theodore

Draper has shown. When American troops landed the junta's overthrow had been all but accomplished, and with little bloodshed. Most of the fighting took place afterward when the military, encouraged first by the U.S. military mission and then by the troop landings, made a comeback. President Johnson defended the intervention by charging that the rebels beheaded fifteen hundred people. The embassy said a thousand bodies were lying about when the American troops arrived. In one account President Johnson had Ambassador Bennett phoning him to ask for Marines while personally under fire. None of this was true. There were no mass executions. The embassy was never hit. Although some five thousand foreigners were evacuated, there was little reason to think them in danger.*

When this became evident the government fell back on another line. The counter*coup* was organized by good Boschistas, it admitted, but they lost control to Castroites. At first the President couldn't name these sinister elements, but Bennett came up with a list, though it was frequently revised. It finally had seventy-seven names which newsmen checked out. Three were allegedly communist sympathizers whom Colonel Francisco Caamano Deno, the leading rebel, supposedly named to his provisional government. The reporters discovered that these men were not communists. Caamano had not appointed them in any case. Other names included people who were in prison or out of the country when the revolt began. Still others were well-known anti-American nationalists with no communist associations. James Nelson Goodsell concluded that 40 per cent of those named couldn't possibly have played any part in the uprising. The administration was not consistent even in its red-baiting. Ambassador Bennett later gave a speech saying that thanks to prompt action "the Communists were prevented from taking over," which hardly squared with the administration's earlier contention that they already had.

This scarcely mattered at the time. By June order was restored and an inter-American occupation force, provided mainly by friendly dictators, established. Another outbreak of violence was put down in October. The next year elections were held and Joaquin Balaguer, a former Trujillo man acceptable to the U.S., became president. The election was free enough, no doubt. The CIA had sufficient confidence to pay the expenses of impartial witnesses (unbeknownst to them, of course) who attested to that fact. But as the Dominicans believed that the purpose of Ameri-

---

* This was known even at the time. Art Buchwald wrote a whimsical column about Sydney, the last American tourist who was kept from leaving by the Marines so they would have someone left to protect. Buchwald was told later by a friend in the USIA that this was almost literally the case. What to do when there were no more evacuees worried government propagandists a lot.

can intervention had been to keep Bosch out, there was not much point in voting for him again. He got half a million votes nonetheless. Afterward Bosch left the country, his faith in democracy destroyed. At the decade's end he was calling for a "dictatorship with popular support" in the Dominican Republic.*

Though it left the Dominican Republic in shambles, President Johnson's policy was a great success at home. Jingoism is always popular when cheap. Anti-communists were heartened by the show of force. Imperialists were assured that America would always rule the waves, Cuba notwithstanding. And the subsequent effort to give the U.S. gunboat a democratic and international superstructure comforted many. Few Americans could support aggression without some queasiness, but a little soothing syrup from Washington set them right in most cases. Not that President Johnson got away with it entirely. Some who had gone along until then, notably Senator Fulbright, turned against him. The credibility gap widened. All the same, it was a famous victory, though cynics were reminded of those American victories in Cuba that preceded Fidel Castro.

Though slight at first, opposition to the war in Vietnam started immediately upon its escalation. The teach-ins were the peace movement's first response. They began at the University of Michigan on March 24, 1965. A faculty group had planned a one-day moratorium during which professors would speak on the war instead of teaching. This caused a great flap, and the anti-war group decided a moratorium would do more harm to the University than to the war party. They decided to have an all-night meeting instead. More than three thousand students attended the marathon seminar. The idea was contagious. Before long almost every large university, and many small ones, held teach-ins. Berkeley's was, of course, the most spectacular. It went on for two days. Twelve thousand students heard Dr. Spock, Senator Gruening of Alaska (the first Senate dove), Norman Thomas, Norman Mailer, I. F. Stone, Isaac Deutscher, Felix Greene, and countless others denounce the war. Entertainment was provided by people like Dick Gregory, folk singers Phil Ochs and Malvina Reynolds, and a satirical group called The Committee.

* John Bartlow Martin underwent an even stranger conversion. President Johnson sent him to Santo Domingo when the trouble began. He used his credit with the democrats to complete their ruin. Then he wrote a magazine article exposing unsavory administration tactics. Finally, in his book he defended its Dominican policies while saying that henceforth America should align itself with the revolutionary and not the reactionary elements in Latin America, even if some were red. He made no effort to reconcile this principle with the opposite one he had defended earlier.

Mailer was so overwhelmed that he dedicated his next book to "Lyndon B. Johnson whose name inspired young men to cheer for me in public." The teach-ins were not confined to multiversities. Marist College in Poughkeepsie, New York, a Catholic school for men, had the radical Jesuit priest Father Daniel Berrigan, Staughton Lynd of Yale, and the venerable A. J. Muste speak against the war, while it was defended by such as Henry Cabot Lodge.

At first the administration ignored the teach-ins, hoping they would go away. They raised problems because even then it was hard to get qualified people to defend the war publicly. Secretary of State Rusk finally took notice, blaming teach-ins on "the gullibility of educated men." That didn't help much, so in May the administration dispatched a three-man "truth team" to carry its message through the Midwest. It was booed at the University of Iowa and shouted down at the University of Wisconsin. Some campuses listened to it, though, and its leader described the tour as "exhilarating." The experience was not repeated, however. On May 15 the movement reached its peak with a National Teach-in at the Sheraton Park Hotel in Washington. McGeorge Bundy, who had declined many earlier invitations, was to defend the administration, but the Dominican crisis called him away. He was replaced by Robert Scalapino, an academic hawk from Berkeley. The anti-war panel, virtually a Who's Who of distinguished Asian scholars, made quick work of him. Later, on June 21, Bundy did surface in a televised exchange with Hans Morgenthau, the country's leading academic authority on foreign policy. Bundy tried to discredit Morgenthau by showing he had erred before on other matters, as if infallibility were the test of legitimate criticism. Yet later when Bundy became a dove he spoke against the war, even though one of its architects.

In the teach-ins and his many articles, Morgenthau stressed certain points repeatedly. He thought the war was based on a false relationship between prestige and public opinion. It had hurt France to abandon Indochina and Algeria. But afterward France's prestige was greater. The Bay of Pigs injured the U.S., but not for long. The fear of a temporary shift in public opinion was leading Washington to pursue a war that would be much more harmful to its standing in the long run. Already many around the world were questioning both its wisdom and morality. Their number could only increase. Morgenthau feared that by personalizing the war Rusk, McNamara, Bundy, Rostow, the President, and others had so committed their own prestige as to make withdrawal impossible. His attack hurt because he was not a pacifist. He had supported most American Cold War policies up to then. His name was synonymous with hardheaded realism in foreign affairs. (American *Realpolitik* was in fact often called "the Kennan-Morgenthau school" after its two most distinguished advocates.) It was precisely for its ineffectiveness that he opposed the war. Wickedness, he insisted, did not pay off in the long run. It loses a country friends abroad and loyalties at home. It ought not to be practiced except when nothing else will save the state. Vietnam was not such a case. The risks run there were greater than any outcome, however happy, could justify.

The teach-ins did not change the government's policy. They did make Washington more defensive. And they goaded the President into further prevarications. On April 7 he announced himself ready for "unconditional discussions" with North Vietnam. While announcing a massive troop buildup on July 28 he said: "I have stated publicly and many times, again and again, America's willingness to begin unconditional discussions with any government at any place at any time." Two weeks later the *Manchester Guardian* reported that Washington had already turned down at least two overtures, the most recent one in September 1964 when Ho Chi Minh agreed to a secret meeting between representatives of both countries. The U.S. rejected this bid for fear Goldwater would learn of it. After the election U Thant, Secretary General of the United Nations, tried to arrange talks. Hanoi agreed; Washington did not.

Ambassador Stevenson was so depressed by this news that he told Eric Sevareid of CBS, shortly before his death, that he considered resigning. U Thant hoped for a cease-fire in Vietnam. Hanoi was interested, but the U.S. would not hear of it. At this time Hanoi insisted that the air war against it must be stopped before negotiations began. It also demanded a place for the NLF in whatever new government was formed in Saigon. The U.S. would not end the bombing without proof that infiltration from the North had stopped. And President Johnson wanted the NLF disarmed before a political settlement was reached. The U.S. saw negotiations as a way of winning in conference what it had failed to gain in battle. If the NLF would only surrender first and talk later, all would be well. Though many Americans thought this reasonable, the DRVN and the NLF did not. But then, they were not expected to. The administration's fictions were strictly for public consumption.

The teach-ins also made dissent respectable. Before them many people who disliked the war were afraid to say so. Joe McCarthy, even in the grave, still scared them. Most teach-ins were organized by a handful of students and faculty. Yet when they struck at the king and lived, others were encouraged to do likewise. Not that they weren't red-baited. Senator Dodd's witch-hunting subcommittee put out a report calling the teach-ins a commie plot. But the old magic no longer worked. Most school administrations ignored the report, some even refuted it. The most celebrated incident took place at Rutgers. During a teach-in Professor Eugene Genovese, a Marxist historian, said that he "welcomed" a

Viet Cong victory. Naturally the New Jersey legislature demanded his head, or at least his job. They got neither. The University protected his right to be foolish in public, though reluctantly. He resigned later, much to its relief, but went on to have a brilliant academic career. In the Mc-Carthy era he would have been fired outright, and probably blacklisted as well.

While the teach-ins' ultimate effects were far from negligible, they did not stop the war. Instead it got worse. This made the anti-war movement more outraged and desperate, especially its left wing. Leftists began to carry VC and DRVN flags in demonstrations. "Hey, hey, LBJ, how many kids did you kill today?" they chanted. One short-lived organization, the May 2nd Movement, collected blood for the NLF. In Berkeley the Vietnam Day Committee made several attempts to block troop trains. During the October 1965 peace demonstrations it marched on Oakland and was attacked by both the police and motorcycle hoodlums. When the VDC planned another march for November 20, the Hell's Angels promised to destroy it entirely. Sonny Barger, their leader, declared the "peaceniks" to be full of chickenshit. Allen Ginsberg, a beat-generation poet turned guru, wrote a long poem asking them not to beat up the marchers. It was read with appropriate solemnity at San Jose State College on the 15th before an audience of students and Angels. More orthodox figures made the same request. On the 19th the Angels, who had become quite pompous and corny (for them) about their reputation, called a press conference. Barger announced they had decided not to attack the marchers for the sake of public order, and to avoid generating sympathy for "this mob of traitors." He also read a telegram they had sent to President Johnson offering to serve behind the lines in Vietnam.*

Individual actions were sometimes even more striking. Following the Buddhist monks' example, two men burned themselves to death in protest against the war. One, Norman Morrison, a Quaker, did so on the steps of the Pentagon. He was soon forgotten in America, though not in North Vietnam. Others took the less drastic step of burning their draft cards. In the manner of symbolic gestures, these acts were thought especially atrocious. One of the peculiar features of nationalism is that while death and mutilation leave its practitioners unmoved, flag desecrations

---

* The President ignored them, more's the pity. Not only would it have gotten them out of Oakland, but the war would have gained a touch of redeeming panache. At the same time, of course, its true nature would have been exposed, which is probably why he turned them down. As Norman Mailer observed at Berkeley, in Vietnam the ideology of the communists was being opposed by the spirit of the Cosa Nostra. Still, the thought of a gang of drug-crazed motorcycle freaks screaming up the Ho Chi Minh Trail was a stirring one. And they would have fit right in with the other "freedom fighters" in Vietnam (CIA assassins, Green Berets, Chinese mercenaries, Montagnard tribesmen, and the like).

144

and the like inflame them. Accordingly, when pacifists started burning draft cards Congress passed a law making it a federal offense ($10,000 fine or five years in jail) to knowingly kill or wound a Selective Service card. David J. Miller, a Catholic pacifist, was the first one arrested under the law. He went to prison for this, and so did others who followed his example. Young men kept on burning their draft cards anyway.

The administration survived these experiences, some of which did peace more harm than not. But opposition was building up in weightier quarters too. The dissenting academy had already been heard from. The cultural community now expressed itself. The White House Festival of the Arts provided the occasion. President Johnson envied his predecessor's skill at cultural politics, and, prodded by Eric Goldman, decided to have a try at it. On May 27 the festival was announced in the *New York Times*. Six days later the *Times* carried an open letter from the poet Robert Lowell politely declining to attend out of his "dismay" at the President's foreign policy. This provoked a crisis of conscience among other artists. Saul Bellow and John Hersey wrote letters agreeing with Lowell but explaining why it was still a good idea to attend. Dwight Macdonald and others sent the President a telegram supporting Lowell. Macdonald, a left-wing political journalist turned film critic, decided to go nonetheless. He could at least record the event, and, perhaps, subvert it too. "On these terms," he wrote later, "I sacrificed, and not for the first time, consistency, and possibly even good taste, in the interest of a larger objective."

The festival went off on schedule and was gratifyingly offensive. John Hersey, who read from his book *Hiroshima*, began by saying that it was especially relevant to the present with its dangers of "miscalculation, of accident, of reliance not on moral strength but on mere military power. Wars have a way of getting out of hand." The President welcomed his guests but did not move among them. He told a reporter that "some of them insult me by staying away and some of them insult me by coming." Macdonald circulated a petition endorsing Lowell's position. Few signed it; not that many disagreed, but they thought it rude or tasteless, or impolitic. Macdonald was undismayed. Lowell's letter had done its work. "Rarely has one person's statement of his moral unease about his government's behavior had such public resonance. I think it was because the letter was so personal, so unexpected and yet so expressive of a widespread mood of 'dismay and distrust.'"

The Johnsonians never realized, until it was too late, and sometimes not even then, what the protest was about. Governors are always self-righteous, and all the more so when embarked on dubious adventures. Few appreciate that there are other standards beside their own. President Johnson was better than most. His career was based as much on empathy as cunning. He understood that a consensus is not built by force. But the early attacks on his war policy came from those he least understood—the young, the intellectual, the cultivated. They had been the most critical of him for his want of grace, wit, and sophistication. He had just about given up on them anyway. Their response to the war completed his alienation. They would pay heavily for having been so snobbish. But Johnson would pay too. What he did not quite grasp then, though he would later, was that it took more support to govern than to win elections. Every time he escalated the war, polls showed that a majority—the silent majority, some would call it—supported him. But the silent majority, being silent, was of little use in a crisis. If the outraged minority were numerous enough, or properly placed, they could make things nearly impossible for a government. It was no use trying, as did Johnson and after him Nixon, to rouse the silent majority. In politics it is not the inert many but the volatile few who count. This was especially true in the Democratic party, where liberals and intellectuals were most active. As propagandists, fund-raisers, and precinct-workers they were indispensable, so they had power in the party far beyond what their comparatively small numbers suggested. When they turned on President Johnson he was finished as party leader. He understood then that there was no point in going on, even if, as was likely, he gained re-election, for he could not govern. He appreciated that the war had lasted too long, cost too much. But he never saw that the resistance began with people who resented having foreigners slaughtered in their name. Lyndon Johnson was the first President since Herbert Hoover to be turned out for moral obtuseness.

PROFILE:
The City

AMONG America's principal institutions were her cities. Most
people lived in or near them. Most great national enterprises depended
on them. In the sixties they deteriorated rapidly. Pollution and
congestion affected the great ones. Essential services decayed. But what
worried city residents was the rising crime rate. At the decade's end law
and order became an obsession. Yet the more people demanded civil
peace, the less of it they got. At first liberals doubted that the rise in
crime was real. The FBI announced new increases annually, but it was
hardly an impartial source as its budget depended on crime and
subversion. Then too, even if honestly done, the FBI's methods of
recording and reporting crimes were subject to change, and the local
sources it relied on were even less consistent. Crimes varied over time,
making comparisons difficult. In 1962 there were 461 bank robberies, a
27 per cent increase over the previous year. Yet in 1932 there had been
609 holdups at a time when there were 5,300 fewer banks to rob. And,
though crime seemed to be up, the prison population was going down.
In 1963 the gross number of inmates declined in twenty-seven prison
systems, and in thirty-two more the ratio of inmates to the whole
population fell off. In 1939 the national rate of imprisonment was 137.6
inmates per 100,000 of population. By 1964 it was down to 118.3 per
100,000.

Many Americans concluded from this that criminals were being too lightly punished. Stiffer penalties would ease the crime rate. Still, American sentences were already as severe as any in the Western world. Only 150 Englishmen each year were sentenced to five years or more in the penitentiary. In the U.S., with less than four times the population, more than fifteen thousand criminals received comparable sentences annually. Some believed that more executions would reduce the homicide rate. But in 1964 a third of all murders were committed by someone in the victim's family, and half by a friend. Thus an American was three times as likely to be killed by a friend or relative as by a stranger. Stronger penalties were of little use in preventing these crimes of passion. More and more states recognized this, and executions became less common—sometimes by executive moratorium and, less often, by the abolition of capital punishment, as in New York.* This was a point gained for civilized values. But it left the larger problem of private violence untouched. Cities became progressively more dangerous to live in. Liberals called for new wars on poverty to destroy the social basis of crime. Conservatives demanded more law and order, meaning, usually, police repression. Both methods were tried, often at once, to little effect. Like poverty, crime defeated the best efforts of Americans in the 1960's. Maybe the problem was insoluble. Or, perhaps, for all the screaming about it, people just didn't try hard enough. Many bought guns (hence the increase in accidental shootings) and dogs. Yet these were no substitute for an effective public policy—whatever it might be. In its absence, things simply got worse and worse. Was the day coming when every well-dressed man would wear a sidearm as in the Old West, and no lady go abroad unescorted? Few were prepared to bet against that possibility. The Great Society was a marvelous idea, but many Americans would cheerfully have settled for a safe one.

Even if there had been no rise in crime, and no fear of riots, city life would still have been unpleasant, even dangerous. New York City,

* No state took the most obvious step to reduce homicides. Murders were usually committed with the nearest weapon at hand. If that weapon was a knife, the victim's chances of survival were six times greater than if a gun was used. Stringent gun-control laws would probably lead to fewer attacks with guns and more with knives. Fewer victims would die in consequence. Such laws would, of course, have been unthinkable and un-American.

being the largest, showed this most clearly. In 1955 a municipal board had proudly announced that "New York City is assured a plentiful supply of the finest water for the rest of this century." Ten years later there was not enough to permit residents to wash cars, sprinkle lawns, or fill swimming pools. Restaurants served drinking water only on request. The immediate cause of this shortage was a predictable decline in rainfall. Bad planning did the rest. Water was still largely free in New York. In consequence, eight million New Yorkers wasted as much water (300 million gallons daily) as seven million Londoners *used*. Mayor Wagner opposed water meters on the grounds that free water was crucial to the city's "social philosophy." The Hudson was full of water, but the city had abandoned its only pumping station on the river fifteen years before. And so it went. Next year the rains came and everyone forgot about water. In due course another drought would probably refresh their memories, no doubt as uselessly as before.

Hard-pressed New Yorkers suffered a more novel inconvenience in the fall of 1965. On November 9 the Northeast lost its electric power. The blackout started at Niagara Falls and reached New York at 5:28 P.M. Everything without an auxiliary power source stopped functioning. Hospitals and radio stations kept going, saving lives and preventing panic. All else stopped. The consequences were not nearly what they might have been. A bright moon helped the planes aloft and none crashed. Emergency safety measures worked on trains, subways, and elevators, though countless thousands were trapped in them for varying lengths of time. In the Empire State Building firemen had to break through a wall to rescue passengers in one stranded elevator. "Are there any pregnant women in this car?" asked one. "We've hardly even met," was the answer. This was typical. New York can take it, was the prevailing mood. Commuters slept in train stations, department stores, and armories (opened by Governor Rockefeller for the emergency). Telephone service continued, which helped everyone stay calm. Even New Yorkers' habitual nastiness, always so noticeable to visitors, declined. They were mostly cheerful and cooperative throughout, showing that there is nothing like a good disaster for bringing people together. Fortunately, this new spirit was not severely tried. The next day power was restored. Not much came of this, though nine months later New York hospitals noted a sudden boom in babies. In the future if a population shortage threatened, the authorities would know what to do.

On investigation it turned out the blackout was caused by a tiny relay that had not been reset for the higher power loads generated since 1963. At 5 P.M. on Tuesday, November 9, electricity was flowing to Toronto over six power lines from the Sir Adam Beck No. 2 distribution station in Queenston, Ontario. At 5:15 the power surged slightly, activating the mis-set relay. It tripped a circuit-breaker, cutting out one line and transferring its power to the other five. These lines instantly became overloaded and were cut out by their own relays. Unable to go north, this river of power automatically surged southward into the connecting U.S. power grid, activating more relays along the way. The northern regions denied power sucked current from the south. The huge drain called more relays into action. This "cascade" effect shut down the entire northeastern grid system.

Who was to blame? Sir Adam Beck No. 2 station was guilty in the first instance. But the power outage would have been localized were it not for the grid's inadequacies. There was simply not enough power on hand to compensate for the initial losses. For one thing, the grid was not big enough. Then too, while power companies in the Northeast had correctly estimated their long-term needs, they had not provided for them. There was, of course, no shortage of excuses for this.* Yet the truth was clear enough. The companies were unable or unwilling to provide enough power, but were strong enough to keep the federal government from doing so. Private power, though inadequate, was essential to the American way. Public power, though necessary, was socialistic and morally enfeebling. No more great blackouts took place in the sixties, but the imbalance between demand and capacity got worse. It was hard not to think that fresh disasters awaited the region, especially long-suffering New York City.

New Yorkers still found things to cheer about. Pope Paul's visit was one. John Lindsay's election as mayor another. Paul paid the city a fleeting visit on October 4, 1965. His main purpose was to address

* The most ingenuous was offered by Consolidated Edison of New York. It wanted to build a power plant on Storm King Mountain. Conservationists, fearing it would ruin Storm King, blocked the plan. Thus, Con Ed implied, the blackout was really the conservationists' fault. Little wonder that Con Ed was the most unpopular power company in the Northeast, scorned even by TV comedians.

the United Nations. There, in the spirit of Pope John, whose great encyclical *Pacem in Terris* had committed the Roman Church, he spoke for peace. "*Jamais plus la guerre,*" he cried out. "No more war, war never again." He also talked privately with Secretary General U Thant and President Johnson. He said mass in Yankee Stadium. And he visited the World's Fair. All day long the cheering never stopped. Millions saw him live, and millions more on TV. He was the first reigning Pope to visit North America, which was gratifying. He gave a ringing endorsement to the United Nations, which was better still. It was one of the brightest days many Americans could remember.

The New York mayoralty campaign was less edifying, though perhaps more important. One of the curious features of American life is that no matter how vile the public job, someone can always be found to take it. Being mayor of a large city used to be good for fun and profit. In those days people were happy if graft was kept at reasonable levels and basic services maintained. Now the problems were worse and the demands greater. Yet there was not much mayors could do. The state governments discriminated against them. The federal government, which alone had the power to help them, was preoccupied with the arms race, the space race, and other costly diversions. New York City was in such bad shape that many doubted it could be saved at all. Mayor Robert F. Wagner had managed to hold things together for three terms, but the strain told. In 1965 he decided not to run again. His system was condemned by Congressman Lindsay for its reliance on "power brokers," a phrase that hardly did justice to the incumbent's complex style. What it involved was a series of exchanges by which Peter was forever being robbed to pay Paul, one problem solved at the expense of another. When the transit workers threatened to strike for higher wages, Wagner would give way. Then fares would be raised, making it harder for the people who most needed public transportation to use it. Other public employees would be encouraged to ask for more money. If they didn't get it they might strike. If they did the cost of doing the city's work went up. This meant more taxes which drove out businesses thus reducing the tax base. There was no escaping the vicious cycle in which city government was locked. Help had to come from outside. Lacking it, all the mayor could do was continue his juggling act and pray.

Why did John V. Lindsay want to inherit this situation? Though a Republican in an overwhelmingly Democratic city, he had a safe congressional district and a brilliant future. The odds against his winning a city-wide election were great, the chances of accomplishing much if he did slight. One reason might have been that there was nothing else to run for. Rockefeller seemed likely to go on forever as governor. Both U.S. Senators (Robert Kennedy and Jacob Javits) were immensely popular. Still, Lindsay was only forty-three. He could afford to wait for something better to turn up. That he didn't, and chose instead to take on the roughest job around, was one measure of the man. He ran as a fusion candidate on both the GOP and Liberal tickets.* Against him the Democrats, puffed up with overconfidence, nominated an obscure machine politician, Abraham D. Beame.

The Conservative party chose William F. Buckley, thus lending dramatic interest to the race. Like Lindsay, Buckley was tall, rich, handsome, and a Yale graduate. Otherwise they had little in common. Buckley was the country's best-known conservative intellectual. Urbane, witty, sometimes eloquent, he had been a fierce and intemperate controversialist for many years. With his gifts he might have been a great scholar, writer, or politician. Instead he spent his life protecting wealth, privilege, and traditional religion with an elegantly baroque prose. This put him in odd company indeed, for one of the chief rules of the Establishment is that, outside the South, those who possess high status do not defend it. Or rather, they keep their position by invoking its opposite. Hence rich men supported the war on poverty, intellectuals called for more open universities, officeholders demanded broader democratic practices, and monopolists extolled competition. None of them lost anything by this. Quite the contrary. It cost little and paid rich dividends in public esteem and acceptance.

Since there was room for everyone in this great consensus, those who chose to remain outside it were abnormal by definition. The militant right especially was full of freaks—Minutemen, John Birchers,

---

* The Liberal party was small but controlled what was sometimes a crucial bloc of votes in New York. It usually supported reform Democrats rather than running its own candidates.

anti-Semites, racists, and what all. There were scarcely any real intellectuals among them, and though Buckley tried hard to give his journal, the *National Review,* a distinguished tone, it was uphill work. So he was surrounded by a motley band of ex-communists, unreformed Catholics, neo-colonialists, and Social Darwinists. And he found himself propounding the merits of strange people and places—the province of Katanga, the late Senator Joe McCarthy, Taiwan, Papal infallibility, and many, many more. The *National Review* lived in a strange, perfervid world, menaced by bizarre threats from the left (Arthur Schlesinger, Jr., for example). It believed the innocuous liberal organization Americans for Democratic Action to be stronger and more wicked than the Mafia.

Yet if the *National Review* seemed absurd, Buckley himself didn't. He was a powerful debater, entirely free of scruple, sentiment, or a debilitating regard for fact. He played to win, and usually did.* Arid polemics did not absorb all his time. A few years before he had helped organize the Conservative party in New York City, and already it was making itself felt in the real world. Buckley's candidacy gave it another boost, though he didn't even live in the city and said what he felt from the beginning, thus showing himself unfit for public office. He had, in a way, the best platform of any candidate. He was the only one to come out for universal water metering (and a sliding scale of charges during droughts), the only honest way of ending water shortages. His transportation program was magnificent by past standards. It involved auto tolls and a good deal of experimentation in regulating car and truck traffic. Best of all was the Buckley Bikeway, a proposed bicycle path that would run above Second Avenue from 1st to 125th Streets. The most vicious plank called for police repression of undesirables, but Buckley was made to pay for that. Both the press

---

* His most famous debates were with Norman Mailer, his opposite number on the left. Afterward each would write an account explaining his victory. Mailer's were the best, since he was incomparably the better writer, but not the most accurate. Buckley almost always beat him because, while Mailer was struggling earnestly for the truth, Buckley wished only to cut him up. Mailer was vulnerable in so many ways that this was easy to do, though it proved nothing except who was most ruthless—and everyone knew that already. In 1968 during the national political conventions, Buckley was paired on TV with the novelist Gore Vidal, an even more cutting and poisonous wit. Vidal made mincemeat of him.

and the candidates vilified and misquoted him to an extraordinary degree.*

This made for a lively campaign. Buckley had no chance to win himself, but in a close race the votes he gained at the expense of one candidate might elect the other. There was considerable doubt as to whom he would injure most. Lindsay suffered from being shown up by him on television. Beame lost normally Democratic white ethnic bloc voters who thought Buckley would be harder on the blacks. Polls showed Lindsay and Beame to be running even, with Buckley expected to get 18 per cent of the vote. As it turned out, Lindsay got 45.3 per cent, Beame 41.3 per cent, and Buckley, because of last-minute defections, 13.4 per cent. What happened, apparently, was that a crucial number of voters who wanted change were scared of Buckleyism and, since Beame represented business as usual, were stuck with Lindsay. All the same, it was Buckley's finest hour. His campaign was divertingly candid, his platform ingenious. The Conservative party grew. Now the question was, would Lindsay, a minority mayor with an unstable fusion organization, be able to govern the city? Most people thought not, but with New Yorkers hope springs eternal. Why else would they live in so trying a place?

Lindsay was hardly elected when on January 1, 1966, the transit workers struck. New Yorkers had at times gone without water, electricity, newspapers, and taxicabs the year before. But nothing hurt it as much as this strike. Over three million workers used the city's buses and subways daily. Without them the city could barely function. Mayor Lindsay walked to work as an example. Others pressed bicycles, roller skates, and even horses into service. Most tried to drive in. On January 10, the worst day of the strike, 850,000 cars crept through Manhattan. Things would have been worse still if many had not simply stayed home. On the first day 10 per cent of Manhattan's department stores failed to open. Businesses that did reported absentee rates of from 25 to 90 per cent. A fifth of the wage earners in Harlem could not get out of the ghetto. City stores lost a billion dollars in sales, it was believed.

---

* Buckley expressed much pious horror at this in his book *The Unmaking of a Mayor*. But as he had been maligning and red-baiting people for years, it was hard to work up much sympathy for him.

The transit workers often threatened to strike, but had not done so before as Mayor Wagner and union head Mike Quill invariably settled the matter between them. This time Mayor Wagner left the problem to his successor. But John Lindsay had expressed a high-minded contempt for the old ways. He preferred conventional bargaining techniques. Mike Quill, a quick-tempered ex-radical, was insulted, especially when Mayor Lindsay announced that negotiations were not being conducted in good faith, hence the strike. Quill, who called on the mayor to show less profile and more courage, had asked for the moon to start with as usual. Among his demands were a four-day work week, a 30 per cent pay raise, six weeks of annual vacation, and other benefits that would cost the city an estimated $680 million in the next two years. When the court issued an injunction against the strike, Quill tore it up on camera and, on January 4, went defiantly to jail. After a series of sixteen-hour bargaining sessions, the union settled on January 13 for a staggered 15 per cent wage increase and fringe benefits amounting to between $52 and $61 million. The terms were about what the union would have gotten without a strike from the old administration. Mayor Lindsay learned a valuable lesson, the first of many such.

The transit strike was followed by a newspaper strike that forced the *Herald Tribune* to merge with the *World-Telegram and Sun* and the *Journal-American*. Many jobs were lost. Later this hybrid failed too, throwing even more people out of work. Nor did the reduction of city newspapers to three—the *Times, Daily News,* and *Post*—raise spirits. Mayor Lindsay tried to cheer New Yorkers by calling the metropolis Fun City. This was received sardonically, especially when the garbage men went on strike in 1967, turning Fun City into Fungus City. 100,000 tons of rubbish piled up on city streets and sidewalks. Trash fires increased by 700 per cent during the nine-day walkout. Under pressure from the state, Lindsay finally agreed to accept arbitration, which gave the workers much of what they asked for. Lindsay wanted to keep taxes down, but in his first two years of office had to grant wage hikes totaling $300 million, and even so teachers, transit and welfare workers, sanitation men, and others went on strike. The teachers increasingly wanted not only more money but more power. Their militancy led to the Ocean Hill dispute that so demoralized liberal blacks and whites alike. Lindsay had more responsibility than power where many of these were concerned. Even if he had made no mistakes things would still have gotten worse. Much of the decay was entirely beyond his grasp. He could do nothing to make the power companies increase their capacity. Nor was there much he could do to prevent telephone service from falling off. As the mail service was deteriorating too, the movement of business and industry out of the city increased, leaving fewer taxpayers to support the rising cost of public services. The soaring crime rate led people to buy dogs for protection. These animals had a habit of defecating in public, further degrading the environment.

Lindsay did have his successes. There were no great riots in New York as elsewhere. This was at least partly because Lindsay did all he could to ease tension, down to and including walking the streets of troubled neighborhoods. No mayor ever worked harder or took more abuse, from black militants, white bigots, and disgruntled liberals who expected miracles and would settle for nothing less. Surprisingly, Lindsay kept his temper and even his sense of humor. More surprisingly still, he ran for re-election in 1969, even though he lost the Republican primary to an aloof conservative, State Senator John Marchi, and had to run on the Liberal ticket alone. His chances of re-election seemed slight at this point. He had offended the silent majority of Democratic voters in many ways. The white working class resented his attentions to racial minorities. The Jews were still unhappy about Ocean Hill. The borough of Queens thought its snow was removed too slowly. There was no end to the agonies of life in New York, all of which were invariably blamed on the mayor. His fate seemed sealed even before Norman Mailer announced his candidacy, thus cutting into what remained of Lindsay's constituency on the left.

Fortunately for Lindsay, the Democratic death wish was still at work. The Democratic candidate Mario Procaccino was inept to the point of absurdity. Speaking to Negro voters he proclaimed his heart to be as black as theirs. He called for law and order at every turn. Conscience obliged Arthur Goldberg and other prominent liberal Democrats to disown him. Few liberals defected to Mailer.* Lindsay

* At another time Mailer might have done better. His running mate Jimmy Breslin was a colorful and beloved New York journalist. He was also the only link between its white proletariat and the intelligentsia. Their program was very inventive. They wanted to make New York City the fifty-first state so as to stop

had armies of volunteers and bags of money. After a long uphill fight he outpolled Procaccino by 160,000 votes. New York was saved, for the moment. Racism was held at bay. Poverty, pollution, and congestion continued. Whether the city would ultimately survive remained doubtful.

---

the tax drain to Albany. Once a month they meant to have a "Sweet Sunday" when automobiles would be banned from Manhattan. Mailer campaigned hard, drunk or sober, but it was no use. The Jews thought Mailer too deracinated. Lindsay was more like what they wanted their sons to become. The white working class preferred law and order to Jimmy Breslin. Liberals feared Procaccino more than they liked Mailer. They didn't actually like Lindsay all that well, but he seemed the only realistic alternative.

6 FROM CIVIL RIGHTS TO BLACK POWER

THOUGH it was often called the Civil Rights Revolution (or the Negro Revolution), there were few revolutionaries in the movement for Afro-American equality. Most blacks asked only for what most whites already had. This seemed startling for two reasons. First because the racial double standard was so old and well established that people thought it part of the natural order. What God had done mere man could not undo. Negroes (and Indians and Spanish-speaking people) occupied those stations in life appropriate to their talents. This was not a matter of prejudice but of justice, for in a free society everyone moved to exactly the level his abilities warranted. The Negro's inferior place was a consequence of his inferior attributes. Then in 1954 the Supreme Court weakened these assumptions. *Brown v. Board of Education* held that the Constitution protected all Americans equally, regardless of race. Worse still, it declared that Negro inferiority was not congenital but induced. In attacking segregated schools the Court also struck at the attitudes justifying segregation. This shocked not only the South but other parts of the country too—though somewhat later. It opened the way for a mass civil rights movement.

The second startling thing about the Negroes' emergence was the nonviolent ethic they developed. This was so contrary to American customs as to be almost revolutionary. Though mainly Christian, Americans did not practice turning the other cheek and loving their enemies. They believed in self-defense. They also believed, less firmly, in obeying the law. Self-defense and respect for law did not go together very well, since to invoke the one was sometimes to violate the other. But this did not trouble many. People were used to applying one principle at a time as needed.

Under Martin Luther King, Jr., the civil rights movement defied both these precepts. Rights workers did not obey the law, neither did they defend themselves. Both these responses were un-American. So was their insistence on redeeming the oppressor through love. People hate those they have wronged, and all the more so when that hate is met with love. Hence the beatings, murders, and other savageries which rights workers experienced after the Montgomery bus boycott of 1955. Dr. King had formed his ethic before going to Montgomery, by reading Ghandi, Tolstoy, Thoreau, and the Bible. It was ideally suited to Southern conditions. Being devoted to the Bible, Southern blacks grasped the idea of nonviolence readily. And as they were so heavily outnumbered, and even more outgunned, nonviolence was the obvious response. It is what the weak use to turn the oppressor's strength against him. White Southerners were slow to understand this. At first they met nonviolent demonstrations with force. This produced martyrs, strengthened the movement, and won outside support. Later the white South turned to more subtle tactics which worked better. But in the late fifties and early sixties guns and clubs were the usual response to nonviolence. The civil rights movement thrived on them, though at a great human price.

After Montgomery, the next great step was taken on February 1, 1960, when four Negro college students sat down at a whites-only lunch counter in Greensboro, North Carolina, and asked for service. There had been sit-ins before with few results. But this one captured the public imagination and it was followed by countless others. At the year's end perhaps seventy thousand blacks and whites had staged sit-ins in more than a hundred communities. They would lead in time to the wholesale desegregation of public facilities throughout the South. They would also produce the Student Nonviolent Coordinating Committee (SNCC, pronounced Snick).

Most Negro leaders endorsed nonviolence, out of enthusiasm or calculation, but a few did not, notably the Black Muslims. This curious sect had been founded in Detroit in the 1930's and was led by one Elijah Poole, called Elijah Muhammad. "The Lost-Found Nation of Islam in the West" numbered about thirty thousand in 1959 when a television documentary entitled "The Hate That Hate Produced" won it many new members. Black Muslim theology derived from Islam, black folkways, and the Protestant Ethic. Muslims believed that the black race ("Negro" was thought a slave term) had once been the only race. But a mad scientist named Yakub had rebelled against Allah and invented the white man, or devil. Someday he would be destroyed. In the meantime the proper strategy for American blacks was to organize a separate state of their own.

Though their theory was based on hatred, the Black Muslims were not usually violent or anti-social. On the contrary, they attracted desperate young blacks who would otherwise have ended up in jail or worse. Many who joined were convicts like Malcolm Little, who as Malcolm X became the Nation's chief spokesman. Black Muslims avoided tobacco, alcohol, narcotics, and "soul food" (another relic of slavery). They were frugal and industrious and where possible founded their own schools and businesses. They never got in trouble with the law, except when harassed by it. This happened fairly often in the early sixties. People fear what they do not understand, particularly when it is armed, disciplined, and hostile. When their mosques were raided by the police, Black Muslims sometimes fought back, as the Panthers would later. This frightened people even more. Negro leaders, committed then to peace and love, feared the Nation would queer their pitch. It seemed at times as if hating the Black Muslims was all that every race, creed, religion, and section of the country had in common.

Rarely has a public judgment been so mistaken. Whatever their faults, the Muslims were true separatists who wanted only to be left in peace. As this became clear, policemen bothered them less and the violence subsided. The Nation's potential for growth proved to be very slight. Its doctrines were too austere for most blacks. Its devotion to self-help and the gospel of work was not only inappropriate but anachronistic. Its rigid discipline, enforced by the paramilitary Fruit of Islam, was equally unattractive. And by remaining aloof from the civil rights struggle it alienated militant youth. Muhammad's leadership suffered when he failed to support his black converts in prison with legal and other forms of aid. Eldridge Cleaver and men like him lost faith. Even Malcolm X despaired and was thrown out for questioning the official line. When he left he took the Nation's future with him. Later, when people learned that Muhammad did not himself practice the sexual austerities he preached, it made little difference. By then the visionaries were long gone and only the sectarians remained. Few found the Nation's decline comforting though, for it was replaced by the Black Panther party which was even scarier.

Robert F. Williams, Jr., drew less attention than the Muslims in those days, which was another mistake. He, not they, foreshadowed what was to come. Williams had become head of the NAACP chapter in Monroe, North Carolina, in 1957. When threatened by the local Ku Klux Klan he organized a rifle club of sixty members and got it chartered by the

National Rifle Association. This was partly to get the free ammunition provided NRA members by a grateful government, partly also, no doubt, a tribute to both groups' joint faith in self-defense. When the Klan organized a motorcade against one NAACP member's house, the club drove them off with gunfire. White Monroe's enthusiasm for vigilante action declined thereafter.° Later Williams was able to get two Negro boys aged seven and nine freed from the state reformatory where they had been sent for long terms after one was kissed on the cheek by a little white girl. Williams went on leading sit-ins and protests until the summer of 1961 when he was charged with kidnaping and driven into exile for eight years.

Everyone but his followers was relieved at this. He had deeply embarrassed the NAACP. It was bad enough that he rejected the nonviolent ethic, worse still that he did so with such success. His was the only armed NAACP chapter and, for its size, the most effective. While he lasted, Williams was a standing challenge to the NAACP's way of doing business. He was a threat to the Congress of Racial Equality also. CORE was more aggressive than the NAACP, but also more dedicated to nonviolence as a way of life. A group of its Freedom Riders were in Monroe when Williams was indicted. His ideas had a lasting effect on them. Some would later help take CORE beyond nonviolence. Of course Williams's experience could be read both ways. Those who opposed armed militancy saw his destruction as proof of its uselessness. Those who favored it argued that his years of success showed its worth. To them his being run out of the country on what was either a frame-up or a technicality was only one unfortunate detail in an otherwise satisfactory pattern. Williams first took the path more disillusioned blacks would follow later, even to becoming a third-world-style revolutionary.

At the time Williams's case seemed freakish. Most militant blacks were still nonviolent, and in the Freedom Rides were performing their most striking feats. CORE organized the rides to test the racial policies of Southern bus terminals and forced the administration to reform them. On May 15, 1961, nine Freedom Riders were attacked near Anniston, Alabama, and their bus burned. Another band went on to Birmingham where two more were beaten. On May 20 at least another twenty were injured when their bus was attacked by a mob outside Montgomery. They included several reporters and John Seigenthaler of the U.S. Attorney General's office. Four hundred federal law officers were sent to Alabama to insure order. Two days later Alabama National Guardsmen with fixed bayonets scattered a mob bent on attacking a meeting where

---

° Whites finally nailed the NAACP member, a physician, more deviously. Though a Roman Catholic, he was sent to prison for allegedly performing an illegal abortion.

Martin Luther King was to speak. On May 28 Attorney General Kennedy asked the Interstate Commerce Commission to end the segregation of interstate buses and facilities. On November 1, 1961, the ICC banned segregation on all interstate buses, trains, and terminals. A thousand people were involved in the rides that made this possible. It cost CORE $300,000 in legal fees alone. The human costs to those beaten and imprisoned were beyond calculation. But they made CORE an important civil rights organization. Its budget in 1962 was $750,000, three times what it had been the previous year.

CORE and its allies won the struggle to integrate public facilities because Robert Kennedy was the Attorney General. His office was the only important one in Washington deeply committed to civil rights. He alone of the administration's great figures had close Negro friends. Even so, his emotions were not uncomplicated. After the University of Georgia was integrated in 1961, despite student rioting, he spoke at its law school and remarked "in the world-wide struggle, the graduation at this university of Charlayne Hunter and Hamilton Holmes will without question aid and assist the fight against communist political infiltration and guerrilla warfare." A dubious proposition, though one he would later outgrow. Kennedy was devoted to racial equality but not to the means used to advance it. His famous meeting with James Baldwin and other Negro spokesmen left both sides angry and baffled. As Attorney General, Kennedy naturally had doubts about civil disobedience. As a Democrat he wanted to strengthen the party while avoiding a white backlash. The administration saw voter registration, not civil disobedience, as the key to black freedom in the South—and to its own future there. It aided the effort in various ways and tried, without much luck, to protect those working for voter registration. The Voting Rights Act of 1965 did so more effectively. The administration was right to emphasize the ballot. The more benign Southern racial climate after 1965 was partly caused by black votes. Yet had it not been for the pressure generated by civil disobedience there might have been no voting rights act. So one hand washed the other, however reluctantly at times.

After the Freedom Rides there were too many incidents to summarize fairly. The Universities of Mississippi and Alabama were integrated, the one violently and the other peacefully, even though Governor Wallace of Alabama had promised to bar school doors personally if need be. He did block the door, but only to make a speech. President Kennedy was irritated anyway and gave one of his best TV talks, asking: "Are we to say to the world—and much more importantly, to each other—that this is the land of the free except for the Negroes; that we have no second-class citizens, except Negroes; that we have no class or caste system, no ghettos, no master race, except with respect to Negroes?" The movement pressed forward though churches and schools were bombed and rights workers beaten and killed.* Dr. King's Southern Christian Leadership Conference staged a great drive in Albany, Georgia, which failed as the local power structure mixed force with cunning for a change. He did better the next year in Birmingham, Alabama, which became a milestone in the history of civil rights. The lame-duck city government responded to black demands with force. Thousands of schoolchildren were arrested. Chief Bull Connor became a household word, especially for using police dogs, cattle prods, and fire hoses against the protesters. Black homes were bombed and blacks rioted in response. Some 2,500 persons destroyed six stores, an apartment house, and many automobiles. The crisis passed thanks again to federal intervention. The administration pulled all the strings it could. National business leaders (including even Roger Blough) talked sense to their opposite numbers in the South. Civil rights actions in Cambridge, Maryland; Greenwood, Mississippi; and Selma, Alabama, during 1963 were more inconclusive, though Selma elevated Sheriff Jim Clark to the racist hall of fame.

The main event that year for rights workers was the great March on Washington for Jobs and Freedom on August 28. It was organized by Bayard Rustin and A. Philip Randolph to help the administration's civil rights bill. Rustin, its principal architect, was a moderate black socialist. Randolph was president of the Brotherhood of Sleeping Car Porters. Though a small union, it was the only one with a black leader. Randolph was, therefore, the country's symbolic black trade unionist (as Ralph Bunche was the symbolic diplomat and Robert Weaver the symbolic federal bureaucrat), without whom no labor function was complete. He and Rustin meant to remind the government of its unmet obligations to blacks. But their proposal aroused such enthusiasm that its original character was lost. The years of struggle leading up to Birmingham had inspired whites as well as blacks. The march gave them a chance to say so comfortably. It offered the appearance, at least, of action, and the assurance of security. The price of admitting so many prominent whites was a mellower tone. John Lewis of Snick had to modify his speech so as to exclude passages like: "We will march through the South, through the heart of Dixie, the way Sherman did. We shall pursue our own 'scorched earth' policy and burn Jim Crow to the ground—nonviolently." What began as a protest ended as a celebration. President Kennedy blessed a delegation of rights leaders. Hubert

---

* The most prominent of these was Medgar Evers of the Mississippi NAACP. Evers's murder had, for Mississippi racists, the unpleasant effect of bringing his brother Charles back home. Charles Evers proved to be as dedicated as and even more resourceful than his brother. Before the decade ended he would become the first black mayor of a Mississippi town since Reconstruction.

Humphrey, one of fifteen U.S. Senators who participated, said that the march would probably change few votes in Congress, but was a good thing for the country anyway. 200,000 people heard Dr. King's most famous address which included the refrain "I have a dream" and ended with the words that would one day mark his grave: "Free at last, free at last, thank God Almighty I'm free at last."

Everyone but racists enjoyed the march. The *New York Times* liked its discipline. *Time* magazine and the *Philadelphia Inquirer* called it a "triumph." Russell Baker of the *Times* described it as a "vast army of quiet, middle-class Americans who had come in the spirit of a church outing." Which was exactly the problem. Who could object to a church outing? Who had ever been moved to action by one? The march had its uses. Negroes saw they had many friends. Politicians endorsed the cause. But mass had been bought at the expense of point. Congress failed to respond. Worse still, the country gained a false sense of where civil rights was going. The march suggested that nonviolence was more popular than ever. In fact, it was already declining. The march was not just another step along the upward trail; it was almost the highest moral point nonviolence would reach. Its organizers wanted to impress everyone with the hour's urgent needs. People were tranquilized instead.

The rioting in Birmingham was one early sign that black patience was wearing thin; the argument in Snick over nonviolence was another. The Student Nonviolent Coordinating Committee had concentrated on voter registration in Mississippi and Alabama. It organized a "freedom ballot" campaign to show how blacks would vote if enfranchised. Despite the usual intimidation, some eighty thousand Negroes cast freedom ballots. This was a good turnout given the circumstances, but many in Snick were dissatisfied. Symbolic votes were not reward enough for the risks run. At Selma and Greenwood they had won much favorable publicity. Celebrities came to see and be seen. But when they left, the danger was as great as before. The Justice Department didn't help rights workers much. The FBI, most activists thought, was against them. It would do nothing to protect their lives, much less their rights. J. Edgar Hoover denied these charges, as was only to be expected from a man who called Martin Luther King "the most notorious liar in the country." In November 1963 thirty-five black and seven white Snick organizers met in Mississippi to plan next year's Freedom Summer. For the first time black organizers asked that white roles in Snick be limited. Some wanted whites to leave Snick entirely and combat racism in their own communities instead. Bob Moses, one of the founders and a legend in his time, led those blacks who still believed in integration. They intended Snick to exemplify the color-blind society of the future. This argument prevailed. Snick would give integration one more chance.

A handful of insiders knew that nonviolence was running out of time. In 1964 Howard Zinn, a radical white academician, wrote a book, *SNCC: The New Abolitionists*, calling for presidential action to save the movement. James Baldwin wrote a more powerful tract that gained a wider audience. *The Fire Next Time* was a great work of prophecy, such as comes along occasionally to give nations a second chance (though, generally, they decline to take it). Baldwin was a black novelist and essayist who still had a foot in each camp. As an American he believed in the promise of American life; as a Negro he shared the black man's rage. The tension between his American sensibilities and black emotions gave *The Fire Next Time* a unique power. The balance was a delicate one, though, and he was not to keep it for long. Time was running out for him too.

In the book, drawing on his own life, Baldwin showed the perils of black life and the failure of Christianity to improve it. Once a boy minister, he had come to agree with Elijah Muhammad that the "white man's heaven is the black man's hell." But he didn't think Muhammad had the answer, nor Martin Luther King either. Whites admired nonviolence as a way of saving their lives and property, not for its own sake. It was their fear of black violence that opened the door to change. "The Negroes of this country may never be able to rise to power, but they are very well placed indeed to precipitate chaos and ring down the curtain on the American dream." That was the threat. The promise was that the country might yet be redeemed. "The price of this transformation is the unconditional freedom of the Negro: it is not too much to say that he, who has been so long rejected, is the key figure in his country, and the American future is precisely as bright or as dark as his. And the Negro recognizes this, in a negative way. Hence the question: Do I really want to be integrated into a burning house?" And so, he concluded, "if we do not dare everything, the fulfillment of that prophecy, recreated from the Bible in song by a slave, is upon us: 'God gave Noah the rainbow sign, no more water, the fire next time.'"

In 1964 that prophecy began fulfilling itself. Even before the ghetto riots things got uglier. In February 464,000 black students boycotted the New York public schools. They wanted an immediate end to "de facto" segregation caused by residential segregation. Busing was the only way to do so. This meant that black students would be transported to white schools and vice versa. The white lower middle and working classes took this badly. They feared school integration would mean housing integration and falling property values. Or, at the very least, that integrated schools would retard their children's education. As Americans they had too much at stake in their schools to allow this, even though the actual risk was slight. Education was seen as the chief element in upward mobility. Parents who had done poorly in life attributed it to their defective schooling. Their own children would go longer and do better. This was why white parents resisted integration so fiercely, and why black parents struggled for it. They too believed education had magical powers. If integrated schools made for better students, blacks would do a lot to get them. In New York and other Northern cities there were many battles over school desegregation during the next few years. Integrationists lost most of them. After a while Negro activists went in for separatism and Black Power. The pressure for integration declined. At just that point courts began ordering school districts, North and South, to integrate. These orders came long after they were needed. Black rage and white backlash had gone too far. It was too late to appease black militants or forestall white reactions. In the North, especially, the failure to secure integrated schools in time had disastrous consequences.

There were other signs of the worsening public temper in 1964. New York had ghetto rent strikes. CORE threatened to block traffic on the city's bridges, and did so at least once. When President Johnson opened the World's Fair on April 22 he was picketed and booed. Some three hundred demonstrators, including James Farmer, then head of CORE, were arrested for demonstrating against hiring policies at the New York fair grounds. In that same month a white minister in Cleveland was crushed to death while protesting at a school construction site. San Francisco militants attacked hiring policies at supermarkets by filling up shopping carts with goods and abandoning them. Adam Clayton Powell saw these as signs that the "black revolution" was moving into a new phase. The first phase in the South had been concerned with middle-class status issues like the right to sit up front in a bus or down in a restaurant. The next stage would be Northern, proletarian, and rough. It would be concerned with "gut" issues like who gets the money.

The nonviolent drama had to be played out first. Even while Southern Senators filibustered against the civil rights bill, the Mississippi Summer Project was organizing. When their filibuster was broken on June 10 after seventy-five days, the nonviolent battalions were already filtering down to Mississippi from their staging area in Oxford, Ohio. Freedom Summer was conceived by Snick but sponsored by the Council of Federated Organizations which included other civil rights groups and the National Council of Churches. Its thousand white volunteers, together with Snick's field force, concentrated on voter registration. By the end of July some forty thousand Negroes had been organized in the Mississippi Freedom Democratic party. Roughly thirty Freedom Schools were operating in nineteen counties. In the fall one hundred black first-graders attended integrated schools. Fifteen people were murdered during the Freedom Summer. Most of the killings attracted little notice until August 4, when the bodies of James Chaney, Andrew Goodman, and Michael Schwerner, missing since June, were discovered in an earthen dam near Philadelphia, Mississippi. In December the FBI arrested twenty-one persons for slaying them, including Sheriff Lawrence Rainey of Neshoba County. The country was appalled, but that did not help the dead, protect the living, nor materially advance the cause.

Though its finest hour, Freedom Summer gravely wounded the non-violent movement. Militant blacks turned against it for many reasons. The strain of repaying hate with love was greater than many could bear. To walk unarmed in the valley of death was an unnatural act for Americans. Nonviolence did not keep blacks from feeling rage, only from expressing it. Being unable to fight the enemy they fought one another, as a physician who treated them later confessed. In time the militants would draw up elaborate balance sheets proving that nonviolence was unproductive. But nonviolence did work, even if at too high a price. Black hostility was not more effective than nonviolence, only more gratifying.

Race relations within the movement were never as smooth as advertised. Blacks required white help, but some resented both the need and those who met it. They were quick to detect white moral pretensions. They felt whites traded on their skin, though perhaps unconsciously. Whites could drop out anytime they wished, but a black was still a black even when inactive. The double standard meant that whites were more newsworthy. Of all the Negroes killed during Freedom Summer, only James Chaney received national attention, and he because two white youths were murdered with him. Whites generated useful publicity this way, but at the cost of wounded black feelings and, it was thought, inflated white egos. Sex was a problem too. Interracial copulation was supposedly evidence of color-blindness. But it was rarely as simple as that. Some white girls believed in the myth of Negro sexuality. The movement let them satisfy the claims of lust in the name of idealism. There were blacks happy to oblige, but they disliked the stereotype even while exploiting it. People want to be loved for themselves, not for what they embody. Some blacks went further and demanded sex as proof of white commitment. This led others to think they were in the movement chiefly "to ball white chicks," as was said. Black women naturally resented these affairs. Joining in did not make things much easier for them. White sexual relations with black females had always been a mark of their oppression. The movement encouraged miscegenation but could not wipe out the memories it recalled. Hence, though interracial sex was meant to be therapeutic, it often had the opposite effect. Not surprisingly, when blacks turned hostile miscegenation was an early target.

Black writers were among the first to go in for separatism and racial hate. In 1960 Le Roi Jones was a fairly typical Negro writer. In 1961 he was already sneering at "white liberalism," though it was not yet the fashion to do so. In 1963 he was still calling himself a Negro while attacking Martin Luther King as an Uncle Tom. When the novelist Philip Roth criticized his play *Dutchman*, Jones called him a racist. Later Jones moved to Newark, divorced his white wife, and organized a community Black Power organization. This did show sincerity. Jones became a real force in the community. But it was nonetheless a morbid sign of the times. Abusing white liberals seemed to many an agreeable substitute for social action, especially when the whites paid for the privilege, as some always would. It was easier to revile critics than to answer them. Even the best Negro writers found this pose tempting. James Baldwin followed *The Fire Next Time* with a play, *Blues for Mr. Charlie* (1964), which attributed anti-Negro feeling to sexual envy. Robert Brustein called it an "inflammatory broadside of race hatred which will profit nobody but the author," and a work of "provocation rather than conviction." The hostility and racial chauvinism of some black intellectuals undermined their collective influence. Those who did not take a violent line were drowned out. Those who did were discredited. They inflamed black tempers and white guilt feelings. Yet they shrank from the conclusions their rhetoric pointed toward, as well they might. It remained for the desperate young to become arsonists and bombers.

Malcolm X was an important exception. As other black intellectuals became more violent and irrational, he grew less so. In his youth Malcolm Little was a petty criminal who hustled his way to prison. There he became a self-made intellectual and a Black Muslim. He rose rapidly in the movement and became its chief spokesman. In 1963 he was driven out, nominally for a tactless remark upon President Kennedy's death about chickens coming to roost, actually because his popularity threatened Elijah Muhammad. Then too, he was increasingly unhappy with the Nation's isolation. Though no integrationist, he felt the Muslims could not ignore a movement so popular among the young. He wanted a popular front while Muhammad cared only for doctrinal correctness. Malcolm also came out more plainly for violence than Muslims were supposed to. After leaving the Muslims he went to Africa and became an orthodox believer in Islam. He made a pilgrimage to Mecca and learned there that Islam made all men brothers. African socialists taught him that capitalism, not color, was what kept the black man down. Thus he shed the prejudices that made black separatists so ineffectual. He returned to America and established the Muslim Mosque, Inc., to prop-agate the true faith, and a secular auxiliary, the Organization of Afro-American Unity, to advance his political ideas.

His work had hardly begun when, on February 21, 1965, he was shot to death, probably by disgruntled Black Muslims. There was a good deal of solemn moralizing in the press at this. It had always treated him as a mad dog anyway. His crack about chickens coming home to roost was recalled. It was duly noted that those who live by the sword shall perish by it. Only after his autobiography was published and a new genera-tion of militants emerged was his importance understood. Black extrem-ists would revere him posthumously. He was the first black revolution-ary. He believed in guns. He put the honky down. This was true enough so far as it went, but there were better reasons for remembering Mal-colm X. Though a brilliant speaker, skilled dialectician, and charismatic figure, he was first of all a man of character. He did not have to wear African clothes, leather jackets, or dark glasses to make his point. He was what the people who admired him would call straight, a quality they scorned in others. At his death he had outgrown most of the affec-tations they were just assuming. With his gifts and new-won flexibility he could have gone anywhere, become anything. He might have even led the rebellious young blacks to less self-defeating positions than those they later occupied. Like Martin Luther King, though in a different way, he was indispensable. His murder was another reason why the sixties turned out so badly.

The impact of Malcolm's death was further muffled by events in Ala-bama soon after. Dallas County was not the worst in Alabama's Black Belt. Snick and the Southern Christian Leadership Conference had got-ten 325 Negroes registered to vote out of some fifteen thousand eligibles. In neighboring Lowndes and Wilcox counties not a single Negro was registered, though they constituted a larger percentage of the whole population than in Dallas County. But Dallas County was especially attractive to rights workers because of its sheriff, James G. Clark, Jr. "Bull Connor gave us the civil rights bill," observed one of Dr. King's aides, "and Jim Clark is going to give us the voting rights bill." They had judged their man correctly. Elsewhere, notably in Montgomery, smooth officials blocked voter registration without seeming to. This was not Jim Clark's style. When blacks protested and demonstrated in Selma, the county seat, he arrested them (more than 3,400 in all). This attracted outside support, but not enough. King spent five days in jail. Congress-men visited the scene. Nothing seemed to capture the public imagi-nation.

Then a protester was shot to death in nearby Perry County. Rights leaders capitalized on this by organizing a protest march on Selma for

March 7, 1965. On "Black Sunday" six hundred blacks and a few whites walked through Selma and onto the Edmund Pettus Bridge. Jim Clark was there to meet them with a line of state troopers. His men attacked the marchers with clubs and tear gas. Selma was in the public eye at last. Dr. King called on the nation's clergy to rally round and some three hundred did. They were joined by other white sympathizers. The marches and meetings went on. On March 9 the Reverend James J. Reeb was clubbed by racists and died soon after. On the 15th President Johnson proposed a voting rights bill to Congress. That same day James Forman led a small march in Montgomery which was scattered by a police charge. After some wrangling with the courts, permission was granted for a march from Selma to Montgomery. President Johnson federalized elements of the Alabama National Guard. On March 21 the great march began. 3,200 people, led by Dr. King and Ralph Bunche of the UN, walked the first seven miles. Thereafter the court permitted only three hundred to continue. It took them four days to cover the fifty miles to Montgomery. When they entered the city, protected by an overwhelming show of military force, 25,000 people joined them. They gathered before the old state capitol, once the Confederate government's seat, to sing and cheer. Dr. King gave one of his best speeches. Afterward Mrs. Viola Liuzzo, a Detroit housewife, was shot to death in her car. She had been ferrying marchers back to Selma from Montgomery. The chain of events that make Selma a part of history was now finished. Tens of thousands had taken part in them. Millions had seen them on television. Three rights workers were killed. The voting rights bill passed. It was a great victory for the nonviolent, integrated civil rights movement—the last such.

On August 11 looting and rioting erupted in Watts, a section of Los Angeles. The next morning Chief William H. Parker of the L.A. police made light of the violence. An aide said, "It was just a night to throw rocks at policemen." Five days later thirty-four people were dead, four thousand more under arrest, and much of Watts in ashes. Stores had been looted and burned. Firemen who tried to save them were driven off by snipers. It took fourteen thousand National Guardsmen to restore order. There were many explanations put forward at the time. Chief Parker blamed civil rights workers and nameless conspirators; Mayor Samuel W. Yorty blamed the communists. As this suggests, Los Angeles was badly served by its officials. It was one of only two major cities in the U.S. without an anti-poverty program that summer. (Chicago was the other, and it had a riot too, though a smaller one.) Its five-thousand-man police force had no more than two hundred Negro officers. Chief Parker opposed gang work, so little was done by police to help potential juvenile delinquents. And because Chief Parker was feuding with

J. Edgar Hoover Los Angeles had the only major police force whose members received no training at the FBI National Police Academy, then the only agency training policemen to control riots. To their institutional defects the L.A. police added a dash of bigotry. Officers in Watts called their nightsticks "nigger knockers." They liked to say to one another, "LSMFT," which meant "Let's shoot a motherfucker tonight." Chief Parker supported his men, and Mayor Yorty supported the chief. With this encouragement, the police tended first to provoke violence, then to overreact to it.

In addition to police brutality and official neglect, even contempt, Watts suffered from other problems. It was more attractive than most ghettos, as visitors never failed to notice (in California even the slums were better), but it was still a ghetto. It had no hospital. Between 1959 and 1965 median income in South Los Angeles had dropped by 8 per cent. In Watts 30 per cent of the adult males were unemployed. Many who had jobs lacked autos and were condemned by the city's shoddy and expensive public transit system to spend dollars and hours each day getting back and forth to work. Yet elsewhere in California there were more cars than families. Hence, while L.A. as a whole was booming (department store sales were up 10 per cent in 1964), blacks were worse off than before. This does not explain why other ghettos with similar problems failed to riot. But these conditions made the Watts riot possible, even if they didn't cause it.

While the riot's origins remain obscure, its consequences were not. Watts finally got some anti-poverty money. Many types of volunteer efforts were launched. The novelist Budd Schulberg established a writer's workshop in the ghetto. Businessmen provided capital to start a baseball bat factory (manufacturing the "Watts Walloper"). Community self-esteem grew. Each year thereafter local people organized a festival to celebrate the uprising. Polls taken later showed that more Watts residents believed it to have been helpful to "the Negro cause" than damaging. Ghetto children reflected this by proudly singing on outings, "We are from Watts, mighty, mighty Watts."* These were real

---

* Follow-up studies made it harder to explain the riots. Some experts thought that newcomers to the city were responsible. But most rioters turned out to have been in Los Angeles for at least ten years. Others believed that lower-class poverty and isolation from white society were crucial. Yet a study made by two UCLA sociologists, Raymond J. Murphy and James M. Watson, found that people in the best and worst neighborhoods of Watts were almost equally involved (25.6 per cent of their respondents from the worst areas and 18 per cent from the best areas participated in the riots). Comparative affluence eased black resentment only slightly. Middle-class blacks, with some notable exceptions like the comedian Dick Gregory who was shot while trying to disperse a mob, were not much of a moderating force. Neither group blamed its problems on the police. They were keenly resented, but more as a symbol of oppression than a cause of it.

gains; the question was, were they worth the price? Thirty-four died that community morale might improve. New jobs were created, others were lost as many burned-out stores never reopened. Watts did not get a hospital or adequate transportation. People became more conscious of Watts's needs, yet those needs remained almost as great as ever. The police did not get any nicer, nor were Mayor Yorty's sensibilities refined. Chief Parker died a few years later, unrepentant to the end.

In a real, if slightly more distant way, Watts had a poisonous effect on the public temper. The white backlash was increased by it (and the other riots that followed). Police departments everywhere equipped themselves with heavy weapons. Private citizens armed themselves in growing numbers. A few joined white terrorist organizations like the Minutemen. More formed gun clubs. Even middle-class housewives were to be found taking pistol lessons. White vigilantism did not increase to the degree these developments suggested. But in politics the backlash became important. Amiable Governor Pat Brown of California was ruined politically by white resentment of rioting blacks (and college students). The next year conservative Ronald Reagan beat him easily. Nor was Brown the only liberal officeholder to go down. Law and Order, the popular way of describing black repression, got Mayor Yorty re-elected a few years later. In 1969 it elected a mayor in Minneapolis, a city with no riots and few blacks. This is not to say that the riots were fatal to black ambitions. Some gains were made despite them. It was uphill work all the same, and needlessly so.

The riots had other negative effects. They encouraged some race leaders to practice blackmail. If we don't get what we ask for someone's going to burn the city down, they would say. Baldwin's *The Fire Next Time* had been a prophecy and a warning. Now it was both a reality and a threat. "Freedom Now" or "Burn, Baby, Burn" (the arsonist's battle cry) were supposedly the only alternatives. Sometimes this worked, and sometimes it didn't. Either way it contaminated the public atmosphere. And even when it did work it was still self-defeating. Riot prevention became the test of effective policy. When riots took place the policy, however fine, was discredited. Thus official decency was conditional on the good behavior of an entire race, and justice hostage to uncontrollable events. Watts and its successors also contributed mightily to the growing cult of violence among militants of both races. To them the disturbances were not riots but uprisings or even rebellions, precursors of the revolution. Revolutionary fantasies were in the air even before Watts.* After it they became commonplace. Gandhi, Thoreau, and

* In February 1965 New York police arrested a band of conspirators who had planned to blow up the Statue of Liberty, the Washington Monument, and the Lib-

Martin Luther King were replaced by Fidel Castro, Chairman Mao, and Ho Chi Minh as minority culture heroes. Looting and arson became revolutionary gestures, streetfighting the ultimate radical expression. A kind of madness was rising, and the thirty-four who died in Watts were only its first victims.

More immediately disconcerting was the emergence of Black Power. It started, oddly enough, during a nonviolent march organized by James Meredith. Little had been heard of Meredith since he graduated from Ole Miss and moved to New York. But on June 5, 1966, he began walking from Memphis to Jackson, Mississippi, a distance of 225 miles. His idea was to show courage and inspire it in other Negroes. "It's the silliest idea I ever heard of," said one civil rights worker. But Meredith pressed on with a small entourage of admirers, FBI agents, and local police. On the second day he was warned of a white man waiting down the road to shoot him. Meredith shrugged it off, as well he might have with all those lawmen on hand. At 4:15 P.M. Aubrey James Norvell, forty-one, a quiet Christian man according to neighbors, popped up from the roadside and put two barrels of birdshot into Meredith before anyone could respond. Meredith was not badly hurt. His march now became an event all the same. Dick Gregory joined it, so did Martin Luther King, Floyd B. McKissick of CORE, and Stokely Carmichael of Snick. King hoped to get publicity for new federal legislation. Carmichael wanted to spread news of the Lowndes County (Alabama) Black Panther party organized by Snick that year. A struggle for power resulted. Snick won. When the marchers reached Jackson they excluded the NAACP for having been insufficiently bellicose. ("It's all right" said Charles Evers, field director of the Mississippi NAACP, "I'll be here when they're all gone." And so he was.)

Snick's rhetoric got meaner as the march went on. At Canton, Mississippi, the marchers tried to set up tents in a schoolyard and were stopped. They massed, 2,500 strong, to shout defiance. "The time for running has come to an end," said Carmichael. But when state patrolmen attacked them with clubs and tear gas they ran just the same. Afterward John Lewis, former chairman of Snick, got up to say, "Fellow freedom fighters. The whole man must say no nonviolently, his entire Christian spirit must say no to this evil and vicious system." Hardly anyone paid attention. They were listening now to Stokely Carmichael. "Black Power. It's time we stand up and take over. Take over. Move on over, or we'll move on over you." Worse was to come, but to nonviolent leaders this was quite bad enough. Some, like John Lewis, dropped out. Others tried to define Black Power, a singularly elusive concept, in ways

---

erty Bell. They included members of a Black Liberation Front and French-Canadian separatists.

that would make it seem less incendiary. Martin Luther King called it "an appeal to racial pride, an appeal to the Negro not to be ashamed of being black, and the transfer of the powerlessness of the Negro into positive, constructive power." Many rejected Black Power altogether. Roy Wilkins of the NAACP called it "the father of hatred and the mother of violence." To A. Philip Randolph it was "a menace to racial peace and prosperity. No Negro who is fighting for civil rights can support black power, which is opposed to civil rights and integration." This last was an especially sore point. Whatever else it might mean, Black Power threatened integration. Carmichael saw integration as a denial of black culture and a way of siphoning the most talented elements out of the black community. It implied that white was good, black inferior, that the only means for black advancement was through white channels. Integration was emasculating. Black Power would win the Negro's freedom while preserving his cultural integrity.

This posed countless problems. For a decade the whole civil rights program had aimed at integration. If little had been gained, it was not for want of trying. Most blacks could not simply abandon what had been so laboriously secured. Yet even though Black Power advocates were few, by raising the cry they made integration even harder to get. Black Power was thought to have some connection with the summer's violence. There were no more Wattses in 1965, but by August assorted small riots had taken seven lives, injured four hundred, and produced three thousand arrests. Because whites believed Black Power was at fault, their own tendency to respond in kind grew. This was most noticeable in Chicago, where Dr. King and his SCLC were working for open housing. Whites met his demonstrations with missiles and assaults. They raised signs appealing to White Power. (Later, in Milwaukee and elsewhere, this would be refined into demands for "Polish Power" and the like.) On August 5 King himself was stoned.

Even so, most Negro activists still favored integration. Black children continued to risk everything by attending white schools in the South. In the North busing remained controversial. The problem was illustrated most dramatically in East Harlem that fall when parents boycotted a brand-new intermediate school solely on account of its racial composition. The school board had spent $5 million to make IS 201 a model of its kind. Instead of winning cheers it got pickets, demonstrations, and a brief teachers' strike. The children finally went back to school, but the problem remained. What was to be done? Without going over to Black Power, some Negro leaders began to think differently about school integration. Dr. Kenneth B. Clark, the only Negro member of New York State's Board of Regents, was one. Though his work had helped inspire the Supreme Court's desegregation decision in 1954, he now wondered if the best course wasn't to improve the segregated schools which black children would attend for many years more.

A kind of convergence took place. Young militants turned away from integration on principle, more moderate leaders gave up on it, to a degree, in practice. Militants made virtues of poverty, isolation, and uniqueness. Moderates, with some pain, recognized their persistence. This did not happen overnight. But during the next few years moderates began using words like "black" and "community" that had neo-separatist implications. Most did not accept the Black Power mystique with its emphasis on armed self-defense and the peculiar virtues of black folk culture. "Soul food" and "soul music," the attributes of this style of life, never appealed to them much, nor did "natural" hair styles, sunglasses, and African clothing. The distance between moderates and militants lessened all the same. This accommodation eased tensions among Negroes. It did not keep relations between the races from deteriorating. Black Power stimulated white resistance and, perhaps, black riots. Blacks rioted because whites were not doing enough. The riots made whites want to do even less. Black resources were not adequate to black needs. Militance alienated the white allies Negroes needed if conditions were to improve. Things therefore worsened, making black militants even angrier.

The House of Representatives did not improve matters by unseating Adam Clayton Powell, Jr., on March 1, 1967. For years he had been the most powerful Negro Congressman, and probably the most flamboyant man in the House. If chastity, sobriety, and fiscal integrity were requirements for membership, the House would have been a smaller body than it was. At least fifty other Congressmen had relatives on their payrolls. Most took sightseeing "junkets" at public expense. Had Powell sinned quietly in the approved fashion, few would have complained. But he went too far. His estranged wife did not work for him, yet he put her on the payroll so as to pocket her salary. He hired beauty queens as staff members and traveled openly with them. When convicted of libel in New York, he refused to settle up and avoided arrest by avoiding New York. Constituents who wished to see him had to go to Washington, or to his retreat on the island of Bimini. This gave his numerous enemies in Congress their chance. First the House Democrats took away his chairmanship of the Committee on Education and Labor. If he had eaten crow at this point they would probably have gone no further. But instead of recanting he denounced them as racist conspirators. Only two men had been excluded from Congress before, one for bigamy and the other for resisting American entry into World War I. Powell became the third, though whether he was punished for arrogance or blackness was never quite so clear as his friends believed. He later got the courts to reinstate him and, after paying the New York judgment, resumed his seat. But his chairmanship was gone for good, and his power with it.

Powell's ouster made Stokely Carmichael, angry young chairman of Snick, angrier still. In his speeches at black colleges that spring he was more inflammatory than ever. Carmichael was a superb orator, as events soon demonstrated. He spoke at Nashville on April 7 and 8. The second night students at Fisk University rioted, crying "Black Power." One black student was wounded, ten policemen and seven more students injured by missiles. There were fifty arrests. At Mississippi's Tougaloo College he spoke proudly of the "Nashville rebellion." In Alabama he said, "To hell with the laws of the United States." In Houston he similarly encouraged the students at black Texas Southern University. A month after his Mississippi tour black students at Jackson State rioted for several days. One man, a truck driver, was killed. Four days later a gunfight between black students and police at Texas Southern ended after one policeman had been killed, and three policemen and one student wounded. 488 students were arrested, fifteen suspended or expelled from the university. These were among the first fruits of Black Power. Carmichael went on urging black students to "fight for liberation by any means necessary."

On July 13, 1967, the next wave of ghetto riots began in Newark, New Jersey. It apparently started after police beat up a Negro cab driver. Vandalism and arson followed. The police began using live ammunition the next night and killed five people. On the third day National Guardsmen were ordered in, though the violence appeared to be subsiding. Over the weekend they and the police killed twenty more. The riot was explained as a consequence of Newark's exceptionally high rate of unemployment and unresponsive government. Blacks composed 52 per cent of the population and experienced four times as much unemployment as the national average. They were underrepresented in what was a notably corrupt city administration.

The Detroit riot was not so easily accounted for. Unemployment was low and wages for unskilled industrial workers the second highest in the country. Nearly 60 per cent of Negro families owned cars, 45 per cent owned their homes. Mayor Jerry Cavanagh owed his job to black voters and had responded energetically to their problems. Detroit had gotten several hundred million dollars from the federal government for anti-poverty and urban renewal programs. It had a riot all the same. The violence began on July 23, 1967, and lasted until July 29. When it was over, forty-three people were dead, hundreds more injured, and seven thousand under arrest. Damage was estimated at a quarter of a billion dollars. Thirteen hundred buildings were destroyed, a thousand of them stores that would probably not reopen. Five thousand people were homeless. Several thousand who had worked in the ruined stores were jobless. As in Newark, most of the deaths were caused by National Guardsmen. The police did not kill many (though several were charged with murdering three youths in the Algiers Motel). The paratroopers who pacified one sector killed fewer still. They did not use machine guns or larger weapons. When fired upon they evacuated the building first, then dug the sniper out by hand. Guardsmen were frightened, badly trained, and undisciplined. They fired on everything that moved or glittered. Yet for want of anything better, governors continued to call them out for riot duty all through the decade and after.

Being more inexplicable than most, the Detroit riot generated even fewer positive responses. President Johnson and Governor Romney quarreled over who was most to blame for not suppressing it quickly. People called for vast new anti-poverty programs. The President observed that fifteen or twenty urban bills were pending in Congress as it was. There was no more money available anyway, thanks to the war in Vietnam. Johnson did appoint a special commission chaired by Governor Otto Kerner of Illinois to study the riots. When the commission turned in a report the next year he would ignore it. Congress was even less helpful. The Senate Permanent Subcommittee on Investigations launched one probe, HUAC another. When the administration asked Congress for $40 million to exterminate city rats the House laughed the bill away. "Why not just buy some cats and turn them loose," one legislator suggested entertainingly. Another House wag urged his fellows to "vote down this rat bill rat now." As no one could show that rats were communist-inspired, the bill might have perished. But the Houses's comedy routine got bad reviews, which so embarrassed it that some rat control money was appropriated later. The urban crisis continued, without, it was true, much resistance from Congress, but also without further displays of legislative wit.

People who believed in democracy were disappointed by the government. Extreme radicals of both races were not. Tom Hayden, a founder of Students for a Democratic Society, announced that the Newark riot was a revolutionary consciousness–raising experience, and the rioters were "people making history." H. Rap Brown, the new chairman of Snick, said the riots were a "dress rehearsal for revolution," and cheerfully advised that "violence is as American as cherry pie." Brown was no summer soldier. He personally went to Cambridge, Maryland, while the Detroit riot was on and helped start another there. When not inciting people to riot he enriched the national vocabulary by calling President Johnson a "mad wild dog" and a "white hunky cracker." (Hunky, or more often "honky," was the favorite black militant epithet that year. It would later be replaced by "pig.") Though Brown was the top black extremist of 1967 (Carmichael had been No. 1 the year before; Eldridge Cleaver succeeded Brown in 1968), he was not alone. At a Black Power conference held in Newark after the riot, a thousand militants approved resolutions calling for a separate black nation, and a black militia. The right of black people to revolt was upheld. By this time Black Power had become so diffuse that it no longer required a headquarters, which was a good thing for it as Snick was fading fast. When it turned from civil rights to Black Power, donations fell off. Then it condemned Israel for conquering Arabs "through terror, force, and massacre." American Jews, who contributed heavily to Snick as to other civil rights groups, took this poorly. CORE declined also, especially after deleting the word "multiracial" from its constitution.

Nothing much was done to stop the riots. They ended, all the same. (The major ones anyway. Rioting itself became part of the American way of life.) How was this paradox to be explained? To begin with, the great riots were all clearly spontaneous. No one knew why they began or why they ended. Like some mysterious natural phenomenon, they started abruptly and stopped the same way. To the degree that conscious thought was involved, the riots' lessons were easily drawn. The blacks rioted and the blacks paid. Very few whites died, scores on scores of Negroes did. Some white businesses were destroyed, many more black homes and shops went up in flames. When white stores were burned out they were not usually rebuilt, so black jobs were lost on top of everything else. Some conscience money drifted into the ghettos afterward. It was small change compared to what was lost. Black morale improved sometimes; black circumstances worsened. White reprisals grew in severity. H. Rap Brown was silenced by the courts and dropped out of sight. Stokely Carmichael left the country for a time. Le Roi Jones remained at large with difficulty. The police, equipped now for combat operations, began exterminating the Black Panthers. Racial violence was so clearly unprofitable that aspiring black rioters were, perhaps, deterred. Or perhaps not. The riots may well have been so impulsive that such calculations played no part in ending them. At any rate, they did stop, to the relief of all but the lunatic fringe of both races.

The riots did not harm black-white relations as much as might have been supposed. In the fall, white backlash movements were put down in Boston and Cleveland. Boston was especially significant. Though it had only eighty thousand Negroes, it was a center of white unrest for many reasons. 45 per cent of the registered voters earned less than

$6,000 a year. 35 per cent had not finished high school. The more prosperous were moving to suburbia, leaving the city with fewer people (the population had declined by 23 per cent in the previous two decades) to meet graver problems. The poor whites lived mainly in ethnic ghettos, threatened by the growing black minority on the one hand and the city's decay on the other. The school systems, which poorer whites thought the key to their children's future, were in desperate shape. In 1963 the Harvard Graduate School of Education said that seventy-one of the two hundred schools in Boston should have been abandoned. But instead of building the fifty-five replacement schools it called for, the city put up only four. At the same time black pressure for school integration mounted.

This was where Louise Day Hicks came in. A lawyer herself, and the daughter of a judge, she emerged in the sixties as the *lumpen*-bourgeois's white hope. As a member of the Boston School Committee in 1963, she led the fight against school integration. She was re-elected that year gaining 73 per cent of the votes cast, becoming the city's biggest vote-getter. In 1965 she fought busing and once more was re-elected at the top of the list. She now aimed for the mayor's office. South Boston was still mainly Irish, resentful that others prospered while it did not, conservative, fearful of both the blacks and the white establishment that was thought, with reason, to worry more about Negroes than poor whites. Her position there was solid. Mrs. Hicks was no raving bigot, but she did represent the defensive, backward-looking spirit of South Boston. Kevin White, the Massachusetts Secretary of State, ran against her. They could hardly have been more different. Mrs. Hicks was dumpy and middle-aged, with a tight little mouth and chin (she looked rather like a female Hubert Humphrey, in fact). White was handsome, young (thirty-eight), well educated, and backed both by the financial community and by younger liberals. He won, getting 53 per cent of the vote, and went on to become an outstanding mayor. All the same, Mrs. Hicks had done very well for a woman (who appealed especially to other women, a rarity in politics) with no money or established organization. She was down but hardly out. If things did not improve in Boston she would be around to ride the backlash into power.

Cleveland was rather different. The Democratic candidate for Mayor was Carl B. Stokes, a Negro who had won the primary despite the machine's opposition. While Cleveland voters were overwhelmingly Democratic, this did not insure his election. No Negro had ever been elected mayor of a great city. The backlash ran strongly in Cleveland, a city whose ethnic minorities had never melted, and who, as in Boston, feared and resented the blacks, and all the more so as Negroes comprised nearly a third of the population. Stokes's Republican opponent, Seth C.

Taft of the famous Tafts, would normally have stood little chance in a place where Democratic registrations outnumbered Republicans 5 to 1. But as the only alternative to a black mayor his position was greatly enhanced. Taft ran a very upright campaign. He neither sought nor wanted the racist votes. He got them anyway. 80 per cent of the city's white voters cast their ballots for him. But a crucial minority voted for Stokes, who slipped in by 1,644 votes out of nearly 260,000 cast. As in Boston, the lesson seemed clear: there was still the promise of a racial settlement in America. But there was not much time left to redeem it.

On March 2, 1968, the National Advisory (Kerner) Commission on Civil Disorders reported to the President. It blamed the recent violence on white racism and called for the usual "massive" programs to allay black discontent. President Johnson called it a "good report by good men of good will," but added that "they always print that we don't do enough. They don't print what we do." Then he buried the report—another reason, it was said, why Robert Kennedy sought the presidency that year. A month later more rioting took place after Martin Luther King, Jr., was assassinated on April 4. Though shocking to the country it was no surprise to King. His life was always in danger and he spoke of death more than once, notably in a prophetic address given the night before he was slain. His life had been threatened that very day, but, he said, "It really doesn't matter with me now, because I've been to the mountain top, and I don't mind." Then with more emotion than was usual, he concluded: "I just want to do God's will. And he's allowed me to go up to the mountain and I've looked over and I've seen the Promised Land. I may not get there with you. But I want you to know tonight that we as a people will get to the Promised Land."

King was in Memphis, Tennessee, almost by accident. The sanitation workers (AFL-CIO), 98 per cent of them black, had been on strike for months. A week earlier King had led them in what was supposed to be a peaceful march that had ended in violence and the death of a seventeen-year-old Negro boy. Though he was busy planning the Poor People's March on Washington, he came back to Memphis to recover the moral ground lost earlier. On his second day there King was shot to death by a sniper on the balcony of his motel.* President Johnson went on television to call for public order. "I ask every American citizen to

---

* Later an escaped convict, James Earl Ray, was identified as his killer and arrested in London, England. He declared himself innocent at first. At his trial he pleaded guilty, then, after being sentenced to life imprisonment, changed his mind. To date his bids for a second trial have failed. Many people, Martin Luther King, Sr., among them, still believe he was, if guilty, part of a conspiracy.

reject the blind violence that has struck down Dr. King, who lived by nonviolence." This had little effect, perhaps because the Vietnam War had undermined Johnson's authority as a foe of violence. He further designated Sunday, April 7, as a day of mourning and ordered the American flag flown at half-staff over federal installations. Rioting erupted anyway, especially in Chicago and Washington, D.C. When it was over, forty-six persons were dead, all but five of them Negroes. One hundred towns and cities had suffered from arson or looting or both. 21,000 federal troops and 34,000 state guardsmen had been called out in the largest military deployment for a civil emergency in modern times.

While the cities burned, preparations for King's funeral went forward. A host of notable Americans, including all the serious candidates for President except Richard Nixon, attended it. Martin Luther King gave his own eulogy. The climax of his intensely moving funeral were his recorded thoughts on the subject. A few months before he had said that when buried he didn't want a long eulogy or a list of prizes and awards. "I want you to say on that day that I tried to love and serve humanity. Yes, if you're going to say that I was a drum major, say that I was a drum major for justice. Say that I was a drum major for peace." 150,000 people saw him laid to rest at Morehouse College in a tomb inscribed with these words from an old slave song: "Free at last, free at last, thank God Almighty I'm free at last." But of course Martin Luther King was free a long time before then. He liberated himself. And because he was free, countless others were too. For King, the means used were as important as the end sought. He got the Nobel Peace Prize for, in the terms of the award, having done the most "for the furtherance of brotherhood among men and to the abolishment or reduction of standing armies and for extensions of these purposes." He never gave up on nonviolence, as did so many of his followers, black and white alike, but he began to feel that time was running out. He had described the Poor People's March as a "kind of last plea for the nation to respond to nonviolence." If it failed, "I would say to the nation, I've done my best." His best was very good indeed, but, as events were soon to show, it was not good enough, nor was any man's. His birthday will no doubt become a national holiday, and, like his predecessors, he will be honored to the degree that his teachings have been ignored.

At the end King's popularity had declined. Black militants called him "de Lawd" and made fun of his traditional speaking style. Hawks, including former allies in government and the labor movement who supported nonviolence at home but not abroad, turned against him when in 1967 King began attacking the war in Indochina. Already the Northern white backlash was reducing his effectiveness, as demonstrated by the failure of his open-housing campaign in Chicago the preceding year.

The Poor People's Campaign was a resounding flop. The Reverend Ralph Abernathy, King's long-time associate who succeeded him as head of the Southern Christian Leadership Conference, lacked charisma. But the campaign failed chiefly because nonviolence was in retreat. The Poor People (mostly black but including other minorities) established themselves in "Resurrection City" by the Lincoln Memorial's reflecting pool at the end of April. The wettest spring in years discouraged many. The campaign's lack of drama and its inability to secure visible gains disheartened others. Only about five hundred stayed on in the little settlement of plywood tents. Solidarity Day, June 19, went off fairly well. Fifty thousand people participated in what was supposed to be a re-enactment of the great March on Washington of 1963. They booed Vice-President Humphrey and cheered Senator McCarthy. Then most went home. A handful of defiant ones, including Ralph Abernathy, were jailed for refusing to evacuate Resurrection City when their camping permit expired.

The dismal end of Resurrection City was part of the general worsening of race relations that continued through 1968. The armed services began to reflect this. There were ugly racial incidents at many installations, especially in Vietnam. While only 12 per cent of American forces in Vietnam were black, Negroes made up 20 per cent of the fighting forces and 25 per cent of the elite combat units. Many felt discriminated against in other ways. There were incidents at bases in both Vietnam and the U.S. The worst was a race riot at the Long Binh Detention Center outside Saigon. This was a prison compound with 720 prisoners, over half of them black, living in facilities designed for four hundred. One night in August after a pot-pill party, black prisoners attacked white prisoners, overcame the prison guards, and set fire to the buildings. One white prisoner was beaten to death, sixty other men were injured including the stockade commander. When the guards restored order they herded 220 black prisoners into a barbed-wire enclosure and waited for them to surrender. A few held out for as long as three weeks. At first the military was able to suppress the news of these events. It continued to pretend that black servicemen were entirely happy with their well-advertised opportunities. As unrest spread to installations in the U.S., this became harder and harder to do.

Equally disheartening was the news from New York. There, for one thing, the welfare system was breaking down. In 1960 the State of New York predicted that by 1970, 700,000 people would be receiving welfare at a cost of $537 million. By the end of 1968 a million people were on the rolls in New York City alone. In 1965 the welfare population was growing by about five thousand people a month. In 1968 the growth averaged twenty thousand a month. Fifty thousand people were added in August. A quarter of the city budget was now spent on welfare. Even so, it was far from adequate. New York gave a family of four $278 a month. This still kept them below the poverty line, yet it was a handsome stipend compared to what the Southern states—from which most of New York's welfare population was drawn—offered. Mississippi estimated that the minimum subsistence for a family of four amounted to $201 a month. A family getting Aid to Dependent Children in Mississippi actually received $55 a month. This was one reason why New York, which paid 100 per cent of estimated subsistence needs, attracted the indigent. Another was that while New York City had recognized the right of needy people to public assistance, it had never publicized that fact before. When Mayor John Lindsay came in the policy was changed. People were made aware of their rights. Relief agencies were encouraged to be more generous. In consequence, the Aid to Dependent Children rate of acceptance rose from 66.5 per cent in 1965 to 81.4 per cent in 1968. Then too, the poor became more militant, encouraged by storefront welfare information centers—many operated with federal money as part of the war on poverty. If things continued at that rate, half the city would be on welfare by 1980. As it was, one of every eight New Yorkers was on welfare. For children the rate was one in five. New York had one-seventh of all the substandard housing in America. A half-million people lived in public housing, yet 135,000 more families remained on waiting lists. Mayor Lindsay asked the federal government for $5 billion a year for five years to meet the crisis. This was a fair claim, as New York's welfare crisis was mainly a result of the failure of other areas, especially in the South, to do their part. Of course he didn't get the money.

The school crisis was almost as bad and even more baffling and provocative, especially where the Ocean Hill experimental school district was concerned. Everyone agreed that the struggle was generated by earlier failures. In 1954 the Board of Education ringingly endorsed the Supreme Court's desegregation order. Yet by 1966 the number of predominately Negro and Puerto Rican schools had increased from 118 in 1960 to 201, while the number of white schools was down from 327 to 237. If the Puerto Ricans, who were more dispersed than blacks, were excluded, the picture was even worse. There were several reasons why integration failed. Residential segregation increased, and this naturally affected the schools. But one big reason was the school system's persistent refusal to integrate. When pressured by civil rights groups it developed an open-enrollment plan, which was not actively promoted and accomplished little. In 1964 and 1965 the school board, after a series of protests and school boycotts, advanced more ambitious plans, including busing. These were not implemented either. The confidence of black people in the system's good will accordingly declined. The New York schools failed to integrate because white parents objected. But the schools were also handicapped by their own fantastic bureaucracy. A million children were enrolled in New York's public schools, more than the total population of most American cities. To cope with them a central structure of great complexity had grown up. Everything was directed from school headquarters at 110 Livingston Street. The result was stagnation, frustration, and inefficiency under the best of circumstances. Under stress the system hardly moved at all. Then too, there were few blacks in the system. Most New York teachers were trained by the city's public colleges, only 3 per cent of whose enrollment was black. Consequently only about 10 per cent of public school teachers and almost no principals and supervisors were Negroes. Hence blacks had little leverage within the system, while the pressure they exercised outside it only heightened its natural resistance to change.

The rise of separatist impulses after 1965 seemed to offer a way out. The school system couldn't give black people integration, but local control was another matter. Everyone disliked the central bureaucracy. Mayor Lindsay was an advocate of decentralization. Frightened whites who had fought integration ought to find decentralization (in one sense an assurance of continued segregation) agreeable. And in the later sixties citizen participation, local control, popular democracy, and such notions were endorsed by radicals and conservatives alike. Even the teachers' union was enthusiastic, and when the Ford Foundation agreed to help pay the costs for a demonstration district to see if decentralization would work, it suggested Ocean Hill.

The United Federation of Teachers (AFL-CIO) already had a teacher-parent joint action group in the district, a decaying area between the slums of Brownsville and Bedford-Stuyvesant.* Less than a third of the adult residents had completed high school. More than half the households subsisted on less than $5,000 a year. Only two-fifths of the population had lived in Ocean Hill as long as five years. About 70

* The Ocean Hill fight was so intense because black militancy met teacher militancy head-on. Teachers always used to be easily pushed around, but in the sixties many, especially in New York and other large cities, joined the American Federation of Teachers. (The UFT was the local affiliate.) It was a real union, not a company union like the old National Education Association. When the AFT got tough it got results. This forced the NEA to do likewise. It too began authorizing strikes (called "sanctions") and walkouts. The status of teachers rose rapidly in consequence. Their pay increased—always a mark of community esteem—and people respected them more, however grudgingly, as they did teamsters and other hard-boiled trade unionists. Teaching became a more desirable profession, and the quality of new teachers improved strikingly. When the teacher shortage ended in 1969 they were ready for it. School boards would no longer be able to take advantage of them, neither would anyone else. Mostly this was to the good, except where the interests of teachers and other militants seemed to clash, as in Ocean Hill.

per cent of the residents were black and 25 per cent Puerto Rican. But the union was not the only educational force in Ocean Hill. Another group, led by a white worker priest, Father John Powis, was working for community control of the schools. Both elements were represented on the planning council that set up the Ocean Hill Demonstration District. The planning council, without the consent of the New York Board of Education, then created a governing board of parents, teachers, and others to make policy for the eight demonstration schools. Ocean Hill got going in the fall of 1967 and was immediately confronted with the city-wide teachers' strike. Local efforts were made to break it. Teachers were harassed. Roving militants came in to cross picket lines and teach classes.

The UFT retaliated by forbidding union teachers to sit on the governing board, and joined with the Council of Supervisory Associations (the principals' union) to have the newly, but also illegally, appointed Ocean Hill principals ousted. In November all the eighteen assistant principals applied for transfer out of the district. Hostilities between union teachers and parents and students became more intense. After Martin Luther King's murder a number of teachers were assaulted. Vandalism, arson, and other abuses were commonplace, especially in the new intermediate school, IS 55. The teachers got angrier. The governing board became more radical. Things got worse when the governing board tried to get rid of nineteen teachers and administrators. Some agreed to accept transfers, but ten held out. Various complex deals and maneuvers were attempted. All failed. When school opened in the fall, the UFT staged four strikes in succession to support the ten. There was some violence. At times as many as a thousand police were needed to keep order. Sometimes the schools had to be closed. In November complicated negotiations between the union, Supervisor Rhody McCoy, the Board of Education, the mayor, and the State Education Department resulted in an interim settlement. It called for the State Supervisory Commission to oversee the entire city system with a special state trusteeship for Ocean Hill. The governing board lost four of the principals it wanted and was itself suspended. Its members were barred from visiting the schools. Observers from the State Education Department were given authority to countermand the local supervisor's orders. Any school where union teachers were harassed would be closed immediately. According to Martin Mayer, this meant that the mayor was prepared to risk even a race riot to prevent another teachers' strike. The enraged Ocean Hill governing board walked out of the negotiations with Father Powis, allegedly calling out, "Hey, baby, now we burn down Brooklyn," to which Whitney Young of the Urban League is supposed to have replied, "It's a pity . . . there are only 2,000 blacks you can get killed in Ocean Hill."

The affair was disastrous for the city. The very white parents whom decentralization was supposed to placate now turned against it. The union, an early advocate of the idea, did so also, and lobbied in Albany to block legislation that would have authorized it. Black militancy in Ocean Hill became more intense. Anti-semitism appeared. The UFT was mainly Jewish. All ten of the Ocean Hill teachers who resisted transfer were Jews. One black teacher read a poem on radio station WBAI dedicated to union head Albert Shanker that began "Hey, Jew boy, with that yarmulka on your head/You pale-faced Jew boy—I wish you were dead." After he read it his host, Julius Lester, said "Beautiful." In consequence, WBAI, an independent, listener-supported radio station, one of three such in the unique Pacifica system, was picketed. Mayor Lindsay was faced with the possible loss of the Jewish vote essential to his re-election. While trying to explain himself he was booed down in a synagogue. Polls taken among Negroes suggested later that black anti-semitism was really negligible. But the fear of it, fanned by the UFT, once a leader in the civil rights struggle, was not.

The most sinister motives were attributed to everyone involved. Jason Epstein, a well-known book editor, accused the union of resisting decentralization for fear that its white members would come under the authority of largely black governing boards. And he further charged that Martin Mayer's account of these events was colored by Mayer's conviction that the gentile establishment was expressing its residual anti-semitism by encouraging militant blacks to attack Jewish institutions as well as individual Jews. Old friends divided on the question. Dwight Macdonald wrote a furious letter to the *New York Review of Books* saying that Michael Harrington, whose *The Other America* ne had made famous, had tricked him into supporting the UFT. Harrington replied, in effect, that Macdonald had been duped by the Establishment. Harrington believed that the Ford Foundation–Urban Coalition–Board of Education axis meant to use Black Power to strengthen the status quo. Community control really meant "black control of black misery and white control of the nation's wealth." The degree of verbal overkill involved can hardly be exaggerated. Macdonald called Albert Shanker a racist demagogue. Jason Epstein compared Ocean Hill to Palestine during the British mandate and called on the imperialists to evacuate it.

The fight over Ocean Hill damaged everyone—the mayor, the union, the school board, the liberal establishment, and the district. It further divided an already polarized city. About the only comfort to be drawn from it was that things did not turn out quite so badly as might have been expected. There was no race riot. Brooklyn was not burned down. The experiment survived, in a truncated fashion, as did Superintendent McCoy. And a year later, when an election was held to determine who should represent the district's teachers' aides, people drawn mainly from the community, the UFT won. Though the bitterness was real, it was apparently not so intense as had been feared. The school system might yet be saved, though no one quite knew how.

Black news was still chiefly bad news in 1969. The energies loosed by civil rights churned on. But division, violence, and confusion still reigned supreme. And the rise of Richard Nixon meant that the federal power could no longer be counted on. Analysis is hardly possible when chaos is king. So it was all that year. There were only a few things that people could agree about. One was the future of the Black Panthers. They did not appear to have any.

At the year's end the Panthers claimed to have had twenty-eight members killed by the police. Even if that total was smaller, the heat was clearly on them. Among their leaders, Huey P. Newton was in prison for manslaughter and Bobby Seale on a charge of murder. Eldridge Cleaver was in exile. David Hillard was free on bond pending his trial for threatening the life of President Nixon. Bobby Hutton had been killed the previous year. The locals were equally burdened. In Denver two Panthers were held in lieu of $200,000 bail for flight to escape prosecution. In April twenty-one Panthers were arrested in New York for conspiring to blow up various things including a police station and the Bronx Botanical Gardens. In May twenty-eight Panthers were arrested in New Haven for the kidnaping and murder of a party member. Enormous bails kept most in jail. In Illinois the party chairman got four years for allegedly stealing $71 worth of ice cream bars. Spiro Agnew called the Panthers a "completely irresponsible, anarchistic group of criminals." J. Edgar Hoover said they were the single biggest threat to the country's internal security. The Justice Department set up a special task force to suppress them. No sensible person doubted that federal and local authorities were conspiring to destroy the Black Panther party. This was clear even before the mayor of Seattle admitted blocking a federal agency's effort to raid the Panthers in his city. Two Chicago Panthers were killed in especially cold blood. Police caught them sleeping and shot them to pieces. Charges were later dropped against the survivors, tacit admission that the police were at fault.

Why were the Panthers singled out for special treatment, though only one of many black nationalist groups? They were, for one thing, the most visible. Their old habit of making armed displays (since abandoned) drew attention. So did their willingness to shoot when attacked. Fortifying their headquarters was provocative too, even though clearly in self-defense. People are not supposed to defend themselves against the police. All these acts of bravado were enough by themselves to explain why the police wanted them dead.

A further reason was the Panthers' developing ideology. Ordinary black racists to begin with, they soon became self-consciously revolutionary. They quoted from Marx, Frantz Fanon, and other authorities. And they put what they learned into practice. Revolutionary discipline was imposed in the bolshevik manner. Efforts were made to secure allies. This meant working with parallel organizations like the Young Lords and the Young Patriots. The Lords were Puerto Rican streetfighters who became radicalized. Their leader in Chicago, Cha Cha Jiminez, was inspired by reading Eldridge Cleaver to politicize his followers. The Young Patriots were poor whites, mostly from Appalachia. The three groups managed to combine "the ambiance of 'West Side Story' with the theory and discipline of the National Liberation Front," the *New York Times* said. The Panthers were ideological and stylistic leaders. Their habit of wearing berets and shouting "Right on" at suitable intervals was quickly adopted. So was their vaguely Marxist-Leninist analysis of American society, and their opposition to "cultural nationalism." Going African, in appearance at least, was scorned by the Panthers. Nor did they have any faith in black capitalism, the Nixon approach to racial betterment. Huey Newton wrote, "There can be no real black capitalism because no blacks control the means of production. All blacks can do is have illusions." Black capitalism was merely "the establishment's way to draw the teeth from black power." The Panthers hoped to go beyond ethnic organization. In the short run Black Power, Brown Power, and such were useful ways of developing a higher social consciousness. In the end they wanted a general revolution by, as they thought, the exploited majority of Americans.

The Panther critique of palliatives like black capitalism was impressive. So was their ability to rise above racism and cultural chauvinism. They were good at spotting internal contradictions in the American system. Inevitably, they were less sensitive to their own. If the pig power structure was as bad as they said, then open threats to destroy it invited retaliation. They made the threats, yet seemed surprised at the response. Their style and poise made them attractive in the ghetto but outraged the police who were so much more powerful than they. Their ideology was their best claim to respect, but it gave the authorities a license to hunt them. Like the radical Weathermen, they were damned if they did and doomed if they didn't. To give up their style and political philosophy would be to stop being the Black Panther party. To retain them was to die. It didn't say much for the American way of life that it could only be saved by killing the Panthers. Yet that was how people felt.

The Black Panther experience was doubly tragic: first because they were blind to the fact that you can't make a revolution in a country where most people support the government; second because the government couldn't see that either, and persisted in treating a head cold as an epidemic.

The Panthers were only a very small part of the black scene in 1969, though among the most publicized. Black action was now so widespread as to defy summary. Every large city and many small ones had black freedom organizations. Scarcely any area of urban life was neglected by them. Some black enterprises were more conservative than not, a fact sometimes hard to grasp for the extravagant language with which they were advanced.

Take CORE for example. James Farmer was considered terribly militant when he organized the Freedom Rides. He was replaced by the seemingly more radical Floyd McKissick. Farmer dropped from sight and emerged years later as a subcabinet officer in the Nixon administration. Then McKissick left CORE to promote black capitalism, assisted by the Chase Manhattan Bank and other institutions. Little was heard of CORE thereafter. The matter of James Forman was even stranger. He began as a Freedom Rider, went on to be executive director of Snick, and then became minister of foreign affairs for the Black Panthers. In 1968 he resigned to lead the Black Economic Development Conference which aimed to shake down religious bodies. As the churches had exploited blacks for so long, Forman believed half a billion dollars in reparations was only fair. He broke into church services and demanded cash on the barrelhead.

Others followed his example, or bettered it in the case of one Philadelphia group which desecrated communion elements in a fit of idealism. Some denominations released funds to blacks on this basis, though rarely to Forman himself, and never as reparations. More benign formulas for admitting white guilt were easily come by. Forman was thought a terrific radical. His "black manifesto" was so revolutionary that it had to be suppressed. All the same, blackmail was not such a radical act. And, propaganda apart, it was not put to remarkably left-wing uses. Paying up apparently made some religious leaders feel better. It did not have an equally cheering effect on moderate blacks. After the Episcopal Church gave Forman $200,000, Roy Wilkins of the NAACP noted dryly that this showed him the error of his ways. No denomination had ever given groups like his that much money, obviously because they asked for justice instead of demanding revolution and black domination.

The rage for Black Studies was equally perplexing. At first the demand for college courses on black history and culture seemed simple enough. Blacks made up more than 10 per cent of the population and they had reason to expect instruction on subjects peculiar to them. Yet it soon was evident that many did not want academic courses but a combination of propaganda and activist training. To these were added demands for control over faculty and curriculum. Some wanted segregated facilities too. Black militants dominated 59 per cent of the 232 campuses that experienced protests in the first six months of 1969. 76 per cent of them involved no violence or property destruction. Separatist or segregationist demands appeared in only 13 per cent of the protests. But they got the most attention, and often the best results.* The eruptions at San Francisco State College and Cornell University showed how this process worked.

San Francisco State's experience was the saddest. Like all the California state colleges, it was fearfully short of money. (Although rich, California was thirty-third among American states in its per capita support of higher education.) Yet it had a superior faculty and a bright, diverse student body. And it was more open to innovation than comparable institutions. But at a time when other schools were increasing their black enrollments, San Francisco State's was declining—mostly because admission requirements had grown stricter. The minority students who did get in were far more militant than before. Tensions grew so in consequence that even liberal presidents had trouble coping. President Robert R. Smith resigned in September 1968 after a black instructor urged students to bring guns on campus and Smith was told to suspend him. The militants threatened him if he did, the regents if he didn't. A violent student strike followed. He was succeeded by the well-known semanticist S. I. Hayakawa, who took a hard line. He brought city police on campus to enforce order. More violence resulted. The tumult went on for months before the striking students and teachers were subdued. By then the student government had been gutted and many experimental programs ended or curtailed. Nathan Hare, head of the Black Studies department, was fired, but remained its guiding spirit as chairman-in-exile. Some of the best faculty resigned. There was less money than before for the rest to manage with. The Black Studies department became a center of extremist agitation. Hare announced that it "will soon blossom to become the most meaningful and relevant institution in educating black people to the contradictions and gross hypocrisy that prevail in this oppressive country." It violated all the rules of academic propriety, but Hayakawa was afraid to discipline it for fear of more violence. Meanwhile, the Association of Western Colleges was threat-

---

* According to the Urban Research Corporation of Chicago, black demands were twice as likely to be granted as other kinds. And, as a rule, the more violent a protest the more likely it was to succeed. So campus radicals were right to say that coercion was better than negotiation—up to a point anyway.

ening to take away San Francisco State's accreditation if Black Studies was not brought under control. Hayakawa had more latitude than most college presidents. His intemperate language endeared him to Governor Reagan and the silent majority. Polls showed him to be the state's most popular Democrat. Conservatives everywhere acclaimed him, though he was still nominally liberal. San Francisco State itself was degraded anyway. Minority enrollments did not go up. A thousand students got to take courses approved by the Black Panthers, to what useful purpose no one else could guess. Radical students wrote a million words describing this revolutionary triumph.*

The best-publicized black protest was at Cornell. Here it was the University's success at recruiting spirited black students that led to trouble. When President James A. Perkins came to Cornell in 1963 there were few blacks enrolled. He established a Committee on Special Educational Projects to recruit them. Soon enough were on campus to form an Afro-American Society. When black coeds wanted a dormitory of their own they got it. When Negroes asked for a Black Studies program the University promised to establish one. In January 1969 it set up a black center with a budget of $175,000. But black demands stayed ahead of the University's ability to respond. Militants wanted a separate degree-granting college. To show their zeal for it, some ran across table tops in a dining hall during mealtime. Later a group barricaded themselves in a campus building. They were finally negotiated out and emerged with guns in hand. Pictures of them festooned with rifles and ammunition belts were shown around the country. The University itself was paralyzed and Perkins forced to resign. (He may have been lucky at that. The President of Swarthmore College died of a heart attack during a confrontation with the black students he had helped bring on campus.) The militants did not get their college, though the Black Studies program was continued.

No one knew what to make of this. Scores of colleges and universities rushed to install Black Studies programs out of fear or enthusiasm. Few were able to recruit enough black scholars to man them. Those that did often had to raid black colleges. This led Vincent Harding, chairman of the history department at Spelman College, a black school in Atlanta, to call Black Studies a racist plot. In the guise of integration Northern schools were drawing off the best professors from impoverished black colleges. Thus higher education got it both ways. Colleges were racist

* At lesser institutions black students often got short shrift for protesting. The Wisconsin State University at Oshkosh summarily suspended nearly a hundred black students after a sit-in. Few of them were reinstated. At Ferris State College in Michigan, when black students occupied a campus building after being beaten by white students, state policemen broke down the doors and hauled them off to a makeshift jail in the local armory.

if they didn't establish Black Studies, but also if they did. The concept of Black Studies remained doubtful. Many Negro leaders (Bayard Rustin, Roy Wilkins) opposed Black Studies. They thought blacks could take courses in the field without harm, but what did they gain from schooling that produced no marketable skills? What blacks needed were degrees in medicine, law, and other useful fields. Black Studies was a luxury that oppressed minorities could not afford. Such majors traded off short-term emotional gains for long-term occupational disadvantages. And, they might have added, Black Studies cost money that might better go to scholarships.

All the same, it was clear that the demand for Black Studies would continue (although the University of California at Riverside dropped its program). Other ethnic groups copied the blacks. Even if minority students could be convinced that ethnic studies were nonproductive, they would probably want them anyhow. It was reassuring to have a warm place to hole up in at the alien, white-dominated university. And at a time when so many things semed hard to get, ethnic studies was something that, for better or worse, could be had. Universities want to be fashionable. The very fact that Black Studies was modish made them desire it. There was a good case to be made for ethnic studies as a subject of academic inquiry, especially as universities already offered courses in every field of human interest from swimming to brake-lining. Blacks rightly questioned why it was proper to offer credit for the theory and practice of basketball while denying it for the theory and practice of ghetto organizing. So, for good reasons and bad, Black Studies grew. Perhaps one of the first signs of racial equality would be its decline. Once Negroes were as satisfied as, say, Irish Americans, then Black Studies would take its place with Gaelic studies. Hasten that blessed day, the universities could only murmur.

Though less publicized, the high schools' problems were perhaps more severe. Racial clashes grew in number and severity and reached further down the grades. School boycotts became commonplace. "Integrated" (actually changing) schools saw more racial polarization than ever. Interracial contacts declined, fist fights increased. Most of the conflicts were produced by black militancy, according to Alan F. Westin of Columbia University. He monitored eighteen hundred local newspapers and found that demands for black cheerleaders, "soul food" in cafeterias, honor to Malcolm X, and such were the usual causes. Most secondary schools were dominated by white middle-class values. It was hardly unreasonable for blacks to want their culture recognized in schools where they were numerous. But as their efforts were invariably resented, and sometimes resisted, trouble often followed. 1969 was the most violent year yet. Most observers thought that worse was to come.

Militancy was still rising, so was the proportion of blacks in many schools.

Another source of trouble was in the building trades. These unions were among the best paid and most conservative in the country. Admission to them was jealously guarded. Members looked after their relatives first and Negroes last (with some notable exceptions like the New York Electrical Workers, who accepted a thousand apprentices in the early sixties, two hundred of them black and Puerto Rican). The result was that most trades had only a few blacks. In 1969 the first major efforts to desegregate these unions produced boycotts in Pittsburgh and white counterprotest marches in Chicago. The Nixon administration finally adopted what was called the Philadelphia Plan. It established racial quotas for construction work forces that contractors and unions alike were obliged to meet. The AFL-CIO condemned this approach but came up with no alternative of its own. Harvard University won some glory by becoming the first big enterprise requiring builders to meet racial quotas as a condition of their contracts. But the issue remained explosive, especially as the economy slackened. It was hard enough to get blacks a thin slice of a fat pie. If the pie shrank, more violence might be expected.

At the decade's end Negroes were better off than before. In 1960 nonwhites earned 52 per cent as much as whites, in 1968, 63 per cent. In 1960, 39 per cent of nonwhite youngsters completed high school, in 1968, 58 per cent. In the same period the number of nonwhites in "craftsmen and foremen" job classifications rose 57 per cent while the number of such jobs increased by only 12 per cent. Nor were blacks unaware of this. According to the Gallup poll the percentage of Negroes satisfied with their work rose from 54 to 76 per cent. They were more satisfied with their income and housing too. Much remained to be done. 12 per cent of the entire population still lived below the poverty line (as against 22 per cent in 1960). The line itself was probably set too low. The distance between black and white median incomes was still too great, except among young families in the North. Housing worsened in the late sixties as inflation and tight money depressed the home-building industry. All the same, it was a decade of remarkable progress for blacks. The figures showed that. So did the rise in black pride and confidence. There were never so many public and private efforts focused on a single problem, even in the South. Whites who murdered blacks were beginning to be convicted, not only in the border states but in Mississippi as well. When the courts ordered Southern school systems to desegregate immediately at the decade's end, most complied, however gracelessly. There was surprisingly little violence.

All this should have occasioned much rejoicing but didn't. One reason was that progress aroused expectations that exceeded the country's ability to respond. Gains were measured against what remained to be done, not what had been accomplished. As the Gallup poll showed, morale did in fact improve. But few could see this because militant blacks were so firmly committed to an angry style. They believed only confrontation politics paid off. No one doubted that without it Negroes would have been in reduced circumstances. But it made whites angry in return. Like all men they wanted to be complimented for doing the right thing, even under pressure. When instead more was asked of them, some rebelled. Many felt threatened. Others were hurt when blacks seemed to reject them. Black militancy was abrasive enough. Black separatism was more trying still. And it offended precisely those whites who were most eager to help. Governor Lester Maddox of Georgia didn't care if Negroes demanded separate facilities. That was what he wanted too. But Northern liberals had staked a lot on integration and many took its decline personally. The ghetto uprisings of the mid-sixties offended more. So did what appeared to be the general increase of black violence, whether criminal, political, or merely verbal.

These reactions were understandable, perhaps even inevitable. During the civil rights movement's great days blacks were promised much more than they got. Much of what they did get in the way of laws and poverty programs accomplished little. They had reason to feel disappointed, if not betrayed as some did. The bitterness they always felt deepened. The early rights movement had generated unreasonable expectations among white liberals too. They thought Negroes would go on turning the other cheek and loving their enemies indefinitely. Many liberals secretly felt that the blacks had let them down by not remaining saints and martyrs. Separatism and Black Power made it easy for them to turn away from civil rights. But though natural, these feelings were extremely ominous. Many of the gains Negroes made resulted from the boom which ended in 1969. Unemployment then began rising. The GNP leveled off. Inflation rose. If a recession came, much of what had been won would be lost. Police repression of the Black Panthers might spread to other militants. President Nixon was busy courting the South. Government officials who showed too keen an interest in civil rights were fired or squeezed out.

Thus, despite all the real progress since 1960, race relations got worse. Black rage grew, so did white apathy and the white backlash. There was no going back where Negroes were concerned. There seemed no way to go ahead either. It did not take a Jeremiah to see in this a recipe for fresh disasters.

PROFILE:
Women's Liberation

ONE MOVEMENT of the late sixties that ran against the grain was women's liberation. Where the counter-culture was hedonistic, the women's liberation movement was Calvinistic in the sense of being disciplined, angry, and work-oriented. The resurgence of feminism took most Americans by surprise. After all, women already had all the rights men did, and privileges they didn't, it was thought. In fact the relative position of women had been deteriorating ever since the old feminist movement died out. Though more women went to college than in 1920, they made up a smaller percentage of the undergraduate population. The proportion of women earning graduate degrees was smaller than in 1930. More women worked, but still mostly at the worst jobs. White women earned less on the average than black men, black women least of all. Despite Title VII of the Civil Rights Act of 1964 which prohibited certain discriminatory practices, women continued to earn less than men with the same training and experience. Yet until the late sixties women did not protest. This helped persuade everyone, themselves included, that women really were as well off as people hoped.*

---

* It was hardly in the male interest to sustain these illusions, for the economic discrimination against women hurt nearly everyone. In the North black poverty was concentrated in families headed by women. 56 per cent of black families with incomes under $3,000 fell in this category in 1968. Conversely, middle-class affluence

Then, without much fanfare, things began to change. In 1961 President Kennedy appointed a committee to investigate the status of women. Many states followed suit. The uneasiness thus betrayed was heightened by the publication of Betty Friedan's famous polemic *The Feminine Mystique* a few years later. Mrs. Friedan forcefully pointed out the discrepancies between what was claimed for women and what they actually enjoyed. She attributed their continuing subordination to the propaganda of educators, women's magazines, and others who successfully brainwashed women into thinking that domesticity plus sex plus consumption equaled happiness. At first Mrs. Friedan was considered eccentric. But soon the charges she made were widely endorsed. Her own National Organization for Women (NOW) was one result. By the end of the sixties there were many feminist groups, mostly local.

One of the peculiarities of modern history is that feminism is always thought ridiculous. The old feminist movement, while a mighty social expression that lasted nearly a century and involved millions of women at its peak, struggled against ridicule to the end. The new feminism encountered it at the beginning. One way to avoid being made fun of was to use different terms. Thus few women called themselves feminists in the old way, nor did they call for emancipation. Women's liberation became the accepted term. It covered a multitude of tendencies. NOW was often compared with the NAACP. It appealed to a broad range of people, especially older business and professional women. It preferred to work through established institutions.

Other feminist groups spun off from the New Left. Sometimes they functioned as women's auxiliaries. Other times they aimed at correcting abuses within the movement as well as outside it. New Leftists did not automatically shed their masculine prejudices by becoming revolutionaries. Sometimes they were even worse than the average man. The prestige of third-world liberators led many to exaggerate traditional masculine traits. This spurious *machismo* was most readily expressed against movement women. Some, especially at first, did accept the Earth Mother role this cast them in. Increasingly,

---

was also a function of feminine employment. In 1955, 53 per cent of all families with incomes of between $12,000 and $15,000 had working wives. Equal pay for equal work would go a long way toward abolishing poverty. It would also do a lot for middle-income families, who had the largest proportion of working wives.

though, they didn't. During the Columbia rising, when assigned housekeeping duties women rebelled and, under the slogan "Free women do not cook," forced an equitable division of revolutionary duties. The most advanced came to feel that women's needs were so unique that they could never be satisfied in a male-dominated movement, however well intentioned. But they clung to New Left rhetoric and tactics all the same. Thus they produced in WITCH and elsewhere a guerrilla theater of their own. It was this tendency that first brought women's liberation national publicity. In 1968 a group of them picketed the Miss America pageant in Atlantic City with signs reading "Miss America Sells It" and other indelicacies. This was a tricky kind of protest. Though meant to be funny as well as tough, it exposed feminists to more of the same ridicule that had always been so debilitating to them. They could never be sure whether people were laughing at them or with them. All the same it did get publicity, which is one thing struggling movements usually need.

Some of the attention was unwelcome. Feminists are always thought to be more sexually accessible than other women. This is rarely the case. But in taking up sexual issues they expose themselves as more timid women do not. Liberated women strongly attacked abortion laws. This was in the great feminist tradition. Emancipated women always wanted to control their bodies. Hence they supported contraception early on, and sometimes easy divorce. Legalizing abortion was another step in the same direction. Feminists regarded it as a defensive measure. But prurient males saw it as a preliminary to sexual license. A few women wanted to do away with the concept of illegitimacy so that unwed mothers would not be discouraged or discriminated against. This too incited lust.

Militant feminists were, and always had been, more suspicious of sex than not. While some practiced, or even advocated, free love, most didn't. More than that, they tended to view heterosexual relations as inherently exploitive of women. Men and women shared the pleasure, but women alone paid the price. The most extreme wing of the women's liberation movement put this line into practice. Though often attractive, they stopped dating men. Some even uglified themselves in protest against the exploitation of feminine charm. A few stopped wearing bras on the mistaken theory that it would reduce their sex appeal. And they raged against the entire male sex, to the point, in some cases, of advocating lesbianism. This was only to be expected. Like all oppressed groups, women were full of suppressed anger. How could it be otherwise when they were at once discriminated against and patronized? Though equal in theory, they were exploited as workers, housewives, and consumers while being assured that the treatment they got was exactly what their own natures entitled them to. At the same time as men suppressed them—perhaps because of it—men resented their complaints.

The violent abuse that feminists everywhere encountered was all out of proportion to what they did. Liberal men like David Susskind invited them on television programs for the sole purpose of insulting them, so it seemed. Everyone with the slightest experience in these matters was struck by how much sheer bigotry men (and brainwashed women too) were willing to express. In fact, among ordinary middle-class people anti-feminism seemed the only remaining respectable prejudice. It was once socially acceptable to hate Jews, Negroes, immigrants, and the like. That was no longer true. Even anti-Catholicism, the "anti-Semitism of the intellectuals" as it used to be called, had become contemptible. Only the hatred of women (and homosexuals) remained. Liberals felt free to comment openly on women's mental and emotional inferiority, and invariably did when feminism came up. Such men commonly denied being sexual bigots on the grounds that they didn't hate women as such, only those who didn't know their place. The wonder was not that so many women were hostile to men, but that so many were not—openly at least. (In fact, there were plenty of ways for traditional women to express resentment, if unconsciously, hence the vast folklore concerning nagging wives and mothers.)

But while women had much to be angry about, and there was some value to admitting it, hate could be self-defeating. It didn't do anyone much good when militants disrupted Senate hearings on the birth-control pill, calling it a plot against women. Nor did prohibiting sexual relations with men make for a healthier society. In the long run what was needed was an integrated social order. Sealing people off in sexual ghettos, even voluntary ones, only compounded existing problems. Hate the sin not the sinner, Christianity instructs, and it is good advice for radicals too. Mainly, however, extremism was dangerous to its practitioners. In the past, feminists on the lunatic fringe had done more harm to themselves than to anyone else. Self-indulgence is self-destructive of any radicalism, especially under modern conditions. Women's liberation got a lot of coverage in 1969. Publicity of a sort the original feminists spent generations to secure could be had practically for the asking. And that was precisely the danger. The hothouse growth the media promoted had a deadly effect on many movements in the sixties. Nobody one day, a celebrity the next, and nobody the day after was a common cycle. Whatever became of Mario Savio, Bettina Aptheker, H. Rap Brown, Stokely Carmichael, and all the rest? Drunk with the sense of power today, stripped of it tomorrow—the media giveth and the media taketh away. Into the pop culture ashcan they went along with yesterday's TV serials. For feminism to avoid becoming just another nonreusable instantly obsolete commodity like the sensations that preceded it would take some doing.

One reason feminism was always taken lightly was that to take it seriously opened up dreadful possibilities. What if feminine equality was incompatible with marriage and the family? Nobody could be sure it wasn't. That was why even moderate feminists had always been viewed by some as potential homewreckers. To confront the woman question squarely meant taking risks. Feminism might well be the most truly radical proposition of them all, one that threatened to reach into secret and intimate places which politics had scarcely touched before. Hence, along with all the other problems they had to deal with, liberated women had to confront this widespread, if seldom admitted, anxiety. And they had to resist the other pathologies to which radical movements were prone in the sixties. They all succumbed to sectarianism, fissioning, rhetorical extravagances, posturing, and obsessiveness. But if liberated women could avoid imitating them they might go far indeed.

7 TWO CULTURES

WHEN THE cultural history of this decade is written, art historians are likely to say that most of it was based on what had gone before. Music, architecture, the dance, poetry perhaps, and literature, were chiefly concerned with ideas and modes developed earlier. Drama, painting, and sculpture attracted the most attention, though critics rarely agreed on what the new forms of expression meant.

Cultivated people used to feel that there was a clear line between high culture and popular culture. True, there were grey areas of insecurity. Some media ignored these distinctions entirely. Perhaps they were false from the start. But given the great rate of cultural change in modern times, it was a comfort to believe there was a difference between the two cultures which one need not be expert to appreciate. In the 1960's this simple faith, already badly strained, collapsed. The resulting inability to distinguish between art and entertainment was one of the two most important cultural facts of the 1960's. The other was the growth of what became known as the counter-culture. It was related to the first in that critical standards had to blur if what the counter-culture did was to be called art. And, as morality followed art, the old moral values had to give way if the new standards were to be called virtuous.*

---

* Scholarly standards changed too, though less conspicuously than artistic ones. The most vivid example of this was the third edition of *Webster's New International Dictionary, Unabridged,* which came out in 1961. It was based on the principle that a dictionary should be "descriptive and not prescriptive." *Webster's Third* did not presume to judge, only to describe. Dwight Macdonald pointed out that the new dictionary "impoverishes the language by not objecting to errors if they are common enough." While adding some words not present in the first edition

In the 1940's and 1950's the abstract expressionists had made New York the world capital of serious painting. Though most people disliked non-representational work—which was why Andrew Wyeth was the single most popular American painter of modern times—critics and patrons admired it. Abstract expressionism continued to thrive during the sixties, judging by the price of major works which kept going up, but public attention was diverted by fresh novelties. An early example of these were the "happenings" that began in 1959. They were inspired partly by the Dadaist movement of the 1920's. Dada had been a violent, nihilistic protest. It was the first art form to use the "found environment," that is, streets, factories, and the like, instead of establishing its own context as in traditional art. But whereas Dada was based on outrage, both given and received, happenings tended toward the merely cute. They drew a little on surrealism, and on the Gutai, a group of Japanese artists in Osaka who put on a Dada-like presentation in 1957 that involved splashing water and paint around. They were influenced also by John Cage, a composer whose effect on a variety of post–avant-garde movements was incalculable.

The happenings were made by artists who reflected these earlier experiences. The first important one was staged by Allan Kaprow, then an art historian at Rutgers, and was called *18 Happenings in 6 Parts*. It had a more elaborately detailed script than most later efforts and took place in several different rooms at once. Even the audience had to behave in prescribed ways. It was followed in the next several years by many others—several artists for a time did nothing but stage happenings. Some were largely improvised, others followed formal scripts. Sites ranging from parking lots to stages to hotel courtyards were used and a great variety of equipment called into play. The most engaging happening was created by the Swiss artist Jean Tinguely. His *Homage to New York*, a self-destroying work of art, was set in motion at the Museum of Modern Art on March 17, 1960. It was twenty-three feet long and twenty-seven feet high and consisted of eighty wheels, a bathtub, a toy wagon, old bottles, and other junk, and was powered by fifteen motors. While sawing, beating, and burning itself to death, this assemblage of scrap also made music of a sort, did abstract paintings, and even reproduced itself when a segment detached from the parent machine and moved about under its own power. Most happenings, however, involved

of 1934, it dropped many more. This meant that half the words in the English language were lost between 1934 and 1961. Lexicography, once a barrier to the decay of language, now contributed to it.

human actors assisted (or overwhelmed) by various artifacts. They amused and irritated people for several years and then faded as a vogue, though people went on staging them.

At the time, happenings seemed related to the plastic arts. Most of their creators were, or had been, painters or sculptors. John Canaday thought the happenings were a reaction against purely abstract art, which had become wearisome. The happenings and other neo-Dadist expressions better satisfied the public's need for a chic new art form. Pop art did this even more satisfactorily, however, and soon eclipsed the happenings. Later events demonstrated that the happenings were more theatrical than not. They were part of a tradition of attempted escapes from formal theater's restrictions. But happenings were not done by professional theater people, which meant that they never became truly affecting or dramatic. They relied chiefly on technical effects, yet their technology was inadequate to the demands made on it. Some day, no doubt, machines will exist capable of doing what the happenings aimed at. The light shows, guerrilla theater, and other unconventional dramatic forms of the late sixties were foreshadowed by the happenings. They also probably better suggested how advanced technologies would be used for aesthetic and entertainment purposes in the future.

Pop art as such hit its stride in 1963. Admirers were quick to establish its pedigree. Picasso's *Plate with Wafers* (1914) was an early precedent, Stuart Davis's *Lucky Strike* (1921) another. Davis's 1924 depiction of a disinfectant bottle, *Odol*, was even more prophetic. The Dadaist relationship was so clear that pop art was often called neo-Dada. But like the happenings, pop was Dada without rage or politics. It also owed something to abstract expressionism, which it aimed to go beyond by developing a less restrictive and more iconographic style. Hilton Kramer called the formula "de Kooning plus Duchamp," which seems about right, though much pop was hard-edged and realistic. Robert Rauschenberg was probably the mode's originator. His first successful object work, *Bed* (1955), consisted of a real quilt and pillow. The quilt went on a stretcher and the pillow over it, then other designs and objects were added. At about the same time Jasper Johns was moving in the direction of his most celebrated work, *Painted Bronze* (1960). It was a casting of two Ballantine Ale cans, with the labels painted on. One had been opened. Another milestone was Jim Dine's *Green Suit* (1959), the first of his large collage-paintings in which actual objects became part of the design.

Pop objects and their creators received great publicity and correspondingly huge fees, not only from collectors and museums but from businesses as well. Demand stimulated output. Andy Warhol was one who early accepted the logic of this situation. At first he painted his soup cans and such. Then he began silk-screening them. At the end he simply made designs which his assistants executed over and over in a cavernous loft aptly named The Factory.

Early success did not turn Warhol's head. He continued to live with his mother and to dress (in dark glasses and leather jackets) as before. Reporters were invariably struck by his sweet disposition. Although nicer than most, he was not unique among pop artists in this respect. As a group they had largely avoided the long period of struggle and frustration through which the abstract expressionists had gone. Most of them were in or near their fifties before they began making big money. But Jasper Johns was living off his work at the age of twenty-nine, and in another five years was getting as much as $30,000 for a single piece. Other pop artists, junk sculptors, and the like did as well. Adversity was supposed to build character, yet obviously it did the affections little good. Abstract expressionists tended to be rough, abrasive characters, suspicious of others, resentful of the young artists who won so easily what they had battled to acquire, and cynical about the commercial context in which they functioned. Pop artists resembled their work in being comparatively open, flexible, tolerant, and accepting. The media liked them because they were good copy, businessmen because they were easy to merchandise, the jet set because they were comfortably fashionable, and the young because they were facile and undemanding.

All the same, pop art was as troubling for moralists as for aesthetes. In the past art had been thought to be both decorative and uplifting. Modern art, beginning in America with the so-called Ashcan School, and especially with the great Armory Show in 1913 which introduced cubism and other advanced European schools to this country, was once resented for being neither. But in time cultivated people accepted each successive avant garde as embodying moral insights more pertinent or valuable than what it displaced. Abstract expressionism, for example, was valid because it was complex, irrational, and freely expressive—like modern life. Since authority was everywhere being discredited, an art form that permitted, indeed demanded, that each man draw his own conclusions from it compelled respect. Pop art could make no such claim. A limp telephone might be witty or telling, but it could not nourish the spirit. Yet while the old notion that art should be elevating no longer carried weight, the moral function of art had become increasingly urgent. For many in the twentieth century, artists and writers had replaced priests and ministers as dispensers of truth. The cult of art (like the cult of psychoanalysis) was based on man's need for moral security in an uncertain time. Abstract expressionism met this need, for some anyway; pop art did not. Pop did not kill off the cult of art. There was still much to venerate. But it did create a moral vacuum and enabled the cynical, the posturing, or the merely addled to flourish as never before. It also provided the counter-culture with useful excuses. When everything became potentially a work of art, and everyman an artist, anyone could claim to be living for truth or beauty without having to prove it. So the collapse of agreed-on standards in art permitted a similar erosion in life.

The most conspicuous development in literature after 1960 was the triumph of sexual freedom. An early sign of this was the surfacing of erotic literature. In 1960 federal courts ruled that D. H. Lawrence's novel *Lady Chatterley's Lover* (1928) was not obscene. The Post Office's long struggle to keep Americans from reading it was abandoned. Few serious people doubted that *Lady Chatterley*, though imperfectly realized, was a work of literature. But its sexual passages were so explicit that obscenity now became entirely a matter of context. Material which of itself was clearly pornographic by older standards ceased being so if properly presented. And the Supreme Court confused the issue even more. On the one hand, a work was acceptable if it did not violate "prevailing community standards," on the other, if it had redeeming social or aesthetic importance. Few books on sex failed to offend Middle America. Few were entirely without social significance. In practice the Supreme Court's rules could not be applied, and very quickly the remaining barriers against erotic literature fell. First *Lady Chatterley* and Henry Miller's long-suppressed *Tropic of Cancer* appeared. Their publishers fought many good fights on every level of government to distribute them. Enough were won to make feasible the release of other literary efforts long thought too stimulating for public consumption. The next step was the publication of books like *The Memoirs of a Woman of Pleasure (Fanny Hill)* and Frank Harris's autobiography *My Life and Loves*. There was something to be said for both of these. *Fanny Hill*, an eighteenth-century *tour de force*, managed to be erotic without using obscene or even coarse language. In its way it was a triumph of delicacy. Harris's book was more earthy and more important. He had figured prominently in turn-of-the-century journalism and literature. He was also a persistent and ingenious womanizer. Hence his memoirs contained much interesting, if unreliable, gossip about men of letters, together with fascinating, and rather more creditable, information on the sexual underground of his time.

Once these books were allowed, literary pornography all but disappeared as a legal concept. No sexy book was so dismal or meretricious that a redeeming spark of social or moral illumination could not be found in it. In a few years everything from the Marquis de Sade on down was freely available. The hue and cry against pornography continued, but, where the written word was concerned, to little effect. College bookstores automatically put the latest Victorian pornography from Grove Press on their shelves. One Ivy League bookshop thoughtfully grouped the most salacious work of every publisher together on a single rack, blandly labeled "Dirty Books." Middle America saw this new freedom as yet another expression of moral decay. Small towns and cities went on censoring books, the Supreme Court notwithstanding. But elsewhere the fight was lost. The functional excuse for censorship had always been that pornography led to self-abuse and sex crimes. Even if God didn't require its suppression, public health and safety did. Many now disputed this. Some argued that masturbation was tolerable, even desirable. The link between pornography and sex offenses was denied. For one thing, there was no proof of it. On the available evidence one could as easily argue the reverse and say that pornography offered a harmless way of discharging frustrations that might otherwise be a problem. From this perspective, pornography as such was socially redeeming. Denmark legalized pornography of all sorts at the decade's end with no apparent ill effects. No one was surprised when under free-market conditions the products' quality improved. Many were when the volume of sales inside Denmark declined. Few Americans were prepared to examine the question on its merits. Yet as plays and movies became progressively more explicit in the sixties, who could say that the Danish solution would never be applied here?

Theatrical developments in the sixties paralleled those in other arts. Structure became less important and sex more so. The cult of youth, romanticism, the preference for instinct and spontaneity, the urge to propagandize flourished. Some found these tendencies amusing, even important, but few serious critics did. Those who once expected the avant-garde theater to redeem the commercial theater were especially depressed. Most had long since given up on Broadway with its glossy musicals and comedies. What was called Off Broadway had higher aims, and sometimes met them. It depended heavily on foreign playwrights (Anouilh, Genet) and a few native talents such as Edward Albee. The Living Theater was a radical company that in *The Connection* (1960) and *The Brig* (1963) was impressive. There were some great moments as when the American Place Theater performed Robert Lowell's *Old Glory* in 1964. It was, perhaps, the most original American work of the decade.

Even so, when Robert Brustein collected his theater reviews for the years 1959–65 he called the book *Seasons of Discontent*. Already it seemed to him Off Broadway was alternating between what was safe and what was sensational. Some plays exploited Negro protest themes (in 1964 alone these included *Blues for Mr. Charlie, The Blacks, In White America,* and *Dutchman*), others repeated the tired formulas of commercial theater. The Lincoln Center Repertory Theater typified the latter. It opened in 1964 amidst great fanfare as a subsidized alternative to Broadway. Lincoln Center was supposed to have Broadway's professional virtues but not its timid box-office orientation. Yet critics found Lincoln Center's first season to be not so much a challenge to Broadway as an echo of it. They were all the more certain when Elia Kazan defended his first offerings by claiming that two were hits. Later the group, under new management, would do better, though not enough better to justify its pretensions.

As Off Broadway grew more like the real thing, its place was filled by what was inevitably called "Off Off Broadway" (or, by Brustein, the Third Theater). But it too suffered from the same vices as Off Broadway, modishness in particular. Vogue followed vogue, theater of the absurd one year, theater of cruelty the next. In the late sixties counter-cultural values became dominant—nudity, sexual perversion, spontaneity, anti-Establishmentarianism, and the like. One of the earliest and most successful attempts to make the counter-culture pay was a musical called *Hair*. It was first produced Off Off Broadway by the La Mama troupe, a penniless avant-garde company. Inspired by the hippie phenomenon, it was billed as the first tribal-love-rock musical and won attention particularly for a scene in which performers of both sexes disrobed. It moved to Broadway, made a mint, and inspired countless imitations.

Hair did not have especially lofty aims. It advanced the usual propaganda of the youth culture, but in a cheerful, entertaining way. Other works were more ambitious. Tom O'Horgan, its director, also brought forth a play called *Futz* about a farmer who loved his pig. This provided the occasion for wild scenes where actors stood on their heads, climbed on each others' backs, droned inaudibly when they were not shouting, and mimed various sexual acts. Playwright, script, plot, and speech itself receded. Improvisation, audience participation, bare flesh, and obscene language prevailed. Sometimes this approach was critically successful, as in *Big Time Buck White*, which was written and first performed in Los Angeles. It did well because improvisation and audience participation were appropriate to a play centered on a meeting of black radicals. But mostly sensation took the place of craftsmanship. Only hard-core partisans of the counter-culture admired *Futz*.

Dionysus in 69 attracted wider audiences, perhaps because better done, maybe because of its grandiloquent claims. About 40 per cent of the dialogue was from Euripides, the balance was supplied by Richard Schechner, a drama professor at New York University and leader of the Performance Group which staged it. The audience sat around on the floor and climbed up on wooden structures representing the towers of Thebes. Sometimes they participated in the show. One character, Pentheus, always selected a girl from the audience to make love to, and went as far with her as she and the law permitted. The play changed constantly. Sometimes the members of the cast disrobed. It was a financial success even though critics were divided. John Simon called it "group therapy for actors" and notable for "bad diction and worse odors." Robert Brustein and Walter Kerr felt the same way, but Clive Barnes, a determined friend of the new, liked it and so did the more traditional Harold Clurman.

The main feature of *Dionysus in 69* was not nudity but the ethic it embodied. Schechner, who received a doctorate from Tulane University and edited the *Drama Review* for six years, was the new theater's leading ideologist. He saw the drama as a "visual-verbal participatory game" as well as a form of communal celebration. The Polish playwright Grotowski was said to have inspired him with a sense of religious dedication to the theater. Schechner's enthusiasm for group therapy was all his own. The Performance Group worked constantly at removing their hostilities and aggressions. They had an encounter group session guided by trained leaders once a week. The result was not so much a theatrical company as a way of life.

The Living Theater went even further. It had been organized by Judith Malina and her husband Julian Beck in the 1950's as an avant-garde theatrical company which expressed its radicalism mainly in aesthetic terms. As the McCarthy era gave way to the new age, the Becks grew more political, participating in sit-ins and anti-bomb protests. Their plays became more deliberately polemical too. Then, for obscure and doubtlessly political reasons of its own, the federal government closed down the Living Theater for nonpayment of taxes. After much harassment the Becks went to court and staged an impromptu drama featuring truth and beauty versus the military-industrial complex, with their troupe serving as Greek chorus. The Becks got short jail sentences, after which the whole company left for Europe. Having been politicized by the Internal Revenue Service, they began living together as a tribe or commune, and solved, as they thought, the problem of how to fuse art with propaganda. Their performances involved radical declarations, a minimum of dialogue, personal encounters with the audience, and the sexual revolution.

In 1968 they came back to America and took their most famous work,

Paradise Now, on tour. It began with the troupe protesting against cloth-ing, drug laws, and other forms of repression. Then the performers par-tially undressed and tried to coerce and seduce the audience into join-ing them. Any kind of audience response, hostile or friendly, became part of the play. At most performances a few audience members were moved to strip, sometimes completely, and join the "flesh pile." Though critics admired the Becks' courage and dedication (by the end of 1968 they had been arrested fifteen times and had had four theaters closed by four different federal agencies), they disliked the Living Theater's new style. Clive Barnes of the *New York Times* applauded it because the young did, and because the troupe, though bad actors, were "physically as highly tuned as dancers."

Richard Gilman thought *Paradise Now* exhibited "everything flaccid and indulgent and embarrassing about their work." At one point Beck cried that there were fifteen hundred prisoners in a nearby jail. " 'We're going to march on the jail and free them later tonight, who will march with us?' Of course no one marches, of course the prisoners remain. Easy, irresponsible, outrageous." It seemed to Gilman that instead of freeing the theater from artifice and unreality, the Living Theater had merely substituted its own conventions while arrogating to itself much unearned moral increment. The players wanted to have it both ways, "to be a theater of public and political use and at the same time to be a community in search of its own salvation." "It's not a show, it's the real thing," a member of the group shrieked during *Paradise Now.* "No, it's not the real thing, it's a show," Gilman concluded.

Of all the critics Robert Brustein, later dean of the Yale drama school, was probably most depressed by the Living Theater. Indeed, he had been discouraged about the theater in general since 1965 when he wrote (of Le Roi Jones, Edward Albee, and William Hanley): "What results is less an artistic quest than a fashionable posture or personal exhibi-tion, with the playwright producing not masterpieces but conversation pieces. This, to be sure, is the characteristic art of our time. Now that the cultural revolution has become an arm of big business, the mass media, and the fashion magazine, values have all but disappeared from artistic creation, and a crowd of hipsters and their agents are cynically exploiting the fears and pretensions of a semi-educated public. Must we choose between a discredited Establishment and a careerist avant garde? Are the only alternatives to be between the collapsed idealism of the old and the secret cynicism of the new?" But things deteriorated even more rapidly than Brustein feared. He had admired the Living Theater before it went into exile, and he saw the new theater as a promising movement. Given its radical and anti-war flavor he thought it in danger of suppres-sion. But to his surprise it flourished. "This development," he wrote early in 1969, "paralleled a failure of nerve among the middle classes, as the forces of conventional culture seemed to grow guilty and weak before the culture of the young, and the American avant garde, for the first time in its history, became the glass of fashion and the mold of form." The Third Theater accelerated the growth of callowness, sloppiness, and arrogance—as had the Black Power and New Left movements. "What once seemed daring and original now often seems tiresome and familiar; stereotyped political assertions, encouraged by their easy acceptance, have replaced instinctive, individual dissent." Increasingly the Third Theater was noteworthy for its anti-intellectualism, sexual obsessiveness, massacre of language, noisy attention-getting devices, and its indifference to artistry, craft, and skill. Its mindless tributes to love and togetherness were "not adversary demands upon the American character but rather the very qualities that have continually degraded us."

The Living Theater, Brustein was sorry to say, not only reflected this change but helped advance it. "The company had become a self-generating and self-perpetuating organism whose existence was more important than any work it performed; and it was infused with a sense of mission that was less theatrical or even political than religious and evangelical." It made meretricious appeals to free prisoners and stop the war, but whenever things threatened to get out of hand it retreated into its theatrical function. The audience was never allowed to change the tone or flow of the performance. It spoke constantly of love though bristling with aggression. "The company had now taken on the very authoritarian qualities it had once denounced; the very repressiveness that had driven it from the country four years before." This was bad news for the theater, and even more for the country. The young loved these performances. "This extraordinary generation, upon whom so much praise and attention have been lavished, cannot help but inspire feelings of respect—but my respect is becoming mixed with great apprehension. At once so vital and idealistic, and so childish, irrational, and overindulged," it now seemed bent on replicating the worst aspects of radical culture in the 1930's. Brustein saw the same "abuse of truths that do not serve political ends, the same contempt for writers who do not try to change their times, the same monolithic modes of thought, the same assaults on any expression that is not a form of consent." And their elders, who should have known better, encouraged the young in their follies.

Brustein concluded: "We honor the young because without them there is no future. But there will surely be no future either unless the more extreme of our young can cease from trying to annihilate the past. With our civilization tottering, the temptation is strong to release our hold on reality and credit the most fantastic flights of absurdity simply because they signify change. But the more radical inventions of the new generation are nothing if they proceed from the same violent and mindless sources that originally brought our civilization to this terrifying juncture. We fail the future when we surrender what we know and value for the sake of fashion and influence, and we fail the theater when we countenance the rejection of language, form, and accomplishment in favor of an easy culture."

Yet worse was to come. In March 1969 the Theater of Ideas, a forum of the New York intellectual establishment, organized a symposium called "Theatre or Therapy." It featured Julian Beck and Judith Malina of the Living Theater, and, among their critics, Brustein and Paul Goodman. Brustein wrote his remarks out in the expectation of being heckled. He was, but managed to finish anyway. Judith Malina spoke briefly after Goodman, then the Living Theater company, leaping and screaming, took over the hall. The audience screamed back. Goodman tried to reestablish communications, but that failing he left. One actor took a woman's purse and emptied it on the floor. Another woman said to Beck, "Today I feel more hate than I have ever felt in my life. I'm going home now. I'm going to write a poem about the hate I feel for you." Richard Schechner of the Performance Group called for five minutes of meditation "to think about the beautiful thing that's happening here." It was too noisy to think though. Norman Mailer tried vainly to still the tumult. Judith Malina regained the microphone and declared everything that had gone on to be beautiful and good as well as spontaneous and authentic. Stanley Kauffmann, the critic, rose up at this to shout, "You're lying. The whole thing was phony! You brought your stooges here tonight and staged the whole dismal affair." Miss Malina replied that on the contrary it was only freedom at work. Another audience member asked, "What about our freedom? We weren't allowed to have what we paid for. Your freedom is our repression!" Beck proclaimed disruption to be the wave of the future. The audience finally dispersed, having paid $10 each for the privilege of being abused, and, unlike the Off Off Broadway audiences, not enjoying it a bit.

Though many felt that creative ferment could hardly go further, it did. The Playhouse of the Ridiculous explored yet another possibility. The *New York Times* began a story on it as follows. "Jackie Curtis, 21, 5 feet 11 inches, gender male, 'not a boy, not a girl, not a faggot, not a drag queen, not a transsexual—just me, Jackie,' grooving down St. Mark's Place in mini-skirt, ripped black tights, clunky heels, chestnut curls, no falsies ('I'm not trying to pass as a woman'), Isadora scarf gallantly breezing behind her, is the newest playwright to make the Off Off Broadway scene. Her first play, 'Heaven Grand in Amber Orbit,' a rock musical written last year on a train on the way home from the

Pornography Festival at Notre Dame where she starred in Ronald Tavel's 'Lady Godiva,' is being performed by the Playhouse of the Ridiculous at the Gotham Art Theater." Any reader who thought this a put-on was soon disabused. Jackie was real, so was the Playhouse of the Ridiculous. It specialized in nonplays, a pastiche of Shakespeare, Aeschylus, old movies, grand opera, commercials, and what all. John Vaccaro, founder and director of the Playhouse, used it to project his bedlamite view of the universe. The stage resembled "an animated Bosch painting with perpetual sexual motion." Sex was shown in so many ways at once as to lose not only all meaning but most other attributes too. It also showed up "the 'radical' sexual pieties of other New Theater groups—the salvation-through-orgasm faith of the Living Theater, and the Performance Group's concept of purification through group grope— as merely the latest packaging of the power-of-positive-thinking for the hip market." The Playhouse specialized in "thalidomide humor." Its players were troll-like creatures, notable for their "buoyant nihilism."

However weird, the Playhouse was most remarkable for having gone beyond what were already the clichés of porno-political theater. Whether separately or together, pornography and politics dominated the "experimental" theater in 1969 even more than in 1968. In *Sweet Eros* a girl was kidnaped, stripped, tied to a chair, and lectured at by her abductor. The female lead, an actress named Sally Kirkland who specialized in these parts, had no understudy. And little wonder, as she had to sit in the nude on a drafty stage for forty minutes without saying a word. Art demanded much of other new-wave performers also. In one play, *The Young Master Dante*, the star got sick and his understudy had to go on unprepared. Walter Kerr thought it one of the really memorable events in recent theatrical history, for the hero had to take off all his clothes while holding a bulky script in one hand. He seemed pleased to reach the big castration scene in which he had no dialogue. In Rochelle Owens' *Belch*, a boy had his loincloth snatched away while he was busy strangling himself. In *Geese* two nude men made love to one another; so did two nude women. What did all this strained, portentous disrobing amount to, Kerr wondered? Was it "the last Puritanism? The ultimate, utterly candid exposure of sex for the ghastly thing it is?"* No it wasn't. *Che* was. *Che* was the decade's last word in pornopolitical theater. It had four characters: Che himself, the American President, a nun, and a woman known as Mr. Fong. The President was naked throughout except for his Uncle Sam hat. The nun was mostly nude too. Che was clothed, though he took his penis out at times to illustrate a philosophical point or advance the action. The actors touched

---

* Helen Hayes said: "We had nudity on the stage in my youth, you know. In the Ziegfeld Follies. But it was beautiful nudity. Now it's sort of grubby."

each others' privates and mimed sex acts. They were all arrested for lewdness, obscenity, and consentual sodomy. Attorney William M. Kunstler, soon to become a household word because of the great Chicago Conspiracy Trial, defended *Che* for its redeeming social value. Richard Gilman thought the worst thing about this pathetic spectacle was that the actors only pretended to commit sex. "There is never the slightest suggestion in this most anaphrodisiac of events that anyone is being aroused; nothing rises or flows, nothing leaps or trembles. The sad, unlovely, unbelievably inept performers, young persons reeling up to the frontier, wander zombi-like through all the proceedings, zonked, most probably, on acid as real persons, and, as performers, flattened by the sheer improbability of what they are being called upon to do."

It was all very liberating, no doubt. But few believed that art gained much in consequence. When Sir Noel Coward visited New York he went to see *Oh! Calcutta!*, a nude review. He announced beforehand that he didn't expect to be impressed much. He had seen plenty of naked people in his long life, and still thought suggestion better than statement. Yet so long as depicting sex was hedged about with thrill-producing restrictions, the theater would continue to exploit it. There was some reason to think allowing sexual intercourse in public might be a good thing, if only to have it done with. Once all the taboos were broken and the novelty diminished, the theater might then return to its proper business. It might anyhow, for nude theater was not very profitable once the initial shock subsided. *Oh! Calcutta!* alone made big money.

Films changed radically during the sixties also. This was of greater moment than theatrical changes, if only because movies had a larger audience. When the decade opened Hollywood was still trying to compete with television. Movie houses were closing and profits going down. Most studios appreciated that movies would have to offer something that TV couldn't. Epics seemed one answer. Wide-screen fables with casts of thousands were too expensive for TV, and too grandiose for the small screen anyway. A remake of *Ben Hur* earned huge profits and was followed by movies like *Solomon and Sheba, Exodus, The Alamo,* and *Spartacus.* Most were as dismal and none so lucrative as *Ben Hur.* The industry did not allow for the fact that its audience was changing. An early hint of this was provided by the success of pictures like *The Apartment, Butterfield 8,* and *Elmer Gantry.* While not particularly distinguished (though Burt Lancaster was splendid as Elmer Gantry), they cost less to make than epics and were often more profitable. They were all "adult" films, meaning more mature or controversial, or at least racy, than television dared to be. Though not especially sexy by later standards, they went as far as the censor allowed.

The most striking example in this vein was a foreign picture, *Never on Sunday*, which was cheap, meretricious, and enormously profitable. It was made by Jules Dassin, who as one of the notorious "Hollywood Ten" had refused to testify before Congress during the McCarthy era and was blacklisted by the industry. Some of the ten were kept on to work under false names at greatly reduced prices. Others like Dassin went to Europe. *Never on Sunday* was his revenge. It used the reliable old "whore with a heart of gold" formula, which made it an adult picture. Actually, the theme was only a pretext for an attack on American values as personified by a tourist in Greece. Whether its smirking approach to sex or its crude anti-Americanisms were more pernicious could hardly be determined. Yet the film was thought witty and daring and made a bundle. Thus Dassin swept the board. He beat the Hollywood moguls at their own game—the mass merchandising of bad taste—defied their efforts to ruin or exploit him, retained his left-wing prejudices, and was applauded for doing so, even by the critics. The film was indeed a *tour de force*, though not for the reasons then given. And, considering the type of men who ran Hollywood in those days, its success was almost merited.

The profits earned from adult pictures, together with the failure of such gimmicks as three-dimensional movies, guaranteed that in the future films would be sexier than ever—Bosley Crowther and the Legion of Decency notwithstanding. Crowther, though he was for most of the decade principal film critic of the *New York Times,* resisted the industry's growing sophistication. The adult pictures of 1960 inspired a vintage Crowtherian protest against "the tendency of producers, made evident in any number of recent films, to go for licentious stories and/or inject extreme and gross sex details in their works." The Legion of Decency, an organization that rated films as to their conformity with Roman Catholic moral standards, handed out its once feared condemnations more often. The Vatican called for an end to "degrading spectacles" in motion pictures, and the National Council of Churches denounced the tendency toward more sex and gore. None of this had much effect.

In 1961 a rash of "nudies" broke out. These were low-budget "sexploitation" films which got progressively gamier. Orthodox morality did not give way all at once. The Supreme Court upheld the right of communities to censor movies. The University of Illinois fired an assistant professor of biology for saying, in a letter to the school newspaper, that premarital intercourse led to better marriages. The American Civil Liberties Union rose glumly to his defense in vain. Despite successful rearguard actions of this type, the trend continued.

The mass media not only got sexier but more political also. John Le Carré's novel *The Spy Who Came In from the Cold* was a great success though it showed the espionage establishments on both sides of the Cold War to be equally vile. Nevil Shute's widely read *On the Beach* had humanity extinguish itself through nuclear war. Films brought the same messages to larger audiences. The novel *Fail-Safe* (accidental war again) became a movie; so did *Seven Days in May*, a fantasy concerning an abortive military *coup* in Washington. The most powerful of all was Stanley Kubrick's *Dr. Strangelove, or How I Learned to Stop Worrying and Love the Bomb*. Kubrick, perhaps the greatest American filmmaker since Orson Welles, had earlier made *Lolita*, a masterpiece of black comedy and even pathos. After *Strangelove* would come his awesome *2001*. *Strangelove* owed something to both of these. It employed black humor techniques and used technological effects to reach for higher levels of reality than films commonly aimed at.

So great a work defies summary, but the plot must be outlined to understand the reactions to it. Accidental war threatens the super-powers when Air Force General Jack D. Ripper (Sterling Hayden) sends his bomber wing to attack Russia. He expects this will force America to launch a pre-emptive strike against the Soviets, whom he blames for poisoning the world's water supplies so as to contaminate man's "precious bodily essences."* Instead President Merkin Muffley (Peter Sellers) gives American military secrets to the Russians so that they may shoot the bombers down, over the protests of General Buck Turgidson (George C. Scott) who suspects a commie trick. But one of the planes does get through, triggering a Russian Doomsday Machine that will make the earth uninhabitable. At this point Dr. Strangelove (Peter Sellers again), an unregenerate ex-Nazi scientist, devises a plan to save the military-industrial elite by building huge bunkers in mine shafts before radioactivity eliminates life above ground. There, aided by nubile females who will greatly outnumber them, the leaders will rebuild the Gross National Product to prewar levels. Certain that the Russians must have similar plans, General Turgidson urges the President not to allow a "mine-shaft gap." The film ends with a beautiful sequence of thermonuclear explosions.

This brilliantly written, acted, and directed picture did not appeal much to patriotic Americans. Bosley Crowther, who viewed it twice, thought the movie subversive. Lewis Mumford saw it differently. Calling it "the first break" in the nation's "cold war trance," he went on to say: "What has masked the hideous nature of our demoralized strategy

---

* This was a common delusion at the time. Extremists in America considered fluoridated water part of the international communist conspiracy. As they were often able to prevent its use, untold millions of dental cavities resulted.

of total extermination is just the fact that it has been the work of other-wise well-balanced, responsible men, beginning with Henry L. Stimson. What the wacky characters in *Dr. Strangelove* are saying is precisely what needs to be said: this nightmare eventuality that we have con-cocted for our children is nothing but a crazy fantasy, by nature as hor-ribly crippled and dehumanized as Dr. Strangelove himself. It is not this film that is sick: what is sick is our supposedly moral, democratic coun-try which allowed this policy to be formulated and implemented with-out even the pretense of open public debate." It was hardly odd to find Mumford saying this. What was unusual was to find such pillars of the Establishment as *Time* and *Life* magazines, faithful soldiers in the Cold War though they were, agreeing in part. *Dr. Strangelove* was not only a cultural triumph but a political, even a psychological, one. It showed what the country's "defense" policy was really like. Many went on be-lieving that the film was crazy and the government sound. But others had their vision changed for good, especially after the Indochinese war drove the point home again.

In the mid-sixties movies were sexier than ever. The star system peaked out. As big names were thought the best insurance against fail-ure, they commanded as much as a million dollars a picture plus a share of the profits. Curiously enough, one of the most compelling stars in this period, Humphrey Bogart, was no longer alive. Yet his films were re-vived again and again with much success. The Brattle Theater in Cam-bridge, Massachusetts, which was thought to have begun the phe-nomenon, held annual Bogart festivals so popular they needed no announcements. The audience for these films was too young to remem-ber Bogart. They saw his wartime pictures, like *Casablanca*, out of con-text. As he died in 1957 many had not even seen his last movies when they were new. The striking thing about the Bogart revival was its moral seriousness. It was not just a pop culture fad (like the passion for Busby Berkeley musicals a bit later). Nor was it aesthetic in the manner of the Charlie Chaplin cult. The young admired Bogart for a style that was also a moral code. In life, as on the screen, he was a good man who suspected the appearance of goodness. He despised pretense. When dying, he was said to have remarked, "What's everybody whispering about? I've got cancer. For Christ's sake, it's not a venereal disease." He maintained this special tone throughout his last year. He entertained visitors martini in hand, though too weak to drink it. On retiring he always kissed his wife, the actress Lauren Bacall, and said, "Good night." The night he died Bogart put his hand on her arm and said, "Good-bye, kid."

His films were informed with this same emphasis on style as a moral statement. Peter Bogdanovich described the essential Bogart character as "a man who tried very hard to be bad because he knew it was easier to get along in the world that way. He always failed because of an innate goodness which surely nauseated him. Almost always he went from belligerent neutrality to reluctant commitment." Bogart played men who lived in a time when the old verities no longer applied. Scoundrels waved the flag and flourished; decent people went under. Bogart's characters wanted to be smart and cynical, but were defeated by their integrity. So, with a dour wisecrack, conceding nothing in principle, they obeyed the dictates of honor. That is what Bogart's life and work were all about, how to live with dignity in hard times. Bogart's admirers were attracted chiefly by Bogart's ethics. In his tough, flippant way, what Bogart said to them was that the world was a bad place and getting worse. No man could live in it exactly as he pleased. Yet he could still be a man, accepting life and death for what they were without giving way before them. If willing to pay the price he could live, and die, with honor.

In admiring Bogart the young showed their need for a believable heroism. Yet this does not wholly explain the Bogart phenomenon. As man and actor Bogart was sophisticated and stoical, a mature figure who lived with his back to the wall, morally speaking. These are not attributes that commonly attract the young. They are thought of (especially by themselves) as "idealistic," meaning endowed with absurdly high, but temporary, moral aspirations. They like dash, romanticism, and simple answers. Their feelings toward Bogart (as later for Eugene McCarthy) hardly squared with their other tastes. Perhaps Bogart appealed only to a discriminating minority. Or perhaps the young are more complex than is thought. In either case, their enthusiasm for Bogart, though it tapered off after the middle sixties, was one of the period's more encouraging vogues.

Three years after *Dr. Strangelove* a film appeared, from outside the star system, that showed another side of the American character. *Bonnie and Clyde*'s director, Arthur Penn, was not yet well known. Warren Beatty, who played Clyde and produced the film, was not a big star. The picture was introduced with little fanfare but soon became the subject of controversy. Though based on a gang of actual bank robbers, it took liberties with historical fact. It was too violent by far. Pauline Kael analyzed the public reaction with the care it warranted. First off, she asked, why do people criticize a fictional work for being inauthentic? "I would suggest that when a movie so clearly conceived as a new version of a legend is attacked as historically inaccurate, it's because it shakes people a little."

In life Bonnie and Clyde were not beautiful people like Faye Dunaway and Warren Beatty. But if the leads had not been beautiful the audience would not have been attracted to them, and their deaths would have been less affecting. Then too, people, though not so many as before, did not see the film as an aesthetic medium. "To ask why people react so angrily to the best movies and have so little negative reaction to poor ones is to imply that they are so unused to the experience of art in movies that they fight it." People objected to all the killing, "but the whole point of *Bonnie and Clyde* is to rub our noses in it, to make us pay our dues for laughing. . . . Suddenly in the last few years, our view of the world has gone beyond 'good taste.' Tasteful suggestions of violence would at this point be a more grotesque form of comedy than *Bonnie and Clyde* attempts." Actually, what was objected to was not the violence itself— many films were more sanguinary—but the way it was presented. The principals were gorgeous and the supporting players warm, funny, and endearing. The movie was full of comic episodes, but the violence under- lying them always came up to jolt the audience. The gang knocks over a bank in a hilariously contrived way with banjos whanging away on the sound track and quaint old cars buzzing about. Suddenly a man jumps on a running board to stop them and is shot in the face. As the film un- winds the comic episodes become fewer. One member, already horribly wounded, dies in a gun battle, another is captured, and a third turns traitor. Bonnie and Clyde are ambushed and in slow motion a thousand bullets tear them apart.

By involving the audience so deeply in these characterizations the film, as Miss Kael pointed out, "puts the sting back in death." Hence, though ostensibly not even about the 1960's, *Bonnie and Clyde* rendered the spirit of the age more finely than any other picture, except perhaps *Dr. Strangelove*. It was one of those very few works that posterity could use to judge the era fairly.

Another influence on films, and even more on the counter-culture, were the underground movies of the late sixties. Cheap, experimental film- making had been going on for years. But in the sixties it acquired a special cachet, thanks especially to Andy Warhol and Norman Mailer. As a pop artist Warhol was remarkable chiefly for his organizing and merchandising skills. In The Factory his assistants turned out pop arti- facts wholesale that retailed for astonishing prices (as much as $1,300 for a single Brillo box). In the mid-sixties he brought these gifts to the film world. The Factory became a studio producing a movie a week. Only one, *The Chelsea Girls*, was a commercial success, but it paid for all the others. On an investment of $1,500 it returned a million and a half dollars by the end of 1968.* Though his films verged on the pornographic (in 1969 his *Andy Warhol's Blue Movie*—perhaps his best, certainly his funniest picture—was banned in tolerant New York for depicting a real sex act), and he was surrounded by a large and bizarre entourage (including his famous superstars like Viva, Ultra Violet, and Ingrid Superstar herself), he lived with his mother and went to mass every Sunday. Such a man was clearly not to be judged by conventional standards, if at all. Stephen Koch suggested that Warhol was the climax of the traditional attack on men of action. With him passivity was carried to machine-like lengths. He admired machines. In a sense he was a machine, that is to say, a celebrity, the ultimate human object. He once said that "in the future everybody will be world-famous for at least fifteen minutes." Warhol himself was famous chiefly for being famous.

In a strange way, Norman Mailer seemed Warhol's mirror-image. Active, masculine, a true genius, the novelist also became a filmmaker (and confessed his debt to Warhol). *Beyond the Law,* his second picture, was released in 1968 and became the first to win some critical approval. It was a fictional documentary concerning one night in a precinct house. Mailer himself played Police Lieutenant Francis Xavier Pope. The cast included professional actors like Rip Torn and Beverly Bentley (his fourth wife), friends, and assorted notables. *Beyond the Law* embodied his theory of feedback. "Feedback is when you're watching the kookie girl and the doctor in 'Petulia,' you're also aware that they're Julie Christie and George C. Scott. . . . Feedback has become the condition of our lives. . . . We've passed the point in our civilization where we can ever look at anything as art work. There is always our knowledge of it and of the making of it."

Feedback was the governing principle in the world the media made. *Beyond the Law* brought it to a culmination of sorts. Norman Mailer the celebrity played a part in a film about people who were really celebrities that was produced and directed by the celebrity Norman Mailer. The

---

* Warhol had other sources of income too. When Valerie Solanos shot him in June 1968 he improved the occasion by dictating a novel, called *a*, while still hospitalized. Solanos was a bit player in one of his movies, who thought Warhol was frustrating her genius. She had also founded an ultrafeminist organization, SCUM (Society for Cutting Up Men), so her act, however irrational, was not without principle. SCUM's manifesto began: "Life in this society being, at best, an utter bore and no aspect of society being at all relevant to women, there remains to civic-minded, responsible, thrill-seeking females only to overthrow the government, eliminate the money system, institute a complete automation, and destroy the male sex." She meant to end Warhol's career but only succeeded in adding a new dimension to it. All the same, he confessed later that being shot had dimmed his view of human nature.

result was a kind of boxes-within-boxes effect that both satirized and embodied the American way. And, as usual with Mailer, one could not always tell what was meant and what was mocked. Even his role as film-maker, to which he devoted great hunks of time and talent, was suspect. "Since I've been a sort of notorious—if you will—character all these years, it was inevitable that I should make movies. I wouldn't be fulfilling my duty as a . . . public character if I didn't." But neither, in a way, would he have been fully discharging his prophetic and aesthetic obligations. For by this time movies had gotten a long way past entertainment. To the young especially, movies carried moral and artistic charges that other institutions had formerly borne.

Though few doubted that films could be great, some critics, like Richard Schickel, wondered if movies were really the central art form of modern times as many claimed. For one thing, Schickel asked, who went to movies? Half the audience for them was under twenty-four years of age, three-fourths was under forty. The regulars who went once a month or oftener were mainly college students or recent graduates. In 1948, 3.1 billion movie tickets had been sold. Since 1963 the annual audience had stabilized at about 1.1 billion. The industry prospered by raising ticket prices and selling films to television. The movies were, by comparison with TV, more a specialized than a mass medium, and the social class they appealed to was "less sure of itself, less intensively educated, more panicky about its status than any we have ever known." It was precisely its weaknesses that drew this class to motion pictures. Movies were easy to consume. Unlike a major novel, a film could be absorbed in a few hours. Movies required little technical knowledge to appreciate, so people who found painting, sculpture, or the dance too demanding naturally liked them. They were, Schickel thought, ideal for the "half-baked intellectuals" generated by the population and education explosions. And, it might be added, as the tools for filming them got simpler, it was never so easy to make the transition from viewer to producer. A little equipment and a few hundred dollars was all one needed to film an underground movie.

Like rock music, films answered young peoples' need for ethical reassurance. Though the churches made extraordinary efforts to attract them, no jazzed-up worship service was half so agreeable as *The Graduate*, for example. This thin, though funny, picture became 1968's most popular movie. More than that, it was almost holy writ for many students who identified with the befuddled anti-hero's efforts to find himself. As films became more moral they also got dirtier, that is to say, sex became more explicit. The youthful audience demanded it, and thanks to liberalized court rulings, filmmakers were able to respond. The results were mixed, on the one hand a rash of cheaply made "skin flicks," on the other a handful of beautifully expressive pictures that could not have been made before. Naturally, the mothers of America protested, especially in the provinces. Their fear that youthful morals would be ruined by the sight of, for example, Jane Fonda peeling off her garments in the science-fiction sex spoof *Barbarella* (in free fall yet) was genuine, if absurd. To solve this problem the Motion Picture Association in 1968 developed its first effective rating system to specify particular audiences for films. The MPA believed that most pictures would be voluntarily submitted for rating, and that most theaters would cooperate. In this manner it hoped to avoid legal censorship. Surprisingly enough, the scheme worked out pretty well, at first anyway. Legal censorship was averted, even though by the decade's end commercial films showed everything except closeup shots of sexual intercourse (and stag film theaters in Los Angeles went all the way). This was important to the industry because there was money in high-quality sex films. If the grindhouse "sexploitation" pictures were suppressed, little would be lost. *Blow-up* made vastly more money than *Moonlighting Wives*, and *Belle du Jour* was a great success while *Orgy Girl* went nowhere, as Stanley Kauffmann pointed out. "The paperbound publishers long ago found out that the really big money is in what they call 'literary pornography' more than in sleazy junk—not only because it is more defensible in court but because more people feel comfortable about buying it and because (the valid aesthetic argument) it is better done and thus more satisfyingly erotic." Hence it was vital to keep the backlash against skin flicks from sweeping away the quality sex films. At the decade's end this seemed to have been accomplished.

In 1969 the young and their counter-culture dominated movies, as viewers and, increasingly, as filmmakers too. A whole series of expensive films bombed; a cluster of cheaply produced, youth-oriented pictures did well. The studios that produced extravaganzas like *Star* and *Doctor Dolittle* lost money. Only a few ended in the black, usually for special reasons. Walt Disney's company monopolized what remained of the family comedy market. United Artists prospered thanks to its low overhead. These were exceptions. While the studios were losing millions on large-budget, big-name pictures, small-budget films were turning a handsome profit. Young Peter Fonda's *Easy Rider* cost a half-million dollars to make and earned many times that back.* *Alice's Restaurant* cost several million, still a pittance by Hollywood standards, and did a fabulous business. Suddenly, independents who had been struggling

---

* The record for multiplication was probably held by Russ Meyer's *Vixen*. This socially unredeeming porn flick was expected to gross $6 million on an investment of $72,000. A genius at titillation, Meyer was thereafter given a fat contract by 20th Century–Fox. Pop culture fanciers were eager to see if his special talent would survive the big time.

along on peanuts found people clamoring to finance them. What that meant for the industry was hard to say. Lack of money was a handicap, yet it also provided a kind of discipline for filmmakers. Who could say what easy money would do to their judgment? For better or worse, the major studio system collapsed, thanks partly to foreign competition, as did the star system.

There was much to admire about the new films. Some were excellently made. Others were morally instructive. *Alice's Restaurant* (directed by Arthur Penn) was anti-war and pro-youth, but in a fresh way. It starred Arlo Guthrie, son of the great folk singer and composer Woody Guthrie, and a singer and composer and counter-culture folk hero in his own right. The title was derived from a real incident, memorialized by Arlo in a talking blues composition (an idiom perfected by Woody) of the same name. He had been arrested for illegally dumping trash and was later refused by the draft on account of it. Both the song and the film made much of the curious fact that having been a litterbug disqualified Guthrie for killing people in Vietnam.* Most of the new films advanced counter-cultural values, yet few were as self-serving as the new theater. Some even managed a little introspection. *Easy Rider* celebrated dope, crime, sex, physical mobility, and such almost to the end. But the last line in the film was "We blew it." *Last Summer* matched youthful truth against adult lies until its violent conclusion showed corruption was in the young too. Whatever their faults—and few of these pictures were so perfectly realized as *Bonnie and Clyde* or *Dr. Strangelove*—they showed again that the film as a medium was still effective. People would go on debating its aesthetic limits. But whether it was too easily absorbed for a fine art was probably irrelevant. At their best movies were so variously exciting as to warrant attention. Many bad and false pictures were made. But what was good redeemed what was not. The film industry kept on surprising people; that was probably the best thing about it.

Only the skin flick failed to surprise. Films were not far behind the theater in exploiting nudity. The most striking example of this in 1969 was a Swedish picture, *I Am Curious (Yellow)*. It dealt with the life and loves of a Swedish hippie in search of truth, and demonstrated how difficult life in a country with no serious problems could be for a radical. There was so much nudity and simulated lovemaking in it that many doubted it would ever be shown in America. The customs did indeed seize it. A U.S. District Court declared it smutty. But this judgment was

---

* Life surpassed art in other ways too. The officer who arrested Guthrie out of hippie-hatred was made famous by the song, played himself in the film, and was reconciled with the counter-culture. Alice herself, who had run a bohemian bistro, profited even more. She wrote a cookbook and licensed a chain of "Alice's Restaurants."

overturned on appeal and the film was widely shown thereafter without much fuss (except in the suburbs where moral mothers rose up against it). The trial was grotesque as usual. The jurors ranged from thirty-two to sixty-eight years of age. The most cultivated was an editor of *Reader's Digest* Condensed Books. Yet the film was aimed at young people and intellectuals. Given a jury composed of people who would not go to such a film anyway, the verdict was never in question. When the higher court approved it and people could judge for themselves, it was hard to see what the fuss was about. Most didn't think it a very good film and imagined that the expert defense witnesses had to strain some to uncover its redemptive merits. On the other hand, it was clearly not pornographic either. Thanks to the publicity, no one who went to it could claim to have had his morals impaired thereby. Presumably the jury had sustained damage, however. This prompted the critic John Simon to suggest that hereafter all dirty movies be viewed by one person who would sacrifice himself for society. When he was totally corrupted he could be deported (to Sweden, no doubt, or perhaps disposed of like radioactive waste).

After *I Am Curious* a wave of culturally pretentious skin flicks saturated the market. Although the silent majority gnashed its teeth in rage, little attention was paid it. The rating system protected the ignorant. The Nixon administration promised a war on smut yet did not immediately launch one. The silent majority was vocal enough for once to win pledges, but not enough to get action. Even if it did, few believed films would change much. Raquel Welch might be dressed more heavily, but there was no family audience to speak of for moving pictures any more. For the industry to survive it would have to go on dealing with subjects that interested the young, sex among them. If Middle Americans wanted wholesome films they would have to start going to movies again. Most still thought that too great a sacrifice.

As the line between high and popular culture eroded and ceaseless change became everywhere the rule, some critics advanced theories that attempted to account for these novelties and provide a framework for judgment. Susan Sontag, the most celebrated younger critic of the sixties, largely abandoned the old aesthetics. She spoke instead of "taste" and "sensibility" as guides to understanding. Her best-known essay, "Notes on Camp" (1964), shows how she meant this to be applied. What took fifty-eight notes for her to define can hardly be summed up in a few words. But, briefly, she said that one way of recognizing camp was when a thing was so bad that it became, in a way, good, like old comic strips and depression-era musical comedies. Camp focused on style at the expense of substance. Senator Dirksen was a camp politician. Camp was exaggerated (Jayne Mansfield) or androgynous (Greta Garbo). Camp was innocent and, indeed, sincere. Self-conscious camp was merely "campy," and rarely as satisfying. The big hit of the 1965–66 TV season was *Batman,* a tongue-in-cheek takeoff on the comic strip that was deliberate and, therefore, campy.

Though Miss Sontag stayed close to books, films, and the usual stuff of culture, her net was large enough to include almost any man or artifact. Nothing that was human, or made by humans, was alien to her philosophy. Marshall McLuhan carried this tendency even further. He wrote more about the media than anything else, particularly television, but like Miss Sontag he was interested in the whole of modern culture, especially its physical manifestations. *Understanding Media* (1964), his most famous book, is about artifacts and ideas as well as modes of communication. McLuhan thought that the old intellectual and aesthetic standards had been nullified by the mass media. As he said over and over, "The medium is the message." Content no longer mattered, only the experience of seeing and hearing. *I Love Lucy* could go forward unashamedly; so could James Bond.*

McLuhan had a simple theory that historical change was caused by new forms of communication. Thus the printing press created individualism, privacy, specialization, mass production, and nationalism. This was the theme of his earlier book, *The Gutenberg Galaxy.* Tribal man had used all his senses in a healthy way. Gutenberg man depended mainly on his eyes, leaving the other senses to atrophy. But the new electronic age was changing all that. The mass media created a new primitivism. As the British philosopher Anthony Quinton put it, explicating McLuhan while attacking him, the new men of the future are our children with their sense-ratios altered by TV-watching, "dedicated to 'cool,' participative enjoyments like the frug [a dance craze of the period], and altogether alienated from the Gutenberg assumptions of traditional instructional schooling. That is why we get on with them so badly. The coming society will be appropriate to this type of human being. It will be a 'global village,' a unitary world of neo-tribesmen, sunk

---

* 1965 was the peak year for James Bond movies. His spy thrillers like *Dr. No* and *Goldfinger* had created a vast market for Bond-associated products. They were now sold in seventy countries. Frenchwomen could have gold underwear that would make them "fit for James Bond." American boys could buy a Bond transistor radio that converted to a toy rifle. The Bond films made Sean Connery rich, famous, and disgusted. Connery was an excellent actor (his portrayal of the manic poet Samson Shillitoe in *A Fine Madness* being especially memorable). Yet none of his other parts earned him a fraction of what he got from the mechanical Bond role. The publicity attending it was so loathsome he stopped speaking to reporters entirely—a typical artistic experience in the age of high mass consumption.

in their social roles and fraternally involved with one another in a way that excludes what their forebears would regard as individuality."

Though ostensibly neutral and speculative about it—"I'm just sending out probes," McLuhan would say to critics—he favored the coming order. McLuhan had been trained as an English scholar, but at some point he decided that the traditional culture was doomed by popular culture and its mechanisms. So instead of bucking the tide like most scholars, he went with it. He showed contempt for pop culture all the same. By refusing to admit the aesthetic merits of any part of it, he reduced the whole to a dead level of uniformity. It was neither good nor bad, it was just there, a fact to be reckoned with, not a subject to be judged. He continued to see art and the media as distinct, even hostile, elements. His reverence for traditional art was obvious and disarming. His disdain for the media was largely ignored. The young believed that rock music, underground movies, pop art, and such were beautiful. Still, to go all the way with McLuhan would be to deny even the possibility of a media aesthetic, so they didn't, though many pretended to. McLuhan satisfied many tastes. Pop culture buffs were enchanted by his lore. Businessmen were assured that the trash they produced did not harm the media experience. The viewer's senses were enriched as much by *The Beverly Hillbillies* as by a stunning production of *Death of a Salesman*. Similarly, young consumers took heart from the same message. They were not wallowing in cultural garbage but rather developing new senseratios appropriate to the electronic era. Parents were relieved of guilt too. Their children were different because of the media, not from any failings of their own.

McLuhanism as a system was absurd. Critics frequently pointed this out. He was dogmatic, contradictory, undocumented, and so on. They were right but irrelevant. People liked McLuhan not because he was coherent but because he was needed. They had to cope with the new technology. McLuhan showed them how. Amazing things are going on, he said, and more amazing things are coming. They are not bad in themselves, and their shock can be absorbed if one is prepared for them. *Understanding Media* was a survival kit for squares, a license to groove for the "switched on." In this sense McLuhan was the first philosopher of pop. He was stylish, apolitical, exaggerated, patronizing of both the past and present, contemptuous of his materials, and, of course, quite fun. But, like the taste for camp, his vogue was too fragile to endure. The mid-decade's enthusiasm for McLuhanism faded as things got more baffling still. Sterner philosophies were called for then, though they were not forthcoming simply because needed.

Perhaps the most useful attempt to make sense of all this was Dwight Macdonald's famous essay on mass culture written just when the new era was beginning. To him mass culture (masscult) was mere *kitsch*, that is to say, art predigested for the spectator. It avoids what is difficult in real art and goes directly to what is pleasant. Further, it "includes the spectators' reactions in the work itself . . . it does his feeling for him." This "Law of the Built-In Reaction" is based on exaggeration mainly. Thanks to it sentiment becomes sentimentality, the modern modernistic, and art arty. Masscult is not just unsuccessful art; it lacks even the possibility of being good. It is anti-art. It claims to entertain but only distracts. Unlike folk art, which grew from below, masscult is fabricated from above. Folk art satisfied the popular taste, masscult exploits it. The best thing, in Macdonald's view, would be to abolish masscult altogether. Since that was plainly impossible, the only alternative was to draw a sharp line between high culture and mass culture.

A relentless war against midcult, the bastardized by-product of the unholy union of high and mass cultures, was especially needed. (Examples of midcult were the *Saturday Review*, Hemingway's *The Old Man and the Sea*, Thornton Wilder's *Our Town*.) Midcult was especially insidious because it debased and absorbed the avant garde. Midcult's historical predecessor as *kitsch* for the elite was academicism. But academicism was culturally less dangerous because it opposed, and thus failed to dilute, avant-garde art. And by educating people's taste it enabled them to go beyond the academy to the avant garde. Midcult was a cultural dead end, yet it was spreading everywhere. Max Lerner and Vance Packard debased scholarship. Action painting mistook absurdity for experimentation. Dada had satirized the academic culture of its day, now artists were offering it as serious work. A "*lumpen*-avant-garde" had come into being.

Many serious people found mass culture threatening. Some even accepted Macdonald's definitions of what was art and what was not. It was clear that high culture and popular culture were interpenetrating one another. Soon pop art offered a striking example of this, rock music another. Yet did it follow that cultural miscegenation was always harmful? Most pop art was junk, but most attempts at high art were pretty bad too. And if one admitted that in Claes Oldenburg and a few others the genre had produced real masters, was it not then an authentic art form? And what did it matter if others were really slick frauds? The people who paid inflated prices for their products could afford it. Those who imitated them hurt no one but themselves. The introduction of commercial techniques into the art world (annual model changes, lavish PR campaigns, fashion exploitation) was disagreeable. Yet some artists made it without pandering to fashion. And pop art was not without redeeming social values. It made a true statement about the deteriorating human environment. That it also repeated itself tiresomely did not make the statement less true. One might even say that it was something like a folk art for the industrial age. Even if it was pure *kitsch*, the threat it posed to art remained unclear. High culture survived pop and later fads. They simply made it harder to identify.

Indeed, the confusion between high art and mass culture was a tribute to the latter's vitality. Whatever its aesthetic merits, pop culture was certainly stimulating. It often said things with such power and moral force as to defy categorization. Was *Dr. Strangelove* a commercial product or a work of art? Did it matter? And what about Dylan songs like "The Times They Are a-Changing" and "Blowing in the Wind," or John Lennon's rolling line, "All we are saying is give peace a chance," which became the anti-war movement's anthem in 1969? *Dr. Strangelove* was certainly not tasteless or predigested. People laughed through it, but not easily. Every joke pulled the audience several ways, making for an extraordinarily complex experience. If that was not a function of art, what was? Even "All we are saying," while simple, was simple in the manner of "We Shall Overcome." And, finally, what about Humphrey Bogart? Bogart's films were produced by the Hollywood *kitsch* mill. Yet they were, if not beautiful, morally compelling. And compelling precisely because the effect was a consequence of form following function. Moviegoers inferred Bogart's sense of honor from his style, not from his declamations. His style, in turn, was made up of many small things— expressions, bits of business, directorial tricks, professional expertise, and such. Was this art or artifice? Once more, did it matter?

Which is not to dismiss Macdonald's views. For one thing, he wrote the essay "Masscult and Midcult" when the popular culture was at a low ebb. Ten years later it would seem much different. After the Beatles and Dylan, *Dr. Strangelove* and *Bonnie and Clyde,* guerrilla theater and black theater, and the rest, mass culture was not so easy to dismiss as before. The returns were not yet in. Macdonald's worst fears might still be realized. All the same, mass culture showed itself in the sixties to be more fertile and full of possibilities than anyone in 1960 could have suspected. It remained largely monotonous and sometimes dangerous, of course. The Bogarts were rare, the merchants of schlock and sensation numerous. Self-indulgence was on the rise. Craftsmanship declined. The invasion of high culture by pop culture promotion techniques (the "hype," as it was called) destroyed avant-garde art as a concept, though it had still seemed viable to Macdonald as late as 1960. He worried lest midcult deaden people's aesthetic senses so that they would be unable to properly value high art. But the hype made the new as marketable as the old, thus eliminating the avant garde. Yet if Macdonald was looking the wrong way as the sixties opened, his fears were not unjustified. Art was threatened, not from the flank, as he thought then, but from below. Pop culture's rude surge would soon break through in many places. The kinds of distinctions Macdonald hoped to establish would be needed more desperately than even he guessed, especially when the counter-culture began gearing up.

PROFILE:
Sports

In the sixties, even more than before, Americans liked to spend money on sports. Activities once reserved for the wealthy—boating and skiing especially—were now enjoyed by plumbers and secretaries. Spectator sports benefited most. Television was crucial here. TV networks offered professional leagues package deals for telecasting rights amounting to tens of millions of dollars. The leagues, in turn, adjusted their schedules and made other concessions to insure a profitable season.*

As the stakes went up, so did player demands. Strikes, once unheard of, were now commonly threatened, usually just before the season's start. In baseball history only Babe Ruth and Ted Williams had earned $100,000 a year; now several players made as much. Johnny Bench of Cincinnati vowed to become the first $100,000 catcher. Wilt Chamberlain and Bill Russell in pro basketball, Bobby Hull in hockey, and tennis players like Rod Laver also cracked the magic figure. No professional golf tournament could offer less than $50,000 in first-prize money and still be thought major.

The age of athletic entrepreneurship began in 1964 when the New York Jets of the American Football League gave Joe Namath a $400,000 contract. This was an early high point in the struggle

---

* Marshall McLuhan thought football especially well suited to TV because of its explosive rhythms. He called it the electronic game.

between the two professional leagues for college talent. Namath had been a great quarterback for the University of Alabama. The Jets hoped to lure New York fans away from the established Giants of the National Football League and give the newer AFL some glamour. Namath did the trick. He became an overnight celebrity, as much for his colorful social life among the Beautiful People as for his play. He rented a luxurious apartment in New York City, grew long hair, bought a shaggy fur coat, and various businesses. One investment in a New York bar got him censured by Commissioner Pete Rozelle, inspiring tearful histrionics from the star. Later "Broadway Joe" turned to movie acting and thought of abandoning sport for art. Football fans and film critics alike hoped he would stick with the game.

Namath was one of several superstars in pro football ("main men," their teammates called them). Even less celebrated players earned more money and showed more style than before. But the game itself became more routine and predictable. This showed the influence of Vince Lombardi, coach of the Green Bay Packers and easily football's most impressive personality in the sixties. As a lineman at Fordham in the thirties Lombardi had been one of the famous "Seven Blocks of Granite." Later he was an assistant coach for the New York Giants. When he came to the Packers as head coach in 1959, this once-legendary team was in last place. He made Green Bay world champion in three years. Eventually Lombardi won five world championships in nine years. His sharp eye for talent helped, but mainly Lombardi counted on drive and discipline to make his teams great. His game plan was not complex: Lombardi thought the best way to break an opponent was to attack his strength, not his weakness. The Packers' élan and professional integrity were such that even in defeat they played with distinction.* Lombardi's plays were simple, but executed with perfect efficiency. The "Green Bay Sweep," an orthodox run off tackle, became the most feared maneuver in pro football.

Lombardi's players worshiped him. It was strange to hear huge

---

* Mostly they won though. The 1967 championship game, played in subzero weather at Green Bay, showed why. The Dallas Cowboys led Green Bay 17 to 14. With only seconds to go the Packers had the ball, fourth down on the Dallas one-yard line. The safe thing was to kick a field goal and send the game into sudden-death overtime. Instead Green Bay went for the touchdown, the players knowing that if they failed they would lose the game and about $2,700 apiece. They made the touchdown.

athletes like all-pro guard Jerry Kramer talk about "love" being important to the Packers' success. Others thought Lombardi a martinet, or worse. He was so intolerant of injuries that players feared to ask for rest short of a broken leg. Yet it was hard to argue with a man who demanded the best from everyone. "He treated us all the same," said Henry Jordan, a Packer lineman, "like dogs." When Lombardi died of cancer in 1970, after having gone to the Washington Redskins as coach and part-owner, he was eulogized beyond belief, and not just by fans. Partly this was because athletics was more important to the national sense of well-being than ever before. As basketball star Oscar Robertson put it, "Sports is the only thing this country holds sacred." If not quite true, there was truth here. In an age marked by fakery, hedonism, and contempt for work, sport was one of the few areas in which hard work and ability were still pre-eminent and unmistakable. Lombardi was revered because Green Bay exemplified those traits, even more because he spoke directly to them. On the banquet circuit and elsewhere he explained that the Packers were great precisely because of their disciplined will to power. There was, he insisted, no higher social goal than victory properly arrived at. He was one of the few celebrities who dared any longer to take such a line, and was especially mourned by people nostalgic for lost values. There was something pathetic about all this. Lombardi was a splendid coach with old-fashioned standards. That because of them he became a culture hero showed too the bankruptcy of a tradition once championed by men like Theodore Roosevelt, and more recently echoed by John F. Kennedy. Sport used to seem a metaphor for such virtues as drive, ambition, respect for standards, and individual excellence. Now many thought it their last resort.

TV stimulated a great expansion of professional sports. More teams meant more stadiums to fill. Better still, they meant more games to sell on television. In consequence the American Football League began competing with the NFL in 1960; an American Basketball Association was founded in 1967 alongside the NBA; and so on. Virtually all these "expansion" teams found the going rough as they were stocked initially with players the established teams could afford to lose.

No expansion team was more inept or beloved than baseball's New

York Mets. When the Giants and the Dodgers went West in 1958, New Yorkers had only the aristocratic, seemingly invincible Yankees to admire. Many found them hard to identify with. In 1962 the Mets opened their first season with Casey Stengel as manager. Having been cruelly fired by the Yankee organization which he had led to so many victories, Stengel was not eager to take the field again, but Mrs. Joan Payson (née Whitney), the Mets' owner and an avid baseball fan, talked him into it. "It's a pleasure to be managing the New York Knickerbockers," Stengel told reporters.

In their first season the Mets tied a National League record by losing the first nine games, then went on to establish an all-time record by losing 120 of 160 games. Yet while their record failed to improve with time, attendance did. Some believed the Mets' following came from novelty-seekers jaded by Yankee victories. Others thought Mets fans had developed a taste for comedy. Recalling his experiences at Mets games, Roger Angell wrote: "Amid deafening pleas of 'Let's go, Mets!,' I suddenly understood why Met fans have fallen into the habit of *permanent* shouting. It was simple, really: Supporters of a team that is batting .215 have no heroes, no mighty sluggers, to save their hopes for. The Mets' rallies fall from heaven, often upon the bottom of the batting order, and must be prayed for at all times." Once when Casey Stengel relieved a pitcher, the man protested, "I'm doing the job, Casey. What else can I do?" "You could strike them out," Casey told him. "You know we can't catch grounders."

The Mets finished last in five of seven years until 1969. The turnover among players was enormous. George Weiss, the general manager who also was a former Yankee boss, hoped eventually to build a winner through a strong farm system. He stayed largely with younger players and paid special attention to pitchers. In 1969 the Mets suddenly had the strongest pitching in the league. Tom Seaver, in fact, was thought to be the best in all baseball. And the rest of the team, though not distinguished, was doing just well enough at bat and in the field to win. Still, as late as August 15, with only about six weeks of the season to play, the Mets were in third place, nine and a half games behind the Chicago Cubs. In a flurry, they won thirty-eight of their last forty-nine games, caught and passed the Cubs, won the Eastern Division title, beat the Atlanta Braves three straight in a playoff for the National League pennant, and took four of five games from the Baltimore Orioles to win the World Series.

At the end of a decade of general misery, the Mets' "impossible dream" was taken as a sign of hope and a victory for the common man over large impersonal forces. Isaac Stern, the violinist, thought that "if the Mets can win the Series, anything can happen—even peace." New Yorkers went wild. They tore up the sod in Shea Stadium and then shut down the city with demonstrations of joy.

The Mets' success marked the resurrection of baseball's popularity. At the start of the sixties many had thought baseball too old-fashioned, too slow a game to compete with pro football as America's No. 1 spectator sport. Even more than Vince Lombardi, the Mets showed that Americans love not just winners but heroes. Outside of sports, there were few to cheer for in the sixties.

8 THE COUNTER-CULTURE

COUNTER-CULTURE as a term appeared rather late in the decade. It largely replaced the term "youth culture," which finally proved too limited. When the sixties began, youth culture meant the way adolescents lived. Its central institutions were the high school and the mass media. Its principal activities were consuming goods and enacting courtship rituals. Critics and students of the youth culture were chiefly interested in the status and value systems associated with it. As time went on, college enrollments increased to the point where colleges were nearly as influential as high schools in shaping the young. The molders of youthful opinion got more ambitious. Where once entertainers were content to amuse for profit, many began seeing themselves as moral philosophers. Music especially became a medium of propaganda, identifying the young as a distinct force in society with unique values and aspirations. This helped produce a kind of ideological struggle between the young and their elders called the "generation gap." It was the first time in American history that social conflict was understood to be a function of age. Yet the young were not all rebellious. Most in fact retained confidence in the "system" and its norms. Many older people joined the rebellion, whose progenitors were as often over thirty (where the generation gap was supposed to begin) as under it. The attack on accepted views and styles broadened so confusingly that "youth culture" no longer described it adequately. Counter-culture was a sufficiently vague and elastic substitute. It meant all things to all men and embraced everything new from clothing to politics. Some viewed the counter-culture as mankind's best, maybe only, hope; others saw it as a portent of civilization's imminent ruin. Few recalled the modest roots from which it sprang.

Even in the 1950's and very early sixties, when people still worried about conformity and the silent generation, there were different drummers to whose beat millions would one day march. The bohemians of that era (called "beatniks" or "beats") were only a handful, but they practiced free love, took drugs, repudiated the straight world, and generally showed which way the wind was blowing. They were highly publicized, so when the bohemian impulse strengthened, dropouts knew what was expected of them. While the beats showed their contempt for social norms mostly in physical ways, others did so intellectually. Norman Mailer, in "The White Negro," held up the sensual, lawless hipster as a model of behavior under oppressive capitalism. He believed, according to "The Time of Her Time," that sexual orgasm was the pinnacle of human experience, perhaps also an approach to ultimate truth. Norman O. Brown's *Life Against Death,* a psychoanalytic interpretation of history, was an underground classic which argued that cognition subverted intuition. Brown called for a return to "polymorphous perversity," man's natural estate. The popularity of Zen Buddhism demonstrated that others wished to slip the bonds of Western rationalism; so, from a different angle, did the vogue for black humor.

The most prophetic black humorist was Joseph Heller, whose novel *Catch-22* came out in 1960. Though set in World War II the book was even more appropriate to the Indochinese war. Later Heller said, "That was the war I had in mind; a war fought without military provocation, a war in which the real enemy is no longer the other side, but someone allegedly on your side. The ridiculous war I felt lurking in the future when I wrote the book." *Catch-22* was actually written during the Cold War, and sold well in the early sixties because it attacked the perceptions on which that war, like the Indochinese war that it fathered, grew. At the time reviewers didn't know what to make of *Catch-22.* World War II had been, as everyone knew, an absolutely straightforward case of good versus evil. Yet to Heller there was little moral difference between combatants. In fact all his characters are insane, or carry normal attributes to insane lengths. They belong to a bomber squadron in the Mediterranean. Terrified of combat, most hope for ground duty and are free to request it, but: "There was only one catch and that was Catch-22, which specified that a concern for one's own safety in the face of dangers that were real and immediate was the process of a rational mind. Orr was crazy and could be grounded. All he had to do was ask; and as soon as he did, he would no longer be crazy and would have to fly more missions. Orr would be crazy to fly more missions and sane if he didn't, but if he was sane he had to fly them. If he flew them he was crazy and didn't have to; but if he didn't want to he was sane and had to."

The squadron's success depends more on having a perfect bomb pattern than hitting the target. Milo Minderbinder is the key man in the Theater, though only a lieutenant, because he embodies the profit motive. He puts the entire war on a paying basis and hires the squadron out impartially to both sides. At the end Yossarian, the novel's hero, resolves his dilemma by setting out for neutral Sweden in a rubber raft. This was what hundreds of real deserters and draft evaders would be doing soon. It was also a perfect symbol for the masses of dropouts who sought utopian alternatives to the straight world. One day there would be hundreds of thousands of Yossarians, paddling away from the crazed society in frail crafts of their own devising. *Catch-22* was not just black comedy, nor even chiefly an anti-war novel, but a metaphor that helped shape the moral vision of an era.*

Although children and adolescents watched a great deal of television in the sixties, it seemed at first to have little effect. Surveys were always showing that youngsters spent fifty-four hours a week or whatever in front of the tube, yet what they saw was so bland or predictable as to make little difference. The exceptions were news programs, documentaries, and dramatic specials. Few watched them. What did influence the young was popular music, folk music first and then rock. Large-scale enthusiasm for folk music began in 1958 when the Kingston Trio recorded a song, "Tom Dooley," that sold two million records. This opened the way for less slickly commercial performers. Some, like Pete Seeger, who had been singing since the depression, were veteran performers. Others, like Joan Baez, were newcomers. It was conventional for folk songs to tell a story. Hence the idiom had always lent itself to propaganda. Seeger possessed an enormous repertoire of message songs that had gotten him blacklisted by the mass media years before. Joan Baez cared more for the message than the music, and after a few years devoted herself mainly to peace work. The folk-music vogue was an early stage in the politicalization of youth, a forerunner of the counter-culture. This was hardly apparent at the time. Folk music was not seen as morally reprehensible in the manner of rock and roll. It was a familiar genre.

---

* Lenny Bruce was a more tragic harbinger of change. He was a successful night club comedian who created an obscene form of black comedy that involved more social criticism than humor. Bruce was first arrested for saying "motherfucker" on stage in 1962. Later he was busted for talking dirty about the Pope and many lesser offenses. He may have been insane. He died early from persecution and drug abuse, and then became an honored martyr in the anti-Establishment pantheon. He was one of the spiritual fathers of the yippies.

Folk was gentle music for the most part, and even when sung in protest did not offend many. Malvina Reynold's "What Have They Done to the Rain?" complained of radioactive fallout which all detested. Pete Seeger's anti-war song "Where Have All the Flowers Gone?" was a favorite with both pacifists and the troops in Vietnam.

Bob Dylan was different. Where most folk singers were either clean-cut or homey looking, Dylan had wild long hair. He resembled a poor white dropout of questionable morals. His songs were hard-driving, powerful, intense. It was hard to be neutral about them. "The Times They Are a-Changing" was perhaps the first song to exploit the generation gap. Dylan's life was as controversial as his ideology. Later he dropped politics and got interested in rock music. At the Newport Jazz Festival in 1965 he was booed when he introduced a fusion of his own called "folk-rock." He went his own way after that, disowned by the politically minded but admired by a great cult following attracted as much, perhaps, by his independent life as by his music. He advanced the counter-culture in both ways and made money too. This also was an inspiration to those who came after him.

Another early expression, which coexisted with folk music, though quite unlike it, was the twist. Dance crazes were nothing new, but the twist was remarkable because it came to dominate social dancing. It used to be that dance fads were here today and gone tomorrow, while the two-step went on forever. Inexpert, that is to say most, social dancers had been loyal to it for generations. It played a key role in the traditional youth culture. Who could imagine a high school athletic event that did not end with couples clinging to one another on the dimly lit gym floor, while an amateur dance band plodded gamely on? When in 1961 the twist became popular, moralists were alarmed. It called for vigorous, exhibitionistic movements. Prurient men were reminded of the stripper's bumps and grinds. They felt the twist incited lust. Ministers denounced it. Yet in the twist (and its numerous descendants), bodies were not rubbed together as in the two-step, which had embarrassed millions of schoolboys. Millions more had suffered when through awkwardness they bumped or trod on others. The twist, by comparison, was easy and safe. No partner was bothered by the other's maladroitness. It aroused few passions. That was the practical reason for its success. But there was an ideological impulse behind it also. Amidst the noise and tumult each person danced alone, "doing his own thing," as would soon be said. But though alone, the dancer was surrounded by others doing their own thing in much the same manner. The twist celebrated both individuality and communality. This was to become a hallmark of the counter-culture, the right of everyone to be different in much the same way. The twist also foretold the dominance of rock, to which it was so well suited.

No group contributed more to the counter-culture than the Beatles, though, like folk music and the twist, their future significance was not at first apparent. Beatlemania began on October 13, 1963, when the quartet played at the London Palladium. The police, caught unawares, were hardly able to control the maddened throngs. On February 9, 1964, they appeared on U.S. television. The show received fifty thousand ticket requests for a theater that seated eight hundred. They were mobbed at the airport, besieged in their hotel, and adored everywhere. Even their soiled bed linen found a market. Their next recording, "Can't Buy Me Love," sold three million copies in advance of release, a new world's record. Their first movie, *A Hard Day's Night* (1964), was both a critical and a popular success. Some reviewers compared them with the Marx brothers. They became millionaires overnight. The Queen decorated them for helping ease the balance-of-payments deficit. By 1966 they were so rich that they could afford to give up live performances.

For a time the Beatles seemed just another pop phenomenon, Elvis Presley multiplied by four. Few thought their music very distinguished. The reasons for its wide acceptance were hard to fathom. Most felt their showmanship was the key factor. They wore their hair longer than was fashionable, moved about a lot on stage, and avoided the class and racial identifications associated with earlier rock stars. Elvis had cultivated a proletarian image. Other rock stars had been black, or exploited the Negro rhythm-and-blues tradition. The Beatles were mostly working class in origin but sang with an American accent (like other English rock stars) and dressed in an elegant style, then popular in Britain, called "mod." The result was a deracinated, classless image of broad appeal.

The Beatles did not fade away as they were supposed to. Beatlemania continued for three years. Then the group went through several transformations that narrowed its audience to a smaller but intensely loyal cult following in the Dylan manner. The group became more self-consciously artistic. Their first long-playing record took one day to make and cost £400. "Sergeant Pepper's Lonely Hearts Club Band" took four months and cost £25,000. They were among the first to take advantage of new recording techniques that enabled multiple sound tracks to be played simultaneously. The Beatles learned new instruments and idioms too. The result was a complex music that attracted serious inquiry. Critics debated their contributions to musicology and argued over whether they were pathfinders or merely gifted entrepreneurs. In either case, they had come a long way aesthetically from their humble beginnings. Their music had a great effect on the young, so did their styles of life. They led the march of fashion away from mod and into the hairy, mustached, bearded, beaded, fringed, and embroidered costumes of the late sixties. For a time they followed the Maharishi, an Indian guru of some note. They married and divorced in progressively more striking ways. Some were arrested for smoking marijuana. In this too they were faithful to their clientele.

John Lennon went the farthest. He married Yoko Ono, best known as an author of happenings, and with her launched a bizarre campaign for world peace and goodness. Lennon returned his decoration to the Queen in protest against the human condition. Lennon and Ono hoped to visit America but were denied entry, which, to the bureaucratic mind, seemed a stroke for public order and morality. They staged a bed-in for peace all the same. They also formed a musical group of their own, the Plastic Ono Band, and circulated nude photographs and erotic drawings of themselves. This seemed an odd way to stop the war in Indochina, even to other Beatles. The group later broke up. By then they had made their mark, and, while strange, it was not a bad mark. Whatever lasting value their music may have, they set a good example to the young in most ways. Lennon's pacifism was nonviolent, even if wildly unorthodox. At a time when so many pacifists were imitating what they protested against, that was most desirable. They also worked hard at their respective arts and crafts, though others were dropping out and holding up laziness as a socially desirable trait. The Beatles showed that work was not merely an Establishment trick to keep the masses in subjection and the young out of trouble.

Beatlemania coincided with a more ominous development in the emerging counter-culture—the rise of the drug prophet Timothy Leary. He and Richard Alpert were scientific researchers at Harvard University who studied the effects of hallucinogenic drugs, notably a compound called LSD. As early as 1960 it was known that the two were propagandists as well as scientists. In 1961 the University Health Service made them promise not to use undergraduates in their experiments. Their violation of this pledge was the technical ground for firing them. A better one was that they had founded a drug cult. Earlier studies of LSD had failed, they said, because the researchers had not themselves taken the drug. In order to end this "authoritarian" practice, they "turned on" themselves. Their work was conducted in quarters designed to look like a bohemian residence instead of a laboratory. This was defended as a reconstruction of the natural environment in which social "acid-dropping" took place. They and many of their subjects became habitual users, not only of LSD but of marijuana and other drugs. They constructed an ideology of sorts around this practice. After they were fired the *Harvard Review* published an article of theirs praising the drug life: "Remember, man, a natural state is ecstatic wonder, ecstatic intuition, ecstatic accurate movement. Don't settle for less."

With some friends Leary and Alpert created the International Foundation for Internal Freedom (IF-IF) which published the *Psychedelic Review*. To advertise it a flyer was circulated that began, "Mescaline! Experimental Mysticism! Mushrooms! Ecstasy! LSD-25! Expansion of Consciousness! Phantastica! Transcendence! Hashish! Visionary Botany! Ololiuqui! Physiology of Religion! Internal Freedom! Morning Glory! Politics of the Nervous System!" Later the drug culture would generate a vast literature, but this was its essential message. The truth that made Western man free was only obtainable through hallucinogenic drugs. Truth was in the man, not the drug, yet the drug was necessary to uncover it. The natural state of man thus revealed was visionary, mystical, ecstatic. The heightened awareness stimulated by "consciousness-expanding" drugs brought undreamed-of sensual pleasures, according to Leary. Even better, drugs promoted peace, wisdom, and unity with the universe.

Alpert soon dropped from view. Leary went on to found his own sect, partly because once LSD was banned religious usage was the only ground left on which it could be defended, mostly because the drug cult *was* a religion. He wore long white robes and long blond hair. And he traveled about the country giving his liberating message (tune in, turn on, drop out) and having bizarre adventures. His personal following was never large, but drug use became commonplace among the young anyway. At advanced universities social smoking of marijuana was as acceptable as social drinking. More so, in a way, for it was better suited to the new ethic. One did not clutch one's solitary glass but shared one's "joint" with others. "Grass" made one gentle and pacific, not surly and hostile. As a forbidden pleasure it was all the more attractive to the thrill-seeking and the rebellious. And it helped further distinguish between the old world of grasping, combative, alcoholic adults and the turned-on, cooperative culture of the young. Leary was a bad prophet. Drug-based mystical religion was not the wave of the future. What the drug cult led to was a lot of dope-smoking and some hard drug-taking. When research suggested that LSD caused genetic damage, its use declined. But the effects of grass were hard to determine, so its consumption increased.

Sometimes "pot" smokers went on to other drugs—a deadly compound called "speed," and even heroin. These ruined many lives (though it was never clear that the lives were not already ruined to begin with). The popularity of drugs among the young induced panic in the old. States passed harsher and harsher laws that accomplished little. Campaigns against the drug traffic were launched periodically with similar results. When the flow of grass was interrupted, people turned to other drugs. Drug use seemed to go up either way. The generation gap widened. Young people thought marijuana less dangerous than alcohol, perhaps rightly. To proscribe the one and permit the other made no sense to them, except as still another example of adult hypocrisy and the hatred of youth. Leary had not meant all this to happen, but he was to blame for some of it all the same. No one did more to build the ideology that made pot-smoking a morally constructive act. But though a malign influence, no one deserved such legal persecution as he experienced before escaping to Algeria from a prison farm.

In Aldous Huxley's prophetic novel *Brave New World*, drug use was promoted by the state as a means of social control. During the sixties it remained a deviant practice and a source of great tension between the generations. Yet drugs did encourage conformity among the young. To "turn on and drop out" did not weaken the state. Quite the contrary, it drained off potentially subversive energies. The need for drugs gave society a lever should it ever decide to manipulate rather than repress users. Pharmacology and nervous strain had already combined to make many adult Americans dependent on drugs like alcohol and tranquilizers. Now the young were doing the same thing, if for different reasons. In a free country this meant only that individual problems increased. But should democracy fail, drug abuse among both the young and old was an instrument for control such as no dictator ever enjoyed. The young drug-takers thought to show contempt for a grasping, unfeeling society. In doing so they opened the door to a worse one. They scorned their elders for drinking and pill-taking, yet to outsiders their habits seemed little different, though ethically more pretentious. In both cases users were vulnerable and ineffective to the extent of their addiction. Of such ironies was the counter-culture built.

Another sign of things to come was the rise and fall of Ken Kesey and his Merry Pranksters. Kesey graduated from college in Oregon in 1958 and came to Stanford University. There he studied creative writing and absorbed the local bohemian atmosphere, which was still pretty traditional. People drank wine, lamented the sad state of American culture, and looked to Europe for relief in the classic manner. Kesey found work in a mental hospital, which was the subject of his first published novel, *One Flew over the Cuckoo's Nest*. It enjoyed a great success in 1962. He also figured in medical experiments conducted at the hospital. One of the drugs tested on him was LSD. Soon he was moving in psychedelic drug circles. In 1963, with the profits from his book, he bought a log house and some land near La Honda, about fifteen miles from Palo Alto.

Among the restless types who joined him was Neal Cassidy, a legendary figure who had been the model for Dean Moriarty in Jack Kerouac's famous beat-generation novel *On the Road*. The Merry Pranksters, as they became known, developed a unique life style. Sex played a part in it (a lean-to called the Screw Shack was added to the cabin for this purpose), but music and drugs more so. Everyone was also involved in The Movie—a continuing film record of their experiences. In the spring of 1964 the Pranksters bought a school bus, fitted it out with camping facilities, loaded the refrigerator with orange juice and acid, painted it in psychedelic colors, wired it for sound, and set off for the World's Fair in New York. One freaked out along the way (suffered a drug-induced breakdown) and was lost, but the rest made it to New York and then to Timothy Leary's borrowed estate in Millbrook. Leary refused to see them, but the contrast in drug subcultures was strikingly demonstrated all the same. Leary's League for Spiritual Discovery was cool and devotional. He was, literally, the high priest of a religious movement. The Pranksters were hot and crazy on principle. They visited the meditation rooms in Leary's basement and promptly termed it the Crypt Trip. They also made fun of the Tibetan Book of the Dead, one of the Learyites' most revered texts. Though a fiasco in one sense, the trip to New York helped define the Pranksters' secular identity in the semi-mystical drug world.

They went back to La Honda and wired it ever more extravagantly for light and sound. The Movie got more elaborate. The group expanded. Then, on April 23, 1965, they entered history with the most psychedelic drug bust ever. The county sheriff, federal agent Wong, eight police dogs, and wave upon wave of cops and squad cars stormed La Honda and arrested thirteen unarmed drug freaks. Eventually charges were dropped against all but Kesey, who was tagged for possession of marijuana. Overnight his status as a folk hero was established. In August he went so far as to invite the Hell's Angels to La Honda, and to everyone's amazement the visit came off nicely. There was only one gang-bang, and that voluntary. The Angels left without smashing everything up, even though high on beer and acid. It was practically an unnatural event. Soon after, Kesey was invited to the annual California Unitarian Church conference, where he seduced the young and appalled the old. An appearance at Berkeley's Vietnam Day in October was less successful. He had a theory about ending the war by having everyone turn his back on it. The Vietnam Day Committee thought stronger measures were in order.

What really put Kesey at the center of the new culture, however, were the "acid tests." These were big public gatherings with light shows, rock music, mad dancing, and, of course, acid-dropping. "Can you pass the acid test?" was their motto. These were the first important multimedia happenings, combining light shows, tapes, live rock bands, movie and slide projectors, strobe lights, and other technical gimmicks. Their climax was reached at the San Francisco Tripps Festival in January 1966. It was meant to release all the new forms of expression in the cultural underground. Bill Graham, who had managed the San Francisco Mime Troupe, was its organizer. Kesey and the Pranksters gave the acid test. The Tripps Festival was a great success. Several rock groups (The Grateful Dead and Big Brother and the Holding Company) proclaimed the emergence of a new musical genre—acid rock. Graham began staging such affairs regularly in the Fillmore Auditorium in San Francisco. Out of this came the "San Francisco Sound," which made the city a provincial capital in the music industry. Hippie culture, with its drugs, rock groups, psychedelic folk art, and other apparatus, was well and truly launched.

None of this did Kesey himself much good. Just before the Tripps Festival he was arrested for possession again. To escape a stiff jail term he fled to Mexico. Thereafter the new culture had to do without him. Mexico was a bad trip and he returned a chastened man. He talked about "going beyond acid" and gave a poorly received Acid Test Graduation. Many thought he was just copping out to avoid prison. Thanks to good lawyers and hung juries he finally got only six months at a work camp near his old place in La Honda. On being released he went back to Oregon with his family and started another novel. (His third. The second, *Sometimes a Great Notion*, was published while he was still a Prankster. It is a lovely book, though not so successful as his first.)

Kesey was not well known outside of California at the time except as a novelist. He owed his nonliterary folk-freak reputation to Tom Wolfe's book *The Electric Kool-Aid Acid Test*, which came out afterward. Hence Kesey was not so much influential as archetypal. His progression from student to artist to acidhead and crazy commune leader to jail and repentance was a course many would later take, in part anyway. He foreshadowed the hippies and yippies. He also showed how hazardous the psychedelic drug life was. Kesey lost his freedom for a while, and only time would tell what remained of his talent. Yet the somber end of his trip did not have much effect. The local media gave his revels much publicity, their dénouement relatively little. Wolfe, his Boswell, added to the Kesey legend by writing it up in the breathless, adulatory, highly colored prose of the "new journalism." It made insanity seem romantic and the tawdry glamorous. Nothing contemporary was alien to it if sufficiently bizarre. Wolfe's book was a best-seller. Kesey's activities sold a lot of newspapers. Everyone made money from his adventures but Kesey himself. This moral was not lost on the folk heroes who came after him. A striking feature of the mature counter-culture was the facility with which its leading figures made deviance pay off, usually by writing nonbooks. Even so, their profits were small compared with what the rock kings made.

Though Kesey and his friends had different hopes for it, the Tripps Festival proved to be a turning point in the history of rock. Bill Graham and other promoters took the idea and institutionalized it. Rock and light shows attracted big audiences for years afterward and helped launch counter-cultural music groups into the pop culture mainstream. "Acid rock" and such brought deviant values to a national audience. Sex, dope, and anti-social notions became so common that many radio disc jockeys finally gave up trying to censor the music, though TV managed to stay pure. Radio did try to draw the line at revolutionary exhortations. Thus in 1968 many disc jockeys played the Beatles' "Revolution No. 1" because of its counterrevolutionary lyrics ("But if you're carrying a picture of Chairman Mao, you ain't going to make it with anyone anyhow") but did not play the Rolling Stones' rebuttal which insisted that "the time is right for fighting in the streets."

But rock as an idiom was more concerned with social and sexual freedom than politics. The Rolling Stones' subversive appeal was more formalistic than not. The group's real power derived from its sexuality. Mick Jagger hopped about, whacking the stage with a leather belt. Jim Morrison of the Doors was arrested twice for indecent exposure. More articulate than most rock stars, Morrison described his group's function this way: "A Doors' concert is a public meeting called by us for a special kind of dramatic discussion and entertainment." And, further, "We make concerts sexual politics. The sex starts with me, then moves out to include the charmed circle of musicians on stage. The music we make goes out to the audience and interacts with them: they go home and interact with the rest of reality, then I get it all back by interacting with that reality, so the whole sex thing works out to be one big ball of fire." Their listeners took the message perfectly. Morrison was famous in the rock underground for supposedly being able to hold an erection through a two-hour performance. The performers attracted young camp followers known as "groupies." Something like the bobby-soxers of an earlier day, the groupies were more obviously sensual. One legendary (perhaps mythical) team of groupies, known as the Chicago Plaster Casters, carried rock-phallic worship to its logical conclusion by making plaster casts of the performers' sex organs.

But not all rock fans were overstimulated teenie-boppers. At its most pretentious the cult laid great moral responsibilities on the backs of rock groups. When the Beatles released a new album late in 1968 (called simply "The Beatles"), one student critic announced that having transformed the male image and performed other great services, it was now their duty to "forge a cultural revolution." There was broad agreement on this, but rock revolutionaries differed otherwise. Some thought the Beatles more truly revolutionary than the Rolling Stones, despite the latters' enthusiasm for streetfighting. The San Francisco music critic Ralph Gleason thought that "Revolution No. 1" and its variations proved they had sold out to the Establishment. The Stones were not only ideologically more correct but sexier too. The Beatles' defenders insisted, however, that such songs as "Why Don't We Do It in the Road?" were more profoundly sexual than anything the crude Rolling Stones were capable of.

To see how far the youth culture had progressed in a few years, one had only to compare the careers of Joan Baez and Janis Joplin. Miss Baez remained as delicately beautiful and as clear-voiced as ever. In 1964 she and Bob Dylan had been the "fantasy lovers of the folk revival." But by 1968 her vogue was long since gone. She still sang in much the same manner as before. She was even more dedicated to peace and nonviolence. Miss Baez was a tax resister on moral grounds, and she married a draft resister who went to prison rather than accept induction. Yet neither her music nor her beliefs nor her style of life was "relevant" to young people any longer. The place she once occupied was taken by Janis Joplin, a wholly different kind of woman. Miss Joplin was a hard-drinking, tough-talking, ugly but dynamic power singer with roots in the blues tradition. She became famous as the singer for a San Francisco rock band called Big Brother and the Holding Company. A wild, passionate, totally involved performer, she was not much different as a person. Miss Joplin was what the groupies would have become if talented. She did exactly what she pleased, took lovers freely, owned a psychedelic sports car and a closet full of costumes, and, when her reputation eclipsed that of Big Brother and the Holding Company, struck out on her own. "If I miss," she told a reporter, "I'll never have a second chance on nothing. But I gotta risk it. I never hold back, man. I'm always on the outer limits of probability." What was her philosophy of life? "Getting stoned, staying happy, and having a good time. I'm doing just what I want with my life, enjoying it." She burned her candle at both ends and it did not last the night.

Miss Joplin was far more candid than many rock stars. One of their most tiresome habits was insisting on having it both ways. They wanted to be rich and famous while also radical and culturally momentous. What made the Beatles so attractive was that having become rich beyond the dreams of avarice, they abandoned it. And (Lennon excepted) they did not moralize much, however seriously they took themselves. The Rolling Stones, on the other hand, called for revolution in 1968 and the following year made millions with a whirlwind tour of the U.S. As time went on, the commercial aspects increasingly dominated rock. Few went so far as the coalition of groups in St. Louis who refused demands that they offer free, or at least reduced-price, tickets to the needy because doing so would be contrary to the American principle of free enterprise. But time was on their side. The evolution of the San Francisco Sound showed how quickly culture could give way to commerce. At their inception the hippie rock groups were products of the Haight-Ashbury subculture and dedicated to its precepts. But those who prospered soon succumbed to the cash nexus. Bill Graham got rich from his rock palaces, the Fillmore West in San Francisco and Fillmore East in New York. The Carousel Ballroom in San Francisco, funded by the indigenous Grateful Dead and the Jefferson Airplane, went broke. Before long San Francisco was only a regional music center, the New Rock's Nashville, as one critic put it. It was not so much an independent musical capital as a branch office of the music industry. As rock became less a movement and more a business, its impact, though not its popularity, declined. It seemed unlikely that rock would soon become a television staple. But some day its fans would be middle-aged, so even that possibility could not be permanently excluded.

The counter-culture's influence on fashion was nearly as great as on rock. Fashions began to change radically even before the hippies and other such groups appeared. An early sign of this was Rudi Gernreich's topless bathing suit for women in 1964. Designed more in fun than avarice, this curious garment (knitted trunks suspended from a cord around the neck) actually sold. Only a few gallant models really bared their breasts in public, yet it was clearly an idea whose time had come. Discothèques (night clubs featuring recorded music) were starting up, and they inspired customers with writhing "go-go" girls who demonstrated the new dance routines. Some of these went topless, and before long, in California at least, others followed. The first thing one saw on leaving the Los Angeles airport was a sign reading "Topless Bowling." This did not mean that customers went half-nude but that cocktail waitresses did. Later bottomlessness was added, even in such unlikely places as Madison, Wisconsin. Although only performers went this far, as a rule, a new exposure prevailed. Rudi Gernreich raised his skirts three inches above the knee and introduced the no-bra bra, a wispy creation appropriate to the new designs.

In London things had already gone further. Skirts were so short that some were calling them "mini-skirts." Young designers like Mary Quant were making Carnaby Street synonymous with fashion. The "mod" look would soon reach New York. Bikinis were now seen on American beaches in sizable numbers. Less abbreviated than the European models, they still astonished people accustomed to the reinforced swimsuits of the fifties. Before long they would be standard among girls and young women. The most striking thing about these changes was that they came from below. Fashion had always been dictated from above, by Parisian couturiers and other authorities. It was a monopoly of the rich. But in the sixties it was the young, and relatively unknown designers like Quant and Gernreich who catered to them, who set the pace. Young people did the twist first, shortened their skirts first, and made being "kicky" and "switched on" desirable. More expensive versions of their styles were then designed for the modish rich. Not since the 1920's had women's clothing changed so radically. No one could remember when the flow of fashion had been reversed on such a scale.

This was all to the good. Few tendencies in the sixties were entirely wholesome. Some were very dangerous. But the breakdown of fashion authority and the stylistic anarchy that followed were wonderful. While skirts went up, they also went down. When the ankle-length "maxi-skirt" came in, the mini did not go out. The result was that a woman might wear a mini-skirt under a maxi-coat, or a late Victorian top over either length. Hair could be long or short. Necklines might touch the throat or the navel. Every kind of color, pattern, and design flourished. Wigs of many shades followed. Even the sober eyeglass became a fashion accessory, being sometimes huge and dark, other times small and wire-framed. Not everyone made intelligent use of her new freedom. As always in modern times, designers liked the young and thin. Less favored people could not always resist wearing styles inappropriate to them. But only individual bad taste or perversity was responsible for this. Fashion's door opened so wide that, properly worn, almost anything went. Never before had women such a range of garments to choose from. Many, particularly older ones, failed to profit from this. They went on wearing conventional garments whether suited to them or not.

It was the rare elderly woman who looked good in deep-necked, bare-armed evening dresses, yet few took advantage of the formal pants suits and party pajamas that enabled older people to be in style without exposing the ravages of time. It was the young, who had no need of them, who ordinarily wore such outfits. The ideal strategy would be to expose oneself when young and firm, and then cover up as needed later. For the first time it became theoretically possible to do this. If such freedom persisted, women might learn to take advantage of it.

By mid-decade even the great couturiers had accepted the new wave. Yves St. Laurent included utterly transparent—save for a few opaque bands—dresses in one collection. Other designers cut large circles out of their garments, usually around the midriff. In 1964 Christian Dior had plunged necklines below the waist. The next year armholes dipped also. André Courrèges developed the first true pop-fashion line. It involved white boots, zombie glasses, astronaut baby bonnets, and a short, boxy silhouette in stark white, pastel, or checked fabrics. One critic thought it resembled architecture more than textiles.

Few girls next door wore clothes that extreme. But in modified and low-priced versions the new styles were very popular. Mini-skirts became common. With them girls wore knee boots and short A-line coats. Boots made whips a suitable fashion accessory. Sadomasochism in dress was further encouraged by one firm which sold a leather or vinyl garment called "The Story of O" dress, after a chic pornographic novel by that name. Betsy Johnson developed the do-it-yourself dress, a clear plastic shell with separate designs to be stuck on as the wearer pleased.

Male clothing changed too. In 1962 Pierre Cardin introduced a male line to complement his clothes for women. At first his tight-waisted, long-jacketed suits seemed peculiar. Only the slightly precious wore them. The Beatles helped change that in 1964 with their Prince Valiant hairdos, suits buttoned to the chin, visored caps, and extravagant haberdashery. Though they later went hippie, the original effect persisted. Young males began to flower. Older ones emulated them, more discreetly of course. Frilly, vivid clothes on the model of Carnaby Street appeared in U.S. department stores. Bonwit Teller added a Cardin male boutique in 1966. The same year fur coats for men appeared, though they were rare until football superstar Broadway Joe Namath bought a mink two years later. Ties, collars, and cuffs widened. Trouser legs flared and belled. Shirts got darker; ties lighter. Sideburns sprouted. Some styles were transient, like the all too forgettable Nehru coats of 1968. But generally male fashions followed the women's lead. Not since the eighteenth century had men been so colorfully arrayed. They never smelled better either. By the mid-sixties American males were spending nearly half a billion dollars yearly on scents and beauty aids. They became almost as gorgeous and sexy as women. Where once at parties men resembled penguins, they now emulated the peacock. And best of all, unlike so much else in the decade, no one was the worse for it.

The rebellion against traditional fashion went in two directions, though both were inspired by the young. The line of development just described emphasized brilliant or peculiar fabrics and designs. Here the emphasis was on costuming in a theatrical sense. People wore outfits that made them look like Mongols or cavaliers or whatever. These costumes, never cheap, were often very costly, though not more so than earlier styles. They were worn by others besides the young. What they owed to the emerging counter-culture was a certain freedom from constraint, and a degree of sensuality. Though the mini-skirt became a symbol of rebellious youth, it was so popular that wearing it was not an ideological statement, even if Middle Americans often thought so.

The other direction clothing took was more directly related to counter-cultural patterns. This mode had two seemingly incompatible elements —surplus military garments and handcrafted ones. Army and navy surplus clothing was the first style to be adopted by young people looking for a separate identity. Socially conscious youths began wearing army and navy jackets, shirts, and bell-bottom trousers in the early sixties. This was not meant to show contempt for the military, for anti-war sentiment was then at a low ebb, but as a mark of ostentatious frugality in the high-consumption society. As these garments became more in demand, the price went up and more expensive commercial imitations appeared. Wearing them accordingly meant less, but a certain flavor of austere nonconformity stuck to them all the same. They remained favorites of dissenting youths thereafter, even though worn by the merely fashionable too.

The hippies made handcrafted items popular. The implication here was that the wearer had made them, thus showing his independence and creativity. In the beginning this may often have been so. Soon, however, the market was so large and the people with skill and patience so limited that handcrafted items were commercially made and distributed, frequently by entrepreneurs among the young, sometimes through ordinary apparel channels. Bead shops and hippie boutiques became commonplace. Though their products were often quite costly, the vogue persisted among deviant youths anyway, partly because it was clear that whatever they wore would soon be imitated, partly because the message involved was too dear to abandon. Wearing beads, bangles, leather goods, fringes, colorful vests, and what all showed sympathy for American Indians, who inspired the most common designs, and fitted in with the popular back-to-nature ethic. When combined with military surplus garments they enabled the wearer to touch all the counter-cultural bases at once. Thus these fashions transmitted, however faintly, signals meaning peace, love, brotherhood, noble savagery, community, folk artistry, anti-capitalism and anti-militarism, and, later, revolutionary zeal.

This hippie *cum* military surplus mode also had a functional effect. It was a great leveler: when everyone wore the same bizarre costumes, everyone looked alike. Even better, it gave the ugly parity with the beautiful for the first time in modern history. Most of these costumes were pretty ghastly. A string of beads or an Indian headband did not redeem faded blue jeans and an army shirt. Long stringy hair or an untrimmed beard only aggravated the effect. Yet the young called such outfits beautiful. In effect, aesthetics were exchanged for ethics. Beauty was no longer related to appearance but to morality. To have the proper spirit, though homely, was to be beautiful. This was a great relief for the poorly endowed and a point in the counter-culture's favor. Yet it enraged adults. Once the association between beads, beards, and military surplus goods on the one hand, and radicalism and dope on the other, was established, Middle America declared war on the counter-culture's physical trappings. School systems everywhere waged a relentless struggle against long hair. To dress this way in many places was a hostile act which invited reprisals. The style became a chief symbol of the generation gap, clung to fanatically by youngsters the more they were persecuted for it, as fiercely resisted by their elders. The progress of the generational struggle could almost be measured by the spread of these fashions.

No doubt older people would have resented the new styles in any case, but the way they emerged made them doubly offensive. They were introduced by young bohemians, mainly in New York and San Francisco, whose deviant attributes were highly publicized. New York hippies were concentrated in a section called the East Village. (Greenwich Village, the traditional bohemian refuge, had gotten too commercial and expensive.) By the mid-sixties a sizable community of radicals, dropouts, youthful vagrants, unrecognized avant-garde artists, and others were assembling there and a variety of cults beginning to flourish. One of the odder was called Kerista. It was a religio-sexual movement that planned to establish a colony in the Caribbean. "Utopia Tomorrow for Swingers," its publication, the *Kerista Speeler*, proclaimed. Kerista invoked a murky, perfectionist theology revolving around sexual love.

Sometimes the members engaged in bisexual gropes to advance the pleasure principle. This sounded like more fun than it actually was, according to visitors.

The mainstream of East Village cultural life was more formally political and artistic. The many activities of Ed Sanders suggest the range of enterprises generated there. He was editor and publisher of *Fuck You: A Magazine of the Arts*. A typical editorial in it began: "Time is NOW for TOTAL ASSAULT ON THE MARIJUANA LAWS. It is CLEAR to us that the cockroach theory of grass smoking has to be abandoned. IN THE OPEN! ALL THOSE WHO SUCK UP THE BENEVOLENT NARCOTIC CANNABIS, TEENSHUN!! FORWARD, WITH MIND DIALS POINTED: ASSAULT! We have the facts! Cannabis is a nonaddictive gentle peace drug! The marijuana legislations were pushed through in the 1930's by the agents and goonsquads of the jansensisto-manichean fuckhaters' conspiracy. Certainly after 30 years of the blight, it is time to rise up for a bleep blop bleep assault on the social screen. . . . But we can't wait forever you grass cadets to pull the takeover: grass-freak senators, labor leaders, presidents, etc.! The Goon Squads are few and we are many. We must spray our message into the million lobed American brain IMMEDIATELY!"

Sanders was also head of the East Village's most prominent rock group, The Fugs. They sang obscene songs of their own composition, and created equally obscene instruments for accompaniment (such as the erectophone, which appeared to be a long stick with bells on it). Among their better efforts were "What Are You Doing After the Orgy?" and the memorable "Kill for Peace." *The Fugs Song Book* described their music thusly:

The Fug-songs seem to spurt into five areas of concentration:
a) nouveau folk-freak
b) sex rock and roll
c) dope thrill chants
d) horny cunt-hunger blues
e) Total Assault on the Culture
   (anti-war/anti-creep/anti-repression)
. . . The meaning of the Fugs lies in the term BODY POETRY, to get at the frenzy of the thing, the grope-thing, The Body Poetry Formula is this:
The Head by the way of the Big Beat to the genitals
The Genitals by way of Operation Brain Thrill to the Body Poetry.

In his spare time Sanders made pornographic movies. His most epic work, *Mongolian Cluster Fuck!*, was described in *Fuck You* as a "short but searing non-socially redeeming porn flick featuring 100 of the lower east side's finest, with musical background by Algernon Charles Swinburne & THE FUGS." Though more versatile and creative than most, Sanders was typical of the East Village's alienated young artists. Tiny papers like *Fuck You* were springing up everywhere. All tried to be obscene, provocative, and, it was thought, liberating. They despised form, caring only for the higher morality and aesthetics it was their duty to advance. Some were more political (porno-political usually) than others. Collectively they were soon to be known as the "underground press."

Several cuts above the underground press were the flourishing little magazines. They were avant garde in the traditional sense and aimed, in their way, for greatness. By 1966 there were at least 250 of these (as against sixty or so in the 1920's). The better financed (*Outsider, Steppenwolf*) were tastefully composed and printed; others were crudely photo-offset (*Kayak, Eventorium Muse*). The *Insect Trust Gazette,* an annual experiment, once published an issue in which the original manuscripts were simply photographed and printed without reduction. About a third of the "littles" were mimeographed. There was even a little magazine for scientists, the *Worm-Runners' Digest,* edited by a droll researcher at the University of Michigan for people of like taste.

Older cultural rebels contributed to the ferment. George Brecht's musical composition "Ladder" went as follows: "Paint a single straight ladder white/Paint the bottom rung black/Distribute spectral colors on the rungs between." Even more to the point was "Laugh Piece" by John Lennon's future wife, Yoko Ono. It went "Keep laughing for a week." Nam June Paik composed a work known as "Young Penis Symphony." He was also an underground film producer and put on elaborate performances resembling the late happenings. One such was given at the Film-Makers Cinematheque using film, live music, and the cellist Charlotte Moorman. The audience saw short segments of a film by Robert Breer, alternating with views of Miss Moorman, silhouetted by backlighting behind the projection screen, playing short phrases of a Bach cello sonata. On completing each phrase she removed a garment. Another film clip would then be shown. This continued until she was lying on the floor, completely nude, playing her cello which was now atop her. Miss Moorman, "the Jeanne d'Arc of New Music," as she was called, appeared in other Paik compositions. She had been trained at the Juilliard School and was a member of Leopold Stokowski's American Symphony Orchestra.

As these few examples suggest, the East Village gained from its proximity to the New York avant garde. The mature counter-culture owed a lot to this relationship, but even in its early stages the East Village suffered from the influx of teenie-boppers and runaways who were to spoil both it and the Haight-Ashbury for serious cultural radicals. The people who were soon to be called hippies meant to build alternatives to the straight world. Against the hostile competitive, capitalistic values of bourgeois America they posed their own faith in nonviolence, love, and community. Drugs were important both as means to truth and advancers of the pleasure principle. The early hippies created institutions of sorts. Rock bands like the Jefferson Airplane, the Grateful Dead, Country Joe and the Fish flourished, as did communal societies, notably the Diggers. They were inspired by the seventeenth-century communists whose name they took. In practice they were a hip version of the Salvation Army.

Hippies lived together, in "tribes" or "families." Their golden rule was "Be nice to others, even when provoked, and they will be nice to you." In San Francisco their reservation was the Haight-Ashbury district near Golden Gate Park. They were much resented in the East Village by the natives, poor ethnics for the most part. In the Hashbury, on the other hand, they were welcome at first. Though peculiar, they were an improvement over the petty criminals they displaced. Even when freaked-out in public from drugs, a certain tolerance prevailed. After all, stepping over a drooling flower child on the street was better than getting mugged. Civic authorities were less open-minded. The drug traffic bothered them especially, and the Hashbury was loaded with "narks" (narcotics agents). Hunter S. Thompson wrote that "love is the password in the Haight-Ashbury, but paranoia is the style. Nobody wants to go to jail."

The fun-and-games era did not last long, perhaps only from 1965 to 1966. The hippie ethic was too fragile to withstand the combination of police surveillance and media exposure that soon afflicted it. The first hippies had a certain earnestness. But they were joined by masses of teen-age runaways. Nicholas von Hoffman observed that the Hashbury economy that began as a fraternal barter system quickly succumbed to the cash nexus. It became the first community in the world to revolve entirely around the buying and selling and taking of drugs. Marijuana and LSD were universal; less popular, but also commonplace, were LSD's more powerful relative STP, and amphetamines. "Speed kills" said the buttons and posters; speed freaks multiplied anyhow. To support themselves some hippies worked at casual labor or devised elaborate, usually unsuccessful schemes to make money out of hippie enterprises. Panhandling was popular, so was theft, disguised usually as communism.

Bohemians invariably deplore monogamy, and the hippies were no exception. As one member of the Jefferson Airplane put it "The stage is our bed and the audience is our broad. We're not entertaining, we're making love." Though committed to sexual freedom on principle, and often promiscuous in fact, the hippies were not really very sexy. Timothy Leary notwithstanding, drugs seemed to dampen the sexual urge. And the hippies were too passive in any case for strenuous sex play. Conversely, the most ardent free lovers, like those in the Sexual Freedom League, had little interest in drugs. Among hippies the combination of bad diets, dope, communal living, and the struggle to survive made for a restricted sex life. Of course the hippies were always glad of chances to shock the bourgeoisie, which made them seem more depraved than they were. Then too, people expected them to be sexually perverse, and the more public-spirited hippies tried to oblige. Like good troupers they hated to let the public down, though willing to put it on.

Hippie relations with black people were worse than might have been supposed. Hippies owed blacks a lot. Their jargon was derived from the ghetto. They admired blacks, as certain whites always have, for being more emotional, sensual, and uninhibited. But there were very few black hippies. Superspade, a beloved Negro drug pusher, was an exception. Most hippies were frightened of blacks. "Spades are programmed for hate" was the way many put it. The Hashbury was periodically swept by rumors of impending black attacks. Some hippies looked to the motorcycle outlaws to protect them from black rage. This was not without a certain logic. Outlaws hated blacks and loved to fight. But they played their role as hippie militiamen uneasily. In truth they were more likely to destroy a hippie than defend him.

In the end it was neither the bikers nor the blacks but the media that destroyed hippiedom. The publicity given the summer of love attracted countless thousands of disturbed youngsters to the Hashbury and the East Village in 1967. San Francisco was not burdened with the vast numbers originally expected. But many did come, bringing in their train psychotics, drug peddlers, and all sorts of criminals. Drug poisoning, hepatitis (from infected needles), and various diseases resulting from malnutrition and exposure thinned their ranks. Rapes, muggings, and assaults became commonplace. Hippies had little money, but they were irresistibly easy marks. Hippie girls were safe to assault. They reacted passively, and as many were drug users and runaways they could not go to the police.

So the violence mounted. On the West Coast one drug peddler was stabbed to death and his right forearm removed. Superspade's body was found hanging from a cliff top. He had been stabbed, shot, and trussed in a sleeping bag. On October 8 the nude bodies of Linda Rea Fitzpatrick, eighteen, and James Leroy "Groovy" Hutchinson, twenty-one, were discovered in an East Village boiler room. They had been murdered while high on LSD. Though pregnant, Miss Fitzpatrick had also been raped. That was how the summer of love ended. Two days earlier the death and funeral of hippie had been ritually observed in San Francisco's Buena Vista Park. But the killing of Linda and Groovy marked its real end. The Hashbury deteriorated rapidly thereafter. Bad publicity drove the tourists away, and the hippie boutiques that serviced them closed. Some local rock groups dissolved; others, like the Jefferson Airplane and even the Grateful Dead, went commercial. The hippies and their institutions faded quietly away. The Hashbury regained something of its old character. The East Village, owing to its more diverse population and strategic location, changed less.

At its peak the hippie movement was the subject of much moralizing. Most often hippies were seen as degenerate and representative of all things godless and un-American. A minority accepted them as embodying a higher morality. The media viewed them as harmless, even amusing, freaks—which was probably closest to the truth. But before long it was clear that while the hippie movement was easily slain, the hippie style of life was not. Their habit of dressing up in costumes rather than outfits was widely imitated. So was their slang and their talk of peace, love, and beauty. The great popularity of ex-hippie rock groups was one sign of the cultural diffusion taking place, marijuana another. Weekend tripping spread to the suburbs. While the attempt to build parallel cultures on a large scale in places like the Hashbury failed, the hippies survived in many locales. Isolated farms, especially in New England and the Southwest, were particularly favored. And they thrived also on the fringes of colleges and universities, where the line between avant-garde student and alienated dropout was hard to draw. In tribes, families, and communes the hippies lived on, despite considerable local harassment wherever they went.

Though few in number, hippies had a great effect on middle-class youth. Besides their sartorial influence, hippies made religion socially acceptable. Their interest in the supernatural was contagious. Some of the communes which sprang up in the late sixties were actually religious fellowships practicing a contemporary monasticism. One in western Massachusetts was called the Cathedral of the Spirit. Its forty members were led by a nineteen-year-old mystic who helped them prepare for the Second Coming and the new Aquarian Age when all men would be brothers. The Cathedral had rigid rules against alcohol, "sex without love," and, less typically, drugs. Members helped out neighboring farmers without pay, but the commune was essentially contemplative. Its sacred book was a fifty-seven-page typewritten manuscript composed by a middle-aged bus driver from Northfield, Massachusetts, which was thought to be divinely inspired. Another commune in Boston, called the Fort Hill Community, was more outward looking. Its sixty members hoped to spread their holy word through the mass media.

Some of the communes or brotherhoods sprang from traditional roots. In New York City a band of young Jews formed a Havurah (fellowship) to blend Jewish traditions with contemporary inspirations. They wanted to study subjects like "the prophetic mind; new forms of spirituality in the contemporary world; and readings from the Jewish mystical tradition." At the University of Massachusetts a hundred students celebrated Rosh Hashanah not in a synagogue but in a field where they danced and sang all night. Courses in religion multiplied. At Smith College the number of students taking them grew from 692 in 1954 to nearly 1,400 in 1969, though the student body remained constant at about 2,000. Columbia University had two hundred applicants for a graduate program in religion with only twenty openings.

Students saw traditional religion as a point of departure rather than a place for answers. Comparatively few joined the new fellowships, but large numbers were attracted to the concepts they embodied. Oriental theologies and the like grew more attractive, so did magic. At one Catholic university a coven of warlocks was discovered. They were given psychiatric attention (thereby missing a great chance. If only they had been exorcised instead, the Establishment would have shown its relevance). When a Canadian university gave the studentry a chance to recommend new courses they overwhelmingly asked for subjects like Zen, sorcery, and witchcraft. A work of classic Oriental magic, *I Ching* or the *Book of Changes*, became popular. The best edition, a scholarly product of the Princeton University Press, used to sell a thousand copies a year. In 1968 fifty thousand copies were snapped up. Sometimes magic and mysticism were exploited more in fun than not. The Women's Liberation Movement had guerrilla theater troupes calling themselves WITCH (Women's International Terrorist Conspiracy from Hell). During the SDS sit-in at the University of Chicago they cursed the sociology department and put a hex on its chairman.

But there was a serious element to the vogue for magic. Teachers of philosophy and religion were struck by the anti-positivist, anti-science feelings of many students. Science was discredited as an agent of the military-industrial complex. It had failed to make life more attractive. Whole classes protested the epistemology of science as well as its intellectual dominion. Students believed the Establishment claimed to be rational, but showed that it was not. This supported one of the central truths of all religion, that man is more than a creature who reasons. Nor was it only the young who felt this way. Norman Mailer was something of a mystic, so was Timothy Leary. And the most ambitious academic effort to deal with these things, Theodore Roszak's *The Making of a Counter Culture*, ended with a strong appeal to faith. Like the alienated young, Roszak too rejected science and reason—"the myth of objective consciousness" as he called it. Instead of empiricism or the scientific method he wanted "the beauty of the fully illuminated personality" to be "our standard of truth." He liked magic as "a matter of communion with the forces of nature as if they were mindful, intentional presences." What he admired most in the New Left was its attempt, as he thought, to revive shamanism, to get back to the sanity and participatory democracy of prehistoric society. But he urged the left to give up its notion that violence and confrontation would change the world. What the left must do to influence the silent majority "was not simply to muster power against the misdeeds of society, but to transform the very sense men have of reality."

The anti-war movement was strongly affected by this new supernaturalism. On Moratorium Day in 1969 a University of Massachusetts student gave an emotional speech that brought the audience to its feet shouting, "The war is over." "He went into a dance, waving his arms," a campus minister said. "It was the essence of a revival meeting, where the audience makes a commitment to Christ at the end." The great peace demonstrations in 1969 were full of religious symbolism. In Boston 100,000 people gathered before a gigantic cross on the Common. In New York lighted candles were carried to the steps of St. Patrick's Cathedral. Candles were placed on the White House wall during the November mobilization. At other demonstrations the shofar, the ram's horn sounded by Jews at the beginning of each new year, was blown. Rock, the liturgical music of the young, was often played. So was folk music, which continued as a medium of moral expression after its popular decline.

Theology reflected the new supernaturalism, just as it had the aggressive secularism of a few years earlier. Harvey Cox, most famous of the contemporary theologians, published a study of the extra-institutional spiritual revival called *The Feast of Fools* in 1969. "God Is Dead" gave way to the "Theology of Hope," after Jurgen Moltmann's book by that title. A German theologian, Moltmann argued that the trouble with Christian theology was that it ignored the future. "The Church lives on memories, the world on hope," he remarked elsewhere. Though he was a Protestant, Roman Catholic theologians in Germany and America agreed with him. Institutional churches responded to the new by absorbing as much of it as they could. Church happenings, rock masses, light shows, and readings from Eastern mystics were used by Protestants and Catholics alike. The home mass gained popularity among Catholics. It gave to formal worship something of the intimate fellowship that the young found so compelling. Thus while church attendance declined from the high levels of the 1950's, this did not mean a decrease in religious enthusiasm. The most striking aspect of the "religious revival" of the 1950's, after all, had been the absence of devotion. Going to church then was more a social than a religious act. In the late sixties faith was expressed by not going to church.

There were many ways of responding to this spiritual revival. Orthodox churchgoers were offended by it, and even more by the efforts of their denominations to win the inspirited young. More flexible religious leaders saw it as a great opportunity. Secular radicals and educators were more often depressed by it. Men whose lives were dedicated to the pursuit of truth through reason were not about to become shamans. If it was true that science and scholarship had not yet brought the millennium, this did not seem good cause for abandoning them.

The most surprising man to protest this new turn was Paul Goodman. Goodman's life and work were more nearly of a piece than most people's. He was a secular anarchist, but while hoping to wreck the old order, he believed that the old tools—reason, expertise, science—would still be needed. Hence, though he was one of the chief intellectual mentors of the counter-culture, its growing spiritualism, indeed anti-intellectualism, disturbed him.

Late in 1969 he wrote that this first became clear to him while giving a graduate seminar on "professionalism." He hoped to teach the difference between careerism and fidelity to a professional calling. To his astonishment the class rejected the notion that there was such a thing as a true profession. All decisions were made by the power structure. Professionals were merely peer groups formed to delude the public and make money. "Didn't every society, however just, require experts?" he asked. No, they insisted; it was only important to be human, and all else would follow.

Suddenly I realized that they did not really believe that there was a nature of things. Somehow all functions could be reduced to interpersonal relations and power. There was no knowledge, but only the sociology of knowledge. They had so well learned that physical and sociological research is subsidized and conducted for the benefit of the ruling class that they did not believe there was such a thing as the simple truth. To be required to learn something was a trap by which the young were put down and co-opted. Then I knew that I could not get through to them. I had imagined that the world-wide student protest had to do with changing political and moral institutions, to which I was sympathetic, but I now saw that we had to do with a religious crisis of the magnitude of the Reformation in the fifteen hundreds, when not only all institutions but all learning had been corrupted by the Whore of Babylon.

This was a strange confession from one who specialized in youth and its discontents, as Goodman fully realized. His most influential book, *Growing Up Absurd* (1960), dealt with generational alienation. But he had thought it a specialized deviance then, and was heartened by the new student radicals "who made human sense and were not absurd at all. But the alienating circumstances had proved too strong after all; here were absurd graduate students, most of them political activists." "Alienation," he continued, "is a powerful motivation of unrest, fantasy, and reckless action. It leads . . . to religious innovation, new sacraments to give life meaning. But it is a poor basis for politics, including revolutionary politics." Mere confrontation was not the answer to society's ills, especially when done hatefully. Gandhi's great point had been that the confronter aims at future community with the confronted. Yet many New Leftists did not regard their enemies as members of the same species. "How can the young people think of a future community when they themselves have no present world, no profession or other job in it, and no trust in other human beings? Instead, some young radicals seem to entertain the disastrous illusion that other people can be compelled by fear. This can lead only to crushing reaction."

The young knew nothing of society's institutions, how they worked, where they came from, what had made them what they were. For many, history began in 1968. "I am often hectored to my face," Goodman said, "with formulations that I myself put in their mouths, that have become part of the oral tradition two years old, author prehistoric." They didn't trust people over thirty because they didn't understand them and were too conceited to try. "Having grown up in a world too meaningless to learn anything, they know very little and are quick to resent it." The most important thing to the young was being together, en masse if possible. At the rock festivals they found the meaning of life which, as they explained it, consisted of people being nice to each other. A group of them passing a stick of marijuana behaved like "a Quaker meeting waiting for the spirit." And, Goodman concluded, "in the end it is religion that constitutes the strength of this generation, and not, as I used to think, their morality, political will, and common sense." Neither moral courage nor honesty was their salient trait, but rather "metaphysical vitality."

Goodman's argument was an exceptionally brave one. No one who had done less for the young could in good conscience have spoken so bluntly of them. And religion as an organizing principle for making sense of the serious young seemed useful. But it didn't help to distinguish what was durable and what merely fashionable in the counterculture. The term itself was hard to define as it embraced almost everything new and anti-Establishment, however frivolous. On its deepest level the counter-culture was the radical critique of Herbert Marcuse, Norman O. Brown, and even Paul Goodman. It also meant the New Left, communes and hippie farms, magic, hedonism, eroticism, and public nudity. And it included rock music, long hair, and mini-skirts (or, alternatively, fatigue uniforms, used clothes, and the intentionally ugly or grotesque). Most attacks on the counter-culture were directed at its trivial aspects, pot and dress especially. Pot busts (police raids), often involving famous people or their children, became commonplace. The laws against pot were so punitive in some areas as to be almost unenforceable. Even President Nixon, spokesman for Middle American morality that he was, finally questioned them. Local fights against long hair, beards, and short skirts were beyond number. The American Civil Liberties Union began taking school systems to court for disciplining students on that account. New York City gave up trying to enforce dress codes. It was all the more difficult there as even the teachers were mod. At one school the principal ordered women teachers to wear smocks over their minis. They responded by buying mini-smocks.

Nor were athletics—the last bastion of orthodoxy, one might think— exempt, though coaches struggled to enforce yesterday's fashions. At Oregon State University one football player, the son of an Air Force officer, went hippie and dropped the sport. His coach said, "I recruited that boy thinking he was Jack Armstrong. I was wrong. He turned out to be a free-thinker." At the University of Pennsylvania a star defensive back showed up for summer practice with shoulder-length hair, sideburns down to the neck, beads, bells, thonged sandals, and a cloth sash round his waist. He was the only man on the team to bring a pet dog and a stereo set to the six-day camp. After a war of nerves culminating in an ultimatum from the coach, he grudgingly hacked a few inches off his mane. And so it went all over America.

Both sides in this struggle took fashion and style to be deadly serious matters, so political conflicts tended to become cultural wars. In the fall of 1969 the most important radical student group at New York University was called Transcendental Students. At a time when SDS could barely muster twenty-five members, five hundred or more belonged to TS. It began the previous semester when a group protesting overcrowding in the classroom staged a series of freak-outs in classrooms. This proved so attractive a custom that it was institutionalized. Rock, pot, and wine parties had obvious advantages over political action. The administration shrewdly made a former restaurant available to TS for a counter-cultural center. The students welcomed it as a haven for "guerrilla intellect" where the human spirit could breathe free. The administration saw it as just another recreational facility, which, of course, it was. And what dean would not rather have the kids singing out in a restaurant than locking him in his office? Sometimes culture and politics were united. When the $12 million center for the performing arts opened in Milwaukee, Wisconsin, on September 18, 1969, six hundred students disrupted the inaugural concert. They rubbed balloons, blew bubble pipes, threw rolls of toilet paper, and demanded that 20 per cent of the seats be given free to welfare recipients.

The greatest event in counter-cultural history was the Woodstock

Festival in Bethel, New York. It was organized on the pattern of other large rock festivals. Big-name groups were invited for several days of continuous entertaining in the open. A large crowd was expected, but nothing like the 300,000 or 400,000 youngsters who actually showed up on August 15, 1969. Everything fell apart in consequence. Tickets could not be collected nor services provided. There wasn't enough food or water. The roads were blocked with abandoned autos, and no one could get in or out for hours at a time. Surprisingly, there were no riots or disasters. The promoters chartered a fleet of helicopters to evacuate casualties (mostly from bad drug trips) and bring in essential supplies. Despite the rain and congestion, a good time was had by all (except the boy killed when a tractor accidentally drove over his sleeping bag). No one had ever seen so large and ruly a gathering before. People stripped down, smoked pot, and turned on with nary a discouraging word, so legend has it. Afterward the young generally agreed that it was a beautiful experience proving their superior morality. People were nicer to each other than ever before. Even the police were impressed by the public's order (a result of their wisely deciding not to enforce the drug laws).

But the counter-culture had its bad moments in 1969 also. Haight-Ashbury continued to decay. It was now mainly a slum where criminals preyed on helpless drug freaks. Worse still was the Battle of Berkeley, which put both the straight culture and the counter-culture in the worst possible light, especially the former. The University of California owned a number of vacant lots south of the campus. The land had been cleared in anticipation of buildings it was unable to construct. One block lay vacant for so long that the street people—hippies, students, dropouts, and others—transformed it into a People's Park. Pressure was brought on the University by the local power structure to block its use, which was done. On May 15 some six thousand students and street people held a rally on campus, then advanced on the park. County sheriffs, highway patrolmen, and the Berkeley police met them with a hail of gunfire. One person died of buckshot wounds, another was blinded. Many more were shot though few arrested. Those who were arrested were handled so brutally that the circuit court enjoined the sheriff to have his men stop beating and abusing them. Disorders continued. Governor Reagan declared a state of emergency and brought in the National Guard. Five days later one of its helicopters sprayed gas over the campus, thus making the educational process at Berkeley even more trying than usual.

Of course the Establishment was most to blame for Vietnamizing the cultural war. But the meretricious aspects of the counter-culture were evident too. If the police were really "fascist pigs," as the street people said, why goad and defy them? And especially why harass the National

Guardsmen who didn't want to be in Berkeley anyhow? This was hardly on the same order as murdering people with shotguns. Yet such behavior was stupid, pointless, and self-defeating, like so much else in the counter-culture. The silent majority was not won over. Nor was the People's Park saved. A year later the area was still fenced in. (Though vacant. The University, having pretended to want it as a recreational area, tried to make it one. But as the students thought it stained with innocent blood, they avoided it.)

The rock festival at Altamont that winter was another disaster. It was a free concert that climaxed the Rolling Stones' whirlwind tour of the U.S. They called it their gift to the fans. Actually it was a clever promotion. The Stones had been impressed with the moneymaking potential of Woodstock. While Woodstock cost the promoters a fortune, they stood to recoup their losses with a film of the event. This inspired the Stones to do a Woodstock themselves. At the last minute they obtained the use of Dick Carter's Altamont Raceway. It had been doing poorly and the owner thought the publicity would help business. Little was done to prepare the site. The police didn't have enough notice to bring in reserves, so the Stones hired a band of Hell's Angels as security guards (for $500 worth of beer). The Stones did their thing and the Angels did theirs.

The result was best captured by a *Rolling Stone* magazine photograph showing Mick Jagger looking properly aghast while Angels beat a young Negro to death on stage. A musician who tried to stop them was knocked unconscious, and he was lucky at that. Before the day was over many more were beaten, though no others fatally. Sometimes the beatings were for aesthetic reasons. One very fat man took off his clothes in the approved rock festival manner. This offended the Angels who set on him with pool cues. No one knows how many were clubbed that day. The death count came to four. Apart from Meredith Hunter, who was stabbed and kicked to death, they mostly died by accident. A car drove off the road into a clump of people and killed two. A man, apparently high on drugs, slid into an irrigation canal and drowned. The drug freak-outs were more numerous than at Woodstock. The medical care was less adequate. Not that the physicians on hand didn't try; they just lacked the support provided at Woodstock, whose promoters had spared no expense to avert disaster. Oddly enough the press, normally so eager to exploit the counter-culture, missed the point of Altamont. Early accounts followed the customary rock festival line, acclaiming it as yet another triumph of youth. In the East it received little attention of any kind.

It remained for *Rolling Stone*, the rock world's most authoritative journal, to tell the whole story of what it called the Altamont Death

Festival. The violence was quite bad enough, but what especially bothered *Rolling Stone* was the commercial cynicism behind it. That huge gathering was assembled by the Stones to make a lucrative film on the cheap. They could have hired legitimate security guards, but it cost less to use the Angels. (At Woodstock unarmed civilians trained by the Hog Farm commune kept order.) They were too rushed for the careful planning that went into Woodstock, too callous (and greedy) to pour in the emergency resources that had saved the day there. And, appropriately, they faked the moviemaking too so as to have a documentary of the event they intended, not the one they got. *Rolling Stone* said that a cameraman was recording a fat, naked girl freaking out backstage when the director stopped him. "Don't shoot that. That's ugly. We only want beautiful things." The cameraman made the obvious response. "How can you possibly say that? Everything here is so ugly."

Rolling Stone thought the star system at fault. Once a band got as big as the Stones they experienced delusions of grandeur, "ego trips" in the argot. And with so much money to be made by high-pressure promotions, "the hype" became inevitable. Others agreed. The *Los Angeles Free Press,* biggest of the underground papers, ran a full-page caricature of Mick Jagger with an Adolf Hitler mustache, arm draped around a Hell's Angel, while long-haired kids gave them the Nazi salute. Ralph Gleason of the *San Francisco Chronicle* explained Altamont this way: "The name of the game is money, power, and ego, and money is first as it brings power. The Stones didn't do it for free, they did it for money, only the tab was paid in a different way. Whoever goes to the movie paid for the Altamont religious assembly."* Quite so. But why did so many others go along with the Stones? The Jefferson Airplane, and especially the Grateful Dead, reputedly the most socially conscious rock bands, participated. So did counter-culture folk heroes like Emmet Grogan of the Diggers. Here the gullibility—innocence, perhaps—of the deviant young was responsible. Because the rock bandits smoked pot and talked a revolutionary game, they were supposed to be different from other entertainers. Even though they made fortunes and spent them ostentatiously, their virtue was always presumed. What Altamont showed was that the difference between a rock king and a robber baron was about six inches of hair.†

---

* Gleason was the best writer on popular music and the youth culture associated with it, which he once admired greatly. For an earlier assessment see his "Like a Rolling Stone," *American Scholar* (Autumn 1967).

† This is to criticize the singer, not the song. Whatever one might think of some performers, there is no doubt that rock itself was an exciting musical form. Adults rarely heard it because rock seldom was played on television, or even radio in most parts of the country. Rock artists appeared mainly in concerts and clubs, to which few over thirty went. Not knowing the music, there was little reason for them to buy

If Altamont exposed one face of the counter-culture, the Manson family revealed another. Late in 1969 Sharon Tate, a pregnant movie actress, and four of her jet-set friends were ritually murdered in the expensive Bel-Air district of Los Angeles. Though apparently senseless, their deaths were thought related to the rootless, thrill-oriented life style of the Beautiful People. But on December 1 policemen began arresting obscure hippies. Their leader, Charles Manson, was an ex-convict and seemingly deranged. Susan Atkins, a member of his "family," gave several cloudy versions of what had happened. On the strength of them Manson was indicted for murder. Though his guilt remained unproven, the basic facts about his past seemed clear. He was a neglected child who became a juvenile delinquent. In 1960 he was convicted of forgery and spent seven years in the penitentiary. On his release he went to the Hashbury and acquired a harem of young girls. After floating through the hippie underground for a time, he left the Hashbury with his family of nine girls and five boys early in 1968. They ended up at Spahn's Ranch in the Santa Susana Mountains, north of the San Fernando Valley. The owner was old and blind. Manson terrified him. But the girls took care of him so he let the family stay on. They spent a year at the ranch before the police suspected them of stealing cars. Then they camped out in the desert until arrested.

Life with the Manson family was a combination of hippieism and paranoia. Manson subscribed to the usual counter-cultural values. Inhibitions, the Establishment, regular employment, and other straight virtues were bad. Free love, nature, dope, rock, and mysticism were good. He believed a race war was coming (predicted in Beatle songs) and armed his family in anticipation of it. Some of the cars they stole were modified for use in the desert, where he meant to make his last stand. And, naturally, he tried to break into the rock music business. One reason why he allegedly murdered Miss Tate and her friends was that they were in a house previously occupied by a man who had broken a promise to advance Manson's career. The Manson family was thought to have killed other people even more capriciously. Yet after his arrest most of the girls remained loyal to Manson. Young, largely middle class, they were still "hypnotized" or "enslaved" by him. Those not arrested continued to hope for a family reunion. Of course hippies were not murderers usually. But the repressed hostility, authoritarianism, perversity, and

---

the records that showed rock at its most complex and interesting. Like jazz, rock became more sophisticated with time and made greater demands on the artist's talent. Even more than jazz, rock produced an army of amateur and semi-professional players around the country. Though often making up in volume what they lacked in skill, their numbers alone guaranteed that rock would survive its exploiters.

mindless paranoia that underlay much of the hippie ethic were never displayed more clearly. The folkways of the flower children tended toward extremes. At one end they were natural victims; at the other, natural victimizers. The Manson family were both at once.

Taken together the varieties of life among deviant youths showed the counter-culture to be disintegrating. What was disturbing about it was not so much the surface expression as its tendency to mirror the culture it supposedly rejected. The young condemned adult hypocrisy while matching its contradictions with their own. The old were materialistic, hung up on big cars and ranch houses. The young were equally devoted to motorcycles, stereo sets, and electric guitars. The old sought power and wealth. So did the young as rock musicians, political leaders, and frequently as salesmen of counter-cultural goods and services. What distinguished reactionary capitalists from their avant-garde opposite numbers was often no more than a lack of moral pretense. While condemning the adult world's addiction to violence, the young admired third-world revolutionaries, Black Panthers, and even motorcycle outlaws. The rhetoric of the young got progressively meaner and more hostile. This was not so bad as butchering Vietnamese, but it was not very encouraging either. And where hate led, violence followed.

Adults pointed these inconsistencies out often enough, with few good results. Usable perceptions are always self-perceptions, which made the *Rolling Stone* exposé of Altamont so valuable. This was a small but hopeful sign that the capacity for self-analysis was not totally submerged, despite the flood of self-congratulatory pieties with which the deviant young described themselves. The decline of the New Left was another. Once a buoyant and promising thing, it became poisoned by hate, failure, and romantic millennialism. Its diminished appeal offered hope of sobriety's return. So did the surge of student interest in environmental issues at the decade's end. These were not fake problems, like so many youthful obsessions, but real ones. They would take the best efforts of many generations to overcome. No doubt the young would lose interest in them after a while as usual. Still, it was better to save a forest or clean a river than to vandalize a campus. No amount of youthful nagging was likely to make adults give up their sinful ways. It was possible that the young and old together might salvage enough of the threatened environment to leave posterity something of lasting value. The generations yet unborn were not likely to care much whether ROTC was conducted on campus or off. But they will remember this age, for better or worse, with every breath they take.

One aspect of the counter-culture deserves special mention: its assumption that hedonism was inevitably anti-capitalist. As James Hitchcock pointed out, the New Left identified capitalism with puritanism and deferred gratifications. But this was true of capitalism only with respect to work. Where consumption was concerned, it urged people to gratify their slightest wish. It exploited sex shamelessly to that end, limited only by law and custom. When the taboos against nudity were removed, merchants soon took advantage of their new freedom. Naked models, actors, even waitresses were one result, pornographic flicks another. Who doubted that if marijuana became legal the tobacco companies would soon put Mexican gold in every vending machine? It was, after all, part of Aldous Huxley's genius that he saw how sensual gratification could enslave men more effectively than Hitler ever could. Victorian inhibitions, the Protestant Ethic itself were, though weakened, among the few remaining defenses against the market economy that Americans possessed. To destroy them for freedom's sake would only make people more vulnerable to consumerism than they already were. Which was not to say that sexual and other freedoms were not good things in their own right. But there was no assurance that behavioral liberty would not grow at the expense of political freedom. It was one thing to say that sex promoted mental health, another to say it advanced social justice. In confusing the two young deviants laid themselves open to what Herbert Marcuse called "repressive de-sublimation," the means by which the socio-economic order was made more attractive, and hence more durable. Sex was no threat to the Establishment. Panicky moralists found this hard to believe, so they kept trying to suppress it. But the shrewder guardians of established relationships saw hedonism for what it partially was, a valuable means of social control. What made this hard to get across was that left and right agreed that sex was subversive. That was why the Filthy Speech Movement arose, and why the John Birch Society and its front groups divided a host of communities in the late sixties. They insisted that sex education was a communist plot to fray the country's moral fiber. They could hardly have been more wrong. As practiced in most schools, sex education was anything but erotic. In fact, more students were probably turned off sex than on to it by such courses. The Kremlin was hardly less orthodox than the Birch Society on sexual matters, sexual denial being thought a trait of all serious revolutionaries. But the sexual propaganda of the young confirmed John Birchers in their delusions. As elsewhere, the misconceptions of each side reinforced one another.

Still, the counter-culture's decline ought not to be celebrated prematurely. It outlasted the sixties. It had risen in the first place because of the larger culture's defects. War, poverty, social and racial injustice were widespread. The universities were less human than they might have been. The regulation of sexual conduct led to endless persecutions of the innocent or the pathetic to no one's advantage. Young people had much to complain of. Rebellious youth had thought to make things better. It was hardly their fault that things got worse. They were, after all, products of the society they meant to change, and marked by it as everyone was. Vanity and ignorance made them think themselves free of the weaknesses they saw so clearly in others. But adults were vain and ignorant too, and, what's more, they had power as the young did not. When they erred, as in Vietnam, millions suffered. The young hated being powerless, but thanks to it they were spared the awful burden of guilt that adults bore. They would have power soon enough, and no doubt use it just as badly. In the meantime, though, people did well to keep them in perspective.

The dreary propaganda about youth's insurgent idealism continued into the seventies. So did attempts to make them look clean-cut. American society went on being obsessed with the young. But all popular manias are seasonal. Each era has its own preoccupations. The young and their counter-culture were a special feature of the 1960's and would probably not be regarded in the old way for very long afterward. And, demographically speaking, youth itself was on the wane. The median age of Americans had risen steadily in modern times, reaching a peak of thirty years of age in 1952. The baby boom reversed this trend, like so many others. In 1968 the median age was only 27.7 years. But as the birthrate fell the median age began to rise. By 1975 it would be over twenty-eight. By 1990 it should be back up to thirty again, putting half the population beyond the age of trust. Their disproportionate numbers was one reason why youth was so prominent in the sixties. It was reasonable to suppose they would become less so as their numbers declined in relation to older people.

Common sense suggested that work and the pleasure principle would both continue. Once life and work were thought to be guided by the same principles. In the twentieth century they had started to divide, with one set of rules for working and another for living. The complexities of a postindustrial economy would probably maintain that distinction. The discipline of work would prevail on the job. The tendency to "swing" off it would increase, and the dropout community too. The economy was already rich enough to support a substantial leisure class, as the hippies demonstrated. The movement toward guaranteed incomes would make idleness even more feasible. A large dependent population, in economic terms, was entirely practical—perhaps, given automation, even desirable. How utopian to have a society in which the decision to work was voluntary! Yet if economic growth continued and an effective welfare state was established, such a thing was not unimaginable, however repugnant to the Protestant Ethic. Perhaps that was what the unpleasant features of life in the sixties pointed toward. Later historians might think them merely the growing pains of this new order. A Brave New World indeed!

A further reason for taking this view was the rise of an adult counterculture. Americans have always been attracted to cults and such. No enthusiasm, however bizarre, fails to gain some notice in so vast and restless a country. Crank scientists and religious eccentrics are especially welcomed. In the 1960's this was more true than ever, and there seemed to be more uniformity of belief among the cults than before. Perhaps also they were more respectable. The Esalen Institute in northern California was one of the most successful. It offered three-day seminars conducted by Dr. Frederick S. Perls, the founder of Gestalt therapy. When his book by that title was published in 1950 it won, as might have been expected, little attention. But in the sixties it flourished to the point where perhaps a hundred Gestalt therapists were in practice. As employed at Esalen, Gestalt therapy involved a series of individual encounters within a group context. Perls tried to cultivate moments of sudden insights that produced a strong awareness of the present moment. Unlike psychoanalysis, Gestalt therapy was directive. The therapist diagnosed the ailment and organized its cure in short bursts of intensive treatment. People were encouraged to act out dreams so as to discover their hidden message. The emphasis was on sensuality, spontaneity, and the reduction of language which was seen as more a barrier to understanding than a means of communication. There was much role-playing, aggression-releasing exercises, and "unstructured interaction." Esalen itself, with its hot sulphur baths where mixed nude bathing was encouraged, combined the features of a hip spa, a mental clinic, and a religious center. It brought social scientists and mystics together in common enterprises. By 1967 Esalen grossed a million dollars a year. Four thousand people attended its seminars. Twelve thousand used its branch in San Francisco.

Though Esalen was the most celebrated center of "Third Force Psychiatry," it was hardly alone. Encounter groups, T-groups, sensitivity groups all practiced variations of the same theme. So, in a more intense way, did Synanon. Synanon was founded in 1958 by an ex-alcoholic named Charles E. Dederich. It began as a way of reclaiming alcoholics, and especially drug addicts, through communal living and group therapy. It aimed to peel away the defenses that supported addiction. The cure was a drastic one and the Synanon ethic extremely authoritarian, as a treatment based not on clinical experience but actual street life would naturally be. Synanon's most popular feature was the Synanon game, a kind of encounter group open to outsiders. From its modest beginning Synanon expanded rapidly into a network of clinics and small businesses operated by members to support the therapeutic program. Already a corporation by the decade's end, Dederich expected it to become a mass movement in time. Others thought so too. Abraham Maslow of Brandeis University declared that "Synanon is now in the process of torpedoing the entire world of psychiatry and within ten years will completely replace psychiatry."

Esalen and Synanon got much publicity, but, though substantial efforts, they were only the tip of the iceberg. Beneath them were literally thousands of groups dedicated to better mental health through de-sublimation, often sponsored by businesses and universities. In a sense what they did was rationalize the counter-cultural ethic and bend it to fit the needs of middle-class adults. For some, expanding their consciousness meant little more than weekend tripping, with, or more commonly without, drugs. If most didn't give up work in the hippie manner, they became more relaxed about it. Some thought less about success and more about fun. Some found new satisfaction in their work, or else more satisfying work. The range of individual response was great, but the overall effect was to promote sensuality, and to diminish the Protestant Ethic. As with the counter-culture, an inflated propaganda accompanied these efforts. Ultimate truth, complete harmony with self, undreamed-of pleasures, and the like were supposed to result from conversion. De-sublimation did not mean license, of course. As the Haight-Ashbury showed, without self-denial there is self-destruction. The cults tried to develop more agreeable mechanisms to replace the fears and guilts undergirding the old morality. They wanted people to live more rich and immediate social lives, but they didn't propose to do away with restraint entirely. Mystic cults promoted self-discipline through various austere regimes. Psychiatric cults used the group as a control. One learned from his fellows what was appropriate to the liberated spirit.

The sensuality common to most of these groups was what the sexual revolution was all about. Properly speaking, of course, there was no sexual revolution. Easy divorce, relatively free access to contraceptives, and tolerated promiscuity were all well established by the 1920's. Insofar as the Kinsey and other reports are historically reliable, there had been little change since then in the rate of sexual deviance. What had changed was the attitude of many people toward it. In the 1960's deviance was not so much tolerated as applauded in many quarters. Before, college students having an affair used discretion. Later they were more likely to live together in well-advertised nonmarital bliss. Similarly, adults were not much more promiscuous in the sixties than in the forties or fifties, but they were more disposed to proclaim the merits of extra-marital sexuality. The sexualization of everyday life moved on. This was often desirable, or at least harmless, except for the frightening rise in the incidence of VD after the Pill made condoms seemingly obsolete.

Fornication, though illegal in most places, was not usually regarded as actionable. But there remained many laws against sexual behavior that were enforced, if erratically. Contraceptives were difficult to get in some places, especially for single women. Legal abortions were severely limited. Homosexuals were persecuted everywhere. Attempts to change these laws were part of the new moral permissiveness. Few legal reforms were actually secured in the sixties. Liberalized abortion laws were passed in Colorado and elsewhere to little effect. Abortions remained scarce and expensive. The overwhelming majority continued to be illegal. Contraceptive laws did not change much either, though in practice contraceptives became easier to get. Nor were the laws prohibiting homosexuality altered much. Here too, though, changes in practice eased conditions. The deliberate entrapment of homosexuals declined in some cities. Some police forces, as in San Francisco, made more of an effort to distinguish between harmless (as between consenting adults) and anti-social perversions.

More striking still was the willingness of sexual minorities to identify themselves. Male homosexuals were among the first to do so. In the Mattachine Society and later organizations they campaigned openly for an end to discriminatory laws and customs. The Daughters of Bilitis did the same for lesbians. Even the most exotic minorities, like the transvestites and transsexuals (men, usually, who wanted to change their sex surgically), became organized. Most of the groups were, their sexual customs excepted, quite straight. The creation of homosexual churches, like the Metropolitan Community Church of Los Angeles, testified to that. They hoped mainly to be treated the same as heterosexuals. But in the Gay Liberation Front the sexual underground produced its own New Left organization. Its birth apparently dated from the night of June 28, 1969, when police raided a gay bar in Greenwich Village called the Stonewall Inn. Homosexuals usually accepted arrest passively. But for some reason that night it was different. They fought back, and for a week afterward continued to agitate, ending with a public march of some one thousand people.

More sober homosexuals greeted this event with mixed emotions. They were astonished to find such spirit among the so-called street queens, the poorest and most trouble-prone homosexuals of all. But they didn't really dig the violence. As one leader of the Mattachine Society (a sort of gay NAACP) put it: "I mean, people did try to set fire to the bar, and one drag queen, much to the amazement of the mob, just pounded the hell out of a Tactical Patrol Force cop! I don't know if battering

TPF men is really the answer to our problem." In any event, the Gay Liberation Front followed these events. Rather like a Homosexuals for a Democratic Society, the GLF participated in the next Hiroshima Day march that summer. It was the first time homosexuals ever participated in a peace action under their own colors. The "Pink Panthers" were mostly young, of course. But whether their movement flourished or, most probably, withered away, the mere fact of its existence said a lot about changing mores in America.

While it was difficult in 1969 to tell where the counter-culture would go, it was easy to see where it came from. Artists and bohemians had been demanding more freedom from social and artistic conventions for a long time. The romantic faith in nature, intuition, and spontaneity was equally old. What was striking about the sixties was that the revolt against discipline, even self-discipline, and authority spread so widely. Resistance to these tendencies largely collapsed in the arts. Soon the universities gave ground also. The rise of hedonism and the decline of work were obviously functions of increased prosperity, and also of effective merchandising. The consumer economy depended on advertising, which in turn leaned heavily on the pleasure principle. This had been true for fifty years at least, but not until television did it really work well. The generation that made the counter-culture was the first to be propagandized from infancy on behalf of the pleasure principle.

But though all of them were exposed to hucksterism, not all were convinced. Working-class youngsters especially soon learned that life was different from television. Limited incomes and uncertain futures put them in touch with reality earlier on. Middle-class children did not learn the facts of life until much later. Cushioned by higher family incomes, indulged in the same way as their peers on the screen, they were shocked to discover that the world was not what they had been taught it was. The pleasure orientation survived this discovery, the ideological packaging it came in often did not. All this had happened before, but in earlier years there was no large, institutionalized subculture for the alienated to turn to. In the sixties hippiedom provided one such, the universities another. The media publicized these alternatives and made famous the ideological leaders who promoted them. So the deviant young knew where to go for the answers they wanted, and how to behave when they got them. The media thus completed the cycle begun when they first turned youngsters to pleasure. That was done to encourage consumption. The message was still effective when young consumers rejected the products TV offered and discovered others more congenial to them.

Though much in the counter-culture was attractive and valuable, it was dangerous in three ways. First, self-indulgence led frequently to self-destruction. Second, the counter-culture increased social hostility. The generation gap was one example, but the class gap another. Working-class youngsters resented the counter-culture. They accepted adult values for the most part. They had to work whether they liked it or not. Beating up the long-haired and voting for George Wallace were only two ways they expressed these feelings. The counter-culture was geographical too. It flourished in cities and on campuses. Elsewhere, in Middle America especially, it was hated and feared. The result was a national division between the counter-culture and those adults who admired or tolerated it—upper-middle-class professionals and intellectuals in the Northeast particularly—and the silent majority of workers and Middle Americans who didn't. The tensions between these groups made solving social and political problems all the more difficult, and were, indeed, part of the problem.

Finally, the counter-culture was hell on standards. A handful of bohemians were no great threat to art and intellect. The problem was that a generation of students, the artists and intellectuals of the future, was infected with romanticism. Truth and beauty were in the eye of the beholder. They were discovered or created by the pure of heart. Formal education and training were not, therefore, merely redundant but dangerous for obstructing channels through which the spirit flowed. It was one thing for hippies to say this, romanticism being the natural religion of bohemia. It was quite another to hear it from graduate students. Those who did anguished over the future of scholarship, like the critics who worried that pop art meant the end of art. These fears were doubtlessly overdrawn, but the pace of cultural change was so fast in the sixties that they were hardly absurd.

Logic seemed everywhere to be giving way to intuition, and self-discipline to impulse. Romanticism had never worked well in the past. It seemed to be doing as badly in the present. The hippies went from flower power to death-tripping in a few years. The New Left took only a little longer to move from participatory democracy to demolition. The counter-cultural ethic remained as beguiling as ever in theory. In practice, like most utopian dreams, human nature tended to defeat it. At the decade's end, young believers looked forward to the Age of Aquarius. Sensible men knew there would be no Aquarian age. What they didn't know was the sort of legacy the counter-culture would leave behind. Some feared that the straight world would go on as before, others that it wouldn't.

PROFILE:
Hell's Angels

ANOTHER STRANGE FEATURE of American life in the sixties was the motorcycle outlaw. There had been motorcycle gangs in California ever since World War II. (Marlon Brando made a famous motion picture about them in the fifties called *The Wild Ones*.) But in 1964 and 1965 they became a popular rage, especially the gang known as Hell's Angels. The Oakland Angels were notable, even among outlaws, for their ferocity. They first attracted public notice during their Labor Day run to Monterey in 1964. It was their custom on state occasions to gather in a scenic place for several days of revelry. Usually no one but the natives took much notice of what went on. This Labor Day run was different in that several teen-age girls claimed to have been raped by a horde of Angels inflamed by beer and rough language. The event was widely reported and set off a public panic of sorts. The media gave the Angels a great play. In November 1965 they made the cover of the *Saturday Evening Post*. The Angels relished this attention, though it raised problems for them and was based, they insisted, on a lie. The girls in question had not been raped. Rather they had deliberately offered their services, only, as sometimes happened, the girls had enough after a time and got scared when the Angels kept piling on. The few outsiders who knew the Angels well thought this had the ring of truth. They rarely attempted rape because there were always women volunteers to accommodate them.

Motorcycle outlaws were a colorful, if disgusting, lot. Little wonder that the media exploited them so. They did not ride the lightweight sport cycles then becoming popular. Instead they bought huge, obsolete Harley-Davidsons, disdained by all save themselves and the police. On delivery these monsters weighed seven hundred pounds and were so slow and bulky that the Angels called them "garbage wagons." They were then cut down to about five hundred pounds and souped up to racing speed. Thus refined they were known as "hogs." The Angels washed themselves rarely, and their cycling costumes never. These garments, called "colors," were befouled during initiation rites and worn thereafter to the point of disintegration. Individually they varied a great deal. Hunter Thompson describes an outlaw gang on a run this way: "It is a human zoo on wheels. An outlaw whose normal, day-to-day appearance is enough to disrupt traffic will appear on a run with his beard dyed green or bright red, his eyes hidden behind orange goggles, and a brass ring in his nose. Others wear capes and Apache headbands, or oversize sunglasses and peaked Prussian helmets. Earrings, Wehrmacht headgear and German Iron Crosses are virtually part of the uniform—like the grease-caked Levis, the sleeveless vests and all those fine tattoos . . . and the inevitable Hell's Angels insignia."

The publicity given this small band of hoodlums had strange consequences. Although the Oakland Angels had no more than eighty-five members, they were certified as a Grade A national menace by the press. Hence about half the working members lost their jobs, fired out of hand by timid employers. Then police, who had been harassing them right along, did so with renewed vigor. On the other hand, their celebrity status brought them so much attention they began holding regular press conferences in the office of their bail bondswoman.* And for a time they won the favor of New Left intellectuals and thrill-seekers—partly, no doubt, because their violent lives appealed to the growing strain of revolutionary *machismo*. Partly too because they seemed the working-class equivalent of the New Left's alienated bourgeois rebels.

* The Angels were chronic deadbeats, but they dared not welch on debts owed those who alone kept them out of jail. Bail bondsmen thus became their only point of contact with the outside world.

This was a mistake. Though rebellious, the motorcycle outlaws had more in common with the radical right than the radical left. They were all instinctive fascists, insanely patriotic, and anti-communist to the bone. When Berkeley's Vietnam Day Committee organized a protest march on Oakland in 1965, the Angels attacked it. This enabled Lucius Beebe, a prominent local reactionary, columnist, and railroad buff, to compare them with Texas Rangers. His enthusiasm was not widely shared. Thereafter both the left and the press lost interest in them, and they faded from public view. Now and again they would crop up, harassing a demonstration here, or policing a hippie be-in or rock festival there. But fresh sensations came so thick and fast in the sixties that the merely picturesque, however degenerate, could not hold the public's attention for long. Still, the Angels helped make violence somewhat more intellectually respectable on the left. And attenuated echoes of their style of life were heard all around the country for years thereafter. They were hardly fatal to the old order, not so much a wound as a hangnail on its aging body. But they contributed something, if only a little, to its decay.

9 THE NEW LEFT COMES AND GOES

W<small>HEN</small> the sixties opened there were two schools of thought on the future of the left. Most intellectuals had recovered from the Mc-Carthy era. They had been public scapegoats in the early and mid-fifties, much as youth was to be in the late sixties, but Sputnik and the demand for excellence—scientific excellence, at least—rehabilitated them. Chastened by what they had gone through, many elevated technique to the level of principle. This convinced some of their sternest critics, like George Lichtheim, that intellectuals had finally come of age. With the decline of political passion, rationality was increasing. As the technical and scientific elite grew, he argued, "the area of mischief still open to political movements of a more primitive type" declined. It was no longer utopian to imagine "a wholly rational, scientifically controlled planetary order." Daniel Bell gave this school a potent slogan in his essay *The End of Ideology.*

While liberals depended increasingly on a benevolent technocracy to solve problems once thought political, a handful of radicals disagreed. H. Stuart Hughes observed that Bell's essay came at just the wrong time. The Eisenhower era had seen the old fighting political faiths die out, but a new age was dawning as the civil rights movement, the Cuban Revolution, and the stirrings of radical youth around the world showed. C. Wright Mills put it more strongly. In his prophetic essay "The New Left" (October 1960), he maintained that intellectuals had been misled by the decline of organized labor into thinking that radicalism was finished. But they were looking in the wrong place. Not the moribund labor movement but the "cultural apparatus" was the key to the future.

275

Students especially, in the American South, even in Russia, were developing fresh momentum. "Let the old men ask sourly, 'Out of Apathy— into what?' The Age of Complacency is ending. Let the old women complain wisely about the 'end of ideology.' We are beginning to move again."

Few agreed with Hughes and Mills. They were thought victims of that wishful thinking unreconstructed radicals fall back on during hard times. The civil rights movement was unexpected, but being concentrated in the South it hardly seemed a portent of radicalism elsewhere. The major parties were more alike than ever. Many liberals felt there was little to choose between Nixon and Kennedy. "Burroughs Against IBM" was how Gerald Johnson described their encounter in the *New Republic*. Kenneth Rexroth accordingly declared in the *Nation* that he meant to "sit this one out," as did Dwight Macdonald in *Commentary*. There was only one significant event in 1960 that foreshadowed what was to come, and it seemed a fluke at the time.

A subcommittee of the House Committee on Un-American Activities had visited California every year from 1951 to 1960. As with the parent committee, these outings were not meant to produce new laws. HUAC had one of the largest budgets and poorest legislative records in the House. Both were tributes to the fear it inspired. Private citizens were afraid that resisting it would mean bad publicity or worse. Screen writers went to prison for being unfriendly to it in 1947. Colleagues did not limit HUAC's budget or powers for fear of political reprisals. All the same, HUAC was in more trouble than it seemed to be. It had been most successful before 1950. After that Senator McCarthy took the play away from it. He was a better propagandist than anyone on HUAC. (Richard Nixon was the only member to advance his career by serving on it.) Worse still, the Communist party of the United States, HUAC's most reliable victim, was withering away. By 1960 it consisted mainly of aging true believers and a corps of FBI informers. HUAC insisted, as did the FBI, that the smaller the party got the more dangerous it became. Even the faithful found this hard to believe. HUAC was reduced to harassing allegedly subversive schoolteachers and did so in California in 1959. These attentions were not well received. When the subcommittee returned to San Francisco the next year it met the stiffest resistance ever. Bay Area students were angry over the execution of Caryl Chessman a few days earlier.* Resentment over the subcommittee's previous visit

---

* The fight to save Caryl Chessman was the most important attack on capital punishment in American history. Chessman was sentenced to death for having forced two women to have oral relations with him. Fellation, even at gunpoint, was not a capital crime, but the "Red Light Bandit" had moved the victims from their car to his, and so was technically a kidnaper. Chessman had many stays of execution, during which he wrote his autobiography, *Cell 2455, Death Row,* and other books

still festered. Hostile witnesses staged demonstrations in the hearing room. A picket line calling for HUAC's abolition marched outside.

On the second day of hearings, May 9, 1960, the picket line was larger. Spectators, denied entrance to the hearing room, clamored for admittance. At 1:15 P.M. city police turned high-pressure hoses on them, washing and dragging them down a long flight of marble steps. A number were roughed up. The next day five thousand people demonstrated in protest. HUAC and J. Edgar Hoover promptly denounced these acts as communist inspired. A movie was hastily assembled, called *Operation Abolition*, to support this charge. The Northern California Civil Liberties Union responded with its own film, *Operation Correction*. It received little attention compared with *Operation Abolition*, which was shown to millions in American Legion halls and such places. HUAC suffered anyway. Congress kept on appropriating large sums for it. But by defying HUAC the students had won a notable victory which foreshadowed the radical springtime to come.

It was, however, a bit slow in arriving. The HUAC demonstrations produced only a short-lived student abolitionist committee. During the next few years students worked for civil rights. A few helped the limping peace movement, mainly in the Student Peace Union which was founded in 1959 and had about three thousand members at its peak in 1961–62. Students for a Democratic Society was quietly laying the groundwork for its later eminence. It had begun as the Student League for Industrial Democracy, the tiny youth wing of the social democratic League for Industrial Democracy.* SLID became SDS in 1960, but did not change much until the next year when Al Haber and Tom Hayden, both of the University of Michigan, began giving it a more activist flavor. Hayden wrote most of the 1962 "Port Huron Statement," SDS's enabling document, which tried to show that national excesses abroad and anti-democratic practices at home were related. It pledged SDS to the creation of a "New Left," and put special emphasis on the university

---

that made him famous. He was hated by some for what was thought to be a want of humility. When he was executed Governor Edmund Brown cited his "lack of contrition" and "steadfast arrogance" as reasons for denying him further stays. This seemed a blow to the cause, for people all over the world had pled for Chessman's life. Even the Vatican's official newspaper, *Osservatore Romano,* called his execution barbaric. The setback was more apparent than real. Chessman's enemies were so obviously malicious, the arguments for killing him so incompetent, and the governor's role so pathetic that states became more reluctant to impose the death penalty and courts to sustain it. In 1960 there were fifty-six executions, in 1968 none. Even more than Sacco and Vanzetti, Chessman accomplished in death what he could not have done in life.

* The LID was a respected but minute organization which since 1921 had been a reflective advocate of democratic socialism. It revived somewhat in the sixties when Michael Harrington, a prominent socialist writer, took charge. It was always anti-communist, and SDS broke away from it later for that reason, among others.

as a radical center. "Social relevance, the accessibility of knowledge, and internal openness—these together make the university a potential base and agency in a movement of social change."

SDS did not act immediately on this perception. White radicals took their cue from blacks, and when Snick moved off campus SDS did likewise. Snick's voter registration drive in the South was paralleled by SDS's Economic Research and Action Project in the North. ERAP aimed to promote self-organization among poor urban blacks and whites. There were perhaps fifteen such projects between 1963 and 1965, but they did not repay the effort invested in them. ERAP's organizers had expected an economic crisis leading to mass unemployment, especially among the young. When instead the great boom continued they turned to encouraging participatory democracy, somewhat on the model of the Mississippi Freedom Democratic party. ERAP declined—poor whites could not readily be organized, blacks were going their own way—but the idea of community alternatives to parliamentary democracy did not.

The chief difficulty that SDS suffered from was not strategic but contextual. SDS had no trouble identifying problems. It did find solutions for them hard to come by, as was only to be expected in a movement's infancy. The real obstacle, an insuperable one as it turned out, was that America had no left. In most developed Western nations there was an institutional left—the British Labour party, the German social democrats, a variety of socialists and communists in France, for example. Young European radicals commonly disdained them in the late sixties. They were important all the same. The organized left provided learning experiences, a tradition, practical support sometimes, and a constituency, or at least potential constituency, that young radicals might hope to win. When the students of Paris rose against the government in 1968 this was important not so much for its own sake as because it triggered a general strike by left-wing trade unions. The students failed to develop much worker support. The strikers were more interested in wage hikes than in overthrowing the government. In the end the students were repressed, the Gaullist government re-elected, and the workers bought off with wage increases. All the same, student radicalism continued to have a certain vitality in Europe, even though unsuccessful, because it operated in a context where left-wing politics and proletarian class consciousness were realities, however attenuated.

American radicals functioned in a more unreal environment. There was no political left, only scattered handfuls of seemingly impotent survivors from the 1930's and a few students like the group which published *Studies on the Left* at the University of Wisconsin. Organized workers were not class-conscious. They had bourgeois aspirations for the most part. Many even identified with authority. At the decade's end

New York construction workers would march in support of war under a banner reading "God Bless the Establishment." The old left had failed so completely that even its memory had been suppressed. Tom Hayden said that to become a radical was like giving birth to yourself. SDS members found this exhilarating at first. But what it meant was that the radical existed in a vacuum. He had no past, no present to speak of, no constituency, just hope and enthusiasm. Together with a certain historical momentum, this was enough to create the illusion of change but not its substance, especially as there was no great class to which these energies could be directed. The major deprived element in America with a shared identity and sense of grievance were the Negroes, and they, as events soon demonstrated, were not responsive to white radicals. SDS thought to remedy this by concentrating on the young, university students especially. But youth and studenthood are not classes, only temporary conditions soon outgrown. The reality of this fact was temporarily disguised, however, by the studentry's growing militance after 1964.

The University of California at Berkeley was the Bastille of the student revolution. It fell for a variety of reasons, none of them very clear at the time. It was only when student uprisings became commonplace that Berkeley could be understood. The events there are quickly summarized, though they took months to act out. In September 1964 a University official ordered student activists to remove their literature tables from a strip of sidewalk before the campus's main gate. Radicals (and some militant conservatives also) used this strip because being, in appearance anyway, off campus, University restrictions on political activity were not applied to it. The ban was thought a reaction to complaints from local right-wingers against student action in the Bay Area, especially the civil rights campaign then underway against former Senator William Knowland's *Oakland Tribune*. Whatever the cause, it drew a predictable response. On September 29 four student groups set up tables in defiance of the ban. Tensions rose until on October 1 campus police arrested Jack Weinberg, twenty-four, a graduate student and CORE activist.* Students surrounded the police car, immobilizing it through the night. The administration then made a deal that took Weinberg off the hook. This was followed by a cheerful victory celebration.

Just when the crisis seemed over, the regents of the University renewed it. Four student leaders were called at the end of November to answer charges that they had committed acts of violence during the

---

* He later said, "You can't trust anyone over thirty," thus creating the generation gap.

October demonstration. Mario Savio, the principal spokesman of what was now known as the Free Speech Movement, was accused of having bitten a policeman on the thigh. Whether motivated by internal resentments or outside pressures, this attempted reprisal was a fatal error. On December 1 student leaders gave the regents twenty-four hours to drop their charges. When they didn't, students took over the administration building, Sproul Hall. Savio gave his famous speech indicting the University as a machine which treated students as raw material. "It becomes odious, so we must put our bodies against the gears, against the wheels . . . and make the machine stop until we're free." Joan Baez sang "We Shall Overcome," and a thousand people trooped into Sproul Hall, the doors of which had been left conveniently unlocked. While the students organized a free university in the building, police were brought up. 814 demonstrators, most of whom went limp in the approved nonviolent manner, were arrested. The police seem to have behaved with only ordinary roughness, so no one was seriously hurt. There were many painful bangs and bruises all the same. The students (590 of those arrested) and their allies were soon bailed out and brought home, often by faculty members. On December 3 a student strike took place. Perhaps more than half the University's classes did not meet. On December 7 President Clark Kerr spoke to eighteen thousand people in the outdoor Greek Theater. When he finished, Mario Savio attempted to address the meeting but was dragged off by the police. This made a poor impression, so he was later given the stage. He then merely announced another meeting to be held later.

Next day the faculty convened and, after a wild debate broadcast to students listening outside the auditorium, voted to place no restrictions on the content of speech or advocacy. The FSM appeared to have won. In fact, nobody had. The chancellor was forced out, and later President Kerr. The new University administration was more patient and responsive, but it too failed to please the militants. From 1965 on there was no end to campus disturbances of one kind or another. Vandalism became commonplace. These circumstances helped elect Ronald Reagan to the governorship. He in turn did what he could to make things worse by harassing University officials, cutting their budget requests, and antagonizing the studentry. Many distinguished professors resigned. The nonstudent population multiplied, turning the South Campus area into a hippie slum. The University of California survived, but its reputation did not. In the fifties Berkeley had symbolized academic greatness. It was the best public university in the country and equal to the finest private universities. In the sixties Berkeley came to stand for student power. It remained a distinguished institution despite everything. Yet to the public Berkeley meant chiefly violence, radicalism, and bohemian license.

People oscillated between the general and the particular in explaining the FSM. One set of explanations had to do with immediate events. Mario Savio had participated in the Freedom Summer of 1964. Many students had been involved in local civil rights demonstrations, especially sit-ins to make San Francisco businesses hire blacks. This had a radicalizing effect on many. A more specific cause was the University of California system. Each branch of the University was answerable to the central administration of President Kerr. This made for a bureaucratic structure so rigid and baffling that it alienated not only students but faculty as well. Below the top it was unclear who had authority over what. Banning the student tables was a mistake which, once made, was aggravated by the University's complex decision-making process. What one administrator did was overruled by another. It took time to work up and down the chain of command. Eventually students became less willing to see delay as inevitable, and quicker to blame it on deceit.

Under President Kerr the University's guiding principle was technocratic liberalism. Kerr was much admired by the Establishment for, among other things, his book *The Uses of the University*. It proclaimed that the age of giants was over. President Hutchins of Chicago was the last Captain of Erudition to run a great university. He was followed by Captains of the Bureaucracy like Kerr. The new man's duty was to mediate among contending factions, both within and without the university. What made this difficult was that while the "knowledge industry" was crucial to the state ("intellect has also become an instrument of national purpose, a component part of the 'military-industrial complex'") few people understood this. Thus a university president had to manage a space-age growth industry while dealing chiefly with horse-and-buggy mentalities. Kerr himself was anything but a despot. He was in fact the Robert McNamara of higher education, a skillful manager of complex systems. Nor did he lack sympathy for the knowledge industry's products. Of the students he wrote, "Recent changes in the American university have done them little good. . . . There is an incipient revolt against the faculty; the revolt that used to be against the faculty in loco parentis is now against the faculty in absentia." He also saw that the "multiversity" tended to exalt science and technology at the expense of the humanities, and even sometimes of the social sciences.

In practice these insights did not help him much. As a captain of bureaucracy it was his job to manipulate people, not to lead or inspire them. This meant creating among students the illusion of autonomy while withholding the substance of it where possible. His predecessor had been a traditional administrator who disliked political activity on campus. Kerr modified his strictures, but in ways so artful and ambiguous as to make little difference. Student groups like the vaguely left-wing SLATE party were driven off campus, and unpopular visiting speakers also. But this system depended on student compliance. When during the FSM controversy they refused to cooperate, it fell apart. The faculty, though occupying a more privileged position, had their resentments too. Berkeley was the only student uprising supported (for a time anyway) by a majority of the faculty. This was partly because the pattern was not yet clear, but also because student resistance mobilized faculty discontent.

To these particular explanations was added the general charge that universities had gotten too big and impersonal and their faculties too remote. This view was popular among liberals, conservatives, and students alike. The *New York Times*, Ronald Reagan, and Mario Savio all endorsed it. Everyone looked back to some imagined golden age when universities were no more than happy families writ large. But a poll taken on campus during the FSM fight showed that the overwhelming majority of students liked the university. What galvanized them was simply the free-speech issue. Once it was resolved there was never again a student majority for radical action. In truth, students at big universities were attracted precisely by the combination of personal freedom and institutional largess that size permitted.

In California, particularly, students good enough to go to Berkeley had their choice of many smaller public college and university campuses with excellent faculties and facilities. They went to Berkeley not despite its size but because of it. Later events showed that few students cared for the corporate life. Dormitories, fraternities, and sororities attracted smaller proportions of them. They struggled everywhere to live off campus in ways of their own choosing. They did not want to see more of the faculty and staff but less of them. Where this was not true it was because the faculty went along with the students on most things, abdicating their authority and responsibility—that is to say, what made them professors instead of friends or lovers. The faculty-student relationship is always unequal, however genially conducted, being founded on what one knows and the other does not. As students increasingly rejected all authority, they had to reject the faculty too. Whether this was good or bad was immaterial. It was the chief fact of life at the best universities especially, and no amount of reviling the professoriat, or calling for stiffer discipline, or attempting to re-create an idealized past could change that.

Most involved in the FSM struggle misread it. Militant students believed they had found a lever to move the world, or at least the academic world. Liberals took much student propaganda at face value. Feeling guilty at having neglected their students, professors were quick to promise a new era of student-teacher intimacy and a new age of academic reform. Some were attracted by the love, peace, brotherhood ethic of the students and, as men will, expected it to last forever. Conservatives thought the end of civilization was near at hand. Student militants reminded them of the Hitler Youth. The more optimistic among them felt that universities would only be Latin-Americanized, turned into staging grounds for revolution. All erred, though not to the same extent. Student activists found that power in the university was hard to grasp. Concessions were made to students at Berkeley, and elsewhere even more, but the balance of power did not tilt much. *In loco parentis* declined. The appointment of token students to university committees became commonplace. Professors and administrators grew more circumspect. No one wanted to bring on another Berkeley through rudeness. Student life got easier, especially as the post-Sputnik drive for excellence declined, and students were catered to more.

Their lack of power spared students a greater disillusionment. Had they actually taken over universities they would have been disheartened to find how marginal they were to the power elite. Few skills taught at, or services rendered by, the university could not be handled in other ways. Later protesters drove many defense-related projects off campus without doing much harm to military research. Most university degrees had little relevance to the work graduates did; they were only mandarin requirements for the most part. If the degree qualification were abolished, employers could still meet their manpower needs through in-house training programs and the like. Radical students attacked the university because that was where they were at, and because the university was especially vulnerable to them. But to justify themselves they had to argue that the university was a vital component of the military-industrial complex; that by threatening its ruin they could turn the system around. In time radical students came to see that neither was possible. The rage and frustration this knowledge produced helped lead to the bombing, arson, and vandalism that marked student protests at the decade's end.

These events weakened liberal optimism also. During the FSM and for some time after, liberals often took the student side. They contributed mightily to what became the conventional eulogy of the young as the best-educated, most altruistic generation in history. When the flower-power ethic declined and militant students adopted the language, sometimes also the tactics, of *Realpolitik*, liberal professors were more discouraged than anyone. Wanting peace, they got violence. Wanting community with the students, they were pushed further away by the counter-culture and its generational exclusiveness. Some kept on trying to follow the students' lead. Others turned against student militance. Many feared that in their zeal to reform the university, radicals would destroy it. Some left-wing students talked casually of closing down the university for its sins. They did not care that the evil done by the university—military research, officer training—could be done anywhere, while the good was peculiar to it. If there were no universities there would be precious little support for disinterested inquiry. The search for truth and beauty, especially in the unpopular arts, would languish. The military-industrial complex would roll on undisturbed.

That was what some faculty conservatives had argued at Berkeley. Many more would do so later. Conservatives greatly exaggerated the threat student radicalism posed, dismissed what was valuable in it, and all too often forgot that angry students were not enemies to be destroyed but members, however unruly, of the university community. Yet conservatives were more accurate about Berkeley than others. They were right, though often for the wrong reasons; just as liberals were wrong for the right reasons. This seemed cold comfort. Fearing the worst was not much help in preparing for it. Conservatives knew no more than anyone else about how to cope with the changing studentry. They kept on invoking past ideals when it was the present turmoil that mattered. They called police power to the aid of scholarship again and again, though the two were ancient enemies. Even when repression worked, as at San Francisco State, it did nothing to rebuild the house of intellect.

Thus while Berkeley was a prototype of the crises to come, it provided no solutions to them. All the subsequent upheavals were much alike. Professors and administrators struggled for compromises which trustees and civil authorities as often as not undermined. After each uprising the students were more alienated than ever, the faculty more humiliated and dismayed. The presidents resigned. Middle Americans and their political representatives increasingly turned against education as such. Before long educators would regard the fifties as a kind of golden age, McCarthyism notwithstanding. The New Left made some changes in the universities, but mainly it produced nostalgia, resentment, and fear among the old, and moral arrogance and a frustrated utopianism among the young.

All this was hardly apparent at first. While the tide of student protest rose, its targets were such that decent men could only make tactical objections. In 1965, 114 students were arrested at the University of Kansas for a sit-in protesting racial discrimination in fraternities and sororities. At conservative Yale the same year, students demonstrated when a popular philosophy professor was let go. At St. John's University in New York City, the largest Catholic school in the country, students denounced campus censorship and a ban on controversial speakers. Three deans at Stanford University resigned during a struggle over student government.

Few of these episodes were self-consciously radical. Students for a Democratic Society was not yet faction ridden. It had no ideology, only a set of elevated principles, chief among which was "participatory democracy." It was the functional equivalent of anarchism. People were to make their own decisions. There would be no leaders as such, only spokesmen for the general will. There were also a few doctrinaire groups in the Old Left tradition. The Young Socialist Alliance carried on the Trotskyist line. The Communist party made a small comeback by organizing the W. E. B. Du Bois Clubs. Though vaguely Marxist, they were hardly extreme. They attracted few members in any case. Most campuses with Du Bois Clubs were more amused than not when Richard Nixon, board chairman of the Boys' Clubs of America, denounced them as a red plot. He feared that innocent youths wishing only to learn paddleball would join them by mistake because Du Bois and Boys sounded so much alike.

Most student activists confined themselves to doing good works locally. But they did contribute significantly to the national peace movement in 1965. The test ban had weakened the peace movement. The war in Vietnam brought it back to life. This time, however, it took a different form. The old peace movement (SANE, Women's Strike for Peace) was made up chiefly of adults and had no real institutional base. The new movement centered on the campus. Both students and professors figured largely in it, hence the teach-in. This was the early Vietnam War protest movement's distinctive contribution. Not that the movement disdained more traditional expressions. On the Saturday before Easter in 1965, twelve thousand protesters staged the largest antiwar demonstration in Washington anyone could remember. In October fourteen thousand marched in New York City. These were insignificant numbers by later standards, but impressively large ones then, even if police estimates were high enough, which they probably weren't.

The New Left, though politically radical, was still culturally pretty straight. SDS was involved chiefly in community organizing. A collection of radical essays, *The New Student Left*, which came out in 1966 could as easily have been written in 1960. A sober, academic, *Studies on* *the Left* tone prevailed. Tom Hayden, his streetfighting days still before him, contributed one of the best pieces. But there were some signs of coming events, most notably the House Un-American Activities Committee hearings on NLF sympathizers. The hearings were repeatedly disrupted. When HUAC called up members of the (Maoist) Progressive Labor party, they proudly declared themselves to be communists and attacked the Committee and the war. One young man wearing a Continental Army uniform distributed parchment reprints of the Declaration of Independence. He objected so strongly to the proceedings that he was arrested. Even Senator Everett Dirksen remarked afterward that "this spectacle can do the Congress no good." HUAC was gutted. After the 1960 demonstrations in San Francisco, the Committee was reluctant to expose itself and seldom did. By claiming to be communists, radical witnesses destroyed its only important weapon. The Committee depended largely on the feeling, shared by members and most witnesses alike, that it was an awesome thing to be communist, and terrible to identify others as such. All through the forties and fifties this common agreement, backed by a frightened public opinion, led to frequent combats with HUAC which witnesses could hardly win with honor, yet dared not lose. A trail of wrecked lives and fortunes marked HUAC's progress in those years, mute testimony to its power. The defiant young witnesses of the sixties ended all that with one stroke by proudly claiming to be communists, especially when they weren't (in the sense of being party members). Public opinion no longer gave the committee a club with which to beat unfriendly witnesses. Even if it had, young radicals did not have careers and so could not be threatened with the loss of them like the older generation of witnesses. So much for HUAC.*

Though larger than the others, SDS was still but one of several New Left organizations. It competed with the Du Bois Clubs, the May 2nd Move-

* Another spectacle that did the government no good was the revelation by the muckraking *Ramparts* magazine in its March 1967 issue that the Central Intelligence Agency had been subsidizing the National Student Association. This relationship was maintained by successive NSA leaders as the organization always needed money, but especially because the NSA pursued an anti-communist policy in the international student movement. Its support by the CIA was kept secret because the NSA liked to contrast its independence to the state-dominated communist student movements. As students everywhere lost interest in the Cold War, and in America became progressively estranged from their government, this connection made less and less sense. The NSA meant to end it in 1968, but a disaffected member told the story to *Ramparts* anyway. Investigations disclosed that the CIA subsidized some forty educational and cultural organizations in the same way (through philanthropic foundations). These subsidies were withdrawn also, but too late to avoid embarrassing the government and further alienating the young.

ment, and the Young Socialist Alliance among others.* What first really distinguished SDS in the public eye was its campaign against the draft. SDS had gotten into this by accident. After Black Power, the failure of community organization, and the war in Vietnam, nonviolence and participatory democracy seemed less relevant. SDS organized some marches and rallies against the war, but this work seemed too bourgeois for many. Then, as the draft quotas went up, spontaneous reactions against the draft began on college campuses and SDS chapters were swept up by them. The national council voted in September 1965 to launch a national anti-draft program, and, though defeated by the membership on referendum, the idea was so widely reported that Attorney General Katzenbach announced he was having SDS investigated. The number of chapters promptly doubled, it was said. SDS hardly knew what to do with this accession of recruits, but as the chapters were mainly self-actuating, indecision at the top mattered very little. Sit-ins, draft-card burnings, and other protests became common. Some were directed against the Selective Service system's attempt to give standardized exams to college students to help determine eligibility for induction. Others were directed against military recruiters, and soon against recruiters for corporations involved in defense work, notably Dow Chemical, the manufacturer of napalm.

This comparatively large and independent membership exposed more clearly than before the inadequacies of SDS's program, such as it was. After participatory democracy collapsed as a guiding ethic, many felt a more coherent, perhaps even traditional, ideology was needed. There were many would-be Lenins eager for this work. M2M had dissolved and its members now constituted a PL caucus within SDS. They favored a worker-student alliance along classic revolutionary lines. Another faction thought SDS should ally itself with the "new working class"—the clerks, technicians, service employees, and so on who were becoming more numerous and important than the production workers on whom Marxists relied. Still other SDSers were becoming captive to the liberation-struggle mystique and searched for some way to become urban guerrillas or streetfighters. The campuses would be their Sierra Maestra, and Tom Hayden or someone their Fidel.

To the confusion within SDS was added the complexities of a nationwide uprising against the war, the Establishment, the white race, capi-

---

* Which proves how misleading the term New Left could be. Only SDS was really new. The Du Bois Clubs were an offshoot of the Communist party. M2M was sponsored by the nominally Maoist Progressive Labor party. As Maoism had nothing to do with American conditions, PL and the M2M were more Stalinoid than not, though leavened with a certain enthusiasm for third-world liberation heroes. The YSA was Trotskyist and, like its parent body, the Socialist Workers party, flavored with depression-era Marxism.

talism, and other odious institutions. Many insurgent groups were thought to have some connection with one another, but all attempts to organize them into a powerful coalition failed. The National Conference for New Politics in 1967 showed why. The awful ghetto riots that year lent urgency to it, but what began in tragedy soon ended as farce.

Two thousand representatives of two hundred organizations met in Chicago's Palmer House over the Labor Day weekend to consider establishing a third party. The organizers were mainly people of considerable experience in radical and pacifist causes, but most delegates seemed to be under thirty. What was in store for them became clear when during Martin Luther King's keynote address black militants started chanting, "Kill whitey." Worse was to come. The black caucus presented a list of thirteen demands including 50 per cent black representation on all committees (about a sixth of the delegates were black), condemnation of the "imperialist Zionist war" in the Middle East ("which does not imply anti-Semitism," they added), and efforts in white communities to humanize their "savage and beastlike" character. Conciliatory whites raised the obvious questions. "How are you going to appeal to liberal Jews for funds and support against the war in Vietnam after that 'imperialistic Zionist' bit? And how do you go and broaden your base among the whites? By . . . telling them: 'Hey, Honkie, I'm here to humanize your savage and beastlike character'?"

Nonetheless, as one conference organizer put it, "an extraordinary development took place. The walls of the Palmer House began to drip with guilt." The thirteen points were accepted by a 3 to 1 majority. James Forman of Snick mounted the stage in triumph, surrounded by colorfully dressed bodyguards. He then told the body off. Some radicals left the room, but according to Walter Goodman's sprightly account, "the remaining whites fairly tingled with pleasure under the lash of his demagogy. H. Rap Brown declined to appear before an integrated audience, thereby depriving himself of an ovation from the honkies." The black caucus then demanded 50 per cent of the convention votes. It was granted this also, as some thought that once in charge the blacks would be more cooperative. Arthur Waskow, one of the founders, responded to this by observing that "if you castrate a man, you don't sleep with him afterwards." Only a third of the delegates took his point. Thereafter the excitement subsided. It was decided not to form a third party. The customary anti-war, pro-black resolutions were briskly voted. The most obvious moral was drawn by Rennie Davis, who said, "We are a movement of people with radically different needs. A super-coalition just makes no sense." Blacks learned anew that there were hardly any limits to the self-abasement of certain liberals. Guilty, or perhaps only masochistic, whites were made to do penance for their sins. Militants enjoyed the agreeable illusion of dominance.

Events, however, did not wait on the movement's ideologists and putative harmonizers. Stop the Draft Week, from October 16 to 21, was marked by demonstrations around the country. Draft cards were collected for transmission to the Justice Department. Protesters besieged the Oakland Induction Center for days, fighting with the police for control of what on Friday was a twenty-block area. Perhaps twenty thousand people were involved. On October 18 a sit-in against Dow Chemical at the University of Wisconsin was broken up by riot police who sustained eighteen injuries, while student casualties came to sixty. Stop the Draft Week was climaxed by the now legendary March on the Pentagon. None of this did SDS much good. Some members went the Marxist route, others became yippies. The Youth International party was a highly publicized example of the New Left's subversion by the counter-culture. It was not a party or an organization in any real sense, only a tendency given the name yippie by a handful of new bohemians. This was done late in 1967 when several people, including Abbie Hoffman and Jerry Rubin, both nearly thirty, both former political activists, signed a manifesto calling for a "Festival of Life" in Chicago at the time of the Democratic National Convention, to coincide with the "Festival of Death" inside the convention hall. The yippies proposed to substitute a cultural revolution for the political rebellion leftists envisioned. They would overthrow the state, it appeared, by talking dirty, fornicating in public, and other defiantly theatrical acts. They did indeed stage a Festival of Life the next year, and thousands of hippies together with many straights participated. But though it was followed by other yippie triumphs, there was no cultural revolution. It took more than obscene language and long hair to seize power from the Mayor Daleys.

By this time the New Left was beginning to disintegrate, a fact masked for a time by the fury with which it was denounced, and especially by the campus uprisings which created the illusion of progress. Between January 1 and June 15, 1968, the National Student Association counted 221 major demonstrations at 101 colleges and universities involving nearly forty thousand students. But Columbia, by far the most spectacular, may stand for all the rest. Several elements combined to inflame passions there. One was a vigorous SDS chapter. Another was the University's pressure against the ghetto. Columbia was an important landlord in Harlem, and was building a lavish gymnasium on city land adjoining the ghetto. Though neighborhood people were to have the use of separate facilities in it, militant black leaders remained dissatisfied. "This community is being raped" was how the chairman of Harlem CORE put it. SDS therefore merged its effort to have Columbia divorce itself from the Institute of Defense Analysis (a university consortium for military research) with black resentment against Columbia's real estate operations. On April 23 a mixed band of SDS and the Students' Afro-American Society members marched on Low Memorial Library. Repulsed by guards, they went to the gymnasium site shouting, "Gym Crow Must Go," and tore down a section of fencing. They then occupied Hamilton Hall, executive center of the undergraduate college. The following day black militants seceded from the allied force. They retained Hamilton Hall while the whites occupied Low Library. There the young idealists ransacked President Grayson Kirk's files, drank his sherry, and smoked his cigars.

In the next few days other buildings were taken and converted into "revolutionary communes," each with its own style and, sometimes, ideology. Against the seven hundred or so insurgents was ranged a "majority coalition" dominated by athletes. They surrounded Low Library to keep supplies out of rebel hands. When the "jocks" threw back a relief column, one veteran observer of Columbia football defeats said, "It's probably the first time Columbia has ever held a line." Negotiations having failed, President Kirk ordered the police in early one morning (when Harlem would presumably be asleep) and the revolution was suppressed. The black students in Hamilton Hall surrendered peacefully, but the other buildings were taken by storm. About seven hundred students were arrested and 150 injured. A student sympathy strike followed, which made it impossible to carry on, and the University closed early that semester. It was another famous victory for SDS and its newest star, Mark Rudd, who became a television personality during these events.

As always, the results were ambiguous. President Kirk resigned soon afterward. He was unpopular to begin with and, by being lenient at the beginning and harsh at the end, managed to alienate all shades of opinion. University policies were liberalized, construction of the new gymnasium stopped. The University chapter of SDS declined as Rudd and seventy-two other students were suspended. It remained troublesome the following year, but accomplished little. The physical damage to University buildings was easily repaired. More permanent was the harm done a history instructor whose research notes and manuscripts were burned. SDS and its supporters bore his loss lightly. He had been hostile to the protest and only got what he deserved. And, as Dwight Macdonald observed, you can't have a revolution without violence anyway.

Though Macdonald was a very old leftist, the Columbia rising thrilled him as much as any undergraduate. The rebels thought themselves to be creating a new order. Macdonald was excited by memories of an older one. To him the occupied mathematics building was "the Smolney Institute of the revolution, the ultra-Left SDS stronghold (said to have been liberated by a task force led by Tom Hayden in person) while Fayerweather was the Menshevik center"—that is, it favored a compromise settlement. "I've never been in or even near a revolution before," Macdonald wrote afterward, "I guess I like them. There was an atmosphere of exhilaration, excitement—pleasant, friendly, almost joyous excitement. Everybody was talking to everybody those days, one sign of a revolution" (and of a disaster he might have added). Students learned more in those six days, he was sure, than in years of classes.

This observation was unfailingly made after every campus protest. But while doubtlessly true, it was certainly irrelevant. What they learned had nothing to do with what universities were designed to teach, and was accomplished at the expense of what the university did best. One can see why students enjoyed these protests. Defying authority in a good cause was fun. So were camping out for a week in university buildings, building temporary utopias, and standing guard dramatically against the enemy without. It was a mixture of living theater, cowboys and Indians, the Russian Revolution, and nursery school. Afterward, everyone got a good spanking for being naughty.

This is not to deny the danger involved. Though no one was killed, the possibility was always there. The police did mistreat people. The university was hurt in ways that would not be fully known for years. But, fundamentally, the rebels were acting out infantile fantasies that were not less childish for being conducted on an adult stage, nor more attractive for being based on such legitimate complaints. That so experienced a man as Dwight Macdonald could be swept along by them was, perhaps, only a further sign of how advanced the national pathology had become. The communes were merely coeducational slumber parties writ large. The occupied buildings were not so much liberated as vandalized. Mathematics was not the Smolney Institute. There was no revolution.*

---

* To be on a troubled campus in those days was to envy the Warden and Fellows of Wadham College, Oxford. In reply to a set of non-negotiable demands, they wrote: "Dear Gentlemen: We note your threat to take what you call 'direct action' unless your demands are immediately met. We feel that it is only sporting to let you know that our governing body includes three experts in chemical warfare, two ex-commandos skilled with dynamite and torturing prisoners, four qualified marksmen

The Columbia uprising, heartening though it was, could not keep SDS afloat. Sectarian diversity and counter-cultural subversion had gone too far, as the national council meeting in October 1968 demonstrated. After a battle over the conditions under which they were to use facilities provided them by the University of Colorado at Boulder, fratricidal warfare broke out. The main fireworks were provided by an anarchist group calling itself "Up Against the Wall: Motherfuckers," and the organization's own Progressive Labor faction. The PL group wanted to reshape SDS along more traditional Marxist lines.

The Motherfuckers hated ideology as such, feeling that an uninhibited mock-proletarian style of life was revolutionary enough. Their vocabulary was limited and obscene, though not inexpressive. One member characterized the PL position as less exciting than "a lukewarm fart in August." Another reacted to what he felt was authoritarian rhetoric in this manner: "What I'm saying is it's bullshit, dig it, bullshit to support repression anywhere. Dig. Look at Cuba, China. The German SDS had its conference in Yugoslavia—that's freedom? That's bullshit, man; you're all fucked up if you can support that in the cause of internationalism. That's bullshit." The College Press Service reported that one member, "a Motherfucker and the stepson of Herbert Marcuse, suggested that everybody in PL go home for a good fuck before they talked any more, and earlier dropped his pants to show one of the accoutrements for his program." Another summed up the Motherfuckers' program thusly: "What we're trying to say is that the whole fucking struggle isn't anti-imperialist, capitalist or any of that bullshit. What we're saying is that the whole thing is a struggle to live. Dig it? For survival. The fucking society won't let you smoke your dope, ball your woman, wear your hair the way you want to. All of that shit is living, dig, and we want to live, that's our thing. Action, not this bullshit rapping."*

What the national council meeting did not reveal of the New Left's progress, the Hemispheric Conference to End the War in Vietnam did.

in both small arms and rifles, two ex-artillerymen, one holder of the Victoria Cross, four karate experts and a chaplain. The governing body has authorized me to tell you that we look forward with confidence to what you call a 'confrontation,' and, I may say, even with anticipation."

* The New Left's developing argot, borrowed largely from the ghetto, needed some translation. "Dig" meant understand. To "ball" was to have sexual intercourse with. To "rap" was to discuss something. Talking dirty is, of course, a common way of expressing childish bravado. And it makes parents mad. The regents of the University of Wisconsin were so angry with the student newspaper for printing the unexpurgated account from which these quotations are drawn that they levied financial penalties against it.

It was held in Montreal in late November to organize further anti-war demonstrations. The conference was intended to be a kind of liberal popular front, but almost immediately it was challenged by a bizarre leftist coalition demanding funds to fly Black Panther leader Bobby Seale to Montreal. The planners had actually invited Seale, but refused to pay the air fare for his bodyguards—a typical example of white racism. At the first meeting radicals took over and declared their intention to reorient the conference. Not peace but victory for people's liberation movements was their ambition. They proposed a new name for it, "The Hemispheric Conference to Defeat American Imperialism." Besides white radicals and black militants, the insurgent forces included Chicanos (Mexican Americans), Latin Americans, and Quebec separatists. The liberal organizers, assisted by orthodox communists, tried to organize a counterinsurgence movement. In the nick of time a delegation from the National Liberation Front arrived to oil the troubled waters. The steering committee was broadened and a new schedule of workshops on imperialism, liberation, and the like developed. A statement was issued expressing support for liberation movements everywhere, but especially in Vietnam. The conference ended with a service, attended by Bobby Seale and his bodyguards, at which twenty draft cards were presented for burning to the NLF delegates. The NLF anthem was played and all rose with clenched fists upheld. Of course none of this made any difference. The war went on. Most Americans were unaware that such a thing as the Hemispheric Conference had ever happened. It was just another piece of role-playing by the revolutionaries *manqués* of the New Left. But it did show how much had changed since the National Conference for New Politics met in Chicago the year before. Then all that was required of a liberal wanting to fellow-travel with the left was lip service to Black Power and a blind eye for anti-Semitism. Now the price had been raised to include universal revolution. Not surprisingly, the number willing to pay it declined. After more such victories the left would have no friends at all, a prospect some radicals seemed to welcome. The young radicals, white and black alike, were becoming more ultra-leftist and adventurous just as the country moved to the right. This made further repression inevitable.

In 1969 the New Left collapsed. It had never been very large or very well focused, but in the early days purity of intention covered a multitude of weaknesses. Partly because of their novelty, partly because of their obvious selflessness, New Leftists were extravagantly admired. I. F. Stone spoke for many in 1965 when he said of Snick, CORE, and SDS:

"This idealistic youth is the same youth already serving in the Peace Corps abroad and the poverty program at home. They are the seed corn of a better future. They embody the strain of idealism which in every generation has written the brightest chapters in our American history. They are the spiritual sons of the Jeffersonians and the abolitionists." He warned the government not to destroy that future by alienating them. Of course it did anyway. But more than official unresponsiveness and the war caused what came after. Snick and CORE succumbed to Black Power. The New Left became increasingly frustrated, not so much because of its failure to win specific goals as from its inability to find constituents. The white New Left was composed largely of well-educated middle-class youngsters from liberal and left-wing families. They early saw the difficulties in using colleges to win sweeping social changes. At the best schools it wasn't hard to bring out students in protest. But students were an unreliable constituency. They were transients. After graduation most got lost.

SDS tried in different ways to create alliances. Many critics ranging from conventional Marxists to black revolutionaries like Julius Lester thought the white working classes suitable. As Lester pointed out, "The student radical is never heard talking about a rise in the price of milk, new taxes, real wages, or doctor bills. The student radical creates his own society in which money is not an overriding problem, and because it isn't the student radical thinks that revolution is all about love, because he has time to think about love. Everybody else is thinking about survival." He advised them to get away from abstract issues like American imperialism and into the questions most working people cared about. Progressive Labor operated on just this principle. PL believed in old-fashioned Stalinist principles like party discipline, inevitable revolution, and the proletariat. Its members looked and talked straight. They saw drugs, rock, long hair, and such as obstacles to the business of radicalizing workers.* But PL was working against the tide. While it was trying to re-Stalinize the left, young radicals were turning on to glamorous third-world revolutionaries like Che Guevara, the Viet Cong, Frantz Fanon, and the Palestinian Liberation Front. A program that meant assuming the drab style of American proletarians had no charms for them. They wanted to be streetfighters and guerrilla warriors (thus fulfilling [Irving] Howe's Law: "Where there is no genuine radicalism, there will be ultra-radicalism"). The problem was to find an American

---

* This excited admiration in strange quarters. John Roche, ex-leftist of the old school, a former presidential assistant, and an ostentatiously tough guy who taught at Brandeis and wrote a column regularly chastising liberals and radicals, was one such. He called PL "the Salvation Army of the Left" for its good work in salvaging dope-maddened nihilists.

equivalent of the third-world peasantry. The blacks were already spoken for. The proletariat seemed hopelessly fascist. By the end of 1968 ultra-left SDS members were calling for "the re-consolidation of the mass anti-war movement under the anti-imperialist, anti-racist banner of support for the Vietnamese people, led by the National Liberation Front, and of all oppressed people in their struggle against imperialism." In practical terms this meant a "mass" movement of alienated teen-agers and college students.

Factionalism within SDS came to a head at its annual meeting in June 1969. SDS was badly divided by then. Groups like the Motherfuckers and the Crazies were almost purely nihilistic. Revolution to them meant dope, sex, and violent gestures. With many it was hard to say where the hippie influence ended and the Hell's Angels' began. At the other extreme were the grim dogmatists of PL organized in worker-student caucuses. Against them were ranged a dozen tendencies, from the National Office faction (itself further subdivided into things like the Klonsky-Coleman groupuscle) to the San Francisco Bay Area Revolutionary Union. Many strange events took place. There was a fight over whether a young man who belonged to the Chinese Red Guard should be allowed to speak. PL opposed him, thinking he would misrepresent the cult. At one point an anti-PL group known as the Action-Faction whipped out little red books (containing the thoughts of Chairman Mao) and staged a mock Red Guard rally. A black nationalist gave what he thought a very funny speech that referred to women's liberation as "pussy power." Some leftists took women's liberation seriously and were not much amused.

The most important document was presented by a National Office faction and was named, after a song by Dylan, "You Don't Need a Weatherman to Know Which Way the Wind Is Blowing." It called on white radicals to support all foreign and domestic liberation movements. A struggle to control the platform followed. PL won; the others then walked out and held their own convention. They called themselves the Revolutionary Youth Movement. But it too soon divided into an ultra-left faction known as Weatherman, and a more conventionally leftist wing called RYM-II. All these groups naturally claimed to be the only true SDS. The precise ideology and personnel of each warring sect made little difference. You couldn't tell the players without a scorecard then; it was even harder afterward to make out who was for what. Sect names kept changing all the time. Many of them were derisively coined by the opposition anyhow. (Thus Weatherman called an RYM-II faction in New York "Running Dogs," perhaps to distinguish them from another sect known as the Mad Dogs.) What all this meant was the end of SDS as anything like a coherent national movement. SDS had been the pivot around which the whole New Left revolved. When it collapsed, the New Left did too.

The subsequent history of Weatherman, most spectacular of the sects, was especially pathetic. Weathermen (who controlled the old SDS National Office, now renamed the Weather Bureau) had come to think that American blacks were joining the world-wide struggle against U.S. imperialism. The duty of white radicals was to help the anti-imperial struggle by opening a new front in this country, behind enemy lines as it were. Most working-class and middle-class whites had already been bought off or brainwashed by the power structure, they admitted. Where then was the new Red Guard to come from? From the alienated young was Weatherman's answer. Dissatisfied young workers, motorcycle outlaws, high school dropouts, street kids, rock freaks, the whole *lumpen*-youth culture was ripe for revolution. The strategy for mobilizing them was worked out in small Weatherman collectives. They decided on instant polarization as the proper mode of radicalizing youngsters. Tough high school kids must be shown that radicals were not hippies or soft intellectuals, but gang members in their own right. Weathermen would accomplish this by picking fights with teen-age gangs, attacking high schools, and otherwise showing heart.* They went into training for their new roles. Once some proficiency had been achieved, trial runs were made. In Detroit Weathermen went to working-class beaches during the summer carrying red flags. Fights resulted and some Weathermen, including Mark Rudd, were badly beaten. But they pressed on and in the fall of 1969 organized the New Red Army for a confrontation with the "pig power structure" in Chicago. In Pittsburgh seventy-five Weatherwomen tied up five uncooperative Quakers and rampaged through a high school shouting "Jailbreak!" This was supposed to catalyze the young. Twenty-six of the women were arrested. In Detroit more Weatherwomen, called the Motor City 9, entered an examination room in Macomb County Community College and began lecturing. Two men students who tried to leave were subdued with karate blows. All the women were later arrested. The Boston collective raided Harvard's Center for International Affairs, beating an instructor and a librarian.

All this was by way of preparation for Chicago. When it gathered in Chicago that October, the New Red Army consisted of about two hundred Weathermen and a hundred Weatherwomen, 4,700 fewer people than expected. On the first day of rage, after appropriate ceremonies,

---

* This showed the pernicious effect of children's literature. The Weathermen had been raised on stories in which manly young chaps always become fast friends after having an introductory fistfight. Alas, on the street sportsmanship was not central to peer relations.

they set off, clad in denim, armed with clubs, and shielded by motor-cycle helmets. As the *New York Times* put it, "The first rock of the revolution went through a window of the Chicago Historical Society." They moved down the street shouting "Long live the victory of the people's war" and creating two, three, many broken windows. The windshields of ruling-class automobiles were shattered too. (Also some Volkswagens.) When the police formed a line they charged it. Sixty Weathermen were arrested when police broke into a church where they were staying, apparently because they had earlier beaten up a police informer. On the last day two hundred survivors marched into the Loop and broke more windows. The police arrested another 103, raising the grand total of arrests to 290. Hardly a Weatherman was left unbooked.

Most radicals opposed what the Weathermen did. One Black Panther went so far as to call their actions "Custeristic" (a reference to General Custer's tactics at the Little Big Horn). Weathermen thought otherwise. They had shed the "white-skin privileges" that made them feel so guilty. The pigs had treated them just like blacks. They had shown up more feeble leftists. They had overcome their fears and doubts just like Che. Once out on bail, some went to Washington for the New Mobe's immense peace demonstration. They were among the few thousand who attacked the Justice Department and ran up the VC flag before being dispersed by tear gas. Attorney General Mitchell watched them from a balcony and told his wife later that it "looked like a Russian Revolution going on." On the plane back to Chicago one Weatherman told a reporter, "You could see the red flags waving over this huge cloud of gas. It looked like the Russian Revolution. Outtasight." (Andrew Kopkind, a radical journalist, was less impressed. The streetfighting in Washington fell way short of his exacting standards.) Thus did the fantasies of left and right converge. Almost the only point on which both agreed was that Weathermen threatened the national security. This wasn't much, just enough for each side to act out the same morality play. Given the shortage of Weathermen, though, it couldn't run for long. Soon the Weathermen went underground and became terrorists, as did others. In New York a band of New Left conspirators were arrested for planting bombs in office buildings. In Madison, Wisconsin, a group calling itself the Vanguard of the Revolution staged a whole series of outrages at the year's end. Draft board offices, Army Reserve and ROTC installations were burned and vandalized. And on January 1, 1970, the Badger Ordinance Plant at Baraboo, Wisconsin, was apparently bombed. If so, this involved stealing a light plane (leased by the Air Force ROTC, as it happened) at night, locating the plant, dropping several time bombs (which failed to detonate), and landing at another airstrip unobserved. A tribute to the bombers' nerve and skill if nothing else.

How was the New Left's demise to be explained? It was only a few years since love, peace, brotherhood, and participatory democracy sprang easily to the radical lip. By 1969 hate, violence, obscenity, and revolutionary role-playing seemed dominant. There were many exterior developments to explain this change. Repeated failure led to bitterness and desperation. Third-world revolutionaries generated an irresistible mystique. Che Guevara had more political sex appeal than Gandhi or Martin Luther King. Then too, a movement wanting revolutionary changes could not stay democratic in a country where most people supported the government. So participatory democracy gave way to revolutionary action. But revolutionary action could not succeed in a country where government monopolized the means of effective violence. Thus the New Left's own logic drove it to madness and despair. There was ample precedent for this. The most striking feature of student political movements is their self-destructiveness, as Lewis S. Feuer pointed out in *The Conflict of Generations*. Student movements that began in exultation have repeatedly ended in martyrdom. Denied victory, young radicals seek death. Assassination, terrorism, and self-immolation are their answers to defeat.

Americans, more than most people, think they can escape history. When the New Left started it made much of the difference between it and earlier radicals. It was open, undoctrinaire, independent where they had supposedly been conspiratorial, dishonest, and sectarian. But in scarcely more than eight years the New Left recapitulated practically the whole history of American radicalism. To the worst features of the old tradition—terrorism, sectarianism—it added refinements of its own —romantic racial theories, obscene invective as a matter of policy, and so on. Even Weathermen were not unaware of this. They practiced self-criticism and warned against "violence-tripping" and "death-tripping." But formal injunctions mattered less than group dynamics. Obsessed with revolutionary fantasies, more and more isolated in their communes from the real world, Weathermen seemed helpless before their passions. They hoped by becoming political criminals to shed their advantages, their odious white-skin privileges. But there is no perfect equality outside the grave, as they seemed unconsciously to sense.

Weatherman was, of course, only one small part of the New Left. Yet the other elements, if suffering from fewer self-inflicted wounds, seemed hardly more real. Progressive Labor ground out a mechanically Marxist line. The Crazies, Mad Dogs, Motherfuckers, and whatnot sacrificed everything to style, making PL seem the very model of a modern revolutionary movement. Most of all, the hippie-yippie syndrome, whose charms older people found so hard to grasp, proved fatally seductive to New Leftists. No one ever made a revolution out of dope, sex, militant gestures, and dirty language. Revolutions are commonly based on discipline and self-denial. The radical style was hedonistic and self-indulgent, hence self-destructive. But in the short run it was so attractive that even high school students succumbed to it. Some two dozen underground newspapers circulated in the secondary schools of New York City alone. On December 2, 1968, these youngest radicals declared a city-wide boycott to protest an extension of the public school year. It was 35 per cent effective. In 1969 Dr. Alan F. Westin recorded 675 secondary-school protests around the country (and his survey was not complete), more than half of which concerned student power and related issues. One sixteen-year-old, speaking of anti-administration activity in his own school, told a *New York Times* writer, "It's beautiful. They play pig-hawk-Nazi and we play oppressed-dove-nigger. As soon as we can show white kids that in this country all students are niggers, then we can take to the streets." So the means became the end. The purpose of streetfighting was to fight in the streets.

Though the New Left failed at all its main projects in the 1960's, it had a large, perhaps permanent, effect on the studentry. At the better schools protest became a normal extracurricular activity. According to the Urban Research Corporation, there were protests on 232 campuses during the first six months of 1969. The New Left was involved in only 28 per cent of these. Thus, while young radicals had invented the art, it was no longer unique to them. In fact, protest itself was rapidly becoming a convention. Next to racial issues, student power was the most important object. For whites it was paramount. Some protests were war-related. But most were aimed at reducing parietal regulations (dormitory hours, visiting privileges, and so on) and limitations on student government. University "governance" (decision-making) was a frequent target.

Men found it hard to explain this. The destruction of parental authority by Dr. Spock was frequently cited. Conservatives also blamed liberal professors, the New Left, and other subversives. Liberals answered that "the students are trying to tell us something." Feeling they had made a mess of things, guilty liberals were vulnerable to youth's claim that it would manage them better. Conservatives ignored the formal content of student protesters altogether; liberals accepted it at face value. Everyone agreed there was a generation gap, though the causes of it remained obscure.

The first attempts to measure student dissent offered another possibility. Some opinion surveys indicated that most youngsters (80 to 90 per cent) agreed with their parents on most things.* This was true of

---

* The polls were hardly consistent with one another. Joseph Adelson, "What Generation Gap?", *New York Times Magazine* (January 18, 1970), summarizes

college students also, but with a difference. Vocationally oriented students, as everyone guessed, were more traditional, liberal arts students less so. Students generally disliked parietal restrictions, and for obvious reasons. They had been established when few attended college. Those who did go were physically less mature. But by the 1960's almost half of those eligible for it had some kind of higher education. And they were at age eighteen several more years past puberty than their Victorian predecessors. Being more highly sexed, and more stimulated by sexually charged media, they were more intolerant of efforts to enforce chastity. And as so many went to college, it seemed unfair to students that they should do without the personal freedom their working peers enjoyed. Most schools when pressed were willing to concede this, so parietal regulations rapidly decayed.*

Most of the young claimed a special maturity and, being united on the point, were often able to carry it. But beyond that, agreement did not go far. Student protesters were concentrated in the liberal arts because in the late sixties enrollments grew more rapidly there than in scientific and technical areas. This was hardly surprising. The college population almost doubled in the decade. Many youngsters with no good reason for going to college now went anyway. Lacking clear professional objectives they naturally gravitated to the liberal arts. Motiveless, sometimes alienated, escaping the draft in many cases, they were predisposed to accept the radical critique of higher education. Then too, as pro- or proto-intellectuals, they naturally took the positions that American intellectuals as a class espoused. So long as these were concerned with off-campus issues—war, racism, poverty—their radicalization posed little more than public-relations problems for the universities.

After Berkeley the focus of student protests was increasingly on campus. And radicals tended more and more to attack not just the university's ties with the military-industrial complex but its very nature. ROTC and defense research were unimportant to most universities. If abolished they would not be greatly missed. But when students began attacking university administrations and trustees for being part of, or pandering to, the military-industrial complex, they grew harder to deal with. So

---

many studies showing there was no generation gap to speak of. But a Gallup poll released on May 30, 1970, showed that 61 per cent of college students described themselves as liberals, while an earlier poll showed that only 34 per cent of adults did so. This suggests that although the distance between students and adults was not as great as was thought, it was still growing at the decade's end.

* This did not mean a great increase in sexual activity, however. The Kinsey Institute found little more sexual experience among students in 1968 than in 1948. Coeducational dormitories and fraternities (serenities, some called them) became common. But propinquity stifled desire, or rather, an incest taboo developed among people living together in what had to be fraternal harmony. Sexual relations seemed to have become more open, but not necessarily more frequent.

the grievances accumulated. Military contractors must not recruit on campuses. Endowments must not be invested in firms doing business with South Africa. Students ought to sit on governing boards and have veto powers over faculty appointments. Inevitably, curriculum and instruction came under fire. Students should not have to take irrelevant courses (like foreign languages and sciences). Requirements as such should be fewer and simpler, and exams and grades too. Perhaps it would be best to do away with them altogether. Thus what began as an attack on the university's complicity in undesirable programs ended by attacking the university itself.

Many protesters, lacking serious reasons for being in college, resented having to study. History was not so onerous as, say, engineering, but to people with little interest in history it was trying enough. And it wasn't "relevant." That is to say, studying history did not promote peace, racial justice, and similar good things. If one could not expose a discipline for abetting the military-industrial complex, one could damn it as "elitist," anti-social, or irrelevant. There were plenty of other rocks lying around for the discontented to throw. Grades were arbitrary, unreasonable, and discriminatory. They impeded learning and kept out the blacks; so did exams, of course. Professors spent too much time doing research on irrelevant subjects. When not wasting their time at this, they were wasting the students' with equally irrelevant lectures.

These attacks were demoralizing in the extreme, even when unaccompanied by threats or violence. Liberal education rested on a very few unexamined, and probably unprovable, assumptions: that learning was a good thing in its own right; that it could be measured by tests and grades with reasonable accuracy; that the mind was a muscle to be strengthened by difficult exercises. As there was no way to verify these propositions, their vitality depended on general agreement. When that consensus was destroyed, faculty morale collapsed. Professors had a bad conscience about much of what they did anyway. Most teachers lectured because that was the cheapest way to handle masses of students. Few scholars, however learned, had enough original ideas to sustain the many lectures they delivered each year. No one knew better than those who gave them how arbitrary grades and examinations were. So too with graduation requirements. Why should students take five courses a semester? Why not four, or even three? Since the universities already gave courses on everything from poultry management to the theory of basketball, why not give courses in ghetto organization, spiritualism, or worse?

As most professors had to admit the need for reform, many campuses saw course loads reduced, pass-fail grades established, graduation requirements eased, and so on. Each step was invariably preceded by much student-faculty committee work. Elaborate apologias were drawn up explaining how the proposed change would lead to fresh triumphs of intellect. Afterward students would pronounce the experiment successful but inadequate. New demands would then be put forward and the process repeated. While many of these changes were intrinsically desirable, getting them involved a maximum of fraud and self-deception. One assertion would be countered with another. (Grades reflect accomplishment. Grades inhibit learning.) The threat of student action was always there to goad the faculty along. Most changes were made to appease students rather than to implement powerfully felt educational principles. Hence students got what they wanted (sometimes), but in such a way as to increase their contempt for the faculty. (Nor did giving way to blackmail enhance the professors' self-esteem.) When students didn't get what they wanted, things grew worse. Then faculties and administrators had to vigorously defend the dubious, for they too were losing confidence in the standards they were supposed to enforce. Even when victorious, faculties gained little from such encounters.

The most defensible aspect of the old system was that to succeed at it usually required hard work. However dull or irrelevant it may have been, to the extent that it fostered self-discipline it gave students the best possible preparation for life. While the "reforms" of the late sixties made education more fun, they did so at the expense of the one thing that traditional schooling did fairly well. And there were no measurable compensations for what was lost. The Protestant Ethic gave way to the pleasure principle in college but not in life. Four years of rapping, marching, and glorious peer-group relationships were poor preparation for a world still organized along sterner lines. Some students discovered this, and rejected the world by dropping out, turning on, or forming communes. Others attempted to prolong the undergraduate experience by entering graduate school, and then agitating to make it more like what they had known before. So the graduate schools too were beset with demands that the doctorate become relevant by being made easier to get.

Only a minority of colleges and universities experienced these pressures, but they tended to be the best ones. The inadequacies of the poorer students, and the moral and ideological prejudices of the better ones, combined to make life for the faculty increasingly uncomfortable at such places. College was becoming a more universal experience. Growing numbers of young people enjoyed longer periods of irresponsibility. The age at which they married, took jobs, and acquired children and mortgages, rose. Thus, while student politicalization in a New Left sense waned after 1968, the colleges were not let off the hook. Student careerism kept declining. The pressure for a fun-filled, autonomous, relevant student life increased. And, though often frivolous in fact, student demands still carried a self-consciously moralistic burden. College life had never been so pleasant, nor students so full of self-pity. No one could guess in 1969 where all this would end. Some, historians especially, took comfort from the knowledge that all things come to an end. Others feared that they would not until colleges became playgrounds. A few expected that universities would go in for "tracking" as many high schools did. Academic work would still be offered to the academically inclined minority, while the rest would enjoy relevant entertainments— suitably disguised, of course, so as to resemble a curriculum. Nearly everyone agreed that the future of higher education would not be clear until the war in Indochina was over. So long as it and the draft went on there would be a despair on campus that lent urgency to even the silliest complaints. Only peace would relieve the strain and illuminate what was to come.

The New Left's passing was a relief, especially to academicians, but hardly a cause for rejoicing. Who could enjoy the sight of all that hope and passion wasted, the burning out of those young lives? Thousands went to jail, or into exile, or underground, or blew themselves up with homemade bombs. Though at the end they did much harm, it was mainly to themselves. And there was a reason for their madness. The evils they attacked were real. Poverty, war, racism, and injustice flourished. It was not sufficient to say, as adults did, that they always had and the thing to do was chip away at them little by little. That was true enough, but not good enough in the world's richest country. The young radicals failed themselves by giving way to unrestrained emotionalism. But adults failed too. Because there were no institutions to link up with, the New Left never really got off campus. It remained a student movement throughout, and student movements in developed countries have little more than the power to disrupt.

The New Left ended when the sixties did. SDS was gone. Other organizations vanished also, or shrank in size. Subscriptions to radical and underground papers declined. Terrorism increased. This too was a sign of failure, for in developed countries terror is the weapon of despair. Not since the early 1920's, when the old left collapsed amidst showers of dynamite, had there been so many bombings as in 1970. These accomplished little even by terrorist standards. The bombers suffered more casualties than they inflicted. Their greatest exploit was especially fruitless. Sterling Hall at the University of Wisconsin was blown up and a young scientist killed. This was an accident, it seemed. The bombers aimed to destroy the Army Mathematics Research Center and got the Department of Physics by mistake. Too bad, their remaining admirers said; still, they meant well.

The New Left's collapse was obscured by events like this. Revolutionary terrorism, pseudo-revolutionary posturing on campus, fresh student protests (as after the Cambodian invasion in 1970) led some to think the New Left flourished, others to think its demise made little difference since trouble did not die with it. The New Left's fate was consequential all the same. For many people, not all of them radical by any means, it was a tragedy. The New Left must answer for its failings, arrogance, self-righteousness, an impatience that led to adventurism first and nihilism later. Young radicals talked much of love, even at the end, but in practice this meant loving one another, plus distant subculture folk heroes like the Viet Cong. There was not much moral credit to be gained from either of these. It is easy to love people like one's self, or those one never sees. The trick, as all good religions teach, is to love those one naturally dislikes.

Still, the New Left's main problems were not personal but contextual. Young radicals made many fine efforts to no avail. Things, the war especially, got worse. This was damaging enough of itself. Worse still was the fact that they had nothing much to fall back on. There was no mature left to offer hope for the future. Liberals were too far behind them politically and too weak and disorganized in any case. Functioning as they did in a political vacuum, young radicals had nowhere to go when their own attempts failed. The New Left was a victim not chiefly of internal weakness but of history, and this in two ways. For one thing, the whole modern experience goes to prove that radicalism does not work in America. This being so, reasonable people accept things as they are (which is another reason why conditions improve so slowly). The New Left appreciated but did not accept this fact. Young radicals instinctively employed Marx's dicta to the effect that philosophers have done much to understand the world; the point, however, is to change it. So they rejected most of America's history and made a virtue of being alone. Instead of foreclosing their possibilities it opened up fresh ones, they argued. With no unimaginative Socialist party to clip their wings, they could fly as radicals never had before. This was not so much a mistake as an essential condition, for without it there would have been no New Left.

The second way history destroyed them was by creating all those events and developments that had such fatal effects on young radicals in the sixties. The Indochinese war set up overpowering emotional shockwaves. Third-world revolutionaries offered seductive models of little relevance to the American scene. The counter-culture was even more destructive, in a way, for it created a false sense of constituency. When millions of youngsters smoked dope and damned the Establishment it was hard for radicals not to think that they might be politicized and turned to good account. Radicals wasted a lot of time and effort proving this couldn't be done. Yet they found the counter-culture so alluring that it drew them in even so. The counter-culture was politically debilitating on the one hand, while on the other it led radicals to adopt a style that most Americans loathed, thus adding to their already formidable difficulties. It also turned them on to utopian community-building, a good thing of itself, but one largely incompatible with political action.

Still, no man could be sure that the left was finished. The New Left was dead, the radical impulse lived on in communes and such. Radicalism in the sixties was mostly localized anyhow, which is why a formal chronicle like this falsifies the experience in a way. The events described here really happened. They are what most people knew the New Left for, and what posterity is likely to remember best. Yet the New Left was not chiefly SDS and other national organizations, but thousands of young people clustered around underground newspapers and similar foci. No one led them in the sense of commanding their behavior, or even their loyalty. One reason why SDS perished was that some of its leaders forgot that and came to think of the national office as an instrument of power rather than a means of getting publicity. When it was gone the local bodies and underground papers remained, though they too changed constantly. Only time would tell what would come of this flux. The most reasonable prediction was that, like all previous radical eras, this one too would fade away, most communes dissolve, the underground papers fail. Still, the history of the left in the 1960's was not made by reasonable people.

PROFILE:
Religion

ON JUNE 2, 1963, John XXIII died. His reign as Pope had been one of the shortest in modern times. Yet his four and two-thirds years in office were more productive than any Pope's since Leo XIII. Leo had brought the Church into the nineteenth century; John brought it into the twentieth. He made the first real steps toward reconciliation with other Christian denominations. He convened the first Vatican Council in many years. Its lengthy sessions opened the Church to changes on a scale unknown since the counterreformation. Pope John's impact was heightened by the contrast with his predecessor. Pius XII had been a distant, aristocratic figure. A man of highly orthodox views, his reign was distinctive mainly for changes that did not take place. Pope John came of peasant stock and never lost his feeling for the things that mattered to ordinary people. Almost immediately after his election he abandoned the tradition of Papal isolation. He visited the Regina Coeli prison at Christmas, gave Communion to the streetsweepers of Rome, and in general conducted himself more like a parish priest writ large than a prince of the Church. At his death he was the best-loved man on earth.

The Roman Catholic Church in America was slow to feel the effects of John's reign. American Catholics were more conservative than any in the West. Immigrants or the sons of immigrants for the most part, they were led by an undistinguished hierarchy.

These predominantly Irish American bishops often possessed the kind of wardheeler's mentality to be expected from a people whose eminence in religion and politics was a consequence of single-minded parochialism. The Irish boss and the Irish bishop were cut from the same cloth. Both were shaped by the same confining anti-Catholic and anti-immigrant prejudices they found in America. The result was a great emphasis on loyalty and conformity in politics and religion alike, but especially in the latter. The authority of the party leader was not absolute—the Pope's was. Hence the American Church, which had been a mission church for so many years, was like a colony of Rome in comparison with the freer Catholic Churches of other advanced countries. Not that the American faithful suffered from divided loyalties, as was often charged. Actually they were patriotic to a fault: equally devoted to Washington and Rome. Since these loyalties existed on different planes, American Catholics found no contradictions between them, whatever others might think.

This was soon to change. Time and prosperity were producing new Catholic generations to whom the attitudes formed by poverty and discrimination were inappropriate. Anti-Catholicism itself was declining, even among liberals and intellectuals who clung to it long after they had discarded other once respectable prejudices. Pope John was one good reason for this, President Kennedy another. Both demonstrated that it was possible to be both free and Catholic. In the sixties politicians like the Kennedys, and Eugene McCarthy, and a host of nuns and clergymen dispelled fears that the growth of Catholicism threatened American liberty. And John F. Kennedy's scrupulous—overscrupulous, some Catholics thought—conduct in office proved to most that a Catholic President would not give special favors to his co-religionists.

When Pope John died, few could have guessed what the effects of his reign would be. The American Church seemed as stodgy and defensive as ever, as was demonstrated by the refusal of Catholic University to allow four distinguished scholars of the Church to teach its students. Catholic U. was the Church's only national university. It was governed by the entire episcopate, and reflected the bishops' views in a particularly direct way. The men barred from lecturing at Catholic University in 1963 showed what these views were. One,

Father John Courtney Murray, was the foremost Catholic theologian in America. He was unacceptable because of his liberal position on certain doctrinal questions. Another was barred because he favored substituting the vernacular for Latin in the liturgy. The University's rector said the men were banned for their involvement in controversial issues, though conservatives spoke frequently on campus. This was how the Church had been run for generations. There was a tiny "underground church." Its existence was a well-kept secret.

The Vatican Ecumenical Council ended on December 8, 1965. Convened under Pope John, completed under Pope Paul, it had taken three years of planning and four years in session to reach this moment. The Roman Catholic Church, to which a quarter of the American people belonged, was never the same again. The Council's statements were themselves of great importance. The Pontiff announced the creation of a synod of bishops to consult with him in the Church's management. Birth control was handled in such a way as to sustain the ban on contraception while leaving the door open to future changes. Nuclear arms were condemned, despite the efforts of American prelates to have American weapons exempted. Priestly celibacy was sustained. Anti-Semitism was attacked and the Jews cleared of any blame for Christ's death (a step irreverently described as "taking the Jews off the hook"). In a conciliatory effort, Pope Paul moved to beatify both his immediate predecessors, the conservative Pius XII as well as the liberal John XXIII. This meant they would probably become saints. At the Council's end Pope Paul and the Patriarch Athenagoras committed "to oblivion" the mutual excommunications that had separated Catholicism and Orthodoxy since 1054.

But though the churches were drawing together, Catholics were drifting apart. The consensus reached by the Vatican Council was more apparent than real. Already the Pope was warning against an excessive enthusiasm for change. He would later proclaim his omnipotence and infallibility in stronger terms. This did little good. Pope John had opened a door that Paul was helpless to close. Apart from specific points at issue—clerical celibacy and birth control especially—freedom of conscience itself was proving irrepressible. In the 1960's every change, however slight, was instantly hailed as "revolutionary." But that much-abused word did seem applicable to Catholicism. The Pope supervised a host of changes in doctrine, liturgy, and practice, but as in all revolutions, change generated an appetite for more change. This was not yet apparent in 1965. Soon it would be unmistakable.

On July 29, 1968, Pope Paul VI released his long-awaited encyclical on birth control, *Humanae Vitae (Of Human Life)*, reaffirming the Roman Church's ban on artificial contraception. Almost immediately it became clear what changes Vatican II had wrought in the Church. Pope Paul meant to suppress the movement among Catholics for repeal of the ban. Instead he undermined the Papacy itself. Many Catholics were especially disappointed that the Pope had not followed the advice given him by two separate bodies of his own choosing. In 1964 he had appointed a sixty-member commission including laymen and married couples to study the issue. In June 1966 it advised that the regulation of birth, short of abortion and sterilization, should be left for married couples to decide. Worse still, from the Papal viewpoint, a commission of sixteen prelates which reviewed the first report endorsed it. The Pope finally packed a twenty-man commission with conservatives and succeeded in getting the advice he wanted. By then, however, the earlier commissions' recommendations had become public, and in October 1967 the Third World Congress for the Lay Apostolate, an important organization of Catholic laity, recommended eliminating the ban on contraception.

The ferment thus occasioned guaranteed that *Humanae Vitae* would be not only disregarded in practice but widely challenged in principle. In the United States nearly eight hundred theologians signed or supported a statement that "spouses may responsibly decide according to their consciences that artificial contraception in some circumstances is permissible and indeed necessary to preserve and foster the values and sacredness of marriage." Loyal prelates counterattacked futilely. Philadelphia's John Cardinal Krol warned the dissenting priests that they were "mounting an insurrection against God," but few accepted this definition. Most laymen tacitly agreed with the protesting priesthood. A study released by the Urban Life Institute of the Jesuits' University of San Francisco showed that 70 per cent of American Catholics approved the use of contraceptives. Priests were about evenly divided, almost exactly along age lines. The Center for the Study of Man at the University of Notre Dame found that 95 per cent of the younger priests opposed the Papal encyclical, and 95 per cent of the older ones supported it. In most dioceses a tacit agreement was reached by which the bishops condemned the use of contraceptives while individual priests advised parishioners as they saw fit.

Those conservatives who attempted to press the issue found themselves in dangerous waters, as the case of Washington's Patrick Cardinal O'Boyle demonstrated. When *Humanae Vitae* was released, 142 Washington priests wrote O'Boyle saying they thought it contradicted the guarantees of freedom of conscience expressed by Vatican II. The seventy-two-year-old O'Boyle was liberal on racial questions, but as a veteran of the American Church's colonial era was a conservative on questions of doctrine and authority. He tried laying down the law to rebellious priests. The Association of Washington Priests, a kind of clerical union, responded that its members still viewed birth control as a matter of conscience. Cardinal O'Boyle lost his temper with one priest and suspended him. The priest was supported by some twelve hundred of his parishioners who held a candlelight rally in his behalf, complete with freedom songs. It was obvious that the old sanctions no longer worked. Young priests were not so easily intimidated, and they knew more about canon law and related matters than earlier generations had. The diocese paid their tuition for courses at Catholic University, now suddenly a hotbed of reform thought. "The worst mistake I ever made was to send you fellows to that university," Cardinal O'Boyle told one dissident priest.

The struggle over birth control was but one sign of the changes among American Catholics. The underground was surfacing. Young priests and laymen challenged many traditional beliefs. The *National Catholic Reporter* of Kansas City flourished. At a time when most Catholic publications were in trouble, the *Reporter* picked up ten thousand new subscribers a year for being independent. Bishop Helmsing of Kansas City condemned it for fostering heresy and scandal. But it went on reporting supposedly secret Church meetings, and questioning and probing all the same.

Next to birth control, priestly celibacy was probably the main point of contention between traditionalists and reformers. By the end of 1968 it was thought that six hundred priests a year were leaving the clergy; perhaps as many as 15 to 20 per cent of all priests ordained since 1964 had dropped out. When the *Gallagher President's Report,* a newsletter for businessmen, surveyed a group of priestly defectors, 73 per cent gave celibacy as their main reason for leaving. The Church, which had once treated defectors as outcasts, increasingly found itself obliged to recognize their existence. Nuns caught the spirit too. Formerly the most docile and submissive of all religious groups, they began doffing their habits, living in slum apartments, and otherwise shattering the "poor little sisters" image that had characterized them for so long. And they were as ready as priests to defy the hierarchy. Even James Francis Cardinal McIntyre of Los Angeles, most reactionary of the great prelates, discovered this when he attempted to limit sisterly reformers in his archdiocese. After years of quarreling with him over changes in their rules and customs, most of the Immaculate Heart of Mary sisters voted to abandon formal religious life and become a secular community. About 315 of the 400 nuns would go on teaching and providing health and social services as before, but in an open community where married people and women who had not previously been nuns would be welcome, and where no one would be subject to Church discipline. Small groups of priests and nuns had resigned from their orders before, but this was the first time such a large body had left with the intention of remaining together.

No one could know where the new ferment would lead. The old prelates kept the upper hand in most places. Their day seemed nearly over all the same. Given the great liberal majority among younger clergymen, it seemed inevitable that the future would bring important changes among the hierarchy too. This suggested that in the short run defections would continue to be frequent. The tendency to establish independent congregations of people who regarded themselves as Catholics while defying the Church's authority would probably continue. And the subservience to Rome that had once distinguished American Churchmen would almost certainly decline. Vatican II's "Declaration on Religious Freedom" had narrowed the distance between Roman Catholics and other Christians. The democratic surge within the Church made Catholics resemble

Protestants even more. Thus, whatever else happened, the prospects for Christian unity seemed brighter than ever. Pope Paul could not undo what John had done. The American Church was not about to revert to its old semi-colonial status.

🎏

The sixties were also important for Protestants, whose controversies were the most intense since the liberal-fundamentalist confrontations of the 1920's. Their theologies were taxed more strenuously than at any time in the twentieth century. The cause of these agitations was not entirely clear. Unlike the Catholic Church, which had long needed reforming, Protestantism was already up to date, or so it seemed. Although many denominations were fundamentalist, or at least uninterested in social problems, most influential denominations adhered to the social gospel. No one needed to tell Methodists, Presbyterians, and Episcopalians, among others, that Christians owed a duty to society as well as to God. They had long since accepted that proposition; so had their collective organ, the National Council of Churches. Theologically the social gospel, or variations of it, still prevailed. Even the vogue for neo-orthodoxy, which had lasted for some decades, made little difference. One could take a conservative view of the human condition and still work for social justice, as did Reinhold Niebuhr, the leading neo-orthodox theologian in America. If attendance proved anything, the churches were doing better than ever. The rate of increase was down a little from the fifties, but even so Americans still went to church more regularly than other peoples.* The growing racial crisis had not found the churches wanting. No other voluntary agencies gave as much help to the civil rights movement. Doubtless it was not enough (later the churches would be

* Gallup surveys in 1968 showed that on Sunday 43 per cent of the adult population went to church, compared with 42 per cent in the Netherlands, the nearest competitor. In Finland only 5 per cent did. Americans were also more orthodox than other peoples. 98 per cent of the population claimed to believe in God, 65 per cent in hell, and 60 per cent in the devil. The only Western country that was higher in any category was Greece, where 67 per cent believed in the devil. In the United Kingdom 77 per cent believed in God and 21 per cent in the devil. One theory explained this as a consequence of there being no state religion in America. State churches seemed to discourage devotion, free competition among denominations to encourage it, not only in the U.S. but in places like Ireland, Switzerland, and Canada, where lay interest in religion also ran high.

severely criticized by black militants seeking "reparations"), but it was still a great deal. The civil rights movement would have had a far rougher time if the black churches in the South had not been able to count on money and manpower from their white counterparts in the North. And everywhere in the North where racial justice was pursued, churchmen were in the vanguard.

Yet the more churches did, the less adequate they seemed. Expectations changed more rapidly than performance, and the lag generated further demands on both the theory and the practice of the churches. This contributed to the New Theology which emerged in 1963 with the publication of a book by Bishop John A. T. Robinson of Woolwich, England, called *Honest to God*. Robinson was particularly occupied with the concept of "immanence," the idea that God dwells in man. Its opposite is "transcendence," or the otherness of God. Traditional Christianity favors transcendence and posits a God who, while he governs the universe, is separate from it. But in recent years the idea of immanence had gained ground. One index of this was the growing appeal of Eastern pantheistic religions. Pantheism is the logical conclusion of immanence. Beginning with the proposition that God is in man, it goes on to say that God is man, and hence God is the physical universe. Immanence also found expression in some of the drug cults. Timothy Leary's League for Spiritual Discovery was an effort to find God through mind expansion. Drug cultists generally believed that "turning on" confirmed the truths of Eastern metaphysics. In a general way the hippies also tended toward immanence. They revered nature (symbolized by the flower), and though they did not often pronounce the name of God, sought him in it.

As time went on, science and rationalism lost ground among the young. The decline of interest in college science majors was one sign of this, a rising interest in the supernatural another. The exchange of science for magic was a further example of immanence at work. Christianity and science had been reconciled to one another by assigning primacy to each in its own sphere. The visible physical universe was the province of science, the invisible of religion. The young, in rejecting orthodox science and religion, rejected also this division. Many came to see the physical and spiritual universes as co-existential; there was but one reality, and the spirit dwelt in it.

Hence magic (or astrology) was as good a guide, and probably a better one, to ultimate truth as either science or religion. Here too, immanence replaced transcendence. Immanence became, in fact, one of the central themes of American life in the 1960's. The religious enthusiasm of the era (often unrecognized as such) came to revolve around it.

Bishop Robinson was one of the first to sense the new direction that belief was taking, and his book contributed to the change, even though he meant to salvage transcendence with it. Robinson borrowed heavily from other theologians. One of them was Dietrich Bonhoeffer, a German martyred by the Nazis. Bonhoeffer wanted the Bible demythologized and called for a "Christianity without religion." Before he was killed he wrote that while man should not stop searching for God, he ought to function as if God did not exist. Then God would be no longer a crutch or an excuse, and man would be free to look for him among the poor and needy. Another influence was Paul Tillich, who defined God as The Ground of Our Being.

The theological ideas and social forces moving Robinson influenced others as well, notably the "God Is Dead" theologians, some of whom went beyond the bishop to embrace immanence. The tag itself was created by Dr. Thomas Altizer of Emory University. He believed that Jesus Christ was indeed the son of God, and that the incarnation and crucifixion were real events. But there was no resurrection. In a sense, God died. Having been transcendent, he became immanent, a part of the universe though not all of it. Since then, however, God had grown ever more immanent, his share of the universe ever larger. Thus to Altizer, "Christ is the God who remains in the world. The death of God was the passage from transcendence to immanence," leading to a new man, a new world, a new life. Because of it, man became truly free. In this way Altizer avoided traditional pantheism. His God was an evolving God, unlike the Eastern mystics whose concept of God was static or reactionary.

Altizer's ideas were not unrelated to the work of Teilhard de Chardin, a Jesuit paleontologist who introduced the spirit of the New Theology into Catholic thought. Teilhard saw the universe in terms of an evolutionary theory based upon "the increasing complexification of inert matter." In it, mankind was moving toward a new godhead which he called the Omega point. The incarnation was, to him, the key event in history. At that moment God immersed himself in creation, unifying it, taking direct control as it were, until, having gathered everything together and transformed everything, "he will close in upon himself and his conquests, there rejoining, in a final gesture, the divine focus he has never really left." Then, as St. Paul says, "God shall be all in all." What this meant, in effect, was not that God was dead, only the traditional view of him. Altizer, and many of the God Is Dead school, seemed also to be saying this. They meant that God is absent, or the ability to experience God is dead, or the word "God" is dead, thus obviating a continued search for his identity and nature. William Hamilton spoke of "waiting for God" as if he would one day return. Much of the New Theology, then, occupied the same ground as Bonhoeffer. Man ought to act as if God were dead, even while believing he was not. Generally this was taken to mean that man had become fully responsible for his own condition and must set about repairing it. Most of the New Theologians and their followers believed that the horrors of modern life—racism, mass murder, the bomb—negated the moral assumptions of traditional Christianity. Science and scholarship increasingly narrowed its historical base. The New Theology's function was to purge religion of whatever was archaic and inhibiting, to free the mind and spirit for fresh assaults on social injustice. These ideas were well received by both Protestant and Catholic activists who pressed with increasing vigor against everything that seemed obsolete and confining in their churches.

For the most part, the proponents of God's death were a sunny group, happy to have metaphysics laid to rest and man freed to get on with the business of reform. They got much attention for a time, and then in May 1969 *Time* magazine announced the death of the God Is Dead theology. According to William Braden, it had been withering away for several years. This was not so much because of the hostile publicity, though it was enormous, as because happy secularism soon appeared untimely. There was, it became clear, less and less to be cheerful about. At the same time people, mainly the young, began turning against secularism. They were also turning against the institutional churches which confused many. Polls taken among Americans of all faiths showed that whereas in 1957 69 per cent believed that religion was increasing its influence in American life, by 1969 70 per cent believed it was losing influence. But in fact religion, or at least a belief in the supernatural, was becoming more common among youngsters who found the secularized mainstream churches, whether oriented toward the social gospel or the Death of God, irrelevant. As hippies, drug cultists, magicians, or whatever, they went their own theological ways.

The combination of ghastly historical events and youthful enthusiasm turned professional theologians against the Death of God rather quickly. Harvey Cox's book *The Secular City* (1965) had been influential in promoting the Death of God. A few years later he was saying, "If theology can leave behind the God who 'is' and begin its work with the God who 'will be' . . . an exciting new epoch in theology could begin" (prompting William Braden to remark that "an epoch in contemporary theology would appear to be about three years"). That exciting new epoch would be based on the Theology of Hope, toward which Cox led the way with his new book, *The Feast of Fools* (1969). Avant-garde American theologians began speaking of God again, and also of metaphysics. The Theology of Hope was appealing to them not only for being timely but for being consistent in a way with God Is Dead. Hopeful theologians did not say that God Is, rather that He Is Not Yet. God awaits man in the future. The Theology of Hope would appeal to radicals, it was said, because like them it pointed away from the present and toward the future. It was consistent with revolutionary aspirations; indeed it was possible to see revolution as the coming of God.

At the decade's end it was still not clear where the Theology of Hope was going. Theologians, having become enamored of the new, might well launch another epoch tomorrow. Nor did the Theology of Hope have anything like the effect of God Is Dead. Radical Catholics, priests and laymen alike, were still moving in a secular direction. The young were still forming religious communes and "submarine" churches. These last bore names like the Ecstatic Umbrella and Alice's Restaurant, as if they were rock bands or discothèques. Their symbol combined a yellow submarine with a cross, a peace symbol, and the word "ecumenical" in Greek. The yellow submarine came from an animated cartoon movie about the Beatles. One leader explained, "In the Beatles' movie the submarine was the place where they loved each other in a groovy way and got strength to do battle with the Blue Meanies. It also shows that a Church has to have flexibility and maneuverability." In this way the counter-culture found God.

At the same time, however, other ex-hippies turned to pentecostal Christianity for spiritual relief. Pentecostalism, with its emphasis on mysticism, direct contact with God, and "speaking in tongues," attracted youngsters who found Eastern mysticism and contemporary Christianity equally unsatisfying. Their theology was Bible-oriented but translated into the counter-culture's argot. As one convert put it, his thing was to rap about Jesus and warn others that drugs and the occult are the "sorceries" spoken of in the Bible. "I went through the political route, and then through the drug trip," he told an interviewer. "Others get into meditation or Hare Krishna. We're all looking for life's reality. Jesus said, 'I am the truth'—and that's where reality is at." Pentecostalism grew not only among Protestants but in the Catholic Church as well, with the hierarchy's cautious blessing.

American religious life was probably more fertile and diverse in the sixties than at any time since the nineteenth century. If all this did not quite amount to an age of faith, it certainly seemed so compared with the 1950's which now looked like merely an age of churchgoing. The old religious revival declined; religion itself did not. The established churches became more secular, unchurched youths more religious. Anti-communism excepted, the 1950's was a time when rational, scientific, and secular ideas dominated. In the sixties romantic, millennial, chiliastic, and utopian impulses undermined them. When the decade began, men proclaimed the end of ideology in religion as in politics, but ideology overcame in both areas nonetheless. Futurists assumed that scientific progress had made the supernatural obsolete. What the sixties showed was that even in a technetronic age, perhaps especially then, men still have need of God, and that if the established churches cannot provide for it others will. That was a sobering lesson indeed, though aspiring social managers paid little attention to it. They kept on drawing blueprints for the year 2000 as if nothing had changed since 1914. Then it made sense to expect the future to be like the present, only more so. But after two world wars, Nazism, communism, and the religious excitements of recent years, to imagine a future dominated by reason, secularism, and the rule of science was to possess a faith as extravagant as, and even more groundless than, that of the submarine churches.

10 TO TET AND BACK

An INNOCENT VISITOR to the United States in mid-decade might well have thought that the chief threat to American security was President Charles de Gaulle. Vietnam was to most in the government still a remote problem, but de Gaulle seemed very close at hand. His unsolicited advice to the U.S. was annoying, his apparent opening to the East outrageous. In 1965 he continued to send ministers throughout Eastern Europe in search of trade and cultural agreements. He visited Moscow. Worst of all, he carried out his promise to withdraw from NATO. On June 30, 1966, American forces began leaving France. 72,000 French troops in Germany were taken out of NATO, though they remained on station under a bilateral agreement between Paris and Bonn. The American response was predictable. Ambassador to France Charles E. Bohlen told a House subcommittee that it was "probably the most serious event in European history" since World War II. Secretary Rusk admitted that the Russian threat to Western Europe had diminished, but only because of the NATO shield that de Gaulle was weakening. American tourism in France continued to decline. There were attempts in the U.S. to boycott French imports. This reaction was explained by David P. Calleo who noted that Gaullist foreign policy "invariably appears puzzling, idiotic, or sinister to those who cannot imagine why anyone except a communist would want to be independent of the United States."

The hue and cry against de Gaulle went on for several more years. Then it was pushed aside by the war in Indochina. By the time student uprisings and a monetary crisis drove de Gaulle from power, few in

America cared much one way or another. French policy after de Gaulle was not greatly different, though less abrasively managed than before. This completed the lesson France taught America in the sixties. The Cold War was over in Europe for the most part. Europeans could afford to pursue their own interests. These were not always the same as America's. If Europe united, the discrepancies might become clearer and Europe's ability to exploit them greater. De Gaulle suggested what a truly independent Europe would be like. Accordingly, when he fell Washington did not again press for a United States of Europe and British entry into the Common Market with its old fervor.

Nor did NATO continue to enjoy the sacred status accorded it in the fifties. NATO had become little more than a dumping ground for surplus U.S. military equipment and a cover for American nuclear weapons, which were never "integrated" into the European force anyway. De Gaulle had shown integration to be even more fragile than American exclusiveness made it seem. The rising costs of the Asian war turned people against keeping an expensive U.S. Army in Germany. Though few any longer believed in it, NATO would survive, if only as a trigger to the American deterrent. The U.S. would go on protecting Western Europe, with or without NATO, because it was in her interest to do so. That was a solid fact. De Gaulle could not change it, nor did he mean to. What he did do was shake the rickety superstructure of pacts and alliances that years of fussing had erected. This was greatly resented by the Rube Goldbergs of diplomacy, but it was a service to them all the same. De Gaulle introduced a note of realism long missing in U.S.-European affairs. And, almost imperceptibly, it began doing its work in Washington and elsewhere.

Such was not the case with Vietnam. Washington was now welded to its illusions by the blood of Americans it sent to die there. The war was no longer debatable. The gamble having been taken, nothing remained but to see it through. Escalation proceeded by stages, separated often by fraudulent peace offensives. The first of these began with an informal Christmas truce observed by both sides in December 1965. Afterward President Johnson grounded his warplanes and filled the air with diplomats. Averell Harriman went off to Poland, Belgrade, and India. Ambassador to the UN Arthur Goldberg was plucked from a vacation in the Bahamas and flown to Rome, where he spoke to Pope Paul and Foreign Minister Aldo Moro. After that he was received by President de Gaulle in Paris and Prime Minister Wilson in London. Under Secretary of State Thomas C. Mann went to Mexico City. Assistant Secretary of State

G. Mennen Williams canvassed Africa. Hardly a capital was left unturned during these few weeks, except, naturally, Hanoi.

What was the point of all this furious traveling? How, indeed, could one find peace by looking everywhere except in Vietnam? To ask the question was to answer it. The President was not working for peace but for better public relations. He made the effort because the latest futile attempt to establish contact with Hanoi had become known. As was so often the case, it had been initiated by private citizens. In November two Italian professors had gone to Hanoi as volunteer peacemakers. President Ho told them he would not insist on the removal of all American troops from Vietnam before negotiating. This seemed to them a concession, though it's not clear that Hanoi ever expected the troops to leave before talks began, and they rushed to tell Amintore Fanfani the good news. Fanfani, then sitting as president of the UN General Assembly, passed the information on to Ambassador Goldberg, who sent it to the President, who sent it to Dean Rusk. Secretary Rusk's office was already piled high with unopened peace bids. But as so many knew of this one, he had to respond to it. So he drafted a cautious letter which was relayed via Fanfani to President Ho. It had barely reached Hanoi when news of it appeared in the *St. Louis Post-Dispatch*. The administration immediately made public the exchange between Fanfani and Rusk. Whereupon Hanoi denounced the whole thing as just another imperialist fabrication.

On January 31, 1966, the bombing of North Vietnam resumed. On February 8 a delegation of five Senators headed by the Majority Leader, Mike Mansfield, after thirty-five days in Vietnam reported that a year of Americanizing the war had changed nothing. "All of mainland Southeast Asia, at least, cannot be ruled out as a potential battlefield," they concluded. Ornithology now dominated the politics of war. The friends of American intervention were called hawks, critics were doves. Senator George D. Aiken of Vermont thought the country needed more owls. Senator Warren Magnuson of Washington proclaimed himself an American eagle. Art Buchwald, noted social philosopher, admitted to being chicken. The Senate was rapidly becoming a nest of doves. Mansfield was uneasy about the war, Morse and Gruening had been against it from the first. But the weightiest criticism came from William Fulbright, chairman of the Senate Foreign Relations Committee.

Fulbright was a most unusual Senator. The son of a prosperous Arkansas businessman, he had gone to the state university and then, in 1925, to Oxford as a Rhodes scholar. No one would have called him an intellectual then. Sports, campus politics, and collegiate life were his main interests. But Oxford had a great effect on him, as Cecil Rhodes meant it to. It awakened his intellect and established his taste. He went on to George Washington University, where he finished second in a class of

135 law students. He taught there for a time, and then at the University of Arkansas. In 1939 he was appointed its president; at thirty-four he was the youngest university president in the country. He was turned out by a new governor two years later. In 1942 he was elected to Congress, where he won immediate attention for a speech rebutting Representative Clare Booth Luce's attack on Vice-President Henry Wallace. In 1943 he became nationally known for his resolution demanding international peacekeeping machinery after the war. The next year he was elected to the Senate.

There his career was at first less brilliant than expected. He did sponsor the student-teacher exchange program that bears his name. He was the only Senator to vote against appropriations for the McCarthy subcommittee in 1954. He was active in the successful fight to censure McCarthy. But Fulbright never made the Senate "club." His position as a border-state politician forced him to vote against integration and related measures. As he was not a conservative in the Southern sense, this left him with no outside constituency to offset his weak position in the Senate. Then in 1959, when he was fifty-four, the seniority system made Fulbright chairman of the Foreign Relations Committee. Some power and much prestige went with the job. Though ability had nothing to do with his selection, Fulbright was a perfect choice all the same. Intelligent, reflective, an expert on foreign affairs and well known abroad (more so than in America probably), he was ideally suited for the work fortune called him to.

What that would be was not immediately evident. Fulbright's sense of his committee's duty had been formed in the 1940's. The great struggle for collective security had made a bipartisan foreign policy what the Senate most desired. Fulbright did too. He believed his committee should advise Presidents but not oppose them. As late as 1963 he still anticipated that the President's authority over foreign policy would grow. When he thought the President mistaken he said so, but not in public. His subcommittees were kept on a tight rein. This position survived the Bay of Pigs (which he opposed) and the Cuban missile crisis (which he favored). What destroyed it was the Dominican affair. When President Johnson invaded the Dominican Republic Fulbright supported him. But he held hearings on the intervention later, and these changed his mind. On September 15, 1965, he gave a notable speech, saying: "U.S. policy in the Dominican crisis was characterized initially by over-timidity and subsequently by over-reaction. . . . Through the whole affair it has also been characterized by a lack of candor. . . . The administration acted on the premise that the revolution was controlled by Communists—a premise it failed to establish at the time and has not established since."

For the sober Fulbright this was comparable to a diatribe. Naturally it inspired sharp reactions. Fulbright was always stubborn. The harder he was pushed, the more resistant he became. Once having broken with custom, he found it easier, even though under heavy fire, to do so again. In January 1966 his committee began its televised hearings on Vietnam. Retired General James M. Gavin explained his "enclave theory," a proposal for de-escalating the war. George Kennan stressed Vietnam's peripheral importance and urged the country to remember where its real interest lay (in Europe). Secretary Rusk was called up three times in three weeks, for as much as seven hours at a time. Fulbright grilled him relentlessly in his soft-spoken way. Secretary McNamara refused to testify except in closed session. Fulbright followed up these hearings with another set on China. In a kind of senatorial teach-in, leading Asian scholars, hawks and (mostly) doves, explored the war's impact on Chinese affairs.

No one knew if any minds were changed by these hearings, but they legitimized the anti-war movement. Now it was no longer a matter of silly housewives, peaceniks, intellectuals, and assorted freaks. The dissenting Senators showed that men of stature and influence opposed the war too. The administration went on the defensive once more. It could pass off the teach-ins lightly. The Senate Foreign Relations Committee, and its expert witnesses, were not so easily brushed aside. Not that the administration didn't try. President Johnson attempted to obscure the Fulbright hearings by hastily flying off to Hawaii for a meeting with the Saigon junta. That encounter generated the customary humbug. President Johnson said, "We are here to talk especially of the works of peace. We will leave here determined not only to achieve victory over aggression, but also to win victory over hunger, disease, and despair." The South Vietnamese militarists dedicated themselves to "the eradication of social injustice" and the building of "a stable viable economy and . . . a better material life for our people." Vice-President Humphrey then went to Vietnam bearing his own message of hope.

The Hawaii meeting drew attention from Fulbright's hearings as intended, but the Senator was not discouraged. On April 21 at the Johns Hopkins University he gave his most famous speech. Later it was published with his other two Christian A. Herter lectures as *The Arrogance of Power*. One of them attacked the Dominican intervention. Of the recent elections there he observed that "recovery from a disaster does not turn the disaster into a triumph." The U.S. must learn, he insisted, that the growing desperation of poor peoples would create more such upheavals. He noted that in 1965 the U.S. proudly hailed the construction of half a million new housing units in Latin America (sixty thousand of them with Alianza help). What the government did not say was that in the same year the number of families in need of housing went up by 1.5 million. The administration pretended things were getting better when actually they were getting worse. The U.S. had a fortunate history, Fulbright went on. Thus it could not understand why less-favored people took desperate steps. When a nationalist uprising had communist elements, the U.S. suppressed it if possible. This was a mistake, Fulbright argued. Communism was not of itself a repellent doctrine. What hurt was the fanaticism with which it was pursued. Some kinds of national communism could be lived with. Attempts to suppress them only made matters worse, as in Vietnam. At bottom, Fulbright argued, America's problems were a consequence of its great ambitions. It wished to set limits for the whole world to abide by. Though not entirely ignoble, this grand scheme led to war and oppression abroad and unrest at home.

He urged another course, a prudent, even conservative one. On its behalf he invoked the names of Burke, Metternich, and Castlereagh "because they believed in the preservation of indissoluble links between the past and the future, because they profoundly mistrusted abstract ideas, and because they did not think themselves or any other men qualified to play God." This was a little disingenuous of Fulbright. He knew that such men fought the great revolution of their time, while he wanted America to do just the opposite. Yet in calling them to his aid Fulbright was not being merely artful. He was at heart a deeply conservative man. Having lived through wave after wave of public feeling over foreign and domestic issues, he no longer trusted passion to guide men's affairs. As a student of history he knew that things rarely turn out as planned. Yesterday's enemy was today's friend. What was heresy to this generation might be the orthodoxy of another. This being so, the sensible man moved slowly and kept his options open. Fulbright subscribed to liberal principles (he would surely have voted for civil rights if Arkansas had let him), and was a great respecter of persons. It was his temperament, not his ideology, that was conservative. In another country Fulbright might have been recognized for what he was. But in America troglodytes, reactionaries, bigots, and true believers of the right monopolized the word *conservative*. An honorable man hardly dared use the term, so Fulbright didn't. Hence he was denounced by rightists for being left, and by leftists for being right.

What he could do he did do, and splendidly. It was as if his whole life had been pointing toward this moment. The years of study and reflection, his long experience as a servant of American power abroad, the political compromises and disappointments, his naturally independent, even difficult, spirit now came together. Having repudiated the present policy, he would teach people to want another. And it was as a teacher, not a politician, that he made his mark. His committee hearings, his lectures, his statements to the press all had this one purpose. Though the White House closed its doors to him, and his enemies sought to ruin him back home, Fulbright persisted. In his mannerly way he repeatedly called the administration to account. He was not scared by its threats nor deterred by its refusal to testify before him. The anti-war Senators took an awful beating, for whatever reasons. Morse and Gruening were turned out of office in 1968. Robert Kennedy was murdered. Eugene McCarthy later gave up his seat. Edward Kennedy was disgraced. But Fulbright held his place and kept the pressure on.

Still, the war ground ahead. The lies about it mounted. Bernard Fall pointed out once more in 1966 how ridiculous the official U.S. figures were. As of January 1, 1965, there were supposed to be 103,000 Viet Cong in South Vietnam; 40,000 more supposedly infiltrated during the year. The VC suffered an estimated 79,000 casualties. Thus, as of January 1, 1966, VC strength ought to have been 64,000. In fact, the government announced, the VC actually numbered 237,000. How had it gotten the additional 173,000 men? By terrorizing them into enlisting. If so, this was a mighty achievement, since each original VC had to continuously terrorize more than two and a half armed conscripts. But anyone who believed that would believe anything, and did.

Such nonsense as this produced a good deal of black humor at home. Buchwald feared that a bridge gap might develop in the North, for the U.S. had bombed so many it was running out of targets. He was reassured by an Under Secretary of Defense who told him that when things got tight the U.S. parachuted more bridges in to keep its bombers busy. Propaganda was another grave problem. Americans could hardly call the enemy "yellow bellies" as in the last war, since its allies were of like complexion. The press hardly ever got to photograph enemy atrocities, whereas the South Vietnamese made theirs distressingly available. And Ho Chi Minh did not resemble a blood-crazed dictator but rather a "starving Santa Claus."

Then there was the fact that complaints about the war, while a sacred American right, encouraged the VC and prolonged the fighting. This put the responsibility for ending the war on the President's critics. Buchwald pointed this out to his friend Polanski. If only Polanski would shut up, Hanoi would negotiate. " 'But I don't like the way the war is going,' he protested. 'No one likes the way the war is going, Polanski, but the more you say you don't like the way the war is going the worse the war gets. At least that's what President Johnson says.' 'But if I don't say I don't like the way the war is going, how will President Johnson know I don't like it?' 'President Johnson knows already that you don't like the way the war is going.' 'Who told him?' 'Probably the FBI. But the important thing is he doesn't care if he knows it. What worries him is that Ho Chi Minh knows it.' 'How could Ho Chi Minh know it?' Polanski wanted to know. 'Because President Johnson keeps talking about U.S. critics helping Ho Chi Minh all the time.' "

Less good-natured was Barbara Garson's satire *MacBird*. Its hero had murdered his predecessor Ken-O-Dunc to gain the throne and launch the Smooth Society. The surviving Ken-O-Dunc brothers mean to destroy him. Other characters include the Earl of Warren, the Wayne of Morse, and the Egg of Head (Adlai Stevenson, of course). The following passage indicates how Miss Garson established MacBird's character.

MESSENGER: "Beatniks burning draft cards."
MACBIRD: "Jail 'em."
MESSENGER: "Negroes starting sit-ins."
MACBIRD: "Gas 'em."
MESSENGER: "Asian peasants arming."
MACBIRD: "Bomb 'em."
MESSENGER: "Congressmen complaining."
MACBIRD: "Fuck 'em. Flush out this filthy scum; destroy dissent. It's treason to defy your President. (His followers start to move doubtfully) You heard me! Go on, get your ass in gear. Get rid of all this protest stuff, y'hear."

This, as Dwight Macdonald pointed out, would have been inexcusable except that was how President Johnson actually spoke. "In sum, *MacBird* is a tasteless, crude, wholly destructive satire which roughs up everybody and everything from Shakespeare to Vietnam . . . and which is extremely funny, especially at its most tasteless, crude, and destructive moments." Oddly enough, President Johnson came through, even in this vicious caricature, as an imposing figure. For all his faults, perhaps because of them, Johnson was larger than life, a kind of Texas de Gaulle. He tended to think of himself as more Lincolnesque than Gaullist, though. Before resuming the air war against North Vietnam he called in a band of congressional leaders and read to them of Lincoln's ordeal from Bruce Catton's *Never Call Retreat*. Other times he thought himself to be Woodrow Wilson, or even Churchill. Yet this was a harmless conceit by comparison with his role as Sheriff Johnson, the lawman of Southeast Asia. Secretary McNamara had put in his hand the greatest military instrument ever made. He was using it to flog the very earth in Vietnam. In 1954 the French had less than 350 aircraft in Indochina. The U.S. now had nearly ten times that number, all vastly superior to what the French used. Bernard Fall, though he wished the communists defeated, was beginning to doubt that South Vietnam would survive its deliverance. American planes defoliated jungle and rice paddy alike. The bombers tore up square miles at a time. Helicopter gunships shot everything that moved in enormous Free Fire Zones.

What of Saigon itself? In thirty months the government had changed hands ten times. In 1966 it was run by Premier Nguyen Cao Ky who had held office since the previous June. Before that he was chief of the air force. Marshal Ky at the age of thirty-four looked like a juvenile delinquent and acted like the fighter pilot he was. He wore flashy black uniforms and jumpsuits, as sometimes did his beautiful young wife, a former airline hostess. Their dress was an early example of what would become known as unisex. Like most Saigon oligarchs Ky was from the North originally. Like most Northerners he was contemptuous of Southerners whom he saw as soft, lazy, quarrelsome, and characterless. For him the country's heart was in the North. Hence he wished always to invade it. He didn't much care for Americans either, though dependent on them. He sometimes hinted that American imperialism was an ever-present danger. Marshal Ky was also remarkably loose-tongued, the male equivalent of Madame Nhu. And he was not an absolute ruler, being only first among his equals in the ruling junta. While not an especially admirable figure, he did have one significant talent: the ability to hold power, a rare one in South Vietnam at that time. He proved it again in 1966.

The Buddhists had never stopped causing trouble since Diem's fall. On March 10 Marshal Ky gave them a new grievance by dismissing General Nguyen Chanh Thi, who commanded the northernmost corps area. He was a particularly loathsome individual who boasted of once killing eight VC prisoners to make the ninth talk. But he went easy on the Buddhists so they liked him. Demonstrations followed his removal, many directed against American power. When riots broke out the next month in Da Nang, where the U.S. had a great air base, Marshal Ky put them down. He did so again in May. Further rioting in Hue, the ancient capital and seat of Buddhist power, erupted in June. Marshal Ky once more suppressed it. When disorder threatened Saigon he used troops again. On June 21 they broke into the Buddhist Institute, silencing that stronghold of anti-governmental agitation. Marshal Ky was too shrewd to think guns solved every problem, and cleverly played off Buddhist factions against one another. He also promised "free" elections later in the year. The U.S., it seemed, had finally found a winner. The countryside was still being pulverized. Of 8,500 strategic hamlets (New Life hamlets, they were now called) only 1,500 were really secure. The VC controlled vast areas by night that the government laid claim to in the day. But Saigon was in good hands, and that seemed enough.

1966 ended with 375,000 American troops in Vietnam, compared with 181,000 at its start. President Johnson said just before Christmas that while "long and difficult days" were ahead, he thought the tide of battle had turned. Secretary McNamara, for whom hope still sprang eternal, announced that progress had "exceeded our expectations" and that draft calls might be halved in 1967. The tonnage of bombs dropped on Vietnam was already equal to the whole amount expended on the Pacific Theater in World War II. Despite this, the U.S. thought that the enemy had added 100,000 men to his effective strength. Where there had been only 11,000 DRVN regulars in South Vietnam the year before, now there were 50,000. VC strength was up from 230,000 to 287,000. All that escalation had done was increase casualties on both sides, while everything else remained the same. Reporters who asked why, in light of this, deescalation or negotiation was not attempted were answered, off the record, as follows. The U.S. could not agree to mutual withdrawal of American and North Vietnamese forces because the VC, though outnumbered, would then easily overrun the feeble ARVN. The U.S. could not accept a settlement that left the National Liberation Front intact because it was the only viable political force in the country. Given a free election it would either win outright or secure a dominating position. American spokesmen phrased it differently, of course. They talked of keeping the NLF from winning by political subversion what it could not gain on the battlefield. But whatever language was used, what it meant was that only U.S. intervention kept the South Vietnamese communists from seizing what was rightfully theirs. This did not leave much room for negotiations with Hanoi.

The DRVN continued to accept peace feelers anyhow, though it expected little from them. Hanoi always understood the American situation better than Washington cared to admit. It appreciated that so long as the U.S. thought it could win the war, serious talks were impossible. But nothing was lost by cooperating with hopeful peace seekers (a point Washington was slow to take), and something might one day be gained from them. One of the most striking examples of how this worked was the "Marigold" initiative of 1966. Marigold sprang, as peace bids always did in those days, from outsiders. One was Giovanni D'Orlandi, a career diplomat who was the Italian ambassador to Saigon and dean of the South Vietnamese diplomatic community. He made a habit of giving asylum to the victims of government *coups*. In consequence, he had one of the few unbugged private residences of note in Saigon. No security officer cared to offend the man on whom his own life might someday depend. The other moving force was Janusz Lewandowski, chief of the Polish mission to the International Control Commission in Vietnam. With the approval of their governments the two men began working on a plan to bring the U.S. and the DRVN together for discussions. In July Ambassador Lodge started meeting them.

Delicate feelers were extended through the summer and early fall. In November roving Ambassador Averell Harriman became interested and the code name Marigold was assigned these conversations. On November 14, though the principals could not know this, President Johnson authorized the first bombing attacks on Hanoi. Bad weather delayed them for several more weeks. On the same day Lodge described the U.S. aims in Vietnam to D'Orlandi and Lewandowski. The latter immediately went to Hanoi and spoke to Premier Pham Van Dong, who agreed to talks with the U.S. if they were kept secret. Lewandowski returned to Saigon and on December 1 presented Lodge with the ten points which he thought summed up the American position. "It will never win the Metternich Award for distinguished diplomatic prose," one American said of the paper (which, given State's customary infelicity, was a damning remark indeed). But it did accurately express Washington's views. The next day Lodge told D'Orlandi and Lewandowski that the ten points could serve as a basis for discussion. Lewandowski suggested that the U.S. have representatives in Warsaw prepared to speak with DRVN envoys by December 6. That very day the heavy U.S. raids, authorized by President Johnson several weeks before but delayed by the weather, took place. Lodge explained that it was impossible to cancel the raids for fear of breaching Marigold's security, a point on which Hanoi had been adamant.

The problem here was that only one man in the State Department knew about both Marigold and the plan to bomb around Hanoi (the Deputy Assistant Secretary of State for East Asian and Pacific Affairs), and he had no authority over the war's conduct. This, in turn, was because President Johnson wanted to run the war himself. All command decisions had to be made on such a high level that it was hard to get any response to events. The main policy body was the Tuesday luncheon group of Secretaries Rusk and McNamara, the President, his press secretary George Christian, Walt Whitman Rostow, and sometimes the Joint Chiefs and the CIA director. A provision existed for diplomatic reviews to coordinate bombing raids with peace feelers, but it had fallen into disuse. The only man in government permanently concerned with such overtures was Ambassador Harriman. He had a tiny staff and no clear mandate. Thus the government's mode of operation nearly precluded negotiations, even if it wanted them. When reporters asked later how it was possible for Hanoi to be bombed on the very day talks were agreed on, they were told by a presidential associate that they would never get the inside story "because it makes our government look so bad."

What made it look even worse were the raids of December 4. Those in the State Department who knew of Marigold and feared the effects of the first raids near Hanoi did not try to stop the next attacks either. They thought it was too late to work up the chain of command. They feared compromising Marigold's security. Rostow, and others near the President, had no interest in the talks anyhow. They believed Ho Chi Minh would talk when he was ready, bombings or no. The official position was that Marigold had little chance to succeed, and if it did the bombings would not matter. The raids continued until on December 13 and 14 Hanoi proper was bombed. Harrison Salisbury of the *New York Times* was there to report the attacks. Among other targets, the Polish Friendship School and the Polish, Rumanian, and Chinese embassies were hit. The Canadian mission to the International Control Commission was damaged slightly.

Salisbury wondered why the U.S. went to such trouble for the sake of a few truck-repair installations with a handful of aging vehicles in them. But the raids were puzzling only if one attached a military significance to them. Once it was realized they had none, everything was perfectly clear. The function of the air war was to coerce Hanoi into accepting American peace terms. That being so, it hardly mattered what was hit once the few obvious military targets were destroyed. Except for the port of Haiphong (full of Russian and other neutral shipping) and the Red River irrigation system (the destruction of which would have killed millions by flood and famine), everything became fair game. Homes, churches, schools, and hospitals, as Salisbury and other witnesses reported, crumbled before the onslaught, not because American pilots sought them out but simply because they were there.

The Hanoi raids killed Marigold. Afterward, Americans offered curious explanations for its failure. Some blamed it on the Poles, others on Harrison Salisbury for describing how civilians had been bombed, though in fact the Polish Foreign Minister had told U.S. Ambassador Gronouski that talks were off ten days before Salisbury's first story appeared in the *Times*. (The administration's outrage at Salisbury's accurate reporting led I. F. Stone to call it "Harrison Salisbury's Dastardly War Crime.") Worst of all, nothing was learned from Marigold. On April 19, 1967, the U.S. proposed that both sides pull back ten miles from the Demilitarized Zone so that it could be truly neutralized. That very evening the power plants in Haiphong were bombed. And so it went. After Marigold, Hanoi insisted for the first time on a complete bombing halt as a precondition for talks.

Much later, reviewing these sordid events, the *Times* (of London) *Literary Supplement* drew the moral "that bad mechanics can destroy good intentions, and perhaps also that a master who does not know his own mind can be frustrated by a servant who does." This was a charitable view indeed. After all, the main problem was not poor organization, sabotage by the hawks, or anything so mechanical. It was simply that the U.S. could achieve its object in Vietnam only by crushing the enemy. The purpose of negotiations, in the American mind, was to hasten that day. Since neither the NLF nor the DRVN was on the verge of surrender, there was nothing to talk about. Washington could hardly say this aloud, hence the endless propaganda about liberty, self-determination, and aggression from the North. Sometimes the administration could not even admit this to itself, which led to more confusion among friends than enemies. So the year ended, like the one before, in a cloud of lies and rumors.

Even after the failure of Marigold all hope was not lost. On January 3, 1967, Premier Pham Van Dong of North Vietnam told Harrison Salisbury that only the bombing of his country prevented negotiations from beginning. U Thant agreed. On February 2 President Johnson said that he was still waiting for a sign from Hanoi. The DRVN Foreign Minister then indicated through the communist journalist Wilfred Burchett that talks would begin when the bombing ended. He referred specifically to Johnson's remarks and said, "Well, he's had the sign." Unfortunately, that was not the sign Johnson wanted. Others kept the heat on him nonetheless. Pope Paul again called for peace in Vietnam. On February 8 Premier Kosygin endorsed the DRVN proposal to begin talks in exchange for a bombing halt. By then President Johnson had sent off a letter to Ho Chi Minh explaining what he meant by a sign. To begin with, the U.S. could not stop bombing the North because the DRVN would use the lull to resupply their troops in the South. If, however, the DRVN first stopped infiltrating men and supplies into the South, the U.S. would "reciprocate" by halting the bombing.

While this letter was in transit the annual Tet truce occurred out of respect for the lunar new year. From February 8 to 11 the U.S. halted its bombings and, apparently, the DRVN ceased infiltrating the South. All the same, on February 13 President Johnson announced that the DRVN had violated the truce by resupplying its troops, and resumed the bombing on an even greater scale. Of course the U.S. had also used the truce to resupply its troops, and had put another seventeen thousand men into the field. Only Washington understood why it was proper for the U.S. to resupply during truces and wrong for the DRVN. To no one's surprise, President Ho rejected Johnson's letter. The real problem, as Theodore

Draper pointed out, was not so much the crude blackmail practiced by Washington as the definition of reciprocity underlying it. The only way North Vietnam could have reciprocated for the bombing raids against it was by bombing the U.S. or at least South Vietnam. Being unable to do this, it had done the next best thing by sending troops south. But the U.S. then demanded that these troops, which Secretary McNamara now admitted had not been there when the raids began, be abandoned by the DRVN, after which the bombing would stop. North Vietnam was not to supply its Southern troops, but the U.S. would continue supplying its own forces while the war in the South continued. One did not have to be a fanatic communist to appreciate the one-sidedness of this proposal. The DRVN was to make all the concessions and abandon its troops. The U.S. would then generously stop its aggression against the North. Hanoi's refusal of these terms was then used to justify further attacks on the North's "infrastructure."

On February 21, just after this latest diplomatic fiasco, Bernard Fall stepped on a land mine in South Vietnam. Of all the brave people killed there he was among the best. Fall was French by birth. During the German occupation he had fought in the underground and then with the Free French. After the war he came to America as a student. His doctoral dissertation was on the first war in Indochina. His feelings about the endless struggle there were complex. As an anti-communist and a French veteran he naturally identified with the French Union forces, whose gallantry he celebrated in a moving book on the battle of Dien Bien Phu. But he also loved the Vietnamese, sympathized with them in their long agony, and yearned to see them have a government worthy of them. Few Westerners understood the complexities of Vietnam better than he. No one living in America (he taught at Howard University) and writing for Americans was better at explaining Vietnamese conditions to them. When the U.S. first entered the war he hoped it would win. But as the awful procession of events developed he despaired of Saigon's ability to form a popular government. And he was increasingly horrified as the immense American military machine ground back and forth across South Vietnam, leveling the towns and jungles with ruthless impartiality. On one of his many visits there Fall contracted a possibly fatal disease. All the same, he went back again in 1967 to write yet another of the great books that are his monument. He was only forty when he died. Among the hundreds of thousands who perished in that inferno, the loss of a single life might seem unimportant. But Fall was truly an indispensable man. No one in America had his depth of knowledge on Vietnam, nor combined the reporter's eye and the scholar's mind as he did. He was desperately missed by everyone who cared about the ravaged land he died in.

In 1967 American casualties reached the 100,000 mark. No one knew how many hundreds of thousands of Vietnamese had been slain. The country was bombed more heavily than either Germany or Japan had been in World War II. Ground operations were equally destructive. That year Jonathan Schell returned to Vietnam. He had previously written a *New Yorker* article (later published as *The Village of Ben Suc*), describing the elimination of a single community. Now he examined the same process on a vaster scale to show "that we are destroying, seemingly by inadvertence, the very country we are supposedly protecting." He concentrated on two mountainous northern provinces, especially the province of Quang Ngai. It had been controlled by the National Liberation Front for years. Saigon had attempted to secure it, first with the Strategic Hamlet program and then with New Life hamlets. In most cases, once the old villages were destroyed and the peasants relocated, the NLF re-established control. In 1967 the Americans sent in Task Force Oregon to break the VC once and for all. As of August 1967 there were 138,000 Vietnamese in the province's refugee camps. Since 1965, when the Marines began operating there, about 40 per cent of Quang Ngai's total population of 650,000 had passed through them. About 70 per cent of the province's villages had been destroyed, mostly by American forces. In the sectors assigned to the ARVN, comparatively few villages were abolished. In U.S.-controlled areas 90 per cent of them were destroyed. As in most parts of South Vietnam, the destruction was indiscriminate.

There was a certain Alice in Wonderland character to the American effort. When a village was destroyed for harboring communists it was said to be the peasants' own fault. Yet villagers rarely had much choice in the matter. The U.S. could not guarantee them security against VC reprisals, so their lives were at hazard either way. No matter, they were still to blame if the Army had to kill them. Schell was struck especially by the American tendency to identify villagers in terms of what was done to them. If a village was evacuated its inhabitants were called VC supporters. When sent to a camp they became refugees. The dead were always confirmed Viet Cong. There was a label for every occasion, but the event came first and the rationale afterward. Stranger still, the people in refugee camps got higher relief payments if they had been injured by the VC than if Allied actions were responsible—that is, when they were paid at all. Much resettlement was really just a matter of redefinition. Refugees would be put in camps, the camps would then be declared hamlets and the refugees denied a resettlement housing allowance on the grounds that they were already resettled. The whole process of de-populating the countryside was called "urbanization."

The air war in South Vietnam was equally seamy. Large areas had restrictions laid on them, which the pilots habitually evaded. Generally they shot up what they pleased, though for some reason they continued to think themselves unreasonably inhibited by higher authority. Given a free hand they would soon put an end to Charlie, as the VC was called. Yet Schell didn't see what more they could do than was already being done, even if their nominal restrictions were lifted. The pilots used their power in different ways. A certain FAC (forward air controller, a pilot in a light aircraft who called in the fighter-bombers) detected the VC by means of intuition, in which he had great confidence. One FAC pilot would call strikes at the sight of an unarmed man, another might not unless actually fired on. Schell flew on one mission where the FAC had two churches destroyed, explaining that the Godless VC were wont to fire from them. Then, perhaps thinking this not quite justification enough, he pointed out that the VC destroyed churches too. "They don't care at all about blowing up a church and killing innocent civilians." Another moral quirk that the pilots had in common with domestic hawks was their feeling that it was ethically better to kill civilians by accident than to assassinate officials. At home, as in Vietnam, people who criticized random butchery by aircraft were always met with the rejoinder that the VC murdered village chiefs. There was something peculiarly American about this. Why was it worse to deliberately kill government agents (guilty men by NLF standards) than to bomb the innocent? Though slain without malice they were dead all the same, and in far greater numbers than the VC was even capable of.

Nor did the American people have to take Schell's word alone. CBC, the Canadian government's broadcasting network, did a documentary on the war called "The Mills of the Gods" which sustained the air war's critics. No American network had the courage to make such a film. It was shown in the U.S. mainly on educational TV, but millions were able to see for themselves how air strikes were handled. A CBC reporter asked one helicopter pilot why he had shot up a particular structure. He said that he saw footprints leading into it that showed the person had been running. Since only a VC would run from a gunship, the building was obviously an enemy structure. What the pilot failed to say was that Vietnamese who did not run were often shot too. Even more illuminating was an actual strike filmed by the CBC team from an accompanying jet. The pilot viewed the operation as a sporting event, whooping and cheering when an especially nice hit was made. He said that he often wished he could walk through a village afterward to see the damage firsthand.

Americans, Schell noted, were especially struck by the peasants' ingratitude. Americans viewed the tremendous destruction as preliminary to the great, democratic reconstruction to come. The peasants' indifference to this prospect was baffling. So was their dumb acceptance of the limited aid available in the refugee camps. Americans invariably pointed out that military operations were only half the story in Vietnam, but it was the only half that most peasants ever saw. Little wonder that they lacked the broad vision U.S. forces thought appropriate. Still, most Americans grimly refused to take the point. Indeed, Schell found the level of self-delusion to be staggeringly high. Perhaps the best instance was his interview with the U.S. senior adviser for Quang Ngai province after its devastation. He explained what a triumph the pacification effort had been. That very night the VC overran Quang Ngai City, freeing twelve hundred prisoners from the provincial jail. Later he heard an important American official in Saigon say that Quang Ngai was going to be one of the big success stories of 1967.

That was how it went throughout the American defense establishment. Ambassador Lodge began the year by saying, "I expect . . . the war to achieve very sensational results in 1967." General Westmoreland, sunny as ever, announced in July that "we have succeeded in obtaining our objectives." In November he declared that "the enemy's hopes are bankrupt." Still, more of everything seemed always to be needed. In August, though 480,000 American servicemen were already in Vietnam, the President proposed to send 50,000 more. Congress was asked for more money—$4.5 billion in March, and then another $12 billion. Most congressional doves voted for these appropriations. They feared being accused of "letting the boys down." It was hard to see why. If Congress withheld funds and the President continued to send men into combat, who would be to blame? Surely not the Congress. Such a thing was inconceivable anyway. No President would for long pursue a war without congressional support. By refusing to vote their consciences these dissident legislators made things much easier for the President. Even so, sixteen Senate doves, including Robert Kennedy and J. William Fulbright, went out of their way to further placate the hawks. On May 17 they addressed a statement to Hanoi proclaiming their own opposition to "any unilateral withdrawal of American troops" and calling on the DRVN to negotiate.

The hawks were not appeased. Congressional fire-eaters wanted a vastly expanded war effort. Strategists like Bernard Brodie were calling for greater coercion of Hanoi, including, perhaps, the use of tactical nuclear weapons in Vietnam. Though the President was in fact observing their strictures on "graduated escalation," and a record 4,668 missions were flown against North Vietnam in August, the escalation still seemed too gradual to them, mainly, of course, because it wasn't working. The Joint Chiefs wanted to bomb yet more heavily. Admiral Sharp hoped to shut down the port of Haiphong, however many Russians and other neutrals were killed in the process. Only Secretary McNamara among the top leaders was losing faith. Everyone else thought a few more turns of the screw would do it. But McNamara told a Senate subcommittee in August that "nothing in the past reaction of North Vietnamese leaders [provides] any confidence that they can be bombed to the negotiating table." Three months later he was no longer Secretary of Defense.

McNamara was the first leading administration official to defect on account of the war, although he helped President Johnson make it seem like an ordinary resignation. Certainly his job was a killing one. He had held it for seven years, longer than any other Defense Secretary. But even then it was clear that Vietnam was responsible for his departure. He had once supported it so vigorously that it was called "McNamara's War." But McNamara finally realized that the more the DRVN was bombed, the more the NLF was helped. He made no secret of this when briefing Congressmen. McNamara now believed that the war had to be won on the ground in South Vietnam, and that bombing the North was "counterproductive." So he had to go, for the President was not about to shift gears. In a final display of loyalty McNamara went along with the fiction that his resignation was merely routine, thus robbing it of considerable impact.

Loyalty was not least among the virtues that made him indispensable to two Presidents. He was brilliant, incredibly hard-working even by Johnsonian standards, and a masterful administrator. But his fidelity was especially prized. When he took office in 1961 he discovered that Eisenhower had been right to say there was no missile gap. Yet when his statement to that effect was reversed by President Kennedy, McNamara dutifully revived the missile gap to justify the huge increase of ICBM's that followed. Later he admitted that in consequence Russia had followed suit, narrowing the U.S. lead in strategic missiles. Again, in 1967 when the military asked for a big anti-missile defense system, McNamara's first response was to oppose it. He pointed out that had President Eisenhower not vetoed the Nike-Zeus system in 1959 the U.S. would have spent $13 or $14 billion for a defense system that would have been obsolete even before completion. The proposed Sentinel ABM offered the same prospect. It would cost $5 billion to begin with and probably wouldn't work. But when President Johnson insisted, McNamara worked up a flimsy excuse for this latest military pork barrel. Though it would not do much good against a Russian salvo, he now argued, China might be deterred by it. Even Senator Russell thought this a fragile argument. The Chinese were hardly so stupid as to send their handful of missiles against a country that could utterly destroy them in return. McNamara ate his earlier criticism all the same.

Replacing McNamara was a difficult business. Logically, his able assistant Paul Nitze, the Deputy Secretary of Defense, ought to have succeeded him. But Nitze was disqualified for having been right too often about Vietnam. In 1961 he had been against Rostow's plan to send American troops in limited numbers to stiffen the ARVN. Nitze described "Walt's Plan Six" as like being a little bit pregnant. To protect the small early drafts, more troops would be needed. America would end up with a major investment in the land war. Then again, in 1965, when President Johnson decided to escalate, Nitze objected. The new commitment was likely to be open-ended. And he knew, from his experience in World War II with the strategic bombing surveys, that limited bombing actually increased morale and production. Nothing short of wholesale destruction of the cities was likely to work. Since he turned out to be right both times he was naturally much resented. Nor did being right qualify him for a job that chiefly demanded the perpetuation of past failures. Having gotten rid of one doubting Thomas, Johnson was not disposed to admit another to his war cabinet. So Clark Clifford, a Washington lawyer and presidential adviser who was considered hawkish, replaced McNamara. That was another of the President's mistaken judgments, though no one suspected it then.

The anti-war movement did not let the administration's strategems go unnoticed. A symbol of what President Johnson had accomplished came in January 1967 when Dwight Macdonald changed the name of his column in *Esquire* magazine from "Films" to "Politics." An old radical, once a Trotskyite and then an anarchist, he had given up on politics when events destroyed the basis of his left-wing anti-communism. He had been attacking Stalinism since the 1930's, but when doing so became the property of rightists and fanatic Cold Warriors, he dropped out. Macdonald remained, as Norman Mailer would say later, America's oldest living anti-Stalinist. Yet he could not fight that battle with a good heart in the company of such as Joe McCarthy, John Foster Dulles, and Hubert Humphrey. So he turned to cultural criticism. The war in Vietnam brought him back to politics, as it did so many others. Nonpolitical people were being radicalized by the war, and ex-radicals repoliticized. Macdonald's return was especially fitting. He had been one of a handful during World War II who thought it wrong to burn Germans in the name of anti-fascism. Burning Vietnamese in the name of anti-communism seemed to him no better. But history had changed him too. He recalled that in his youth he had sneered at those who sought "the lesser evil" in complex political situations. Now he searched earnestly for it, along with millions of others whom Lyndon Johnson brought together.

On April 15, 1967, police estimated that 125,000 people demonstrated for peace in New York City, and another 30,000 in San Francisco. The big politicians were still lying low, but Martin Luther King, more influential than any officeholder, threw his weight against the war. On April 4 he demanded a unilateral cease-fire and described the U.S. as "the greatest purveyor of violence in the world today." Most orthodox civil rights leaders were not ready to go so far, nor did they wish to compromise their movement by linking it with peace. But all around the country individuals were taking action in their own way. Most were still little known, except for Cassius Clay, heavyweight boxing champion of the world. Clay had been converted by the Black Muslims who gave him the name Muhammad Ali and made him a minister. Ali claimed to be exempt from the draft both as a minister of religion and as a conscientious objector. When the government took him anyway, he refused induction and was subsequently convicted and sentenced to five years in jail and a $10,000 fine. He appealed, and years later was still free on bond. This ended his fighting career (temporarily, as it turned out). The World Boxing Association declared his title vacant, so did most state boxing associations. Thus did professional boxing, the most corrupt of all major sports, establish its patriotism. No one had known until then that there were political requirements for athletes. The legal justification for taking away Muhammad Ali's livelihood remained unclear. He was KO'd all the same.

Because his reasons for refusing induction were so peculiar, being based on Muslim doctrines, Ali's gesture did not have the moral resonance it might otherwise have had. More notable in this sense was the refusal of Captain Howard Levy to train Special Forces medical corpsmen in the treatment of skin diseases. Levy headed the dermatology clinic at Fort Jackson, South Carolina. He based his refusal on the grounds that the Green Berets were "murderers and liars and thieves," and that their corpsmen were really combatants in violation of professional ethics and the Geneva Convention. At his court-martial the so-called Nuremburg doctrine, which held that soldiers had a duty not to commit war crimes, was raised. Levy believed that the Green Berets were "killers of women and children," and felt obligated under international law not to help them. The presiding officer challenged Levy's defense lawyer, Charles Morgan, Jr., a Southern liberal and staff member of the American Civil Liberties Union, to produce evidence that atrocities were committed in Vietnam as a matter of general policy. This was impossible.

The worst thing in Vietnam was the air war, and that was not considered criminal. The Green Berets did commit murder, but Morgan couldn't prove it (nor could General Abrams, who succeeded Westmoreland in Vietnam, though he tried to later). Soldiers did butcher civilians, as the My Lai massacre of 1968 showed, but it hadn't happened yet, and even if it had no one could prove that atrocities were a matter of deliberate policy. Unlike the Nazis, American soldiers did not record their criminal acts, even when proud of them. Levy was duly court-martialed and spent several years in jail. Dissension kept rising in the services nonetheless. Punishing GI's opposed to the war made them more cautious, but not less numerous or determined.

Growing numbers of young men refused induction and went to Canada or to jail. Thousands more organized to stop the war. Their biggest single enterprise that year was called the Vietnam Summer. It was modeled on the Freedom Summer of 1964. Though it had failed, the Freedom Summer was a legend among radical youths, and they remembered it when organizing anti-war projects in 1967. Some twenty thousand young people participated in the Vietnam Summer. Its national headquarters had two hundred workers who spent perhaps a half-million dollars. Nominally the effort was directed by a steering committee of adult pacifists, liberals, and academic radicals. But increasingly real authority flowed from the young, activist cadre in the national office. Kenneth Keniston made a study of them, so we know far more about the psychodynamics of the national office than is usually the case with such movements. Keniston was more interested in sociology than politics. He saw his subjects mainly as representatives of the budding youth culture. Still, his book *Young Radicals* manages some political comment despite itself.

It makes clear that the summer of 1967 was a crucial turning point for the New Left. Some young radicals already disdained this sort of promotional activity. They were in the Vietnam Summer because they wanted to prove it wouldn't work. Not that they meant to sabotage the program. But they were convinced that after a fair trial it would collapse, thus radicalizing the participants. Others hoped it would be effective. Yet they were prepared to concede in advance that it might fail and force them leftward. The project did fail and the young radicals did become more extravagant. The March on the Pentagon in October showed that. But ultra-radicalism was more than just a calculated response to the worsening situation. Keniston pointed out that "the issue of violence is to this generation what the issue of sex was to the Victorian world." While sexually freer than previous generations, they were more obsessed by violence. The great massacres of World War II haunted them; the prospect of nuclear war had shadowed their entire lives.

Accordingly, resisting violence had become central to their way of life. They had prized the nonviolent ethic of Martin Luther King so long as it seemed effective. They made great efforts "to overcome in themselves any vestige of sadism, cruelty, domination, or power-seeking in human relationships." But their tactics aroused violence in others which increased their own rage and hostility. And when the slaughter grew in Vietnam they began to think of American violence as so potent that only counterviolence would end it. Already they were citing the Jewish example in World War II. If the Jews had fought back at the start, Nazism might have been contained, they thought. Thus "for all his efforts to control violence, cataclysm, and sadism, the young radical continually runs the danger of identifying himself with what he seeks to control, and through a militant struggle against violence, creating more violence than he overcomes." In this one sentence Keniston anticipated the end of the New Left.

The fall showed more clearly what was ahead. In Oakland, California, throngs of demonstrators besieged an induction center for five days, stopping buses and fighting with the police. On many campuses recruiters for the military, the CIA, and Dow Chemical were harassed. Some schools were forced to cancel interviews. In December four hundred people were arrested across the country during four days of anti-draft demonstrations and sorties. But the most dramatic event of 1967 was the great March on the Pentagon on October 21. Anywhere from thirty to 75,000 demonstrators crossed the Arlington Memorial Bridge, some to picket and demonstrate against the Pentagon, others to storm it. The demonstrators got a bad press for the most part. But radical anti-militarists were heartened by the show of spirit. It further widened the gap between hawks and doves, and it inspired one of the great books of the sixties, Norman Mailer's *Armies of the Night*.

To understand this remarkable document one has to know something of Mailer's earlier life and work. As he was the most confessional writer in American history, the facts are easily come by. What they mean is something else again. In the 1950's Mailer was generally thought to be wasting himself. The critics didn't like the novels that followed his *The Naked and the Dead*. His radicalism, though bizarre and personal, was considered passé. America had moved beyond ideology, but Mailer had not. He insisted on finding truth through better orgasms. He drank too much, experimented with drugs, and was frequently divorced—all signs of impending ruin. And he insisted on making a fool of himself in public. Clearly, he was not a person to take seriously, though he might once have been, it was agreed. In retrospect these objections, while true, seem irrelevant. In the fifties Mailer was simply out of phase with the times. An age of orthodoxy, sobriety, and self-restraint does not admire excess, even in geniuses. For another, Mailer was a long time in the making. At the end of the sixties he was still unfinished and unpredictable. No two of his novels are alike. This was much resented, though critics ought to have been glad of the extra employment. But like most people critics want to have everything neatly sorted. Mailer was always having to be relabeled, which was bothersome. Many would have liked to write him off as some kind of freak. Yet his power was such that few did, to their secret relief probably when the sixties came. For in this decade Mailer flowered more brilliantly than before.

One novel, *The American Dream*, was a thriller about an intellectual who murders his wife (Mailer had stabbed one of his) and experiences unusual sex and violence. It was published chapter by chapter in *Esquire* magazine as Mailer wrote it, a piece of bravado which irritated critics no end. Mailer compared himself to Dickens, who did the same thing. People thought it unbearably vain of him to take such chances in public anyway. His next fictional work, *Why Are We in Vietnam?*, was not about Vietnam but concerned some Texans hunting big game in Alaska. The book featured the most elaborate and inventively obscene language ever used in an American novel. And because it dealt with violence it really was about Vietnam after all.

But whatever posterity might think, the books that counted most in these years were not his novels. Beginning with *Advertisements for Myself* in 1959, Mailer had been developing a literary genre peculiar to himself. It included essays, doggerel verse, fictional experiments, and much self-exposure. Woven through it were his views on current problems and ultimate questions. He was his own most exhaustive critic, sometimes finding faults, sometimes greatness in works whose merits escaped most others. He dissected even his worst or most ridiculous acts for the light they shed on the human condition. As the books piled up (*Presidential Papers, Cannibals and Christians, Idols and Incense*) it got harder and harder to attribute all this to mere self-esteem. Autobiography is always written because the author thinks his life the stuff of truth or art. But few autobiographies are genuinely instructive or illuminating, often because the natural desire to make one's self look good subverts the larger design. Mailer's first virtue was that he did not fear to look bad.

He insulted Jacqueline Kennedy, feuded with other writers, tried to organize a championship boxing match, bit an actor on the ear, and made obscene speeches in public while drunk—the list of his follies seemed endless. These were often discreditable to the man (foolish, criminal, degrading, they were called), but they were all grist to the writer's mill. Afterward he took them up, examined them, drew out such morals from them that it was hard to tell where life ended and art began. In truth, they were all of a piece. The man was absurd, prone to danger, offensive, childishly violent, and exploitive of women; so was the writer. The end result, the books the life made, were increasingly rich, pregnant with strange insights and associations. Though Mailer often seemed bent on destroying himself, his writing gained in force. Critics thought this a paradox when they recognized it at all. But with *Armies of the Night* many grasped what a few knew already, that in a strange way his life fed his art, that what seemed weaknesses were somehow necessary to his genius.

What is in the book that made it penetrate the critical brain as his earlier works had not? It is written in the first person, beginning when Our Hero receives a call at home asking him to be in the March on the Pentagon. Should he take time from his labors as Greatest Living American Novelist and self-made film producer, he wonders? After weighing the rival claims of honor and ambition he decides to go. Book I, "History as a Novel: The Steps of the Pentagon," tells what befell him in consequence. Book II, "The Novel as History: The Battle of the Pentagon," tells what happened later. In his role as historian Mailer carefully presents the facts. The march was originally planned by a mobilization committee of adults, including the veteran pacifist David Dellinger. Things lagged at first, then Jerry Rubin was appointed project director. Rubin had been a leader of the Free Speech Movement at Berkeley and of the Vietnam Day there. He had status among the alienated young, so "to call on Rubin was in effect to call upon the most militant, unpredictable, creative—therefore dangerous—hippie-oriented leader available to the New Left." Prospects for the march improved; so did the risks. To mitigate these the mobilization worked out ground rules for the police that Mailer summed up as follows: "We, the government, wage the war in Vietnam for our security, but will permit your protest provided it is only a little disorderly. The demonstrators: we still consider the war outrageous and will therefore break the law, but not by very much." Accordingly, speeches were made, fifty thousand people marched on the Pentagon, a few attacked it and were arrested or beaten or both. Mailer got himself jailed. That night a small band stayed on and were worked over by some of the 1,500 police, 2,500 National Guardsmen, 200 U.S. marshals, and assorted military personnel gathered for the occasion.

Put so baldly, *Armies of the Night* doesn't sound like much. But Mailer developed this thin scenario into an elaborate, complex screenplay. The meeting of protesters takes on a mythic quality at his hands. The great dissenters were out in force—Dr. Spock, Dagmar Wilson of Women's Strike for Peace, Paul Goodman, and many more. Mailer meets Chaplain Coffin of Yale, "one full example of the masculine principle at work in the cloth," for the first time. In jail he finds himself with Noam Chomsky, a brilliant linguist then rapidly become the anti-war movement's foremost intellectual. Dwight Macdonald was there, and so was Robert Lowell, a natural aristocrat and prince among men.* Mailer works his ambivalent relationship with these two for all it is worth, especially his complex feelings toward Lowell. Lowell seems always to be one-upping him in a mild, distinguished way. Mailer doesn't know if he's being put down or put on. Or perhaps Lowell is only the innocent-wise child he appeared to be. In contrast, *For the Union Dead*, Lowell's mighty poem, is always in the back of Mailer's mind, though he never speaks of it directly. This most powerful encounter between poetic imagination and the nation's tragic past seems strangely fitted to the moment. So, beginning with Lowell's effect on his vain, competitive spirit, Mailer ends by subtly calling history to the side of art—and all in the guise of journalism.

To these mythic characterizations Mailer adds extraordinarily vivid descriptions of the Fugs entertaining the crowd, Ed Sanders announcing a grope for peace, and Abbie Hoffman, the future yippie leader, leading a mass attempt to levitate the Pentagon. Of that brilliantly attired band Mailer says, "The dress ball was going into battle."

Two passages in particular suggest the deepest level at which Mailer operated. On his release from jail he said this to the press: "Today is Sunday, and while I am not a Christian, I happen to be married to one. And there are times when I think the loveliest thing about my dear wife is her unspoken love for Jesus Christ. Some of us were at the Pentagon yesterday, and we were arrested in order to make our symbolic protest of the war in Vietnam, and most of us served these very short sentences, but they are a harbinger of what will come next, for if the war doesn't end next year, why then a few of us will probably have to take longer sentences. Because we must. You see, dear fellow Americans, it is Sunday, and we are burning the body and blood of Christ in Vietnam. Yes, we are burning him there, and as we do, we destroy the foundation of this republic, which is its love and trust in Christ."

Near the book's end Mailer speaks of a few Quakers who were arrested, refused to wear prison clothing, and were stripped and thrown in the Hole. Mailer asks if in their torment they prayed for the country, and the men it sent to Vietnam who knew not what they did. "The prayers are as Catholic as they are Quaker, and no one will know if they were ever made, for the men who might have made them were perhaps

---

* Macdonald returned the compliment in *Esquire*, where he reviewed the book and the events it celebrated. He notes that when Lowell told Mailer that he was the best journalist in America, Mailer was annoyed. "But what neither of them could have realized, since the present work hadn't been written, was that Mailer was about to carry journalism into literature in the way that Agee had done in *Let Us Now Praise Famous Men*: by planting himself squarely in the foreground and relating the whole composition to his own sensibility."

too far out on fever and shivering and thirst to recollect, and there are places no history can reach. But if the end of the March took place in the isolation in which these last pacifists suffered naked in freezing cells and gave up prayers for penance, then who was to say they were not saints? And who to say that the sins of America were not by their witness a tithe remitted?"

Both these quotations are authentic Mailer, but the first seems self-mocking. Few reporters could have thought that Mailer really believed the Republic to be based on the love of God. Yet, as the second quotation shows, he did. The last page in *Armies of the Night* is a prayer (called "The Metaphor Delivered") for the country's future.

Mailer was many things—clown, poet, brawler, genius perhaps—but mystic does not ordinarily appear on the list. Still, he was that too, though rarely seen as such. The one thread that seemed to bind his scattered acts together was the search for that truth he sometimes gave the name of God. That was both what redeemed and informed his apparent madness. Mailer veered crazily through life under full canvas, ballasted by his great talent, sights set on a polestar that only he could see. If a fool, he was a holy fool. Even his enemies, and they were legion, sensed the power in him. If given a choice, he was not the prophet Americans would have asked for in those years. But he was what they got, and they were lucky to have him—though rarely grateful.

Posterity will doubtless think the March on the Pentagon remarkable mainly for the book it inspired. Impressive as the numbers involved were, neither this nor any subsequent demonstration seemed to have had any effect on policy-makers, which was why the extreme left turned to violence and terror soon afterward. The administration continued to insist that all was well. Maxwell D. Taylor, who had done so much to make the war, published an article in the *New York Times Magazine* called "The Cause in Vietnam Is Being Won" that appeared simultaneously with the march. It included this astonishing statement: "Probably the most serious liability which we must offset is the *illusion* [my italics] that the United States is deeply divided over Vietnam and, in the long run, will abandon its present policy." The customary round of assurances followed this march. The summer before, Dean Rusk had made clear that he had learned nothing from the war. He said that no aggressor should think that the absence of a "defense treaty, Congressional declaration, or a United States military presence grants immunity to aggression." Of course, few countries failed to enjoy one or another of these blessings. The U.S. had since World War II made security agreements with forty-two countries in NATO, SEATO, and the like. Bilateral agreements had been signed with others. Thirty-eight nations benefited from U.S. military advisory teams, and there were major American bases in twenty of them. But the U.S. saw its role in grander terms than even these figures suggested. That same summer President Johnson told White House visitors that America had "a whole world to guard."

Congress was increasingly reluctant to concede this. If it would do nothing about the current war, it hoped at least to avoid future ones. In April the Senate refused to give President Johnson what it regarded as a Latin American Gulf of Tonkin resolution for a meeting of hemispheric chiefs of state at Punta del Este. In May Congress rejected a new weapons system for the first time in a decade. It involved a $1 billion appropriation for "fast deployment logistic ships" designed to give emergency support to American troops anywhere in the world. The Senate Armed Services Committee pointedly remarked that by making U.S. intervention easier, the system would also make it more likely. In June Congressmen met with administration officials to discourage American intervention in the Middle East crisis. On July 20, 1967, many Senators, hawks and doves alike, criticized the administration for sending three U.S. transport planes and 150 men to the Congo. In August the Senate Foreign Relations Committee, with conservative support, began hearings on the general subject of American commitments abroad.

The anti-interventionist sentiment in Congress made itself felt particularly on foreign aid. Foreign aid had been losing favor for years, though the U.S. still provided some assistance to seventy-six countries. But the percentage of national wealth spent on aid was small and getting smaller. Japan spent a larger proportion of its national income on foreign aid, and so did other countries. Nor was American aid so selfless a program as Congress liked to pretend. Aid was usually restricted to purchases in the U.S., so the goods and services went overseas while the dollars stayed at home. As American products were often more expensive, recipient countries got proportionately less for the money than if they had been able to buy freely in the world market. Sometimes aid benefited American business more directly. India had insisted on distributing fertilizer produced there by American companies, and also on setting the prices for it. In 1966 Standard Oil of Indiana refused to accept such restrictions any more. To back Standard, the U.S. Agency for International Development put food shipments to India on a month-to-month basis. India with its starving millions was in no position to play politics with food, though America was. Accordingly, it gave way. In 1967 AID requested $50 million for India to buy American fertilizer at American prices.

Except for military aid, most support to underdeveloped countries was in the form of loans. The poorer third-world countries were already paying more to the World Bank in principal and interest on past loans than they were receiving from it in new loans. In 1965 Latin American debt payments equaled the total of public development loans and grants received that year. Between 1955 and 1964 the amount of export earnings that went to maintain national debts there rose from 6 to 15 per cent. At the same time that payments on past loans ate up present ones, Latin America was suffering a net loss in skilled personnel. In the decade before 1964, 13,800 Argentinian engineers migrated to the U.S. 90 per cent of all Asian students in America did not return home. The U.S. and other developed nations raised tariff walls against finished goods from third-world states, while international prices for many of their raw exports declined. In 1965 the UN's Food and Agricultural Organization pointed out that malnourishment in the underdeveloped countries was greater than before World War II. In 1966 the UN's World Economic Survey revealed that third-world purchasing power had declined. The net outflow of interest and profit from them to the rich nations was increasing.

In attacking foreign aid for its entangling possibilities, then, Congress chose the poorest reason for condemning it. The aid programs were bad because they were too few and too self-serving. Aid benefited the American economy more than the recipients. Often it didn't work at all. Where it did work its tendency was to reinforce local oligarchies. When the Alliance for Progress was begun much brave rhetoric was uttered about the "peaceful social revolution" it would inaugurate. But while the Alianza was supposed to generate social reform, in practice it became a way of bailing out distressed ruling elites. This further offended anti-American students, intellectuals, and left-wing politicians. Surprisingly, in some countries even the military, traditionally pro-American and richly rewarded for being so, grew restive. In Peru and Bolivia they would soon take power, not to crush the left or restore order but apparently to implement that very social revolution which the Alianza had failed to inspire. As foreign aid was so ineffective, even retrogressive for the most part, its continuing decline in the later sixties was no great loss to the world. Still, it might have been better to reform the aid programs than undermine them. But as so much else was being sacrificed to the gods of war, aid could hardly be exempted.

On January 31, 1968, on the second day of Tet, the lunar new year, the Viet Cong struck at thirty-six (of forty-four) provincial capitals, sixty-four district towns, countless villages, and a dozen American bases. Perhaps 60,000 men were involved in these assaults. Before Saigon was quiet 150,000 more refugees had been created and Cholon, the Chinese quarter, mostly leveled. It took six hours to secure the American embassy alone. Elsewhere the fighting was equally savage. Ben Tre, a town of 35,000, was occupied by an estimated three battalions of Viet Cong. They were driven out after artillery and air attacks that demolished at least half the town's structures. "It became necessary to destroy the town to save it," explained an American officer afterward. Hue, the ancient capital of Annam, was not secured until February 25. By then 70 per cent of its homes lay in ruins. The American military announced that a famous victory had been won. The invaders had lost 33,000 men. (Going by rule of thumb, three wounded to every enemy killed, this meant that the 60,000 attackers had suffered over 120,000 casualties, a discrepancy left unexplained by the military.) In April General Westmoreland announced that "we have never been in a better relative position."

The Tet offensive demonstrated anew the poverty of official thought on Vietnam. The VC were supposed to be too weak to mount a major attack. When they did strike and were beaten off the military announced once more that they were now definitely finished. But it was clear that the NLF had never expected to seize control of the country. Only 4,500 VC attacked Saigon. About 6,000 enemy troops occupied Hue. What the Tet offensive showed was that the VC was still a power, would remain so for years to come, and that the people of South Vietnam were not loyal to their government. The VC had infiltrated combat units into Saigon and elsewhere, and laid plans that hundreds of thousands, perhaps millions, of people had to know about. Yet the regime only learned of the offensive when it began. The major cities were quickly regained, but the pacification program in the countryside was profoundly disrupted. A year later many areas secured by the VC during Tet were still in enemy hands. In their narrow way the military, seeing the cities safe again, proclaimed victory. What they could not understand was that the U.S. had suffered a great political defeat. For years the administration, while paying lip service to the political question in Vietnam, had relied entirely on armed force to answer it. The folly of that course was now apparent to nearly all reasonable men, in office and out.

Coming as they did on the heels of Tet, Johnson's narrow victory in New Hampshire and the prospects of certain defeat in Wisconsin convinced him not to run for re-election, and to call a partial bombing halt. As always with so complex a man, the reasons for his decision were hard to determine. It was clear that he would lose other primaries, if not to Eugene McCarthy certainly to Robert Kennedy. This would not keep him from being renominated as he would still control the convention, nor would it prevent his re-election. He said later he was sure he could win again, and given Richard Nixon's tiny margin of victory that was probably true. But it was also clear to him that he could not expect to govern successfully since his own party would be torn apart by then. It was to Johnson's credit that he did not want the presidency for its own sake, but for what he could do with it. The ashes of victory were hardly more to his taste than the ashes of defeat.

His decision to de-escalate was more complex. Like everyone else, President Johnson had been astonished by the Tet offensive. He was even more disconcerted when General Westmoreland asked for another 206,000 troops to make the inevitable victory more certain. Always before when the military asked for more they got it. This time a funny thing happened. On March 18 a blue-ribbon panel convened to discuss the prospect. It included Dean Acheson, Douglas Dillon, McGeorge Bundy, George Ball, Arthur Dean, and others. They got the usual optimistic briefing by Dean Rusk and other high administration hawks. But they also heard from lower-ranking officials in the State Department, the CIA, and the Pentagon, without their superiors being present. For the first time, in many instances, the panel members got an unvarnished analysis of the dismal post-Tet condition of South Vietnam. The result was that the panel, all of whom had previously been hawks, recommended that the U.S. abandon its hopes of a military victory, de-escalate the war, and try seriously for a negotiated settlement.

Johnson was understandably surprised at this. And even more so when he heard from the junior officials. For the first time he learned what people close to the action really thought. Secretary of Defense Clifford improved the shining hour by asking the President for three things: not to send more troops, to Vietnamize the war as much as possible, and to call a limited bombing halt. Clifford's recent tour of Asia had persuaded him that the military's World War II tactics were not working in Vietnam, and that other Asian states had little stomach for the war. He also saw that the whole middle level of the war-making bureaucracy was rotten with doubt. As Townsend Hoopes, Under Secretary of the Air Force, pointed out later, many second-echelon figures were thinking of resigning, perhaps in a block, if changes were not made. The war had already driven some from the government; it was only a matter of time before resignations were made specifically to protest the war.

The Pentagon's request for more troops was decisive in several respects. It forced a review of the entire war, the first ever to be done open-mindedly. It implied that the generals did not really think Tet such a splendid victory after all, thus discrediting them. Most of all, it forced the President to see that the war could not be won at a reasonable cost. To put several hundred thousand more men in the field meant drafting

200,000 troops and calling up 250,000 additional reservists to support them. This would cost billions and lose more votes. Worse still, experience showed that to neutralize 200,000 American soldiers the North Vietnamese needed only to send 50,000 troops south. In addition to its large standing army the DRVN could draw on a pool of 200,000 young men who reached military age every year. For all practical purposes North Vietnam had an inexhaustible supply of military manpower with which to counter American troop increases. The alternative, bombing enemy supply lines, was already a proven failure. This too was a matter of simple arithmetic. The DRVN imported about eight thousand tons of supplies a day. Intensive bombing might reduce this by half, or even by three-quarters, but the DRVN's forces in South Vietnam needed only one hundred tons of supplies a day. This was so little that no amount of bombing could prevent its getting through, by foot if need be. In effect then, North Vietnam was impervious to anything less than genocide— which was out of the question, even, perhaps, for Walt Rostow.

Thanks to Secretary Clifford, President Johnson finally accepted, if halfheartedly, the logic of these figures. They were real, unlike the phony numbers ground out by the military—the body counts, the estimated casualties, the hamlets pacified, the square miles liberated—that had fooled McNamara for so long, though based on little more than the military's need to impress him. No one had expected Clifford to turn the tide. On the contrary, he had been chosen to replace McNamara, it was thought, because he was a hawk and wouldn't go over to the nervous nellies as McNamara seemed on the verge of doing. Clifford was alleged to be a legal wheeler-dealer and Washington influence peddler. Such men do not get ahead by offending Presidents. But while he may still have been a hawk when sworn in, Clifford did not remain one for long. He had no responsibility for past errors and so no need to defend them. Once he grasped the facts he worked patiently and skillfully, using all those conciliatory skills that made him a successful lawyer, to get the administration to face them. President Johnson's startling announcement on March 31, 1968, that he would not run for re-election and was ordering a partial bombing halt in North Vietnam was Clifford's work more than any other man's.

Although Johnson appeared sincere about leaving the presidency, his enthusiasm for a negotiated settlement was less clear. The partial bombing turned out to be very partial indeed, as it excluded an area extending two hundred miles above the Demilitarized Zone separating North and South Vietnam. Senator Fulbright and others, pointing out that Hanoi had always insisted on a complete bombing halt before opening negotiations, feared this was only another Johnsonian trick, a way of seeming to want peace without actually having to try for it. To their surprise, and maybe the President's, North Vietnam responded favorably. After much backing and filling on both sides, it was agreed on May 3 that talks would begin in Paris. This was the first real break in the long, dismal chain of events since the war was enlarged in 1965. Yet it did not signify any reduction in combat levels. The bombing went on as intensively as before, and was perhaps even more effective for being concentrated in a narrower area. American propaganda remained as belligerent and obtuse as ever.

The only additional sign of American sincerity was the appointment of Averell Harriman to head its delegation to Paris. Harriman was by this time the most experienced negotiator in American history. John F. Kennedy had noted years before that under three Presidents Harriman had held as many important jobs as any American diplomat except John Quincy Adams. During President Johnson's administration he moved into a class by himself. The remarkable thing was that though he had served four Presidents, Harriman started from scratch with each of them. He was useful to Presidents because he had a talent for knowing the right people and studying the right subjects. He started out in domestic affairs with Franklin Roosevelt during the New Deal, then switched to foreign affairs as war impended. By 1943 he had shifted from dealing with the British to negotiating with the Russians. He was one of the first important Americans to favor a tough line with Stalin.

When President Kennedy took office Harriman told a friend that he had started as a private with both Presidents Roosevelt and Truman, and ended up on top. He expected to do the same with Kennedy. Sure enough, though he seemed to have been appointed as roving ambassador mostly out of charity after Nelson Rockefeller ended his political career, Harriman came back. In short order he received several promotions, negotiated the test-ban treaty and the cease-fire in Laos, became an expert on Southeast Asian affairs, and was a close adviser to President Kennedy. President Johnson demoted him to roving ambassador again. But he too soon learned that Harriman was indispensable. In debate Harriman was ferocious. His friends called him "the old crocodile," but many who were bitten by him came to admire Harriman all the same. One political associate said of him, "The only insincere thing Averell ever did in his life was shake the hand of a voter." In diplomacy he was not so constrained. He once replied to a Congressman's question with the remark, "I'm glad you're not Secretary of State." Though tough and outspoken, Harriman was an insider's insider. If he opposed a policy he did all he could to change it. But when he could not he accepted the inevitable, kept his own counsel, and lived to fight another day.

When President Johnson sent him to Paris in 1968 he was nearly eighty years old, somewhat deaf, but as formidable as ever otherwise. In an essay on him some years before, Joseph Kraft said Harriman had "looks, health, an exciting job, and eighty million dollars. He can afford to thumb his nose at anybody." That was still true. But Harriman did not thumb his nose at the North Vietnamese. Close acquaintance with the Saigon regime had made him despise it—a view he hardly troubled to conceal. From a technical standpoint he was the best man Johnson could have appointed, if not the most faithful to his chief's errors. Harriman did not make clear how much he disagreed with the official line until the administration was out of power, but it seems likely that he was privately informing the President early on of the need to make real concessions if the negotiations were to succeed. He was tired of the war too. Without liking the North Vietnamese he respected them, and thought their case a reasonably good one. Given a free hand he might well have worked out a settlement and made a graceful American withdrawal from Vietnam possible. Even so, he moved things to the point where on November 1 President Johnson finally had to end the air war against North Vietnam entirely. So after a long and probably unnecessary delay, serious negotiations began. At that point something like half a million tons of bombs had been dropped on the DRVN. At least nine hundred U.S. planes were lost over it. The chief result was that infiltration from the North increased, by the administration's own figures, from 12,000 men in 1964 to more than 200,000 in 1968. Rarely had so much slaughter and destruction produced so few visible results.

Nothing came of the Paris talks, apparently because the administration still denied reality. The first condition for peace in Vietnam was to accept that the long American effort to reverse the tide of events there had failed. The NLF continued to be the only political organization with a popular following. The Saigon regime still depended entirely on the U.S., despite the vast quantities of blood and treasure spent to make it viable. It followed that to have peace South Vietnam must have a government acceptable to the NLF, not necessarily dominated by it, but one to which it was a party. The Saigon regime refused to entertain even the prospect of such a coalition, as it had to. Even though it had rigged the previous election by excluding most neutral and leftist candidates, it had still not managed to win a popular majority. Afterward the opposition leader was imprisoned. Free elections would end the generals' reign, so would a coalition government. Perpetual war was their only means of staying in power. So long as the U.S. supported them the fighting would go on. The administration could not win in Vietnam because it was politically impossible to send the million or more troops victory required. And it could not withdraw as that would mean confessing errors that had cost hundreds of thousands of lives. For the U.S., as for Saigon, the only remaining alternative was eternal combat, but at a more bearable (for Americans) level of intensity. That seems to be what Johnson had in mind, and why there was so little progress in Paris despite Harriman's desire to start things moving. It was the policy that Nixon inherited from President Johnson, and which he improved upon, as we shall see later.

So the Johnson administration ended with the ashes of defeat strewn all around. Defeat in Vietnam (for when a small power fights a great power to a draw, that is the equivalent of victory for it), defeat in the war on poverty, and defeat at the polls. The last was probably the least serious. Though Hubert Humphrey was Johnson's man, in a way, the President had consistently damaged his campaign. He seemed to find the prospect of Nixon's replacing him far from repugnant. Nixon would continue his foreign policies. His domestic programs were hopelessly wrecked anyhow. And he may have suspected that the contrast between his administration and Nixon's would make him look better in history's eyes than if he were succeeded by Humphrey. In the event, when it came time to relinquish his power he did so with more grace than any President in modern times under similar circumstances. Many stories came out of Washington in the twilight of the Johnson presidency on the philosophical manner in which he accepted retirement. He admitted few mistakes. The party's division was all the Kennedys' fault, not his own—or even McCarthy's. History would absolve him because of "what I did for the Negro and seeing it through in Vietnam for all of Asia." Walt Whitman Rostow, whom many thought his most sinister adviser, was equally complacent. When asked later by the *New York Times* if any mistakes had been made, he could hardly think of one.

Dean Rusk was equally stubborn, "a captive of the past, doggedly misapplying its lessons," as the *New Republic* observed. Even out of office he kept on attacking his critics as isolationists who threatened the marvelous world order constructed by America after World War II. He and Rostow were virtually the only key Johnson men loyal to their errors, and the only ones to suffer for them. Most ex-officials got good jobs outside the government when the Republicans came in. Rusk was unemployed for a time. Then he was hired, after much opposition (arising, of all things, from his alleged liberalism), to teach law at the University of Georgia. Rostow was rejected by his old school, MIT, and ended up helping Johnson edit his papers at the University of Texas. There was much hand-wringing at these reprisals, yet though exiled to the provinces both men got handsome salaries. For war criminals (which was how they were regarded by many) this was decent treatment indeed. The only real injustice was that their partners in crime got off scot free. But perhaps even these mild penalties did some good. The trouble with warfare is that generally those responsible never have to pay. The innocent die but the guilty are only turned out of office, if that. It would not be a bad thing to have the risks divided a bit more equitably.

It is still too early to sum up the Johnson presidency. As David Wise observed in a shrewd essay on him, there are two extreme views maintained by serious people about Johnson. "To his admirers, Johnson is a complex, misunderstood, and noble figure who bound up the wounds of the nation after the tragedy at Dallas by sheer force of will, pushed more needed social legislation through Congress than any of his 34 predecessors, who saved freedom in Southeast Asia and then made the supreme sacrifice of his own political career in a bold move to win the peace.

"To others he is a character out of a Greek Western. At first, he is the man in the big ranch house, elected by the largest popular majority in history, rich, powerful and seemingly invincible. Then, felled by hubris, a victim of his own tragic flaws, impaled by war, he rides off forever into Credibility Gap, his name to bleach in the desert with the bones of the Great Society beneath the merciless glare of history."

Most liberals were willing to admit that he was magnificent after Dallas, during the 1964 election, and in the Great Society's glory days. Relatively few accepted his view of what was at stake in Vietnam. Even some who did thought the price too high. Most disagreement concerns the reasons for his fall. Eric Goldman, a professional historian who saw the President close up, blamed it on character defects. In his view President Johnson was forever barred from greatness by his provincial origins and domineering temperament. This is, curiously enough, a point that Johnson himself partially agreed with. He often remarked that, having been raised outside the liberal establishment, he could never be President of all the people as he wanted to. This seems unduly fatalistic. Johnson had many well-advertised weaknesses, but he was a man of many strengths as well. What did him in was not so much vanity, Texas homeliness, or bad diction, but several great errors—escalating in Vietnam, taking too long to see it wouldn't pay, refusing to conciliate the liberal opposition in his own party, and so on. These are mistakes of a sort that greater men than President Johnson have made before. It is conceivable that President Kennedy, who was advised by the same people who urged Johnson into the war, would have acted much as he did. And the most serious of these mistakes was a result not of any defect unique to the President, but of the whole approach to foreign affairs that dominated public men after World War II. Believing that there was a Cold War which the U.S. must win, fearing Munichs, seeing dominoes in every threatened backwater, the Establishment supported escalation in 1965. When it failed, Johnson was left to take the blame. Most advisers washed their hands free of blood, but there was no way the President could. Those many hundreds of thousands gone because of him—how could he say it was all in vain and still sleep at night? This is not to excuse the President. Men are responsible for what they do. Lyndon Johnson sought the power of life and death, and when it was his he used it brutally. But he only did what most of his highly placed critics would have done had they the means. The tragic flaw was not in the President but in the structure of national decision-making. It would remain when he was gone. That was the chief lesson Eugene McCarthy meant to teach the country. His counsel was rejected because otherwise the American people would have to admit their responsibility for what had become of them. How much easier to blame it all on President Johnson's character! What better way of insuring that all the bloody history recounted here would be for nothing!

PROFILE:
Organized Medicine

THE FIRST GENERAL session of the American Medical Association in 1969 began as usual with a Marine band rendering the national anthem. Then a group of dissenting physicians seized the podium. One of them, Dr. Richard Kunnes, declared that AMA really stood for the American Murder Association. "You're the criminals who rather than developing a preventive health program have prevented health programs. You're the criminals, who through your monopolistic, exclusionary, and racist practices, have created a vast shortage of health manpower, resulting in a needless death of countless millions." Demonstrators marched down the aisles chanting "Hip, Hip, Hippocrates . . . Up with the service, down with fees." They made their points in other ways too. Some picketed with signs reading "Caution, the AMA may be hazardous to your health." One burned his AMA card.

Afterward, business continued, but not quite as usual. James H. Cavanaugh, the administration's Deputy Assistant Secretary for health and scientific affairs, gave the assembled doctors notice. President Nixon, to whose lips the dread words "socialized medicine" had once come so easily, was "appalled" by the national health crisis. On taking office he had found it worse than he thought. "Revolutionary changes" were needed. Every cherished belief must be called into question.

355

There was a special irony about Cavanaugh's remarks, for he was addressing the AMA only because it had defeated the nomination of HEW Secretary Finch's first choice for his position. The AMA had thought Dr. John H. Knowles of Massachusetts General Hospital too radical, and their lobby, as powerful as any in Washington, had blocked his appointment. Now they found that change was not to be escaped so easily. It was not just that some young doctors had been radicalized. Medical care had grown so scarce and expensive as to alarm the silent majority too. When it was only the poor who suffered, physicians were free to do as they pleased. But the outrage of Middle America, though slow to gather, was a fearsome thing. Not even the mighty AMA could withstand it entirely.

The crisis was easy to measure. The U.S. once had had the fourth lowest infant mortality rate in the world. Now it lagged behind fourteen other nations. (It was seventeenth in life expectancy for men over sixty-seven years of age.) There were so few physicians being trained that America imported seven thousand a year from other countries, mostly poor ones, and even they were not enough. At the same time health costs soared. Between 1957 and 1967 they went up three times as fast as the general price level. In 1967 alone hospital prices increased by 20 per cent. In Baltimore there were only one hundred general practitioners to care for 550,000 slum dwellers, and all but ten of them were over sixty years of age. There was a shortage of nurses too. In New York City 75 per cent of the positions for registered nurses were unfilled. On weekends most of the nursing was done by untrained nurse's aides, with an annual turnover rate of close to 100 per cent.

This did not happen by accident. The AMA and its satellites liked things that way. The AMA had once been a progressive agency. In 1917 it supported a compulsory national health insurance system. But in later years it became largely concerned with protecting the physician's income. The medical profession operated like a classic monopoly, restricting output so as to raise prices. Medical schools turned down most applicants, thus maintaining a high physician-to-patient ratio. (In 1968 the University of Chicago Medical School accepted 75 of 2,400 applicants.) Licensing procedures were designed to restrict competition further. Two-thirds of all the health occupations required licenses, which the health guilds alone controlled. Where a guild did not set its own standards it was because of domination by a higher one. Thus dentists controlled the licensing of dental hygienists, registered nurses of licensed practical nurses. Each guild tended to exploit the one below it. Physicians got fees while nurses earned salaries. The lower the occupation, the greater the inequity. Self-employed physicians earned $35,000 a year on the average while unskilled hospital attendants made as little as $40 a week.

Licensing was crucial because it was the means by which people were kept from moving up. It concentrated on formal training and ignored experience. A practical nurse could not become a registered nurse without taking a full course in nursing school. A registered nurse could not become a physician without going all the way through medical school. As there was no allowance made for experience, and no financial assistance, few ever made the jump from a lower guild to a higher. Worse still, like other exploited groups, the various guilds tended to identify with their oppressors. Nurses rarely formed unions or went on strike. Instead their professional association tried to lengthen the formal training period so as to restrict output in the manner of physicians.

Medical reformers had plenty of good ideas for solving these problems. One was to abolish diplomas and make performance on standard qualifying exams the only criterion for licensing. Given the AMA's political power this was not likely to happen. Other reforms were more practical. It might be possible to have previous experience count toward admission to a higher guild. New paramedical specialities might be developed to do the routine work now performed by nurses and physicians. This seemed especially feasible as it would enable doctors to treat more patients and hence earn more money. Some such payoff was probably essential to any reform the AMA could be made to accept. The AMA itself flirted with the notion of giving nurses more responsibility and allowing them to receive fees. This would raise the income of nurses and attract more recruits to the profession. It was doubtless utopian to imagine that more laymen would be put on hospital and licensing boards to give the public interest a voice. It might, however, be possible to expand the group practice and prepaid medical-care programs already in being. Both lowered the unit cost of medical care and encouraged preventive medicine, the most neglected aspect of health service. As the decade ended, little had been done to reform the health industry. It was clear that far more pressure would have to be generated, and the AMA's fear of income declines assuaged, before important changes could be made.

The other half of the medical crisis was the insurance question. Medical reforms might end the manpower shortage, but almost certainly costs would keep rising. Indeed, raising the pay of low-income health workers would probably raise medical costs even more. Yet health insurance was already moving beyond the reach of some Middle Americans—another reason for their anxiety. In 1969 Blue Cross tried to raise its rates 50 per cent in New York. Its rates went up 25 per cent in Connecticut, 44 per cent in New Jersey, and 33 per cent in Rhode Island, among other places. Given the rise in medical, especially hospital, costs, it was inevitable that Blue Cross would have to charge more. It was by far the most important form of hospitalization insurance available. 68 million people were directly insured by it, and another eighteen million through a supplement to Medicare. Nearly half of all Blue Cross operations involved federal programs of some kind.

Blue Cross was, of course, a nonprofit agency. But while it didn't pay dividends to stockholders, there was no incentive on the part of its operators to reduce costs. Since it paid only in-patient benefits, physicians had people hospitalized who could have been treated as out-patients if their insurance permitted. This increased hospital costs. So did the failure to cover preventive medicine. Blue Cross was controlled by physicians and hospital administrators, so it did not make accounting difficulties for them. When prices for hospital services went up, Blue Cross sought ways to reduce its own rather than the hospitals' costs. Its local affiliates tried increasingly in the 1960's to get away from the old "community rating" system by which local rates were set on the entire community's use of hospital services. What the affiliates wanted was "experience rating" in which low-risk health groups (the young, the rich) would get lower rates and high-risk groups (the aged, the poor) would get higher rates. This would eliminate the social aspect of Blue Cross and make it a strictly payment-for-service operation like commercial insurance.

Skyrocketing health insurance costs led President Nixon to appoint an investigating committee soon after taking office. At the same time Congressmen and private citizens organized campaigns for national health programs on a scale not seen since the 1940's, and under more favorable circumstances. What would come from this would most likely be some kind of federal support for health insurance, though not a compulsory national system as laymen hoped. Federal support would involve federal auditing procedures, and probably the setting of fiscal performance standards which would force many administrative changes. What hospital administrators wanted to do was go on as before, but with government footing the extra bills. Their chances of getting this were good. For one thing, the head of Nixon's investigating committee was none other than the president of the Blue Cross Association. For another, the central principle of American reforms, especially medical reforms, is the payoff principle. Just as Medicare was made acceptable to physicians by making it profitable for them, national health insurance would probably be arranged so as to maximize hospital income. Even so, it would probably be worth having. And once installed it might improve the chances of getting more economical hospital practices and socially desirable changes like preventive medicine and out-patient care. Some day American health services might be as good as England's. But here, as in so many other areas, things would surely get worse before they got better.

11 1968: THE HARD YEAR

THOUGH HARDLY anyone guessed it in January, 1968 was to be Eugene McCarthy's year. While practically the whole Establishment tried to keep him from dominating it, he did so anyway. Afterward he would call it "the hard year."* That year of disaster was indeed hard for most Americans, but especially for Senator McCarthy who ran such a race and bore such burdens as no man in recent memory had. He made it look easy, and, wanting no sympathy, got none. Yet from the first he was subject to strains that few politicians, hardened as they were to the high-risk game, could long have endured.

It began the previous November when he proposed to campaign against President Johnson in selected primaries. Those who did not sneer, laughed. Everyone knew you couldn't deny renomination to an incumbent President. The last time it had been seriously attempted was in 1912 when Theodore Roosevelt nearly wrecked the GOP. And TR had been an immensely popular man. Who was Gene McCarthy to dare what greater men (Robert Kennedy, for example) feared to try? He was witty, a good speaker, and popular in his native Minnesota. But what were these small assets when set against the presidential power? As it turned out, quite a lot. McCarthy did not have a national constituency like Robert Kennedy, or even Hubert Humphrey. He was not influential in the Senate, being outside the club which ran it. In fact, he had probably enjoyed more weight earlier as a House member when he organized the liberal Democratic caucus that became known as McCar-

---
* That would have been the title of his book, had his publishers not perversely insisted on calling it *The Year of the People.*

thy's Marauders. But he alone of the major Democratic politicians who disliked the war believed that something could be done about it. So he had vision and, what was better, the nerve to act on it. When Allard K. Lowenstein approached him, McCarthy was ready for the call.

As much as any one man could be, Lowenstein was founder of the dump-Johnson movement. A slight, intense, bespectacled man in his thirties, he was already an experienced liberal. Though passionate, he did not entertain extreme political views. Lowenstein had specialized in youth work and hated the war especially for its effect on the young. He decided early that President Johnson had to go if the alienated young were to be saved from dropping out or sliding off into the lunatic fringe. He began traveling around the country to focus anti-war sentiment on political objects. Advertisements against the war by college editors, Peace Corps returnees, and others sprang up behind him. In the summer of 1967 he began urging Robert Kennedy to run for President. Senator Kennedy's own staff was for it, so was his wife Ethel. But the Camelotians advised him to wait until 1972. Only Arthur Schlesinger, Jr., and Richard Goodwin, both former special assistants to President Kennedy, of the old official family favored his candidacy, and for reasons that were more moral than practical. Sorensen, Salinger, *et al.*, who in the spirit of Camelot were more interested in seizing power than scoring moral points, were not impressed. They persuaded Robert Kennedy, who was, after all, a Camelotian himself. And he understood that Lowenstein, John Kenneth Galbraith, and the other dump-Johnson leaders hoped he would run for their own purposes, not his. They wanted him because he had the biggest personal following of any available politician. Many were outside the Kennedy connection and so not interested in restoring Camelot. In the Kennedy manner, Robert heeded the family loyalists and party professionals who told him to wait, though his instinct was to run. Lowenstein told him, "The people who think that the future and the honor of this country are at stake because of Vietnam don't give a shit what Mayor Daley and Governor Y and Chairman Z think. We're going to do it, and we're going to win, and it's a shame you're not with us because you could have been President."*

Lowenstein then began knocking on the doors of anti-war Senators. McCarthy was not his first choice, nor even his second. But McCarthy told Lowenstein that if no one else would go he would, because "there comes a time when an honorable man simply has to raise the flag." And that was the whole of his reasoning and strategy for the campaign. Many

---

* Robert Kennedy took his point later, and acknowledged it handsomely. He sent Lowenstein a note reading, "For Al, who knew the lesson of Emerson and taught it to the rest of us . . . 'that if a single man plant himself on his convictions and there abide, the huge world will come round to him.'"

pressures had been working on him—his daughter Mary, an eloquent and forceful college student, his own doubts, and an arrogant appearance before the Senate Foreign Relations Committee by Nicholas Katzenbach, the Under Secretary of State. But there were more reasons for staying out, not least of which was that he might look foolish. Still, honor could be satisfied in no other way, so he ran. As he indicated, however, he did not mean to run flat out in the Kennedy way. He would "raise the flag" and see what happened. If the anti-war sentiment was there waiting to be mobilized, as he suspected, he would not need to beat on every door in the country to rouse it. If it wasn't there, no amount of campaigning by him would create it. Then too, if things worked out the campaign would be a long one, and he didn't mean to burn himself out as Nixon had in 1960. In any case, whirlwind campaigns were not his style. As he puts it in his best-known poem, "Are You Running with *Me*, Jesus?", which begins with a short list of famous joggers including Senator Proxmire:

> I'm not matching my stride
> With Billy Graham's by the Clyde.
> I'm not going for distance
> With the Senator's persistence.
> I'm not trying to win a race
> Even at George Romney's pace.
>
> I'm an existential runner,
> Indifferent to space.
> I'm running here in place.

That was how the legendary New Hampshire campaign began. Senator McCarthy seemed merely to be strolling around the state, aided only by Robert Lowell and Paul Newman. Lowell, whose talents as a public speaker were considerably inferior to his poetic gifts, was there mainly to refresh the candidate. Newman, an articulate, politically knowledgeable man in addition to being one of the country's most popular male movie stars, was more formidable. Still, the professionals reasoned, one swan does not a summer make. Johnson men predicted that McCarthy would be lucky to get 5 per cent of the vote (a figure which they revised upward at regular intervals thereafter). Most agreed that McCarthy's vanity, and his old grudge against Johnson for keeping him on the vice-presidential string so long in 1964, had led him into folly. The general amusement was not shared by Senator Kennedy. At first McCarthy had hinted that his campaign was designed only to make Kennedy declare himself. It soon appeared Kennedy would not, and McCarthy started running in earnest. Kennedy naturally resented this. It was bad enough that he had suppressed his own desires and stayed out. But it was gall and wormwood to see McCarthy doing what he ought to have done. On the very day that Tet, the lunar new year festival, began in Vietnam, Kennedy told reporters at the National Press Club that McCarthy's campaign "so far has been very helpful to President Johnson." He knew better, though most people still did not. Allard K. Lowenstein had already committed the First People's Volunteer Brigade to battle. All over New England the students were rallying to McCarthy's standard. They poured into New Hampshire and by election day hardly a registered Democrat had escaped their attentions. Working with them were indigenous liberals who meant to displace the Johnson men who controlled the New Hampshire Democratic party. Richard Goodwin shared their spirit. When he joined McCarthy's staff he turned to another speechwriter and said, "With these two typewriters we're going to overthrow the government." Even before Tet the basic pattern was established. McCarthy made the soft sell while the students sold him harder. Insurgent liberal Democrats infiltrated the party structure. There were few precedents for this quiet revolution. Little wonder that the press, and hence the nation, was slow to grasp what was happening in New Hampshire.

Then came the Tet offensive. Tet had a mixed effect on the McCarthy campaign. On the one hand, it made his candidacy seem real for the first time (to realists), and the money started coming in. On the other, it convinced Robert Kennedy that he had to run. He was wobbling even before it. His instincts, his wife, his staff kept pressing him. Just before New Hampshire Jesse Unruh, Speaker of the California House and one of the few state legislators with a national reputation, asked him to run. This assured Kennedy of organization support in a key state. He was further upset when President Johnson blandly disregarded the Kerner report. Then too, it was obvious that the young, a vital part of his constituency, were being lost, perhaps for good, while he sat on the fence. Tet pushed him off it. It is still unclear why he waited until after New Hampshire to say so. Even just before it, there was a dim chance that the support coalescing around McCarthy might yet be diverted to him. But by declaring after the New Hampshire primary he seemed an opportunist who had let McCarthy take the risks so he could skim off the profit, or, in Murray Kempton's bitter analogy, like a scavenger come down from the hills after a battle to shoot the wounded. Worse still, he leaked his intentions early, before, as one McCarthy student said contemptuously, enough money had come in to pay their bills. Hence his announcement was both too late and too early. He compounded his error with a further dash of Camelot hokum. Though proven wrong, the Camelotians still influenced him and he let Theodore Sorensen write this phrase into his declaration of candidacy: "At stake is not simply the leadership of our party and even our country, it is our right to the moral leadership of this planet." To McCarthyists, and even to his own staff, this was just the sort of thinking that had gotten America into Vietnam to begin with.

But those, like Kennedy himself perhaps, who thought McCarthy would now give up his vain efforts and rally behind the only "serious" anti-administration candidate were quite wrong. McCarthy had done fabulously well in New Hampshire. He not only received 42.2 per cent of the Democratic votes, but 5,511 Republican ones as well. He got only 410 fewer votes than the President. The campaign, which had seemed so amateurish at the time, had been very cleverly handled. His low-key, issue-oriented approach was exactly right for New Hampshire. His students had also appealed to the most thoughtful voters. At the same time New Hampshire liberals were so well organized that while Johnson got more votes, McCarthy got most of the national convention delegates. And they took over the state party organization. The same things were happening in Wisconsin and elsewhere. His followers had worked out a successful strategy, and in doing so obliged McCarthy to go all the way. Almost no one defected to Kennedy, though he made great efforts to win back the students particularly. Later he ruefully observed that he had the B and B— students, while McCarthy had the A students. This was about right. The best students went to McCarthy and stayed with him. Those who followed Kennedy were as much fans as political activists.

Once Kennedy started bombing around the country the differences between the two men became more apparent. Kennedy descended on college campuses and their hot receptions turned him on. He was more volatile than John Kennedy had been, and audience feedback pushed him to the edge of demagoguery at times. He seemed to think President Johnson responsible for every national ill down to and including drug addiction. He said the administration was "calling upon the darker impulses of the American spirit." Reporters took him to task for this, and he was more careful later. But his whole strategy hinged on exploiting his magnetism and glamour, and made certain excesses inevitable. His aides organized vast crowds, whose excitement often threatened people's safety, children especially. He emerged from these ordeals with torn clothes and bleeding hands. After Martin Luther King's death and President Johnson's withdrawal, Kennedy calmed down a lot. But the frenzy was always there in the audience, as it had to be if he was to win.

McCarthy never changed. Tranquil to a fault, he just kept running there in place, though in the end he campaigned longer and harder than anyone else. Wisconsin was like New Hampshire, only more so, the campaign even more self-supporting. Some outside students came in, though they were not really needed. The state's own colleges, led by the great campus of the University of Wisconsin at Madison, were equal to the task. Wisconsin was heir to a tradition of progressive politics that found modern expression in the Democratic party. Both U.S. Senators from Wisconsin were liberal Democrats, and though Johnson men controlled the party apparatus, McCarthyists were infiltrating it. Nationally the President's popularity was at its lowest point since he assumed office. Only about 35 per cent of those polled supported his policies. Kennedy wasn't on the ticket in Wisconsin, so the anti-administration vote would not be split. Local polls showed that Johnson was going to be beaten badly.

Before that could happen the President spoke to the nation and, to general amazement, announced that he would not be a candidate for re-election. It was the most startling declaration of noncandidacy in American political history. Johnson didn't want his search for peace hampered by politics, he said. And he thought his renunciation would have a unifying effect. He also limited the air war against North Vietnam.

McCarthy won big in Wisconsin as expected, though perhaps not so big as he might have if Johnson had not withdrawn. Then he went on to Indiana and the first direct confrontation with Kennedy. It was not the ground either would have chosen if he could have helped it. The Klan had once run Indiana, and it was still chauvinistic and provincial. As a celebrity, Kennedy had the best chance there. The suburbs, where McCarthy was most popular, were not very important in Indiana, and so he had the worst prospects. Afterward he was to say, "They kept talking about the poet out there. I asked if they were talking about Shakespeare, or even my friend Robert Lowell. But it was James Whitcomb Riley. You could hardly expect to win under these conditions." The ground between them was occupied by Governor Branigin, the Democratic incumbent who originally ran as a stand-in for President Johnson. He had a well-disciplined but unenthusiastic party machine backing up a naturally hokey political style. They finished in just that order with Kennedy getting 43 per cent of the vote, Branigin 31, and McCarthy 27. The press corps following Kennedy wrote a good-natured parody about him called "The Ruthless Cannonball" that summed things up in one verse:

> He has the Poles in Gary
> The Blacks will fill his hall
> There are no ethnic problems on the Ruthless Cannonball.

Just to make certain, the Kennedys spent a great deal of money. And Robert took a somewhat lower road than before, citing his record as Attorney General to prove his soundness on the law-and-order question (a euphemism throughout the year for repressing blacks). As the black vote was solid for him already, he could afford to flirt with bigotry a little. On the other hand, while playing up to Hoosier chauvinism he also spoke plainly to hostile medical students of their profession's failings. And he gave the best impromptu speech of his life to a black audience in Indianapolis the night Martin Luther King was murdered. In a simple, moving way he tried both to comfort and advise them. He too had had a brother killed, by a white man, he reminded his stricken auditors. But great sorrow ought to promote rededication, not violence or racial hatred. And he ended by quoting from Aeschylus on tragedy's effects. No doubt few listeners knew who the Greek poet was, or grasped exactly the burden of Kennedy's remarks. But it was marvelously winning, nonetheless, especially for being so direct and unaffected. A part of it was shown on television, and one could see why good men loved him so.

The most important thing about the Indiana campaign was not its outcome but what it showed the national prospects to be. Kennedy was still locked into a black-ethnic–teenie-bopper pattern. They made him look good in certain primaries, but they were too few to win a national election with. A detailed Gallup poll released on April 28 was particularly revealing. Among voters under thirty, Kennedy was favored over Humphrey 41 per cent to 16 per cent. But McCarthy was not terribly far behind as 32 per cent of them liked him best. McCarthy was ahead among voters aged thirty to forty with 35 per cent favoring him, 27 per cent liking Kennedy, and 23 per cent supporting Humphrey. He also was favored by voters over fifty, getting 32 per cent of them to Humphrey's 29 per cent and Kennedy's 25 per cent. Kennedy was ahead among grade-school graduates. 36 per cent of them preferred Kennedy while 23 per cent liked McCarthy. But among college graduates the imbalance was much greater. They favored McCarthy over Kennedy by a margin of 26 per cent. Kennedy was ahead with Catholic voters—36 per cent to 29 per cent—but led only slightly among trade-union families, 31 per cent to 29 per cent (Humphrey had 27 per cent). Even more strikingly, Kennedy had made no inroads at all into the peace vote. People who supported the war would give McCarthy only 26 per cent of their votes, while among those opposed 41 per cent would go for him. Kennedy's support among both groups was exactly the same—28 per cent. Of the major Democratic candidates, McCarthy was clearly ahead in the country at large. College graduates and anti-war voters were the core of his strength, but McCarthy was also popular among older voters, not terribly behind Kennedy with the younger ones, and nearly even with him among trade-union families. He also appealed to Republicans and even, oddly enough, to followers of George Wallace who admired him for bucking the Establishment. Kennedy's problem was to create a popular base sufficiently broad to impress Democratic regulars. McCarthy's was to get beyond the Democratic primaries, where the black-ethnic axis hurt him, into the national arena where his strength lay. Both, of course, suffered from Humphrey's appeal to the party organization that would control the convention. In the spring that was a less pressing matter, though finally it would be crucial.

The next few primaries were indecisive. Kennedy won handily in Nebraska, partly because of dissatisfaction with the administration's farm policy. McCarthy's old ties with Hubert Humphrey, and especially Secretary of Agriculture Orville Freeman, hurt him. And while there weren't many blacks in Nebraska, neither were there many suburbs. Kennedy glamour had, in consequence, an especially clear field. Oregon was another story. Depressed Kennedy supporters condemned the state for being one vast suburb. What they meant was that Oregonians were mainly native-born whites in comfortable circumstances. They were independent. The anti-war spirit was especially strong among them. The state was tailor-made for McCarthy's low-key, sardonic approach. His nonpartisan status helped him too. While Kennedy was forced to challenge regular Democrats in 1968, Camelot had been based on them. This old association clung to Kennedy even while the regulars were going over to Humphrey in a body. In Oregon McCarthy had the better organization. Under these circumstances the effort to make Kennedy seem the country's only possible savior fell flat. "Bobby threatened to hold his breath unless the people of Oregon voted for him" was how McCarthy described it. Then too, McCarthy simply hit harder. He was especially pointed when asking if Kennedy, whose whole political career was based on the very men responsible for the Vietnam War, was exactly the right man to end it.

In consequence, Oregon was where the Kennedy family lost its first election. Losing a primary does not mean much as a rule. McCarthy had lost three already with few ill effects. But Kennedy was not an ordinary politician. Charisma was the largest part of his appeal, and as the English authors of *An American Melodrama*, the best account of the 1968 election, noted, charisma is peculiarly evanescent. It means more than just attractiveness or popularity. To have it is to be clothed with a special grace as hero, prophet, or savior. It is an extraordinary quality evoked by extraordinary circumstances. But being unstable it must be continually replenished with fresh victories. And it does not often survive defeat. The magic cloak once torn dissolves quickly. Oregon diminished Kennedy and made victory in California essential. California was anything but a typical state. Yet it was huge, hence vital, and more than any other it represented the future. Despite its anachronisms—John Birchers, aging Midwesterners, ex-Oakies—this was where the new America was being shaped. Kennedy had to win it.

McCarthy's situation was more complex. If he won in California, as he very well might, Kennedy would probably drop out and many of his delegates would go to Humphrey, who would then certainly be nominated. But if McCarthy lost badly his funds would dry up and, probably, his candidacy also. The best thing that could happen, then, would be for him to lose by a hair. This would keep him alive until Chicago where, if Humphrey and Kennedy deadlocked, he might be chosen out of desperation. The President hated Kennedy most, and might support McCarthy if he were the only alternative. This was not a terribly likely prospect, but it was the best one McCarthy's advisers could foresee. As there was no way of arranging to lose narrowly, however, they had to play to win. Which was just as well as McCarthy's followers intended to win and nearly did. McCarthy summoned them to battle in his usual stirring way. "My strategy is to walk through the Red Sea dry-shod. Any of you who want to follow me before the waters close in are welcome to do so." All the same, McCarthy had an excellent organization in California. His people had gotten him the top line on the ballot by ingenious means. In a single night, petition-signing parties were held all over the state that produced more than enough signatures to get him registered first. Students provided him with virtually unlimited manpower. And, as his daughter Mary put it, they were more effective than Kennedy's. "They have the jumpers and squealers—we have the thinkers and doers." Kennedy depended heavily on paid professionals. McCarthy had 150 local headquarters established and manned by local volunteers. And, for once, McCarthy may have had the edge in celebrities. Hollywood turned out a glittering contingent on his behalf, headed by Paul Newman who went all the way with McCarthy from New Hampshire to Chicago. And though almost no orthodox Democratic politicians supported McCarthy, he had the California Democratic Council, the largest liberal Democratic citizens' group in the country, behind him.

To combat these obstacles Kennedy pulled out all the stops. The usual shower of gold fell on California. All the family's political debts were called in. One of the most genuine and attractive things about Robert Kennedy was his passion for obscure minorities. If there were any Indians in the country he had not spoken to, it was only by accident. Yet the Indian vote was insignificant. The Mexican-American vote was also small, but Kennedy was a tireless friend of the "Chicanos" (as brown militants were calling themselves). He had been especially helpful to Cesar Chavez and the striking grape-pickers. But Chavez was also indebted to the AFL-CIO for steady financial support, and the unions supported Humphrey. Chavez wanted to stay neutral. Kennedy, rightly as it turned out, felt his endorsement was essential and made Chavez back him. Mainly, though, Kennedy relied on the *blitzkrieg*. Advance men lined up big crowds, and he would then drive through them for hours at a stretch amidst scenes of frightful enthusiasm. The old charisma was still working but, as polls showed, it was not enough. McCarthy was running a very skillful television campaign. Leaving the canvassing to his volunteers, he concentrated on getting interviewed. McCarthy looked good on TV, where his naturally quiet, reflective manner came through best. Thus his biggest handicap, the inability to inspire vast ovations, became an asset. The evening news would show a typical Kennedy mob scene set against a thoughtful McCarthy interview. Kennedy's men tried to get interviews for their candidate with little luck: the crowds were what was most newsworthy about him. So they decided, in desperation, to accept McCarthy's old challenge to debate.

McCarthy had used Kennedy's refusal to debate him successfully in Oregon, and it was working for him again in California. Kennedy's men had followed the maxim, proven out in the famous TV debates of 1960, that such exposure helps the lesser-known candidate. They didn't wish to use Kennedy's great reputation to advance McCarthy's. But by California the differences between them had narrowed to the point where Kennedy's charisma was being offset by McCarthy's mature, experienced image on television. When it came, the debate was a considerable disappointment. McCarthy was unprepared, and no one could see why he'd wanted it in the first place. Kennedy was armed to the teeth with materials demonstrating experience and grasp of the issues. It tended toward formlessness. There was little real difference between the candidates except that McCarthy was usually on the defensive. Kennedy accomplished this by dubious means. He got McCarthy to admit that some of his advertising had been withdrawn for being unfair to Kennedy. But when McCarthy tried to point out that some of Kennedy's ads were even more unfair, Kennedy blandly replied that he didn't know what McCarthy was talking about—which was plainly false.

Kennedy's worst ploy involved the racial question. This was Kennedy's special province, and he resented McCarthy for taking issue with him over it. McCarthy was always being criticized for not going into the ghettos more. He did visit some, but the point of his campaign was to escape the old politics based on racial, class, and ethnic appeals. This did not mean that McCarthy didn't care about the Negro question, nor that he had no ideas about it. Quite the contrary. On May 28 in Davis, McCarthy spelled out his position on the ghetto more clearly than ever. Kennedy's approach, epitomized by his Bedford-Stuyvesant project of self-help plus white capital, was tacitly to accept segregation while trying to make poverty areas more livable. "Gilding the ghetto," his critics called it. This was where McCarthy disagreed. His program involved better mass-transit systems so that inner-city people could get out to the suburbs where the jobs were. He wanted plenty of public housing, some of it outside the center city, to bring the worker and the job together but also because he still believed in integration as the ultimate goal for America. And he didn't think black capitalism and involving private enterprise in ghetto affairs would help much, Bedford-Stuyvesant notwithstanding.*

There was room for disagreement among honorable men on the ghetto question, as over integration itself. But Kennedy took a queer way to express his doubts. He accused McCarthy of being at once insensitive to black needs and a danger to white suburbanites. "I mean, when you say you are going to take ten thousand black people into Orange County . . . ," he began, when in fact McCarthy had never proposed any such thing. Nor would any sane man knowing how hostile that stronghold of the John Birch Society would be to black immigrants. It was, of course, just this kind of thing that had given Kennedy his reputation for ruthlessness. It did seem to work though. In California Kennedy cut into the undecided vote which usually went to McCarthy. His aides thought the debate responsible. But his margin of victory was provided by the blacks, who in some areas broke precedent by voting in greater proportions than whites. The Mexican-Americans voted for him practically to a man. So he won, to his great relief, and perhaps to McCarthy's also, for the margin between them, 4.5 per cent of the total vote, was just about right to give McCarthy the near win his candidacy needed most. Then the assassin's bullet struck down Kennedy and the race was over for both of them.

It was assumed at the time that Kennedy would have gone on to capture the New York delegation. But McCarthy's followers, who actually took it, might well have done so anyway. The New York regulars disliked Kennedy more than McCarthy. He had been, as was always said, a "carpetbagger" to start with, winning election to the Senate from New York without really living there. The professionals bowed to his power at the polls, but they never liked it. And they naturally favored Humphrey for President. McCarthy had fine organizers in New York, whose complex primary system was well adapted to their talents. They boned up on the rules and fielded more delegate slates than any of the other factions. Even children helped out. People would talk to the Junior Students for McCarthy who wouldn't speak to any normal canvasser, and

---

* Later events showed he was right on that count. After Kennedy's death, support for his Bedford-Stuyvesant project declined. It was as much a consequence of his personal reputation as the needs of the ghetto. Even if it had worked, the chances of its being imitated on the necessary scale were slight.

their opening line, "Do you believe in death?" was a grabber. The Mc-Carthyists won 63 out of 123 delegate seats (with 30 going to the late Senator), and probably would have done almost as well had Kennedy lived. But of course it made no difference. With Kennedy gone there was no chance of the convention stalemate that was McCarthy's only hope.

As all the world knows, Robert Kennedy was shot down in a hotel kitchen minutes after giving his conciliatory victory statement in Los Angeles.* What followed were the by now traditional post-assassination events. President Johnson sent an official jet to fly the body to New York where hundreds of distinguished people stood vigil by the bier. The President and other great men and women came to the funeral mass. It was led by Richard Cardinal Cushing, who had done the same for President Kennedy, with the Pope's own representative Angelo Cardinal Dell'Acqua attending. Leonard Bernstein conducted. Senator Edward Kennedy read a moving eulogy asking that his brother be remembered "as a good and decent man who saw wrong and tried to right it, saw suffering and tried to heal it, saw war and tried to stop it." Andy Williams, a popular singer and family friend, sang the "Battle Hymn of the Republic." Afterward came the long train ride down the Penn Central's main line to Washington. Huge crowds lined the way. Two people were killed before all traffic was halted along the line. It took eight hours to make the 226-mile trip. The family's agony, made all the worse by these deaths, can scarcely be imagined. There were a thousand people— friends, relatives, reporters—aboard the train, drinking, sweating (most coaches were not air-conditioned that hot June day), and despairing.

Reporters especially gave way to cynicism. To the English authors of *An American Melodrama*, "The afflicted train limping through urban America became a moving focus of absurd morbidity, thoroughly mixed with banality by the communications media and disseminated throughout America, to no beneficial result. Aboard the train, those who could not contrive the resource of black humor vied with each other in maudlin exaggerations about the national predicament." Which only went to show how difficult it is for foreigners to gauge another people's emotions. *An American Melodrama* was the best book about the 1968 elections, partly because the authors' cold foreign eyes pene-

---

* The man charged with his murder, Sirhan B. Sirhan, was a Palestinian refugee with no clear motive, unlike previous assassins. If one was pro-Cuban the death of John F. Kennedy had some purpose. Racists did not have to explain why Martin Luther King died. But Robert Kennedy's murder was pointless, seemingly the consequence of a pathetically deranged mind (though it was thought initially that Sirhan acted against Kennedy's pro-Israeli statements). Dr. Martin M. Schorr who examined Sirhan said, "By killing Mr. Kennedy, Sirhan B. Sirhan kills his father and takes his father's place as the heir to his mother." His act was much admired by Arabs all the same.

trated the defensive fictions and sentiments that Americans surround themselves with. But it was precisely their detachment that kept the English newsmen from understanding what it was like to live through that seemingly endless chain of assassinations in the sixties, or to grasp how shocking it was to have this greatest of all modern electoral dramas end so tragically. Nor could they realize how much Robert Kennedy was liked, in the center and on the left, even by those who did not care for his politics. (Tom Hayden, a founding father of SDS, wept at the funeral.) And finally, no one living through purgatory on the train could judge its effect on television.

For viewers with any degree of sympathy it was terribly affecting. To sit before the flickering screen for hours, days perhaps, on end, to see the stately movement of events interspersed with clips of the living Robert Kennedy, was to experience again the murder and burial of John F. Kennedy. It was all the worse the second time around, and worse still for happening to a man who was in so many respects more vital and passionate than the late President. Thus to *déjà vu* and remembered sorrow was added a special sense of loss. It made people despair for the future of a country whose best men were being murdered, or sent to Vietnam to kill and be killed senselessly, or jailed, or driven into exile. *An American Melodrama* mocks, and properly so in a way, the excessively gloomy editorializing that followed Robert Kennedy's assassination. Though desperate enough, things were not quite so bad as James Reston and his fellow Jeremiahs claimed. It was easy for the English to recognize that, not so easy for a people who had seen their hopes for America destroyed by war, racial strife, political division, and repeated assassinations. As the funeral train wound its slow way down the Eastern seaboard, it carried to the grave not just the dream of another Camelot and the ambitions of Kennedy loyalists but the whole renewal of American political life that had begun in snowy New Hampshire such a short time before.

Liberal Americans had good reason to weep then, and millions did. The train, so ghastly to be on, was a perfect symbol for everything that had just ended in Los Angeles. The people who lined the tracks, waving, and sometimes in their embarrassment cheering feebly, mourned not just the man but what in that moment he symbolized. Those in the train could not see their faces, as TV viewers did. They could not hear the thousands softly singing the "Battle Hymn of the Republic" in Baltimore long before the train came by, their voices rising and falling in the silent air. And they could not have been moved as other Americans were to see the dark train sliding through the station, with the crowds singing and Senator Edward Kennedy, sitting on the rear platform as he did most of the journey, often in shirtsleeves with his arms around a child, raising a weary hand to them. And the funeral party was surely too exhausted on the gentle night when Robert Kennedy was laid to rest in Arlington cemetery, next to his brother John, to grasp the somber beauty of that moment. Eyes thought to be drained of tears wept again.

How will history judge Robert Kennedy? It is still too soon to say, no doubt. But to hazard a guess, probably his foremost quality will seem to have been his capacity for growth. He began public life as a young enthusiast on Senator Joe McCarthy's subcommittee staff. In those days he appeared to possess little more than the terrible ambition Joseph Kennedy gave all his sons, together with an unbecoming desire to persecute suspected communists. Later he attacked union racketeers with the same lack of scruple. He already had a reputation for ruthlessness when he became Attorney General, and though able, was not considered particularly literate or intelligent. While he continued to show little interest in civil liberties (allowing the FBI to tap Martin Luther King's phone, for example), he developed a great interest in civil rights and to most people's surprise became an outstanding Attorney General. After President Kennedy's assassination his character mellowed and deepened. His sympathy for distressed minorities, already strong, became stronger still. He struggled with the great questions of life and death, read Aeschylus and Camus, and exchanged his instrumental optimism for a more stoic philosophy. He wished to do good more than ever, yet he was less sanguine about its possibilities. Because to get a little done you must dare a lot, he became less conservative politically. "I can't be sitting around here calculating whether something I do is going to hurt my political situation in 1972," he once remarked. "Who knows whether I'm going to be alive in 1972?" This was not morbidity but realism. His favorite poem was Alan Seeger's "I Have a Rendezvous with Death," in which the poet romantically goes off to war expecting to die but thinking it worthwhile anyway.

Kennedy became, if anything, more witty in his later years. At Wahoo, Nebraska, in his last campaign a high school reporter showed him the result of a student poll and asked if he had any comment. "RFK: Yes. Tell those who voted for me, thank you. Q: What about those who voted against you? RFK: Tell them I'll get them. (Laughter from the press corps.)" Once he spoke across the street from a movie marquee advertising "The Happiest Millionaire." He pointed to it and said, "Make that come true on election day." Robert Kennedy was more moody, intuitive, impulsive, and emotional than President Kennedy had been. He was more Boston, more Catholic, and, in the Irish way, more puritanical too. All this made for a complex, intriguing, attractive personality. Everyone who knew him agreed that the more you saw of him the more you liked him. Even the press corps, long since inoculated against personal and political enthusiasms, were drawn to him, so much so that the more honest struggled constantly to preserve some measure of detachment, usually with diminishing success. One cannot think of another politician for whom the press would have composed an affectionate parody like "The Ruthless Cannonball."

It was just because of these qualities that Robert Kennedy's death was such a loss. He was always in the process of becoming. No one will ever know what kind of man he might ultimately have been. And it was doubly tragic because his last race, for all its gallantry, was founded on a betrayal of his best instincts. If he had run for President in McCarthy's stead, or if he had declared before New Hampshire, he would have scored a moral triumph such as few could remember. A man who had more to lose than any other major politician would have risked everything in one magnificent gesture. But the fatal Kennedy ambivalence between morality and reality did him in. Like most serious politicians the Kennedys believed that winning came first. But, again like most politicians, they found that to win one must take out mortgages with bosses, interests, and factions. Winning that way left little room for the causes one had presumably gained office to advance. This is the classic dilemma of democratic political leaders, but it was especially acute in the case of men who, like the Kennedys, had great pretensions. Robert Kennedy wanted to walk hand in hand with Mayor Daley and Martin Luther King. The thing could not be done, and by the time he realized that, and made the proper decision, it was too late. All he did was split the anti-war movement and assure the nomination of Hubert Humphrey, the President's own deputy. As a historic figure, then, Robert Kennedy is likely to be best remembered for what he might have been. If he had been less than what he was, history would focus on his brilliant record as Attorney General, and his prudent counsel during the Cuban missile crisis. But he aimed so high that he must be judged for what he meant to do and, through error and tragic accident, failed at. On the other hand, he will also be remembered as an extraordinary human being who, though hated by some, was perhaps more deeply loved by his countrymen than any man of his time. That too must be entered into the final account, and it is no small thing. With his death something precious disappeared from public life.

What of Eugene McCarthy? Kennedy's assassination marked the real end of his "magical mystery tour," or "children's crusade," or whatever one chose to call it. He would go on to Chicago to play out his personal drama, but it was largely over by then. Both the run and the man are extraordinarily difficult to assess. More nonsense, much of it vicious, was written about McCarthy in 1968 than about any man in recent years. The *New Republic* summed it up nicely afterward in an editorial called "Showing You Care." A common criticism of McCarthy's candidacy by liberals was that he didn't care about the job enough to make a "strong" President. The *New Republic* called this the "passion-for-office" test of presidential fitness, the theory being, apparently, that if the candidate didn't want the office bad enough to lie, cheat, and steal, he wasn't qualified to have it. This was a curious enough position in itself, but more so given the fact that Lyndon Johnson was an especially strong President —hence the reaction against him. Even Senator George McGovern, an unusually sensible politician, offered his potential strength as the chief virtue of his belated candidacy.

The *New Republic* said of McCarthy's followers: "The most stunning argument in favor of their man's seriousness of purpose—that he had entered the lists when all others had declined to do so—was turned against him, in another of the remarkable feats by which wine is transformed into water in politics: 'Don't call it courage, call it foolishness.' Everyone knew that it was impossible to tumble an incumbent President from within his own party, let alone to stop a war. Thus the man who tried to do so, far from offering testimony to his faith in the democratic process, proved simply that he did not really care enough to be President. The only conclusion to draw was that McCarthy found some special and perhaps perverted pleasure in helling around New Hampshire in the winter with only a crowd of newly shorn college students for company— or had 'nothing to lose.' " Nothing to lose except face, almost the most important of all commodities for a professional politician. Then again, when asked by a reporter if he would make a good President, McCarthy replied that he thought he would be adequate. This showed his frivolity. Another count against him was that he did not "build bridges," that is to say, he didn't appeal to people like Mayor Daley who would not normally support him. This again showed his want of seriousness. Every serious politician sells out to a degree, it was understood; the whole trick was to sell at the best possible price.

McCarthy's failure to captivate the press was also cited. "His inability or refusal to be 'visibly moved' was legendary. There is no instance on record of his crying in public. He generally appeared more impatient than gratified when his speeches were interrupted by applause." This showed his lack of compassion. But what really hurt him with newsmen, hardly notable for compassion themselves, "was his refusal to respond in kind to ersatz seriousness and spurious conscientiousness." Reporters expect politicians to be hypocrites, and resent it when they aren't. Then too, during a campaign most newsmen are expected to turn out a story every day, and friendly politicians cooperate by staging non-events or pseudo-interviews to meet this need. Presumably both sides benefit from these fraudulent encounters. The politician gets more free publicity. The reporter satisfies his editors. By failing to conform, McCarthy showed again his self-destructive political tendencies, while injuring, or so they must have thought, the reporters' careers. They paid him back by emphasizing his arrogance and insensitivity, and the amateurish character of his campaign.

By and large, both the press and the Kennedy Democrats were victims of their prejudice. McCarthy was an exceptionally daring politician. He was one of the first to openly attack Joe McCarthy when the Wisconsin Senator was thought to be both invulnerable and capable of wrecking any enemy. And he was, of course, first to challenge the presidential power over Vietnam. He was also among the early critics of the CIA, the only important politician to urge the firing of General Lewis Hershey (Selective Service director) and J. Edgar Hoover. No Kennedy could say as much. But McCarthy was also a shrewd politician. It was the unorthodoxy of his campaign that kept his enemies from seeing that. McCarthy understood early on that Johnson was vulnerable, which was why he went to New Hampshire. He also understood that the constituency which would rally round him was tired of the old politics with all its humbug. The best students, the well educated, and the independents would work for him to the degree that he contrasted to other Democratic leaders. They didn't like Johnson's combination of patriotic corn and arm-twisting. Yet they also disliked Kennedy's pitch to blacks and ethnics, his wooing of the established pols, and the deliberate charisma which his advertising exploited.

It was precisely because McCarthy avoided all these pitfalls that he was admired. What he proved was that plain speaking, nerve, and a low profile appealed to a constituency that no one believed existed, or that if it did exist was unimportant. He also picked up votes from alienated conservatives who admired him not so much for his specific policies as for his independence. McCarthy never made the slightest effort to win votes from George Wallace. He got some anyway. And, as we saw earlier, though his base was in the suburbs he had strong support among trade-union families and the very young. Since he got it without pandering to any interest group, McCarthy was in a position to innovate, and he did. As David Halberstam, who really liked Kennedy best, observed, McCarthy was charting a course for the future while most politicians were still hung up on the past—Kennedy included. Though in many respects a conservative, which was why he ran in the first place—to sustain confidence in the system among the young and alienated—McCarthy's campaign was the most radical of all. His racial proposals aimed at integration when liberals like Kennedy were falling back on separatism. His foreign policy was not isolationist, as Dean Rusk seemed to think, but it did involve a drastic reordering of international affairs. Though he was often sharp with newsmen, he understood the uses of television better than almost any politician. However badly the newspapers treated him, McCarthy knew that television counted most, and he came across beautifully on it. The understatement and wry humor that were his stock in trade were not really reportable. His best remarks had a way of being mangled by the press.

TV showed him as he was: witty ("They're [Republicans] somewhat like the lowest forms of plant and animal life. Even at their highest point of vitality there is not much life in them; on the other hand, they don't die"), learned ("One of the things that I object to about the Kennedys is that they are trying to turn the presidency into the Wars of the Roses"), and fast on his feet. He had a marvelous technique with hecklers. Once in California he trapped them as follows: "They say I'm a stalking horse for Kennedy. [YEAH.] And they say I'm a Judas goat for Johnson. [YEAH.] Awful hard to be both." Nationally the McCarthy organization was faction-ridden. His Senate staff distrusted the newcomers. There were countless rivalries and personality clashes. McCarthy was frequently criticized for this. But as Jay Sykes, his manager in Wisconsin, pointed out later, there was a method even here. While McCarthy ignored upper-echelon factionalism, he was attentive to the local organizations. He believed, and rightly as it turned out, that in his campaign it was the grass roots that counted. He once disposed of questions about why a staff member had resigned by saying that the loss was trivial, nothing like the damage he would have sustained had his driver quit. This was unbearably flippant from the newsmen's viewpoint, but it summed up his campaign. The important thing was that he cast his bread upon as much water as he could. Thanks to his army of volunteers, the rest would take care of itself. And so, to a surprising degree, it did.

Both the man and his campaign were best captured by Hans Morgenthau in, of all places, the *New York Review of Books*. After talking at length with Senator McCarthy, Morgenthau reported that the private man and the public man were identical. Unlike the usual campaign in which it was understood that what followed would be quite different, McCarthy's candidacy embodied his views on how policy should be conducted. Morgenthau wrote that McCarthy had three precise ideas about what he could do as President. "He can restore a philosophy of government and of the American purpose which suits the genius of the American people. By doing this, he can move large masses of Americans and, more particularly, of the younger generation back into active participation in the democratic processes. Finally, he presents clear-cut alternatives to the policies of the present administration as well of his competitors, especially in the field of foreign policy." McCarthy, he noted, had an "instrumental and restrictive conception of presidential power."

His foreign policy was "common sense restored to its rightful place." He saw the American mission as not to dominate but to lead. It was more important to set a good example at home than to try and reform the world by force—thus racial justice in America was more desirable than trying to coerce South Africa into changing its ways. NATO was obsolete, but this did not mean that the U.S. should abandon its European presence, which was desirable if only to sustain the Western orientation of Germany. China ought to be recognized, but Taiwan could not be ignored. In Latin America McCarthy understood that revolution was coming and that the role of the U.S. was not to suppress it but to see that basic American interests were preserved. On Vietnam McCarthy had the courage and honesty to realize that the war was lost and that the U.S. had to make the best terms it could—which probably meant a coalition government with the NLF. Morgenthau concluded: "That so many Americans seem willing to put their trust in a man of such qualities, who has come to them without money, without organization, and without prestigious sponsorship, honors them perhaps more than it honors him. Win or lose in August and November, Eugene McCarthy will have this historic achievement to his credit: to have made active and visible qualities of goodness and sanity latent in the American people, to have revealed a face of America that was concealed beneath the distorting mask of its political practices, and to have given us an intimation of what the American people could be like if they had a leader worthy of them."

Kennedy's death and the ruin of McCarthy's fortunes guaranteed that no great changes would take place in 1968, but the election itself was yet to be held. And to have the election it was necessary first to endure the nominating conventions. Of all the trying features of American political life, conventions are easily the worst. Though streamlined a bit for television, they remain long, boring, and incomprehensible for the most part. Endless speeches and roll calls stupefy viewers, while the real convention takes place behind closed doors where the deals are made. The Republican convention in Miami was very traditional. "Nixon Girls" paraded winsomely, balloons rose in the fetid air while Rockefeller fell. His campaign had little chance to begin with. He only launched his last-ditch effort because, for the first time in his career of pursuing the Republican nomination, he had solid Establishment support. Richard

Nixon, having made the most remarkable political comeback in recent history, was comfortably in the lead, George Romney, his main challenger, having disqualified himself by saying that he had been "brainwashed" into supporting the war earlier. Yet many businessmen doubted Nixon could win and, more out of despair than enthusiasm, asked Rockefeller, still perhaps the country's most popular Republican, to tackle him once more. Accordingly, the Rockefeller machine ground out a PR blitz designed to prove that though Nixon had run in the primaries and Rockefeller had not, "Rocky" remained the people's choice. It failed. When he came to the convention, then, Rockefeller's only chance was that a last-minute Reagan boom might divide conservatives, enabling him to slip through.

This was not so forlorn a hope as it seemed later. Nixon was, next to President Johnson, the most distrusted figure in national politics. Conservatives supported him not because of his ideology, for he had none, but because he supported the ticket in 1964. The pros appreciated that too, and even more his great contribution to the GOP comeback in 1966 when the party had picked up seven additional governorships and forty-seven more seats in Congress—almost exactly the number Nixon had predicted. Nixon was going to be nominated because of what he was owed, not for the affection he was held in. Ronald Reagan was the conservatives' new darling. He was personable, good on TV, and quick to exploit student protests, Black Power, welfare measures, and everything else that conservatives despised. And he was more professional, for all his late entry into politics, than Goldwater had been. But the Reagan candidacy flopped, taking Rockefeller with it, thanks mainly to Senator Strom Thurmond of South Carolina.

Thurmond was a strange figure. A militarist (and reserve general), a segregationist (who had been the Dixiecrat candidate for President in 1948), he was revered in the South for championing war and racism. With most Southern Republicans (the bulk of them, like Thurmond, recent converts), he preferred Reagan. But he was convinced that Reagan would only produce another debacle. So he used his influence to hold the South for Nixon, who, though a weak conservative, was better than none at all. He was immediately rewarded when Nixon, having won on the first ballot, chose Spiro Agnew of Maryland as his Vice-President. Agnew was, in his own words, "stunned." So was the country. He had no visible qualifications to be next in line for the presidency. All most people knew about him was that, having run for governor of Maryland against a racist, he had become one himself. Black votes put Agnew in the statehouse, but when riots erupted in Maryland he blamed them on the Negro leadership and raised the cry for law and order. But his obscurity and backward sentiments were exactly what commended him

379

to Nixon. Nixon did not want another running mate like Henry Cabot Lodge, who had gone pretty much his own way in 1960. As a political cipher, Agnew could be depended on to take orders. And, as a border-state governor, Agnew was acceptable to the South. This last was vital. Thurmond was owed a favor. More than that, the GOP was flirting with a "Southern strategy." The Democrats were to be displaced as the nation's majority party by a new coalition of businessmen, farmers, and Western and, especially, Southern bigots. Nixon himself denied there was a Southern strategy. And though he appealed to the South, his signals were ambiguous. But in selecting Agnew he sent it a message that no one could mistake.*

Still, it was hard to tell from his convention performance exactly what sort of candidate (or President) Nixon would be. His style was more slick and convincing than before. In his acceptance speech he made the usual appeal for law and order, but also promised to end the war in Vietnam ("honorably," of course). The old mawkishness was still there (he invoked as always his humble origins and Quaker mother). But the speech was more conciliatory than not. Norman Mailer, who covered both conventions, found the new Nixon baffling. "There had never been anyone in American life so resolutely phony as Richard Nixon, nor any one so transcendentally successful by such means—small wonder half the electorate had regarded him for years as equal to a disease. But he was less phony now, that was the miracle, he had moved from a position of total ambition and total alienation from his own person (at the time of Checkers, the dog speech) to a place now where he was halfway conciliated with his own self. As he spoke, he kept going in and out of focus, true one instant, phony the next, then quietly correcting the false step." That blurred quality was to be the new Nixon's hallmark. Strom Thurmond might know where Nixon was going, but no one else seemed to, then or later.

---

* Actually, the Southern strategy was more apparent than real in 1968. Nixon made a few gestures toward the South, but in the main his campaign was straight Madison Avenue. This disappointed Kevin Phillips, a brilliant young Republican strategist who wanted seriously to exploit ethnic hostilities. He believed there were twenty major ethnic groups, and twenty minor ones, ripe for a carefully planned appeal to their worse natures. On this basis a great new coalition could be built. The party did take his advice in one important respect. It concentrated on the border states rather than the Deep South, on the grounds that moderate Democrats were easier to convert. If the border went Republican, the Deep South would have to come along eventually as there would be no place else for bigots to go. It was unlikely, however, that Phillips' complete strategy would ever be implemented. For one thing, it required a bold commitment such as politicians hate to make. They like to cover their bets, Nixon especially. As Milton Viorst pointed out, the Nixon administration was a caretaker government, not a coalition-builder. Even if it wasn't, Viorst argued, Phillips' scheme would not work. "I don't think great coalitions can be built on cynicism."

Hubert Humphrey's nomination was even more inevitable than Nixon's. While Kennedy and McCarthy were storming through the country, Humphrey was quietly lining up delegates. He didn't run in the primaries. The polls showed him way behind McCarthy and Kennedy. He was assured of nomination all the same, especially after Kennedy's death. The hawks were for him as one of their own. Labor backed him as a long-time champion of their interests. The regular civil rights organizations could not turn their backs on one who had led the fight for civil rights at the Democratic convention in 1948. President Johnson seemed to be for him. The professionals owed him for his years of speaking and fund-raising on their behalf. They were terrified of the citizens for McCarthy. In this respect the McCarthy surge was much more threatening than Kennedy's had been. Kennedy was a party man by choice, a rebel only by necessity. His support came from within the party structure, and he never stopped hoping that the big pols like Mayor Daley would come over to him. Had he lost the nomination everyone knew he would have campaigned loyally for the ticket. McCarthy was another matter. He owed the party nothing. No one knew what he would do if denied the nomination. Worse still, his followers were not under orders. He might change his mind, but that didn't guarantee they would. They meant not just to nominate McCarthy but to capture the party. They had already done so in some states (New Hampshire), and obtained a piece of the action in others (New York, Connecticut). Thus while the polls still showed McCarthy to have the best chance of any Democratic candidate in November, nominating him would mean a loss of professional control over the party apparatus. Politicians are in business to win elections, but not at such a cost. If the price of victory was less power in the party, they wouldn't pay it. It was, and they didn't.

Humphrey had once been an insurgent himself, which made his position as the bosses' candidate seem incongruous. But the fit was more comfortable than it appeared. Though he had broken ranks over civil rights in 1948, and been an aggressively independent Senator at first, he had learned early that to get ahead you must get along. He became a Johnson protégé in the Senate, and, without giving much away in principle, joined the club. As a Senator he was able to balance realism and progressivism successfully. But once he became Vice-President that was no longer possible. Vice-Presidents do what they are told. What Humphrey was told to do was sell the war, which he did with his usual gusto. Rhetorical excess was always his problem. He talked too much too often. He got carried away. In 1964 he once enjoined Ohioans to redeem their failure to vote for Kennedy in 1960 by going Democratic in 1964, "so that John Kennedy in heaven will know we won." And he promised a "nuclear reign of terror" if Goldwater was elected. Humphrey's background made it easy for him to justify the war in Vietnam. As a young politician he had helped purge the Minnesota Democratic Farmer Labor party of communists in the 1940's. As a Senator in 1950 he had voted for the Internal Security Act, and later proposed an amendment to it that would have made membership in the Communist party punishable by five years in prison. He was a Cold War liberal and red-baiter for most of his career.

So Humphrey's position as the Establishment's candidate was not so strange as it seemed. He had become a good party man since 1948. He would put his arm around Lester Maddox, the segregationist governor of Georgia, if that helped the ticket. Little wonder that the young and pacific despised him. Little wonder too that he failed to understand why. After all, his record on civil rights was impeccable. And he had backed the test-ban treaty in the Senate. Indeed, his liberal enterprises were practically without number. But the long and short of it was that in 1968 he wielded the administration's hatchet. His job was to hold the line for war and party regularity and break the resistance. Given the McCarthyist refusal to accept what was inevitable, this meant a rough convention.

Others were conspiring to make it rougher still. One of these was Mayor Daley himself, a big-time city boss who had survived the last hurrah by allying a wickedly efficient machine with the business establishment. He had insisted on getting the convention for Chicago even though millions of dollars and endless trouble would have been saved by having it in Miami. The networks could have televised two conventions there for hardly more than the price of one. And Miami was far from the maddened anti-war throng. Daley knew trouble was coming. But he thought his big, brutal police force could handle it, and if not, his man in Springfield would call out the National Guard. Just to be safe, though, he managed things so that the networks would find it hard to televise whatever disturbances did take place.

Daley's *lumpen*-bourgeois prejudices were exactly what some troublemakers counted on to make the convention memorable. Their labors began a month before, when Abbie Hoffman and his friends founded the Youth International party. The difference between the yippies and other leftists, according to Hoffman, was that they were "revolutionary artists. Our concept of revolution is that it's fun." Yippie leaders decided to stage a Festival of Life in Chicago to counterbalance the Democratic convention which would, naturally, be a celebration of death. Meanwhile, the less psychedelic National Mobilization to End the War in Vietnam was planning to demonstrate in Chicago also. The joint yippie-Mobe program was heavily publicized in the underground press. Ed Sanders of the Fugs, a yippie founder, wrote a piece for *The Fifth Estate* of Detroit called "Dope, Peace, Magic, Gods in the Tree-Trunk and Group-Grope."

It explained that the festival meant "poetry readings, mass meditation, flycasting exhibitions, demagogic Yippie political arousal speeches, and rock music and song concerts." An elite force of 230 sexy yippie males would seduce the wives, daughters, and girl friends of convention delegates. Paul Krassner of *The Realist*, the country's oldest underground paper, threatened to put LSD in Chicago's water supply. All these preliminaries were designed to offend Chicago's provincial sensibilities and insure the best possible confrontation.

This was not difficult to arrange. As Norman Mailer pointed out, the slaughterhouse showed the spirit of Chicago. "In any other city they would have technologies to silence the beasts with needles, quarter them with machines, lull them with Muzak, and have stainless steel for doors, aluminum beds to take over the old overhead trolley—animals would be given a shot of vitamin-enrichment before they took the last ride. But in Chicago, they did it straight, they cut the animals right out of their hearts—which is why it was the last of the great American cities, and people had great faces, carnal as blood, greedy, direct, too impatient for hypocrisy, in love with honest plunder. . . . Yes, Chicago was a town where nobody could ever forget how the money was made. It was picked up from floors still slippery with blood."

So that was how it would be in August. The yippies goaded Daley and his minions to rage and madness. Expecting the worst, McCarthy urged his people to stay home. In the event, only about 2,500 yippies came to the convention, but that was more than enough. Dave Dellinger of the Mobe assumed that Daley would play it smart, give the protesters a parade permit, "and let us get swallowed up on the South Side." But Daley didn't want to outmaneuver the demonstrators; that was not Chicago's way. He meant to smash them to bloody bits. Fury and prejudice were two reasons for the violence to follow. But another was the peculiar psychology seeping into police work. As big-city police became more militarized, they acquired the military's enthusiasm for intelligence work. It is the nature of intelligence services to enlarge themselves. Where trouble does not exist they invent it; where it does, they magnify it. The Chicago intelligence apparatus conditioned policemen to react not to what was actually happening but to what yippie boasts made them think would happen. Thus in looking at the Festival of Life they didn't see a handful of put-on artists but rather the entering wedge of riot and rebellion.

Everyone knows what happened when the beards and bigots met that week. Despite Daley's best efforts, much of it was shown on television. Afterward it was written up in great detail. The President's own National Commission on the Causes and Prevention of Violence issued a special report titled *Rights in Conflict* (the Walker Report) that called the worst violence a police riot. The protesters, not only yippies but the more sober elements of the Mobe, were denied permits to sleep in the parks and make protest marches. When they did so anyway they were beaten, gassed, and Maced. No one was safe from the policemen's frenzy. Their sergeants lost control of them repeatedly, and they beat reporters, bystanders, and yippies with equal abandon. Six hundred demonstrators were arrested and several hundred injured badly enough to need medical attention. (About a hundred policemen suffered injuries too, mainly cut knuckles.) The police crowned their triumph by raiding Senator McCarthy's campaign headquarters from which, they insisted, garbage and insults had been showered on them.

Not that it was all a matter of humorless brutality. There were amusing moments too. The yippies had their own candidate for President, a real live pig named Pigasus. Police penetration was so inventive that one agent became an aide of yippie leader Jerry Rubin before arresting him for sedition. Allen Ginsberg lent color to the events by chanting to promote tranquility. It seemed to affect the police little, though.* Jean Genet, the radical French writer, was tear-gassed, and afterward he, William Burroughs, and Terry Southern, all of whom covered the events for *Esquire* magazine, marched regularly with the yippies. Hugh Hefner of *Playboy* was whacked on the bottom by a police club, which was not so much an affront to his personal dignity as to the entire structure of consumer capitalism which he so brilliantly adorned. Abbie Hoffman, a keen student of Marshall McLuhan, painted an obscene word on his forehead as insurance against unwanted photographs. But he encouraged the yippies to give obscene interviews. He knew the dirty words would be blipped out, but he felt blipping was the moral equivalent of the blank spaces in censored Saigon newspapers. At such times emptiness spoke more eloquently than words.

All in all, the total effect was more ghastly than not. Especially for the insurgent Democrats at the convention who knew that those who were, in a sense, their constituents were getting beaten in the streets even as they were being crushed by the Johnson-Humphrey steamroller. But before that, the preliminaries had to be gotten through. Credentials and platform planks had to be fought over, and delegates solicited. The California delegation was especially prized. With Ken-

---

* This remark is not meant frivolously. Ginsberg was not only a good poet (the only important figure in the beat generation to remain pertinent to the sixties) but a true mystic. He devoted years to the study of Mantra Yoga, practiced its austere disciplines, and trained himself to chant, as he did at Chicago, for seven hours at a time. Though Ginsberg lent himself to the yippie put-on, he was himself in earnest and took the Festival of Life to be just that. He also possessed a very sweet character and an exceptionally fluent and expressive speaking manner, as he showed later in testifying for the defendants at the conspiracy trial which followed these events.

nedy dead it might go either way, so the three major candidates, McCarthy, Humphrey, and McGovern, all spoke to it. McGovern's candidacy was hard to figure. Earlier he had almost endorsed McCarthy, and might have had McCarthy's neglect not offended him. McGovern was a good liberal and a dove. Except on the issue of presidential strength he generally agreed with McCarthy. But he was part of the Kennedy connection, and when the Kennedy followers asked him to run at the convention he did. It's not clear why. Some thought it was a spoiler candidacy to save Kennedy delegates from having to vote for McCarthy. Others thought just the opposite, that McGovern ran to keep from Humphrey the delegates who hated McCarthy so much that they would go with the Vice-President if he was the only alternative. As the Kennedy following was based more on personality than principle, these were vital considerations. In the event, it hardly mattered as the combined McCarthy-McGovern vote was only a fraction of what either needed to scare Humphrey. McGovern's intentions were thus never put to the test.

Apart from providing a haven for Kennedy soreheads, McGovern gave reporters an agreeable figure to write about. He said all the right things, unlike McCarthy who, as Norman Mailer put it, "was damned if he would move a phony finger for any occasion." And he said them without the maddening discursiveness that made even Humphrey's friends despair at times. When the Vice-President spoke to the California delegates he took three times as long as McCarthy, "trudging through an imprecision of language, a formal slovenliness of syntax which enabled him to shunt phrases back and forth like a switchman who locates a freight car by moving everything in the yard." Afterward the press agreed that George McGovern, the beau ideal of orthodox liberalism, looked the best. McCarthy, in contrast, was even more himself than usual. His contempt for sentimentality, political rituals, and liberal cant was never displayed to better effect. Naturally this turned off the California delegates, but it appealed greatly to Mailer who had not really liked McCarthy before. As a swinger, and with charisma of his own, Mailer naturally favored Kennedy. He liked tough guys and Beautiful People, and McCarthy's operation seemed short of both. But McCarthy's splendid consistency at Chicago won Mailer's heart. He could see why "Negroes in general had never been charmed with McCarthy. If he was the epitome of Whitey at his best, that meant Whitey at ten removes, dry wit, stiff back, two-and-a-half centuries of Augustan culture and their distillate—the ironic manners of the tightest country gentry: the Blacks did not want Whitey at his best and bonniest in a year when they were out to find every justification . . . to hate the Honkie." Nor was such a man the type to gain Mailer's favor under normal circumstances. But circumstances were far from normal. The police were rioting in the streets. The festival of death was grinding down the best Democrats. The "reign of piety and iron" that Robert Lowell had predicted earlier seemed well under way.

Amidst this moral squalor, rendered especially grotesque by the trappings of a political convention, McCarthy stood even taller than before. While his supporters raved and wept, and the ship foundered, he paced the quarterdeck as he had all that year. The sails were in tatters, his standard nailed to the mainmast, but he had one gun left to fire and he discharged it at the California delegates. It took some brass to summon him in the first place. He had campaigned mightily in California and they all knew where he stood. He was not going to play games with them, nor save their faces with some fake gesture at the last minute. If they voted for him it would be for what he had said and done all along. He began by observing that his position on Vietnam was too well known to bear repeating. Then, as Norman Mailer tells it, he turned to the absurd criticisms that had been made of him, " 'most recently the suggestion that I would be a passive President. Well, I think a little passivity in that office is all right, a kind of balance, I think. I have never quite known what active compassion is. Actually compassion, in my mind, is to suffer with someone, not in advance of him.' He paused, 'or not in public necessarily.' He paused again. Here came the teeth. The voice never altered. 'But I have been, whether I have been passive or not, the most active candidate in the party this year.' He brought the curtain down with that dignity which was his most unique political possession. 'Many stood on the sidelines, as I said earlier, on the hilltops, dancing around the bonfires. Few came down into the valley where the action was. And I said then that if one challenged the President he had to be prepared to be President. It is like striking at the King—it is a dangerous thing.' How dangerous only he could know." "Yes," Mailer concluded, "the reporter had met many candidates, but McCarthy was the first who felt like a President."

Of course McCarthy was not going to be President, as he admitted in a typically impolitic interview that very evening. But before that was made official, more outrages had to be committed. The next day, when the minority anti-war plank was defeated, the convention band played "This Could Be the Start of Something Big," while the insurgent delegates, led by Theodore Bikel of New York, sang "We Shall Overcome." They voted that night at the height of the police riot downtown. Senator Abraham Ribicoff of Connecticut made his feelings clear while nominating McGovern: "With George McGovern as President we would not have to have such Gestapo tactics in the streets of Chicago. With George McGovern we would not have to have the National Guard." There were cheers and boos at this. The Illinois delegation rose to scream insults at him, and no one will ever forget the sight of Mayor Daley shaking his fist and mouthing what seemed to be obscenities at Ribicoff, who looked directly at him, smiled, and said quietly, "How hard it is to accept the truth." Then Humphrey was nominated handily, and the delegates adjourned to their hotels, which reeked of tear gas for the most part.

The next day Humphrey chose his friend, Senator Edmund S. Muskie of Maine, to run with him, and accepted the nomination in a speech that touched every base. On the one hand he deplored anarchy in the streets and called for law and order. On the other, he expressed a dislike of police states. And Humphrey thanked the absent President Johnson for all the blessings he had showered on Democrats. Then the band played "Happy Days Are Here Again," and Humphrey beamed away, his great round face shining in the TV lights.* McGovern loyally trooped up and congratulated him, McCarthy didn't. Humphrey seemed to find his nomination no less enjoyable for the way he had gained it. He was ruined all the same. The party lay in shambles around him. The whole country had seen the violence in Chicago, some of it within the convention hall itself where ubiquitous security guards roughed up delegates and newsmen alike. (One delegate cried out that he had been elected to attend the convention, not sentenced to it.) People had seen the insurgents cry after a moving filmed biography of Robert Kennedy was shown, and heard them sing the "Battle Hymn of the Republic" until Daley shut them up, cleverly for a change, by having a Negro delegate give an unscheduled tribute to Martin Luther King. Only Humphrey retained any illusions about the coming election.

The Democrats would lose, though not because of the police riot in Chicago. What Nixon was soon to call the "silent majority" liked to see hippies and such beaten up. Law and order could hardly be too viciously applied to suit people demoralized by years of war, protest, and youthful contempt for the bourgeois life. Mayor Daley got a lot of fan mail. The newsmen who had been outraged, especially when beaten themselves, soon fell into line. Walter Cronkite of CBS, who had gotten so carried away as to complain of the police brutality (especially to CBS reporters), had an abject interview with Mayor Daley who straightened him out. Within a few weeks most newspapers and magazines saw how

* One of Humphrey's least-discussed liabilities was the fact that he didn't look like a President. He was overweight, and with his big balding dome, square little chin, and rat-trap mouth offered a rather comic appearance. This was, of course, not a good reason for voting against him, but it must surely have cost him votes all the same. The country had had unprepossessing chief executives before, yet no one could remember when such a funny-looking man had been nominated for, let alone elected to, the highest office. The problem was especially acute in an age when TV mercilessly exposed a man's physical shortcomings. It was not yet necessary to be, as Nixon put it, "a pretty boy," still, average looks were probably a minimum requirement for future candidates.

the wind was blowing and came out fearlessly against streetfighting and for law and order. All this was grist to Nixon's mill because Humphrey could never top him on that issue, try as he might. The more demands for repression, the better off Nixon was. Like anti-communism in the 1950's, law and order was (Wallace excepted) a Republican monopoly. So although Democrats had suppressed the revolution in Chicago, the GOP gained most from it. On the other hand, the people who were offended by the Daley-Humphrey pogrom were nearly all Democrats, and energetic ones at that. Liberals, intellectuals, and the active young were a minority in the party, but they were crucial to any Democratic victory in national elections. Without their help as fund-raisers, publicists, and precinct-workers a Democrat did not become President of the United States. They were alienated by Chicago. Many never returned to the fold. Those who did, after Humphrey realized his mistake, returned too late to alter events.*

Accordingly, after Chicago the question seemed to be not would Humphrey win, but would Wallace draw off enough votes to throw the election into the House of Representatives. The Wallace threat was not so serious as it seemed then, but it was real enough. George Wallace was the first genuine demagogue since Huey Long with presidential aspirations. (Joe McCarthy, for example, never tried to organize his following into a coherent movement. Though demagogic, he was not a true demagogue.) And, also like Long, Wallace was not chiefly a racist. In fact, he was once quite the opposite by Alabama standards. He got elected to the state legislature in 1946 at a time when he was too poor to afford a car. He canvassed his rural district by walking and hitching rides. He was then an admirer of Jim Folsom, a populist insurgent who was elected governor that year by defying the "bourbon" Establishment, the "Big Mules" as he called them. But they continued to control the legislature so Folsom did not get the reforms he wanted, like reapportionment and repeal of the poll tax. Folsom was very moderate on the race question. During his second term after *Brown v. Board of Education* he resisted the white backlash and hoped for compliance with the law. A huge (six feet, eight inches), colorful, independent man, he completed his downfall by inviting Adam Clayton Powell to the executive mansion for a drink. Wallace then got reluctantly off his bandwagon. But the big change in Wallace came in 1958 when he tried to succeed Folsom and was beaten by a rabid but obscure segregationist. Wallace is alleged to have said afterward, "John Patterson out-nigguhed me. And boys, I'm

---

* Some people argued that McCarthy's defeat showed the futility of politics. But his campaign forced Johnson to leave office and Nixon to gear down the war. These were the most substantial accomplishments of any peace movement in American history. To despise them was to abandon all hope for popular action.

not going to be out-nigguhed again." And he wasn't. In 1962 he defeated Folsom in the primary, assisted by the fact that Folsom showed up drunk for a state-wide TV program. Then he out-segged his opponent in the runoff.* His promise to stand in the schoolhouse door if desegregation threatened was especially admired.

Race apart, Wallace was a good governor. He largely succeeded at what Folsom had hoped to do. He built fourteen junior colleges and fifteen new trade schools. He put through a $100 million school construction program, got free textbooks for Alabama schoolchildren, combated water pollution, and much else, all in the best populist tradition. The tax system stayed regressive, a certain amount of corruption continued (for the sake of his organization, not himself; he was always financially scrupulous). But otherwise Wallace built up a fine record. Still, when the University of Alabama was desegregated, he did stand in the door and thus became a national figure. He got many invitations to speak at college campuses thereafter and accepted all he could. They enhanced his appeal to the backlash, for everywhere he was disrupted. (At Harvard two of his aides were caught in a band of pickets outside the auditorium who were singing "We Shall Overcome." One turned to the other and muttered fiercely, "Sing, you fool. Sing! I'm too old to run.")

It was in Wisconsin that an admirer persuaded him to enter the presidential primary. At the time he had only $800 and no organization, but he got 35 per cent of the vote in Wisconsin and then went on to get 30 per cent in Indiana and 45 per cent in Maryland. When Goldwater was nominated, Wallace dropped out so as not to split the conservative vote. But the experience gave him national ambitions. Though he called himself a conservative, Wallace was far from ideological. His adviser on theory and part-time speechwriter, John Kohn, a crusty old racist, thought Wallace didn't even dislike Negroes. But he saw that others did and used the race issue much as Joe McCarthy used anti-communism, without having any personal feel for what the rage was all about. Since his candidacy was based on exploiting negative emotions, and was meant to attract conservative Southerners and bigoted working-class Northerners, it was impossible for Wallace to have anything resembling a program. Instead he went around the country smashing straw men like the "left-wing theoreticians, briefcase totin' bureaucrats, ivory-tower guideline writers, bearded anarchists, smart-aleck editorial writers and pointy-headed professors." "There are more of us than there are of

* Alabama prevents governors from succeeding themselves, so popular ones can run only in every other election. Folsom was not the only humane Southern politician to be ruined by the reaction against school desegregation. It played a part in the downfall of Governor Earl Long of Louisiana too.

them," he reminded his audiences. And he had a few simple prescriptions for every ill. Bureaucrats would be stripped of their briefcases. Looters would be shot. "If I become President and some anarchist lies down in front of my automobile, it's going to be the last automobile he lies down in front of," he invariably remarked. This sort of thing paid off. So did his identification with humble folk, the steelworkers, barbers, and so forth who were thought to be his constituents. Wallace did not make bluntly racist appeals. He didn't need to. Instead he promised to win the war in Vietnam, restore states' rights, secure law and order, repeal open-housing laws, and in general restore the country to its rightful owners—assuming that the rightful owners were bigots, warmongers, and illiterates.

Wallace faced two big problems in 1968. One was outflanking Spiro Agnew. The other was selecting a running mate. The problem here was that no one else in the country occupied his peculiar position. No other Southern racist had a following in the North. No Northerner of any standing was willing to run on such a ticket. He held off choosing a vice-presidential candidate as long as he could. Finally he persuaded retired General Curtis LeMay to go with him. It immediately became obvious that this was a mistake, if an inescapable one given the dearth of possibilities. LeMay was a famous warrior, a good thing for a Wallace man to be, but his bloodthirstiness was extreme even for such company. At his initial press conference he said that it would be "most efficient" to drop nuclear weapons on North Vietnam. The more he and Wallace tried to explain what he meant, the worse it sounded. Afterward he predicted dolefully, "I'll be damned lucky if I don't appear as a drooling idiot whose only solution is to drop atomic bombs all over the world."*

Spiro Agnew, whose name, as his wife observed, was hardly a household word, became equally troublesome for Wallace. Nixon's strategy was to seize the middle while Agnew captured as much of the right as could be gotten from Wallace. Agnew was not always as skillful at this as he later became. He declined to visit a ghetto on the grounds that they were all alike. On conservation his position was that if you've seen one tree you've seen them all. He referred to Polish-Americans as "Polacks," which was hardly the way to win ethnic votes. But as Muskie was of Polish origin and most Polish-Americans would vote for him anyway, this probably did the ticket no great harm. He once described a corpulent Japanese-American reporter as a "fat Jap." But again, the

---

* Actually, LeMay was one militarist who was every bit as bad as he seemed. During World War II he had ordered, on his own initiative, fire raids against Japan that killed more people than the atomic bombs. Had the Japanese won he would have been first on their list of war criminals. Later he was an advocate of pre-emptive war. The country that staged a Pearl Harbor need never fear one, was apparently his motto.

Japanese-American vote was not large, so little harm was done. And Agnew was protected by his Greek ancestry from charges of WASPish chauvinism. He was more on target when he said that Humphrey was "squishy soft" on communism, which was certainly news to the people who remembered Humphrey's witch-hunting days. Though false, it pleased the right, as it was meant to. Agnew was an important reason why Wallace carried only five Southern states.*

As the campaign developed a surprising thing happened. Humphrey started gaining. In August the Gallup poll put him sixteen points behind Nixon. On October 21 Humphrey had cut that lead by half. There were many reasons for this. The initial gap was unnatural and bound to diminish in a country where a majority of registered voters were Democrats. The memory of Chicago dimmed. Nixon made no effort to win over dissident liberal Democrats. Having plotted out a campaign based on the Southern strategy, the backlash against students, hippies, and blacks, and a series of slick, bland television promotions, Nixon stuck to it. On Vietnam he accomplished the remarkable feat of not having a position of any kind. He had a plan to end the war, he said, but could not reveal it until after the election. For sheer gall it surpassed all previous political hoaxes. Nixon had no plan, as time showed, but claiming to have one was enough to muffle the issue, though it didn't appeal to those Democrats who knew that a Republican would be freer to end the war than a Democrat. Many remembered that when Eisenhower made peace in Korea, President Truman said that he could have done so on the same basis long before, which was technically true, but politically false. The Democrats then, as in 1968, were the victims of their own policy. They could not end the war on terms good enough to save them from charges of appeasement and being soft on communism. Eisenhower could and did. Nixon could have done the same in Vietnam had he wanted to.

His evasion provided Humphrey with a chance to win some dissidents back, and at Salt Lake City on September 30 Humphrey took it. His concession was not very great, merely a pledge to end the bombing in Vietnam if the communists showed a willingness to restore the Demilitarized Zone. It was the kind of thing that Johnson was forever promising and forever failing to do. But Humphrey had to defy the President to say it, thus showing his independence. And it gave discouraged anti-war Democrats an excuse for endorsing him. McCarthy finally

---

* Agnew really scared many. This made Edmund Muskie, an attractive figure to begin with, look even better. One of the most effective Democratic advertisements was a sign that flashed on TV reading "Spiro Agnew for Vice President," followed by hysterical laughter. Then these words appeared: "This would be serious if it wasn't so funny." Picking Muskie was the smartest thing Humphrey did all year.

came over with his customary enthusiasm. At the end of October he said, "I believe the Vice-President is a man who can be relied upon to tell the difference between the pale horse of death and the white horse of victory. I am not sure Mr. Nixon can make that distinction." It wasn't much, but it was all Humphrey had coming to him. And it was nearly adequate.

On the day before the election Gallup reported that Nixon was only two points ahead of Humphrey. When the balloting was over the distance had narrowed even more. Humphrey got only seven-tenths of 1 per cent less of the popular vote than Nixon. Nixon was elected with the smallest percentage of the vote since Woodrow Wilson won a three-cornered race in 1912. He had a comfortable majority in the electoral college, though, so there was no constitutional crisis. (All the same, George Wallace's 13.5 per cent of the popular vote was very respectable. It was the best showing of any third-party candidate since 1924.) Now Richard Milhous Nixon was President at last. Luck, accident, and his own fantastic resilience had put him in charge. But the country whose leadership he had so painfully acquired was not quite the prize it had once been. Its future was still being squandered in Vietnam. It was more divided than in many years. Inflation and unemployment were rising together. Most kinds of environmental pollution were getting worse. There were hard decisions to be made about all these matters and more. Should work continue on the Supersonic Transport, MIRV, and other projects? And what of the urban crisis, the health crisis, and too many others to mention? It seemed as if no major groups were without grave problems that Washington was supposed to solve. Nixon had won, but what had he won?

PROFILE:
Cesar Chavez

"LA CAUSA" was the happiest cause of all. It began with a grape-pickers' strike in Delano, California, in September 1965. The grape-pickers were among the most deprived and exploited workers in America. Their annual income averaged between $2,000 and $2,300 a year. They were lucky to have work for six months of the year, and enjoyed no job security, fringe benefits, or retirement program. Thanks to the farm lobby in Washington and Sacramento, growers were not required to bargain collectively. The strike, "La Huelga," began with Filipino workers organized by the Agricultural Workers' Organizing Committee of the AFL-CIO. Eight days later they were joined by the Mexican-American National Farm Workers Association led by Cesar Chavez.

Chavez was then forty-one years old. He had begun life as a migratory farm laborer and for ten years worked with Saul Alinsky's Community Services Organization. He absorbed Alinsky's technique of building a local organization from the inside out, which could then work to better local conditions. Chavez left the CSO and moved to Delano to apply these lessons to his own people. Working as a laborer, he had been three years in the field when La Huelga began. His organization was not ready for so big a challenge yet, but Chavez could not stand aside on account of that. Of five thousand vineyard

workers in the Delano area, Chavez had organized three hundred and
AWOC two hundred. That they were not immediately swamped by
strike-breakers was due to outside help. Liberals, youngsters,
clergymen rallied round. The strike rapidly became a civil rights
movement for Mexican-Americans. Six months later ten thousand
people marched to the steps of the state capitol in Sacramento to
support what was no longer merely a strike but a cause, "La Causa,"
as well. The United Auto Workers began contributing $5,000 a month.
In December 1965 the AFL-CIO recognized the Chavez group, now
called the United Farm Workers' Organizing Committee, and merged
the AWOC with it. Union support rose to $10,000 a month. Churches
and other groups contributed also.

In 1966 the UFWO organized a boycott against the principal wine
grape growers, notably the great Schenley and DiGiorgio corporations.
This hurt their business somewhat, and their reputations even more.
They soon negotiated union contracts, and the other major wine grape
growers with them. The table grape growers proved more obstinate.
The Joseph Giumarra Corporation which led them denied Labor
Department studies that showed labor costs amounted to only two to
five cents out of every dollar spent by growers. The growers insisted
on their need for some 350,000 Mexican nationals who had California
work permits. Chavez wanted these so-called "green-carders" sent
home and the immigration laws strictly enforced. As his administrative
assistant, a young minister, put it, "The growers are using the poorest
of the poor of another country to defeat the poorest of the poor in this
country. That's about as low as you can get."

As the fight deepened, "Brown Power" militants became involved.
Chavez was dedicated to nonviolence and protested this development
by a twenty-five-day fast. This permanently injured his health, but it
worked. Nonviolence triumphed, and one March day four thousand
supporters saw Chavez end his fast at an ecumenical mass in a
Delano city park. Senator Robert Kennedy attended, broke bread with
Chavez, and proclaimed him "one of the heroic figures of our time."
Chavez continued to run the strike from his bed. The publicity all this
gained led the UFWO to launch a national boycott against the table
grape industry. Liberal and left-wing volunteers, and union pressure
even more, persuaded the mayors of half a dozen large cities,

including New York, to cancel city purchases of table grapes. The growers hung on even though grape prices began to fall. Many food store chains also stopped carrying table grapes. The growers insisted they were doing almost as well as ever. The Pentagon helped them out with large orders. Then, in the middle of 1969, ten growers producing about 10 per cent of the California grape crop negotiated with the union. Prices for their grapes then went up, as they could be sold anywhere. The Giumarra group expressed continued defiance and pressed ahead with court actions against the strikers. But the next year they gave way too.

It was a victory for which credit was broadly shared. Cesar Chavez and his devoted followers won their freedom despite beatings, arrests, and the usual intimidations. Even better, they did so without resorting to counterviolence. But they could not have prevailed without the unions and the churches. Though the AFL-CIO had a poor track record in the sixties, on this occasion it spent a great deal of money and much effort over a long period to organize workers whose union dues would probably never amount to very much. The California Council of Churches helped too, and agreement was finally reached through the good offices of a team of bishops. Volunteers in many parts of the country picketed stores in support of the boycott. Tens of thousands of consumers went without table grapes for years to make the threat credible. Altogether it was one of the most satisfying labor struggles in American history. And more was to come, for when the grape growers signed, Cesar Chavez turned his eyes toward the lettuce industry. No one really knew what foods he would be asked to give up next. Abstinence was worthwhile. Small sacrifices were the salvation of an entire class. And grapes never tasted so sweet as they did afterward.

12 EPILOGUE: THE REVOLUTION IS OVER

As MANY HAD HOPED and a few had feared, Richard Nixon's election meant some lessening of the national frenzy. Polarization did not abate. There were more campus outrages in 1969 than in 1968. Yet the temper of public life seemed to ease a little. To a measure this was because the war in Vietnam diminished, partly because of presidential cleverness, and partly because everyone was exhausted from the turbulence of 1968. Nations, like men, cannot live off their nervous energy indefinitely. Times of great tension and stress give way to calmer periods. Change does not stop even though men tire of it, yet the forms it takes alter. People can bear to address profound—therefore stormy and divisive—problems for only so long. When that time is up, regardless of what has been accomplished, private matters reassert their authority. Sometimes the corner is turned in a single year. 1919 was one such year. 1969 seemed another.

The decline of politics may have been inevitable, but the shape and pace it took were strongly influenced by Nixon's presidency. Both he and the country were fortunate in the timing that brought him to power. Had he been elected President in 1960 the consequences might have been ghastly. He was then, though an experienced politician, still a provincial in the world of affairs. His emotions were not yet under control (as his farewell address to reporters after the 1962 California gubernatorial election showed). He was still a witch-hunter at heart. His judgment was faulty, yet he insisted on making decisions, agonizing all the while and trusting no one to execute them. Had he presided over the decade, things would no doubt have been even worse than they were. Luckily, Nixon had learned a lot in exile. Just how much was soon evident.

He made much during the campaign of his unifying potential. "Bring us together again" was a plea he promised to answer. But he was not so foolish as to believe that the warring elements in American life could actually be reconciled. The John Birch Society was not going to join hands with SDS. The peace-movement lamb was not about to lie down with the military-industrial-complex lion. What he could do, however, was buy off the right while undercutting the left. His cabinet appointments foreshadowed this strategy. For liberals there were Robert Finch at Health, Education and Welfare, George Romney at Housing and Urban Development, and, perhaps, William P. Rogers at State. Conservatives got Melvin Laird at Defense and John Mitchell at Justice. Some members, like Walter Hickel of Interior, were hard to place. He was in oil among other things, and as governor of Alaska had managed to hide his passion for the environment. But as time was to show, he was a man of the center. Indeed, that was what almost all of them became, whatever they had once been. Melvin Laird, for example, as a member of the House Armed Services Committee was a ferocious hawk and put his name to an exceptionally bloody-minded book on strategy. But once in office he became a typical Secretary of Defense, and less bellicose than many. John Mitchell, as his wife's candid disclosures made evident, belonged to the radical right in theory. But in practice he ran the Department of Justice much as earlier Republicans had. Before the year was up it was obvious that President Nixon got from each department exactly what he wanted. What he wanted for the most part was a slightly right-of-center program.

Not that it lacked imagination. Nixon proclaimed that his would be a reforming administration. What he meant by this was that it would be, Agnew and other throwbacks notwithstanding, a technocratic one. The government's enthusiasm for civil rights and moral principles (this last always more apparent than real in previous administrations) declined. Its interest in problem-solving did not. And given the fact that President Nixon owed so little to the blacks and the ethnics and labor unions and such, he had more freedom to experiment. The first consequence of this was a set of welfare proposals more radical and sweeping than any offered before. He proposed that the federal government take over much of the welfare burden from the states and establish an income floor below which no family would be allowed to sink. The minimums were inadequate, but the main thing was to get the principle of federally maintained uniformity established. Once done, the standards of support could always be raised. It was not so ingenious a program as the negative income tax proposed by conservative economist Milton Friedman, but it was daring enough in its own right to undermine the liberal will to resist. Nixon proposed also to reform the Post Office by taking it out of politics. His Postmaster General, Winton M. Blount, president of the National Chamber of Commerce, was chosen specifically for this mission.

Events quickly demonstrated that President Nixon did not want a government of reconciliation. Vice-President Agnew went out of his way to alienate the left and the peace movement. In one speech he characterized the peace forces as "effete snobs." In another he seemed to threaten television networks with censorship if they didn't treat the administration better. The Justice Department helped local police forces in their campaign to destroy the Black Panthers. Nor did the President leave all his dirty work to Agnew and Mitchell. He went to an obscure college in the Midwest to condemn student protesters. In his televised addresses on Vietnam he attributed various base motives to the anti-war movement. As a candidate he had shown his contempt for Cesar Chavez and the grape strikers by eating grapes in public. As President he had the Defense Department purchase vast quantities of non-union grapes.

The main thrust of the President's grand strategy was directed at Middle America, "the silent majority," as he called it. Middle America was worried most of all about crime, inflation, pollution, civil unrest, and the war—not necessarily in that order. Nixon moved vigorously to meet each of those concerns. Anti-crime bills were introduced. The war was scaled down. Protesters were indicted. Tight money and a balanced budget were supposed to curb inflation. Prices went up anyway, so did unemployment. The GNP leveled off. Many feared it would soon decline.

He was most resourceful when it came to pollution, and not only pollution but the whole "quality of life" question that bothered Middle America. For perhaps a majority of Americans the affluent sixties had been disappointing. Thanks to the long boom, real incomes went up (until the war brought inflation and income stagnation in its train), but life did not seem all that better. More people could go to national parks, which became more overcrowded. The freeway system spanned the country, enabling people to travel in ease and comfort from one congested point to another. Airline facilities nearly collapsed under the awful strain, soon to be made worse by jumbo jets. Railroad passenger service decayed. The air and the water got fouler. Adequate housing, even for the middle class, got scarcer. By 1969 old housing was deteriorating faster than new housing could be built. The Nixon administration attacked these problems in several ways. HUD organized "Operation Breakthrough" to solve the housing problem.* It aimed to subsidize experiments in home-building so as to put it on a mass-production basis. Late in the year President Nixon announced a long-range program (very long range as little money was involved) to deal with air and water pollution. In a dramatic gesture the Florida Everglades, threatened with destruction by a proposed international jetport, were saved.

Of course the usual payoffs continued. To please Southerners the government tried to delay school desegregation, though the courts stopped that soon enough. The ABM, greatest defense pork barrel in history, went forward. So did the SST. This last was an especially mad scheme. The supersonic transport was to be bigger and faster than the Anglo-French and Russian models so as to save the country's honor. It would cost untold billions, pollute the air on a monstrous scale, and drag a fifty-mile-wide sonic boom across the ground behind it.

Despite these and other iniquities, at the end of its first year the Nixon presidency was a genuine success. Elected by a minority of the voters, faced with a Democratic majority in both Houses of Congress, the administration still managed to get most of what it wanted. And it generated enough original programs to unman the liberal opposition. Its most disgraceful enterprises—the SST and the ABM, for example—were holdovers from the Democratic era. Its best ideas were its own. Of course, there was always its bad taste to fault. Tastelessness was one of the things that liberals disliked most about Richard Nixon. People remembered his bathetic Checkers speech in 1952, and his criticism of Harry Truman's salty language in 1960. Eating grapes showed a want of feeling in 1968. And his appeal to the GOP after his nomination to "win this one for Ike" as the former President lay dying was really too much. His speeches remained dreary and predictable. He always prefaced his most obscure remarks by saying, "Let me make this perfectly clear . . ." Every time he made a decision he always explained that doing the opposite would have been easy and popular, especially when he was making an easy and popular decision. On his trip to Europe after being inaugurated, he left no national stereotype uninvoked. In Britain he expressed his affection for the English "sense of history." In Germany he spoke favorably of the "economic miracle." In France he praised General de Gaulle's greatness. All this was inexcusable, except by comparison with his predecessor.

---

* Congress had passed the Housing and Urban Development Act in 1968 to deal with the crisis. It called for building or rehabilitating 26 million housing units in the next decade. By 1969 it was already clear this couldn't be done. Six million of the 26 million units would have to be subsidized for low-income groups; this was ten times the number subsidized in the previous decade. The rate of housing starts would have to be twice as great as in the previous decade. Yet because of the economic sag there were fewer housing starts in 1969 than in 1968.

399

On the other hand, the President had smoothed off many of his old rough edges. More even-tempered and affable, as well he might be, he executed his new duties with ease, and sometimes even wit. Shortly after the election his wife was asked who would be invited to their purely social affairs in the White House. She replied that it would be mainly their old friends, "none of your so-called big shots." Mr. Nixon quickly added: "Just for the record, all our friends are big shots." He bought lovely homes in Florida and California. He met guests and hosted functions with some gusto. And while no one accused him of being a lazy President (as Eisenhower had been thought to be), he perhaps had more fun than ever in his life. It was hard to begrudge him the pleasure. Most Presidents leave office on a dimmer note than they take it with. History would, no doubt, be as hard on President Nixon as on his predecessors. But in the first year it was all wine and roses at the White House. The Executive's gaiety contrasted with the rest of the country. People still worried about war, inflation, and the rest. Liberals suffered withdrawal pains. The long Kennedy-Johnson binge was over. What would come after was still unclear.

The great test of Nixon's presidency would be the war, and though it went on most Americans came to think of it in the past tense. This was his greatest achievement in 1969. Nixon promised to withdraw American troops whatever happened in Paris. Some did leave. The fighting was scaled down. Casualties declined. All that remained, it seemed, was to proclaim victory and try the war criminals. The first was delayed when the enemy obstinately refused to admit defeat. The trials were held anyway. What made them remarkable was that the criminals in question were American. After World War II only enemy war criminals had been tried. Now for the first time the U.S. confessed, to a degree, its own sins. This was a novel break with tradition and difficult to explain. Americans had committed atrocities before and gone unpunished. Vietnam was the scene of many such. The indiscriminate destruction of villages by aerial and artillery fire was commonplace. Perhaps 300,000 civilians had been killed that way since 1965. No one was ever punished for their deaths. But the slaying of a few hundred Vietnamese at Pinkville seemed different.

Pinkville (as the troops called it) was actually the village of My Lai. On March 18, 1968, an infantry company was helicoptered in to destroy hamlets for harboring Viet Cong. This was done all the time in Vietnam. But instead of evacuating the population first, or wiping it out at long range with big guns and planes, the troops eliminated it by hand. Nothing came of the massacre for a time. But about a year later a discharged American soldier who had heard rumors of the event wrote letters to government officials telling what he knew. They demanded answers.

What the Army turned up in consequence was so damning that charges were brought against a number of men. Though many legal points were still to be settled, the main facts seemed clear enough. C Company had suffered many losses, especially from mines thought to be emplaced by Vietnamese civilians. In a guerrilla war it was hard to make distinctions between civilians and combatants anyway. Women supported the Viet Cong and sometimes fought with them. Children could throw grenades and plant mines, it was said. Infants would grow up to become soldiers. The official policy of random bombardment hardly inspired respect for the lives of civilians, especially in combat zones. So out of rage, fear, and prejudice, C Company killed five or six hundred people.

As massacres go in the modern world, it was a small thing. Half a million were slain in Indonesia when Sukarno fell. Few Americans protested that. No one knew how many had died in Africa during the repeated slaughters that followed independence there. They too were unmourned in the U.S. And, of course, Indochina was deliberately ravaged by fire, the sword, and chemical poisons. But it was not yet government policy to murder civilians by hand, so C Company had definitely overreached itself. What followed the Army investigation was even more strange than the massacre itself. Some Americans denied the facts, though participants attested to them. Ex-Private Meadlo, who admitted killing many, described it on national television. Sergeant Michael Bernhardt, the only soldier who refused to fire his weapon during the half-hour of slaughter, was equally candid. (Others, to their credit, had only pretended to fire at people. One apparently shot himself in the foot so as to escape involvement.) The Army itself showed an uneasy conscience, giving the Distinguished Flying Cross to Warrant Officer Hugh C. Thompson, a helicopter pilot, for saving sixteen hamlet children. This may have been the first time that an American soldier was honored for gallantry in action against his fellows, as he was said to have trained his ship's guns on the crazed troops to make them give way.

Most Americans reacted like good Germans to the news. When the *New York Times* sent a reporter to Meadlo's home town, he found general support for the garrulous ex-soldier. "He had to obey orders," was the common response. The only thing they blamed him for was confessing on TV. It was just one of those things that happen in war, nearly everyone agreed. The principal exception was Meadlo's own father, a sixty-seven-year-old former miner. "If it had been me," he said, "I would have swung my rifle around and shot [Lieutenant] Calley instead— right between the God-damned eyes." But otherwise, what Americans used to think of as the instinctive morality of an individualistic people was notably lacking. Meadlo himself was embittered at not getting paid for his TV interview. He had done it out of guilt, but discovering too late that remorse wasn't marketable depressed his spirits. "I ain't talking to nobody now unless they pay," he muttered later in a sullen parody of Milo Minderbinder.* As went New Goshen, Indiana, so went the country. *Time* magazine commissioned the pollster Louis Harris to find what people thought of the incident. Most were sympathetic to the accused men. Most blamed the media for reporting it. Few found the massacre upsetting.

Perhaps most surprising of all was Sergeant Bernhardt's response. He protested when it happened. Earlier he had saved the life of an interpreter who reported three other soldiers for raping a Vietnamese girl. The American tendency to regard the natives as subhuman "gooks, slants, or slopes" bothered him too. It was on account of this that he testified, even though most of his comrades criticized him. Bernhardt saw the atrocities as exceptional events. Yet even if they were routine, he said, he would go on supporting the war. He favored President Nixon over any possible peace candidate. This is not to blame Bernhardt. He had kept his moral sense in the most desperate circumstances. No one expects serving soldiers to deny the value of what they do. For them to reject the war was to say that their own sweat and blood, and the lives of their friends, were all shed in vain. Few men can bring themselves to admit such waste, whatever logic might demand.

The American reluctance to condemn My Lai was not entirely without merit. As Milton Mayer pointed out, "When our agents land on the moon, it is 'we' who did it, but when they kill villagers it is 'they.'" Wars brutalize, colonial wars most of all. When ordinary American boys were given guns and sent to kill an enemy indistinguishable from the people he moved among, who could be surprised that many came to think of the people as the enemy? Massacres are never excusable, but the final responsibility belonged to those who committed men to such dubious battle. It was unbecoming of officials who authorized mass murder by bombardment to flinch at a comparative handful of executions. Governors are responsible for the outcome of their policies, especially when they lead to devastation and death. Nuremburg established that it is a crime to obey criminal orders. Those who execute them must pay the penalty. But those who presided over the war were criminals too, even though none of them would ever be tried.

What made the American response to Pinkville so disappointing was

---

* Another echo of *Catch-22* was that American combat soldiers in Vietnam, known as "grunts," could choose between serving their one year in the field, where the odds of being hit were high, or re-enlisting, which meant being sent back to the States, retrained, and then returned to Vietnam in a safe job. As between two years in the Army with the risk of death, and five years with the certainty of life, it's not surprising that many did re-enlist—especially after bad patrols when the re-enlistment officers descended hungrily on them.

just this failure to admit responsibility. Russell Baker saw the excuses—"war is hell," "an isolated incident," "look at the behavior of other countries in the same circumstances"—as proof that nations like people live by their illusions. A belief in one's moral excellence was chief among them. Its leaders blocked the effort to induce mass guilt in Germany after World War II. The Nixon administration was quick to reassure Middle America in the same way. "Messrs. Nixon and Agnew are telling us not to believe such things. They are telling us to go ahead believing we are just as excellent as we have always believed we are. Good people, decent people whose society is under attack by a bumptious minority and whose essential goodness is not being celebrated by the organs of information." The strategy worked. But no one would ever again be able to dwell on the unique moral defects of the German people. One could only hope that Baker was right to say, "In the long run we are likely to want, not only rhetoric, but also deeds that assert our national decency with such firmness that we no longer have to write letters to ourselves about our excellence."

The search for peace went badly too. Mainly this was because the U.S. government still backed Saigon. When Averell Harriman returned from Paris after Nixon's inaugural, he made that clear enough. He stumped the country saying de-escalation leading to a cease-fire was essential. Peace would require a coalition government including the NLF. Everyone knew that the Saigon regime could not survive a reasonable settlement. Only military victory would keep so corrupt and despised a clique in power. That failing, perpetual war was its best hope. Saigon tried to sabotage the talks at first by not participating. Little progress was made once it did give way. Harriman thought that was because President Johnson did not reduce the fighting. When the bombing halt was announced, Hanoi started pulling its troops out of South Vietnam. The American military responded by shifting combat operations. When the enemy moved out of the I Corps area in the North, the First Cavalry was sent elsewhere for offensive operations. Search-and-destroy missions increased, so did B-52 raids. A valuable chance to scale down the fighting was thrown away. President Johnson disdained a peace on the only terms then available.

There was reason to think President Nixon might take a different line. Though previously a hawk, he was not bound to the war like Johnson. He could end it if he chose. During the campaign he claimed to have a secret plan to that effect. More encouraging was his appointment of

Henry Kissinger as presidential assistant on national-security affairs. Kissinger was a Cold War strategist and former hawk. But just before taking office he published an article in *Foreign Affairs* calling for an evacuation of American forces from Vietnam and a negotiated settlement between Saigon and the NLF. One widely quoted passage was especially lucid: "The North Vietnamese and Vietcong, fighting in their own country, needed merely to keep in being forces sufficiently strong to dominate the population after the United States tired of the war. We fought a military war; our opponents fought a political one. We sought physical attrition; our opponents aimed for our psychological exhaustion. In the process we lost sight of one of the cardinal maxims of guerrilla war: the guerrilla wins if he does not lose. The conventional army loses if it does not win." He seemed to be saying that having lost the war it remained only for the U.S. to surrender as advantageously as possible. The appointment of Ambassador Lodge to replace Harriman in Paris was encouraging too. He had been a hawk, but not a foolish one. He once told reporters in Paris, "Of course I'm on the record as saying there could never be a negotiated settlement, but I'm also on the record as saying there never could be a military victory." Whatever this delphic formula meant, it did not seem to preclude reasonable adjustments.

Yet, as so often before, hope soon withered. Nixon never did unveil his secret peace plan. Instead he chose "Vietnamization." This meant beefing up the ARVN so it could do most of the fighting. American infantry would be withdrawn. The Air Force and other specialized units would remain—perhaps a quarter of a million men all told. Vietnamization was "irreversible," the administration declared. It was also imperceptible at first. Some troops came home, but American strength was still well over 400,000 a year later. Casualties declined, so did costs. The level of combat was reduced. By the end of 1969 most critics assumed that Vietnamization meant a continued U.S. involvement. Instead of ending the war, President Nixon meant to wage it on the cheap. When, shortly before his death, President Ho Chi Minh answered an American letter, Nixon read his reply on TV to show how stubborn Hanoi was. Yet Harriman thought it a soft and encouraging response. So did Jean Sainteny, a Frenchman who had facilitated the exchange of letters. Given the President's uncompromising attitude, the Paris talks languished. Ambassador Lodge resigned in despair. Loyal to the last, he blamed Hanoi. This did not disguise the fact that the U.S. had made no concessions to match the other side's.

In the short run Vietnamization was a great success. The war was less expensive in lives and dollars. President Nixon changed the draft, though in such a devious way that no one could be sure exactly what the new lottery's effect was. All the same, it sharply reduced middle-class anxiety.

His promise to create an all-volunteer Army some day was even more reassuring. Opposition to the war continued, but it lacked focus. In the fall of 1969 giant peace rallies were organized. On October 15 millions of people responded to the New Mobilization Committee's call for a Vietnam Moratorium. A hundred thousand people gathered on Boston Common in support of it. New York City had a whole series of rallies. Senator McCarthy and Mayor Lindsay spoke at one. Wall Street had another. A third was organized by people in the publishing industry. In hundreds of smaller places the pattern was repeated. It was the greatest organized expression of pacific sentiment in American history. A month later the New Mobe focused on Washington, D.C., where from a quarter to half a million people gathered for a second moratorium and a "March Against Death." It was the largest demonstration of any sort ever held in Washington.

None of this had the slightest effect. While the March Against Death moved past the White House, President Nixon watched football on TV. Vice-President Agnew went around the country denouncing anti-war supporters as "effete snobs," "supercilious sophisticates," and worse. In Agnew the silent majority found its voice. The more he abused blacks, intellectuals, and the young, the more popular he became. Soon he was the GOP's best fund-raiser and a threat to George Wallace's popularity in the South. "Spiro Is Our Hero" read the signs welcoming him. "Agnew in 76" became a real possibility. Heartened by this display of support, Nixon continued to Vietnamize the war. By March 130,000 tons of bombs a month were being dropped—the greatest aerial bombardment in history. Laos, where the communists were moving again, was Laotianized. (In 1970 Cambodia would be Cambodianized.) At the year's end 12,500 sorties a month were flown against the Pathet Lao and DRVN regulars. General Westmoreland hatched schemes for an automated battlefield with computers, electronic sensors, and other gimmicks that would largely eliminate U.S. casualties while destroying all human and animal life. An area the size of Massachusetts was defoliated. As always, chemical warfare was said to be temporary. But as the poisons moved through the chain of life they concentrated, so no one knew what their ultimate effects would be. Government advisers called the process by which the peasants were eliminated "urbanization." Some were killed, others were relocated in refugee camps and the larger cities. One day, it was hoped, no one would be left in the country but Viet Cong, who could then be exterminated at will. Science, technology, and Vietnamization combined to make such a vision possible.

Vietnamization did not make the war less surrealistic. On the highest level an air of strenuous unreality prevailed. One staff officer summed up life in Army headquarters thusly: "Often it reminded me of the caucus race in 'Alice in Wonderland.' Everyone runs in circles, no one really gets anywhere, and when the race is over, everybody gets a medal." Indeed, the worse things got, the more promotions were handed out. General Westmoreland was made Army Chief of Staff after the Tet offensive. Self-deception could go no further. Under his successor the reality principle appeared now and then. B-52 raids were notoriously ineffective in Westmoreland's day. As one civilian adviser described them, "It was like Orvieto in 'Catch-22.' They missed the target, but had a great bombing pattern." In 1969 the air raids were often targeted in flight and sometimes managed to catch the VC. As a weapon of war they still remained pretty clumsy, like shooting ducks with a howitzer, but as a terror device they had some value. They also contributed to the high cost of dying in Vietnam since B-52 raids were expensive when mounted against lightly populated jungle areas. Their "cost effectiveness" must have been sensationally bad.

General Creighton Abrams, Westmoreland's replacement, managed to get away from the airborne mystique to a degree. Vietnam was partly a consequence of the infatuation with leaping from airplanes so noticeable among Taylor, Westmoreland, and their like. Guerrilla warfare was thought to be especially suited to airborne troops. Abrams belonged to a group known as the "Old Scruffies," who thought battles were won by infantrymen and that leaping out of aircraft was puerile. He also was more critical of atrocities. Counterinsurgency warfare as practiced by airborne and Green Beret units encouraged torture and such. Being old-fashioned, Abrams thought that despicable. He tried to get Green Berets who had murdered a double agent court-martialed. And he was determined to prosecute more homely slayings as well. It was uphill work. Washington didn't like bad publicity. Vietnam attracted the most bloodthirsty professional soldiers—Colonel George S. Patton III, for example. One Christmas, until Abrams made him stop, he sent out greeting cards inscribed "Peace on Earth" and decorated with color photographs of dismembered VC corpses. At his farewell party on leaving Vietnam, Patton wore a peace symbol around his neck and carried the polished skull of a Viet Cong with a bullet hole above its eye socket. Ghoulish humor was peculiar to Patton; the pathology it reflected was not.

Vietnamization was even more trying. General Abrams knew the ARVN was a mess, though everyone denied it. Of an American adviser to one ARVN division, Abrams said, "I know all I can expect from that guy is good news. That guy has been lying to me for two years." But the truth was so dispiriting, and so contrary to official dogma, that it was hard for any soldier to face. A year of Vietnamization expanded the local military without improving it. A million South Vietnamese were under arms compared with perhaps 200,000 VC and DRVN troops. But no one doubted that without U.S. help they would be quickly overrun. The militia units (called Regional and Popular Forces, or Ruff-Puffs) got little support and were inclined to make deals with the VC by which each left the other alone. The ARVN had an annual desertion rate of perhaps 25 per cent. And little wonder. The troops got paid about $20 a month and were hardly ever furloughed. When they died their families got a year's pay, if they bribed the right person. They were trained by men who had never seen combat (since training assignments were much sought after, they naturally went to those with the best connections). Their officers were upper-class profiteers motivated by bribery, favoritism, and politics. The function of the army was to enrich its leaders and keep the Saigon clique in power. Fighting the VC was a distinctly secondary mission. A rather typical case concerned the ARVN's 25th Division. It was thought to be the worst military unit in Vietnam, and probably in the world. The U.S. military finally got its commanding general relieved. He was then put in command of the vital III Corps area north of Saigon.

The more things changed, the more they remained the same. Vietnamization was a fraud because to reform the ARVN would take a revolution of sorts. But the whole reason for American intervention was to prevent one. President Johnson had proved the war could not be won. President Nixon meant to show that it could be waged indefinitely if the price was right. The ARVN would be better equipped. Mercenaries would be used where possible. Critics complained that it cost a billion dollars a year to support the Thai division in Vietnam. President Nixon answered that it was money well spent to keep American boys out of combat. Other "Allied" troops, except the Australians, were maintained in the same lavish way. Even so, they cost less than American troops, and their deaths caused no stir at home. How long would Vietnamization remain an acceptable substitute for peace? In 1969 Nixon had it all his own way. Yet that was how it always went when new strategies were employed in Vietnam. Johnson was applauded when he escalated in 1965, and when he seemed to de-escalate in 1968. But fresh hope soon went stale when new policies brought the same old results.

President Nixon's Vietnamization strategy depended on everything but American troop levels remaining constant. Yet Vietnam was inherently unstable. How could fewer troops accomplish what more had failed to do? The Viet Cong might gain strength. General Thieu, whom the junta had placed above Marshal Ky, might lose his grip. In 1969 the regime more and more resembled Diem's administration. Opponents, however moderate, were put in jail. Yet new men rose to take their place, even in the legislature. In December Thieu demanded that his critics in the House be impeached or "the people and the armed forces will cut off these deputies' heads. Our duty is to beat such dogs to death." Months later recalcitrant deputies were still defying him, drumhead courts-martial and long prison sentences notwithstanding. Being built on such fragile pillars, how long could Vietnamization stand? Long enough for Nixon to be re-elected perhaps. Richard Nixon was a clever man. But he had to be lucky too. And the more he replayed his predecessors' hands, the more luck he needed. Of course the lives and money he risked belonged to other people, which was what made the Vietnam gamble attractive to each new President. Best of all, except for Senator Fulbright and a few other effete snobs, no one said they were corrupted by power. They were able to lie at home and butcher abroad in the name of patriotism in the one case, and philanthropy in the other.

One of the main side-effects of the Vietnam War was its tendency to discredit the military-industrial complex as a whole. Peace sentiment cropped up in strange places. Retired officers like former Marine Commandant David Shoup moved from condemning the war to condemning the military system. Serving soldiers, including officers, had to be court-martialed for refusing to support the war. Enlisted men distributed anti-military tracts. Stockade prisoners (in the Presidio and at Fort Dix especially) rebelled. Announcers in the armed forces' own broadcasting network complained of censorship while on the air. The troops in Vietnam smoked pot.

More and more universities made ROTC voluntary, denied academic credit for taking it, or abolished it altogether. Scientists refused to do defense research. Most schools where CBR (chemical, biological, radiological warfare) research was conducted had to phase out their programs. University-operated centers like MIT's Lincoln and Instrumentation labs and the Stanford Applied Electronics Laboratory started getting out of the arms research business that had previously sustained them. By May 1969 the Defense Department had cut its secret or classified research-and-development contracts on campus from four hundred to two hundred. The government had spent billions on CBR research without much complaint. Now the whole program had to be practically abolished. The impetus for this came from a single Congressman at first. Representative Richard D. McCarthy of New York and his family were horrified by a TV documentary on chemical and biological warfare. McCarthy was inspired by it to make inquiries. The first result was that senior members of the House Armed Services Committee insulted him. A younger member said if he didn't stop, the FBI would investigate him. Republican Minority Leader Gerald Ford accused him of favoring unilateral disarmament. The military would not cooperate. This only stiffened his resolution, and he began getting some answers. Though the military claimed CBR research was purely defensive—a matter of finding antidotes to possible weapons—it had stockpiled more than 100 million lethal doses of nerve gas. The State Department claimed to adhere to the 1925 Geneva protocol banning poisonous gases and chemicals (which the U.S. never signed), but gases and chemicals were used in Vietnam that were deadly under certain conditions.

In May 1969 McCarthy exposed a secret plan to ship 27,000 tons of unwanted chemical warfare agents for burial at sea after a cross-country rail trip. 908 freight-car loads were to be sent through major cities. Yet in the previous four years thirty-nine communities had had to be evacuated because of derailments involving toxic chemicals and gases. The railroad accident rate was getting worse. There had been three cases of gas leakage recently. McCarthy finally got the hearings he wanted, and they established that 6,400 sheep were killed by nerve gas near the Dugway proving grounds in Utah the previous March. Surprisingly, given the past record of such exposés, this one did some good. The plan to ship nerve gas from the Rocky Mountain Arsenal was temporarily blocked. More importantly, President Nixon ordered an end to the manufacture of chemical and biological warfare weapons. Much remained to be done; other dangerous chemicals were still routinely used, as McCarthy pointed out. But one of the most ghastly defense programs of modern times was sharply diminished. Without the climate of suspicion and alarm created by the Vietnam War, this could hardly have happened.

The *Pueblo* affair was not directly related to the war. Yet the harm it did was a function of the media's tendency to report anti-military news more intensively than before. The *USS Pueblo*, a Navy spy ship, had been seized by North Korea on January 23, 1968. That made the Navy look bad. Why was it spying on North Korea with electronic gear in the first place? And if it was going to spy, why didn't it protect the ships involved? The Navy looked even worse when, after the crew returned, it launched an investigation designed, so it seemed, to blame the ship for the high command's mistakes. Commander Lloyd M. Bucher had surrendered without a fight on the grounds that, as he was armed with only two machine guns, resistance would have been costly and futile. This did not impress the admirals. Though it was the Navy that had sent an unarmed, unescorted vessel to spy on North Korea, and had failed to respond to its call for help, only Bucher and the ship's intelligence officer were censured. Navy investigators wanted them court-martialed. The Secretary of the Navy declined on the grounds they had suffered enough. All the same, their careers were ruined while the men responsible for their disgrace went unrebuked. If Bucher had been like Lords Raglan and Cardigan, and sent his men to certain death as they had Britian's Light Brigade so many years before, he would have been a hero. In a changing world only the military mind remained constant, it seemed.

Still, the military-industrial complex suffered less than might have been expected. Even scaling down the war proved a blessing in disguise. The war generated a certain replacement business for supplies and equipment. But its running expenses blocked the new research-and-development contracts so essential to a healthy economy. President Nixon was alert to the needs of defense contractors and rushed aid to them even before taking office. The TFX was one example. It had been almost the biggest technical mistake of McNamara's reign. Intended as a fighter-bomber for use by all the services, it turned out to benefit none of them. It was so unsuitable for carrier use that the Navy finally was relieved of it. When the Air Force used it against North Vietnam, three of the first six F-111's (as they were now called) were lost in a few weeks. Among their defects was a tendency for the wings to fall off. They had to be recalled from combat, and later, when they kept crashing, grounded altogether. Candidate Nixon had been intensely critical of the F-111's. They were supposed to cost $2.4 million apiece, but when delivered they cost over $6 million, and if the whole contract of seventeen hundred aircraft were completed costs would rise to $9 million each. The total expense would be $15 billion, nearly three times the original estimate. Candidate Nixon also pointed out that the contract went to General Dynamics although the military preferred Boeing. General Dynamics got the contract because it was on the verge of bankruptcy, not because of its brilliant record. Being located in Texas which had twenty-five electoral votes helped too. Despite all this, on November 2, 1968, in a last-minute bid for Texas votes, Richard Nixon ignored his own staff reports and said that the F-111 would continue to be one of the "foundations of our air supremacy." As I. F. Stone put it, the lesson was that "any major new plane must show it can fly successfully through the electoral college."

There were three things wrong with the F-111. It ought not to have been assigned initially to both the Air Force and Navy. The contract should not have gone to General Dynamics. And it shouldn't have been built at all. One justification for it was that as the Soviets were building an advanced supersonic bomber, the U.S. needed one too. But in fact Russia never did build one, the ICBM having made strategic bombers obsolete. The Navy version was designed to protect the fleet against this same nonexistent threat. The hope was, apparently, that if the Navy built a defense the Soviets would feel obliged to come up with the threat it was meant to avert. Alas, they didn't. When Senator Stuart Symington, former Air Force Secretary, pointed this out, the military replied that building a defense against a threat that didn't exist insured that the Soviets would never bother creating the threat. Or, if they did, they would waste a lot of money, which was a good thing as they had less of it than the U.S.

The F-111 was bad enough, but this line of reasoning promised that worse was to come. The Air Force still wanted the ultimate bomber, called the Advanced Manned Strategic Bomber. It would be as pointless as the F-111 and would cost even more—$24 billion, Senator Proxmire thought. And to prevent nonexistent Soviet bombers from sneaking in under U.S. radar the Air Force wanted a new over-the-horizon warning system called AWACS. As of 1969, $18 billion had been spent for SAGE (AWACS's predecessor) and AWACS to avert this nonthreat. And AWACS had only just begun. It would cost $15 billion or so when completed. The Navy was getting a new torpedo, originally budgeted at $680 million, that would cost more than $4 billion on delivery. Then there were the new fighter planes. The Navy's F-14 would cost a billion dollars in 1970, $36 billion when fully deployed. The Air Force's F-15 would cost $25 billion all told.

Nor should the unforgettable C5A be omitted. It was a giant transport plane that was supposed to cost $3 billion or so. This was small beer indeed, even when cost overruns pushed its estimated cost up to $5 billion or more in 1969. What gave the C5A its special interest were congressional hearings that exposed how the contract was handled. Senator Proxmire, who was a bulldog on military cost overruns, investigated the C5A and was told by A. Ernest Fitzgerald, a Pentagon efficiency expert, that it would cost several billion more than planned. This so piqued the Pentagon that Fitzgerald was taken off weapons systems and assigned to study bowling alleys in Thailand. Even so, he apparently remained a menace, so his job was eliminated for, as the Pentagon unblushingly explained, reasons of economy. But more was to come. An Air Force colonel testifying before the House Government Operations Committee admitted that his civilian superiors had approved the doctoring of Air Force documents to hide the C5A overruns. This was done to avoid putting Lockheed Aircraft's common stock in jeopardy, he explained. But later testimony showed this was in error too. When the appropriate memos were put in evidence, it turned out that Air Force generals had actually fed false data to Pentagon officials. Apart from Fitzgerald losing his job, there were two consequences of this affair. The first C5A to be put in service was defective and had to be grounded. And the Defense Department stopped talking about cost overruns. They were now described as "cost growths."

Yet these tawdry scandals were mere peccadillos. All they involved was bribery, deception, corruption, vilification, the looting of the public purse, and perhaps manslaughter. (A lot of men died from the defective products of these contracts, some of them foreigners. The German Air Force lost entire squadrons of American-built F-104's that crashed on routine flights.) The Budget Bureau issued a report in January 1969 that showed what the government got for its money from the aerospace industry. The study covered thirteen major aircraft and missile programs since 1955. They cost a total of $40 billion. Only four of them, costing $5 billion, could be relied on to perform at more than 75 per cent of specifications, and "less than 40 per cent of the effort produced systems with acceptable electronic performance." Yet the contractors profited hugely from these defective systems. North American earned profits of 40 per cent above the industry average. Its score on six military programs was one success, one cancellation, and four that broke down four times as frequently as promised. General Dynamics made more than the industry average though none of its seven weapons systems performed as specified. Secretary of Defense Laird disparaged the Budget Bureau report as only a "graduate thesis." Later he called Bernard D. Nossiter, the enterprising *Washington Post* reporter who excelled at these disclosures, and warned him that publishing the data might weaken U.S. negotiators in arms talks. As well it might, especially since the armaments industry seemed much more of a threat to American security than to Russia's.

A greater threat to national security was the strategic missile race. Other weapons systems could only bankrupt the country; ABM and MIRV might destroy it. The anti-ballistic missile system had an especially curious history. From the outset it promised to be expensive and ineffective. Even if it worked, which was doubtful, it might lead Russia to fear a U.S. first strike. Hence it was either another defense pork barrel or a menace to national survival, or both. Enthusiasm for it persisted anyway. In America the mere possibility of a new weapons system was enough to win it partisans. Each one promised so much money that matters of utility became almost irrelevant. In the case of ABM, the first reason for having it was that it could be built. The second reason was that the Army was being edged out of the missile business and ABM would put it back in contention. ABM technology was so frail and costly that President Eisenhower had vetoed the first scheme. Improvements did nothing to commend the ABM to Secretary McNamara either. The Joint Chiefs finally persuaded President Johnson to accept it. McNamara had to give way though he feared it would cost $40 billion or so, might not work, and could provoke the Russians. He announced his acceptance of it in a speech condemning the arms race.

Sentinel, as the Johnson system was called, would supposedly protect twenty-five (later fourteen) cities. This was hardly enough to deter

Russia, so it was billed simultaneously as a reprisal against Russia for installing an incomplete ABM system (called Galoosh) and as a protection against a small attack by China. Of course China didn't have ICBM's yet, but some day it might. Anyway, the Joint Chiefs insisted, Sentinel was so thin that it would not provoke Russia. ABM critics pointed out that Galoosh had certainly provoked the Joint Chiefs, though only two Russian cities were involved. How much more provocative might Sentinel be? And it was hard to imagine China attacking the U.S. even if it did get ICBM's, since the U.S. could still destroy it many times over. The Senate quarreled about it for a time. Russia's invasion of Czechoslovakia finally turned the tide. If Sentinel was supposed to deter China, there was not much point in building it to get revenge against Russia, but that was how the arms game was played. More complications developed when communities began objecting to having nuclear armed missiles located near them.

That was the situation when President Nixon took office. Careful politician that he was, Nixon canceled Sentinel. Instead he proposed a new system, Safeguard, that would protect ICBM installations. It would cost a little more money at first ($7 billion as against $5.5 billion for Sentinel) and a lot more later if it was fully deployed. As no one expected that China would ever have enough missiles to attack American ICBM sites, the ABM was now once more to be directed against Russia. At this point ABM was more obviously a weapons system in search of a mission than even the F-111. But by main force President Nixon got it through the Senate with a one-vote margin. Thus a potentially unlimited new drain on the public purse was created at a time when civilian programs were being slashed to combat inflation.

MIRV was a more straightforward technical matter. No one knew if ABM would work. There was little doubt that Multiple Independently Targeted Re-entry Vehicles were perfectable. By enabling a missile in flight to launch many warheads, it would enlarge the American strategic missile force by perhaps a factor of ten. That would be more than enough to smash through Galoosh. Even better, the relation of cost to effective striking power made MIRV a comparatively cheap weapons system. But as always, there were drawbacks. Multiplying the U.S. strategic capacity raised the first-strike question again. To counter it the Soviets would have to MIRV their own missiles. This meant another great escalation in the arms race, and a further expansion of ABM if it was to be taken seriously by anyone. Worse still, MIRV missiles would be impossible to monitor, making arms-control agreements less likely. Missile sites could be detected by spy satellites and such. But no spy system could tell how many warheads a missile carried. The U.S. and the USSR went ahead with plans for Strategic Arms Limitation (SALT) conferences. They also proceeded to develop MIRV's. Once done it was scarcely plausible that MIRV could be undone. The best to be hoped for was a new balance of terror on a vastly larger scale.

The world had survived earlier escalations, but this one was different. It blurred the distinction between first- and second-strike systems. While no one was entirely sure of the difference before, strategists on both sides at least believed they knew one from the other, and that in building them countries were sending signals. With MIRV, signaling could no longer be done that way. Worse still, MIRV came along just when the Soviets were achieving parity in strategic weapons.* The balance of terror worked partly because the U.S. always had a clear edge. This vital margin made the otherwise dangerous ideas of strategists irrelevant. Now they had become real menaces, because in urging the deployment of ABM and MIRV they threatened the psychological status quo. The U.S. could not afford to act as if parity didn't exist. And it couldn't afford to try and regain its old lead. The Nixon administration spoke of maintaining a "sufficiency" of nuclear weapons. No one, least of all the Soviets, knew what that meant. On the other hand, parity offered the first real opportunity for strategic arms limitations, as neither side had to bargain from weakness. That was what made SALT so vital. If that chance were lost, who could say when another would come again? As of 1969 the government was going both ways at once. SALT moved forward, so did MIRV. Since they were mutually incompatible, one would have to be sacrificed. Past experience did not suggest that it would be MIRV.

Still, the arms situation was not entirely hopeless. Rising costs and disenchantment with the military produced the first real Senate debate on armaments in memory. Where before the Senate had sometimes passed major arms bills in a single day, it took eight weeks to get a $20 billion arms bill through late in 1969. Chairman Stennis of the Armed Services Committee was on his feet for thirty-eight days. Critics reduced the bill by only $71 million (most of it intended for Pentagon "social research"). But the glove was thrown down in earnest for a change. Anti-military boldness went much further than before in other ways. Some critics even questioned the Navy's carrier program. Attack

---

* Actually, the Soviets did not enjoy real equality with the U.S., despite having about the same number of ICBM's. Total U.S. striking power from all sources was much greater (4,200 to 1,350), and American missiles were more advanced. Russia depended on liquid-fuel missiles while the U.S. had shifted mainly to faster-firing and less vulnerable solid-fuel missiles, many of them with multiple warheads. The U.S. was also ahead on MIRV. Russia was still developing Multiple Re-entry Vehicles (MRV), which could not be aimed at separate targets like MIRV. Thus Russia was substantially behind the U.S. in every respect, but it did have a "sufficiency" of ICBM's. It could deter an American first strike, at least until MIRV became fully operational.

carriers took up 40 per cent of the naval budget, yet they were an obsolete weapon. Like the B-52, they could only be used against primitive countries. Even so, they were very costly in men and money. The accident rate for carrier launchings was much higher than in land-based operations. The price per sortie was higher too. It was hardly surprising that the Soviets had no attack carriers. Compared with missile cruisers, nuclear submarines, and other advanced weapons, they were a poor buy. But the admirals were mad for them, as they had been for battleships earlier.

Arms makers got some nasty shocks too. Apart from the slings and arrows of outrageous Congressmen, they were faced with John Kenneth Galbraith's plan for nationalization. This prominent liberal economist argued that as business risks were already socialized, profits should be too. The biggest contractors often used plants owned by the government. The government helpfully provided them with operating capital in the form of progress payments. It rarely asked for competitive bids. When it did, firms were compensated for underbidding in various ways. Arms making was consequently not free enterprise but rather welfare for the rich. Nationalizing these companies would end that anomaly. It would save money and eliminate much lobbying. Given the companies' frightful performance records, it might also lead to a better product. The old government manufacturing arsenals were as efficient as most private concerns. And they were cheaper to operate. In the age of Nixon no one believed that the corporate welfare system could be reformed. But the proposal was, perhaps, a firebell in the night.

One result of these attacks was that the government became more devious about military spending. The Nixon administration's first original (as against inherited) budget gave no figures for Vietnam at all. On the one hand, it was implied, the war's cost depended on what the other side did and thus couldn't be estimated. On the other hand, it seemed, there was a project which had to be kept secret for fear of tipping the President's hand. It was certainly necessary to keep his critics guessing. Then there was the disappearing "peace dividend." At first the government insisted that as the war ebbed money would be released for domestic use. Secretary Laird mentioned a saving of $13 billion at one point. But when the 1971 fiscal-year budget emerged, $5.5 billion of that saving was absorbed by increased non-Vietnam military expenditures. Senator Proxmire thought that as much as $10 billion had been filched from the peace dividend. He noted that President Nixon had earlier canceled a hypothetical war. In the Kennedy-Johnson years defense planning was based on the need to fight two and a half wars at once. Nixon decided to prepare for only one and a half wars. There ought to have been some saving there too, but it proved hard to find. Apparently new military hardware had eaten it up. The administration responded by abandoning the term: where cost overruns had been renamed cost growth, the peace dividend simply vanished. It was "a rather oddball concept" anyhow, according to Budget Director Mayo. All this was very confusing, and meant to be. The only certainty was that whatever happened in Vietnam military spending would continue on the vastly enlarged post-Eisenhower scale.*

By 1969 the failure of the Alliance for Progress was entirely clear. American policy in Latin America had always been exploitive. Castro frightened the U.S. for a time, hence the Alianza. But when no further socialist revolutions took place, the government relaxed. In 1968 Congress appropriated only $336.5 million for the Alliance, the lowest figure yet. This was not because of the program's success. In March 1969 the Agency for International Development reported that the gains made by Latin countries since the Alianza began had been negligible, despite U.S. expenditures of $9.2 billion. The Alliance had aimed at an annual increase in real productivity of 2.5 per cent. In its first seven years the gross increase was actually 4.5 per cent, but the high birthrate reduced per capita increase to only 1.5 per cent. So the original ten-year goals were abandoned and AID established an eighteen-year timetable. Its success also depended on the birthrate's going down, which seemed unlikely. In the meantime, loans to Latin America had mounted to the point where 75 per cent of incoming bank funds went to pay the interest on old debts. Primary school enrollments were up by 50 per cent from 1960. But, thanks to the birthrate again, the gross number of school-age children not enrolled was up also. There was no land reform to speak of. Income distribution remained about the same.

Senator Fulbright's Foreign Relations Committee issued a staff report showing what this meant for a single country. Colombia received $732 million in aid between 1962 and 1967. President Kennedy intended it to be a "showcase" for the Alianza. Yet its GNP increased only 1.2 per cent a year. Land reform gave property to 54,000 out of 400,000 landless

---

* Or even beyond it. The facts were buried in various reports, but were pieced together by I. F. Stone. The administration expected to spend $415 billion on defense during the years 1970 to 1975. This compared with a total of $300 billion during the first six fiscal years of the 1960's, which had itself been a period of rapid increase. Even assuming that the Vietnam War was ended, the government still meant to spend as much on defense from 1971 to 1975 ($342 billion) as had been spent when the war was at its peak from 1965 to 1969.

families, but their number rose by 10 per cent a year, a rate far in excess of the progress of land reform. There were a million more functional illiterates. Fulbright announced that he would not vote for another aid bill until the money was spent through multilateral agencies like the World Bank. It was obvious that unilateral U.S. assistance didn't work. Much of the aid was military anyway, which did the economy no good. Much of the rest was wasted or stolen. No one knew how much AID money ended up in Swiss bank accounts, where the region's elite sent funds that ought to have gone for taxes and capital development in their own countries. And though aid was supposed to be predicated on local reforms, it wasn't. The U.S. gave the money, after all, not to promote revolution but to prevent it—all the brave rhetoric notwithstanding. So long as there were no more Castros, the policy could be said to work. That it didn't benefit the region was a secondary concern. Some of the aid was profitable: loans had to be repaid with interest; supplies bought with aid funds had to be purchased in the U.S. even though available more cheaply elsewhere. In this sense, aid was good business for the U.S. It was not charity but a subtler form of exploitation.

Peru and Bolivia showed that once again the U.S. was pursuing short-term satisfactions at the expense of its long-term interest. In October 1968 a military *coup* toppled the government of Peru. This was unremarkable enough. What was odd was that the new regime nationalized the local subsidiary of Standard Oil, captured American fishing boats within two hundred miles of its coast, and established diplomatic and commercial ties with Russia. This seemed the worst sort of ingratitude. Peru had gotten U.S. aid. Its military had profited from American training and equipment. Moreover, the historic duty of Peru's military was to prevent the left-wing APRA party from taking office. It had done so repeatedly before. Now it was apparently taking a leaf from APRA's book. In fact, General Juan Velasco Alvarado was more of a Gaullist than a Marxist. But many younger officers, as elsewhere in Latin America, were turning against the established elites and the tradition of complicity with American economic and diplomatic interests that they represented. The result was a policy of internal reform and diplomatic realignment. The International Petroleum Company was expropriated for nonpayment of what was said to be $690 million in back taxes. (Alvarado's predecessor had forgiven IPC its back taxes, which was one reason for his overthrow.) Steps were taken to confiscate the great private landholdings and redistribute them to peasants. There was talk of buying French military jets instead of American planes.

The U.S. reacted cautiously to all this, and with reason. Peru was not the Dominican Republic. It would take more than a few regiments to break its spirit. On the other hand, economic sanctions were not likely to work either. In 1968 it got only $18.5 million in U.S. aid. The loss of it would not make much difference. (U.S. aid had been reduced to force President Belaúnde to forgive IPC's back taxes.) Cutting Peru's sugar quota would cost it more—$45 million. But 90 per cent of all Peruvian sugar imported by the U.S. was owned by an American firm, W. R. Grace. One U.S. ambassador allegedly called for an "Iranian solution" (after the CIA-backed *coup* in the fifties which overthrew Premier Mossadegh). But as the opposition in Peru consisted chiefly of the even more left-wing Apristas, this didn't quite seem the answer.

While the State Department dithered, Bolivia fell. General Alfredo Ovando Candia, chief of the armed forces, replaced the civilian leadership with a military government. He led a motley group of military old-guardists, nationalists, and leftists, committed to what was termed "leftist nationalism." General Ovando expressed hope for an "ideological confederation" with Peru. One of his cabinet members announced that "the time has come for Latin America to make its stand against American diplomatic and economic imperialism." The American-owned Bolivia Gulf Oil Company was threatened with expropriation. Overtures were made to East European countries. Worse still, the new government seemed willing to restore relations with Cuba if it stopped trying to subvert Bolivia. This was indeed the last straw. After all, had it not been for American military advisers, Che Guevara might never have been caught in Bolivia. Now the very people who had hunted him down were cozying up to the man who'd sent him. Things could hardly get worse, and for the rest of the year they didn't.

But it seemed unlikely that the U.S. would find things easier in Latin America very soon. The Alliance's failure made more heroic solutions necessary. Washington continued to insist that only private investments would stimulate economic growth in Latin America. But decades of American investment had accomplished little. Indeed, the need to protect those investments was responsible for U.S. support of reactionary governments everywhere. Americans who did invest there insisted on very high returns to justify the supposed risk (though in fact the U.S. government insured their investments). Hence in Peru alone between 1950 and 1965 U.S. investments had totaled less than $300 million and earned profits of nearly a billion dollars. In view of this it was hard for progressive Latin Americans to understand why more of the same was essential to their well-being. They could scarcely be blamed for looking elsewhere, and for wanting more control over their economic destinies. Whether this new departure worked out or not, the military-industrial complex would probably find Latin America more trying than ever in years to come.

1969 was a lean year for politics. The great explosion of 1968 had exhausted most people. President Nixon's clever tactics kept the opposition off base. The Democrats suffered also from want of leadership. Lyndon Johnson was busy rewriting history in Texas. Hubert Humphrey was out of office. Senator McCarthy maintained a low profile. Senator Edward Kennedy was nearly ruined by an automobile accident. Apparently he went for a late swim after a party with friends and supporters on Chappaquiddick Island off Martha's Vineyard. Somehow he drove off a bridge and his woman companion, a former secretary to Robert Kennedy, was drowned. Senator Kennedy failed to report the accident for some nine hours, long after there was any chance of saving the victim—if there had been any to begin with. Then he went on television and, in Theodore Sorensen's overripe prose, asked the voters of Massachusetts for their advice. They urged him to run again for the Senate. There was little doubt he would be re-elected. But his stature as a party leader was badly damaged. He had just been made Democratic whip in the Senate. The polls showed he was the favorite candidate of most Democrats to run against President Nixon in 1972. As the last male Kennedy it was, of course, his dynastic obligation to do so. Now those prospects seemed permanently blighted. If so, it was a sorry end to the Kennedy saga. It was bad enough that the family had suffered so; worse still that Edward Kennedy should lose in a moment's folly what had taken years of labor to attain.

In his youth he had seemed the least gifted Kennedy. He was expelled from Harvard for cheating. Later he was elected to the Senate solely on account of his name. But after that he became the best-liked and most effective Kennedy to serve in the upper house. He was the only one to be accepted by the club. And he proved a loyal party speaker and fund-raiser. Like John, and more than Robert, he appealed to both Democratic liberals and regulars. Thus what he gained by inheritance he improved on by application. Now it appeared that a malign fate was determined to make every member of that brilliant family pay for his or her talents. Each new tragedy seemed more perverse than the last. Misfortune dogged them so that even Kennedy's enemies kept silent, for the most part, after his disgrace. A few could not resist the chance for easy moralizing. The local district attorney persecuted him for some time afterward. But most Americans seemed properly awed. Yet the family might rise again. Senator Kennedy could be rehabilitated. And there were all those promising males in the next generation to reckon with. There might still be another President Kennedy.

The 1960's saw the physical condition of America's people improve. Real income went up substantially, especially among blacks. So did educational levels. The work force continued to shift toward skilled and white-collar occupations. Poverty, particularly among blacks again, declined. People derived less satisfaction from this than might have been supposed. Black progress was accomplished by forceful tactics that offended whites. At the same time, by proclaiming wars on poverty and prejudice, officials generated unreasonable expectations. When these evils persisted, many blacks felt cheated. The more schools were desegregated, the less grateful blacks seemed, and the angrier whites got. Universities grew as never before. But many students began treating what had previously been thought a privilege as a curse. Universities were damned as racist and authoritarian. The more blacks they recruited the more discriminatory they were accused of being. White radicals claimed they were imperialistic knowledge factories. Adults, staggering under increased tuition and tax payments to sustain these institutions, turned against them on account of their failure to put down student complaints. All this was puzzling enough. Everyone knew that money did not buy happiness, but it was always thought to help. Now it seemed that the more affluent the country got, the more sullen and resentful Americans became. Worse still, most of the real progress in the sixties came from the great boom. By 1969 it was clearly over. The war produced an inflation that eliminated most income gains. In 1969 some fully employed workers had less real income than in 1968. To combat inflation the Nixon administration cut spending and tightened the money supply. This stopped economic growth and stimulated unemployment. Corporate profits, which had grown by 71 per cent in the four years before 1966, rose only 9.2 per cent from 1966 through 1969. The stock market sagged. A recession could hardly heal the wounds prosperity had failed to treat.

Other changes were harder to assess. Corporate domination of the economy increased. There were 4,500 corporate mergers in 1968, 40 per cent more than the year before. In 1967 the one hundred biggest manufacturing corporations held 47.6 per cent of all the assets in this area, as against 35.1 in 1925. The seventy-eight largest manufacturers earned nearly half of all manufacturing profits in 1968. And this underestimated the degree of centralization. Many big corporations were interlocked with one another through shared officers or boards of directors—General Motors with sixty-three other companies (including seven of the top one hundred manufacturing companies), U.S. Steel with eighty-nine companies. Others were parts of giant bank holding companies or "conglomerates" which evaded the anti-trust laws by merging with or buying up unrelated firms. Thus while businessmen continued to praise competition and individual enterprise, there was less and less of both. Everyone spoke for decentralization, local autonomy, and the like. Little was done to save what remained of them. The rhetoric of both liberals and conservatives pointed in one direction, reality in another.

The family farm was another national institution cherished by both ends of the political spectrum. It too vanished. More than a million family farms were lost between 1959 and 1969. The three million that survived were 30 per cent larger on the average than ten years before. The farm population was down to about ten million, or about 5 per cent of the national total. It was not expected to decline much more. Between 1967 and 1968 the farm population changed little. Everyone who intended to leave the land had done so. Some small farms were still run by aged proprietors. When they died, agriculture would be just another mechanized industry. The farmer's praises would still be sung though he had gone to join the mountain man and other extinct human species. The federal subsidies that had done so much to eliminate him would still enrich the big producers whose sturdy yeoman virtues would be invoked to ward off reductions. Thus the dead protected the living. It was all in the best national tradition. No one proclaimed the merits of free enterprise like the monopolistic, privately owned utilities. No one admired farmers more than the Department of Agriculture that presided over their demise.*

Another great area where old trends persisted was the physical environment. Most kinds of pollution increased. Air pollution defied efforts to abate it. Auto engines got slightly cleaner, but there were many more of them than before, so total exhaust emissions grew. Prosperity was the main contributor to environmental decay. More goods were produced and consumed. Making them polluted the air and water, so did their consumption. People could afford to wash more, so more detergents were flushed into water systems. Even where per capita consumption did not go up, population growth sped the flow of garbage. The birthrate declined, but the base was so large to begin with that the population in-

* In 1950, when there were twenty million people living on farms, the Department of Agriculture had appropriations of $1.5 billion and 84,000 employees. In 1970, when there were ten million people living on farms, the Department had appropriations of $7.4 billion and 125,000 employees. This was a classic example of Parkinson's Law. In 1969 the Department spent $3.5 billion on crop subsidies, while the Bureau of Reclamation spent $85 million for irrigation projects to bring arid western lands into production. Most of the subsidies went to the one million "serious commercial producers," the big growers who earned most of the $16 billion a year in net farm income. The fourteen million poor people who remained in rural areas got virtually no help at all. Yet the Department of Agriculture liked to call itself the "Department of Rural Affairs."

creased. There were 200 million Americans in 1969. Some feared there would be 300 million in twenty years' time. Environmental reform became a popular mania at the decade's end, but between rising living standards and population growth it seemed a lost cause. It was hard enough to win individual combats with private greed. To save a threatened beach or wildlife sanctuary involved fierce struggles with powerfully motivated interests. These were more often lost than not.

But it was harder still to get changes that cut into personal income. Pollution abatement cost a lot, and it would be paid for, if at all, through increased prices and taxes. How much of an increase would the people accept? And how many personal sacrifices could reasonably be expected? Would students give up their motorcycles, noisy and foul though they were? Would sportsmen give up their equally noxious outboard motors? How much more would they pay for nonpolluting equivalents if such could be made? And beyond these comparatively small problems were the big ones. Agricultural output depended on insecticides and fertilizers that over time threatened human life. But dispensing with them obviously did too.

Then there were the oceans. Half the seaborne traffic involved oil tankers. Thanks to accidents, bilge pumpings, and such, a thin film of oil covered all the oceans. It would get thicker as affluence and population growth increased the need for petroleum. Offshore drilling leaks and oil spills that ruined beaches got much publicity, and rightly so. But they were trivial incidents compared with the possibility that all the seas would become contaminated. Nor was air pollution just a local threat. As it went up, the earth's capacity to renew its air declined. Scientists spoke of an end to all life on earth within fifty or a hundred years.

No doubt this was overdrawn. Man had often shown himself capable of living under the most appalling circumstances. But it did seem as if the American way of life was endangered. Up to the sixties the ecological price for higher living standards seemed right, but no longer. Even if human life were not extinguished, the quality of life might well decline. If so, higher incomes would no longer translate automatically into higher living standards. No one could buy cleaner air. Before long it might be impossible to escape pollution by moving to "better" neighborhoods. Abundance had been the American dream. Now it threatened the hopes it was supposed to realize. There was more irony here than people could bear. Many denied the problem by insisting as before that pollution and despoliation were essential to "progress." More paid lip service to ecology while maintaining their old habits. Some gave way to despair, others to the manic optimism that had preceded the era's other short-lived social enthusiasms.

The rage for ecological reform had a dual effect. It added to the national despondency, but it also served as a national rallying point. Nearly everyone could agree on saving the environment. Radicals and conservatives alike deplored pollution. Sometimes they even agreed on specific projects. This was no small thing at a time when feelings were so polarized. And being benign it was especially welcome.

Mostly, though, the new consensus was made of uglier stuff. What intense polarization usually provokes in a conservative country like America is a turn to the right. As the left became more strident and absurd, the silent majority found its voice. George Wallace spoke for some, Vice-President Agnew for many more. Black militancy, student protests, and the apparently rising crime rate provoked fresh cries for law and order. The law obliged. Black Panthers were killed, various New Left, Old Left, and hippie leaders were tried for conspiracy. The Johnson administration's effort to gag the peace movement had failed. Trying Dr. Spock and Reverend Coffin for conspiracy proved a mistake. Their dignified conduct was widely admired. The Court of Appeals reversed their conviction. Dissent increased.

The new administration was more successful. For one thing, President Nixon picked his domestic targets better. Instead of going after the respectable opposition he isolated the anti-war movement's most vulnerable element. Eight men were indicted for conspiracy to cause the Chicago convention riots in 1968. Except for David Dellinger, a middle-aged pacifist, and Bobby Seale of the Black Panthers, they were mostly New Leftists. Tom Hayden and Rennie Davis were founders of SDS. Abbie Hoffman and Jerry Rubin helped organize the yippies. The other two, Lee Weiner and John Froines, were radical young academicians. All defended themselves by showing the trial to be absurd. Their ridicule and abuse unbalanced Judge Julius Hoffman. He had Bobby Seale bound and gagged. When that failed Hoffman gave Seale four years for contempt of court and declared a mistrial in his case. Before the trial ended, Hoffman gave the other defendants and their attorneys similar penalties. The jury was out for days and then returned a compromise verdict. Everyone was acquitted of conspiracy, and Weiner and Froines of all charges. The rest were convicted of lesser crimes and sentenced to varying prison terms. Few believed they would serve them. Though they were denied bail as dangers to society, a court injunction soon had them out on bond. The contempt sentences were unprecedentedly severe and might not survive appeal. Judge Hoffman's prejudice made a reversal of their convictions seem likely. Everyone was damaged by the case anyway. The government appeared stupid or malicious, or both. The defendants and their attorneys found few admirers except among their own kind.

Many conservatives thought it a mistake to turn vandals into martyrs by persecuting them. But the government meant to isolate and intimidate the extreme left. Convictions for littering were not enough. By pressing the gravest charges it assured the defendants of years of litigation at best. Whether convicted or not they would pay a large price for being rude and noisy. The silent majority would be appeased. Trying the Chicago 8 made the government's point. Whether it would be taken was another question.

Repression advanced on the legislative front too. Early in 1970 the Senate, with only one dissenting vote, passed a "crime control" bill that eroded more constitutional rights than any measure since the Espionage and Sedition Acts of World War I. Next it passed a drug-control law that allowed police to enter homes without warning. The House passed a bill introduced by the Internal Security Committee (formerly HUAC) that gave the Executive authority to bar accused subversives from defense plants. Only sixty-five members voted against it. Thus, as in the McCarthy era, most liberals on Capitol Hill became parties to the witch-hunt (while hoping, no doubt, that the Supreme Court would quash it).

In a way history seemed to be repeating itself. Korea brought General Eisenhower to the presidency, Vietnam did the same for Richard Nixon. After the New Dealers and the Fair Dealers of the thirties and forties came the car dealers of the fifties. After the New Frontier and the Great Society came—what? There was Richard Nixon again, the very epitome of life in the 1950's, the man (after Joe McCarthy) liberals most loved to hate. As President he sometimes followed the Eisenhower line. There would be peace in Asia, and curbs on government spending. The old morality was proclaimed once more. When Julie Nixon married David Eisenhower, Norman Vincent Peale officiated. Nixon lay low as General Eisenhower had. "Ike" used to keep people like Nixon around to draw enemy fire and take the rap when things went wrong. He got the credit when things went well. And he had liberals like Lodge and Rockefeller to cover his left flank. President Nixon did the same even more deliberately. Agnew and Attorney General Mitchell were his lightning rods. His personal staff was full of conservatives. To redress the balance he had Romney and Finch in the cabinet and Moynihan in the White House. He could go in any direction whenever he chose. Obviously he had not been understudy for eight years to President Eisenhower for nothing. Though Nixon was more obvious than his mentor, he was slicker too. But he would need more than that to match the old general. *

---

* A little modesty would not have hurt either. Even for a President, Nixon's vanity was remarkable. He found historic significance in his most trivial acts, and liked to call them presidential firsts. One he did not lay claim to was that he was the first President to give his own name to a policy statement. The Monroe, Truman, and Eisenhower doctrines, for example, had been so designated by others. But Nixon announced that his plans for the Far East constituted the Nixon Doctrine. (The

Other items pointed to a return of the 1950's, or at least its worst features. Dress designers ruled that skirts must lengthen. Obediently, female trend-setters fell in line. Actually, designers had been trying to
bring skirt lengths down for years, without success. But after Nixon's
election their prospects improved. The middle-aged look featuring wide
shoulders and very long flowing skirts returned. No one could say how
far this would go. The most striking fashion development in the 1960's
had been not so much the mini-skirt itself as the new freedom it represented. A variety of skirt lengths from knee to haunch prevailed. The
range of acceptable costumes extended from sculptured elegance at the
one end to military-surplus garments on the other. Would this spectrum
now diminish? Or would women hang on to their variations, perhaps
even extend them so that skirt lengths and such would no longer be decreed but adapted to individual need? If not, the mini-skirt would be
missed, and the free spirit it symbolized even more. It was especially
fitting that John Lennon got his hair cut about then. Soon fashion stylists
issued a directive that long skirts meant short hair.

Of course the 1970's would not be exactly like the 1950's, the silent
majority notwithstanding. One of the few certainties in recent history is
that social freedoms once gained tend to persist. The 1920's made the
pleasure principle central to the American way of life. Depression and
war curtailed hedonism. In the 1950's women were persuaded to wear
drab clothes and have too many children. But these phases passed away,
and the drive for personal freedom and self-indulgence, never entirely
repressed anyway, was renewed. It would survive the seventies too. The
government might encourage McCarthyism, perhaps Comstockery also.
But the old morality had been dying for fifty years, and no one could
breathe new life into it for long. The silent majority might dream of a
golden age when blacks and females and youngsters knew their place.
But they were too fond of the high-technology, consumer-oriented mass
society that destroyed it to re-create the past. Like everyone, they
wanted more money for less work. They expected the stream of new
goods and services to go on growing and would turn out any government that threatened it. They would go on sending their children to college. They might prefer repression to reform. But in the long run they

---

Nixon Doctrine decreed that henceforth American policy in the Orient would be
the same as before.) He also suffered from a defective self-image, as had President
Johnson. Nixon usually was a Rotarian, Honest-Dick-your-friend-in-the-White-
House, but under stress he became General George Patton. Before invading Cambodia he saw the movie *Patton* several times for inspiration. What was even scarier
was that he thought the film glorified Patton, whereas in fact it showed him to have
been a dangerous war-lover. General Eisenhower had handled Patton brilliantly because he knew what Patton was. This was only one of many lessons Nixon did not
learn when he was understudy to President Eisenhower. Another was that fostering
discord, as Nixon would do in the 1970 elections, rarely pays off.

would take the path of least resistance. Employers had found it easier in the end to accept labor unions than to break them. The silent majority would probably find it simplest to allow blacks a fairer slice of the national pie. And it might be more convenient to legalize marijuana, abortion, and other forbidden things than to suffer the consequences of prohibiting them.

Little morality plays would have to be acted out first. The sixties had been a kind of binge, and people would not go on another until its hangover wore off. But many of the conditions that produced it still remained. They would reassert themselves in time. And, as in the past, something would be done about them, though, as always, too slowly no doubt. The sixties would be remembered for combining the prosperity and social novelties of the twenties with the politics of the thirties. Like those two eras, much of what was done would survive. But also like them, the objects sought would turn out to be less satisfying than expected. Women were liberated, after a fashion, in the 1920's. This did not seem to improve their morale strikingly. Sexual morality was revolutionized without enlarging the sum of human happiness by very much. In the 1930's labor unions finally organized the big industries, and the foundations of the welfare state were laid. Yet want and social inequities continued long after. The unions disappointed their most ardent partisans. The welfare state failed to grow as planned. And both decades were marked by terrible upheavals. The red scares, race riots, and lynchings of the twenties were appalling. The depression and its labor wars brought intense suffering to millions. Measured against these decades, the 1960's didn't look so bad. Its domestic horrors were not worse than theirs, its real progress perhaps more impressive. Civil rights and liberties increased. Poverty diminished. Yet no one mourned the decade's end. Conservatives thought it an age of riot and license. It could not pass into the ashcan of history soon enough for them. Radicals saw it as a moment when the system broke down. Like bolsheviks contemplating the First World War, they found the sixties horrible in themselves but desirable for bringing the revolution closer. Hence they were more ambivalent than most. The prospect of apocalypse encouraged them. Bring on repression, they cried, for afterward comes revolution. This was nonsense of course. It was partly because radicals had overreached themselves that the decade ended so badly. And they would find, like the Wobblies and communists before them, that repression works as often as not. Especially when foolish radicals assist it.

The failure of nerve at the decade's end was, therefore, confined mostly to liberals. Conservatives and radicals had confidence in the future; only liberals faced it with dismay. The springtime of reform had been so fleeting that it passed almost without their knowing it.

They hardly had time to learn "We Shall Overcome" before being read out of the civil rights movement. The cheers for Lyndon Johnson's mighty tide of reform bills in 1964 and 1965 were soon drowned by the sounds of war and riot. The whole reform era lasted scarcely four years. It began with the test-ban treaty in 1963 and was over by 1967. The student movement was equally evanescent and disappointing. One moment liberals were applauding the Peace Corps, participatory democracy, and curriculum reform. The next they were seeing famous universities become battlegrounds while their children dropped out or turned on. To have hopes raised so high and dashed so quickly was bad enough. Worse still was the fear that they themselves were at fault. Their readiness to confess error was the most endearing trait of American liberals. When militant blacks charged them with de facto racism they vied with one another in admitting it. For a time no radical could accuse the liberal establishment of racism and imperialism without being offered a job. The very students who gave up study for agitation were acclaimed the best-educated generation in history. The more anti-intellectual they became, the more perceptive they were said to be.

Inevitably, when the decade ended in a shambles, liberals were the first to examine their conscience. They blamed themselves for not protesting the war soon enough. The fight against poverty was now seen as superficial. Student irrationality was attributed to poor middle-class child-rearing techniques. As liberal administrations had made such a mess of things, perhaps it was only fair to give conservatism a chance. When President Nixon said it was time for people to lower their voices, many complied. More would have if only Spiro Agnew had let them. Still, the amount of guilt, apathy, and despair they manifested was extraordinary. Even the *Wall Street Journal* thought so. Without conceding anything in principle, this conservative organ totted up the gains made since 1960 and congratulated liberals on them. It suggested they snap out of their funk. Few took this good advice. Yet liberals would not have been true to form had they responded differently. Having failed to transform the human condition in a decade, they felt guilty and ashamed. Good riddance to the 1960's they all said, "this slum of a decade" as Richard Rovere called it, and braced themselves for the coming age of piety and iron. A hundred flowers had bloomed in vain.

But the soldiers would come home one day. After winter comes the spring. Until then it helped to remember that the era was not all of a piece. There had been folly, madness, and blight in plenty. Standards decayed. The condition of the people improved nonetheless. Justice was done sometimes. And through it all Americans remained turbulent, creative, surprising. As much a danger to themselves as to others certainly. A nation caught up in a manic-depressive cycle that was trying at both extremes. But not a people to write off too soon. Life was in them yet, and with it hope. Statesmen invoked past glories to justify present squalor. Patriotism was corrupted by imperialism. The nation's heritage was wasted. Yet if no longer ma..kind's last, best chance for freedom, as politicians liked to think, America was still a place worth saving. Romanticists scorned the American dream; materialists soiled her way of life. America was beautiful all the same.

A Note on Sources

1. Prologue: Eisenhower's Year

Life magazine published many statements deploring the want of direction in American life. They were reprinted as *The National Purpose,* John K. Jessup, ed. (New York, 1960). Richard E. Neustadt, *Presidential Power: The Politics of Leadership* (New York, 1960) is an especially cogent declaration of liberal enthusiasm for strong Presidents. It was said to have been much admired by President Kennedy, and Neustadt later became director of the Institute of Politics in the John Fitzgerald Kennedy School of Government at Harvard. Among the many books by discontented intellectuals these were especially effective: David Riesman, *The Lonely Crowd* (New Haven, 1950); William H. Whyte, *The Organization Man* (New York, 1956); and John Keats's two entertaining polemics, *The Insolent Chariots* (Philadelphia, 1958) and *The Crack in the Picture Window* (Boston, 1956). John Kenneth Galbraith, *The Affluent Society* (Boston, 1958) remains the most compelling attack on growthmanship. C. Wright Mills was the foremost radical critic in the 1950's. See especially his *The Power Elite* (New York, 1956). James B. Conant's string of books on public education reflect the anxiety Sputnik aroused. But many criticisms of modern education appeared earlier, notably Arthur E. Bestor, Jr., *Educational Wastelands* (Urbana, Ill., 1953), and especially Paul A. Woodring, *A Fourth of a Nation* (New York, 1957). The consensus historians are justly dealt with by John Higham in "Beyond Consensus: The Historian as Moral Critic," *American Historical Review* (April 1962). Daniel Bell, *The End of Ideology: On the Exhaustion of Political Ideas in the Fifties* (Glencoe, Ill., 1960) was premature, though still a useful source of ideas and criticisms. John W. Gardner's *Excellence: Can We Be Equal and Excellent Too?* (New York, 1961) sums up the post-Sputnikian conventional wisdom. President Eisenhower's own views appear in Volume III of his White House memoirs, *Waging Peace, 1956–61* (New York, 1965). The most revealing insider's account of his methods is Arthur Larson, *Eisenhower: The President Nobody Knew* (New York, 1968). It suggests the care Mr. Eisenhower took to preserve his reputation for dullness. Murray Kempton, "The Underestimation of Dwight D. Eisenhower," *Esquire* (September 1967), makes the same point, though it shows the President to be more Machiavellian than perhaps he really was. Richard Rhodes, "Ike: An Artist in Iron," *Harper's* (July 1970), is friendlier to the President but equally astute. There are too many books on strategy to summarize here. They include Walt Whitman Rostow, *The United States in the World Arena* (New York, 1960); Maxwell D. Taylor, *The Uncertain Trumpet* (New York, 1959); Herman Kahn, *On Thermonuclear War* (Princeton, 1960) and *On Escalation* (New York, 1965); and Robert Strausz-Hupé, William Kintner, and Stefan T. Possony, *A Forward Strategy for America* (New York, 1961). Even more horrible is Melvin Laird, *A House Divided: America's Strategy Gap* (Chicago, 1962). The future Secretary of Defense did not write it himself, and he repudiated much of it later anyway. It remains a melancholy example of what passed for strategic thinking at the time. See also the many books by Bernard Brodie and Henry Kissinger. On the future see Editors of Fortune, *America in the Sixties* (New York, 1960). James MacGregor Burns, *John Kennedy* (New York, 1959) is still best on the subject, though it deals only with the pre-presidential years. Richard Nixon, *Six Crises* (New York, 1962) is probably more revealing than was intended. David Wise and Thomas B. Ross, *The U-2 Affair* (New York, 1962) is comprehensive. Michel Tatu, *Power in the Kremlin: From Khrushchev to Kosygin* (New York, 1968) contains brilliant speculations by a French Kremlinologist about the U-2 affair's impact on Russian politics. Theodore H. White, *The Making of the President 1960* (New York, 1961) is the standard account.

Profile: The Supreme Court

Murray Kempton's observations on the prayer ruling are in "Vessels of Christ," *New Republic* (May 16, 1964). Two general accounts of the Court are Alexander M. Bickel, *Politics and the Warren Court* (New York, 1965) and Milton R. Konvitz, *Expanding Liberties* (New York, 1966). Anthony Lewis, *Gideon's Trumpet* (New York, 1964) is an admirable book on one landmark decision. Charles Rembar, *The End of Obscenity: The Trials of Lady Chatterley, Tropic of Cancer, and Fanny Hill* (New York, 1968) is one of many helpful books on the pornography issue. The Court's achievements are excellently summarized in Joseph W. Bishop, "The Warren Court Is Not Likely to Be Overruled," *New York Times Magazine* (September 9, 1969).

2. Building Camelot

The two standard accounts of the Kennedy administration are Arthur M. Schlesinger, Jr., *A Thousand Days* (Boston, 1965), and Theodore C. Sorensen, *Kennedy* (New York, 1965). Schlesinger is strongest on foreign policy, Sorensen on domestic affairs. Both are court histories, but sometimes revealing even so. As might be expected from a distinguished historian, Schlesinger's is the more artful. I. F. Stone, "Arms Talks: Theatre of Delusion," *New York Review of Books*, April 23, 1970, brilliantly explains President Kennedy's armament and disarmament policies. There are many books exposing the military-industrial pork barrel. H. L. Nieburg's *In the Name of Science* (Chicago, 1966) is especially useful as it concentrates on the research-and-development side where most of the waste occurs. Tom Wicker, *JFK and LBJ: The Influence of Personality upon Politics* (New York, 1968) tells how President Kennedy's domestic program was lost. Herbert L. Matthews, *The Cuban Story* (New York, 1961) describes the early phase of the Cuban Revolution. Of Theodore Draper's several outstanding books on Cuba, *Castroism: Theory and Practice* (New York, 1965) deals best with its evolving ideology. The Bay of Pigs fiasco is described in Tad Szulc and Karl E. Meyer, *The Cuban Invasion* (New York, 1962). Victor Bernstein and Jesse Gordon, "The Press and the Bay of Pigs," *Columbia University Forum* (Fall 1967) indicts the news profession for failing to report it properly. One of the rare contemporary books by a political scientist to expose the contradictions in America's European policy is Fred Warner Neal, *War and Peace and Germany* (New York, 1962). In this same vein is John Lukacs, *A History of the Cold War* (Garden City, 1961). Since those early days a school of diplomatic historians (sometimes called the Wisconsin School) has grown up critical of American foreign policy in the nineteenth as well as the twentieth century. Its leader is William Appleman Williams, whose best-known work is *The Tragedy of American Diplomacy* (New York, 1962). The most sweeping narrative history to come from it is Walter LaFeber's *America, Russia, and the Cold War, 1945–1966* (New York, 1967), which quietly corrects the official line on many points. A helpful short collection of essays on civil defense is Eugene P. Wigner, ed., *Who Speaks for Civil Defense?* (New York, 1968). How the nuclear fallout problem seemed then is shown by the contributors to John M. Fowler, ed., *Fallout* (New York, 1960). The best evidence linking testing with infant and prenatal deaths is in Ernest J. Sternglass, "Infant Mortality and Nuclear Tests," *Bulletin of the Atomic Scientists* (April 1969). Fred J. Cook tirelessly exposed the radical right. See, for example, his *The Warfare State* (New York, 1962). The *Nation*, to which he regularly contributed, was the liberal magazine most alarmed by it. William Buckley's *National Review* magazine has for many years been the most important effort to make conservatism seem real. John G. Fuller, *The Gentlemen Conspirators: The Story of the Price-Fixers in the Electrical Industry* (New York, 1962) shows what some businessmen take free enterprise and competition to mean.

Profile: Space

Writing about the space program became a substantial industry in its own right. Most books advance the NASA line. An early example is Jay Holmes, *America on the Moon: The Enterprise of the Sixties* (Philadelphia, 1962). A good book in this vein is Richard S. Lewis, *Appointment on the Moon* (New York, 1968). There are also a fair number of critical works, beginning with Amitai Etzioni, *The Moondoggle* (New York, 1964). H. L. Nieburg, *In the Name of Science* (Chicago, 1966) sees NASA as only another form of welfare for the rich. The most recent exposé is Hugo Young, Bryan Silcock, and Peter Dunn, *Journey to Tranquility* (New York, 1970). Two good essays written before the moon landing, but after the cuts in NASA's budget, are Ralph E. Lapp, "Send Computers, Not Men, into Deep Space," *New York Times Magazine* (February 2, 1969), and Richard S. Lewis, "Our Terra-Luna Transit System: Where Will It Take Us?", *Bulletin of the Atomic Scientists* (March 1969).

3. Completing the Myth

A full account of the steel crisis is Grant McConnell, *Steel and the Presidency, 1962* (New York, 1963). Hobart Rowen, *The Free Enterprisers: Kennedy, Johnson and the Business Establishment* (New York, 1969) is instructive, especially when read in connection with Galbraith's *The Affluent Society*. David Wise and Thomas B. Ross, *The Invisible Government* (New York, 1964) details the CIA's contribution to Laos. Elie Abel, *The Missile Crisis* (Philadelphia, 1966) embodies the conventional wisdom. Of the personal testaments, Robert F. Kennedy, *Thirteen Days: A Memoir of the Cuban Missile Crisis* (New York, 1969) is most useful. Roger Hilsman offers a somewhat different explanation of its origins in his *To Move a Nation: The Politics of Foreign Policy in the Administration of John F. Kennedy* (New York, 1967). James W. Silver, *Mississippi: The Closed Society* (New York, 1964) puts the Meredith case in perspective. David Halberstam, *The Making of a Quagmire* (New York, 1965) is excellent on the early stages of U.S. intervention in Vietnam. John Mecklin, *Mission in Torment: An Intimate Account of the U.S. Role in Vietnam* (New York, 1965) is an insider's bizarre story. All of Bernard Fall's books are essential reading, beginning, perhaps, with *The Two Viet Nams: A Political and Military Analysis* (New York, 1963). For a hostile but shrewd assessment of de Gaulle's character and tactics, see Robert Murphy, *Diplomat Among Warriors* (Garden City, 1964). On the test ban see I. F. Stone's bitter "The Test Ban Comedy," *New York Review of Books* (May 7, 1970). Joseph Kraft, "Riot Squad for the New Frontier," *Harper's* (August 1963), describes the Justice Department under Robert Kennedy. Sander Vanocur, "Kennedy's Voyage of Discovery," *Harper's* (April 1964), deals with the President's last Western trip. Harry M. Caudill, bard and historian to the region, describes the mountain people's tragedy in "Misdeal in Appalachia," *Atlantic* (June 1965). Mailer's essay on Kennedy appeared first in *Esquire,* and is conveniently available in *The Presidential Papers of Norman Mailer* (New York, 1964). The late President's most engaging traits are best described in Tom Wicker, "Kennedy Without Tears," *Esquire* (June 1964).

Profile: The Warren Report and After

The most judicious book on the Warren Report is Edward Jay Epstein, *Inquest: The Warren Commission and the Establishment of Truth* (New York, 1966). "A Primer on Assassination Theories," *Esquire* (December 1968), is essential. Of these theories, Richard H. Popkin, "The Second Oswald: The Case for a Conspiracy Theory," *New York Review of Books* (July 28, 1966), is especially ingenious. Norman Podhoretz's prophetic editorial is "The Warren Commission," *Commentary* (January 1964). Ovid Demaris and Garry Wills, "You All Know Me! I'm Jack Ruby!," *Esquire* (May–June 1967), is a superb, even moving reconstruction of the life of Oswald's assassin. William Manchester, *Death of a President* (New York, 1967) is discussed in Edward Jay Epstein, "Manchester Unexpurgated," *Commentary* (July 1967), and in Elizabeth Hardwick, "The Death of a President," *New York Review of Books* (August 20, 1967). The Garrison affair is reviewed in Edward Jay Epstein, *Counterplot* (New York, 1969) and "The Final Chapter in the Assassination Controversy," *New York Times Magazine* (April 20, 1969), and also in two stories from the Washington Post Service: John P. Mackenzie, "What Did Garrison Prove?", (Madison) *Capital Times* (February 25, 1969), and William Greider, "White Still Black for Garrison," *Capital Times* (March 11, 1969).

4. Johnson in Power

The best account of Johnson's career, even though it contains little on his presidency, is Rowland Evans and Robert Novak, *Lyndon B. Johnson: The Exercise of Power* (New York, 1966). Eric F. Goldman, *The Tragedy of Lyndon Johnson* (New York, 1969) attempts to blame everything dismal that followed his election to defects in the President's character and background. Theodore H. White, *The Making of the President 1964* (New York, 1965) is the standard account of that election year. Richard H. Rovere, "The Minds of Barry Goldwater," *Harper's* (September 1964), is a penetrating description of the Republican candidate. I. F. Stone's election-year commentaries are available in his collection of essays and reportage, *In a*

Time of Torment (New York, 1967). Norman Mailer's vivid account of the GOP convention, "In the Red Light," appeared first in *Esquire* magazine and is reprinted in *The Presidential Papers of Norman Mailer*.

Profile: Ralph Nader

See Elizabeth Brenner Drew, "The Politics of Auto Safety," *Atlantic* (October 1966), and Paul Dickson, "What Makes Ralph Nader Run?", *Progressive* (January 1970).

5. The Desperate Years Begin

For a description of the generals who stumbled into the Vietnam War see "The Never Again Club" in Joseph Kraft, *Profiles in Power: A Washington Insight* (New York, 1966). How President Johnson's advisers (mostly holdovers from the Kennedy administration) encouraged him to escalate is discussed in Edward Weintal and Charles Bartlett, *Facing the Brink: An Intimate Study of Crisis Diplomacy* (New York, 1967). Many Camelotians would later repudiate the war and blame it all on Lyndon Johnson. Tom Wicker, *JFK and LBJ: The Influence of Personality upon Politics* (New York, 1968) attributes escalation more to impulse than premeditation. Wicker thinks the President began moving toward it within forty-eight hours after taking the oath of office in Dallas. Henry A. Kissinger shrewdly evaluated the war in "The Viet Nam Negotiations," *Foreign Affairs* (January 1969). His views seem to have had little to do with how the war was run by President Nixon, even though Kissinger was on the White House staff. Louis Menashe and Ronald Radosh, eds., *Teach-ins USA* (New York, 1967) includes some of the best speeches. I. F. Stone wrote so many items on Vietnam as to constitute a running exposé of the credibility gap. Most were originally published in *I. F. Stone's Weekly*, a treasure house of such material. See especially his account of how the troop buildup began, "The Best Kept Secret of the War" (April 21, 1969). Theodore Draper, *The Dominican Revolt: A Case Study in American Policy* (New York, 1968) is brilliant. It should be read in connection with John Bartlow Martin, *Overtaken by Events: The Dominican Crisis from the Fall of Trujillo to the Civil War* (Garden City, 1966), which shows how readily benign moral and political sentiments could be put to the service of gunboat diplomacy. The subsequent devolution of Juan Bosch is analyzed in Howard J. Wiarda, "The Crisis of the Latin-American Democratic Left," *Dissent* (November–December 1969). Dwight Macdonald describes his attempted subversion of the Festival of the Arts in "A Day at the White House," *New York Review of Books* (July 15, 1965).

Profile: The City

Harper's published a special supplement on crime just when it was becoming a national obsession. See especially James V. Bennett, "A Cool Look at the 'Crime Crisis,'" *Harper's* (April 1964). The 1965 mayoralty campaign in New York City is described in William F. Buckley, *The Unmaking of a Mayor* (New York, 1966), the 1969 campaign in Peter Manso, ed., *Running Against the Machine* (New York, 1969).

6. From Civil Rights to Black Power

Merely reading all the books on racial matters that appeared in the sixties would be a full-time job. They appeared at the rate of eight or ten a week. Here are a few

I found useful. On the Muslims see C. Eric Lincoln, *The Black Muslims in America* (Boston, 1961). Robert F. Williams, *Negroes with Guns* (New York, 1962) is incomplete but shows what a poor job the press did on him. His book is written in a relatively fresh, straightforward way, though his later statements rely on the standard third-world revolutionary cant. Perhaps the most illuminating of Martin Luther King's books is *Stride Toward Freedom* (New York, 1958). Russell H. Barrett, *Integration at Ole Miss* (Chicago, 1965) is a first-person account of the Meredith affair by a faculty member. James W. Silver, *Mississippi: The Closed Society* (New York, 1964) puts it in a larger context. Anthony Lewis, *Portrait of a Decade: The Second American Revolution* (New York, 1964) describes the first ten years of the civil rights movement just before the climate changed. The nostalgic will enjoy Martin Oppenheimer and George Lakey, *A Manual for Direct Action* (Chicago, 1965) which embodies the lessons of a vanishing strategy. William McCord, *Mississippi: The Long Hot Summer* (New York, 1965) is less despairing than one might expect. Stokely Carmichael and Charles V. Hamilton, *Black Power: The Politics of Liberation in America* (New York, 1965) reviews some key events in militant terms. Hamilton was an academician who with Carmichael produced a book that is less inflammatory than a Snick meeting, less cogent than a scholarly work, while preserving the worst features of each. Le Roi Jones's deterioration may be conveniently traced in *Home: Social Essays* (New York, 1966). The most extravagant poseur among militant black intellectuals was probably Julius Lester. His *Look Out Whitey! Black Power's Gon' Get Your Mama!* (New York, 1968) anticipates the coming of apartheid with some relish. James Baldwin, *The Fire Next Time* (New York, 1963) first appeared in two parts in the *New Yorker* magazine. It should be read after the splendid essays in *Notes of a Native Son* (Boston, 1959) and *Nobody Knows My Name* (New York, 1961). Baldwin's poise deserted him thereafter, and his subsequent writings have not had much influence, for reasons Robert Brustein made clear with brilliance if not generosity in his review of *Blues for Mr. Charlie*. See "Everybody's Protest Play" in Brustein's *Seasons of Discontent* (New York, 1965). Malcolm Little, *The Autobiography of Malcolm X* (New York, 1964) is invaluable. The special flavor of the old civil rights movement is captured in Elizabeth Hardwick, "Selma, Alabama: The Charms of Goodness," *New York Review of Books* (April 22, 1965). On the transformation of Snick see Paul Good, "Odyssey of a Man—and a Movement," *New York Times Magazine* (June 25, 1967). The Watts riot is described in Robert Conot, *Rivers of Blood, Years of Darkness* (New York, 1967). Black attitudes toward it are analyzed in Robert J. Samuelson, "Riots: The More There Are, the Less We Understand," *Science* (August 11, 1967). For the New Left line on the riots see Tom Hayden, "The Occupation of Newark," *New York Review of Books* (August 24, 1967). The Detroit riot is interpreted through its principal atrocity in John Hersey, *The Algiers Motel Incident* (New York, 1968). Berkeley Rice, "In Cleveland and Boston the Issue Is Race," *New York Times Magazine* (November 5, 1967), describes the key mayoralty races of that year. Kay Boyle, "Notes on Jury Selection in the Huey P. Newton Trial," *Progressive* (October 1968), describes Oakland, where the Black Panther was tried, as "less a city than a shocking state of affairs." The making of a Panther is recounted in the best-selling autobiography by Eldridge Cleaver, *Soul on Ice* (New York, 1968). The failure of school integration in New York is one of the many important matters discussed in David Rogers, *110 Livingston Street: Politics and Bureaucracy in the New York City Schools* (New York, 1968). Zalin B. Grant, "Whites Against Blacks in Vietnam," *New Republic* (January 18, 1969), deals with racial tensions among the military. Alex Campbell, "Lindsay's Poor, Rich City," *New Republic* (November 16,

1968), is illuminating on the school and welfare crises. Martin Mayer, "The Full and Sometimes Very Surprising Story of Ocean Hill, the Teacher's Union, and the Teacher Strikes of 1968," *New York Times Magazine* (February 2, 1969), blames Superintendent McCoy and the local board especially. Jason Epstein, "The Real McCoy," *New York Review of Books* (March 13, 1969), takes the opposite tack, less convincingly but with more passion. The easiest way to approach the Black Panther question is to read their publications, which combine invective, encouragement, and neo-Marxist slogans. A peculiar feature of black militants was that though articulate and expressive in ordinary speech, their formal statements were horridly wooden and bureaucratic. In this, if nothing else, they were faithful to the Marxist tradition.

Profile: Women's Liberation

Betty Friedan, *The Feminine Mystique* (New York, 1963) is still the best explanation of why women need to be feminists. The women's liberation movement attracted much publicity in the late sixties, of which the following are typical: "Women's Lib: The War on 'Sexism,'" *Newsweek* (March 23, 1970); Peter Babcox, "Meet the Women of the Revolution, 1969," *New York Times Magazine* (February 9, 1969); Susan Brownmiller, "Sisterhood Is Powerful," *New York Times Magazine* (March 15, 1970). A remarkable personal account is Sally Kempton, "Cutting Loose," *Esquire* (July 1970). There are many feminist periodicals, including *Up from Under* (Boston), an especially well-edited journal, and *Off Our Backs* (Washington), which suffers from internal contradictions.

7. Two Cultures

There are not many art critics who write intelligently for a lay audience, and most of them work for the *New York Times*. Its Sunday art section is, therefore, the single most important source for understanding what was new and important in these years. Ada Louise Huxtable was unfailingly instructive on architecture and urban design. Some fine things were built during the sixties, many more were destroyed. As neither of these developments was peculiar to the decade, they are not discussed here. Hilton Kramer and John Canaday are invaluable guides to painting and sculpture. Canaday's provocative essays on abstract expressionism are reprinted in *Embattled Critic: Views on Modern Art* (New York, 1962). The sociology of the New York School is described in Bernard Rosenberg and Norris Fliegel, *The Vanguard Artist: Portrait and Self-Portrait* (Chicago, 1965). Michael Kirby, *Happenings* (New York, 1965) includes a history and some scripts of these events. Among many books on pop art, two I found helpful are Mario Amaya, *Pop Art . . . And After* (New York, 1966) and Lucy R. Lippard *Pop Art* (New York, 1967). On the theater Robert Brustein is indispensable. His columns for the *New Republic* are reprinted in *Seasons of Discontent: Dramatic Opinions, 1959–65* (New York, 1965). He contributed irregularly thereafter to the *New Republic* and the *New York Review of Books*. His "The Third Theater Revisited," *New York Review of Books* (February 13, 1969), is especially eloquent. The Playhouse of the Ridiculous is described by Rosalyn Regelson in the November 2, 1969, issue of the *New York Times*. Many fine minds were attracted to film reviewing in the sixties. Dwight Macdonald had a monthly column in *Esquire* on films for most of the decade. Stanley Kauffmann's observations in the *New Republic* were always reliable. His *A World on Film* (New York, 1966) makes them conveniently available. The most provocative and idiosyncratic reviewer was probably Pauline Kael, as can be seen from

I Lost It at the Movies (Boston, 1965), *Kiss Kiss Bang Bang* (Boston, 1968), and *Going Steady* (Boston, 1970). Peter Bogdanovich described the Bogart phenomenon in "Bogie in Excelsis," *Esquire* (September 1965). Vincent Canby, "When Irish Eyes Are Smiling It's Norman Mailer," *New York Times* (October 27, 1968), includes the subject's views on his role as filmmaker. Richard Schickel, "The Movies Are Now High Art," *New York Times Magazine* (January 5, 1969), is especially penetrating. Stanley Kauffmann's analysis of the rating system is in "Sex Symbols," *New Republic* (November 2, 1968). "Notes on Camp" is reprinted in Susan Sontag, *Against Interpretation* (New York, 1966). Anthony Quinton's evaluation of McLuhan is "Cut Rate Salvation," *New York Review of Books* (November 23, 1967). Dwight Macdonald's essay "Masscult and Midcult" first appeared in the spring of 1960 and is reprinted in his *Against the American Grain* (New York, 1962).

Profile: Sports

A close look at Vince Lombardi, and one of the best books ever done on a professional sport, is his own *Run to Daylight!* (Englewood Cliffs, 1963), written with W. C. Heinz. George Plimpton offers a droll personal view in *Paper Lion* (New York, 1966). The Mets' triumph was followed by a rush of books. Leonard Koppett, *The New York Mets* (New York, 1970) is a full history; Joseph Durso, *Amazing: The Miracle of the Mets* (Boston, 1970) concentrates on the 1969 season. Roger Angell, "S Is for So Lovable," *New Yorker* (May 25, 1963), is perceptive and amusing.

8. The Counter-Culture

The best description of the traditional youth culture is James S. Coleman, *The Adolescent Society* (New York, 1961). The standard account of the beat generation is Lawrence Lipton, *The Holy Barbarians* (New York, 1959). Norman O. Brown, *Life Against Death* (Middletown, Conn., 1959) was an underground best-seller before there was an underground. Brown's subsequent influence is hard to trace because the book is such difficult reading that most who thought themselves carriers of his word had gotten the message secondhand. He was to Abbie Hoffman what Freud was to Abbie Van Buren. Lenny Bruce's memoirs are *How to Talk Dirty and Influence People* (Chicago, 1965). On Zen Buddhism in America see the many books by Alan Watts. Joan Baez, *Daybreak* (New York, 1968) is a pleasant if uninformative autobiography. Hunter Davies, *The Beatles: The Authorized Biography* (New York, 1968) is complete on the early years, but does not explain or anticipate their breakup. Timothy Leary, *The Politics of Ecstasy* (New York, 1968) is typical. Ken Kesey and the Merry Pranksters achieved national renown because of Tom Wolfe, *The Electric Kool-Aid Acid Test* (New York, 1968). There are many books on rock which seem to laymen much the same. John Gábree, *The World of Rock* (Greenwich, Conn., 1968) is agreeable. Carl Belz, *The Story of Rock* (New York, 1969) is more comprehensive as the author is an art historian. Dave Laing, *The Sound of Our Time* (Chicago, 1970) is a British interpretation. Janis Joplin was a wonderful subject to interview, as can be seen in Michael Lydon, "Every Moment She Is What She Feels," *New York Times Magazine* (February 23, 1969). High fashion and the jet set are described in Marylin Bender, *The Beautiful People* (New York, 1967). One of the first books to detect the renewal of bohemianism was John Gruen, *The New Bohemia: The Combine Generation* (New York, 1966). The best book on hippies is Nicholas von Hoffman, *We Are the People Our Parents Warned Us Against* (Chicago, 1968). Also instructive is Hunter S.

Thompson, "The 'Hashbury' Is the Capital of the Hippies," *New York Times Magazine* (May 14, 1967). Religious communes are described in "Many Religious Communes of Young People Are Under the Sway of Compelling Leaders," *New York Times* (December 14, 1969). On magic see Andrew M. Greeley, "There's a New-Time Religion on Campus," *New York Times Magazine* (June 1, 1969). Theodore Roszak, *The Making of a Counter Culture* (New York, 1969) is a friendly academician's vain effort to make sense of all this. The religious aspect of the Vietnam Moratorium is described in Edward B. Fiske, "War Protest Viewed as 'Civil Religion,'" *New York Times* (October 19, 1969). William Braden pursues these themes in *The Age of Aquarius* (Chicago, 1969). Paul Goodman, "The New Reformation," *New York Times Magazine* (September 14, 1969), is remarkable. See also Daniel P. Moynihan, "Nirvana Now," *American Scholar* (Autumn 1967). The People's Park scandal is described in Sheldon Wolin and John Schaar, "The Battle of Berkeley," *New York Review of Books* (June 19, 1969). The Altamont Death Festival was exposed in "Let It Bleed," *Rolling Stone* (January 21, 1970). Steven V. Roberts, "Charlie Manson: One Man's Family," *New York Times Magazine* (January 4, 1970), is excellent. James Hitchcock, "Comes the Cultural Revolution," *New York Times Magazine* (July 27, 1969), deals nicely with the false association of cultural with political change. Rasa Gustaitis, *Turning On* (New York, 1969), describes adult counter-cultural phenomena. Guy Endore, *Synanon* (New York, 1968) is sympathetic to this very controversial institution. The new homosexuals are described in Claudia Dreifus, "Gay Power: The Birth of the Pink Panthers," *Cavalier* (December 1969). *Playboy* magazine offers a continuing record of sexual change throughout the period. Little has been done to explain the latent effects of television. Charles Sopkin, *Seven Glorious Days, Seven Fun-Filled Nights: One Man's Struggle to Survive a Week Watching Commercial Television in America* (New York, 1968) amusingly describes the garbage available to steady TV viewers. Marshall McLuhan's work puts this in a cheerier perspective. But no one really knows what happens to the moral imagination of people raised from infancy in the world television made.

Profile: Hell's Angels

Hunter S. Thompson, *Hell's Angels: A Strange and Terrible Saga* (New York, 1967) is fascinating.

9. The New Left Comes and Goes

A fine bibliographic essay is James O'Brien, "A History of the New Left, 1960–1968," *Radical America* (May–June, September–October, November–December 1968). On the perils of prophecy see George Lichtheim, "The Role of the Intellectuals," *Commentary* (April 1960). Closer to the mark were H. Stuart Hughes's review of *The End of Ideology* for *Partisan Review* (Summer 1960), and C. Wright Mills, "The New Left," *New Left Review* (October 1960). There are many books exposing HUAC. The best is probably Walter Goodman, *The Committee* (New York, 1968), which is, if anything, too generous to its subject. David Horowitz, *Student* (New York, 1962), describes the city hall affair as it seemed to a Berkeley graduate student on his way to becoming radical. *Student* is also useful as an account of the frustrations that later produced the Free Speech Movement. Two useful anthologies are Michael V. Miller and Susan Gilmore, eds., *Revolution at Berkeley* (New York, 1965), and especially Seymour Martin Lipset and Sheldon S. Wolin, eds., *The Berkeley Student Revolt* (New York, 1965). A spirited account by an adult sympathizer is Hal Draper, *Berkeley: The New Student Revolt* (New York, 1965). Draper's earlier analysis of Clark Kerr's ideology was crucial to the FSM's critique of the University. Kerr did not help matters by having been so candid in his *The Uses of the University* (Cambridge, Mass., 1963). On the early history of SDS see Jack Newfield, *A Prophetic Minority* (New York, 1966). The Conference for New Politics is described in Walter Goodman, "When Black Power Runs the New Left," *New York Times Magazine* (September 24, 1967). A memorandum called "The New Left," prepared for the Dodd subcommittee on the Senate Committee on the Judiciary, and released November 10, 1968, is also useful. It contains a predictably dim-witted staff analysis, together with many interesting articles and documents on the movement, mostly critical. The Columbia rising is described with all the gravity appropriate to a world war by Jerry L. Avorn and his fellow staff members of the Columbia student newspaper. See Avorn, *et al., Up Against the Ivy Wall: A History of the Columbia Crisis* (New York, 1968). John Kifner, "Vandals in the Mother Country," *New York Times Magazine* (January 4, 1970), is a splendid account of Weatherman. Though marred by the author's intense partisanship, and a tendency to shape the evidence to fit his theories, Lewis S. Feuer, *The Conflict of Generations* (New York, 1969) is very valuable. He shows how much student movements in different cultures and historical periods have in common, self-destructiveness especially. An astute and more friendly, though critical, analysis of SDS before it broke up is Tom Kahn, "The Problem of the New Left," *Commentary* (July 1966). On the high school radicals, Nicholas Pileggi, "Revolutionaries Who Have to Be Home by 7:30," *New York Times Magazine* (March 16, 1969), is excellent.

Profile: Religion

Commonweal magazine and the *National Catholic Reporter* are good guides to the changing Church. The oldest established underground Catholic periodical is the *Catholic Worker,* an anarcho-Christian-pacifist monthly paper selling still for twenty-five cents a copy. On the condition of the Church just before renewal see Jon Victor, "Restraints on American Catholic Freedom," *Harper's* (December 1963). Cardinal O'Boyle's tribulations are described in Thomas J. Fleming, "Confrontation in Washington: The Cardinal vs. the Dissenters," *New York Times Magazine* (November 24, 1968). The Los Angeles Times Service told the *National Catholic Reporter* story in D. J. R. Bruckner, "Catholic Weekly Delights, Enrages Its Readers," (Madison) *Capital Times* (December 27, 1968). On clerical dropouts see Colman McCarthy, "Priests Who Live in Sin," *New Republic* (March 1, 1969). See also John Corry, "The Style of the Catholic Left," *Harper's* (September 1966), and John C. Cort, "The Turmoil in the Catholic Church," *Progressive* (December 1968). Edward Fiske, "God Is Alive and Well in America," *New York Times* (December 29, 1968), summarizes the Gallup polls on religion. Two very useful books by William Braden on theology and contemporary affairs are *The Private Sea: LSD and the Search for God* (Chicago, 1967) and *The Age of Aquarius* (Chcago, 1970). The submarine churches are described in Edward Fiske, "Yellow Submarine Is Symbol of Youth Churches," *New York Times* (April 20, 1970).

10. To Tet and Back

David Kraslow and Stuart H. Loory, *The Secret Search for Peace in Vietnam* (New York, 1968) describe many abortive peace bids. Haynes Johnson and Bernard W. Gwertman, *Fulbright: The Dissenter* (New York, 1968) is the best biography of this complex man, even though not especially searching. J. William Fulbright, *The Arrogance of Power* (New York, 1966) shows him at his best. Excerpts from his committee's hearings were published almost immediately in paperback as *The Vietnam Hearings* (New York, 1966). Right-wing criticism of Fulbright was so common as to need no identification. The left's reservations were not so well known. Fulbright was always letting I. F. Stone down, it seemed, though Stone never gave up hoping for his redemption. A typical critique is in the December 29, 1966, issue of *I. F. Stone's Weekly*. Dwight Macdonald's review is "Birds of America," *New York Review of Books* (December 12, 1966). Bernard Fall's piece showing the administration's phony arithmetic is in his *Viet-Nam Witness* (New York, 1966). Marigold is discussed by Kraslow and Loory, and also by Theodore Draper in *The Abuse of Power* (New York, 1967). Or see his "Vietnam: How Not to Negotiate," *New York Review of Books* (May 4, 1967). Jonathan Schell, *The Military Half: An Account of Destruction in Quang Ngai and Quang Tin* (New York, 1968) is chilling. Song My, scene of a ghastly massacre later, was in Quang Ngai province. The strategists who called for nuclear weapons in Vietnam and urged "competitions in risk taking" there and elsewhere are dissected in Ronald Steel, "Recent Fiction," *New York Review of Books* (April 6, 1967). McNamara's career was evaluated soon afterward by I. F. Stone in "McNamara and the Militarists," *New York Review of Books* (November 7, 1968). His fall was described at the time by Stewart Alsop, *The Center: People and Power in Political Washington* (New York, 1968). Insider accounts subsequently confirmed this analysis. Kenneth Keniston, *Young Radicals* (New York, 1968) describes the New Left activists at a crucial turning point. The growing hostility to foreign adventures in Congress is described in Don Oberdorfer, "Noninterventionism, 1967 Style," *New York Times Magazine* (September 17, 1967). Ernest Halperin, "Bad Neighbor Policy," *New York Review of Books* (December 29, 1966), is excellent on U.S. relations with Latin America. Chapter 7 of Michael Harrington, *Toward a Democratic Left* (New York, 1968) explains how foreign aid was manipulated. The struggle within Washington to de-escalate has been frequently described. Two excellent syndicated news stories are Anthony Howard (London Observer Service), "The Year LBJ Lost Gamble with History," (Madison) *Capital Times* (January 1, 1969), and George C. Wilson (Washington Post Service), "How Clifford Shed Hawk Feathers for Role as Dove," *Capital Times* (January 2, 1969). Townsend Hoopes enlarges on these accounts in his *The Limits of Intervention* (New York, 1969), which, though a self-serving and self-indulgent book, is one of the best by an insider. The worst is probably Phil G. Goulding, *Confirm or Deny: Informing the People on National Security* (New York, 1970). Goulding was the Defense Department's chief PR man. He found lying for the government more onerous than expected and came to hate the newsmen, especially Harrison Salisbury, who made it so. He agrees with Hoopes that Clifford was most responsible for turning President Johnson halfway round on Vietnam. Joseph Kraft's piece on Harriman in *Profiles in Power: A Washington Insight* (New York, 1966) is outstanding. President Johnson's uncertain course after talks began is analyzed in Anthony Howard (London Observer Service), "Vietnam: The Policy That Failed," *Capital Times* (November 5, 1968). After Harriman left Paris he repeatedly asked for substantive concessions to advance the negotiations with Hanoi. President Nixon's Vietnamization program was attacked by him as an evasion of the hard realities. He was widely condemned by Spiro Agnew for this. Johnson's last days are brilliantly summed up in David Wise, "The Twilight of a President," *New York Times Magazine* (November 3, 1968). Walt Rostow's thoughts appear in "Rostow Reflects on the Sixties," *New York Times* (January 2, 1969). His self-righteousness was such that even the *Times*'s interviewer noticed it. The *New Republic* disposed of Secretary Rusk in "Goodbye, Mr. Rusk" (January 18, 1969). Eric Goldman's views are in his *The Tragedy of Lyndon Johnson* (New York, 1969).

Profile: Organized Medicine

Two excellent articles are John Ehrenreich, "The Blue Cross We Bear," *Washington Monthly* (November 1969), and David Hapgood, "The Health Professionals: Cure or Cause of the Health Crisis," *Washington Monthly* (June 1969).

11. 1968: The Hard Year

Eugene J. McCarthy, *The Year of the People* (Garden City, 1969) is not very illuminating, though there are good lines in it as might be expected from a poet. The best book on the subject is Lewis Chester, Godfrey Hodgson, and Bruce Page, *An American Melodrama: The Presidential Campaign of 1968* (New York, 1969). On Robert Kennedy, David Halberstam, *The Unfinished Odyssey of Robert Kennedy* (New York, 1968), Jules Witcover, *85 Days: The Last Campaign of Robert Kennedy* (New York, 1969), and William V. Shannon, "Said Robert Kennedy, 'Maybe We're All Doomed Anyway,'" *New York Times Magazine* (June 17, 1968), are all useful. Jay Sykes describes the McCarthy campaign in Wisconsin in the (Madison) *Capital Times*. See especially his piece in the June 7, 1969, issue. Wilfred Sheed writes of his California experience with McCarthy in "The Good Old Days in California," *Atlantic* (September 1968). The *New Republic*'s analysis of McCarthy's critics is "Showing You Care" (December 7, 1968). Hans Morgenthau sums up his foreign policy in "A Talk with Senator McCarthy," *New York Review of Books* (August 22, 1968). On the conventions, Norman Mailer, *Miami and the Siege of Chicago* (New York, 1968) is superb. Tom Buckley, "The Battle of Chicago: From the Yippies' Side," *New York Times Magazine* (September 15, 1968), is instructive. The Walker Report, *Rights in Conflict* (New York, 1968) is magisterial. Kevin Phillips outlines the Southern and other strategies in *The Emerging Republican Majority* (New Rochelle, N.Y., 1969). His ideas are analyzed cogently in James Boyd, "Nixon's Southern Strategy: 'It's All in the Charts,'" *New York Times Magazine* (May 17, 1970). For a brilliant study see Marshall Frady, *Wallace* (New York, 1968). Joe McGinniss, *The Selling of the President, 1968* (New York, 1969) shows how the winning candidate was marketed. McGinniss notes, however, that the book would not have been much different had it been about the merchandising of Hubert Humphrey instead.

Profile: Cesar Chavez

On the grape strike see Dick Meister, "'La Huelga' Becomes 'La Causa,'" *New York Times Magazine* (November 17, 1968); John Gregory Dunne, *Delano: The Story of the California Grape Strike* (New York, 1967); and Peter Matthiessen, *Sal Si Puedes: Cesar Chavez and the New American Revolution* (New York, 1969).

12. Epilogue: The Revolution Is Over

This chapter of necessity is based largely on newspapers and periodicals. On the housing crisis see Gerd Wilcke, "Housing Act Expected to Fail," *New York Times* (March 16, 1969). Peter Arnett of the Associated Press describes the casual way in which it was decided to eliminate a village in "Decision in Vietnam: Death of a

Hamlet," *New York Times* (June 1, 1969). On My Lai see, for example, Henry Kamm, "Vietnamese Say GI's Slew 567 in Town," *New York Times* (November 17, 1969); J. Anthony Lukas, "Meadlo's Home Town Regards Him as Blameless," *New York Times* (November 26, 1969); Joseph Lelyveld, "The Story of a Soldier Who Refused to Fire at Songmy," *New York Times Magazine* (December 14, 1969); and Noam Chomsky, "After Pinkville," *New York Review of Books* (January 1, 1970). Russell Baker analyzed the American response in "Mr. President, Save That Illusion," *New York Times* (November 30, 1969). The Nuremberg precedent is discussed in Telford Taylor, *Nuremberg and Vietnam* (Chicago, 1970). On Harriman's post-Paris statements see I. F. Stone, "An Appeal to Averell Harriman," *New York Review of Books* (June 19, 1969). See also Sanche de Gramont, "The Paris Talks," *New York Times Magazine* (March 16, 1969). Henry Kissinger's famous article is "The Viet Nam Negotiations," *Foreign Affairs* (January 1969). It seems not to have affected President Nixon, though Kissinger was said to have much influence with him. On the war itself see Kevin B. Buckley, "General Abrams Deserves a Better War," *New York Times Magazine* (October 5, 1969), and Tom Buckley, "The ARVN Is Bigger and Better, But—," *New York Times Magazine* (October 12, 1969). On dissent see Robert C. Jensen (Washington Post Service), "Army System on Trial Along with Presidio 'Mutineers,'" (Madison) *Capital Times* (March 22, 1969), and Victor Cohn (Washington Post Service), "The Scientists Rebel," *Capital Times* (May 19, 1969). The saga of Representative McCarthy is told in Seymour M. Hersh, "Germs and Gas as Weapons," *New Republic* (June 7, 1969). Bernard Weintraub, "In the Matter of Lloyd Mark Bucher," *New York Times Magazine* (May 11, 1969), explores the *Pueblo* affair's many ironies. On the F-111 see I. F. Stone, "Nixon and the Arms Race: The Bomber Boondoggle," *New York Review of Books* (January 2, 1969). Typical of Bernard Nossiter's splendid pieces on the C5A for the Washington Post Service is "Blew Whistle on C5A: May Lose Job," *Capital Times* (January 2, 1969). The analysis of deficient weapons systems is summarized in "Inside the Arms Gravy Train: The Poorer the Weapons the Higher the Profits," *I. F. Stone's Weekly* (February 10, 1969). On the ABM, MIRV, SALT, and the deceptions of two administrations, see "Sorry, It's the Same Old Tricky D—ky," *I. F. Stone's Weekly* (March 24, 1969); I. F. Stone, "The War Machine Under Nixon," *New York Review of Books* (June 5, 1969); I. F. Stone, "Memo to the AP Editors: How Laird Lied," *New York Review of Books* (June 4, 1970); Ralph E. Lapp, "A Biography of the ABM," *New York Times Magazine* (May 4, 1969); Ralph E. Lapp, "The Vicious Acronyms," *New Republic* (June 21, 1969); and Robert L. Rothstein, "The Scorpions in the Bottle," *Washington Monthly* (January 1970). These are helpful on Latin America: "Fulbright Scores Aid in Colombia," *New York Times* (February 2, 1969); "Peru Blows the Lid Off a Critical Situation," *New York Times* (February 23, 1969); Felix Belair, Jr., "Aid Agency Reports Birth Rate Offsets Latin Alliance Gains," *New York Times* (March 16, 1969); David Morris, "Bad Neighbor Policy," *Hard Times* (March 24–31, 1969); Susanne Bodenheimer and Alex Georgiadis, "Peru: The Foreign Managers," *Leviathan* (July–August 1969); "Bolivia Takes an Anti-U.S. Lesson from Peru's Colonels," *New York Times* (October 5, 1969). "Farm Policy Is Making Rural Rich Richer," *New York Times* (April 5, 1970) exposes the Department of Agriculture. There were countless pieces on the environmental crisis. See, for example, Barry Commoner, "Can We Survive?", *Washington Monthly* (December 1969). Here are three cheerful notes on which to end. Integration did progress in the South as is shown in Roy Reed, "Mississippi No Longer Heeds Barnett's Defiant Cry of 'Never,'" *New York Times* (November 2, 1969). Despite the rise in violence, there was also, curiously enough, something of a rise in nonviolence at the decade's end. See "Nonviolence Making Quiet Gains in U.S. as a Protest Technique," *New York Times* (April 5, 1970). Ben Wattenberg, "The Nonsense Explosion," *New Republic* (April 4 and 11, 1970), argues cogently that the population increase will be smaller than expected.

Index

INDEX

Food and Agricultural Organization
(UN), 346
Football, 228–230, 232
Ford, Gerald, 25–26, 95, 408
Ford Foundation, 184, 186
Ford Motor Company, 30, 125
Foreign Affairs, 404
Foreign policy: compared with Russian,
137–138; criticism of, *see* New Left;
during Eisenhower administration, 3,
5–9, 20; in Europe, 320; of France,
319–320; during Johnson administra-
tion, 120–121, 131–141, 143, 319–
321, 344–346, 352–354; during
Kennedy administration, 23–24, 29,
35–44, 65–73, 75–87, 92; of Mc-
Carthy, 377, 378; during Nixon
administration, 416–418; Russian, *see*
Russia
Forman, James, 170, 189, 288
Formosa Straits, 6
Fort Dix, 408
Fort Hill Community, 254
Fortas, Abe, 27
Fortune, 13
Forward Strategy for America, A
(Strausz-Hupé, *et al.*), 12
France, 83–84, 86, 319–320; in Indo-
china, 142; in Vietnam, 326
Free love. *See* Sexual freedom.
Free Speech Movement, 280–283, 342
Freedom ballots, 164
Freedom Rides, 89, 161, 162, 189
Freedom Summer, 164, 167
Freeman, Orville, 367
French Indochina. *See* Cambodia; Laos;
Vietnam.
Friedan, Betty, 196
Friedman, Milton, 398
Froines, John, 423
Fruit of Islam. *See* Black Muslims.
Fuck You: A Magazine of the Arts, 250,
251
Fugs, The, 250, 343, 382
Fugs Song Book, The, 250
Fulbright, William, 39, 121, 141, 321–
325, 335, 349, 408, 416–417
Fundamentalism, 153
Futz (Owens), 206

Gaither Commission, 8
Galbraith, John Kenneth, 4, 30, 64, 361,
415
Gallagher President's Report, 311
Galoosh. *See* Missiles, anti-ballistic.
Gandhi, Mohandas, 172, 258, 298

Gangs, 188, 296; motorcycle, *see* Hell's
Angels
Garbage. *See* Strikes, garbage.
Garbo, Greta, 223
Garrison, Jim, 100–103
Garson, Barbara, 326
Gates, Thomas S., Jr., 9
Gavin, James M., 323
Gay Liberation Front, 269–270
Geese, 211
Gemini program, 53, 55, 56, 58
General Dynamics, 410, 412
General Motors, 124, 127, 420
General Services Administration, 126
Generation gap, 233, 236, 239, 240, 249,
264, 266, 299–300. *See also* Counter-
culture.
Genet, Jean, 205, 384
Genovese, Eugene, 143
Georgia, University of, 162, 352
Germany, 41–44, 48, 378; air force, 412
Gernreich, Rudi, 245–246
Gestalt therapy. *See* Esalen Institute.
Ghettos: as election issue, 369–370,
390; white, 179. *See also* Poverty;
Watts.
Gideon decision, 27
Gilman, Richard, 208, 212
Gilpatric, Roswell, 68
Ginsberg, Allen, 144, 384
Ginzburg, Ralph, 26–27
Giumarra Corporation, 394, 395
Gleason, Ralph, 244, 262
Glenn, John H., 53
"Global village." *See* McLuhan, Mar-
shall.
God, 312–313, 314–316. *See also* Re-
ligion.
"God Is Dead" theology, 256, 314–316
"Go-go" girls, 245
Gold, Herbert, 4
Goldberg, Arthur, 156, 320, 321
Goldfinger, 223
Goldman, Eric, 113, 145, 353
Goldwater, Barry, 90, 107–111, 114,
117–118, 119, 381, 389; popularity
of, 108; and Vietnam, 143
Golpistas, 139
Goodman, Andrew, 167
Goodman, Paul, 210, 257, 342
Goodman, Walter, 288
Goodsell, James Nelson, 140
Goodwin, Richard, 361, 363
GOP. *See* Republican party.
Gordon, Richard, 55
Grace, W. R., 418
Grades, university, 301–302

ix

Ruth, Babe, 228
"Ruthless Cannonball, The," 365, 374

Sacco, Nicola, 277
Safeguard. *See* Missiles, anti-ballistic.
Safety: automobile, 123–127; of space flights, 55–58. *See also* Crime; Fallout; Nuclear weapons.
SAGE, 411
Sahl, Mort, 101
St. John's University, 285
St. Laurent, Yves, 247
St. Louis Post-Dispatch, 321
St. Paul, 315
Sainteny, Jean, 404
Salinger, Pierre, 361
Salisbury, Harrison, 138, 330, 331
San Francisco, 110, 166
San Francisco Bay Area Revolutionary Union, 295
San Francisco Chronicle, 262
San Francisco Mime Troupe, 242
"San Francisco Sound." *See* Music, acid rock.
San Francisco State College, 190–191
San Francisco Tripps Festival, 242, 243
San Jose State College, 144
Sanders, Ed, 250–251, 343, 382
SANE, 285
Satellites, 8. *See also* Missiles; Space program.
Saturday Evening Post, 100, 272
Saturday Review, 225
Savio, Mario, 199, 280–282
Scalapino, Robert, 142
Schechner, Richard, 207, 210
Schell, Jonathan, 333–335
Schenley Corporation, 394
Schickel, Richard, 219
Schlesinger, Arthur, Jr., 39, 71, 83, 153, 361
Schools. *See* Education.
Schorr, Martin M., 371
Schulberg, Budd, 171
Schwarz, Fred, 48
Schwerner, Michael, 167
Science, 23, 275, 281, 300, 301, 425; and counter-culture, 255, 257, 267; and religion, 313–314, 317–318; and Vietnam, 405
Science magazine, 59
Scientific American, 44
Scientists and Engineers for Johnson-Humphrey, 114
Scott, David, 55
Scott, George C., 214, 218
Scranton, William, 110, 111

Sculpture, 200
SDS (Students for a Democratic Society), 177, 255, 259, 277–279, 285, 286–287, 289–292, 293–295, 303, 305, 397; German, 292. *See also* Weatherman.
Seale, Bobby, 187, 293, 423
Seasons of Discontent (Brustein), 206
SEATO, 345
Seaver, Tom, 231
Secular City, The (Cox), 316
Seeger, Alan, 373
Seeger, Pete, 235
Segregation, 369; in colleges, 73–75; in education, 25, 27, 158, 165–166, 174–175, 193, 399, 402; in housing, 181; and Johnson, 118–119; of public transportation, 89, 159 (*see also* Freedom Rides); and the Supreme Court, 25; and Wallace, *see* Wallace. *See also* Mississippi Freedom Democratic party.
Seigenthaler, John, 161
Selective Service. *See* Draft.
Sellers, Peter, 214
Selma, Alabama, 129, 163, 164, 169–170
Senate: and armaments, 414; and crime, 424; Johnson's influence in, 105–106; and Joseph McCarthy, 105; peace movement in, 323, 325, 361; and riots, 177; and Supreme Court, 28; and Vietnam, 321, 323–325
Senate Armed Services Committee, 345, 414
Senate Foreign Relations Committee, 322–323, 345, 416
Senate Preparedness Subcommittee, 10
Sensitivity training, 267
Sentinel. *See* Missiles, anti-ballistic.
Separatism, black, 160, 164, 166–168, 174–175, 178, 190, 194, 377 (*see also* Decentralization of schools); black, in colleges, 191; in Quebec, 293
"Sergeant Pepper's Lonely Hearts Club Band," 237
Sevareid, Eric, 47
Seven Days in May, 214
Sex education, 265
Sexual freedom, 254, 263, 268–270; in colleges, 300; and counter-culture, 252–253, 265; in films, 205, 212–213, 215; in literature, 204–205; in the 1950's, 234; in plays, 205, 206–212; and rock music, 243–244; and women's liberation, 197–198
Sexual Freedom League, 253
Sexual relations, interracial, 167–168

A Note on the Author

William L. O'Neill was born in Big Rapids, Michigan, and studied at the University of Michigan and the University of California, Berkeley, where he received a Ph.D. in history. His many books in American history include *A Democracy at War: America's Fight at Home and Abroad in World War II*; *American High: The Years of Confidence, 1945–1960*; *Everyone Was Brave: A History of Feminism in America*; *A Better World: Stalinism and the American Intellectuals*; *Echoes of Revolt: The Masses, 1911–1917*; *Divorce in the Progressive Era*; and *American Society Since 1945*. Mr. O'Neill is professor of history at Rutgers University and lives with his wife in Highland Park, New Jersey.